# Microsoft® Project 2000 Bible

asy-sus@yahoo.com

Chiara_718
babymia

linda_cu2002@yahoo.com

poca627@hotmail.com

lesik8@yandex.ru

# Microsoft® Project 2000 Bible

Elaine Marmel

Hungry Minds™

HUNGRY MINDS, INC.

New York, NY ◆ Cleveland, OH ◆ Indianapolis, IN

**Microsoft® Project 2000 Bible**

Published by
**Hungry Minds, Inc.**
909 Third Avenue
New York, NY 10022
www.hungryminds.com



ISBN: 0-7645-3319-3

Printed in the United States of America

10 9 8 7 6 5 4

1B/SS/QV/QR/FC

Distributed in the United States by Hungry Minds, Inc.

Distributed by CDG Books Canada Inc. for Canada; by Transworld Publishers Limited in the United Kingdom; by IDG Norge Books for Norway; by IDG Sweden Books for Sweden; by IDG Books Australia Publishing Corporation Pty. Ltd. for Australia and New Zealand; by TransQuest Publishers Pte Ltd. for Singapore, Malaysia, Thailand, Indonesia, and Hong Kong; by Gotop Information Inc. for Taiwan; by ICG Muse, Inc. for Japan; by Intersoft for South Africa; by Eyrolles for France; by International Thomson Publishing for Germany, Austria and Switzerland; by Distribuidora Cuspide for Argentina; by LR International for Brazil; by Galileo Libros for Chile; by Ediciones ZETA S.C.R. Ltda. for Peru; by WS Computer Publishing Corporation, Inc., for the Philippines; by Contemporanea de Ediciones for Venezuela; by Express Computer Distributors for the Caribbean and West Indies; by Micronesia Media Distributor, Inc. for Micronesia; by Chips Computadoras S.A. de C.V. for Mexico; by Editorial Norma de Panama S.A. for Panama; by American Bookshops for Finland.

For general information on Hungry Minds' products and services please contact our Customer Care Department within the U.S. at 800-762-2974, outside the U.S. at 317-572-3993 or fax 317-572-4002.

For sales inquiries and reseller information, including discounts, premium and bulk quantity sales, and foreign-language translations, please contact our Customer Care Department at 800-434-3422, fax 317-572-4002, or write to Hungry Minds, Inc., Attn: Customer Care Department, 10475 Crosspoint Boulevard, Indianapolis, IN 46256.

For information on licensing foreign or domestic rights, please contact our Sub-Rights Customer Care Department at 212-884-5000.

For information on using Hungry Minds' products and services in the classroom or for ordering examination copies, please contact our Educational Sales Department at 800-434-2086 or fax 317-572-4005.

Please contact our Public Relations Department at 212-884-5163 for press review copies or 212-884-5000 for author interviews and other publicity information or fax 212-884-5400.

For authorization to photocopy items for corporate, personal, or educational use, please contact Copyright Clearance Center, 222 Rosewood Drive, Danvers, MA 01923, or fax 978-750-4470.

Library of Congress Cataloging-in-Publication Data
Marmel, Elaine J.
Microsoft Project 2000 bible / Elaine Marmel.
p. cm.
ISBN 0-7645-3319-3 (alk. paper)
1. Microsoft Project 2000. 2. Industrial project management--Computer programs.
HD69.P75 M368 1999
658.4'04'02855369--dc21 99-088435

# About the Author

**Elaine Marmel** is president of Marmel Enterprises, Inc., an organization that specializes in technical writing and software training. She routinely employs project management software and skills to manage critical business projects, and otherwise spends most of her time writing. Elaine has authored or coauthored more than 20 books about software, including Word for Windows, Word for the Mac, Quicken for Windows, Quicken for DOS, 1-2-3 for Windows, Lotus Notes, and Excel. Elaine is a contributing editor to the monthly magazines Inside Peachtree for Windows, Inside Timeslips for Windows, and Inside QuickBooks for Windows.

Elaine left her native Chicago for the warmer climes of Florida (by way of Cincinnati, Ohio; Jerusalem, Israel; Ithaca, New York; and Washington, D.C.) where she basks in the sun with her PC and her cats, Cato and Watson. Elaine also sings in the Toast of Tampa, an International Champion Sweet Adeline barbershop chorus.

# Credits

**Acquisitions Editor**
Laura Moss

**Development Editors**
Alex Miloradovich
Sara Salzmann

**Technical Editor**
Dennis Cohen

**Copy Editors**
Nancy Rapoport
Michael D. Welch

**Project Coordinators**
Linda Marousek
Louigene A. Santos

**Quality Control Specialists**
Laura Taflinger
Chris Weisbart

**Graphics and Production Specialists**
Robert Bihlmayer
Jude Levinson
Michael Lewis
Ramses Ramirez
Victor Perez-Varela
Dina F. Quan

**Book Designer**
Drew R. Moore

**Illustrators**
Mary Jo Richards
Ramses Ramirez

**Proofreading and Indexing**
York Production Services

**Cover Design**
Kippy Thomsen

*To my mom with love for all her understanding and support.*

# Preface

Managing projects can be as exciting as scheduling the next space shuttle or as mundane as planning routine production-line maintenance. A project can be as rewarding as striking oil or as disastrous as the maiden voyage of the Titanic. Projects can have budgets of $5 or $5 million. One thing all projects have in common, however, is their potential for success or failure — the promise that if you do it right, you'll accomplish your goal.

## Why You Need This Book

Microsoft Project is a tool for implementing project management principles and practices that can help you succeed. That's why this book provides not only the information about which buttons to press and where to type project dates, but also the conceptual framework to make computerized project management work for you.

### How it's designed

This book strives to offer real-world examples of projects from many industries and disciplines. You'll see yourself and your own projects somewhere in this book. A wealth of tips and advice show you how to address, control, and overcome real-world constraints.

- **As a tutorial.** You can use the Microsoft Project 2000 Bible as a linear tool to learn Project — from the ground up.
- **As a reference.** You can put it on the shelf and use it as your Project reference book, to be pulled down as needed — for advice, information, and step-by-step procedures.

Either way, this book is designed to enrich your Microsoft Project experience and make you a better project manager.

### Who it's for

Unlike word processing or spreadsheet software, many of you may have come to project management software never having used anything quite like it before. You may also have used earlier versions of Project or other project management software.

- **If you're new to project management.** This book is for you. The early chapters explain the basic concepts of computerized project management and what it can do for you, so that you have a context for learning Project.
- **If you're experienced with project management.** This book is also for you. It explains what's new in the latest version of Project and shows you techniques for using the software that you many not have considered before.

You will benefit most from this book if you have at least a basic understanding of the Windows environment, have mastered standard Windows software conventions, and are comfortable using a mouse. But beyond that, you need only the desire to succeed as a project manager, which this book will help you do.

# The Special Features of This Book

To help you maximize your use of this book, we've included many special features in its design and conception. The following sections show you how they work.

## Formatting conventions

To streamline your learning experience, we've used the following formatting conventions:

- **Text you're asked to type.** When you're asked to enter text into a Project schedule, for example, it appears in **boldface**.
- **When using the mouse.** A click indicates a left mouse-button click and right-click indicates a right mouse-button click. Double-click designates two quick, successive clicks of the left mouse button.
- **Keystroke combinations.** These look like this: Alt+Tab. Hold down the first key and, without letting it go, press the second key.
- **Menu commands.** These are shown with the command arrow — for example, Choose File ⇨ Open.
- **New terms.** When a new term or concept is introduced, it appears in *italic.*

## Margin icons

Throughout the book we've included special icons in the margins to call your attention to added information, shortcuts and advice, warnings about potentially disastrous courses of action, the new features of Project 2000, references to additional wisdom, and how to access the wonderful software on the CD-ROM that accompanies this book. Here's how they look:

### Sagacious Sidebars

Sidebars, such as this one, are departures into background details or interesting information. They're designed so you may read around them if you're in a hurry to accomplish a specific task.

When you have the time for a more comprehensive approach to the subject, however, the concepts you find in sidebars may prove invaluable—providing the context and depth necessary to a fuller understanding of Project's functions.

The Note icon signals additional information about a point under discussion or background information that might be of interest to you.

A tip is a bit of advice or a hint to save you time and indicate the best way to get things done.

Cautions are warnings about procedures or steps that could cause problems, such as a loss of data or an irrevocable change to your file.

This icon highlights a new feature in Project 2000.

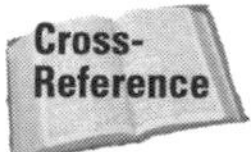


These helpful icons clue you in to sources of additional information on a topic under discussion. They point to another chapter or a specific heading elsewhere in the book.

The CD-ROM icon flags helpful software and templates that you'll find on the accompanying CD-ROM.

# How This Book Is Organized

This book is organized in the way that you will use Microsoft Project. It begins with some basic concepts, progresses through the features you need to build a typical schedule, and then track its progress. The later chapters provide more advanced information for customizing Project, using it in workgroup settings, and taking Project online.

## Part I: Project Management Basics

Part I of the book explains the basic project management concepts and terminology that you'll need in order to learn Project. In Chapter 1 you take a look at the nature of projects themselves, how Microsoft Project can help you control them, and the life cycle of a typical project. In Chapter 2 you get your first glimpse of the Project software environment.

## Part II: Getting Your Project Going

Here's where you learn about the type of information Project needs to do its job. This is where you begin to build your first schedule, adding tasks in an outline structure in Chapter 3. In Chapter 4 you assign timing and construct timing relationships among those tasks. Chapter 5 is where you begin assigning people and other resources to your project; this chapter is also where you learn to determine how these resources add costs to a project and how to handle issues such as overtime and shift work.

## Part III: Refining Your Project

Before your project is ready for prime time, you need to tweak things, just as you check spelling in a word processed document. Chapter 6 explains how to view that information to gain perspective on your project, and Chapter 7 helps you manipulate and customize views to make them work for you. Chapter 8 shows you how to make your project schedule look more professional by formatting the text and modifying the appearance of chart elements. The next two chapters delve into the tools Project provides to resolve conflicts in your schedule. Chapter 9 explores resolving conflicts in the timing of your schedule, so you can meet your deadlines. Chapter 10 considers the issue of resolving resource conflicts, such as overworked people and underutilized equipment.

## Part IV: Tracking Your Progress

Here's where you get the payoff for all your data entry and patient resolution of problems in your schedule. After you set your basic schedule and the project begins, you can track its progress and check data on your status from various perspectives. Chapter 11 gives you an overview of the tracking process. Chapter 12 shows you how to track progress on your individual tasks and view that progress in various ways. Chapter 13 is where you explore the power of generating reports on your projects for everyone from management to individual project team members. Chapter 14 gives advice and methods for analyzing your progress and making adjustments as needed to stay on schedule and within your budget.

## Part V: Working in Groups

Most projects worth the effort of tracking in Project aren't done by a single person: Workgroups, teams, and committees often form a day-to-day working project team. Chapter 15 shows you how to keep members of your workgroup in touch and how to keep your project files secure. Chapter 16 describes how to use Project on the Web. Learn how to coordinate multiple projects to run concurrently or to consolidate smaller projects into larger schedules in Chapter 17.

## Part VI: Advanced Microsoft Project

Part VI provides advice and information to make your use of Microsoft Project easier. Learn about customizing the Project environment in Chapter 18. Chapter 19 provides information on macros — simple programs that enable you to record and automatically play back series of steps that you use frequently, saving you time and effort. Chapter 20 deals with importing and exporting information into and out of Project. Importing information from other software can save you the time and expense of reentering existing data.

## Appendixes

The first three appendixes provide resources and other additional materials to make your work easier. Appendix D covers the contents and installation for the companion CD-ROM that contains trial software, time-saving templates, and a Web page with links to sites of interest in the project management world — including sites to partners of Microsoft Project.

## Project Management Glossary

The glossary at the end of the book contains many project management-specific terms and concepts that have evolved over time. These terms are defined when they are first used in the book, but you may want to look them up at a later date. Use this handy alphabetical listing to do so.

# Acknowledgments

No man (or woman) is an island, and this book is the product of the efforts of several people. Thank you, Laura Moss, for your support and for making things easier in general. Thank you, Alex Miloradovich, for keeping me sane. Thank you, Sharon Eames, for helping me through the final phases of the project. Thank you, Dennis Cohen, for keeping me technically accurate and for adding insight. Thank you, Nancy Rapoport and Michael Welch, for keeping the manuscript readable. And thank you, Steven Noetzel, Jake Mason, and Jason Luster for all the support from your department in setting up an NT Server and producing the Web page for the CD. Last, thank you to the contributors who provided sample software for the readers on the book's CD. You all helped me make this a better book than I could have produced by myself. I'd also like to thank my mom, Susan Marmel, and my friend Sue Plumley for their encouragement and support—you two have no idea how much it means to know you're there.

# Contents at a Glance

# Contents

P A R T

I

# Project Management Basics

✦ ✦ ✦ ✦

**In This Part**



✦ ✦ ✦ ✦

CHAPTER 1

# The Nature of Projects

✦ ✦ ✦ ✦

**In This Chapter**

Understanding projects

The life cycle of a project

✦ ✦ ✦ ✦

Everybody does projects. Building a tree house is a project; so is putting a man on the moon. From the simplest home improvement to the most complex business or scientific venture, projects are a part of most of our lives. But exactly what is a project, and what can you do to manage all of its facets?

Some projects are defined by their randomness. Missed deadlines, unpleasant surprises, and unexpected problems seem to be as unavoidable as the weekly staff meeting. Other projects have few problems. Nevertheless, the project that goes smoothly from beginning to end is rare. Good planning and communication can go a long way toward avoiding disaster. And although no amount of planning can prevent all possible problems, good project management enables you to deal with those inevitable twists and turns in the most efficient manner possible.

In this chapter you begin exploring tools and acquiring skills that can help you become a more efficient and productive project manager. The goal here is to provide a survey of what a project is, what project management is, and how Microsoft Project 2000 fits into the picture.

## Understanding Projects

When you look up the word "project" in the dictionary, you see definitions such as "plan" and "concerted effort." A project in the truest sense, then, isn't a simple one-person effort to perform a task. By this definition, getting yourself dressed, difficult though that task may seem on a Monday morning, isn't a project.

A project is a series of steps, often performed by more than one person. In addition:

- **A project has a specific and measurable goal.** You know you have finished the project when you have successfully met your project goal.
- **Projects have a specific time frame.** The success of a project is often measured by how successfully the project has been completed within the amount of time allotted to it.
- **Projects use resources.** Resources aren't just people; resources can include money, machinery, materials, and more. How well these resources are allocated and orchestrated is another key measure of a project's success or failure.
- **All projects consist of interdependent, yet individual, steps called tasks.** No piece of a project exists in a vacuum. If one task runs late or overbudget, it typically affects other tasks, the overall schedule, and the total cost.

By their nature, projects are dynamic. They can last for months or even years. In addition, projects tend to grow, change, and behave in ways that you can't always predict. Consequently, you, as a project manager, have to remain alert to the progress and vagaries of your projects, or you will never reach your goals. Documentation and communication are your two key tools for staying on top of a project throughout its life.

## Exploring project management

Project management is a discipline that looks at the nature of projects and offers ways to control their progress. Project management attempts to organize and systematize the procedures in a project to minimize the number of surprises you encounter.

Project management and project managers concern themselves with certain key areas:

- Scheduling
- Budgeting
- Managing resources
- Tracking and reporting progress

To manage these aspects of projects, certain tools have evolved over the years. Some of these are conceptual, such as the *critical path;* others involve specific formats for charting progress, such as a *Gantt chart.* The following sections introduce some key project management concepts and tools.

## Critical path and slack

The critical path marks the series of tasks in a project that must be completed on time for the overall project to stay on time. The following example illustrates this concept.

Suppose you are planning a going away party at your office. You have three days to plan the party. Here are some of the tasks involved and their time frames:

| *Task* | *Duration* |
|---|---|
| Signing the good-bye card | Three days |
| Ordering food | One day |
| Reserving a room | One hour |
| Buying a good-bye gift | One day |

The longest task involves getting everyone to sign a greeting card. The shortest task, reserving a room, takes only one hour. Assuming that plenty of rooms are available for holding the party, you could delay reserving the room until the last hour of the third day. Delaying this task won't actually cause any delay in holding the party, as long as you accomplish this task by the end of the longest task, getting the good-bye card signed. Therefore, the task of reserving a room isn't on the critical path. However, you can't delay the task of signing the good-bye card, which is projected to take three days to accomplish, without delaying the party. Therefore, the card-signing task is on the critical path. (Of course, this example is very simple; typically, a whole series of tasks that can't afford delay form an entire critical path.)

To further define and clarify these concepts:

- ✦ *Slack* is the amount of time you can delay a task before that task moves onto the critical path. Another name for slack is *float.* In the preceding example the one-hour-long task, reserving a room, has slack. This task can slip a few hours, even a couple of days, and the party could still happen on time. However, if you wait until the last half hour of the third day to reserve a room, that task would have used up its slack; it would then move onto the critical path.
- ✦ *Critical path* changes as the project progresses. Knowing where your critical path tasks are at any point during the project is crucial to staying on track. A critical path is a means of prioritizing tasks that have no leeway in their timing to make sure they don't run late and affect your overall schedule. Figures 1-1 and 1-2 show the same schedule — first with all tasks displayed and then filtered to show only those tasks on the critical path.

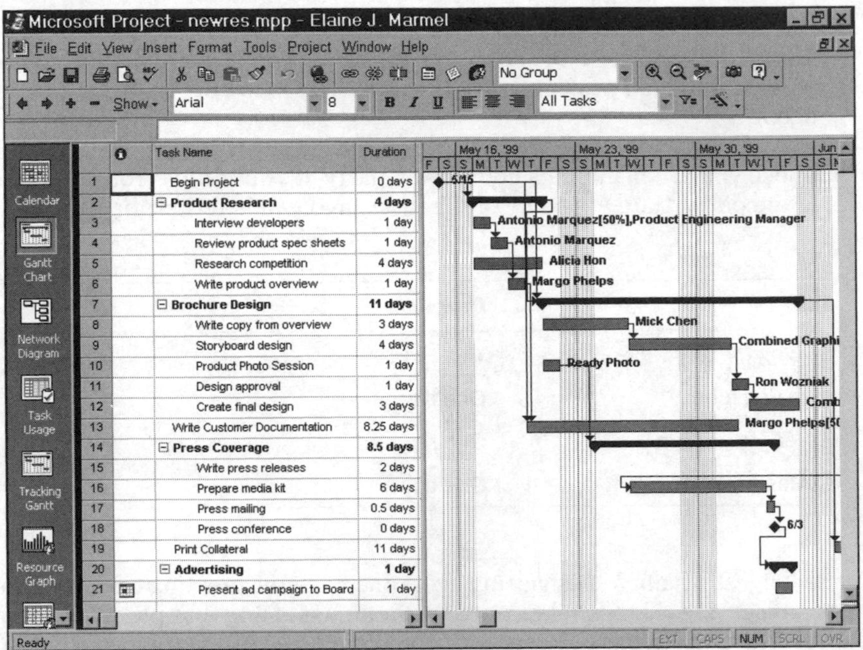


**Figure 1-1:** Tasks with slack display alongside those on the critical path.

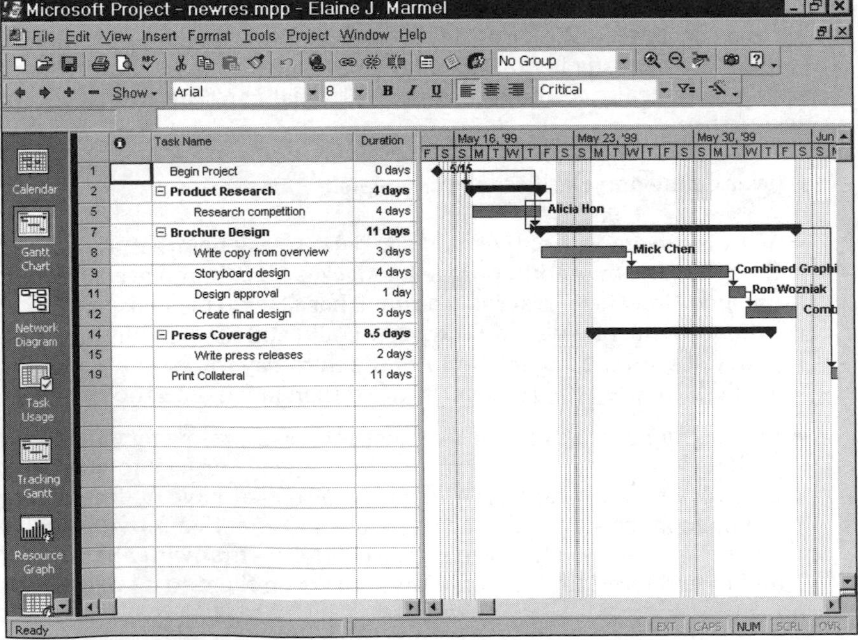


**Figure 1-2:** With the appropriate filter applied, only tasks that can't afford any delay appear in your schedule.

## Durations and milestones

Most tasks in a project take a certain amount of time to accomplish. Tasks can take five minutes or five months. The length of time needed to complete a task is called the task's *duration.* You should always try to break long tasks in a project into smaller tasks of shorter duration so that you can track their progress frequently; for example, break a five-month-long task into five, month-long tasks. Checking off the completion of the smaller tasks each month reduces the odds of a serious surprise five months down the road — and makes you feel like you're actually getting something done.

Some tasks, called *milestones,* have no (zero) duration. Milestones are merely points in time that mark the start or completion of some phase of a project. For example, if your project involves designing a new brochure, the approval of the initial design might be a milestone. Although you can assign a duration to the process of routing the design to various people for review, assigning a length of time to the actual moment when you have everyone's final approval is probably impossible. Therefore, this task has a duration of zero — that is, approval of the design is a milestone that simply marks a key moment in the project.

## Resource-driven schedules and fixed-duration tasks

Some tasks take the same amount of time no matter how many people or other resources you throw at them. Flying from San Francisco to New York is likely to take five hours no matter how many pilots or flight attendants you add. You can't speed up a test on a mixture of two solvents that must sit for six hours to react by adding more solvent or hiring more scientists to work in the laboratory. These tasks have a *fixed duration;* they are also called *fixed tasks,* and their timing is set by the nature of the task.

On the other hand, the number of available resources does affect the duration of some tasks. If one person needs two hours to dig a ditch, adding a second person usually cuts the time in half; two people can dig the same ditch in one hour. The project still requires two hours of effort, but two resources can perform the task simultaneously. Tasks whose durations are affected by the addition or subtraction of resources are *resource-driven tasks.*

In real-world projects, the calculation is seldom so exact. Because people have different skill levels and perform work at different speeds, two people don't always cut the time of a task exactly in half. In addition, the more people you add to a task, the more communication, cooperation, and training may be involved. Although Microsoft Project handles additional assignments of resources as a strictly mathematical calculation, you can still use your judgment of the resources involved to modify this calculation somewhat (see Chapter 10).

## Diagrams that aid project management

Gantt charts, network diagrams, and work breakdown structures (WBS) are tools of project management that have evolved over many years. They are simply charts that you can use to track different aspects of your project. Figure 1-3 shows a Microsoft Project Gantt chart, and Figure 1-4 shows a Microsoft Project network diagram. Figure 1-5 shows a typical WBS, but Microsoft Project does not include a WBS chart as one of its standard views.

You can purchase an add-on product, WBS Chart for Project, to create a WBS chart from a Microsoft Project file. The CD-ROM includes a sample of the program.

Before people used computers to manage their projects, managers drew these charts by hand. Any self-respecting project war room had a 10-foot network diagram, WBS, or Gantt chart tacked to the wall. By the end of the project, this chart was as marked up and out of date as last year's appointment calendar. Thankfully, project management software makes these charts easier to generate, update, and customize.

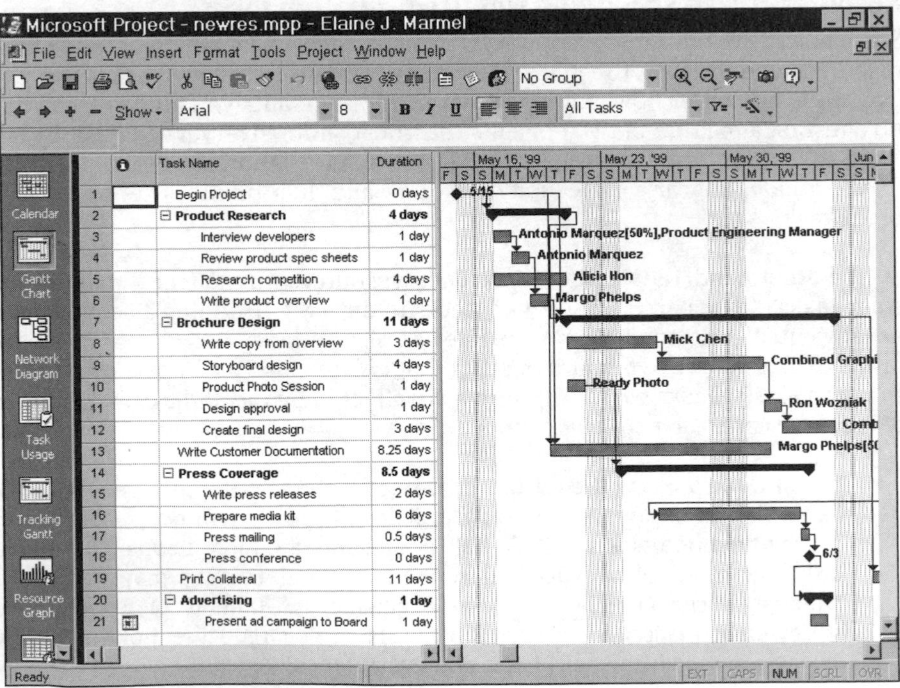


**Figure 1-3:** The Gantt chart bars represent timing of tasks in a project.

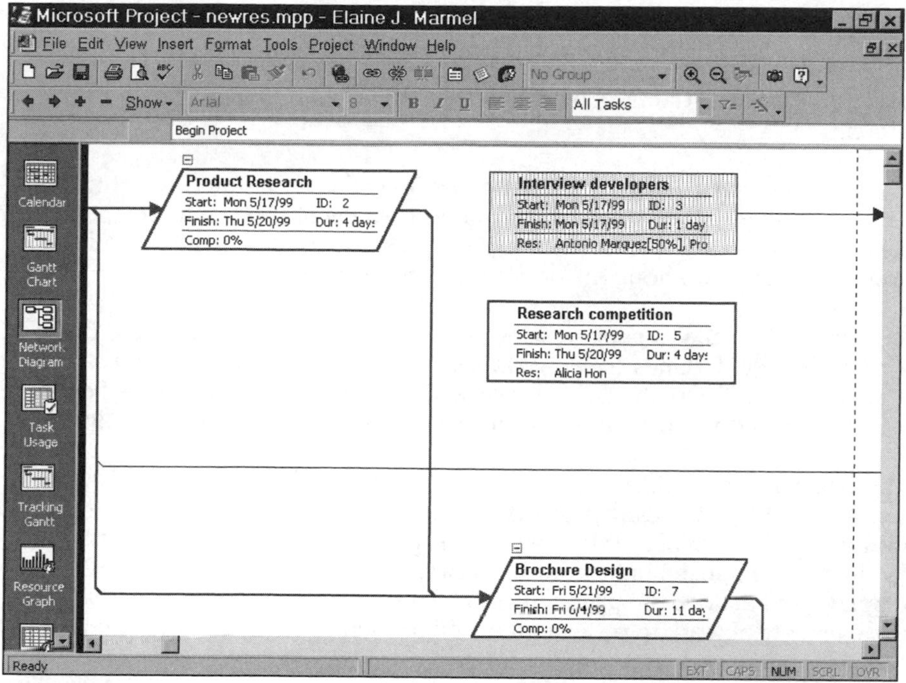


**Figure 1-4:** The network diagram resembles a flowchart for work in a project.

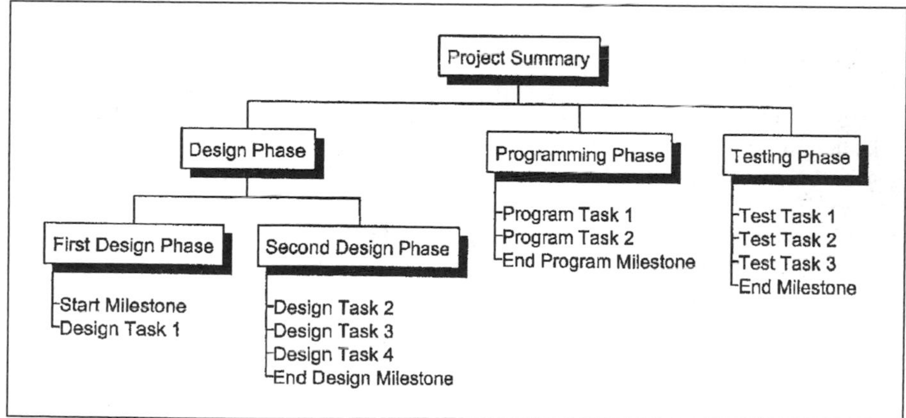


**Figure 1-5:** The work breakdown structure chart reminds you of a typical company organization chart.

A Gantt chart represents the tasks in a project with bars that reflect the duration of individual tasks. Milestones are shown as diamond-shaped objects. You learn more about the various elements of the Gantt chart in Chapter 2. For now, what's important is that a Gantt chart enables you to visualize and track the timing of a project.

Network diagrams, on the other hand, don't accurately detail the timing of a project. Instead, a network diagram shows the flow of tasks in a project and the relationships of tasks to each other. Each task is contained in a box called a *node,* and lines that flow among the nodes indicate the flow of tasks.

Note

In Project 98 and prior versions of Project, network diagrams were called PERT charts. PERT stands for Program Evaluation and Review Technique. The Special Projects Office of the U.S. Navy devised this method for tracking the flow of tasks in a project when it was designing the Polaris submarine in the late 1950s.

The U.S. defense establishment uses the "work breakdown structure" (WBS) as its primary tool for managing projects and describes the WBS in Military Standard (MIL-STD) 881B (25 Mar 93): "A work breakdown structure is a product-oriented family tree composed of hardware, software, services, data and facilities. . . . [it] displays and defines the product(s) to be developed and/or produced and relates the elements of work to be accomplished to each other and to the end product(s)."

Project doesn't contain a PERT chart view; however, on the CD-ROM you'll find a PERT Chart EXPERT sample program that converts the information in any Project file to a PERT view.

## Dependencies

The final project management concept you should understand is *dependencies.* The overall timing of a project isn't simply the sum of the durations of all tasks, because all tasks in a project don't usually happen simultaneously. For example, in a construction project, you must pour the foundation of a building before you can build the structure. You also have to enclose the building with walls and windows before you lay carpeting. In other words, project managers anticipate and establish relationships among the tasks in a project. These relationships are called *dependencies.* Only when you have created tasks, assigned durations to them, and established dependencies, can you see the overall timing of your project.

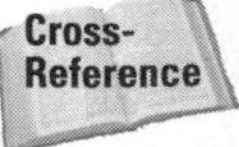


Chapter 4 covers several kinds of dependencies.

## Managing projects with project management software

Many people manage projects with stacks of outdated to-do lists and colorful hand-drawn wall charts. They scribble notes on calendars in pencil, knowing that, more often than not, dates and tasks change over time. They hold meetings, meetings, and more meetings to keep everyone in the project informed. People have developed these simple organizational tools because projects typically have so many bits and pieces that no one can remember them all.

To manage any project, you need some set of procedures. Project management software automates many of these procedures. With project management software you can:

- **Plan up front.** By preplanning the various elements of your project, you can more accurately estimate the time and resources required to complete the project.
- **View your progress.** By looking at your progress on an ongoing basis, from various perspectives, you can see whether you are likely to meet your goal.
- **Recognize conflicts.** By identifying time and resource conflicts early, you can try out various what-if scenarios to resolve them before they get out of hand.
- **Make adjustments.** You can make adjustments to task timing and costs, and automatically update all other tasks in the project to reflect the impact of your changes.
- **Generate professional looking reports.** You can create reports on the status of your project to help team members prioritize and help management make informed decisions.

With improved workgroup, intranet, and e-mail capabilities, Microsoft Project also makes communication and cooperation among workgroup members much easier and more productive.

### What's required of you

Many people contemplate using project management software with about as much relish as they do a visit to the dentist. They anticipate hours of data entry time before they can get anything out of the software. To some extent, that vision is true. You have to provide a certain amount of information about your project for any software to estimate schedules and generate reports, just as you have to enter numbers for a spreadsheet to calculate a budget or a loan pay-back schedule.

On the other hand, after you enter your basic project information into Microsoft Project, the ongoing upkeep of that data is far easier than generating handwritten to-do lists that become obsolete almost immediately after you've made them. In addition, the accuracy and professionalism of reports that you generate with Project can make the difference between a poorly managed project and a successful one. And, as with a quarterly budget you create with spreadsheet software, after you enter the data, Project performs its calculations automatically.

So, exactly what do you have to do to manage your project with Microsoft Project? To create a schedule in Microsoft Project, you must enter the following information about your tasks:

- Individual task names
- Task durations
- Task dependencies

To track the costs of those tasks, you add certain information about resources, including:

- The list of human and material resources and their costs for both standard and overtime hours
- The assignment of resources to specific tasks

To track a project over its lifetime, you need to enter this information:

- Progress on tasks
- Changes in task timing or dependencies
- Changes in resources — that is, resources that are added to or removed from the project
- Changes in resource time commitments and costs

## What Microsoft Project can do to help

Even though you still must enter a great deal of information into your project schedule, Microsoft Project has various shortcuts that can help you automate this chore.

- **Project templates.** If you often do similar types of projects, you can create project templates with typical project tasks already in place; you can then modify the templates for individual projects.

You can take advantage of sample project templates on this book's companion CD-ROM. These templates represent a cross section of typical industries and project types.

✦ **Automating repeated tasks.** If you have tasks that repeat throughout the life of a project, such as weekly meetings or regular reviews, you can create a single repeating task and Project will duplicate it for you.

✦ **Workgroup tracking.** You can use workgroup features that enable individual team members to enter and track progress on smaller pieces of the project. By tracking in this way, no individual person has an overwhelming amount of data entry to do. Also, team members feel more accountable and involved in the project.

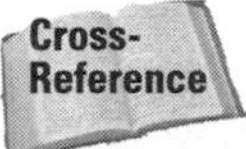


See the chapters in Part V of this book, "Working in Groups," for detailed information on working in groups.

✦ **Macros.** You can take advantage of Microsoft's Visual Basic language to build macros that automate repetitive tasks, such as generating weekly reports.

See Chapter 19 for more information on using macros to speed your work.

# The Life Cycle of a Project

Projects typically consist of several phases. Understanding the nature of each phase can help you to relate the features of Microsoft Project to your own projects.

## Identifying your goal and the project's scope

Before you can even begin to plan a project, you have to identify the goal, which isn't always as obvious as it sounds. Various participants may define a project's goal differently. In fact, many projects fail because the team members are really working toward different goals without realizing it. For example, is the goal to perform a productivity study, or to actually improve productivity? Is the outcome for your project to agree on the final building design, or is it to complete the actual construction of the building? As you analyze your goal and factor in the perspectives of other team members, make sure that your project isn't actually just one step in a series of projects to reach a larger, longer-term goal.

To identify your goal, you can use various communication tools, such as meetings, e-mail, and conference calls. The important thing is to conduct a dialogue at various levels (management through front-line personnel) that gets ideas on the table and answers questions. Take the time to write a goal statement and circulate it among the team members to make sure that everyone understands the common focus of the project.

Be careful not to set a long-range goal that is likely to change before the project ends. Smaller projects or projects broken into various phases are more manageable and more flexible.

After you understand your goal, you should also gather the information you need to define the project's scope. This endeavor may take some research on your part. The scope of a project is a statement of more specific parameters or constraints for its completion. Project constraints usually fall within the areas of time, quality, and cost, and they often relate directly to project deliverables.

Here are some sample goal and scope statements:

### Project A:

- **Goal:** To locate a facility for our warehouse.
- **Scope:** By October 15, to find a modern warehouse facility of approximately 5,200 square feet, with a lease cost of no more than $3,000 per month, in a location convenient to our main office.

### Project B:

- **Goal:** To launch a new cleaning product.
- **Scope:** Includes test marketing the product, designing packaging, and creating and launching an advertising campaign. The launch must be completed before the end of the third quarter of 1999 and must cost no more than $750,000.

Notice that the second scope statement designates major phases of the project (test marketing, designing packaging and an ad campaign); the statement provides a starting point for planning the tasks in the project. In fact, you might eventually decide to break this project into smaller projects of test marketing, designing packaging, and launching an advertising campaign. Writing out the scope of the project may encourage you to redefine both the goal and scope to make the project more manageable.

Keep your goal and scope statements short and to the point. If you can't explain your goal or scope in a sentence or two, then your project may be overly ambitious and complex. Consider breaking it into smaller projects.

Writing a simple goal and scope statement ensures that you've gathered key data—such as deliverables, timing, and budget—and that you and your team agree on the focus of everyone's efforts. These activities are likely to occur before you ever open a Microsoft Project file.

## Planning

When you understand the goal and scope of a project, you can begin to work backwards to determine the steps you need to take to reach the goal. Look for major phases first. Then break each phase into a logical sequence of steps.

Planning for resources is one aspect of planning the entire project. Resources can include equipment of limited availability, materials, individual workers, and groups of workers. Take into account various schedules and issues such as overtime, vacations, and shared resources between projects. Time, money, and resources are closely related: You can save time with more resources, but resources typically cost money. You need to understand the order of priority among time, quality, and money.

**Note**

There's truth to the old joke: Time, budget, or quality—pick two. Throwing resources (which usually become costs) at a schedule can shorten the time but can also cause loss of quality control. Stretching out the time can improve quality but usually causes resource conflicts and added costs. Microsoft Project helps you see the tradeoffs among these three important criteria throughout the life of your project.

Planning is the point at which you begin to enter data in Microsoft Project and see your project take shape. Figure 1-6 shows an initial Microsoft Project schedule.

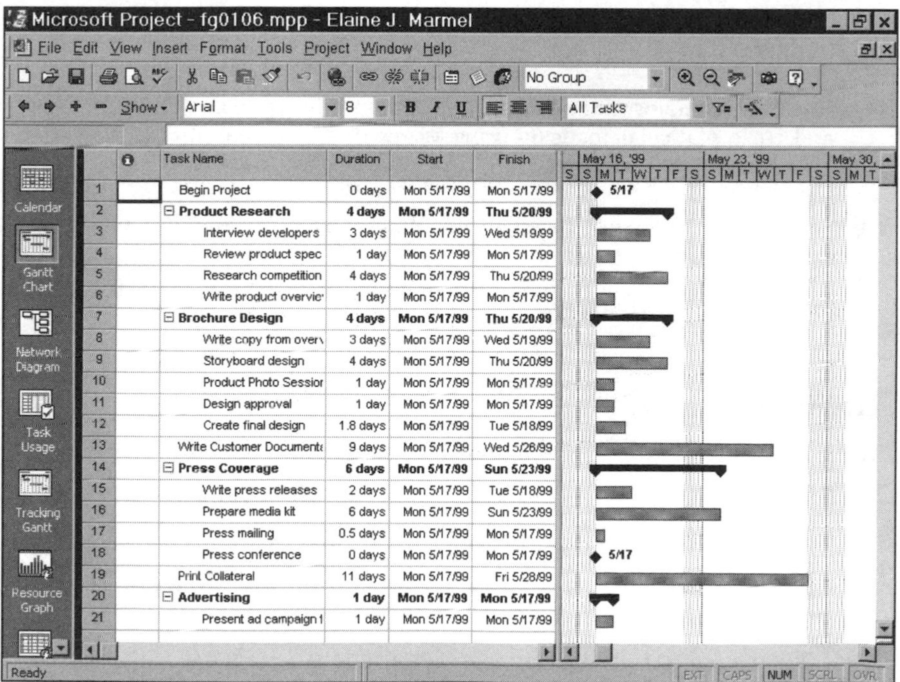


**Figure 1-6:** The outline format of a Project schedule clearly shows the various phases of your project. Notice that dependencies among tasks have not yet been established.

## Revising

Most of the time, you send an initial project schedule to various managers or coworkers for approval or input so that you can refine it based on different factors. You can use the reporting features of Microsoft Project to generate several drafts of your plan.

Be prepared to revise your plan after everyone has a chance to review it. You might want to create and save multiple Project files to generate what-if scenarios based on the input you receive. Seeing your plans from various perspectives is a great way to take advantage of Project's power.

Finding resolutions to conflicts in timing and resource allocation is another aspect of planning and revising. Project helps you pinpoint these conflicts. For example:

- ✦ A team member or resource booked on several projects at once
- ✦ A task beginning before another task that must precede it
- ✦ Unusually high use of expensive equipment in one phase that is throwing your budget out of whack

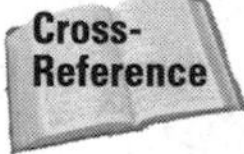


This book contains many tricks and techniques for resolving conflicts. Chapters 9 and 10, in particular, focus on using Microsoft Project features to resolve scheduling and resource problems.

When your project plan seems solid, you can take a picture of it, called a *baseline,* against which you can track actual progress.

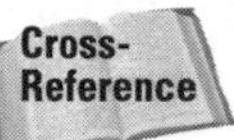


Chapter 11 explains how to set — and, if necessary, clear — baselines.

## Tracking

You should try to determine your tracking methods before your project ever begins:

- ✦ Do you want to track your progress once a week or once a month?
- ✦ Do project participants actually track their own work or merely report their progress to you?
- ✦ Do you want to roll those smaller reports into a single, less-detailed report for management?

Knowing how you will track your project's progress, and who needs to know what and when, helps your team establish efficient tracking mechanisms from the outset.

You can save interim baselines of a schedule at various points during your project. This approach helps you see where major shifts occurred and shows how you accommodated those shifts.

The Microsoft Project schedule in Figure 1-7 shows the original baseline tracked against actual progress.

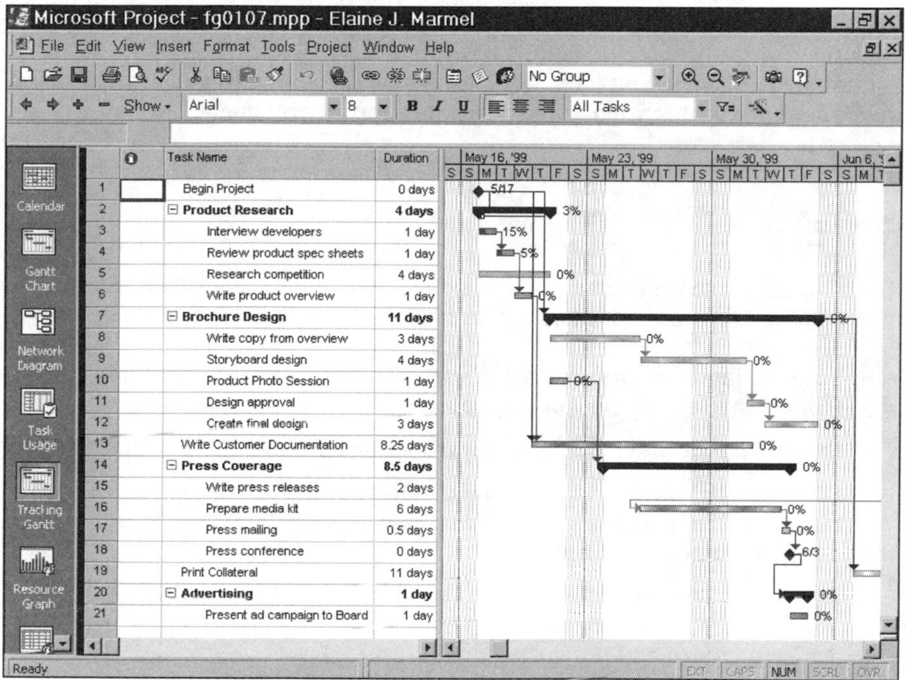


**Figure 1-7:** The darker portion of each bar and the percentage figure to the right of each bar indicate the percentage of each task that is complete.

## Learning from your mistakes

Learning project management software isn't like learning to use a word processor. Project management entails conceptual layers that transcend the tools and features of the software. Having the experience and wisdom to use these features effectively comes from repeated use. You probably won't be a proficient Microsoft Project user right out of the gate. You have to work through one or more projects before you really know the most effective way to enter information about your project. You can expect to develop efficient tracking methods over time. Don't worry: It took you time to learn all you know about managing projects. If you pay attention to what goes on during your projects when you first implement Microsoft Project schedules, you can learn from your mistakes.

Microsoft Project enables you to review your first few projects and see clearly where you estimated incorrectly, made adjustments too slowly, or didn't break phases into manageable chunks. Project keeps your original schedule's baseline in a single file along with your final tracked schedule. When planning future projects, you can use these older baselines to help gauge the duration of tasks, how much things cost, how many resources are too many resources, and how many resources aren't nearly enough.

In the end, you'll be a more successful and efficient project manager. You can easily show your boss the specific actions you've taken to avoid problems and provide solutions. In addition, you'll have the tools you need to help you and your manager understand the issues you face and get the support you need.

# Summary

This chapter presented a survey of the discipline known as project management and explained how project management software can help you manage projects.

- ✦ Projects involve a stated goal, a specific time frame, and multiple resources (which can include people, equipment, and materials).
- ✦ Project management seeks to control issues of time, quality, and money.
- ✦ Critical path, slack, task durations, milestones, fixed tasks, resource-driven tasks, and dependencies are project management elements that help you build and monitor a project.
- ✦ Project management software can assist you in planning, tracking, and communicating with team members and reporting on projects with tools such as Gantt charts and network diagrams.
- ✦ Although using Project takes some effort on your part, this effort pays off in increased productivity and efficiency.
- ✦ Projects typically have five phases: setting the goal and defining scope, planning, revising, tracking, and reviewing to learn from your mistakes.

Chapter 2 takes a closer look at the Project environment and provides information on some of the tools that you can use to manage a project.

✦ ✦ ✦

CHAPTER 2

# Exploring the Microsoft Project Environment

✦ ✦ ✦ ✦

**In This Chapter**

Taking a first look at Project

What's new in Project 2000

✦ ✦ ✦ ✦

Microsoft Project has come a long way in the past few years. It now sports an interface that makes managing a project almost as easy as maintaining your personal calendar. If you're a user of other Microsoft products, such as Word or Excel, the menus and tools in Project will, happily, look like old friends. And although Project's many views can be a bit overwhelming at first, they enable you to choose the perspective you need to monitor the progress of your project at any given time.

This chapter introduces Project's environment as well as the powerful tools Project puts at your disposal. You practice moving among different views and work with some of the tools and onscreen elements that you can use to create schedules.

## Taking a First Look at Project

Although Microsoft Project doesn't come with Microsoft Office software, it is a member of the Microsoft Office family. Consequently, Project uses the standard Microsoft Office menu and toolbar structure and contains some of the familiar Microsoft Office tools.

If you've used Outlook, Microsoft's organizer and calendar program, you'll recognize several features of Project, including the bar on the left of the screen that enables you to switch among views and functions in the software. Project calls this feature the *View bar.*

## Starting Project

The first time you choose Microsoft Project from the Programs section of the Windows Start menu, Project displays both Project and the new Help system on the right side of the screen (see Figure 2-1). This particular help topic offers some useful choices for the user who is new to Project software or to this version of Project.

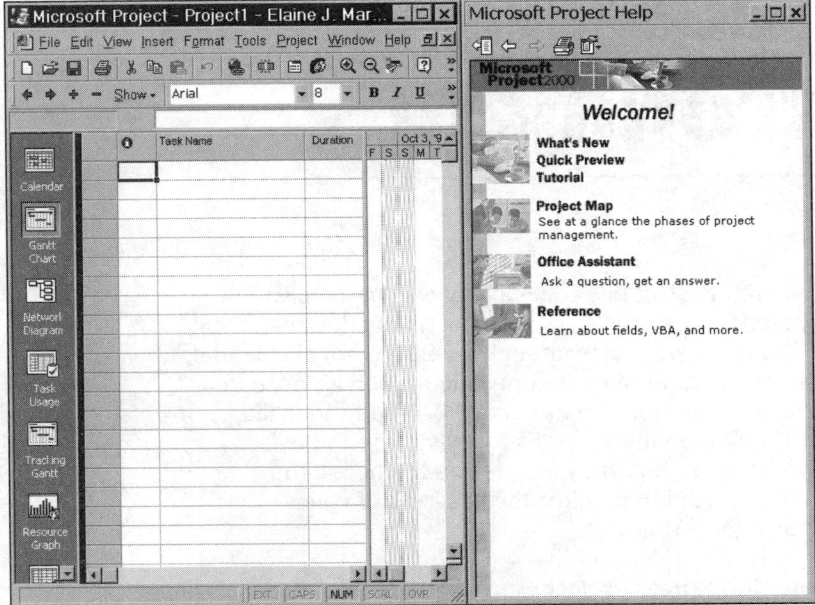


**Figure 2-1:** Project uses the new HTML-based Help system you'll also find in Office 2000.

If Project does not appear on your Windows Start menu, you can use the Run command on the Start menu. Run the file Winproj.exe, which is found in the Microsoft Project folder on your hard drive. You can also open Project by double-clicking a project file in a directory contained in the My Computer area. Project files are saved with the extension .mpp.

At this point you have the following possible actions:

- ✦ **What's New.** Select this to see information about the new features in Project 2000.
- ✦ **Quick Preview.** Select this to see a quick, visual depiction of the electronic project management process.
- ✦ **Tutorial.** Select this to see a demonstration of major Project features.

- ✦ **Project Map.** Select this to display a map of the steps typically involved in managing a project.
- ✦ **Office Assistant.** Select this to display the animated character that you can ask questions of and get help from about Microsoft Project.
- ✦ **Reference.** Select this to view a wide variety of source material, such as troubleshooting information; mouse and keyboard shortcuts; developer information on resource, assignment, task, and time-phased fields; and Visual Basic for Applications and Microsoft Project.

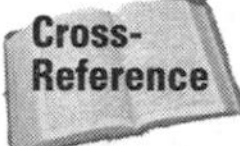


Chapter 3 covers Help options in greater detail.

- ✦ **Help Close button.** You can choose not to take advantage of any of these options and proceed to a new, blank Project schedule by clicking the Close button in the top-right corner of the Help window. When you do, you see a blank project, as shown in Figure 2-2.

You can redisplay this window any time by choosing Help ➪ Contents and Index. In addition, you can view the Quick Preview, the Tutorial, and the Project Map by choosing Help ➪ Getting Started.

In Project 2000, you'll find a fill handle in most table views. You can use the fill handle to populate columns, just as you use a fill handle in Excel.

Project always opens a new project schedule in the Gantt view. You see other views throughout this book, but you're likely to spend a great deal of your time in the Gantt view. This view offers a wealth of information about your project in a single snapshot.

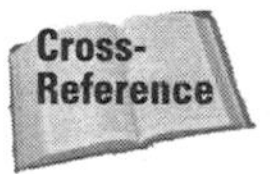


For a detailed look at the other views available in Project, see Chapter 6.

In Project 2000, you'll find a significantly increased number of screen tips. Point and pause at almost any screen part, and Project displays a screen tip and a link to a Help topic (see Figure 2-3).

## Examining the Gantt Chart view

The Gantt Chart view has two main sections: the Gantt table and the Gantt chart. After you enter task information, the Gantt table (in the left pane) holds columns of information about your project, such as task name, duration, start date, and more. The Gantt chart (in the right pane) is a graphic representation that helps you see the timing and relationships among tasks, as shown in Figure 2-4.

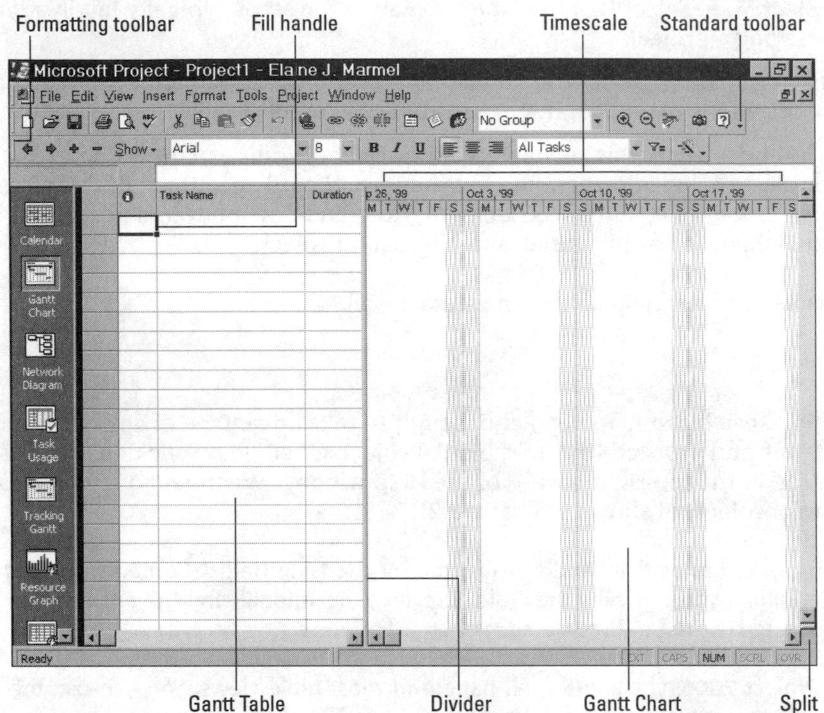


**Figure 2-2:** A blank project contains no project information; when you enter information in the Gantt view, the split pane displays the data both textually and graphically.

The timescale along the top of the Gantt chart acts like a horizontal calendar. Think of it as a ruler against which you draw the tasks in your project. However, instead of marking off inches, this ruler marks off the hours, days, weeks, and months of your project. Notice that the chart displays two timescales: the major timescale along the top and a minor timescale beneath it. These two timescales help you see two levels of timing at once, such as the day and hour or the week and day.

You can customize your timescale to show unusual time increments, such as thirds of months, or make the timescale display larger on your screen. In Figure 2-3, I customized the timescale to show week increments. Double-click the timescale itself to display the Timescale dialog box. You can adjust these and other settings for the major and minor timescale on the Timescale tab. Also note that Project uses default settings for the number of hours in a workday, days in a week, and so on. To adjust these settings to display or hide nonworking days, you can use the settings on the Nonworking Time tab in the Timescale dialog box. In Chapter 3, I explain how to modify the calendars that control a project.

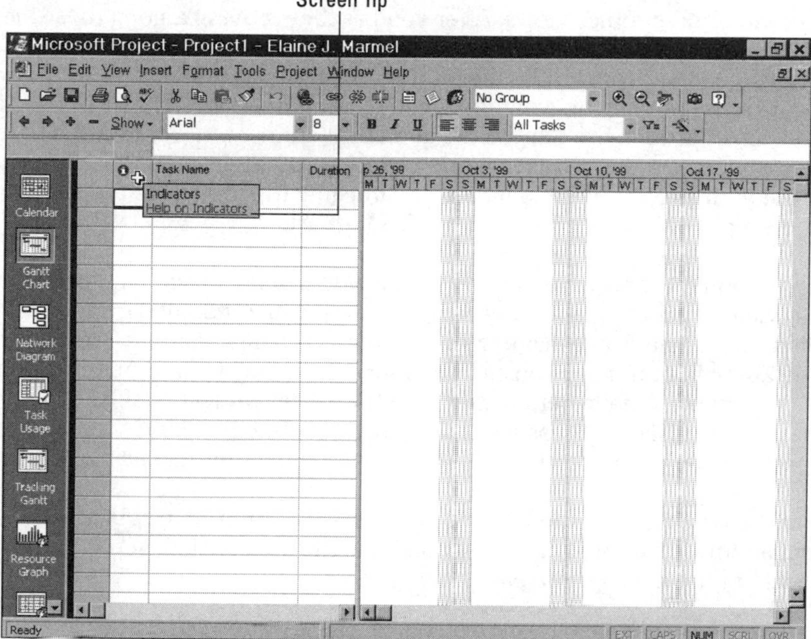


Figure 2-3: New screen tips in Project 2000 provide more help.

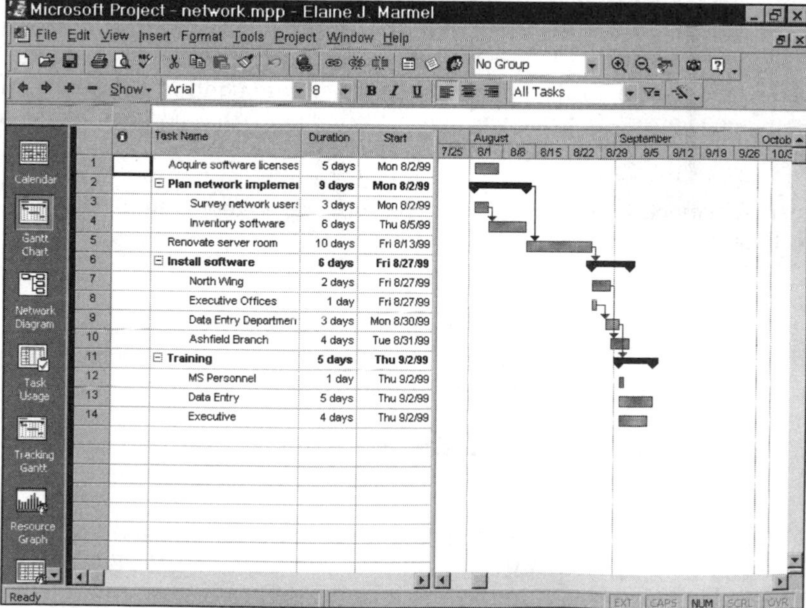


Figure 2-4: A sample project with task details in the Gantt table and bars representing tasks in the Gantt chart.

One of Project's strong points is that it enables you to modify what you see onscreen in the Gantt view and in other views. After you practice moving among these views, you'll be able to see information about timing, budget, or resource assignments in detail, or you can look at just the big picture. You can also customize what each view shows you, depending on what you need to see. For example, you can use the divider that runs between the Gantt table and Gantt chart to adjust how much of the window each pane occupies. Dragging this divider to the right reveals more columns of data about your project in the Gantt table. Dragging the divider to the left displays more of the task bars in your project in the Gantt chart.

In addition to modifying how much of each pane you display onscreen, you can zoom in or out to view larger or smaller time increments, seeing different perspectives of your project's schedule. You can show smaller time increments in the Gantt chart by clicking the Zoom In button, or you can show larger increments of time by clicking the Zoom Out button. A daily perspective on a three-year project enables you to manage day-to-day tasks, whereas a quarterly representation of your project might be more useful when you're discussing larger issues with your management team.

Notice that the two panes of the Gantt Chart view have their own sets of scroll bars. To perform actions on information, you must use the appropriate scroll bar and select objects in the appropriate pane.

## Using Project menus

Project's menus now work like Office 2000 product menus; commands are available "on demand." That is, when you open a menu, you'll see a small subset of commands that Microsoft believes you'll use most often. In addition, at the bottom of the menu, you'll see a pair of arrows (see Figure 2-5). If you highlight the pair of arrows (or pause for a few moments), Project displays the other commands that usually appear on the menu (see Figure 2-6). Once you select a command, that command appears on the menu as soon as you open the menu.

On demand menus (described in this section) are a new feature of Microsoft Project 2000.

You can change this menu behavior to the menu behavior of previous versions of Project, in which all commands appeared on a menu when you opened the menu. To do this, use the Customize dialog box.

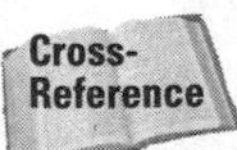


The Customize dialog box is described in detail in Chapter 18.

Several of Project's menus, accessed through the menu bar at the top of the screen, offer commands that are probably quite familiar to you, such as Save, Print, and Copy. Other menus on the menu bar are very specific to the tasks you perform with Project.

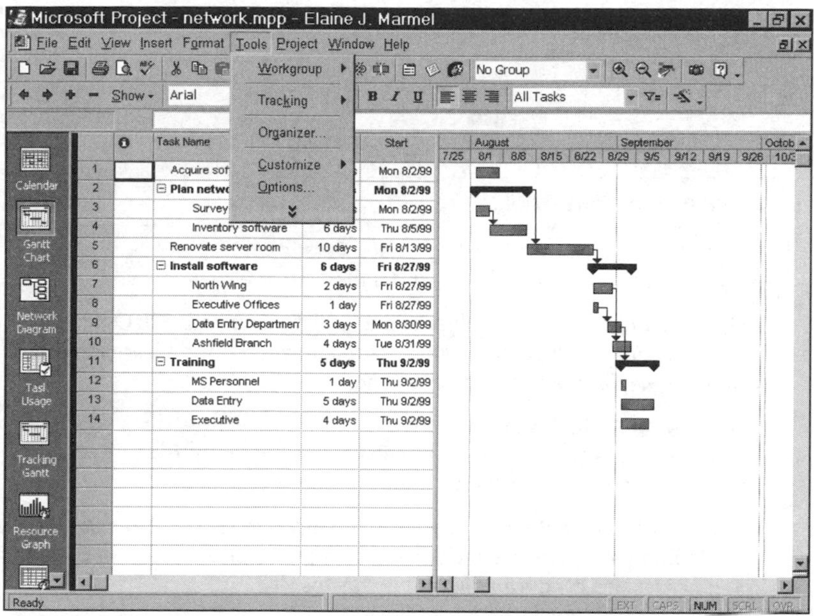

**Figure 2-5:** Initially, only a subset of commands appears on a menu.

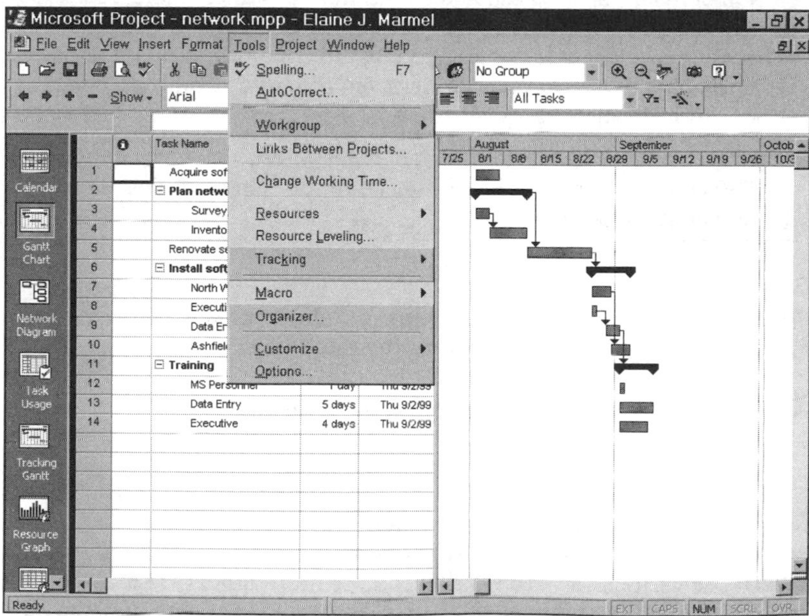

**Figure 2-6:** When you pause or click the down arrow at the bottom of the menu, the rest of the menu commands appear.

Table 2-1 shows the various types of functions you can perform from each menu.

**Table 2-1**
**Microsoft Project Menus**

| *Menu* | *Types of Functions Available* |
|---|---|
| File | Open and close new and existing files, save and print files, adjust page setup and document properties, and route files to e-mail recipients. |
| Edit | Cut, copy, and paste text or objects; manipulate data with Fill, Clear, and Delete commands; link and unlink task relationships; and locate information with Find, Replace, and Go To commands. |
| View | Select various default views of your project, access standard report formats, choose to display or hide various toolbars, use the Zoom feature, or enter header and footer information. |
| Insert | Insert new tasks, another Project file, or columns in views; also insert various objects into your schedule, including drawings, Excel charts, Word documents, media clips, and even hyperlinks to Web sites. |
| Format | Adjust the appearance of text, task bars, the Timescale display, or the overall appearance of a view's layout. |
| Tools | Run or modify Spelling and AutoCorrect functions to proofread your schedule, access workgroup features, establish links between projects, and modify your working calendar or resources. You can also customize standard views and functions with the Organizer, Options, or Customize commands, or record macros and initiate tracking functions. |
| Project | Display task or project information or notes, or use commands to sort or filter tasks to see specific details. You can also control outlining features of your project tasks from here. |

The remaining two menus, Window and Help, contain commands to arrange windows onscreen and access Help features, respectively.

See Chapter 3 for more information on Project's Help system.

As you can see in Figure 2-7, Microsoft has placed corresponding tool symbols and keyboard shortcuts (such as Del or Ctrl+F) next to the menu commands. This display helps you learn the various ways to get things done more quickly in Project. Notice also that the main menus sometimes open up side menus (also called *submenus* or *cascading menus)*. A black arrow to the right of a command indicates the presence of a side menu.

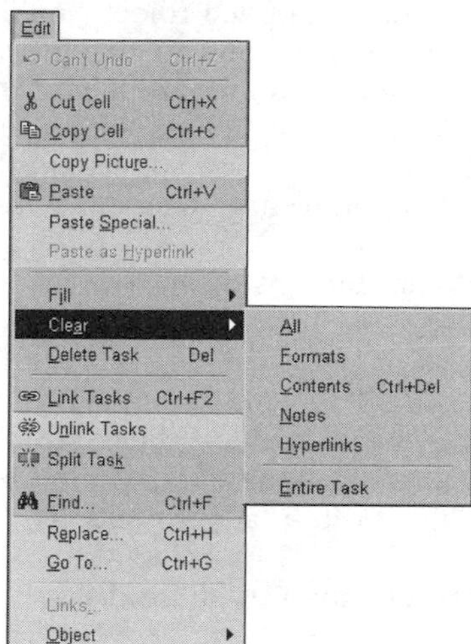


**Figure 2-7:** Tool symbols appear to the left and keyboard shortcuts to the right of commands on Project menus. Side menus offer more choices.

# Examining the toolbars

You're probably already familiar with tools in Windows programs and the way in which they appear by category on toolbars. When you open Project, two default toolbars are visible: the Standard toolbar and the Formatting toolbar, as seen in Figure 2-8.

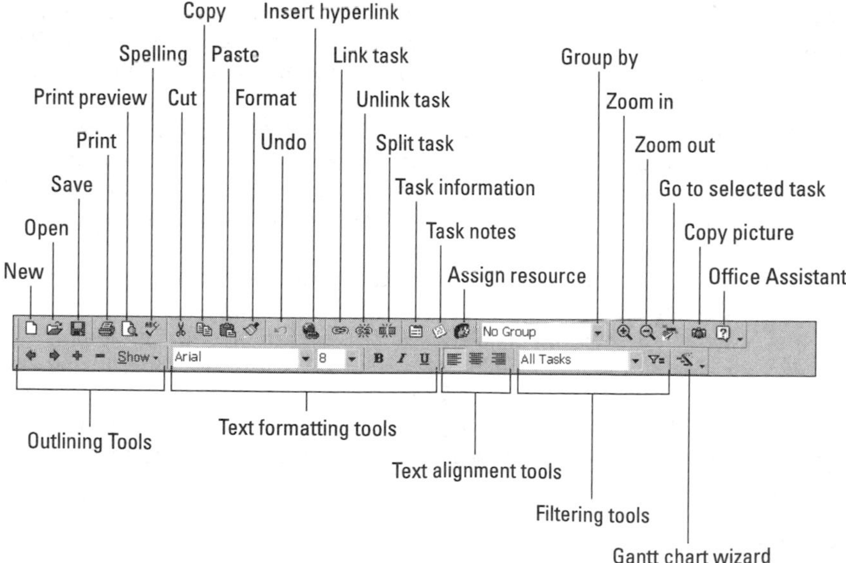


**Figure 2-8:** The Standard toolbar and the Formatting toolbar are Project's default toolbars.

You may see both toolbars appearing on one row when you open Project; you'll also notice that you don't see all the tools displayed in Figure 2-8. You can change the appearance so that the toolbars appear on two rows, as I've done throughout this book. If you choose to keep both toolbars on one row, you can access the buttons that don't appear by clicking the More Buttons down arrow, which appears at the end of each toolbar, and then clicking the button that you want to use.

A screen tip appears to help you identify the More Buttons down arrow if you point at the More Buttons down arrow and pause.

Depending on your operating environment, you may be able to use the Customize dialog box to make Project toolbars operate like Office 2000 toolbars, where they appear on one line and only the buttons you use "most often" appear initially.

To change the appearance of Project's toolbars, use the Customize dialog box, which I discuss in Chapter 18.

In some software programs, the tools available to you are context sensitive; that is, they change according to the function you're performing. In Project, the default toolbars are fairly consistent. Some tools become unavailable when you perform different functions or change views; in such cases, the tools appear grayed out, and nothing happens when you click them.

If you insert an object from another Microsoft application, such as Excel or PowerPoint, into your project, the other program's environment replaces Project's toolbars and menus when you select that object. Therefore, you can use the other program's tools to modify the object without having to leave Project. Project toolbars and menus reappear when you click anywhere outside the inserted object.

In addition to the Standard and Formatting toolbars, Project contains several other toolbars, which sometimes appear automatically when you're performing certain types of activities. However, you can also display any of these toolbars at any time by choosing View ➪ Toolbars and choosing from the toolbar side menu.

These toolbars appear as floating toolbars when you choose to display them. You can move floating toolbars anywhere on your screen by dragging them. To move a toolbar, drag its title bar. Alternatively, you can anchor any floating toolbar at the top of your screen near the default toolbars; simply drag the toolbar (using its title bar) to the top of the screen. Conversely, you can convert the Standard and Formatting toolbars into floating toolbars; just click anywhere on a toolbar (not directly on a tool, however) and drag it to any position on your screen.

## Entering information

Several views or portions of views in Project, such as the Gantt table, use a familiar spreadsheet-style interface. Information appears in columns and rows. The intersection of a column and a row is an individual cell. Each task in your project has an ID number, indicated by the numbers that run down the left of the spreadsheet. You can enter information either in dialog boxes (see Chapter 4) or directly into cells. When you select a cell, the Entry bar displays the information in the cell.

Project 2000 uses "in-cell" entry and editing.

If you've ever used Microsoft Excel or other popular spreadsheet programs, you already know how to enter and edit information in Project. When you begin typing in a cell, the insertion point appears in the cell to the right of any text you enter. To edit text in a cell, click once to select the cell; then, press F2 or click a second time at the location in the cell where you want to begin editing. The insertion point appears at the right edge of the text in the cell if you pressed F2; if you click a second time, the insertion point appears in the cell at the location where you clicked the second time.

As you enter information into a cell, the information also appears in the Entry bar, which runs along the top of the screen, directly under the Formatting toolbar. The Entry bar in Project serves the same purpose as the Entry bar in Excel. You can type new text or edit existing text by clicking anywhere within the text in the Entry bar. Two buttons on the left of the bar enable you to cancel or accept an entry (see Figure 2-9).

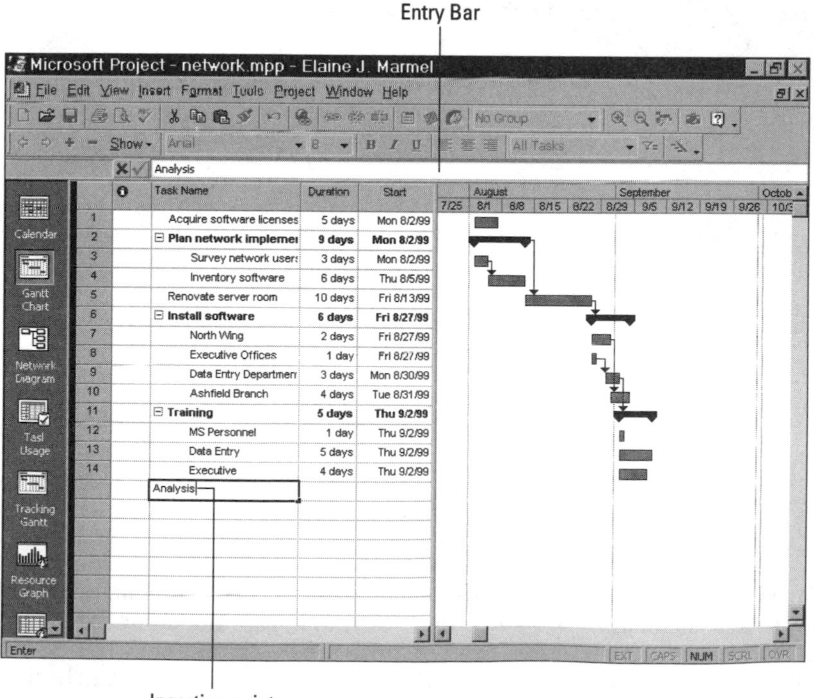


**Figure 2-9:** You can enter or edit text in individual cells or in the Entry bar.

Chapter 4 covers entering and editing text in greater detail.

## Changing views with the View bar

Project offers multiple views in which you can display project information. A single view cannot possibly show all the information you need about timing, relationships among tasks, resource allocations, and project progress; in fact, each type of information requires special kinds of graphical and textual displays for you to interpret them accurately. Think of a project as a small business. As in any business, different people attend to various aspects of the work. The accounting department thinks mainly of the costs of doing business. The plant supervisor focuses on deadlines and having enough machinery to get the job done. Your human resources department thinks of people: their salaries, hours, benefits, and so on. As the owner of your project, you are likely to wear all these hats and more during the project. Rather than changing caps as you move from one responsibility to another, in Project you simply switch to another view to see your work from a different perspective. Each view helps you focus on a different aspect of your project. The View bar shown in Figure 2-10 enables you to jump from view to view.

**Figure 2-10:** The View bar offers several predefined views of your project.

The View bar contains icons for eight views; click the down arrow near the bottom of the bar to see them all. When you move down the View bar, an up arrow appears near the top of the bar so that you can return to the top of the View bar. You can display any of the views listed here by clicking it in the View bar. At the bottom of the View bar is an item called More Views. Click More Views to open the More Views dialog box, shown in Figure 2-11.

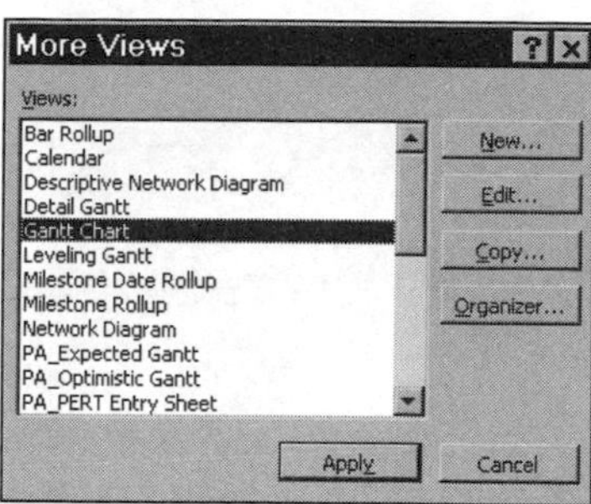


**Figure 2-11:** The More Views dialog box lists 24 built-in views — and you can add your own as well.

In Chapter 6, you learn more about which view you should use to gain a specific perspective on your project. You also can create custom views by clicking New in the More Views dialog box (see Chapter 7).

# What's New in Project 2000

Rather than describe all the new features in Project 2000 here, I'm going to describe just a few — and then provide a table that shows you where you can find more information in this book on other new features.

You can easily find the new features in the chapters in which I discuss them. Simply look for the New Feature icon that appears next to this paragraph.

As I mentioned earlier, Project is not part of Office 2000, but Project is part of the Office family. For this reason, the goals for this upgrade to Project bear a strong resemblance to the goals for Office 2000, and Project shares the approach used in Office 2000 to meet these goals, which are detailed in the following list:

- ✦ First, Microsoft wanted users to be able to easily share information and collaborate online. For this reason, you can save any Project file (or any Office document) in HTML format so that you can share the file with anyone who has a Web browser. You'll find a new Save As Web Page command on the File menu (see Figure 2-12). You'll also find that you can use Project to edit Web pages created in Project — without losing formatting or functionality.

- ✦ To decrease installation and deployment costs, Microsoft has created the Windows Installer, which enables Information Technology (IT) departments to easily customize installations. The Windows Installer enables you to identify features you want to "install on demand." A command appears on a menu but, when the user chooses the command, a dialog box appears, stating that the feature isn't currently installed and providing the user with the option of installing the feature. Typically, features such as templates fall into the "install on demand" category. In addition, IT departments can customize installation so that features run from a local hard disk, a server, or a terminal server.

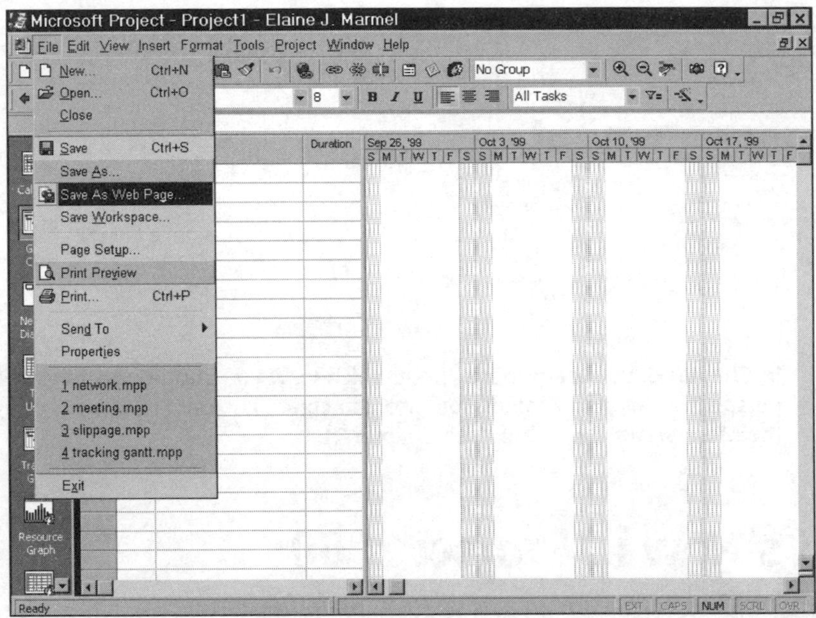


**Figure 2-12:** You can easily share a Project file with anyone who has a Web browser by saving the file as a Web page.

✦ To decrease administrative costs, Project 2000 and Office 2000 support the *roaming user*—a user's profile (documents, Desktop, and application settings) follow him as he moves from machine to machine in the corporate network. One caveat here: a user can roam between Windows 9*x* machines or Windows NT/2000 machines, but her profile will not follow her if she crosses operating system platforms.

✦ To decrease end-user support costs, Project 2000 and Office 2000 applications are self-repairing; that is, they can detect if essential files or registry entries are missing or corrupted, and they will reinstall the necessary files or registry entries. You'll also find a Detect and Repair command on the Help menu that you can run to "fix" a problem application.

✦ Project 2000 sports a new database format that supports SQL 7, Access 2000, and Oracle 6 and eliminates the MPX file format. However, to keep the total cost of ownership down, you can save Project 2000 files in Project 98 format. Therefore, an organization does *not* need to upgrade everyone at the same time because users can share files; you can set Project 2000's Save command to automatically save files in Project 98 file format.

✦ To increase international support, Microsoft has simplified worldwide deployment by creating a single executable that can be used for the United States, Europe, the Far East, and countries that use bidirectional languages such as Hebrew and Arabic.

✦ Project shares one other Office 2000 feature: adaptive menus and toolbars. You've already seen how these work earlier in this chapter. Commands don't appear on menus when you first open the menu; after a short delay or if you point at the double arrows on the bottom of the menu, all commands appear. If you choose a command that didn't appear initially, it will appear initially the next time that you open the menu.

Table 2-2 provides a list of other new features in Project — and the chapter in which you can find information about the new feature.

Table 2-2
**New Features in Project 2000**

| *Feature* | *Chapter* |
|---|---|
| In-cell editing | 2 |
| Fill handle | 2 |
| Number (and renumber) tasks | 3 |
| Outline numbering | 7 |
| WBS numbering | 7 |
| Set a project priority | 3 |
| Setting task calendars | 3 |
| AutoSave | 3 |
| Set deadline dates | 4 |
| Set estimated duration | 4 |
| Month duration unit | 4 |
| Material resources | 5 |
| Network Diagram view | 6 |
| New Rollup behavior | 6 |
| Custom Field enhancements | 18 |
| Grouping | 7 |
| Variable row height | 7 |
| Contoured availability | 10 |
| Leveling improvements | 10 |
| Clearing the baseline | 11 |
| Fiscal year available in timescale | 6 |
| Project Central & Project Central Server | 16 |
| Master calculation of subprojects | 17 |

# Summary

This chapter introduced the Project environment and the many ways in which you can display project information. The chapter described the following techniques:

- ✦ Understanding the Project screen
- ✦ Using Project menus and toolbars
- ✦ Entering information in your project

Chapter 3 covers how to get help in Project and how to save Project files.

✦ ✦ ✦

P A R T

# II

# Getting Your Project Going

✦ ✦ ✦ ✦

## In This Part



✦ ✦ ✦ ✦

# Creating a New Project

✦ ✦ ✦ ✦

**In This Chapter**



✦ ✦ ✦ ✦

Now that you have some project management concepts under your belt and you've taken a stroll around Project's environment, you are ready to create your first schedule. Before you type even a date into a Project schedule, first assemble the relevant information about your project. Then you can open a new Project file and begin to build your project tasks using a simple outline structure.

In this chapter you begin to build your first Project schedule and learn how to take advantage of Project's various Help features. At the end of the chapter, you learn how to save your project.

## Gathering Information

As you learned in Chapter 1, several elements must be in place before you can begin to build a project schedule. First, you must understand the overall goal and scope of the project so that you can clearly see the steps that lie between you and that goal. You'll find delineating the major steps involved a good place to start. Don't worry about the order of the tasks at this point — just brainstorm all the major areas of activity. For example, take a project such as organizing an annual meeting for your company. Here are some possible steps:

- Book the meeting space
- Schedule speakers
- Arrange for audiovisual equipment
- Order food
- Send out invitations
- Mail out annual reports

Now that last item brings up the question of scope: Is it within the scope of your project to create the annual report or simply to obtain copies from, say, the marketing department, and mail them out to stockholders before the meeting? In some corporations, the person responsible for organizing the annual meeting is also responsible for overseeing the production of the annual report. Be sure you answer these questions of scope and responsibility at this stage of your planning.

For this example, you can assume that another department is creating the annual report. You simply need to make sure that someone mails copies of the report to all stockholders before the annual meeting.

## Determining detail tasks

After you have prepared a list of major tasks, break them down into more detailed tasks. Take one of the items on the list — "Order food," for example — and consider how you can break down this task. How detailed should you get? Here's one possible breakdown of the "Order food" task:

### Order food

- ✦ Create a budget
- ✦ Determine a menu
- ✦ Select a caterer
  - Send out requests for bids
  - All estimates received
  - Review estimates and award contract
- ✦ Final headcount to caterer
- ✦ Confirm caterer one week ahead

Could you do without the detailed tasks under Select a caterer? Do you need more detail under Create a budget? Those decisions are up to you, based on your knowledge of your project and procedures. However, here are some points to keep in mind:

- ✦ Create tasks that remind you of major action items, but don't overburden yourself with items of such detail that keeping track of your schedule becomes a full-time job. That's the purpose of daily to-do lists.
- ✦ Include milestones to mark off points in your project. For example, the "Review estimates and reward contract" task under the summary task "Select a caterer" is a milestone — it marks a point in time by which you want to have made a major decision. If that time comes and goes and you haven't selected the caterer, will missing the deadline affect other subsequent tasks? If so, including that milestone could be vital to your success.

- Include tasks that management will want to know about because you'll use the Project schedule to report progress. If your boss wants to see that you've sent out a purchase order to the caterer per your new Accounting department procedures, you might want to include the task, even if you don't think that level of detail is important.

## Establishing time limits

Once you have an idea of the tasks involved in your project, you need to have some idea of their timing. Should you allow two weeks for caterers to come back with bids? Not if you have only three weeks to organize the meeting. You might approach determining task timing by building an initial schedule in Project, assigning time to tasks, and seeing how close you can come to your deadline. If you're way off, you can go back and tweak the timing for individual tasks until your schedule works.

You might be tempted to trim time off your tasks to make them fit a deadline, but this approach can produce an unrealistic schedule. The solution? Use the initial schedule to convince your boss that you need more time, money, or resources to complete this project on time. If he or she wants to trim time from a specific task to meet the deadline, you may have grounds to ask for more help.

At this early planning stage, get any information you need to assign timing to tasks; for example, contact vendors or subcontractors to get their timing estimates, which you need to reflect in your schedule. If your project has a drop-dead completion date, you should be aware of it. However, leave it to Project to show you whether your estimates work in an overall schedule.

## Lining up your resources

Before you can build a Project schedule, you must understand what resources are available to you as well as their costs. You don't necessarily have to know these resources by name, but you should know that your project needs three engineers at a cost of $75 per hour and one piece of earth-moving equipment at a daily rental cost of $450, for example.

You need to identify these resources and assign them to individual tasks early in the project-planning process. Find out anything you can about the availability of these resources: Are some resources available only half-time for your project? Will all of the engineers be unavailable during the third week of August because of a professional conference? Research the cost and availability of resources as much as possible as you begin to build a project.

For more information on identifying resources and assigning them to individual tasks, see Chapter 5.

### Looking at dependencies

Finally, before you enter project information into a schedule, be aware of relationships among tasks. Does the CEO have to approve the menu before you book the caterers? Are you required to wait three weeks after applying for a permit before starting construction on a building? If your project faces issues involving the order and relationships of tasks, you will save yourself some headaches down the line and build a more realistic schedule if you can identify these obstacles now.

## Opening a Project File

Okay, you've done your homework. You've made some notes about your upcoming project's tasks, timing, resources, and dependencies. You're ready to start building your first schedule in Project. On the Windows Start menu, highlight Programs, and then choose Microsoft Project to begin building a task outline.

When you first open Microsoft Project, Project Help appears down the right side of the screen, showing a Welcome screen. If you are building your first project, you might want to view the Quick Preview or glance at the Project Map, shown in Figure 3-1. This map shows you the logical order in which you can build a schedule; you can click various links in this window to get advice about project management and planning.

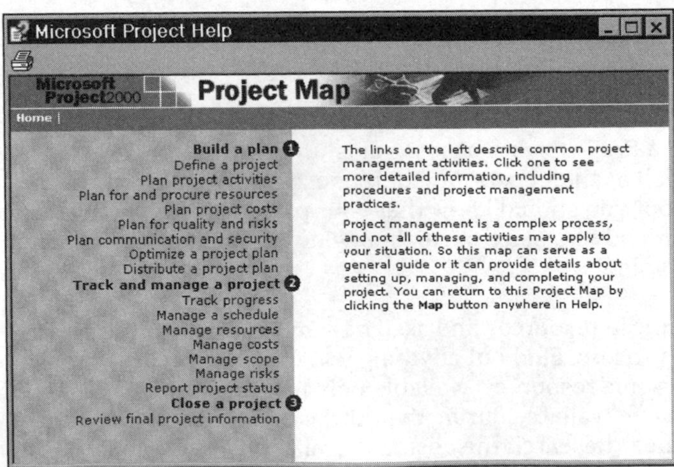


**Figure 3-1:** Click the links on the left to learn more about building a project in Project.

When you close the Welcome window (or any Help window), your screen displays a blank schedule. When you want to work with a schedule in Project, you have three options:

✦ You can open an existing Project file by choosing File ➪ Open.

✦ You can start a new Project file by choosing File ➪ New. Project displays the New dialog box, from which you can select a template on which to base your Project; or, you can choose Blank Project. When you click OK in the New dialog box, Project creates a new file for you and opens the Project Information dialog box.

Project 2000 enables you to base projects on templates. Templates contain "standard" information to help you get started quickly. Instead of entering tasks, you may need only to edit tasks. Choose File ➪ New and click the Project Templates tab to see the available templates.

✦ You can begin your new project using the blank schedule that Project opens for you when you first enter Project.

# Entering Project Information

With the blank schedule onscreen, choose Project ➪ Project Information to start defining your project. The Project Information dialog box shown in Figure 3-2 appears.

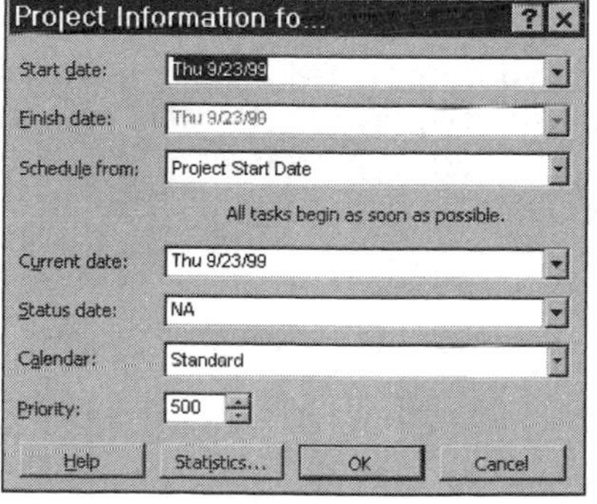


**Figure 3-2:** The Project Information dialog box is the starting point for every project.

The Project Information dialog box appears automatically whenever you start a new project.

You can enter seven pieces of information in the Project Information dialog box:

✦ **Start date.** If you set a start date for the project, all tasks begin on that date until you assign timing or dependencies to them.

✦ **Finish date.** If you know a final deadline, you can enter it here and then work backward to schedule your project. You must change the setting in the Schedule from field to make this option available.

✦ **Schedule from.** You can build schedules from completion to start by setting this field to Project Finish Date. Alternatively, you can build your schedule from the start date forward by accepting the default setting, Project Start Date.

✦ **Current date.** Project uses your computer clock for the default entry in this field. If you want to use a different date, change the date in this field. You can adjust this setting to generate reports that provide information on your project as of a certain date or to go back and track your project's progress from an earlier date.

✦ **Status date.** This field performs earned-value calculations and identifies the complete-through date in the Update Project dialog box; Status Date also enables Project to place progress lines in your project. If you leave the status date set at NA, Project sets the status date equal to the current date set on your computer clock and calendar.

✦ **Calendar.** You can select the calendar on which to base your schedule. The Standard calendar is the default — it schedules eight hours of work, five days a week.

In Project 2000, you can establish a priority for each project in addition to setting priorities for tasks.

✦ **Priority.** You can establish a priority for your project — a numerical value between 1 and 1,000. The project level priority plays a role when you use shared resources across multiple projects. Setting a project priority helps you better control how resource leveling adjusts tasks when you share resources across projects.

You should enter either a start or finish date, but not both. Only one will be available to you, depending on the choice you've made in the Schedule from field. To enter one of these dates, click the down arrow next to the text box. (The arrow is not available if the Schedule from field isn't set for that choice.) Select a date from the pop-up calendar, as shown in Figure 3-3.

If you decide to schedule backwards from the Finish date, Project cannot use tools such as resource leveling to resolve conflicts in your schedule.

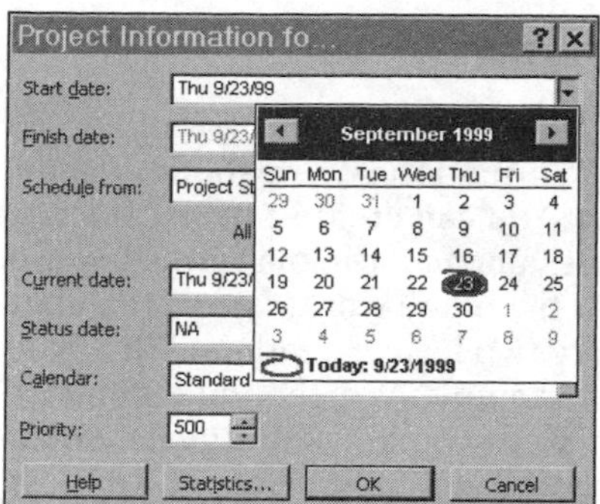


**Figure 3-3:** Use the arrow keys at the top of this calendar to choose other months.

You can change the project's start date during the planning phase, trying out alternative what-if scenarios by modifying this field. As you build your tasks going forward, Project indicates the finish date dictated by the length of your tasks and their timing relationships. When you're satisfied with the overall time frame, you can set the start date that works best when you're ready to begin.

If you have already begun the project, you can set the start date to a date in the past to accurately reflect the real start date. Tasks on the Gantt chart appear to have occurred before the current date line.

If you know the date by which something must be completed (as with the annual meeting project, for example, or a Christmas party that must happen on December 25), you can schedule tasks moving backward from the finish date. When you do so, Project builds the tasks going back in time. You might be surprised when Project generates a schedule telling you that you should have started three weeks earlier to finish in time. In that case, you can either add resources to get the work done faster or reduce the scope of the project.

In Chapters 9 and 10, you'll read about techniques that you can use to help you resolve scheduling and resource problems.

When beginning a new schedule, you would typically accept the default settings for Current date and Status date. Once your project is underway, changing these default settings affects project tracking and the material generated in project reports.

For now, you can leave all the default settings (that is, scheduling from the start of the project, having the current date be today, and starting the project today, as well as basing your schedule on the standard calendar). Click OK to close the Project Information dialog box.

# Looking at Project Calendars

The Project Information dialog box enables you to set the basic parameters of the project's timing. Those parameters and the information you're about to enter for specific tasks are based on the base calendar. You can create a base calendar for each group of resources in your project. For example, if the plant workers work a nine-hour day from 6:00 a.m. to 3:00 p.m. and the office workers work an eight-hour day from 8:00 a.m. to 5:00 p.m., you can create two base calendars. When you assign one day of an office worker's time, for example, Project understands it to be an eight-hour day. In the Project Information dialog box, you designate whether you want your project to use a standard, 24-hour, or Night Shift calendar for most of your work assignments.

In Project 2000, you can also establish task calendars.

Project also supports resource calendars and task calendars in which you can set exceptions to base calendars for specific resources or tasks in your project whose work hours are different from the rest of the resources or tasks.

You learn more about task calendars in Chapter 4 and resource calendars in Chapter 5.

## Setting calendar options

Project makes default assumptions about certain items that form the basis for the default base calendar (or the project calendar). For example, Project assumes that the default week contains 5 working days and 40 working hours. Project uses this calendar for resources unless you assign a different calendar to them. You can see Project's assumptions — and change them if necessary — in the Options dialog box.

To customize the standard calendar to your own working schedule, choose Tools ➪ Options. Select the Calendar tab in the Options dialog box (see Figure 3-4).

Caution

Any changes you make to these options apply to the current schedule only. To save your changes across all schedules, click the Set as Default button on the Calendar tab.

You can select any day of the week as your start day. For example, if you run a restaurant that closes on Sundays and Mondays, you might want to designate a work week of Tuesday through Saturday. In that case you would set the Week starts on field to Tuesday.

If your company uses a fiscal year other than the calendar year (January through December), you may want to set the Fiscal year starts in option. This setting is especially useful when you generate reports showing costs per quarter or year.

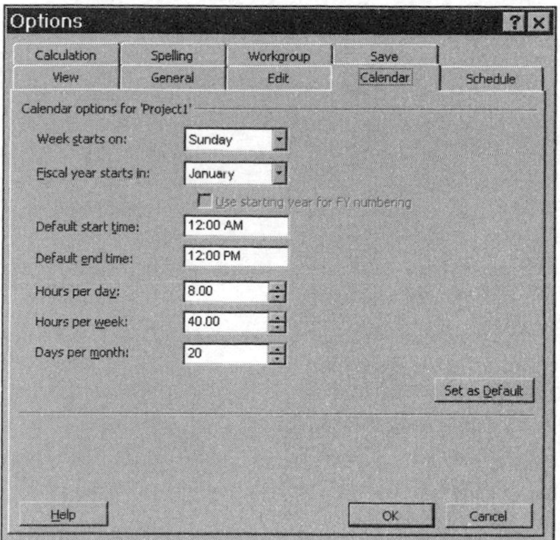


**Figure 3-4:** By reviewing the settings on the Calendar tab in the Options dialog box, you ensure that you and Project are speaking the same language when you enter task duration information.

The final five settings on the Calendar tab of the Options dialog box enable you to designate specific start and end times for each day, the number of hours in a day and in a week, and the number of days in a month. You could set the workday to start at 9:00 a.m. and end at 6:00 p.m., assign nine hours to your workday (no lunch for you!), and end up with a 45-hour week, for example.

## Creating a new calendar

The Standard calendar may not work for your project under all circumstances. You may find that all members of a specific group of resources work on the same calendar — but their calendar is different from the Standard calendar. For a group like this one, you can create a special resource calendar.

Starting in Project 2000, you can assign calendars to tasks.

Or, suppose that you run a print shop and each project you complete requires that you use the printing press, but the press requires cleaning and maintenance each week for two hours on Thursday afternoon. To make sure that each printing project considers the maintenance requirement of the printing press, you can create a "Press" calendar that considers the need to shut the press down to clean and maintain it. Then you can assign the Press calendar to the Press Time task you create for each project.

You use calendars to manage task schedules; you can also modify the calendars of resources to mark time when they aren't available. In Chapter 4, you'll read more about task calendars; in Chapter 5, you'll learn more about resource calendars.

To create a new calendar, choose Tools ➪ Change Working Time to display the Change Working Time dialog box shown in Figure 3-5.

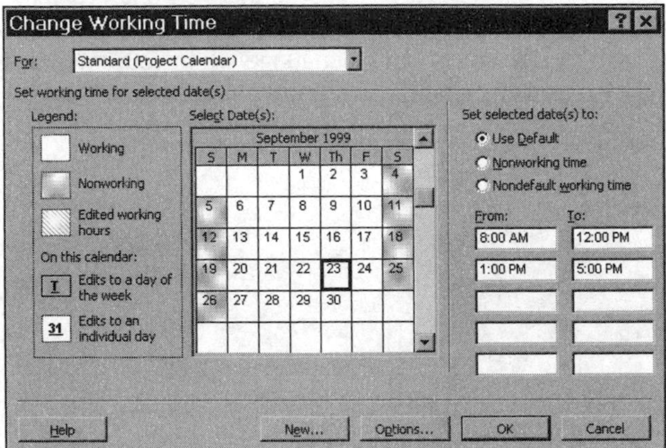


**Figure 3-5:** By default, Project displays the settings for Standard (Project Calendar) in the Change Working Time dialog box.

If other calendars exist, you'll see them listed in the For list box. You can create a custom calendar by clicking the New button. Project displays the Create New Base Calendar dialog box (see Figure 3-6).

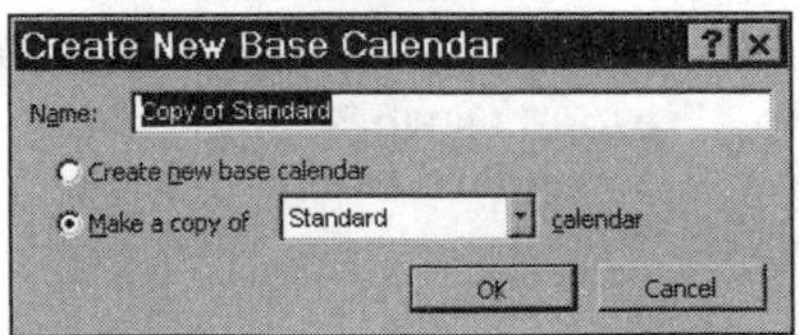


**Figure 3-6:** From the Create New Base Calendar dialog box, you can create a copy of an existing calendar or you can create a new Standard calendar.

If you want to model your calendar on an existing calendar, select the existing calendar from the Make a copy of drop-down box. Provide a name for the new calendar in the Name box.

By default, Project suggests that you copy the calendar you were viewing when you chose the New button. In particular, I suggest that you make a copy of the Standard calendar rather than modifying it. That way, you'll always be able to use the original Standard calendar if you need it.

Click OK to create the new calendar and then make changes to it in the Change Working Time dialog box. To change the working hours for a particular day, make sure you use the For list box to select the calendar you want to change, and then make changes. The Legend on the left side of the dialog box identifies Working days, Nonworking days, Nondefault working hours, and Nondefault days or hours for this calendar.

Using standard Windows selection techniques, select the dates the resource will be on vacation.

To select contiguous days, click the first day. Then press the Shift key as you click the last day you want to select. To select noncontiguous days, press Ctrl as you click each day you want to select. Scroll up to see an earlier month; scroll down to see a later month. To select all Sundays, click the letter that corresponds to the day. Project selects all Sundays in all months.

To change working hours, click the Default Working Time button and then make the necessary changes in the From and To text boxes. Because you set an exception to the regular schedule, the dates you selected appear underscored in the calendar (see Figure 3-7). Even if you don't select the date, you can tell that the day contains nonstandard working hours by comparing the date to the Legend.

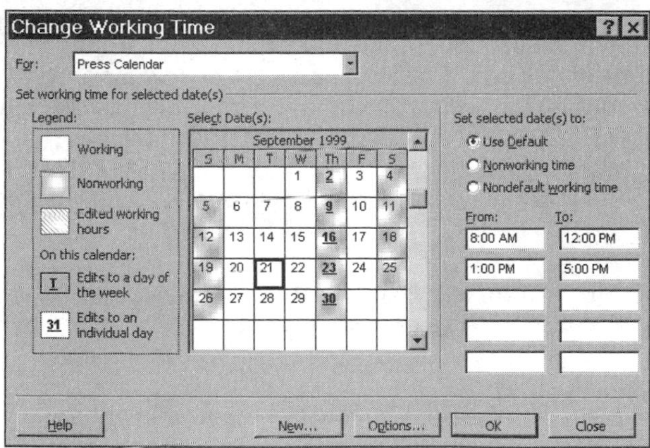


**Figure 3-7:** Project marks exceptions to the typical schedule with an underscore.

Reselecting a date and clicking the Default Working Time button returns the date to its original scheduled time on that date; therefore, selecting Default Working Time for Sundays means "don't schedule work on Sundays."

# Entering Tasks

To start building a project, enter the major steps to reach your goal in roughly the order in which you expect them to occur. (Don't worry if you're not quite accurate about the sequence of events; Project makes it easy to reorganize tasks in your schedule at any time.)

For the sample project — organizing a corporate annual meeting — follow these steps to create your first task: booking the meeting space.

1. Click the Task Name column in the first row of the Gantt table.
2. Type **Book Meeting Space.** The text appears in the cell and in the entry bar above the Gantt table.
3. Press Enter to accept the text.

You can also accept an entry in a cell by clicking the checkmark button to the left of the entry bar, pressing a directional arrow key on your keyboard to move to another cell, clicking another cell with your mouse pointer, or pressing Tab.

Notice that information is starting to appear in your schedule (see Figure 3-8). For example, Project lists the task name in the Task Name column and makes a corresponding entry in the Duration column; the question mark in the Duration column represents an estimated duration. (Remember the default setting in the Schedule tab of the Options dialog box? The default length of new tasks is estimated at one day.) According to the Start column, the task begins today; in addition, a task bar reflects the one-day duration of the task graphically.

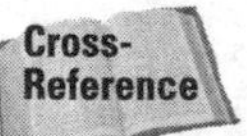


Chapter 4 contains more information on "estimated durations," a new feature in Project 2000.

If you use the scroll bar at the bottom of the Gantt table to move to the right, you see the Finish date entry. Because this is a one-day task, it will be completed by the end of the day.

Using either your mouse pointer or the down-arrow key on your keyboard, move to the second row in the Task Name column and enter **Schedule Speakers** as the next task. Then enter the following tasks in the next four rows: **Arrange for Audio/ Visual Equipment**, **Order Food**, **Send Invitations**, and **Mail Annual Reports**. Your schedule should now look like the schedule in Figure 3-9.

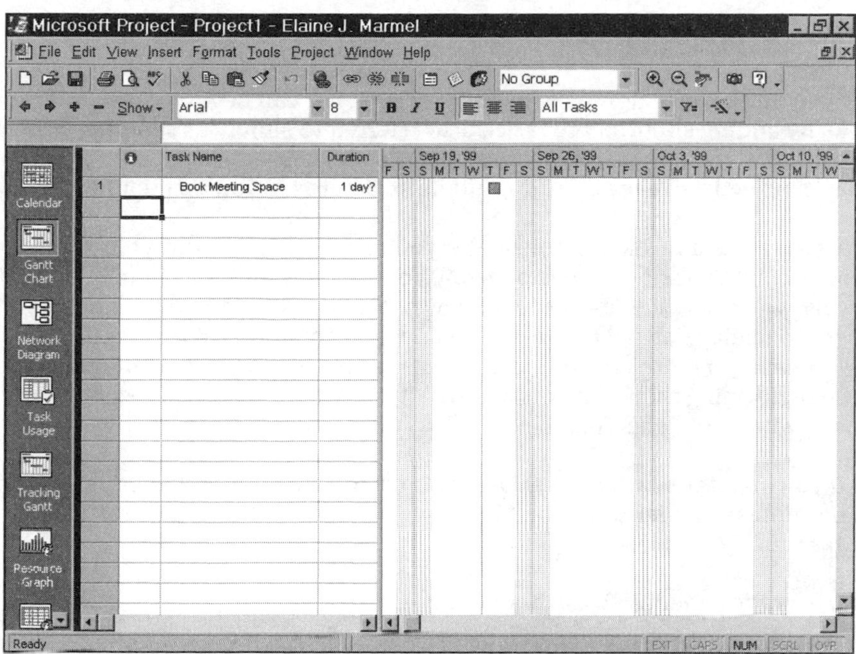


**Figure 3-8:** The task begins on the project start date automatically, although you could use the Options dialog box to have it start on the current date.

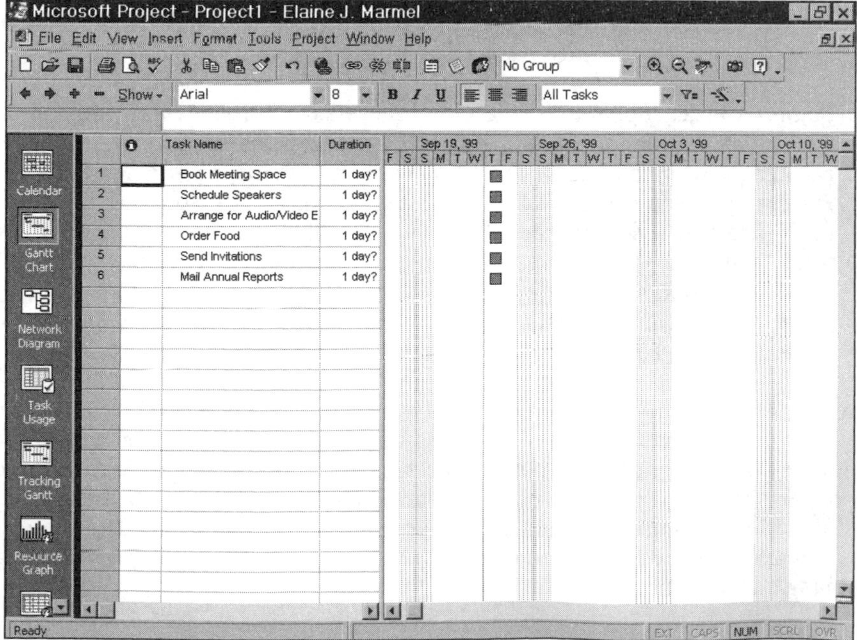


**Figure 3-9:** Note that each task is the same length by default, and each begins on the project start date.

# Adding Subtasks

After you enter the major tasks in your project, you can begin to flesh out the details by adding subordinate tasks, also referred to simply as *subtasks*. When you add subtasks, the upper-level task becomes a summary task. Summary tasks and subtasks provide an easy-to-apply outline structure for your schedule.

Project's outline approach also enables you to display and print your project information with various levels of detail. For example, with only summary tasks showing, you see a higher-level overview of the project than you might want to present to management. On the other hand, you could reveal the details of only one or two phases of a project so that you can discuss those tasks with the people who will be performing them. The outline structure gives you a lot of flexibility in working with your schedule.

When you insert a new task, it appears above the currently selected task. Begin by adding subtasks under the Book Meeting Space task. Follow these steps to insert a new task:

1. Click the Schedule Speakers task.
2. Choose Insert ➪ New Task. Row 2 becomes a blank row, and all the other tasks move down one. Your cursor rests in the new task row.
3. Type **Request purchase order** and click the checkmark button to accept the new task.
4. Click the Indent button on the Formatting toolbar (it looks like a right-facing arrow) to indent the subtask, as shown in Figure 3-10.

Summary tasks appear in boldface and subtasks in normal type by default; however, some people like to differentiate these task types even more. In traditional outlining you sometimes vary the capitalization of items depending on their level. For example, you can capitalize the first letters of all the words in the summary tasks (headline style) and capitalize only the first letter of the first word in the subtasks (sentence style), as in this example. The choice is yours; however, if you decide to use some special effect as you enter text, be consistent so others looking at your schedule can recognize your system. And if others are to work on your schedule, make sure that they follow the formats you have established.

Notice that the summary task now displays a solid black line on the Gantt chart with a downward arrow shape marking its beginning and end. When a task becomes a summary task — that is, when it contains subtasks — the timing of the summary task reflects the total amount of time required to complete the subtasks. If a task has a duration assigned to it and you make it into a summary task, the timing of the subtasks overrides the assigned duration. If you change the timing of a subtask, the summary task duration changes to reflect the change.

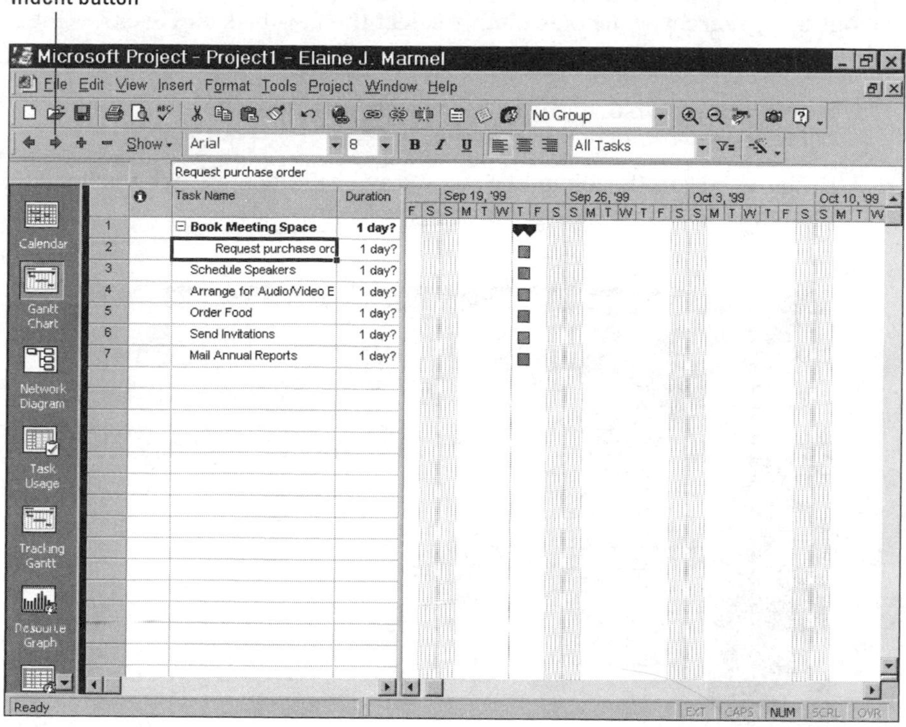


**Figure 3-10:** The summary task now appears in boldface type.

You can add other subtasks by following these steps:

1. Click the Schedule Speakers task.
2. Press the Ins key on your keyboard (which is a shortcut alternative to using Insert ➪ New Task). A new blank row appears.
3. Type **Select room** and press Enter to accept the new task. The new task uses the same level of indentation as the task above it.
4. Press the Ins key on your keyboard. A new blank row appears.
5. Type **Confirm space** and press Enter to accept the new task. The new task uses the same level of indentation as the task above it.
6. Click the Schedule Speakers task to select it if necessary.
7. Press Insert.
8. Type **Order flowers** and press Enter to accept the new task.

The third new task also indents to the subordinate level. To move the task higher in the outline hierarchy, you could simply select the new task and use the Outdent button on the toolbar, but try using your mouse to move it as follows:

1. Move your mouse over the Order flowers task until the mouse pointer becomes a two-way pointing arrow.
2. Drag the task to the left until a thick gray line indicates that it is lined up with the upper-level tasks in the outline (see Figure 3-11).

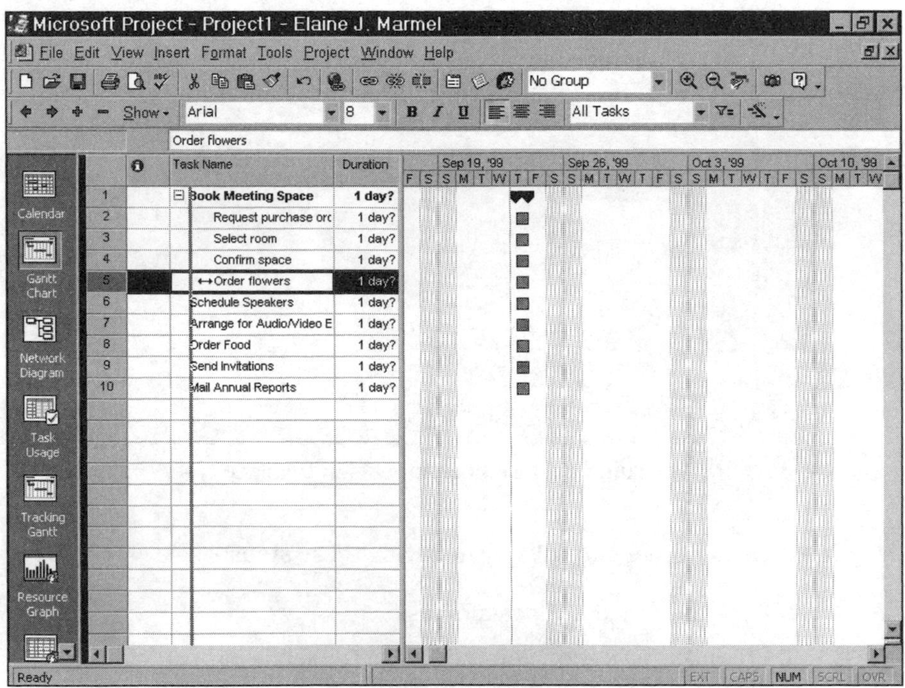


**Figure 3-11:** You can use your mouse to drag tasks in or out in the outline hierarchy.

3. Release the mouse button to complete the move.

Your schedule now looks like the schedule in Figure 3-12. Adding details is as simple as inserting new tasks wherever you want them and then moving them in or out in the outline structure.

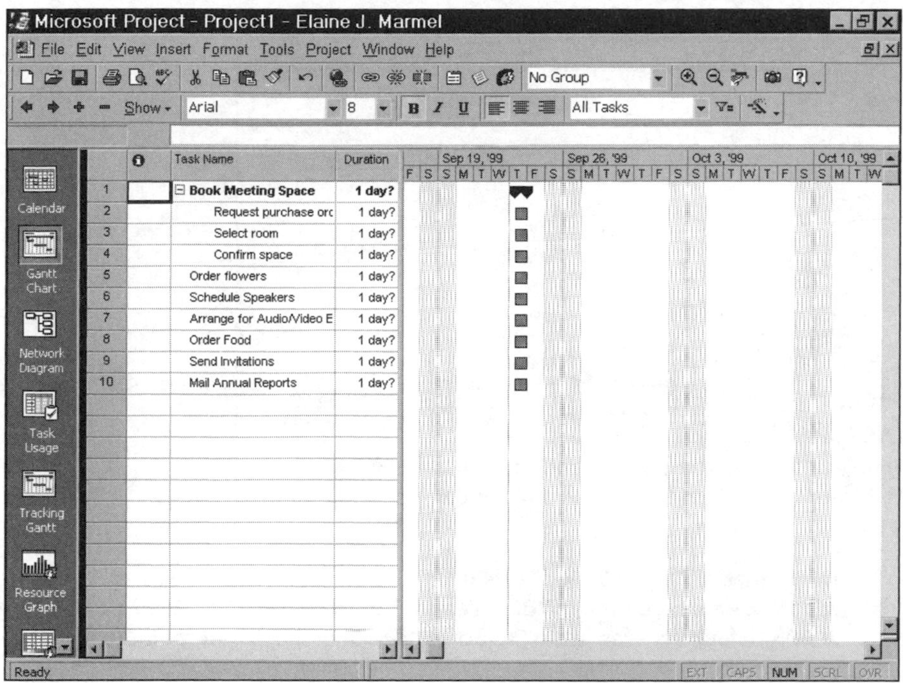

**Figure 3-12:** The outline structure enables you to see summary and subtasks as manageable chunks of work.

# Saving Project Files

Of course, you should always save your work frequently. With the often mission-critical information centralized in a Project file, frequent saving is even more important. When saving Project files, you have the option of setting up protection for them. You can also save your files as *templates,* that is, files on which you can base other schedules.

## Saving files

To save any Project file for the first time, choose File ➪ Save or click the Save tool on the Standard toolbar. Using the new Save As dialog box that Project sports, you specify where to save a file and what format you want to use (see Figure 3-13).

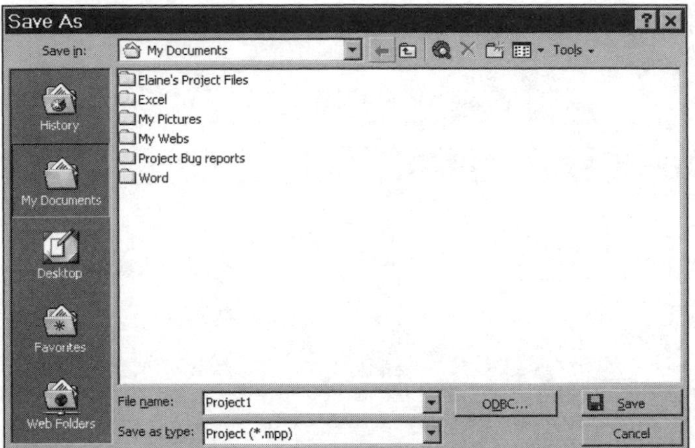


**Figure 3-13:** Use the buttons and tools of the File Save dialog box to tell Project where to save a file and what format to use.

The format of Project 2000 files is different from the format of Project 98 files; you can, however, save Project 2000 files as Project 98 files. You even can set Project 2000's default save format to Project 98 files. See Chapter 18 for more information.

Click the arrow at the right edge of the Save in list box to display a hierarchy of your computer's drive and directory organization. Click the Up One Level tool to move up one level in that hierarchy. Or use one of the Save in buttons (History, My Documents, Desktop, Favorites, or Web Folders) to select a folder in which to save the file. To place this project file in a new folder, navigate to the drive or folder in which you want Project to store the new folder and then use the Create New Folder tool.

After you save a project for the first time, you can simply click the Save button to save the file; Project won't display this dialog box. If you want to change a setting or save the file with a new name, choose File ➪ Save As to display this dialog box again.

By default, Project saves files in Project 2000 format with the extension .mpp. If you want to save a file in a different format, such as a Microsoft Access database (.mdb) or a Project 98 file (also .mpp), you can select that format in the Save as type drop-down list. After you enter a filename and designate its location and file type, click Save to save the file.

Clicking the ODBC button enables you to export Project data to an ODBC database.

Project displays the Planning Wizard if you haven't set a baseline for the project. If you're ready to set a baseline, change the option in the dialog box to save your file with a baseline; otherwise, accept the defaults and click OK to save your project without setting a baseline.

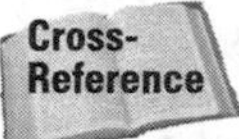


To read more about baselines, see Chapter 11.

## Saving files as templates

One format in the Save as type selection is Template. Template files have an extension of .mpt. The template feature is especially useful in project management because your projects are often similar to ones that precede or follow them. A template file saves all the settings you may have made for a particular project, such as formatting, commonly performed tasks, and calendar choices. Keeping template files on hand can save your coworkers (and yourself) from having to reinvent the wheel each time you want to build a similar project.

You may ask, "Can't I just save my previous project's file with a new name and use that for my next project?" Yes, you can, but after you track progress on tasks, opening that final project file and stripping it back to its baseline settings is a cumbersome routine.

Saving the initial schedule as a template on which you can build new schedules is a much better approach. To create a new schedule, simply open the template and save the file as a standard Project file with a new name.

## Protecting files

Some projects are as top secret as an FBI file. In this case some people within the organization, and certainly people from outside the organization, should not have access to the details. If your projects fit this mold, you need a way to keep your Project files secure from prying eyes. You can set a measure of security for Project 2000 files by clicking the Tools button in the File Save dialog box and choosing General Options to display the Save Options dialog box in Figure 3-14.

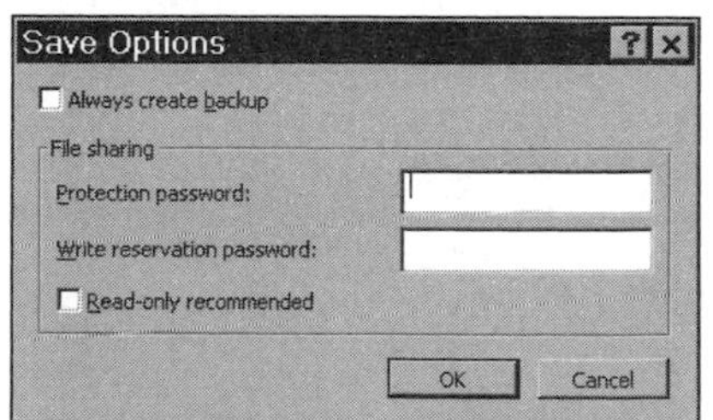


**Figure 3-14:** Don't use your phone extension, birthday, or spouse's name as a password – such passwords are much too easy to break!

What kind of passwords should you use? Consider two factors: you must be able to remember the password, and you must make it something the average person won't guess. (No password is perfect; if someone really wants to break into your files, he or she will.) Try using passwords such as an address or phone number you had as a kid; information you remember but others are not likely to know.

Assigning the Protection password protects the file from being opened. Only someone with the assigned password can open a file protected this way. The Write reservation password, on the other hand, permits anyone to open the file without a password, but as a *read-only* file (that is, no one else can make any changes to the file). Finally, if you check the Read-only recommended option, Project displays a message recommending that anyone opening the file not make changes to it. This choice doesn't actually prevent someone from making changes, however.

Both the Protection and Write reservation passwords are case sensitive. If you assign a password of JoeS, you cannot open the file if you type in joes.

### Closing Project

When you're finished working in Project, you can save your files as described previously and then use one of the following methods to close the program:

✦ Click the Close button in the upper-right corner of the Project window.

✦ Choose File ⇨ Exit.

If you haven't saved any open files, Project prompts you to do so.

## Working with a Project Outline

After you build the outline, reorganizing the sequence of individual tasks is easy. You can also manipulate the outline to show more or less detail about your project. Outlining features work the same way in many software products; for example, Word for Windows, PowerPoint, and Project, all Microsoft products, have the same outlining tools and features. In Project, you can, as you might expect, move and copy tasks; you also can hide and display tasks.

### Adjusting tasks in an outline

To move tasks in an outline, you can cut and paste as you see in Steps 1 through 4 below, or you can drag and drop, as you can see in Steps 9 and 10 below. You also can change the relative position of tasks in the hierarchy of the outline by promoting or demoting them (outdenting or indenting). In Steps 5 through 8 and 11 and 12 below, you see examples of promoting and demoting tasks.

To move tasks, you must first select them. Use any of the following techniques to select tasks:

You can select a task by clicking its Gantt bar.

✦ To select a single task, click its ID number.

✦ To select several contiguous tasks, select the first task. Then hold down the Shift key and click the last task you want to select.

✦ To select several noncontiguous tasks, hold down the Ctrl key as you click the ID numbers of the tasks that you want to select.

It's important to remember that, although you can move tasks wherever you like, when you move a summary task, its subtasks move with it. So, to move a subtask on its own to another location in the outline, you first must promote (outdent) it to the highest task level.

Moving subtasks up one level can be a little tricky. For example, to move the task "Request purchase order" under the task "Order Food," you must first promote "Request purchase order" to the highest level. When you do so, however, the other subtask under "Book Meeting Space" (that is, "Confirm space") becomes subordinate to "Request purchase order." Moving the upper task also moves its subordinate. To avoid this problem, promote the "Confirm space" task so that it is no longer subordinate, move the "Request purchase order" task where you wish, and then go back and demote "Confirm space" to be subordinate, once again, to the "Book Meeting Space" task. In the beginning this process is a little confusing, so you should get some practice by trying the steps that follow.

**Tip** To move a summary task on its own, you must first promote all its subtasks to a higher level.

Try reorganizing tasks using both the toolbar tools and your mouse by following these steps:

1. Click the ID number (in the leftmost column) for the task Order flowers. Project highlights (selects) the entire row.
2. Click the Cut tool on the Standard toolbar.
3. Click the ID number for Send Invitations. Project selects the row.
4. Click the Paste tool on the Standard toolbar. The Order flowers task appears selected in its new location above the task Send Invitations.
5. Move the mouse pointer over the subtask name, Request purchase order, until the pointer becomes a double arrow.

**Tip** When you first place the mouse pointer over the task name, you won't have much time to view the double arrow; Project displays a gray screen tip containing the task name. If you're patient, the double arrow will reappear.

6. Press and hold down the left mouse button while you drag the task to the left. A gray vertical line appears onscreen, indicating you are promoting a task in the outline hierarchy. When you release the mouse button, your schedule should look like the schedule in Figure 3-15.

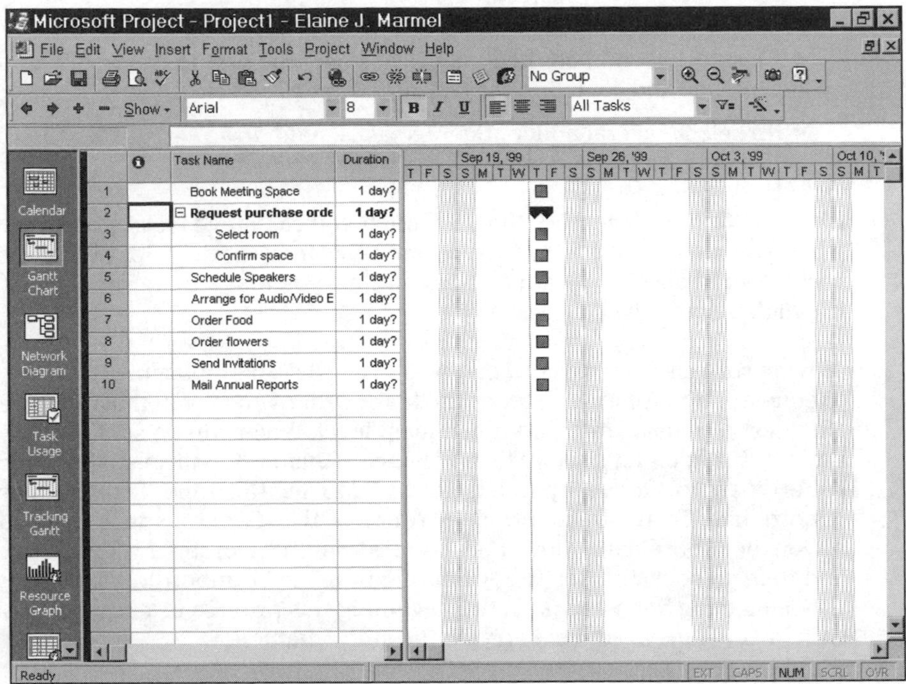


**Figure 3-15:** When you outdent a task, you may shift the hierarchy structure of subtasks beneath it.

Dragging a task to the right demotes the task in the project outline. You'll see the same gray vertical line when you promote or demote tasks.

7. Select both Select Room and Confirm space. Move the mouse pointer over either of the subtask names until the pointer becomes a double arrow.
8. Drag the tasks to the left to outdent them.
9. Click the Gantt bar or the ID number of the task Request purchase order.
10. While using the mouse to point at the ID number, drag the Request purchase order task below the Order food task. A horizontal gray line indicates the new position as you drag.
11. Click the Indent button on the Formatting toolbar to make the task subordinate.
12. Select the Select Room and Confirm space tasks and click the Indent button.

Your schedule now has two tasks with subtasks beneath them (see Figure 3-16). As you can see, moving subtasks around your outline can be a little cumbersome. Don't despair, however—in a well-planned outline, you are much more likely to move summary tasks and their subtasks as a unit.

Tip: You also can move a subtask without taking other subtasks with it by moving the designated task to the bottom of the list of subtasks before outdenting it. This approach saves you the step of outdenting subsidiary subtasks.

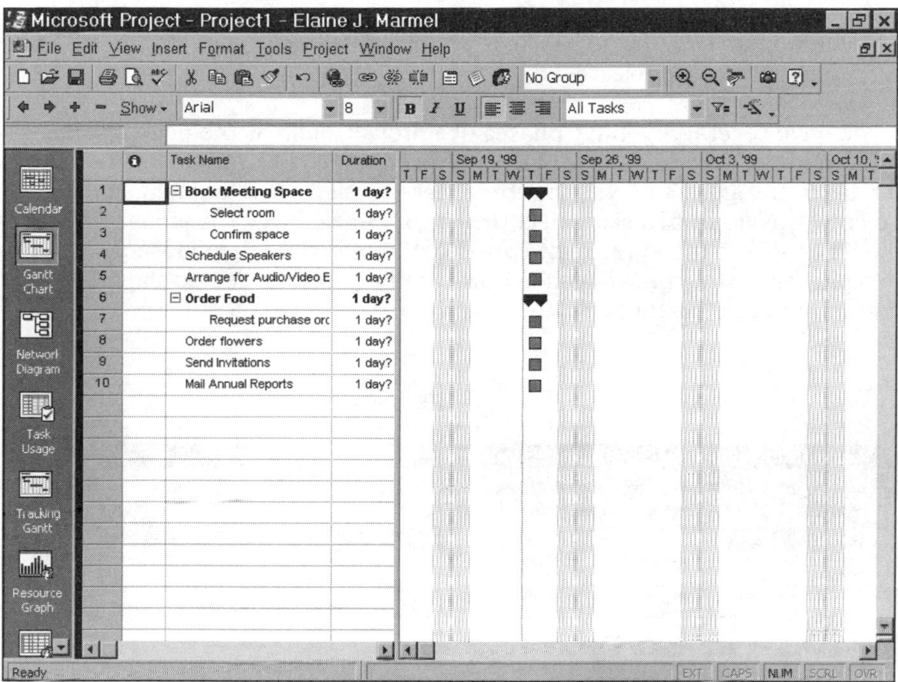


**Figure 3-16:** Both "Book Meeting Space" and "Order food" have subtasks beneath them.

## Copying tasks

Copying tasks is also simple to do and can come in very handy while building a project outline. For example, suppose you were entering tasks in a project to test various versions of a compound to see which works best as a fixative. You might repeat the same series of tasks — Obtain compound sample, Test in various environments, Write up test results, Analyze results, and so on — several times. Instead of typing those tasks 10 or 20 times, you can save time by copying them.

To copy tasks, you must first select them. Use any of the following techniques described in the previous section. You can copy tasks two ways:

✦ Use the Edit ➪ Copy and Edit ➪ Paste commands (or their corresponding tools on the Standard toolbar) to copy the selected task(s) to another location.

Tip

Remember, to copy a summary task and its subtasks, you need only select the summary task and copy it. Project automatically copies the summary's subtasks for you.

✦ Hold down the Ctrl key while you drag the task(s) to another location. Release the mouse button to complete the copy.

New Feature

In Project 2000, the fill handle is available in all views, not just the time-phased view as in earlier releases.

If you have several repetitive phases of a project, such as the development and production of several models of a single product, you can use the fill handle to copy the tasks. In Figure 3-17, you see three tasks: Design, Development, and Production. To copy the group of tasks, select their task names. Place the mouse pointer over the fill handle in the lower-right corner of the selection; the mouse pointer changes to a plus sign. Drag the fill handle down until you have selected the group of rows you want to contain the repetitive tasks.

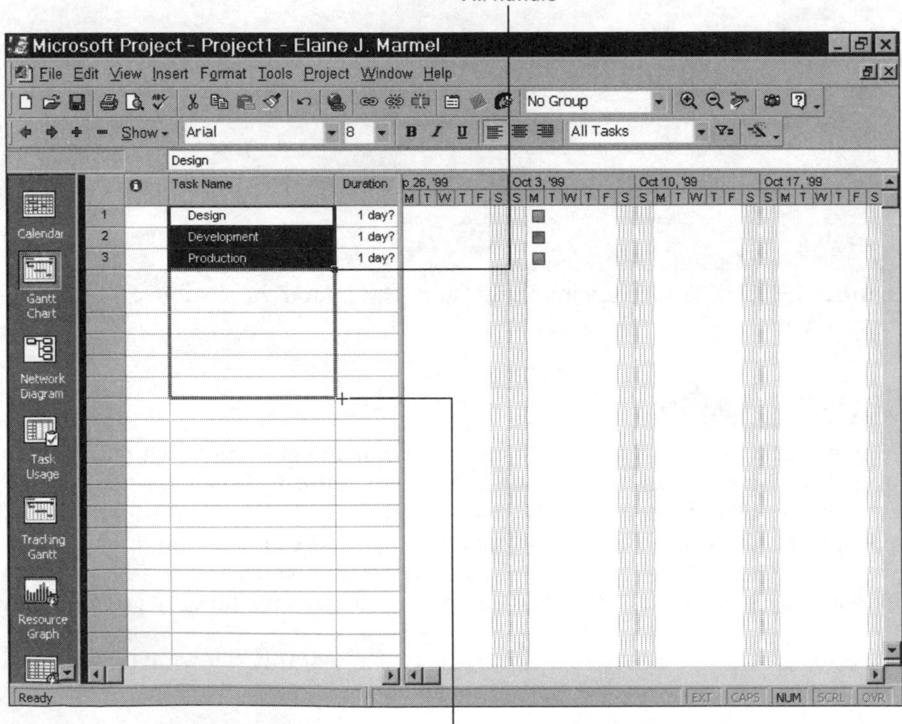


**Figure 3-17:** Take advantage of the fill handle for contiguous copy tasks.

The fill handle copies tasks into a contiguous range; if the range already contains information, using the fill handle to copy overwrites the existing information. To avoid the problem, insert blank rows in the project before using the fill handle. Select the task you want to appear beneath the new row and choose Insert ⇨ New Task. To insert more than one blank row, select the number of rows you want to insert before choosing Insert ⇨ New Task.

When you release the mouse pointer, Project copies the tasks into the selected range (see Figure 3-18).

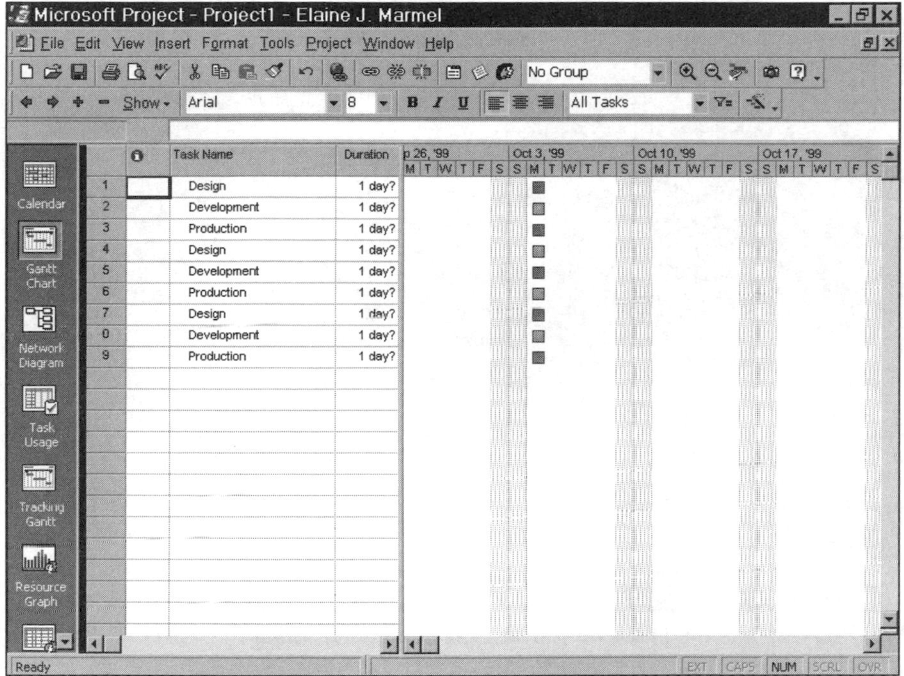


**Figure 3-18:** Project fills the range with the selected tasks.

Suppose you're using WBS codes and you set up the WBS codes to automatically assign codes when you create new tasks. When you copy tasks using any of the methods described, Project automatically assigns incremental WBS codes to the new tasks.

## Displaying and hiding tasks

The outline structure enables you to view your project at different levels of detail by expanding or collapsing the summary tasks. You can use the Show button on the Formatting toolbar to quickly hide or display subtasks based on their outline level (see Figure 3-19). Using the Show button, you also can quickly display all the detail tasks in your schedule.

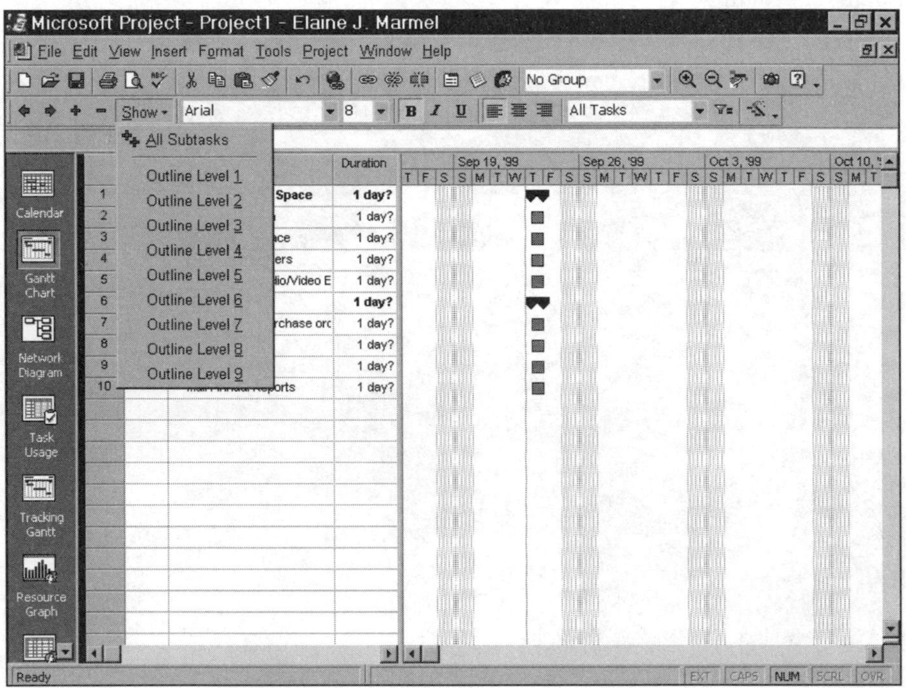


**Figure 3-19:** Use the Show button on the Formatting toolbar to easily determine the level of detail you want to view in a project.

In Figure 3-20, a small box with a minus sign appears to the left of each summary task. This symbol indicates that all subtasks are in view. If you click the minus sign, any subtasks disappear from view and a plus sign appears next to the summary task name. The plus indicates that the task is associated with some hidden detail tasks. Click the plus sign to reveal the "hidden" subtasks.

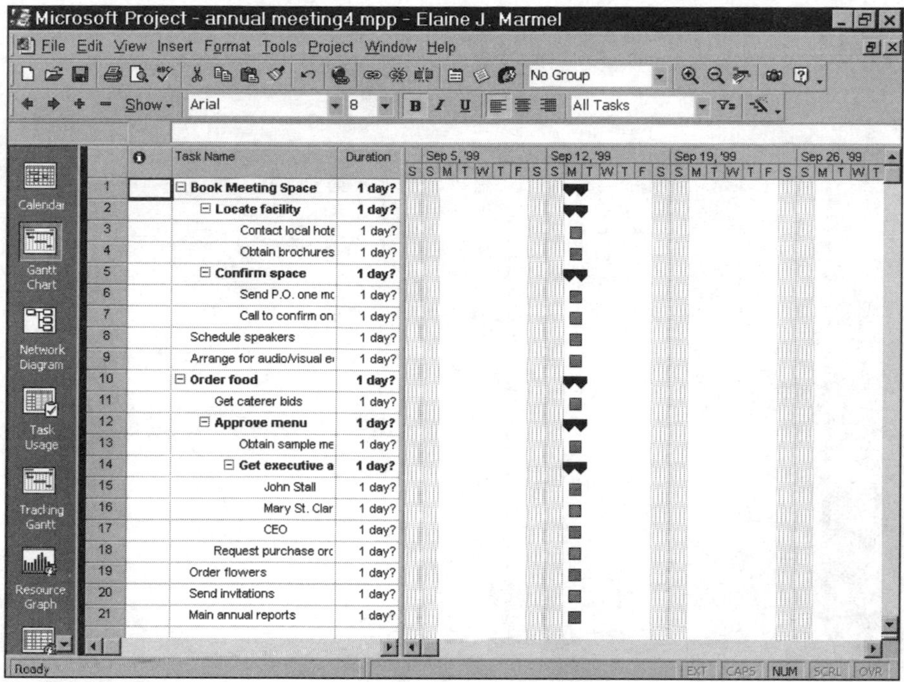


**Figure 3-20:** You can expand or collapse any task that has a subtask.

How many levels of detail can an outline have? Just about as many as you need. For example, the schedule shown in Figure 3-20 has several levels of detail regarding the annual meeting example. Any task that has subtasks also has the plus and minus mechanism for displaying or hiding them.

Using too many levels of outline indentation (usually more than three or four) makes it hard to see your entire schedule onscreen. In fact, a very detailed project outline may indicate that you need to rethink the scope of the project and break it into smaller, more manageable projects.

You can use the hide and show features of the outline to focus on just the amount of detail you wish. You can take the same schedule in Figure 3-20, for example, and show just the highest level of detail for a report to management to summarize project activity, as shown in Figure 3-21.

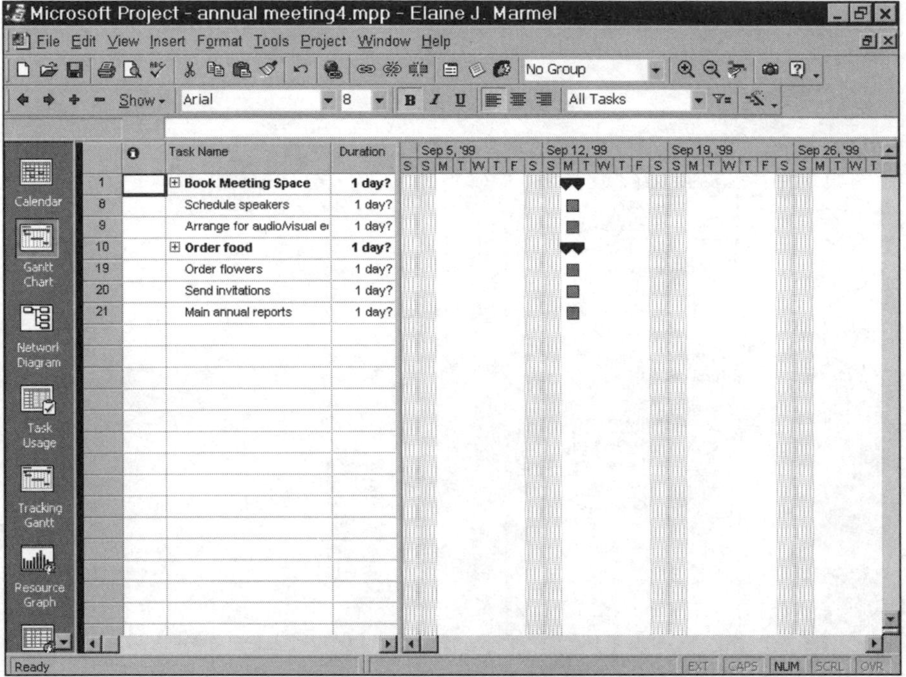

**Figure 3-21:** The detailed tasks are now hidden. But the plus symbols and the summary-style task bar indicate that more is here than meets the eye.

# Getting Help

As you begin to build tasks in a schedule, you're likely to have questions about using Project 2000 that its Help system can answer. Project's Help is similar to the Help feature in Office 2000 products. If you've used any Microsoft Office product, the Help environment in Project will be very familiar.

If you click the Office Assistant button on the end of the Standard toolbar, you'll see an animated Paperclip and a bubble in which you can type an English-language-like question (see Figure 3-22).

The help character annoys many people. In Project, you can avoid it in two different ways:

✦ **Bypass it.** You can choose Contents and Index from the Help menu (see Figure 3-23).

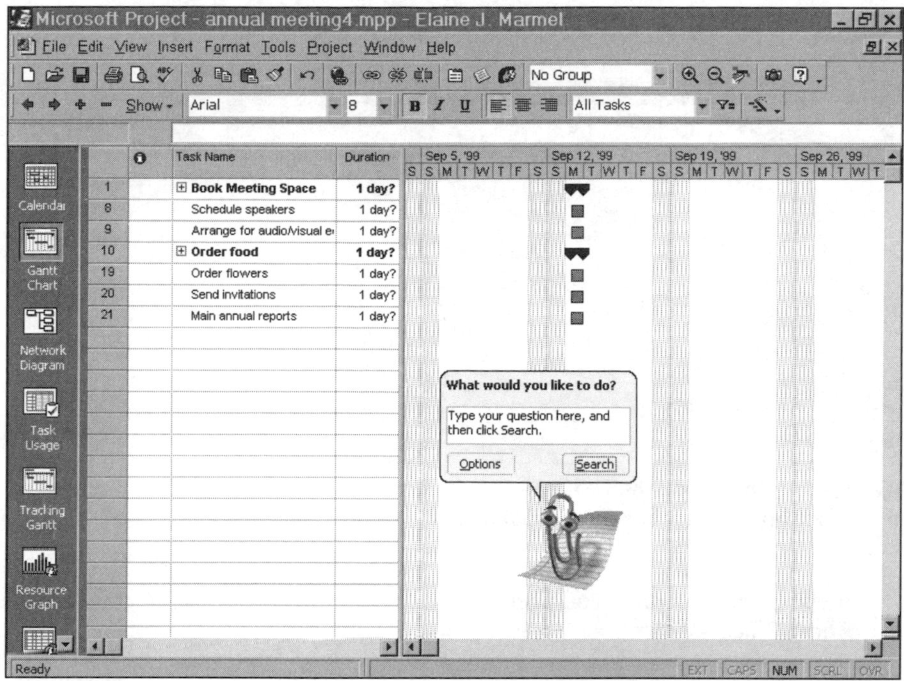


**Figure 3-22:** The Paperclip, which answers questions typed into its thought balloon

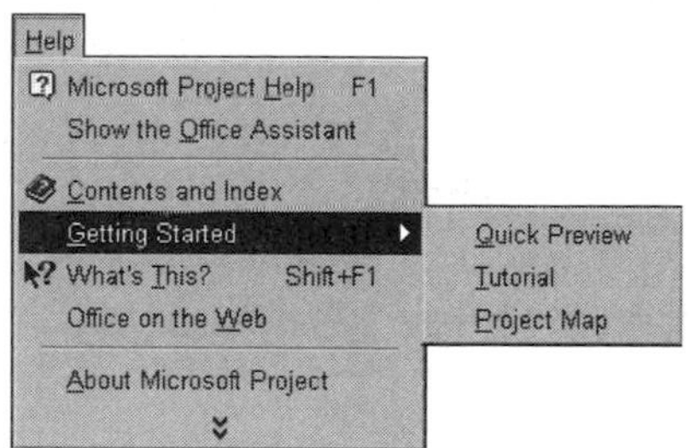


**Figure 3-23:** Use the Help menu to get Help in a variety of ways from Project; you can review the Quick Preview, Tutorial, or Project Map at any time, or you can open the Help system directly – without viewing the Office Assistant.

✦ **Turn it off.** You can turn off the Office Assistant; clicking the Office Assistant button becomes the equivalent of choosing Help ➪ Contents and Index. To turn off the Office Assistant, click the Office Assistant button on the Standard toolbar to display the Office Assistant. In the bubble, click the Options button to display the Office Assistant Options dialog box (see Figure 3-24). Remove the check from the Use the Office Assistant checkbox on the Options tab.

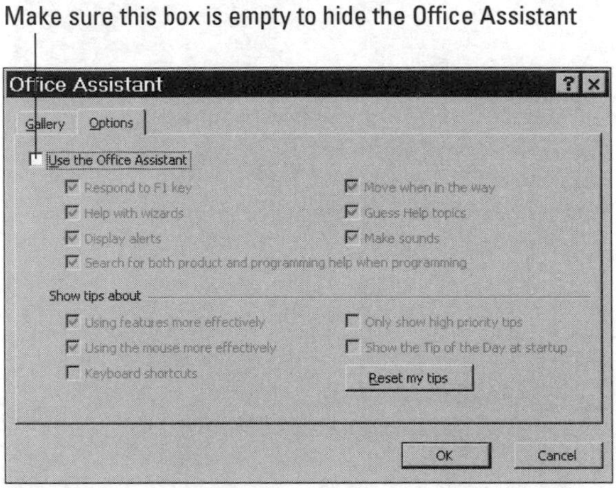

Make sure this box is empty to hide the Office Assistant

**Figure 3-24:** To turn off the Office Assistant, remove the check from the first box in this dialog box.

If you decide later that you again want to use the Office Assistant, choose Help ➪ Show Office Assistant.

## Using the Help system

The Contents and Index option on the Help menu takes you to the Help Welcome window. You find three tabs in the Help window:

- ✦ **The Contents tab.** Lists topic areas that you can open, level by level, until you reach the specific information you require. This feature is similar to working your way through a table of contents in a book to find a particular topic.
- ✦ **The Index tab.** Provides a searchable index of topics and subtopics. Like a book index, you can look up a specific term or phrase by finding it in an alphabetical listing.
- ✦ **The Answer Wizard tab.** Enables you to type questions and search for Help topics.

### The Contents tab

Figure 3-25 shows the first tab of the Help Topics dialog box: Contents. You can use this tab to locate information by general topic areas. When you open any of these topics, Help takes you to a list of subtopics. By narrowing down these subtopics, you eventually get to the information you want.

**Figure 3-25:** The Contents tab provides general topic areas to help you locate what you need.

The Contents tab is simply a way to get help if you know the general topic you want to learn about but perhaps aren't familiar enough with the terminology to type a specific phrase or term in the Index. The Contents tab and the Index tab often bring you to exactly the same information screen. For example, if you select the topic Creating a Project Hierarchy Using Outlining, double-click to display subtopics, and then select the subtopic "Indent and outdent tasks into summary tasks and subtasks," the Contents tab displays the same information as the Index tab displayed in the earlier example.

Use the buttons across the top of the Help information screen. You can display or hide the Contents, Answer Wizard, and Index tabs; go Back to the previously displayed screen; print a topic; or display Options for Help.

## The Answer Wizard tab

When you select the Answer Wizard tab of the Help window, you see a pane where you can type a question (see Figure 3-26). When you click Search, Help displays topics relevant to your question. You can then select a Help topic to display.

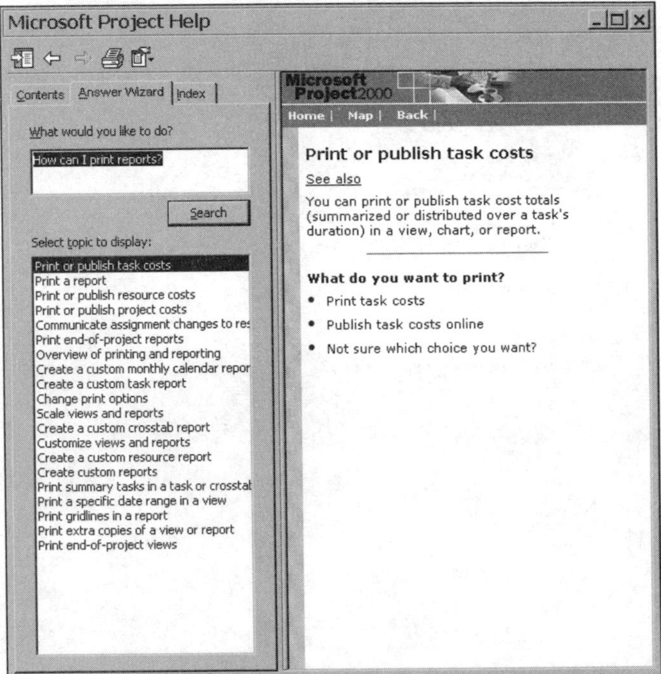


**Figure 3-26:** Use the Answer Wizard to get help by posing a question.

## The Index tab

The Index tab shown in Figure 3-27 enables you to type or choose a keyword and then display information about it.

Follow these steps to locate information on Project's outlining feature. (If you haven't already opened the Contents and Index area of Help, do so now by choosing Help ➪ Contents and Index and then selecting the Index tab.)

1. Type the letters **ou**. Help displays keywords in the middle of the tab that begin with the letters you typed; the first is "outdent."
2. Type the letters **tl**. Project narrows down to the topic "outline." This "quick pick" functionality enables you to type only as many letters as Project needs to identify the topic. You can also use the scroll bar and mouse to scroll through keywords and select topics.
3. Click the Search button at the top of the Index tab. Help displays the topics associated with the keyword, and the actual Help information for the first topic in the list, as shown in Figure 3-28.
4. Click a topic to read the Help information for it.

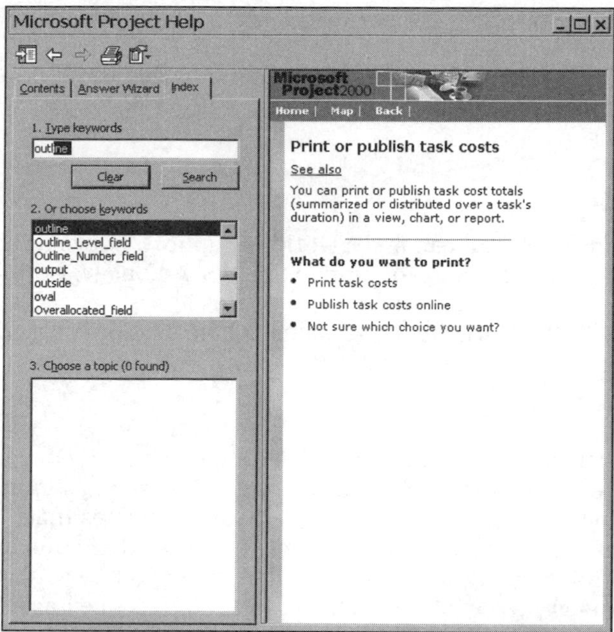


**Figure 3-27:** Use the Index tab to search for help using keywords, much the way you'd use the index of a book.

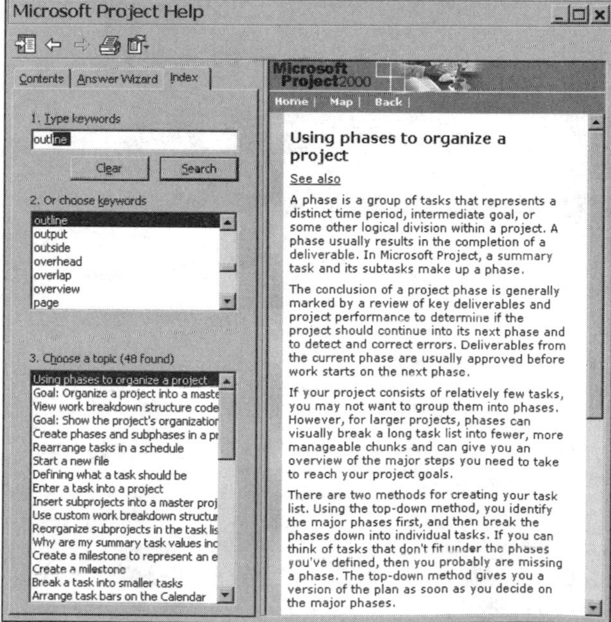


**Figure 3-28:** Several topics might exist for any keyword in the Help Index.

Help information often contains steps required to complete a procedure. In addition, a "Find related help" hyperlink takes you to related topics when you click it. Finally, the Help text might contain hyperlink text, a button to show you how to accomplish some task, and even demos.

## Finding online help

If you're connected to the Internet, you can find a world of support, information, and even freeware, shareware, or products-for-a-price that work along with Project.

This book's companion CD-ROM includes several products from third-party vendors.

Choose the Office on the Web command to follow a link to the Microsoft Office Update Web site (see Figure 3-29). At this site, you can find things such as update information, files to download, and a link to a list of software companies that provide add-on products or specialize in the use of Microsoft Project. If you have a technical question about Project, you can click Assistance to use Online Support or to look up articles on Microsoft Project stored in Microsoft's Knowledge Base. You can also find links on this page to the Microsoft Project Newsgroups, the Microsoft Project Resource Kit, and the Solution Provider Database.

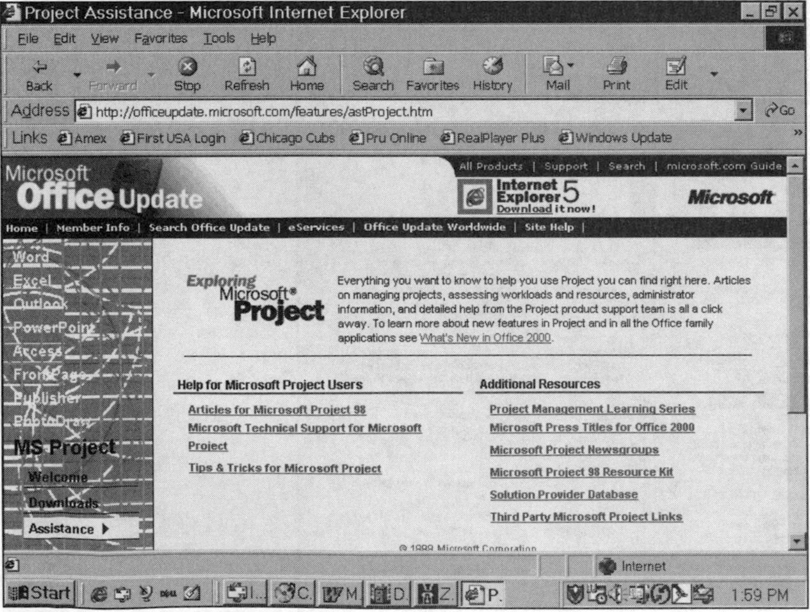


**Figure 3-29:** The Office Update Web site for Microsoft Project provides a wealth of information as well as access to Project newsgroups.

The image you see in Figure 3-29 represents the way the Web site looked on November 11, 1999.

# Summary

In this chapter you started to build your first project by creating summary tasks and subtasks. You learned about the following aspects of Project:

- ✦ Gathering the data you need to begin creating your schedule
- ✦ Entering Project information and setting up some calendar defaults
- ✦ Creating summary and subtasks
- ✦ Saving files and closing Project
- ✦ Working with the outlining hierarchy to assign WBS codes and move, copy, and display subtasks
- ✦ Using the Help system to search for information and obtain online help

In Chapter 4 you start to add details about task types, add timing, and establish relationships among your tasks.

✦ ✦ ✦

# Building Tasks

Hessiod, that classic Greek project manager, once said, "Observe due measure, for right timing is in all things the most important factor." You could do worse than to use this truism from around 700 B.C. as your personal project management mantra today. When it comes to projects, timing is, indeed, all.

In Chapter 3 you created several tasks and used the outlining feature of Project to organize them. But every task in your schedule has the default length (one estimated day), and they all occur on the very same day. In essence, you have listed the steps to get to your goal, but with no related timing; your schedule might as well be a shopping list.

You have to add durations to your tasks; that is, you must establish how long (or how many hours of effort) each task will take. But timing consists of more than determining how many hours, days, or weeks it takes to complete each task. Timing for your project becomes clear only when you've set a duration for each task and when you've established the relationships, called *dependencies,* among the tasks. Only then can you accurately predict the amount of time that you will need to complete the project.

✦ ✦ ✦ ✦

**In This Chapter**

Establishing timing for tasks

Assigning task timing

Using recurring tasks

Establishing constraints and deadline dates

Manipulating the Gantt chart to view timing

Entering task notes

Establishing dependencies among tasks

Viewing dependencies

Deleting dependencies

✦ ✦ ✦ ✦

## Establishing Timing for Tasks

Your boss asks how long it will take to write that report, and you tell her it'll be about a week. Your coworker calls and asks when you'll finish repairing the computer network, and you tell him it'll take another day. You make estimates about task durations every day. You know your own business, and you're probably pretty good at setting the timing for everyday tasks based on many factors.

Exactly how do you figure out the timing for a task in a project? The method is virtually identical to the seemingly automatic process you go through when someone asks you how long it will take to complete a task, such as placing an order for materials. For example:

1. You estimate that you will spend about 40 minutes to do the research and perform the calculations to determine how many square feet of lumber you'll need for the job.
2. You consider how long the actual task—placing a phone order for materials—will take. This duration could be a matter of only minutes, but if you factor in playing a few rounds of phone tag, you might want to allow half a day.
3. You also think about what's involved in getting a purchase order. With your system, cutting a purchase order can take up to four days. Some of that time requires your presence, but most of it consists of waiting.

So how long is your task? You could say you need exactly four days, four hours, and 40 minutes; but just to be safe, you should probably allow about five days. In addition, Project has some issues specific to task timing that you need to understand to estimate task durations accurately.

By default, Project creates *resource-driven* tasks. Here's a simple example. You have to plant a tree. One person needs two hours to plant a tree. If you add another person (another resource), together they need only one hour to complete the task. That is, two resources, each putting in an hour of effort, complete the two hours of effort in only one hour. With resource-driven scheduling, when you add resources, the task timing becomes shorter; if you take resources away, the task takes longer to complete. The resource-driven method is Project's default scheduling method, and Project refers to these resource-driven tasks as *fixed-unit tasks*.

The reduction of time required on a resource-driven task is strictly a mathematical calculation in Project: Ten people get work done in one-tenth the time of one person. However, whenever two or more people work on a task, the time savings are seldom so straightforward. You must also factor in the time for those people to communicate, miscommunicate, hold meetings, and so on.

## To Pad or Not to Pad?

Although most people agree that delays are inevitable and that you should allow for them, people who schedule projects accommodate these delays in various ways.

Some schedulers build in extra time at the task level, adding a day or two to each task's duration—just in case. Unfortunately, padding each task may leave you with an impossibly long schedule, and may suggest to your boss that you're not very efficient. Why should it take two days to run a three-hour test? It doesn't—but because you know that setting up the test parameters properly the first time is an error-prone process, you allow a couple of workdays to complete the testing. Just make sure your boss understands that you're building a worst-case scenario; when you bring the project in early, he or she will be glad to share the praise.

Some project managers add one long task, maybe two weeks or so in duration, at the end of the schedule, and they name it something like Critical Issues Resolution Period. This task acts as a placeholder that covers you if individual tasks run late. This approach can help you see how the overall time left for delays is being used up as the project proceeds. For example, if the final two-week task is running a week late because of earlier delays, you know that you've eaten up half of the slack that that task represents.

Or, you can build a schedule with best-case timing. Then you can document any problems and delays that occur, and request additional time as needed. In the case of a project that you must complete quickly, you may need to work this way. However, best-case timing sets you up for potential missed deadlines.

Which approach should you use? Possibly a combination. For example, try building a best-case schedule. If the completion date is one week earlier than your deadline, by all means add a little time to the tasks most likely to encounter problems, such as those performed by outside vendors.

## Fixed-work and fixed-duration tasks

You also can use the *fixed-duration task* in Project. The number of resources does not affect the timing of this type of task. If you want to allow a week for a committee to review the company's new ad campaign, no matter how many people are on the committee, the task has a fixed duration. You cannot shorten the task's duration by adding resources to it. In fact, adding people to the review process might lengthen it because their effort has no impact on getting the work done more quickly, but coordinating their efforts could add time.

The *fixed-work task* was a new setting that became available in Project 98. When you create a fixed-work task, you set the duration of the task, and Project assigns a percentage of effort sufficient to complete the task in the time allotted for each resource you assign to the task. For example, if you assign three people to work on a one-day task, Project would say that each person should spend 33 percent of his or her time on the task to complete it in one day.

## Effort-driven tasks

For fixed-duration and fixed-unit tasks, you can tell Project to modify the percentage of total work allocated to each resource based on the number of assigned resources if the number of resources changes. In effect, you create an *effort-driven task.* The work required to complete the task remains the same, but Project redistributes the work equally among all assigned resources.

By default, fixed-work tasks are effort-driven. You can choose to make fixed-duration and fixed-unit tasks effort-driven if you want, or you can make Project retain the original allocation of work.

In this chapter, I use Project's default settings: the durations you assign to tasks are resource-driven. Therefore, a five-day task requires five days of resource effort to complete.

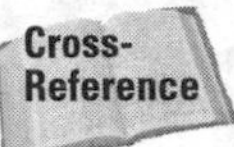


In Chapter 5 you learn more about how resource assignments modify task timing.

# Assigning Task Timing

You now understand the basics of estimating task timing, and you understand how task timing relates to effort expended on the task by resources. The actual process of assigning durations is quite simple. To assign a duration to a task, you can use one of three methods:

- ✦ Enter a duration in the Duration column of the Gantt table.
- ✦ Use your mouse to drag a task bar to the required length, or use a dialog box to enter duration information.
- ✦ Use the Task Information dialog box to enter and view information about all aspects of a task, including its timing, constraints, dependencies, resources, and priority in the overall project.

## Using the Task Information dialog box

Follow these steps to assign durations from the Task Information dialog box:

1. Display the Gantt Chart view. Double-click a Task Name to open the Task Information dialog box shown in Figure 4-1.

You also can click the Task Information button on the Standard toolbar, or right-click either the Task Name or the task's Gantt bar and select Task Information to display this dialog box.

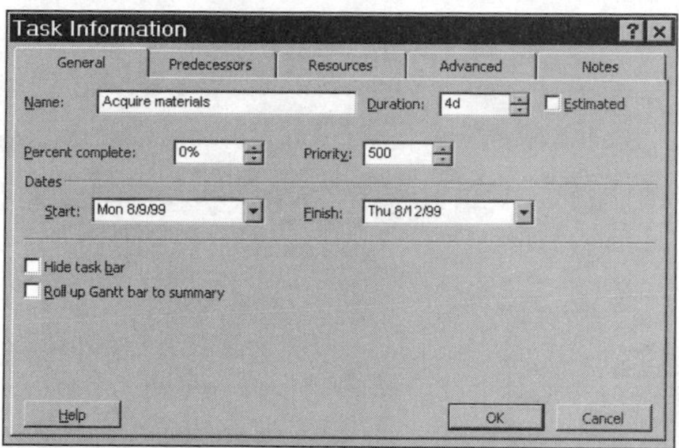


**Figure 4-1:** If you double-click an already-entered task name, that name appears in the Name field in this dialog box; if you double-click a blank task name cell, you can fill in the name here.

2. Use the arrows in the Duration field to reduce or increase the duration from the default setting of 1 day. Each click changes the duration by one day.

You may have noticed earlier that Project uses estimated durations by default for tasks when you type the duration into the Gantt table—you saw a question mark (?) next to each duration. When you establish a task's duration in the Task Information dialog box, place a check in the Estimated box to make the duration of the task estimated. Use estimated durations when the time frame for the task isn't firm; you can easily display tasks with estimated durations using a new filter in Project (see Chapter 6 for more information on filters).

3. Click the Duration field and highlight the current entry to enter a duration in increments other than a day.

Project 2000 enables you to specify a duration in months. Project uses the Calendar tab of the Options dialog box to determine the number of days in a month.

4. Type a new duration using the following abbreviations: *m* for minutes, *h* for hours, *w* for weeks, and *mo* for months.
5. Click OK to establish the task duration. For example, the Gantt chart task bars in Figure 4-2 reflect the new task lengths.

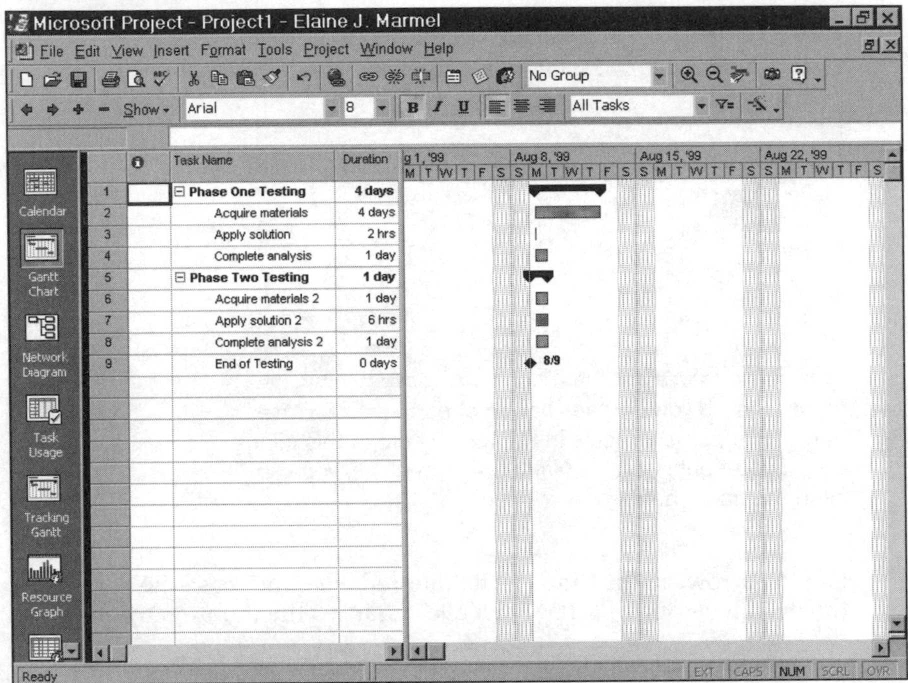


**Figure 4-2:** Task bars become more meaningful after you assign durations.

## Start and Finish Versus Duration

You could use the Start and Finish fields in the Task Information dialog box to set a start date and finish date for the task, rather than entering a duration. However, if you use the Start and Finish dates, Project uses only working days in that date range. If you enter a duration, Project calculates the beginning and end of the task, taking into consideration weekends and holidays for you. These two methods could have different results.

For example, suppose you have a four-day task that starts on December 21, 2000. Here's how that week looks on a calendar:

| *Mon* | *Tues* | *Weds* | *Thurs* | *Fri* | *Sat* | *Sun* |
|---|---|---|---|---|---|---|
| 18 | 19 | 20 | 21 | 22 | 23 | 24 |

December 25, 2000 falls on a Monday. If you entered 12/21/00 as the Start date and 12/26/00 as the Finish date, Project would calculate that as a three-day task (assuming that your company closes for Christmas) with work on December 21, 22, and 26. However, if you enter four days in the Duration field, the calculated Start and Finish dates would be 12/21/00 and 12/27/00, respectively, taking into account both the Christmas holiday and a weekend. The workdays in this instance would be December 21, 22, 26, and 27.

If a task has immutable timing, such as a Christmas celebration on Christmas day, use the Start and Finish fields. If you're definite about how many workdays a task will require, but not the days on which the work will occur, use the Duration field to set timing and let Project calculate the actual work dates based on the calendar.

## Using the Gantt table

To enter a task's duration on the Gantt table, simply click the Duration column and type in the duration. Even though you've set the default to use estimated durations, when you type a duration on the Gantt table, Project assumes you want an actual instead of an estimated duration — unless you type a question mark (?).

You can change Project's default behavior (and use actual instead of estimated durations) on the Schedule tab of the Options dialog box — see the next section for more information.

You can type in a duration in a few different ways. For example, Project recognizes all three of the following entries as three weeks: 3 w, 3 wks, 3 weeks.

If you want to assign the same duration to several contiguous tasks, type the duration once and then use the fill handle in the Duration column to copy the duration to the other tasks.

## Using your mouse and the task bar

Finally, follow these steps to adjust a task's duration using your mouse and the task bar:

1. Place your mouse pointer on the right edge of a task bar until the cursor becomes a vertical line with an arrow extending to the right of it.
2. Click and drag the bar to the right. As you do, Project displays the proposed new task duration and finish date (see Figure 4-3).
3. Release the mouse button when the duration you want appears in the information box.

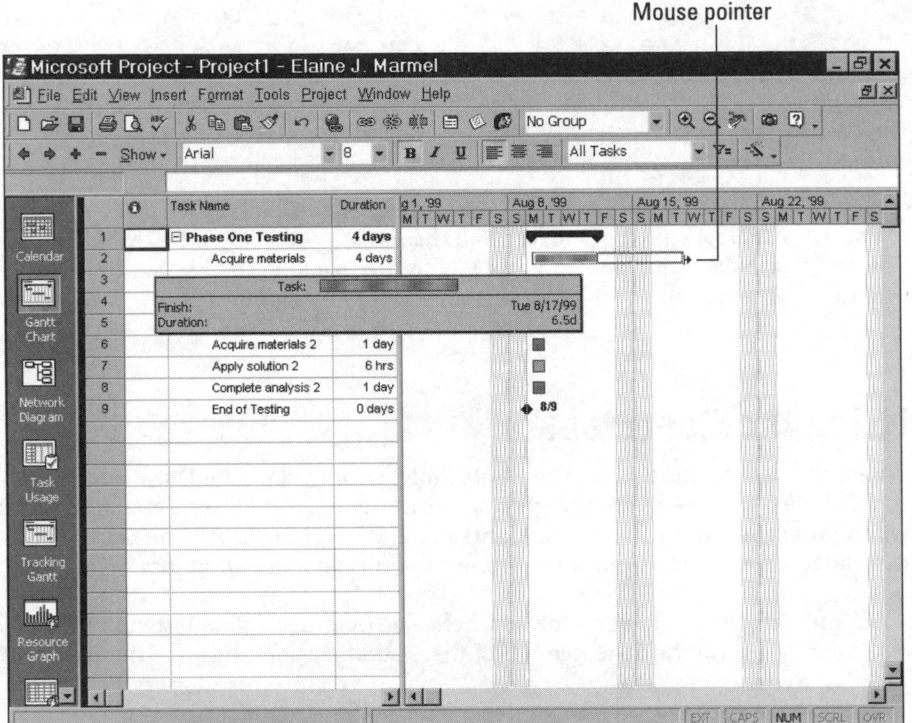


**Figure 4-3:** If you're a visually oriented person, dragging task bars to change durations might be the best method for you.

## Setting scheduling options

You aren't limited to entering resource-driven tasks or estimated durations on the Gantt table. You can change the default task type and other default scheduling settings for your project. Choose Tools ➪ Options and click the Schedule tab of the Options dialog box to change the default settings for entering tasks (see Figure 4-4).

Here you determine the default unit of time for entering task durations (the default is days), work time (hours), and whether new tasks start on the project start date or the current date. For example, if you are working on a five-year project in which most tasks run months, not days, you may want to change the default setting for the "Duration is entered in" field. If you prefer to have any new tasks begin no earlier than the current date, you can adjust the setting for New tasks. To enter actual durations instead of estimated durations, remove the check from the last checkbox on the Schedule tab.

As you gain experience in entering information, you will find ways to customize Project to match your work style. When you are satisfied with the settings in the Schedule tab, click OK to close the Options dialog box.

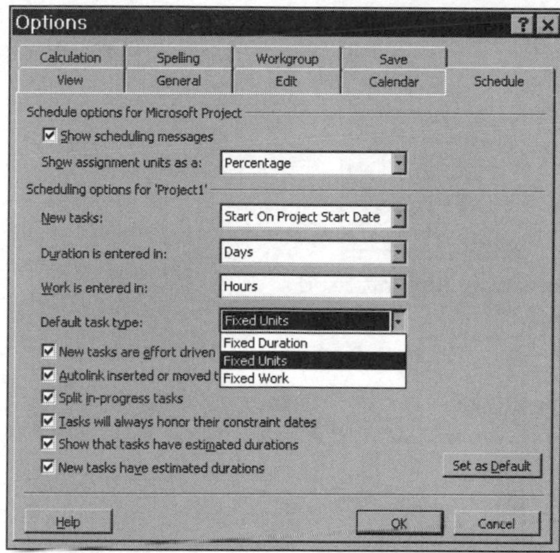


**Figure 4-4:** Use the Schedule tab of the Options dialog box to change Project's default behavior for scheduling.

## Assigning a calendar to a task

You can assign a calendar to a task using the same steps to create a Press calendar described in Chapter 3; choose Tools ⇨ Change Working Time to display the Change Working Time dialog box. Click the New button to create the calendar and provide a name for the new calendar. Select the dates that won't be "standard" and make the appropriate changes. Click OK to save the calendar.

For more detailed steps on creating a new calendar, see Chapter 3.

To assign a calendar to a task, double-click the task to open the Task Information dialog box for that task. Click the Advanced tab and open the Calendar list box to a special calendar for the task (see Figure 4-5).

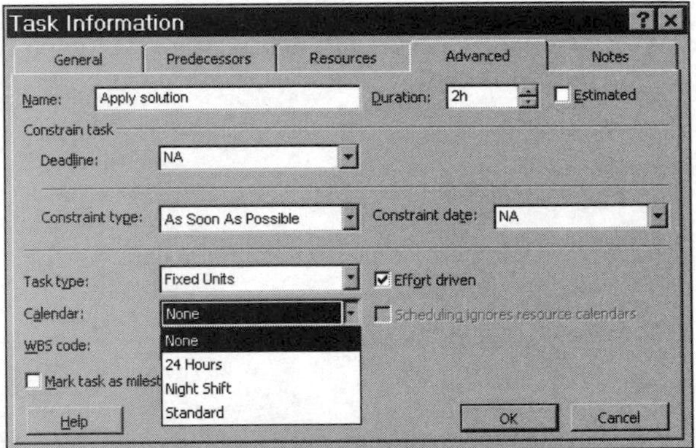


**Figure 4-5:** Assign a calendar to a task from the Advanced tab of the Task Information dialog box.

Task calendars are new to Project 2000.

## Creating milestones

Milestones are tasks that usually have zero duration. Managers often use milestones to mark key moments in a project, such as the completion of a phase or the approval of a product or activity. To create a milestone, you simply assign a duration of zero to a task. The symbol for a milestone on the Gantt chart is a diamond shape. For example, the diamond in the Gantt chart in Figure 4-6 indicates that the End of Testing task is a milestone.

You can mark any task as a milestone without changing its duration to zero. On the Advanced tab of the Task Information dialog box, place a check in the Mark Task as Milestone checkbox. In this case, the task duration won't change to zero; however, the element representing it in the Gantt chart changes from a bar, reflecting the task's duration, to a milestone diamond symbol, representing the task as a moment in time.

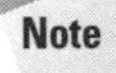


For milestones with durations longer than zero, the diamond appears at the end of the duration.

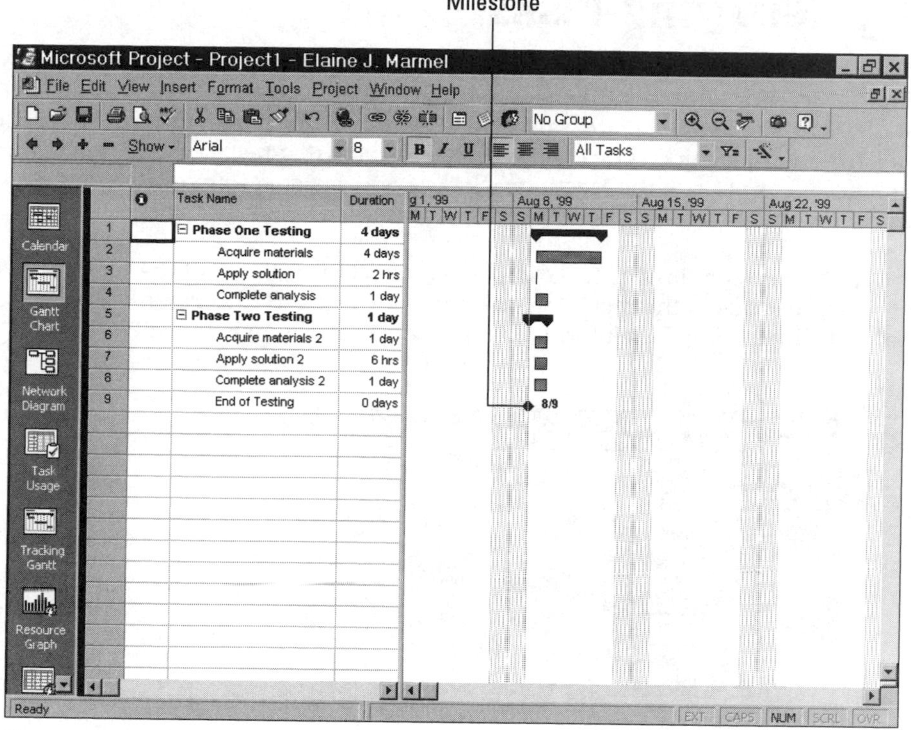


**Figure 4-6:** A milestone is typically a task of no duration; it simply marks a noteworthy point in your project.

## Timing for summary tasks

How do you assign durations for summary tasks? You don't. Remember, summary tasks simply roll up the timing of their subtasks. Therefore, they don't have any timing of their own. If three subtasks occur one right after the other and each is three days long, the summary task above them takes nine days from beginning to end. If you open the Task Information dialog box for a summary task, most timing settings appear gray, indicating that they're not available.

# Using Recurring Tasks

Projects quite often have tasks that occur on a regular basis: weekly staff meetings, quarterly reports, or monthly budget reviews are examples of these recurring tasks. Rather than have you create, say, 20 or so weekly staff-meeting tasks over the life of a five-month project, you can use Project's recurring-task feature. This feature enables you to create the Meeting task once and assign a frequency and timing to it. Follow these steps to create a recurring task:

1. Since Project inserts tasks above the selected task, select the task you want to appear below the recurring task and choose Insert ➪ Recurring Task to open the Recurring Task Information dialog box shown in Figure 4-7.

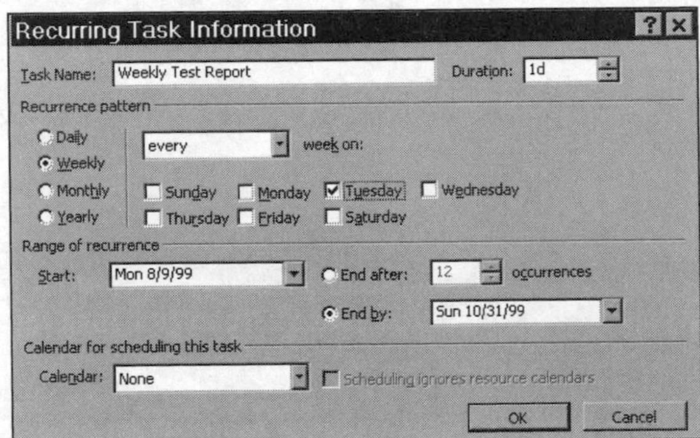


**Figure 4-7:** If a task occurs at regular intervals during the life of a project, you can save yourself time by creating it as a recurring task.

2. Set the task duration in the Duration field; for example, does the meeting run for two hours, or does a report take a day to write?

3. Set the occurrence of the task by selecting one of the Recurrence pattern option buttons: Daily, Weekly, Monthly, or Yearly. Depending on the recurrence you select, the timing settings to the right of the control buttons change. Figure 4-8 shows the Monthly settings.

4. Select the appropriate settings for the recurrence frequency. For a Weekly setting, place a check next to the days of the week on which you want the task to occur; for example, the task in Figure 4-7 occurs every Tuesday. For Monthly or Yearly, set the day of the month on which you want the task to occur; the task in Figure 4-8 occurs on Day 9 of every month.

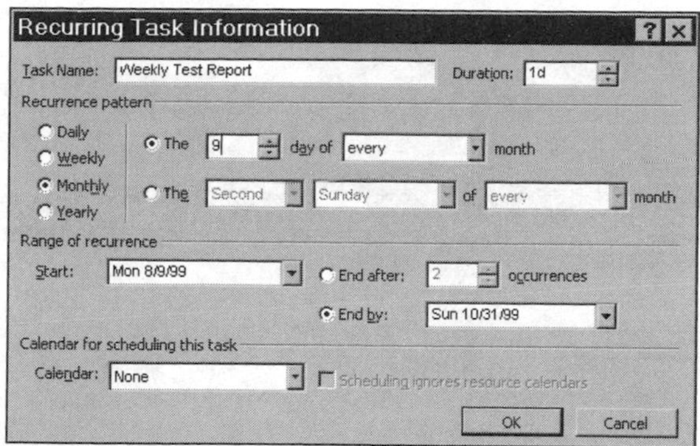


**Figure 4-8:** Daily, Weekly, Monthly, and Yearly occurrences require you to make slightly different choices.

For a Daily task, you have only one choice: whether you want it to occur every day or only on scheduled workdays. For example, if you want to schedule a computer backup for every day of the week – regardless of whether anyone is at work – you could have the task occur every day. (Ask your MIS department how to automate the process so that it occurs even when nobody is at work.)

5. Set the *Range of recurrence* — the period during which the task should recur — by entering Start and End after or End by dates. If you need to repeat a test weekly for only one month of your ten-month project, you could set Start and End after or End by dates that designate a month of time.

If you set the End after number of occurrences, Project calculates the date range required to complete that many occurrences of the recurring task and automatically displays the ending date in the End by box. This method can be useful if one of these events falls on a holiday: Project schedules one extra occurrence of the task to compensate. For a weekly staff meeting, you probably don't want to schedule an extra meeting because of a holiday; you can just skip that meeting or schedule it on a different day. On the other hand, if you must repeat a test 16 times during the project cycle, you would want to add one more occurrence of the Test task to compensate for the holiday. Therefore, set the number of occurrences rather than the time range.

6. Click OK to create the task. Project creates the appropriate number of tasks and displays them as subtasks under the summary task, Meeting; note the recurring task symbol in the Indicators column of the Gantt table in Figure 4-9.

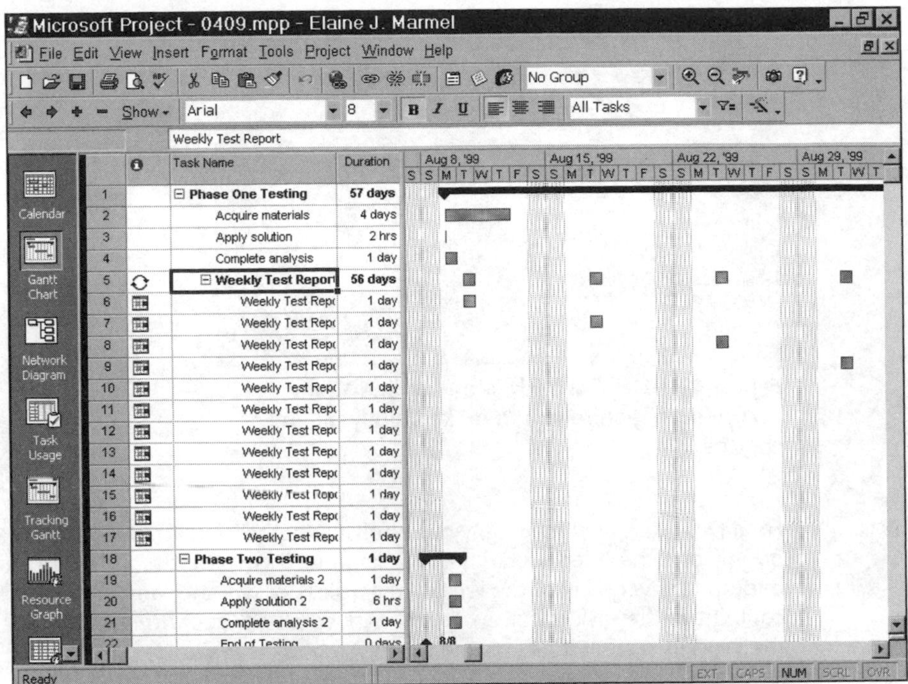


**Figure 4-9:** Task bars appear for each occurrence of the recurring task in the Gantt chart.

The symbol next to each Weekly Test Report task in the schedule in Figure 4-9 represents a task with a timing constraint applied. Project applies this constraint automatically as you enter settings for the recurring task. If you move your mouse pointer over one of these symbols, you can see an explanation of that constraint; for example, the first Weekly Test Report task has a Start No Earlier Than constraint, based on the timing you set in the Recurring Task Information dialog box. The first recurring task can start no earlier than the From date entered there, and each task occurs weekly thereafter. You learn more about setting timing constraints in the next section.

# Establishing Constraints and Deadline Dates

Constraints affect the timing of a task relative to the start or end of your project or to a specific date. Setting a deadline date in Project provides you with a visual reminder if you don't complete a task by the deadline date you establish.

## Understanding constraints

Project sets all tasks you create to start, by default, with an As Soon As Possible constraint. Barring any dependency relationships with other tasks (see "Establishing Dependencies Among Tasks" later in this chapter), the task would start on the first day of the project. You can set other constraints:

✦ **As Late As Possible.** This constraint forces a task to start on a date such that its end occurs no later than the end of the project.

✦ **Finish No Earlier Than/Finish No Later Than.** This constraint sets the completion of a task to fall no sooner or later than a specific date.

✦ **Must Finish On/Must Start On.** This constraint forces a task to finish or start on a specific date.

✦ **Start No Earlier Than/Start No Later Than.** This constraint sets the start of a task to fall no sooner or later than a specific date.

Only the Must Finish On/Must Start On settings constrain a task to start or end on a particular date; all the other settings constrain the task to occur within a certain time frame.

## Using deadline dates

You can also establish a deadline date for a task. The deadline date differs from a constraint because Project doesn't use the deadline date when calculating a project's schedule. Instead, the deadline date behaves as a visual cue to notify you that a task finished after the deadline date (see Figure 4-10). Be aware that you won't see any indicator if you complete the task prior to the deadline date.

Project 2000 enables you to set a deadline date for a task.

While deadline dates won't affect the calculation of a project schedule, they will affect a Late Finish date and the calculation of total slack for the project. Also be aware that you can assign both a deadline date and a constraint to a task. In a project that you schedule from a beginning date, a deadline date has the same effect as a Finish No Later Than constraint. If you assign deadline dates to tasks in projects that you schedule from an ending date, those tasks will finish on their deadline dates unless a constraint or a dependency pushes them to an earlier date.

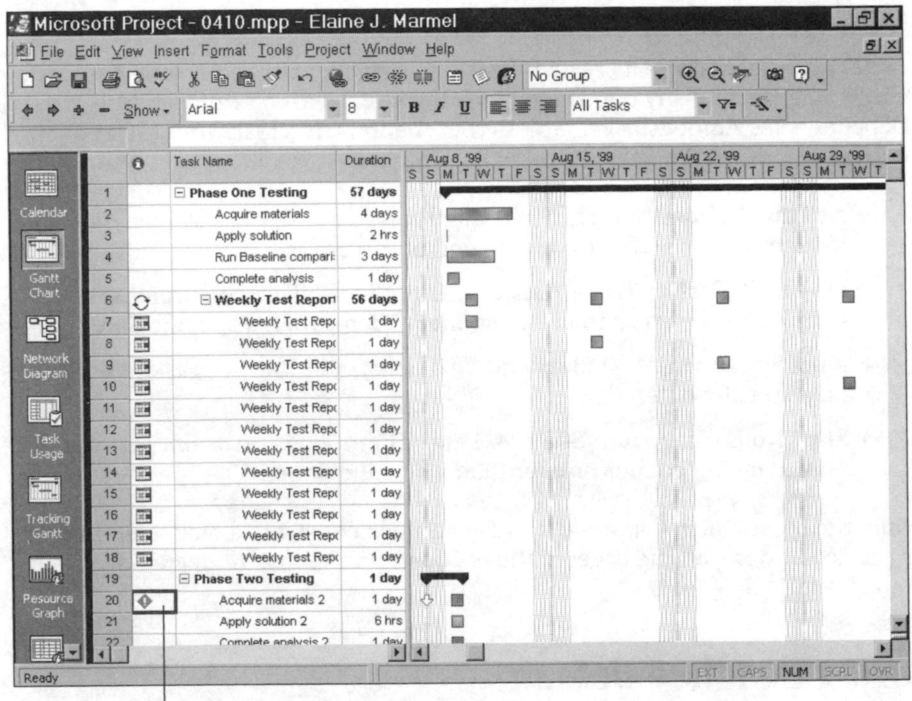


**Figure 4-10:** When you set a deadline date for a task and you don't finish the task before the deadline, Project displays an indicator to alert you that the task finished later than you specified.

# Setting constraints and deadline dates

You set constraints on tasks in your project using the Advanced tab of the Task Information dialog box, shown in Figure 4-11. Select a constraint type in the Constraint Type drop-down list. For all settings in the Type list other than As Late As Possible and As Soon As Possible, designate a date by typing in a date or by clicking the arrow next to the Constraint Date field and choosing a date from the drop-down calendar that appears. Set a deadline date by clicking the arrow next to the Constraint Date field and choosing a date from the drop-down calendar that appears.

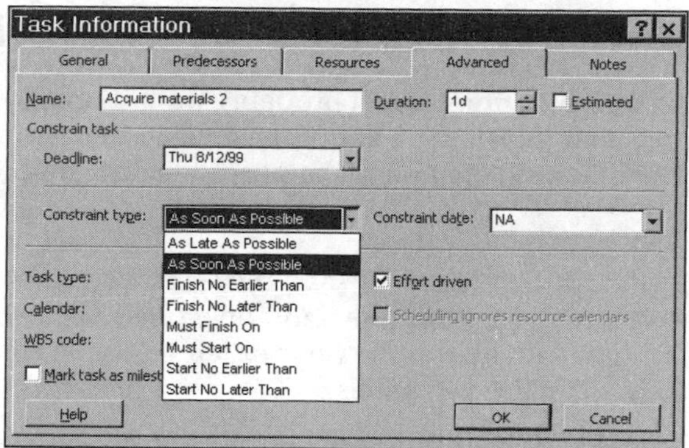


**Figure 4-11:** Click the arrow next to the Constraint type field to see the various constraints.

When might constraints be useful? Consider these situations:

- ✦ A project involves preparing a new facility for occupancy, and you want the final inspection of that facility to happen as late as possible.
- ✦ The approval of a yearly budget must finish no later than the last day of the fiscal year, ready to begin the new year with the budget in place.
- ✦ Billing of a major account must start no sooner than the first day of the next quarter so that the income doesn't accrue on your books this quarter.
- ✦ Presentation of all severance packages for laid off employees must finish on the day a major takeover of the company is announced.

Deadline dates might be useful when:

- ✦ You need to prepare the annual budget by a deadline date to ensure approval in time to begin the new year with the budget in place.
- ✦ You need to prepare severance packages for laid off employees so that you can present them on the day a major takeover of the company is announced.

You see how constraints and dependencies interact in establishing the timing of tasks later in this chapter in the section "Establishing Dependencies Among Tasks."

# Manipulating the Gantt Chart to View Timing

After you enter several tasks and task durations, you'll probably want to manipulate the timescale in the Gantt chart to view information about these tasks using different increments of time. Use any of the following methods to modify the appearance of items in your Gantt chart:

- ✦ Adjust the amount of the window the Gantt table and the Gantt chart use by moving your mouse pointer over the divider line until it becomes the two-directional arrow cursor. Drag the divider to the right or left to adjust the amount of the window taken up by the two panes.
- ✦ Modify the width of columns in the Gantt table so you can see more columns onscreen by moving your mouse pointer over a column's right edge until you see the two-directional arrow cursor. Drag the column edge to the right or left to adjust its width.
- ✦ Double-click the column heading and change the column width in the Column Definition dialog box that appears. Also use this dialog box to change the title and alignment of the column title.
- ✦ Modify the increments of time displayed in the timescale itself either by double-clicking the timescale or by choosing Format ➪ Timescale. The Timescale dialog box, shown in Figure 4-12, appears. You can change the units for both the major timescale (shown on the top) and minor timescale (shown just beneath the major timescale). These adjustments enable you to concentrate on a particular period in your project or to view larger increments with less detail. The Count field controls how many instances of the unit Project marks off on your Gantt chart.

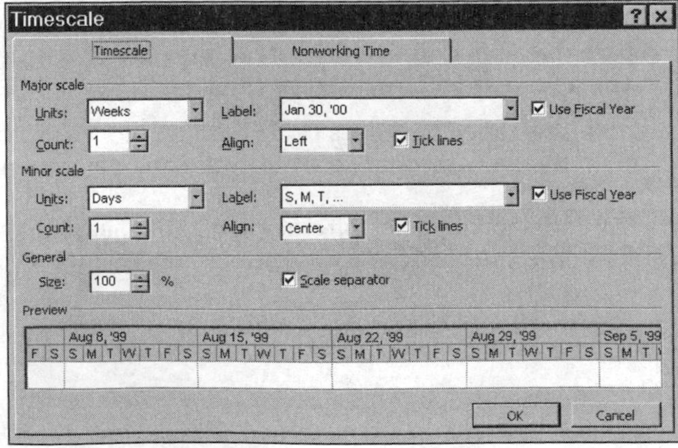


**Figure 4-12:** In the Timescale dialog box, adjust the units to display and how many to include.

Figure 4-13, for example, shows a major timescale in months and a minor timescale in weeks. The Count for each is 1: one month with each of its four or five weeks shown. If you change the Count for weeks to 2, the weekly timescale marks display in two-week increments, as shown in Figure 4-14.

To shrink the timescale even more—that is, to see more of your project onscreen—use the Size setting in the Timescale dialog box. This setting enables you to view the timescale at a percentage of its full size.

Figure 4-15 shows one timescale using a fiscal year while the other timescale uses a calendar year; the fiscal year begins in June. Notice the crossover of the two timescales. Using different fiscal/calendar bases on the timescales makes most sense if all other scale settings are identical; that is, compare months or quarters using the same count in *both* scales.

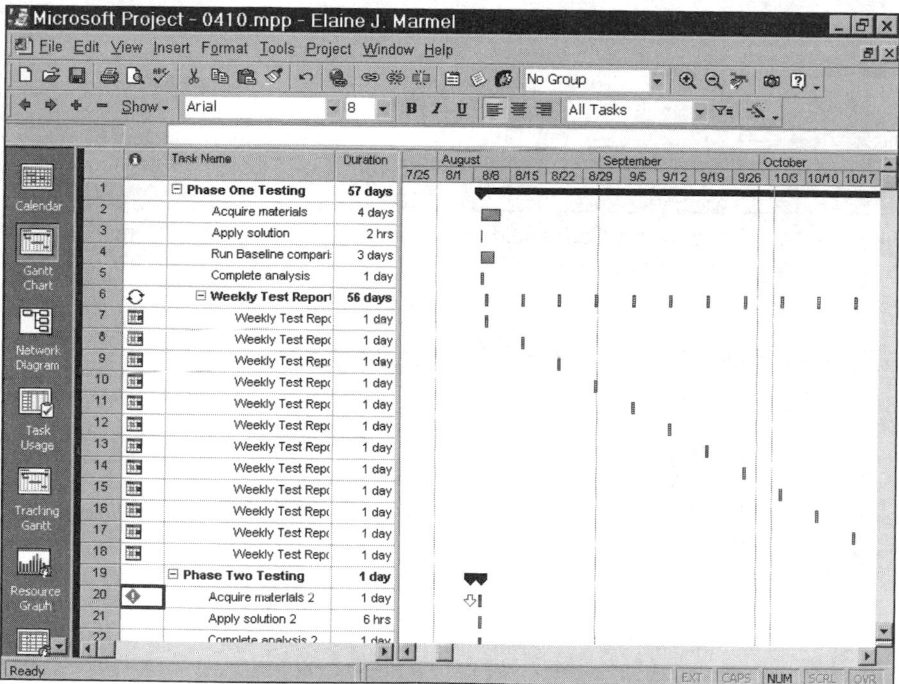


**Figure 4-13:** When you specify one week in the Count field of the Timescale dialog box, Project marks off every week on the minor timescale.

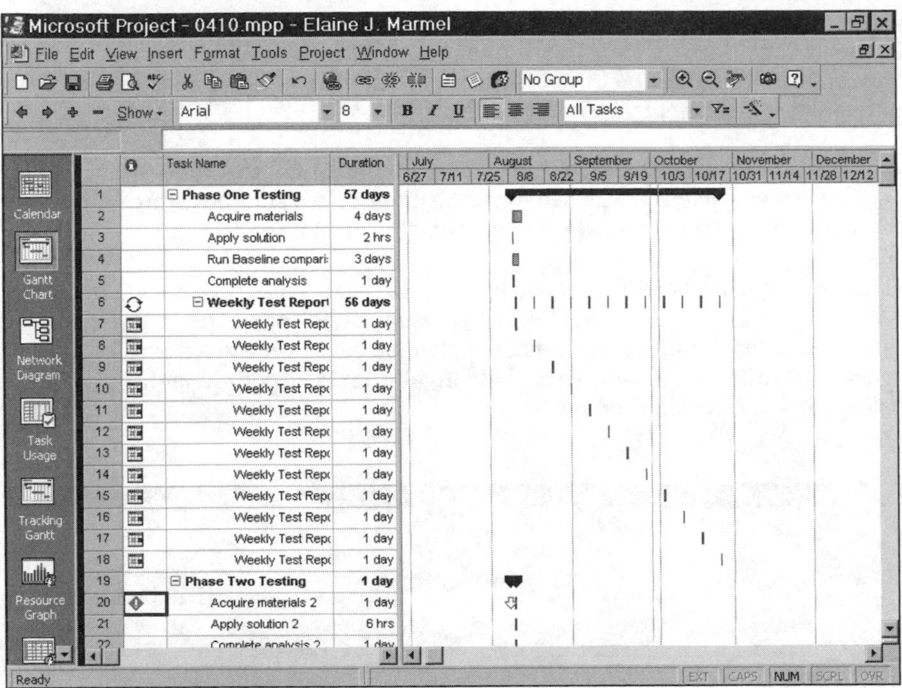


**Figure 4-14:** Changing the Count field for weeks to 2 causes Project to mark off weeks in two-week chunks.

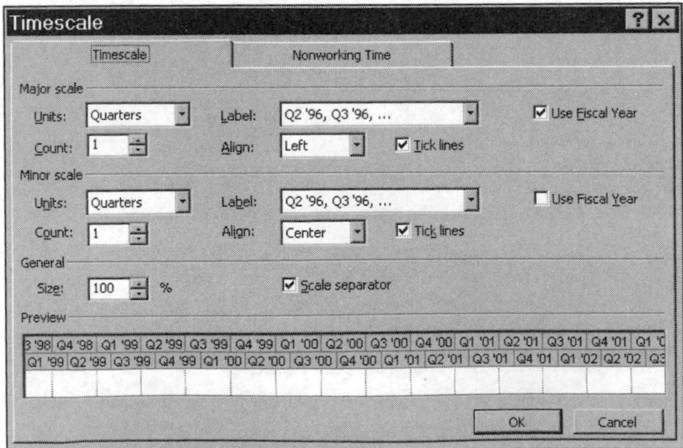


**Figure 4-15:** You can compare fiscal and calendar years for the same schedule.

In Project 2000, you can independently set the use of the fiscal year for both the major and the minor timescale so that you can compare fiscal year information with calendar year information.

To make this feature work, you must set up a fiscal year calendar. Use the detailed steps you found in Chapter 3 or the overview steps reviewed earlier in this chapter. As you create the new calendar, make sure you click the Options button in the Change Working Calendar dialog box to display the Calendar tab of the Options dialog box. Then, change the starting month from January to your fiscal year's starting month.

# Entering Task Notes

You can attach notes to individual tasks to remind you of certain parameters or details for the task. For example, if a task involves several subcontractors, you might want to list their contact information here so it's close at hand when you're working on the project schedule. Or use the Notes field to note company regulations relative to that type of procedure. When you add a note to a task, you can display the note onscreen and include the note in a printed report.

You can also attach notes to individual resources and to their assignments, as you learn in Chapter 5. To enter a note for a task, follow these steps:

1. Double-click a task to open the Task Information dialog box.
2. Click the Notes tab to display it (see Figure 4-16).

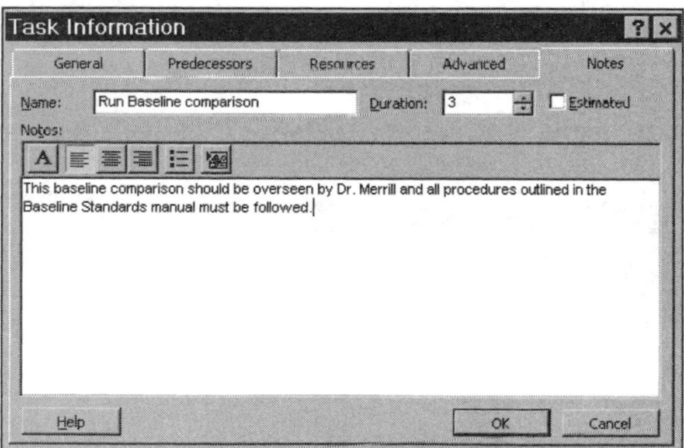


**Figure 4-16:** The Notes tab provides simple word processing—such as tools for formatting your notes.

3. Type your note in the area provided. You can use the tools identified in Figure 4-16 to format your note text.
4. Click OK to attach the note to your task.

A Note icon now appears in the Indicators column of the Gantt table, as shown in Figure 4-17. Move the mouse pointer over this icon to display the note.

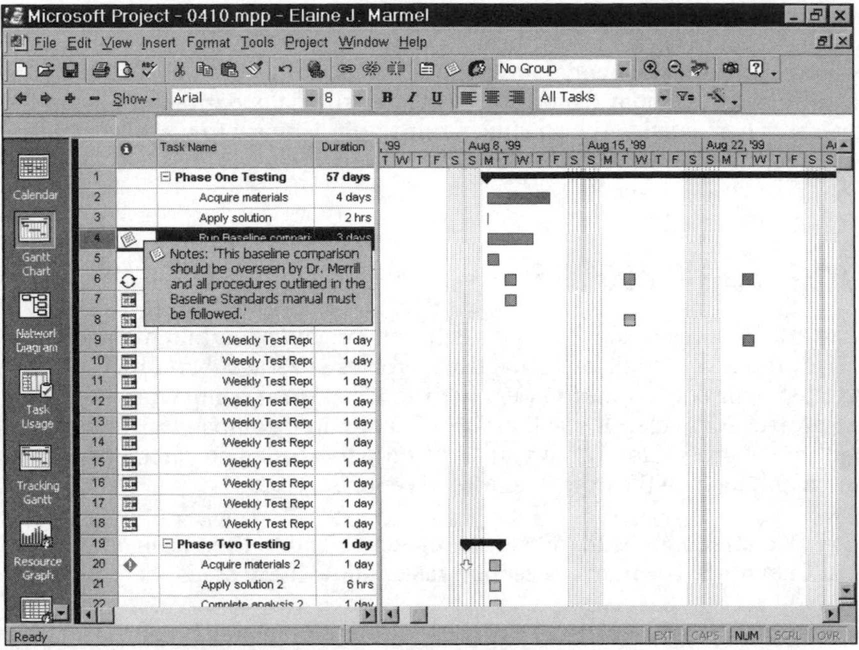


**Figure 4-17:** Project automatically adds an icon for the note to the Indicators column.

You can print notes along with your schedule. To do so, follow these steps:

1. Choose File ➪ Page Setup.
2. Click the View tab to display the settings shown in Figure 4-18.

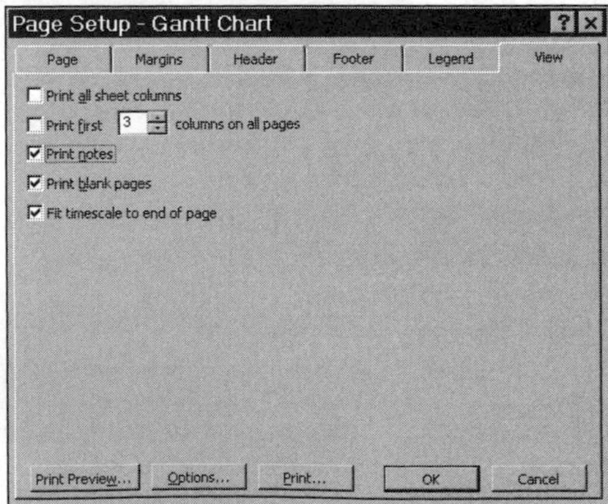


**Figure 4-18:** Notes appears as the right-most column in your Gantt table when you place a check next to Print notes.

3. Click the Print notes checkbox to have Project print notes for tasks.
4. Click OK.

You learn more about printing schedules in Chapter 7.

# Establishing Dependencies Among Tasks

Whereas constraints tie tasks to the project start or end or to particular dates, dependencies tie tasks to the timing of other tasks in the project. Dependencies are central to visualizing the true length of a project.

Dependencies exist because all tasks in a project rarely can happen simultaneously; usually, some tasks must start or finish before others can begin. Tasks overlap for many reasons: the inability of resources to do more than one task at a time, the lack of availability of equipment, or the nature of the tasks themselves (you can't start construction until you receive a construction permit). You can't really know the total time you will need to complete a project until you establish durations and dependencies. For example, a project that comprises five 10-day-long tasks with no dependencies among the tasks takes ten days to complete. But, if the tasks must happen one after the other, the project requires 50 days.

## Understanding dependencies

Let me take a moment to define some terms. A task that must occur before another task is a *predecessor* task. The task that occurs later in the relationship is a *successor* task. A task can have multiple predecessors and successors. Tasks with dependency relationships are *linked*. Gantt charts show these links as lines running between task bars; an arrow at one end points to the successor task. Some dependency relationships are as simple as one task ending before another can begin. However, some relationships are much more complex. For example, if you're moving into a new office and the first task is assembling cubicles, you don't have to wait until all the cubicles are assembled to begin moving in furniture. You might work in tandem, using the first morning to set up cubicles on the first floor. Then you can begin to move chairs and bookcases into the first-floor cubicles while the setup task continues on the second floor.

## Understanding the interactions between constraints and dependencies

Both constraints and dependencies drive the timing of a task. Consider for a moment how constraints and dependencies might interact when you apply one of each to a task. Say that you have a task—to open a new facility—that has a constraint set so that it must start on June 6. You then set up a dependency that indicates the task should begin after a task—fire inspection—that is scheduled for completion on

June 10. When you try to set up such a dependency, Project displays a Planning Wizard dialog box, like the one in Figure 4-19. This dialog box indicates a scheduling conflict. Project displays this dialog box when a conflict exists among dependencies or between constraints and dependencies.

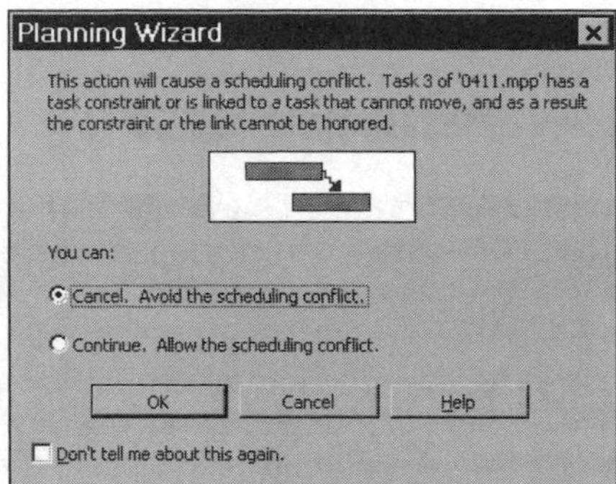


**Figure 4-19:** Multiple dependencies or a combination of dependencies and constraints can cause conflicts in timing.

If a conflict exists between a constraint and a dependency, the constraint drives the timing of the task; the task bar does not move from the constraint-imposed date. You can modify this functionality by choosing Tools ➪ Options. On the Schedule tab of the Options dialog box, remove the check from the Tasks Will Always Honor Their Constraint Dates checkbox. When you change this option, dependencies, rather than constraints, determine timing.

See Chapter 9 for more about resolving timing conflicts.

You can create dependencies in one of three ways:

✦ You can select two tasks and use the Link Tasks command on the Edit menu or the Link Tasks button on the Standard toolbar. The first task you select becomes the predecessor in the relationship.

✦ You can open the successor task's Task Information dialog box and enter predecessor information on the Predecessors tab.

✦ You can use your mouse button to click the Gantt bar of a predecessor and drag to the Gantt bar of a successor to create a link to a successor task.

If you want to link a whole range of tasks to be consecutive (one finishes, the next begins, and so on down through the list of tasks), select the range of tasks (drag from the ID number of the first task to the ID of the last task). Then use the Link Tasks button or the Link Tasks command in the Edit menu to create a string of such relationships at one time.

## Allowing for overlap and delays

Although many dependency relationships are relatively clear-cut — Task A can begin only when Task B is complete, or Task C can start only after Task B has started — some are even more finely delineated. These relationships involve overlap and delay (delay is also called *lag time*).

To understand these two concepts, let's look at examples. Your project tests a series of metals. In the first task, you apply a solution to the metal, and in the second task, you analyze the results. However, time can be a factor, so you want the analysis to begin only when several days have passed after the application of the solution. You build in delay between the finish of the first task (the predecessor) and the start of the second (the successor). Figure 4-20 shows a relationship with some lag between two tasks; the line between the two tasks indicates the dependency, and the space between the bars indicates the gap in time between the finish of one and the start of the next.

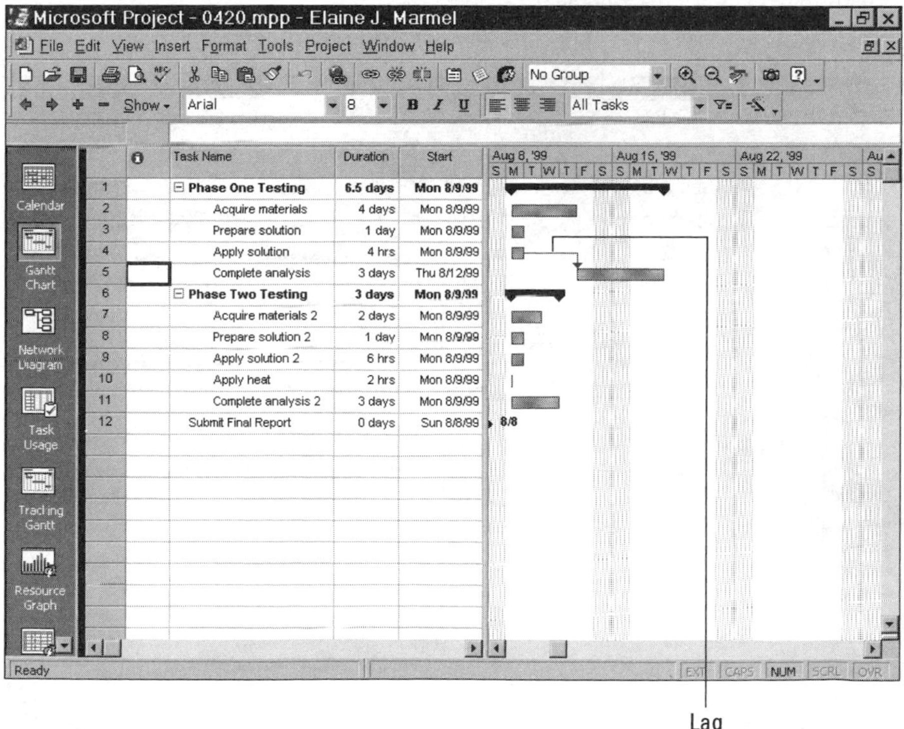


**Figure 4-20:** After you apply the solution, you must wait four days to analyze the results.

Some people prefer to build a task to represent lag, rather than to establish a dependency relationship. For example, instead of placing a dependency between application of the solution and analysis, you could create a three-day-long task–Solution Reaction Period. Then create a simple dependency relationship between Solution Reaction Period and the analysis so that the analysis task won't begin until Solution Reaction Period is complete. Adding the lag tasks can generate a very long schedule with multiple tasks and relationships to track. But in a simpler schedule, this approach enables you to see relationships as task bars. You can try both methods, and see which works best for you.

Another test in your project involves applying both a solution and heat. You first want to apply the solution for three hours and then begin to apply heat as well. Notice the overlap between the tasks: the predecessor task—applying the solution—begins at 8:00 a.m. and runs to 2:00 p.m.; the successor task—applying heat—begins three hours after the start of the predecessor task, at 11:00 a.m. The project in Figure 4-21 has some overlap between tasks.

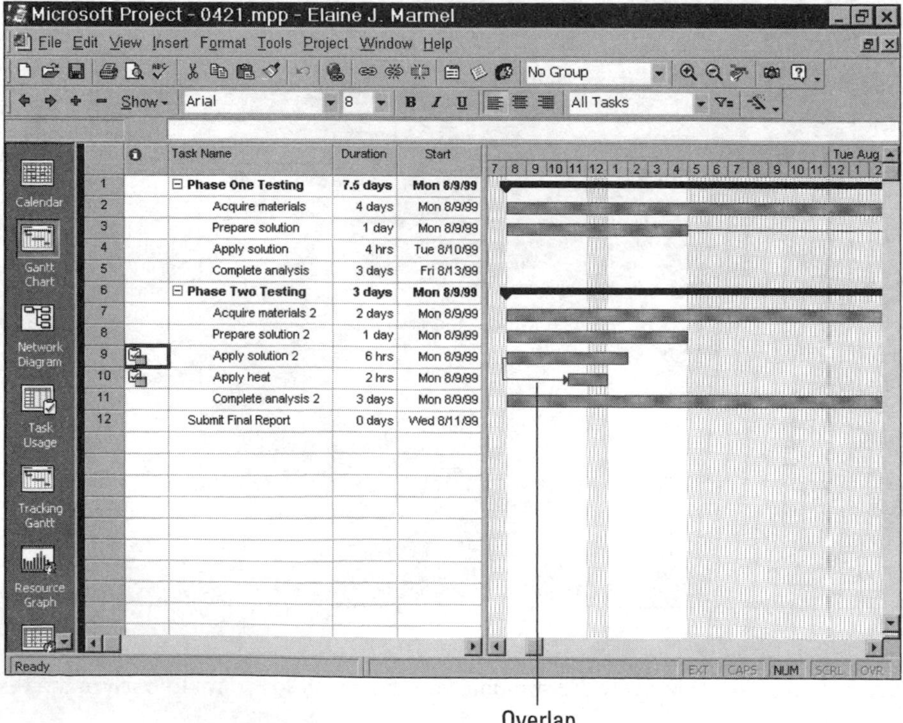


**Figure 4-21:** Some overlap occurs between the application of the solution and the application of the heat in this testing project.

I set up a task calendar that ignores lunchtime so that both tasks could continue uninterrupted (the icons in the Indicator column represent the task calendar), and I changed the timescale so that you can see the hours of a day.

## Dependency types

Four basic dependency relationships define the relationship between the start and finish of tasks: start-to-finish, finish-to-start, start-to-start, and finish-to-finish. You can set these dependency relationships on the Predecessors tab of the Task Information dialog box, shown in Figure 4-22.

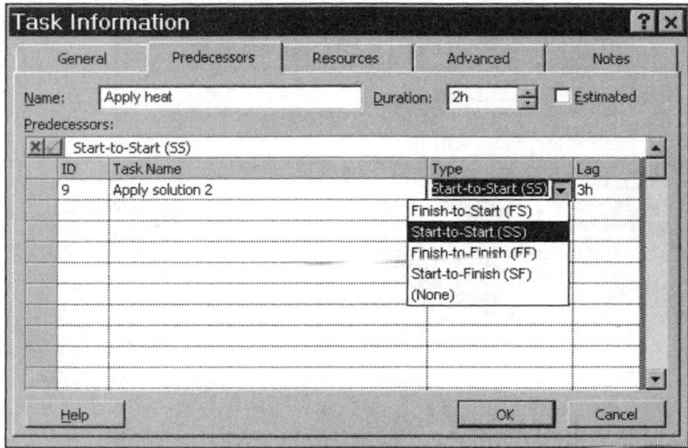


**Figure 4-22:** Four types of dependencies enable you to deal with every variable of how tasks can relate to each other's timing.

The first timing mentioned in each relationship name relates to the predecessor task and the second to the successor. Therefore, a start-to-finish dependency relates the start of the predecessor to the finish of the successor, and a finish-to-start relationship relates the finish of the predecessor to the start of the successor. Project refers to these relationships by their initials, such as SS for a start-to-start relationship.

### Finish-to-start (FS)

A finish-to-start relationship is the most common type of dependencies and is, in fact, the only relationship you can create using your mouse or Link Tasks tool or command. In the finish-to-start relationship, the successor task cannot start until the predecessor task finishes. Examples of this relationship are:

- ✦ You must write a report before you can edit it.
- ✦ You must have a computer before you can install your software.

In Figure 4-23, you see examples of the FS relationship in which the successor task can start as soon as its predecessor is finished. The following tasks have a finish-to-start relationship:

Task 2 and Task 3

Task 3 and Task 4

Task 4 and Task 5

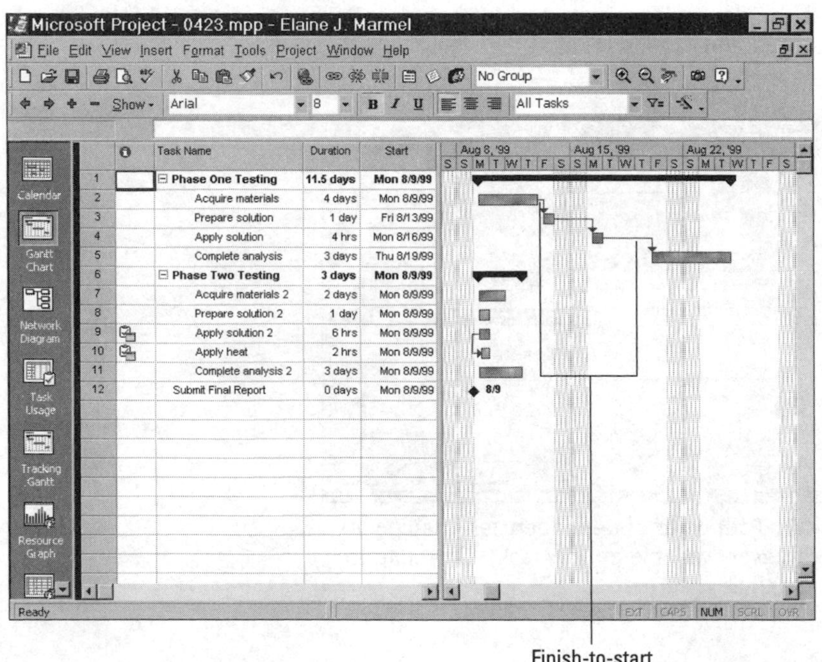


**Figure 4-23:** In the FS relationship, successor tasks cannot start until predecessor tasks finish.

The relationship between Tasks 4 and 5 also contains some lag time added in the previous section, "Allowing for Overlap and Delays."

## Start-to-finish (SF)

With the start-to-finish relationship, the successor task cannot finish until the predecessor task starts. Here are some examples:

✦ You can finish scheduling production crews only when you start receiving materials.

✦ Employees can start using a new procedure only when they have finished training on it. If the use of the new procedure is delayed, you also want to delay the training so that it occurs as late as possible before the implementation.

Could you set up this start-to-finish example as a finish-to-start relationship? Not really. The idea is to allow no delay between training and implementation. If you set the new procedure to start only when the training finishes, the new procedure could start any time after the training ends, depending on how other relationships might delay it. If the training task has to finish just before the other task starts, delays of the later task (implementation) also delay the earlier task. This fine distinction will become clearer when you see projects in action.

Figure 4-24 shows a start-to-finish relationship between acquiring materials for Phase 2 Testing and completing the analysis of Phase One Testing. Assuming the test results of Phase 1 determine the materials you'll need for Phase 2, you really can't begin acquiring materials for Phase 2 Testing until you have completed the analysis of Phase 1 Testing.

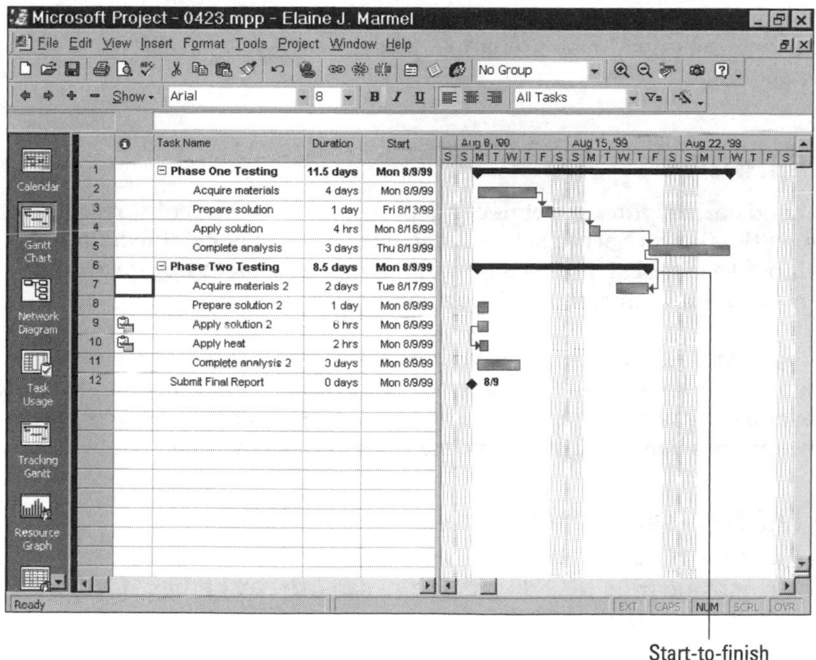


**Figure 4-24:** The successor task cannot finish until the predecessor task starts.

## Start-to-start (SS)

In a start-to-start relationship, the successor cannot start until the predecessor starts. Consider these examples:

- ✦ When you start getting results in an election, you can begin to compile them.
- ✦ When the drivers start their engines, the flagger can start the race.

Refer to Figure 4-21 to see a start-to-start relationship with some built-in lag time.

### Finish-to-finish (FF)

In the finish-to-finish dependency, the successor task cannot finish until the predecessor task finishes. For example:

- ✦ You finish installing computers at the same time that you finish moving employees into the building so that they can begin using the computers right away.
- ✦ Two divisions must finish retooling their production lines on the same day so that the CEO can inspect them at the same time.

Suppose, in Phase Two of the testing in Figure 4-25, you can begin preparing the solution (Prepare solution 2) while you're still acquiring materials (Acquire materials 2); however, you cannot finish preparing the solution until you finish acquiring the materials. Therefore, set up a finish-to-finish dependency between the two tasks to make sure that you don't finish preparing the solution if you experience a delay acquiring materials.

## Establishing dependencies

As mentioned earlier, you can set dependencies in a few different ways. If you use the tasks on the Gantt chart to set dependencies, you must establish finish-to-start relationships. To establish more complex relationships, including delay and overlap, use the Task Information dialog box.

You can set dependencies between two summary tasks or between a summary task and subtask in another task group using a finish-to-start or a start-to-start dependency. You cannot use any other type of dependency, and you cannot set dependencies between a summary task and any of its own subtasks.

### Setting finish-to-start dependencies

With the Gantt chart displayed, you can use your mouse, the Link Tasks tool, or the Link Tasks command from the Edit menu. You can use any of these methods to set a simple finish-to-start relationship:

1. Place your mouse pointer over the predecessor task until the cursor turns into four arrows pointing outward.
2. Drag the mouse pointer to the second task. An information box describes the finish-to-start link you are about to create, as shown in Figure 4-26.
3. Release your mouse button when you're satisfied with the relationship, and Project establishes the link.

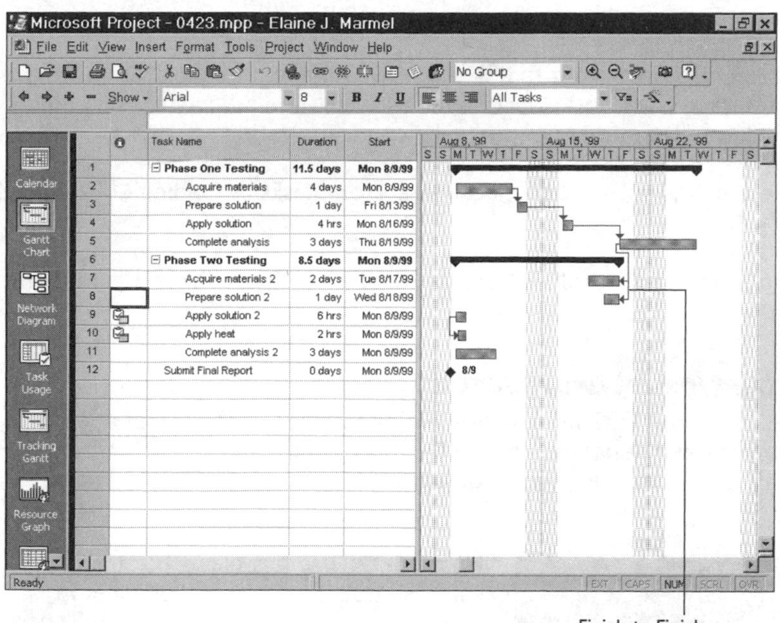


**Figure 4-25:** The successor task cannot finish before the predecessor task finishes.

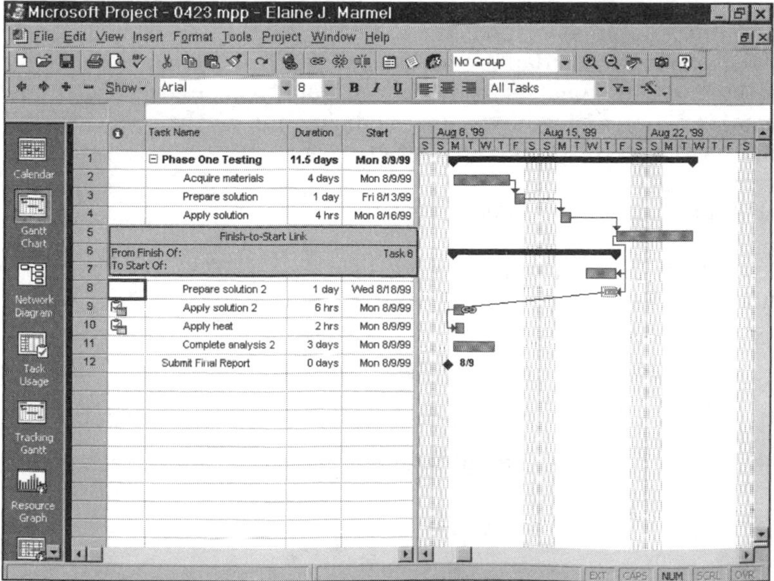


**Figure 4-26:** The relationship isn't established until you release the mouse button. If you have second thoughts, just drag back to the predecessor task before releasing your mouse.

To use the Link Tasks tool or command, simply follow these steps:

1. Select the tasks you want to link. To select adjacent tasks, drag through their ID numbers in the Gantt Chart table. To select non-adjacent tasks, hold Ctrl as you click the ID numbers of the tasks you want to link.

In Project 2000, you also can select non-adjacent tasks by holding Ctrl as you click their Gantt bars.

2. Click the Link Tasks tool, or Choose Edit ➪ Link Tasks. Project establishes the link.

## Setting other types of dependencies

You can use either the Task Information dialog box or the Task Dependency dialog box to set any type of dependency. Use the Task Dependency dialog box (see Figure 4-27) to establish dependency types or lag times between tasks.

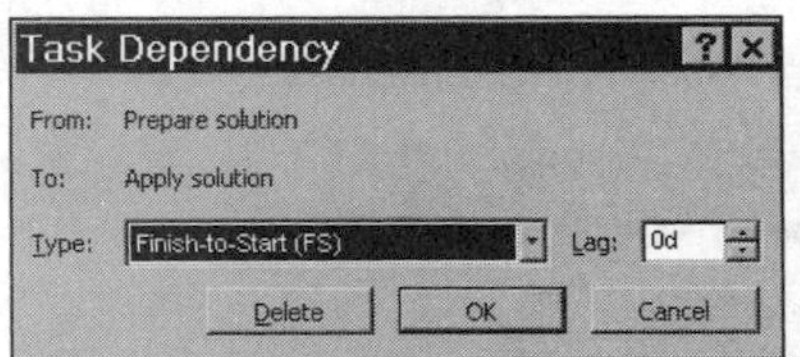


**Figure 4-27:** Use this dialog box to establish task dependencies or lag time.

From the Task Information dialog box, in addition to establishing dependencies and lag times, you also can set overlap times. To open the Task Dependency dialog box, double-click the line that connects the tasks you want to change. If you choose to use the Task Information dialog box, open the dialog box for the successor task and build the relationship on the Predecessors tab.

Follow these steps to create a task dependency:

1. Double-click the task you want to make a successor. When the Task Information dialog box appears, select the Predecessors tab if it's not already displayed.
2. Click the Task Name column; an arrow appears at its far end.
3. Click the arrow to display the drop-down list of task names shown in Figure 4-28.
4. Click the task you want to identify as the predecessor to this task.

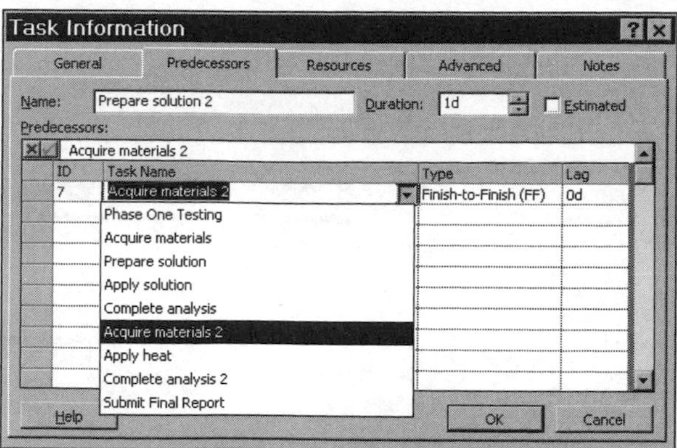


**Figure 4-28:** Every task you create for your project appears on this list.

5. Click the Type field; a list box arrow appears.
6. Click the arrow to display a list of dependency types.
7. Click the type of dependency you wish to establish, such as start-to-start or start-to-finish.

To establish a dependency with no delay or overlap, click OK at this point to create the relationship. If you want to establish any delay, click the Lag column and supply an amount of time for the delay. If you want to establish overlap, simply enter a negative number in the Lag column. For example, if you want the successor to finish one week before the predecessor finishes, use a finish-to-finish relationship and type **1 week** in the Lag column.

# Viewing Dependencies

When you've established several dependencies in a project, you can study them in several ways. You can, of course, open each task's Task Information dialog box and look at the relationships listed on the Predecessor tab. You can also view the lines drawn between tasks to see dependencies. Finally, you can scroll to the right in the Gantt table to display the Predecessors column, as in Figure 4-29. This column lists any relationships, using the two letter abbreviations for the dependency type and positive and negative numbers to show lag and overlap.

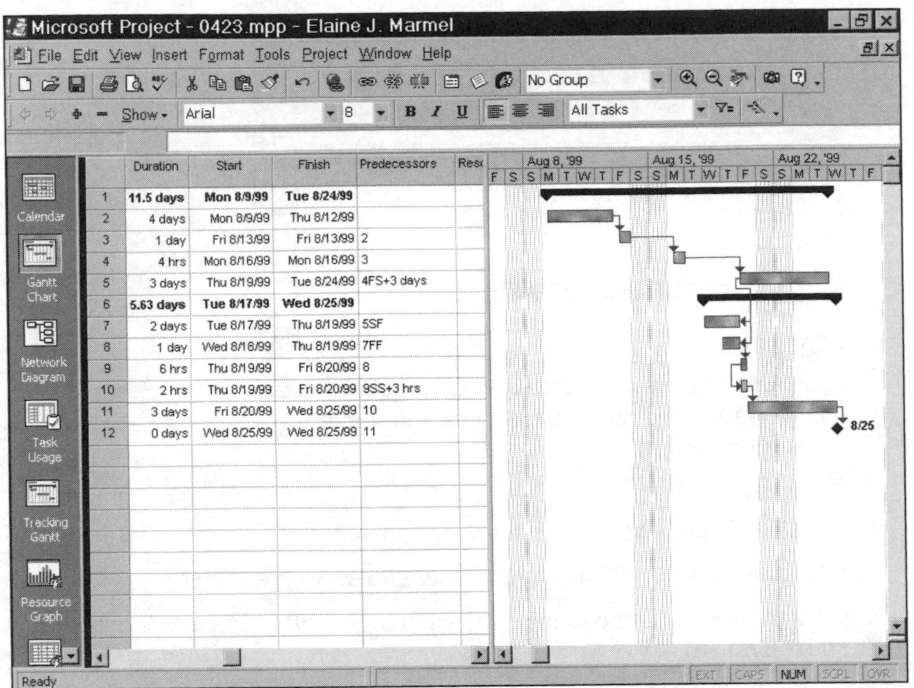


**Figure 4-29:** Display the Predecessors column to show all the relationships for a task.

# Deleting Dependencies

Here are several techniques for deleting dependencies:

- ✦ Open the Task Information dialog box for the successor task, select the Predecessors tab, click the task name for the link to be broken, and press Delete on your keyboard.
- ✦ Display the Predecessors column in the Gantt table, click that column for the successor task, and either press Delete to delete all relationships or edit the predecessor information in the cell or in the entry bar.
- ✦ Select the tasks involved in the dependency you want to delete and click the Unlink Tasks tool, or choose Edit ➪ Unlink Tasks.
- ✦ Double-click the dependency line and click the Delete button in the Task Dependency dialog box.

If you delete a dependency, the task bars may shift accordingly to reflect any new timing.

# Summary

In this chapter you read more about the timing of tasks, including how to set task durations and dependencies. You know how to:

- ✦ Differentiate between resource-driven and fixed scheduling
- ✦ Establish task durations
- ✦ Assign calendars to tasks
- ✦ Create recurring tasks
- ✦ Establish constraints and deadline dates
- ✦ Adjust the timescale to view task durations
- ✦ Add and view task notes
- ✦ Set, view, and delete dependencies

In Chapter 5 you begin to assign resources to tasks and to learn more about the relationship between resource assignment and task timing.

✦ ✦ ✦

# Creating Resources and Assigning Costs

✦ ✦ ✦ ✦

**In This Chapter**

Understanding resources

Creating a resource list

Modifying resource information

Using resources and tasks

Handling unusual cost situations

✦ ✦ ✦ ✦

The management portion of the term "project management" suggests that you are overseeing and, supposedly, controlling what goes on during the project's lifetime. In the last chapter you learned how to build the tasks that make up the project. Now you need to identify the resources for each task. Some tasks require people only; other tasks may also require equipment.

As you create resources, you'll see that various rates are associated with a resource. As you assign the resource to a task in your project, Microsoft Project automatically begins to calculate the cost of your project.

## Understanding Resources

Resources are the people, supplies, and equipment that enable you to complete the tasks in your project. Resources cost money and therefore affect the cost of the project. To manage a project effectively, you should define resources and assign those resources to tasks in the project. Thus, you need to know how Project uses those resource assignments to change the duration and length of your project.

If you expect to use the same resources for several projects, consider setting up the resources in a special project that contains no tasks. Then you can use Project's resource pooling feature and the "resource project" to share resources across multiple projects. This approach enables you to set up resources once but use them repeatedly on many different projects. For more information on resource pooling, see Chapter 10. For more information on managing multiple projects, see Chapter 17.

## How resources work

By defining and then assigning resources, you accomplish several goals:

- ✦ You can keep track of the tasks being performed by resources — because Project identifies the resources assigned to each task.
- ✦ You can identify potential resource shortages that could force you to miss scheduled deadlines and possibly extend the duration of your project.
- ✦ You can identify underutilized resources. If you reassign these resources, you may be able to shorten the project's schedule.

When the tasks you create are effort-driven — and Project defines all new tasks as effort-driven by default — the resources you assign to a task affect the duration of the task. For example, if you assign two people to do a job, the job typically gets done in less time than if you assigned only one person to the job. But, you ask, what about the cost? Does the use of additional resources increase the project's cost? Perhaps yes; perhaps no. You may find that completing the project in less time (by using more resources) saves you money because you can accept more projects. Or you may be eligible for a bonus if you complete the project earlier than expected.

## How Project uses resource information to affect the schedule

For effort-driven tasks, Project uses the resource information you provide to calculate the duration of the task and, consequently, the duration of the project. However, if you set up a task with a fixed duration (refer to Chapter 4), Project ignores the resources assigned to the task when calculating the duration of the project. Similarly, if you don't assign resources, Project calculates the schedule using only the task duration and task dependency information that you provide.

See Chapter 4 for information on task durations and task dependencies.

Assigning a resource to a task can affect the duration of the project because work on the task cannot begin until the resource is available. Project uses a resource calendar to define the working days and times for a resource, but the resource's availability also depends on other tasks to which you assigned the resource.

If the work assigned to a resource exceeds the time available, Microsoft Project assigns the resource to the task and indicates that the resource is overallocated. This technique enables you to see the problem and decide how to fix it.

You also have the option of assigning costs to resources when you define them. The next section, "Creating a Resource List," explains how Project uses the cost information you supply.

### How Project gathers cost information

When you assign costs to resources and then assign resources to tasks, Project can calculate the cost of a project. In addition to resource-associated costs, Project also handles fixed costs, which you learn more about near the end of this chapter.

Assigning costs enables you to monitor and to control the money you're spending on a project. Project shows you where and how you are spending your money; this information enables you to control when a project's costs accrue, which, in turn, helps you schedule your bill payment. The cost-related information that Project provides helps you verify the following items:

- ✦ The cost of resources and materials for any task
- ✦ The cost of any phase of your project as well as the cost of the entire project

Cost information that you gather on one project may help you calculate bids for future projects.

## Creating a Resource List

Project gives you the option of creating resources one at a time, as you think of them, or of entering all (or most) resources using the Resource Sheet. To display the Resource Sheet, click the Resource Sheet button on the View bar (see Figure 5-1) or choose View ➪ Resource Sheet.

In Project 2000, you can define two different types of resources: human (called "Work") and material. Human resources are the resources you've always been able to define in Project. Use material resources to define items you consume while working on a project.

If you use the Resource Sheet to define most of the resources for your project, the actual process of assigning resources goes much faster because you don't have to stop to create the resource first. Also, using the Resource Sheet is a safe way to define resources; the visual presentation helps you avoid accidentally creating the same resource twice. For example, if you define Vickey and Vicki, Project sees two resources, even though you might have simply misspelled the name the second time.

You can create the basics for the resource by filling in the Resource Sheet; press the Tab key to move from field to field (cell to cell). The Resource Sheet in Figure 5-1 does not show all the fields described in this section; scroll to the right to see the rest of the Resource Sheet.

A field is a cell in a table into which you type appropriate information. All table and form views contain fields. You can also add fields to any table or form view to customize it. You can learn more about fields and adding them to views in Chapter 7.

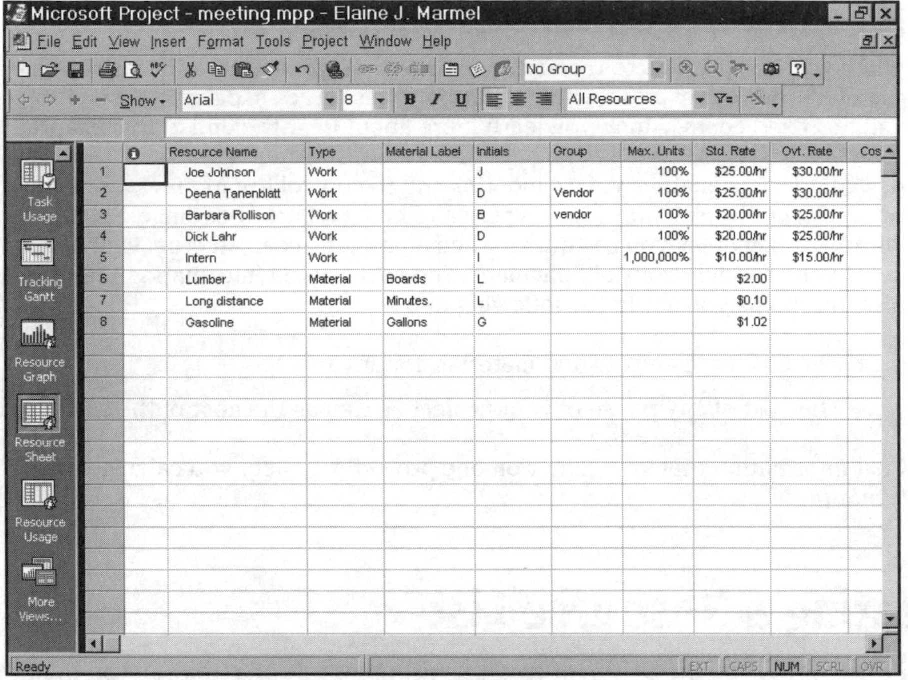

**Figure 5-1:** The Resource Sheet displays a list of the resources available to your project.

Each field on the Resource Sheet serves a specific purpose:

✦ **Indicators.** Although you can't type in the Indicators field, icons appear here from time to time. Some of the icons appear as Project's response to an action you've taken. For example, you may see an indicator for an overallocated resource. In other cases the indicator appears because you entered a note about the resource (see "Adding Notes to a Resource" later in this chapter).

Tip

If you point at an indicator, Project displays the information associated with the icon.

✦ **Resource Name.** Type the name of the resource. For manpower, you might type a person's name or you might type a job description, such as Product Analyst 1 or Product Analyst 2.

✦ **Type.** Use this column to specify whether you're defining a human or material resource. Project refers to human resources as "Work."

✦ **Material Label.** For material resources, specify the unit of measure. You can set up any label you want; you might use minutes for long distance, feet for lumber, or miles for gasoline.

✦ **Initials.** Type initials for the resource, or accept the default Project provides, which is the first letter of the resource name. This designation appears on any view to which you add the Initials field. Typically, a resource's name appears, but you can customize the view to display initials if you prefer.

✦ **Group.** Assign resources to groups if they share some common characteristic, such as job function. Then you can use this field as a filtering or sorting mechanism and display information about the group (a particular job function) as opposed to a specific resource. Just type a name to create a group.

Be sure to spell the name the same way each time if you want to filter or sort by group.

✦ **Max. Units.** Project expresses the amount of the work resource you have available for assignment as a percentage. For example, 100 percent equals one unit, or the equivalent of one full-time resource; 50 percent equals one-half of a unit, or one-half of a full-time resource's time; and 200 percent equals two full-time resources.

✦ **Std. Rate.** The standard rate is the rate you charge for regular work for a resource. Project calculates the default rate in hours; you can, however, charge a resource's work in other time increments (for work resources, you can use minutes, days, weeks, or years; for material resources, think of the charge as per unit based on the Material label). To specify a time increment other than hours, type a slash and then the first letter of the word representing the time increment. For example, to charge a resource's use in days, type /d after the rate you specify.

✦ **Ovt. Rate.** The overtime rate is the rate you charge for overtime work for a work resource. Again, Project calculates the default rate in hours, but you can change the default unit the same way you changed it for the Standard Rate.

✦ **Cost/Use.** In the Cost/Use column (read that as "cost per use"), supply a rate you use to charge a one-time rate for a resource. Use this rate for costs that are charged on a per/unit basis (such as material costs), rather than on some time-related basis.

✦ **Accrue At.** This field specifies how and when Microsoft Project charges resource costs to a task at the standard or overtime rates. The default option is Prorated, but you also can select Start or End.

- If you select Start and assign that resource to a task, Project calculates the cost for a task as soon as the task begins.
- If you select End and assign that resource to a task, Project calculates the cost for the task when the task is completed.
- If you select Prorated and assign that resource to a task, Project accrues the cost of the task as you complete scheduled work.

If you set a cost per use rate for a resource and assign that resource to a task, Project always charges the cost of the resource at the beginning of a task.

✦ **Base Calendar.** Base calendar identifies the calendar that Project should use when scheduling the resource. The calendar identifies working and nonworking time. Project assumes each resource uses the Standard calendar, but, as you'll read later in this chapter, you can create calendars for resource groups — perhaps to handle shift work — or you can modify an individual resource's calendar to reflect vacation or other unavailable time (such as jury duty).

✦ **Code.** You can use this field as a catchall field to assign any information you want to a resource, using an abbreviation of some sort. For example, suppose your company uses cost-center codes; you may want to supply the cost-center code for the resource in the Code field. You can sort and filter information by the abbreviations that you supply in the Code field.

After you create a resource, Project displays the resource's ID number on the very left edge of the Resource Sheet, to the left of the Indicators column.

# Modifying Resource Information

You just learned a quick way to set up a resource — by typing on the Resource Sheet. In addition, you can use the Resource Information dialog box to fine-tune your resource's definition.

Use the Resource Information dialog box to modify resource information. To display the Resource Information dialog box, double-click any resource on the Resource Sheet or choose Project ➪ Resource Information. Then click the General tab.

You already provided most of the information on this tab on the Resource Sheet, so this section discusses the fields in the dialog box that weren't available on the Resource Sheet.

## Assigning a communication method

Use the Email field (see Figure 5-2) to supply the e-mail address of a resource. You must fill in this field if you want to use Project's workgroup feature, which enables users to assign, accept, or decline work electronically. You can make a selection from the Workgroup drop-down list to specify an electronic communication method.

If you're using a MAPI-compliant e-mail program and you've stored the resource's e-mail address in your Address Book, you can click the Details button to have Project look up the e-mail address for you. You can then copy the address from the Address Book, close the address book and, in the Email field, press Ctrl+V to paste the address into the Resource Information dialog box. See Chapter 15 for more about the workgroup feature.

## Specifying resource availability

Suppose you set up a resource to represent a specific job — such as Intern in Figure 5-1. And suppose you have more than one of this resource, but not at all times. Using the Resource Availability section shown in Figure 5-2, you can specify the time periods for which the resource will be available. In Figure 5-2, five interns are available from August 19 through August 31, two interns are available for the first two weeks of September, and five interns are available from September 16 and October 15.

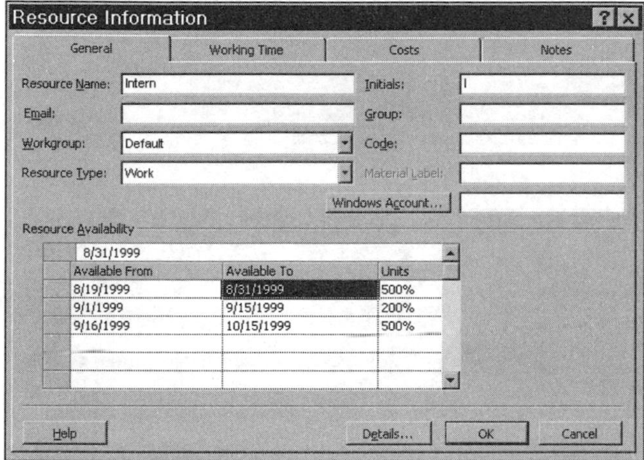


**Figure 5-2:** Use the General tab of the Resource Information dialog box to add information about a resource such as an e-mail address or availability.

With Project 2000, you can contour the availability of resources.

## Adding notes to a resource

Click the Notes tab of the Resource Information dialog box. The Notes text box in Figure 5-3 is a free-form text box in which you can type any information you want to store about the resource. For example, you might want to store a reminder about a resource's upcoming vacation or an explanation about resource availability.

After you type text in this box and click OK, a Note indicator icon appears in the Indicators column on the Resource Sheet (see Figure 5-4).

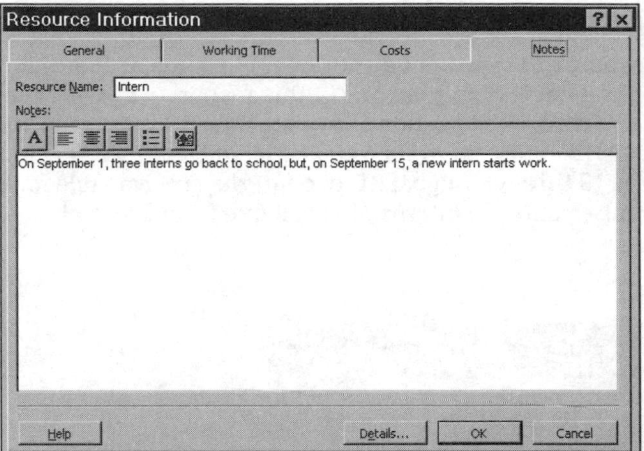


**Figure 5-3:** Use this text box to store any information about a resource.

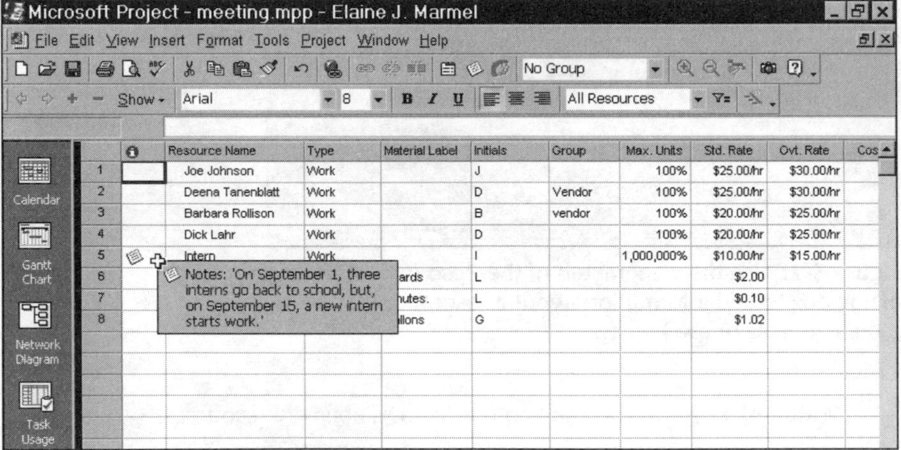


**Figure 5-4:** You don't need to reopen the Resource Information dialog box to read a note; instead, use the mouse to point at the indicator icon, and Project displays the contents of the note.

# Calendars and resources

As you learned in Chapter 3, Project uses a base calendar called the Standard calendar to calculate the timing of the project. When you first create a resource for your project, Project uses the Standard base calendar as the default (8-hour day, 40-hour week if you haven't changed that setting in the Project Information dialog box). As you saw in the preceding section, you can modify the dates a resource is available; you also can modify working times. For example, you may want to change a resource's working hours, or you may want to block off a period of time — such as vacation time or a business trip — for a resource, making it unavailable during that period.

The entire project has a Standard calendar, and each resource also has his or her own Standard calendar.

## Modifying a resource's working hours

Suppose that a specific resource won't be available all day on a given day, or even on several specified days. For example, all the interns may work from 1:00 p.m. to 6:00 p.m. To change the working hours of a resource, use the Working Time tab of the Resource Information dialog box. Double-click the resource on the Resource Sheet to open the dialog box. The resource's calendar appears with today's date selected. The Legend on the left of the dialog box identifies Working days, Nonworking days, Non-default working hours, and Exceptions.

Using standard Windows selection techniques, select the dates your resource will be on vacation.

To select contiguous days, click the first day. Then press the Shift key and click the last day you want to select. To select noncontiguous days, press Ctrl as you click each day you want to select. To select all of any day – say Sunday – click the letter of the day. Project selects all of those days, in all months.

To change a resource's working hours, click the Default Working Time button and then make the necessary changes in the From and To text boxes (see Figure 5-5). As soon as you click any other date, the dates you selected appear underscored in the individual's calendar because you set an exception to the regular schedule (see Figure 5-6); the Legend shows you that the exception involves nondefault working hours.

To avoid overallocating a resource that works part of a day, level the resource on a day-by-day basis. You'll read more about handling overallocations in Chapter 10.

## Blocking off vacation time

Human resources do take time off from work and, to avoid overallocating a person by assigning work during a vacation period, you should mark vacation days on the resource's calendar.

Double-click the resource to display the Resource Information dialog box and click the Working Time tab. Find the date or dates you want to block for vacation time using the scroll bar next to the calendar. With the vacation dates selected, select the Nonworking time option. Click any other date on the calendar to cancel the selection; each date you marked as vacation time appears with an underscore. Again, by comparing the date to the Legend, you can tell the reason for the exception.

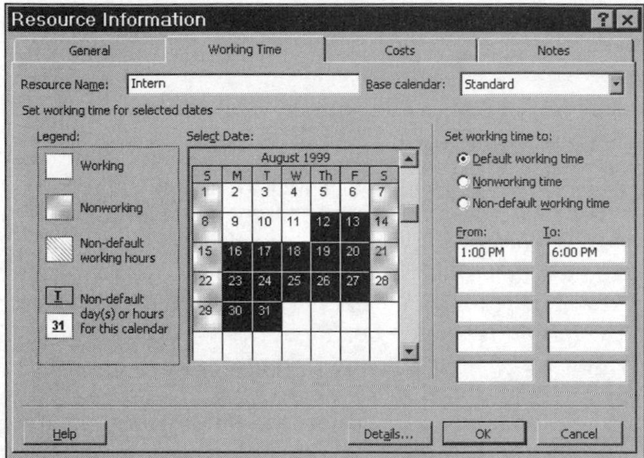


**Figure 5-5:** Select the dates you want to change.

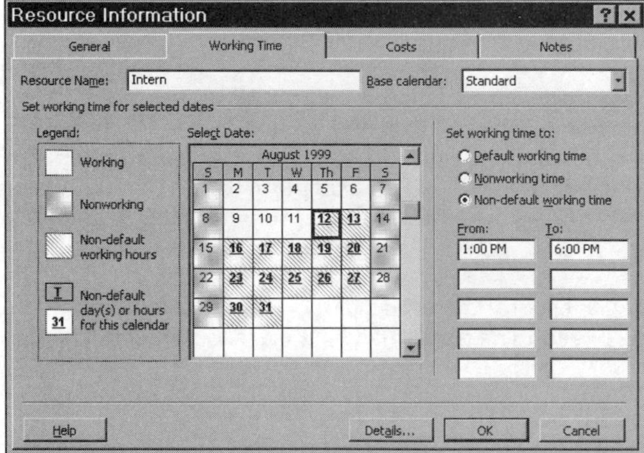


**Figure 5-6:** Project marks exceptions to the typical schedule with an underscore.

# Using Resources and Tasks

You've spent a lot of time in this chapter learning to define resources and fine-tune your resource definitions. Now you can finally assign resources to tasks. As noted earlier in this chapter, defining resources helps you manage your project more effectively, both in scheduling and in cost.

## Assigning resources to tasks

You can easily assign resources to tasks from the Gantt Chart view. Use the View bar to switch to the Gantt Chart view and then follow these steps:

1. Select the task to which you want to assign a resource. You can click the task bar on the Gantt chart or you can click any column in the Gantt table.
2. Click the Assign Resources button or choose Tools ➪ Resources ➪ Assign Resources to open the Assign Resources dialog box (see Figure 5-7).

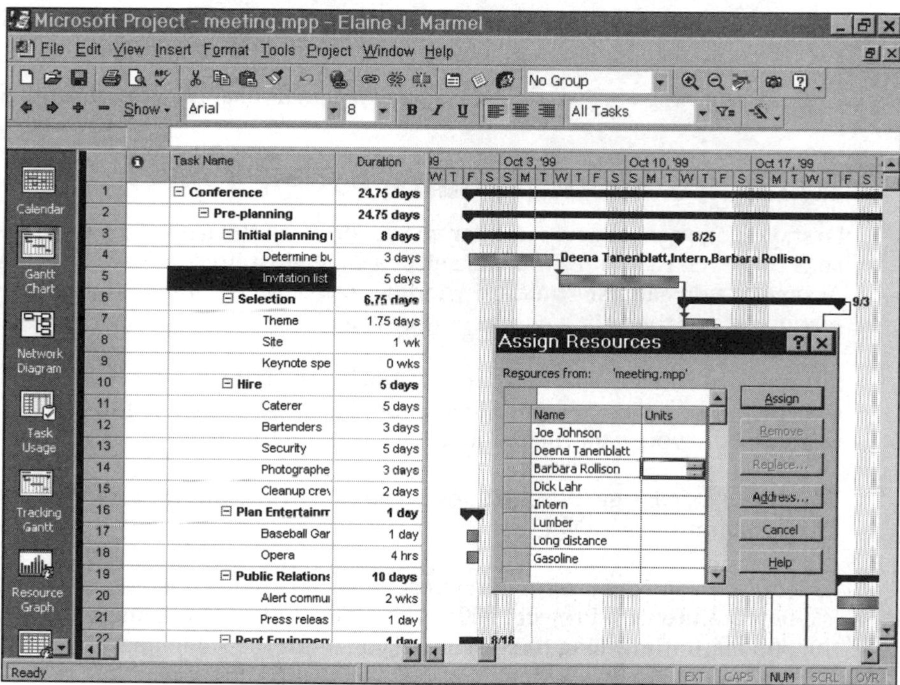


**Figure 5-7:** Use the Assign Resources dialog box to assign a resource to a task.

3. Select the resource you want to assign from the Name list of the Assign Resources dialog box. If you use a MAPI-compliant e-mail program such as Microsoft Outlook, the Address button is available. You can click the Address button to select a resource from your address book.

Did you forget to define a resource? You don't need to return to the Resource Sheet. Just type the name of the resource in the Name column of the Assign Resources dialog box.

4. Do one of the following to assign the amount of a resource:

- To assign any amount other than 100 percent of a resource, type the quantity of the resource as a percentage in the Units column. (Project defines units as percentages, so 100 percent equals one unit of the resource.)
- To assign 100 percent of a resource, leave the Units column blank. Project assigns 100 percent by default.

Note: You don't need to type the percent (%) sign; Project assumes percentages. Also, if you type .5, Project converts your entry to 50%.

5. Click Assign. Project places a check in the left-most column of the Assign Resources dialog box to indicate the resource is assigned to the selected task.
6. Repeat Steps 3, 4, and 5 to assign additional resources or click Close.

## Some tips about resource assignments

First, you can assign several different resources to the same task by simply selecting each resource. You can select a single resource and immediately click Assign, or you can use standard Windows selection techniques to select several resources and then click Assign only once.

Second, you can assign a resource to a task on a part-time basis by assigning less that 100 in the Units column. The number you type represents the percentage of working time you want the resource to spend on the task.

Third, you can assign more than one resource by assigning more than 100 in the Units column.

Fourth, you can consume material resources in two ways: fixed and variable (this is a new feature with Project 2000). When you use fixed consumption, you indicate that, no matter how long the task lasts, you'll use the same quantity of the material. For example, to build a swimming pool, you'll need two tons of concrete — no matter how long it takes you to pour the concrete. When you use variable consumption, you indicate that the length of the task does affect the amount of the material you will use. For example, when you mow the lawn with a gas mower, the amount of gas you'll consume depends on how long you run the mower.

You designate fixed or variable consumption in the Units column of the Assign Resources dialog box. To differentiate between fixed and variable consumption, supply the rate at which you consume a variable resource. In Figure 5-8, gasoline is a material resource being consumed at a variable rate because I included the time frame used to measure consumption — the "per hour" designation.

After you assign a resource to a task, the resource name appears next to the task bar on the Gantt chart by default. Depending on the task type you set, you may be able to use resource assignments to modify individual task lengths and the entire project schedule. For example, if you assign additional resources to an effort-driven fixed-unit task, Project shortens the duration of the task. As you learned in Chapter 4, the amount of work to be done doesn't change, but the extra concurrent effort shortens the time necessary to get the work done. Or if you assign a resource to work part-time on an effort-driven task, you might find that you can complete several tasks at the same time.

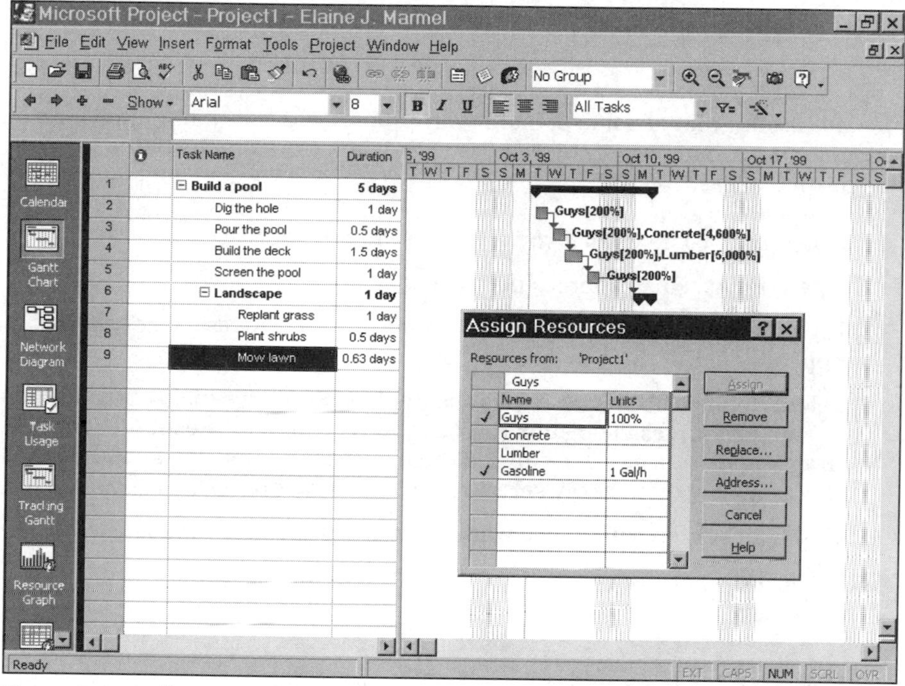


**Figure 5-8:** Indicate variable consumption by supplying the rate when you specify the amount you'll use.

Tip

If you overallocate a resource by assigning more than you have available, Project displays the resource in red on the Resource Sheet view. Chapter 9 explains how to handle these problems.

## Removing or replacing a resource assignment

To remove a resource assignment, select the task from which you want to remove the resource assignment — using the Gantt Chart view. Then click the Assign Resources button or choose Tools ➪ Resources ➪ Assign Resources to display the Assign Resources dialog box. Highlight the resource you want to remove from the task; you should see a check next to the resource in the left-most column of the dialog box. Click Remove (see Figure 5-9).

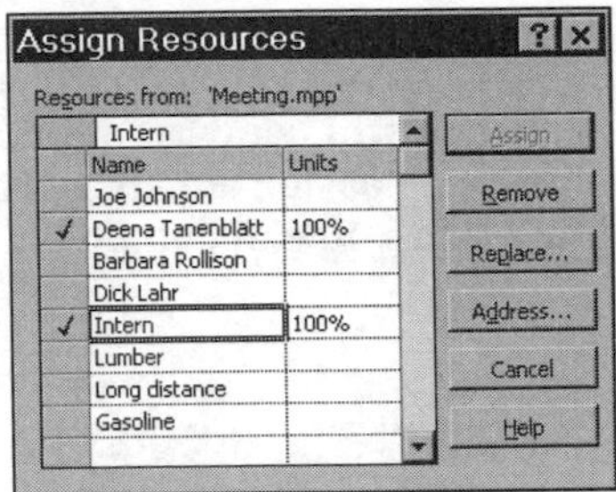


**Figure 5-9:** Remove resources from tasks by selecting them in the Assign Resources dialog box and clicking Remove.

You can be sure that at some point in your project you will want to move resource assignments around. Here's the easy way to switch from one resource to another on a particular task:

1. Select the task for which you want to switch resources.
2. Open the Assign Resources dialog box.
3. Highlight the resource you want to remove from the task; a checkmark appears next to the assigned resource.
4. Select Replace. Project displays the Replace Resource dialog box on top of the Assign Resources dialog box (if you move the Replace Resource dialog box by dragging its title bar, you can see them both). The Replace Resource dialog box enables you to easily select replacement resources (see Figure 5-10).
5. Highlight each resource you want to assign and supply units.
6. Click OK.

# Handling Unusual Cost Situations

Resources go hand in hand with tasks if you're trying to figure out how long it will take to complete a project. If you assign costs to your resources, those costs also affect the cost of your project. But assigning a cost to a resource is not the only way to assign a cost to a project. For example, projects can have fixed costs associated with them. This section starts with a quick look at overall project costs and then focuses on handling unusual cost situations.

## Looking at the project's cost

You've seen how to assign costs to resources. You've also seen how to assign resources to tasks — and, by the transitive property of equality (remember that one from high school algebra?), assigning a resource to which you have assigned a cost will cause your project to have a cost. Are you wondering what that cost is? From either the Gantt Chart view or the Resource Sheet view, choose Project ⇨ Project Information to open the Project Information dialog box. Select Statistics to open the Project Statistics dialog box (see Figure 5-11).

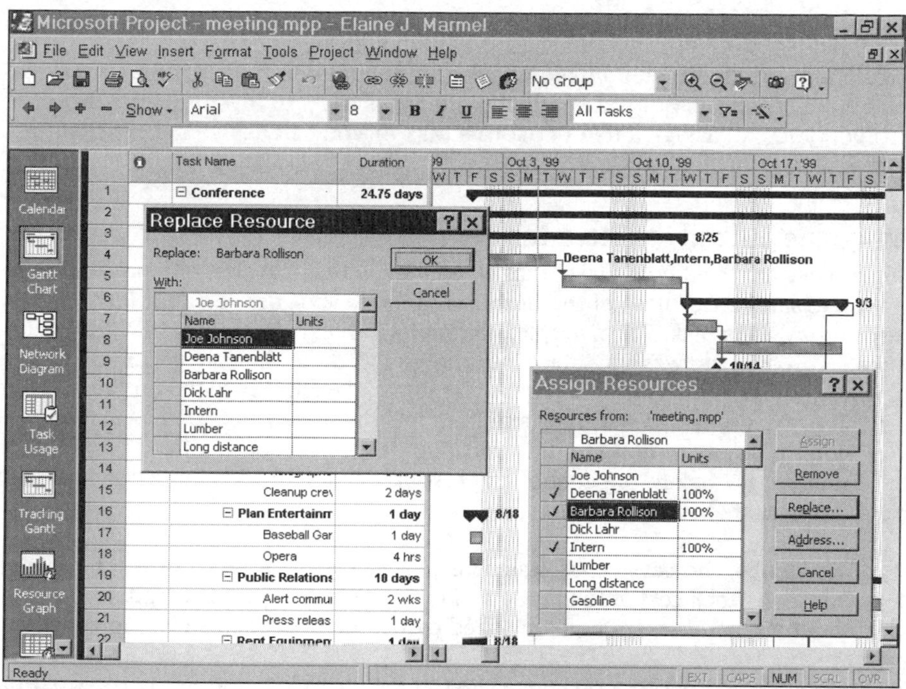


**Figure 5-10:** The Replace Resource dialog box looks very similar to the Assign Resources dialog box.

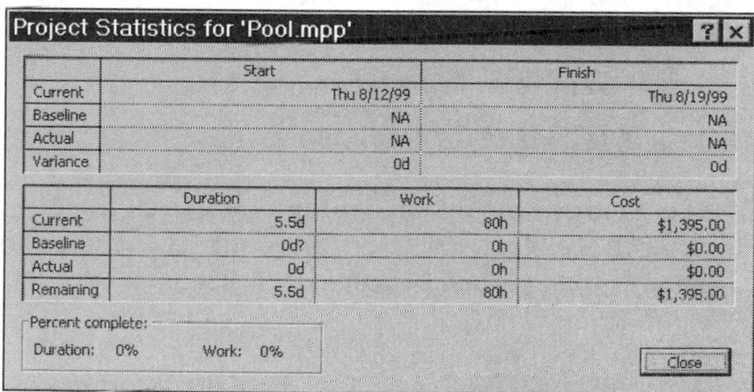
Project Statistics for 'Pool.mpp'

| | Start | Finish |
|---|---|---|
| Current | Thu 8/12/99 | Thu 8/19/99 |
| Baseline | NA | NA |
| Actual | NA | NA |
| Variance | 0d | 0d |

| | Duration | Work | Cost |
|---|---|---|---|
| Current | 5.5d | 80h | $1,395.00 |
| Baseline | 0d? | 0h | $0.00 |
| Actual | 0d | 0h | $0.00 |
| Remaining | 5.5d | 80h | $1,395.00 |

Percent complete:
Duration: 0% Work: 0%

Close

**Figure 5-11:** Check the cost of your project in the Project Statistics dialog box.

Part IV covers tracking, recording actual work done, and analyzing and reporting on progress. Chapter 14 explains additional ways to view project costs. The following sections consider ways to assign unusual costs to a project.

## Assigning fixed costs

This chapter has, so far, focused on resources, and you have learned how to assign costs to a resource. But the costs of some tasks need to be calculated differently. In Project, you can assign a fixed cost to a task or you can assign a fixed resource cost to a task.

### Assigning a fixed cost to a task

Some tasks are fixed-cost tasks; that is, you know that the cost of a particular task stays the same regardless of the duration of the task or the work performed by any resources on the task. For example, your catering service, as part of each job, washes linens. You own the washing machine, and you've done the calculation on the amount of water plus electricity (plus wear and tear) used each time you run the machine for a wash cycle. Or, you're renting a site for a meeting for a flat fee. In cases like these, you assign the cost directly to the task. If you assign a cost to a task, Project adds the fixed cost of the task to the cost of any resource work you assign to the task when calculating costs for the project.

Remember, however, that assigning a fixed cost to a task does not necessarily make the total cost of the task equal to the fixed cost you assigned. You could, for example, assign more than one fixed cost as well as variable costs to a task.

To assign a fixed cost to a task, use the Gantt Chart view and apply the Cost table. Follow these steps:

1. Use the View bar to switch to the Gantt Chart view.
2. Choose View ➪ Table:Entry ➪ Cost to switch to the Cost table view of the Gantt chart (see Figure 5-12).
3. Select the task to which you want to assign a fixed cost.
4. Type the cost for that task in the Fixed Cost column and press Enter.

You can control the way Project accrues the fixed cost for a task from the Fixed Cost Accrual column. Your choices are Start, Prorated, and End. These choices have the same meaning as the accrual choices for resources discussed earlier in this chapter.

To control the way Project accrues all fixed costs, use the Calculation tab of the Options dialog box (choose Tools ➪ Options).

### Assigning a fixed resource cost to a task

Suppose you hire a consultant to perform a task for a fixed amount of money; you can assign the consultant to the task as a fixed-cost resource.

1. Use the View bar to switch to the Gantt Chart view.

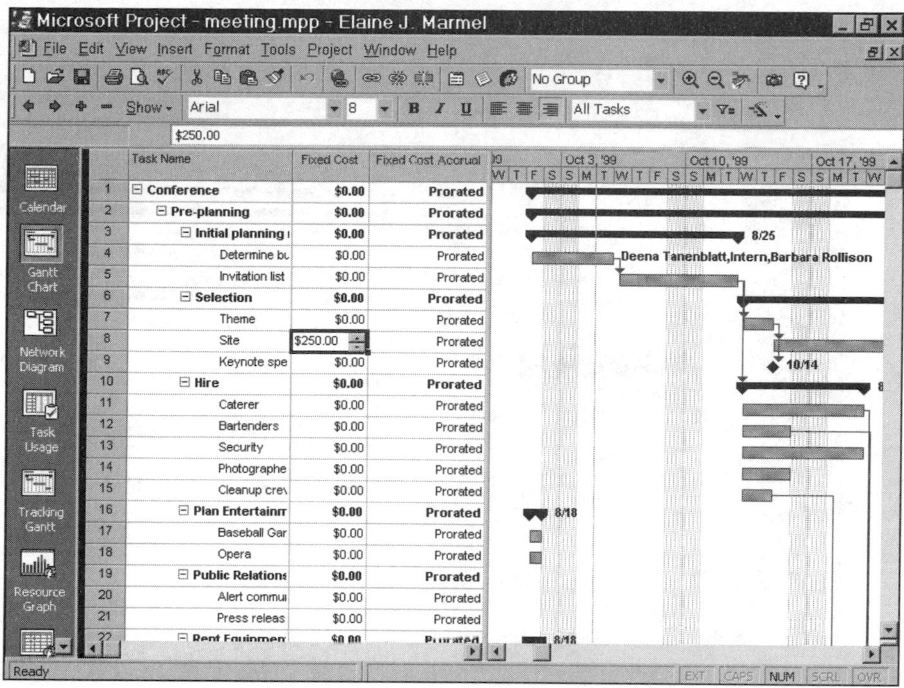


**Figure 5-12:** Use the Cost table view of the Gantt chart to assign costs to tasks.

2. Choose View ➪ Table:Cost ➪ Entry to switch to the Entry table view of the Gantt chart.
3. Select a task from the Task Name column.
4. Assign the resource to the task using the steps explained earlier in this chapter. Don't worry about the number of units you assign.
5. Choose Window ➪ Split.
6. Select the resource from the Resource Name column in the bottom pane.
7. Choose Format ➪ Details ➪ Resource Cost. A pane appears at the bottom of the Gantt chart.
8. Type **0** (zero) in the Units column for the resource.
9. Type the fixed-resource cost in the Cost field. Figure 5-13 shows a fixed-resource cost for Dick Lahr.
10. Click OK.

Project adds a fixed-resource cost to other resource costs when calculating the total cost of a task, but the cost does not depend on the time a resource spends working on the task.

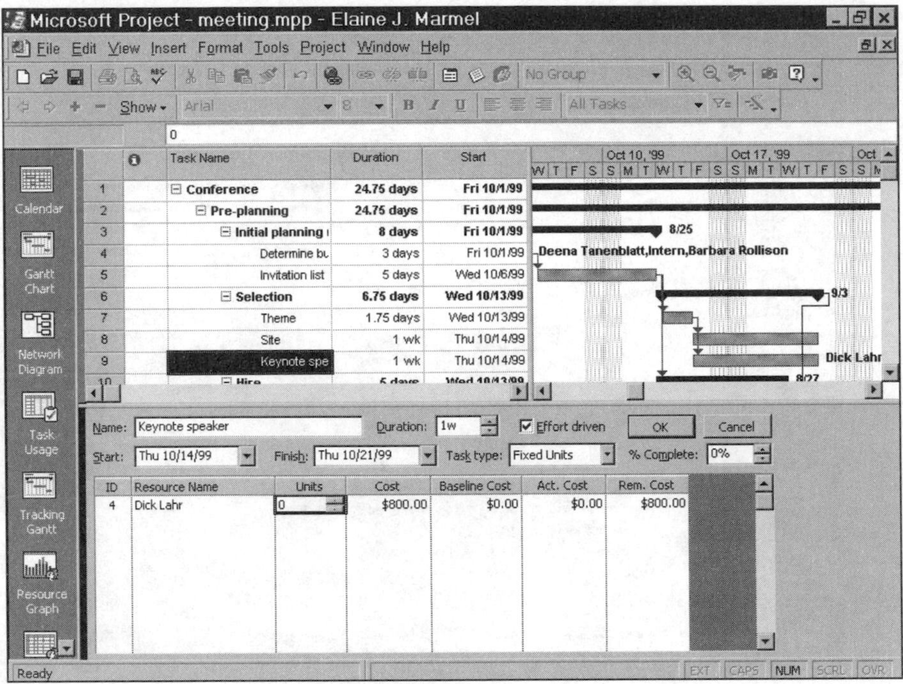

Figure 5-13: Adding a fixed resource cost

Tip

Choose Window ➪ Remove Split to close the bottom pane in the Gantt Chart view or drag the Split Bar.

## Accounting for resource rate changes

In some situations you must charge different rates on different tasks for the same resource. Or possibly, you expect a resource's rate to change during the life of your project. Project uses cost rate tables to accurately reflect resource costs as they change. On cost rate tables you can identify up to 125 rates for a single resource, and you can identify the effective date of each rate. Cost rate tables help you account for pay increases or decreases to resources during the life of your project and enable you to charge the same resource at different rates, depending on the task.

To assign multiple rates to a resource, use the Costs tab of the Resource Information dialog box. On the Resource Sheet view, double-click the resource for which you want to assign multiple rates. Click the Costs tab in the Resource Information dialog box (see Figure 5-14).

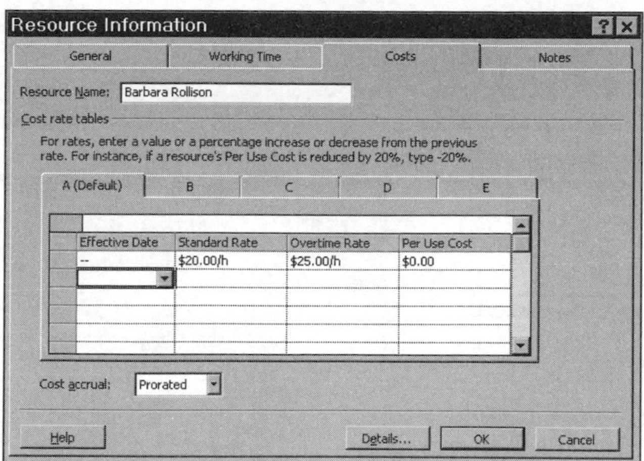


**Figure 5-14:** Use cost rate tables to assign different rates to a resource.

The Costs tab displays five cost rate tables (tabs A through E) that you can use to assign different rates to a resource for use on different dates throughout a project's life. On each cost rate table, you can enter up to 25 rates for the selected resource and indicate an effective date for each rate. Project uses the effective dates you supply to apply the correct rate to a resource at different times during the project.

**If you are specifying a new rate as an increase or decrease of an existing rate, you can specify the new rate in a percentage (+10% or –10%); Project calculates the value of the rate for you. You must enter the percent sign.**

If you charge different amounts for resources depending on the type of work they perform, you might want to use each cost rate table tab to represent sets of rates for different kinds of work.

To assign the correct resource cost rate table to a task, follow these steps:

1. Assign the resource to the task using the Assign Resources dialog box, as you learned earlier in this chapter.
2. Use the View bar to switch to the Task Usage view (see Figure 5-15).
3. In the Task Name column, select the resource for which you want to select a cost table.
4. Click the Assignment Information button on the Standard toolbar to display the Assignment Information dialog box. Click the General tab (see Figure 5-16) to select a cost rate table.

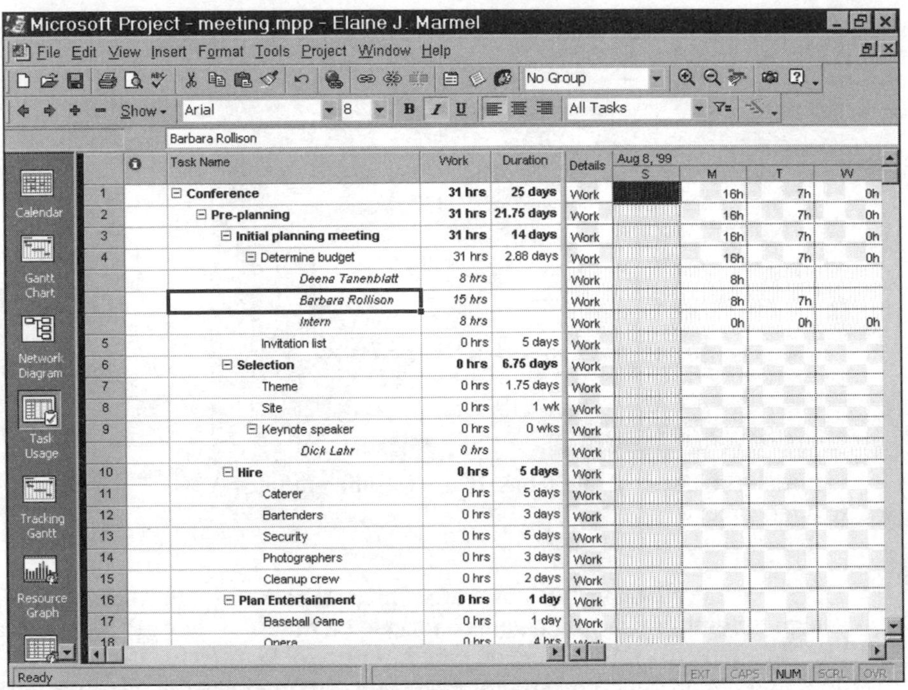


**Figure 5-15:** Task Usage view shows you the amount of time a resource is assigned to a particular task.

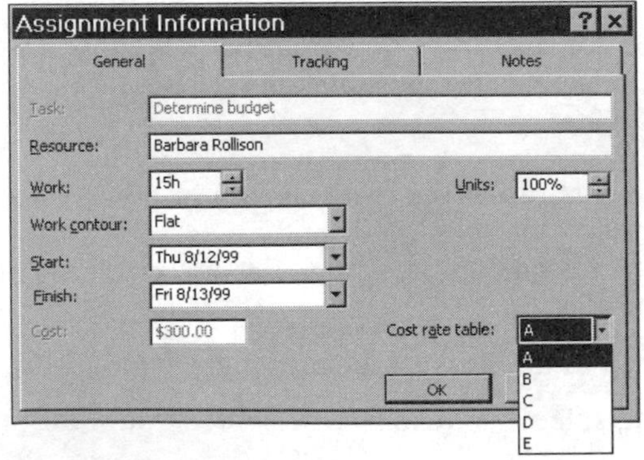


**Figure 5-16:** Use the General tab of the Assignment Information dialog box to select a cost rate table.

**5.** Select the correct cost rate table from the Cost rate table drop-down list.

**6.** Click OK.

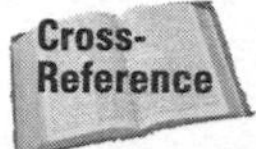

Chapter 12 covers project costs in greater detail.

# Summary

This chapter detailed more about using resources in Project, including how to create and assign resources. You've learned how to:

- Create a resource list
- Modify resource information, including using calendars for resources
- Assign resources to tasks and remove resource assignments
- Handle fixed costs, both for individual tasks and for resources
- Assign either a fixed or variable cost to a material resource
- Set up different rates for resources to account for pay increases or decreases or for charging resources at different rates on different tasks

In Chapter 6 you learn the basics of using the standard views in Project.

✦ ✦ ✦

P A R T

# Refining Your Project

✦ ✦ ✦ ✦

## In This Part



✦ ✦ ✦ ✦

# Understanding the Basics of Views

✦ ✦ ✦ ✦

**In This Chapter**

What is a view?

What views are available?

Examining indicators

Admiring the views

Printing your project

✦ ✦ ✦ ✦

Views in Project enable you to enter, organize, and examine information in various ways. Consider this analogy to help you understand why a project needs multiple views: A project is like a small business. As in any business, different people attend to various aspects of the work. The accounting department thinks mainly of the costs of doing business. The plant supervisor focuses on deadlines and having enough machinery to get the job done. Your human resources department thinks of people: their salaries, hours, benefits, and so on.

As the owner of your project, you are likely to wear all these hats — and more — during the project. Rather than changing caps as you move from one responsibility to another, in Project you simply switch to another view to see your work from a different perspective. Each view helps you focus on a different aspect or aspects of your project.

Project provides a variety of views, and this chapter provides you with a basic understanding of the default views in Project; the next chapter covers techniques you can use to customize views and make them work for you.

## What Is a View?

A view is a way to examine your project. Different views enable you to focus on different aspects of the project. Project uses three types of views, and typically uses them in combination with each other:

✦ **Chart or graph views.** Present information by using pictures. You've already seen the Gantt Chart view, which is a chart view.

- **Sheet views.** Present information in rows and columns, similar to the way a spreadsheet program presents information. The Task Sheet view and the Resource Sheet view are both sheet views, and each row on the sheet contains all the information about an individual task or resource in your project. Each column represents a field that identifies the information you're storing about the task or resource.
- **Forms.** Present information in a way that resembles a paper form. You saw the Task Form view in Chapter 4; a form displays information about a single item (task) in your project.

Shortcut menus are available in many views. Right-click the view to see a shortcut menu.

# What Views Are Available?

The following is a list of the default views available in Project:

- Bar Rollup
- Calendar
- Descriptive Network Diagram
- Detail Gantt
- Gantt Chart
- Leveling Gantt
- Milestone Date Rollup
- Milestone Rollup
- Network Diagram
- Expected Gantt (PERT)
- Optimistic Gantt (PERT)
- PERT Entry Sheet
- Pessimistic Gantt (PERT)
- Relationship Diagram
- Resource Allocation
- Resource Form
- Resource Graph

- Resource Name Form
- Resource Sheet
- Resource Usage
- Task Details Form
- Task Entry
- Task Form
- Task Name Form
- Task Sheet
- Task Usage
- Tracking Gantt

The PERT views will not appear initially in the More Views window; once you use them, you will see them in the More Views window.

You can modify the default views by switching what appears onscreen. You can also create custom views. The two sections that follow describe some common ways of manipulating views:

- Switching the table of any view that includes a table
- Adding or changing the details that appear in any view that contains a Details section

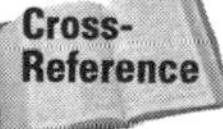

You also can create a combination view in which you actually see one format in one pane of the window and another format in another pane. Read about creating custom views and combination views in Chapter 7.

## Changing a table

If a view contains a table, you can use the Select All button to quickly switch to another table. The Select All button appears in the upper left of the table portion of the view. Right-click the Select All button to open the menu that appears in Figure 6-1.

Project displays different choices on this menu, and the choices you see depend on the view displayed when you opened the menu.

Choose More Tables to open the More Tables dialog box, which displays all the tables available in Project (see Figure 6-2).

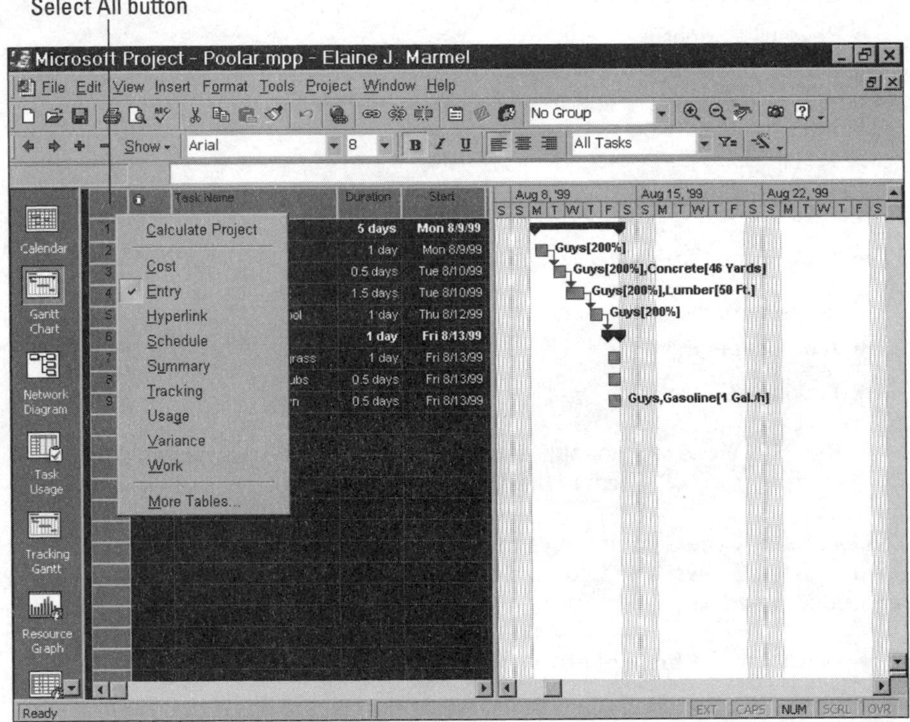


**Figure 6-1:** Switch tables by choosing from the menu that appears when you right-click the Select All button.

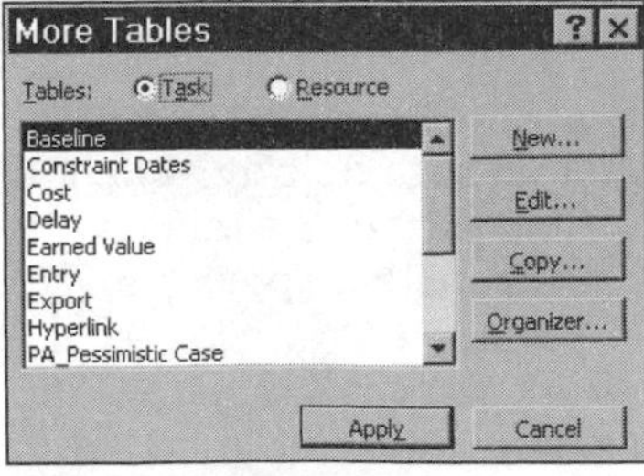


**Figure 6-2:** The More Tables dialog box shows the tables to which you can switch in the Task Usage view.

The PERT tables won't appear in the More Tables dialog box until you've displayed PERT views. Read more about PERT views later in this chapter.

## Changing a details section

You also can change the information that appears in the Details section of any view that displays a Details section (such as the Task Usage view). Choose any item from the list that appears when you choose Format ➪ Details (see Figure 6-3).

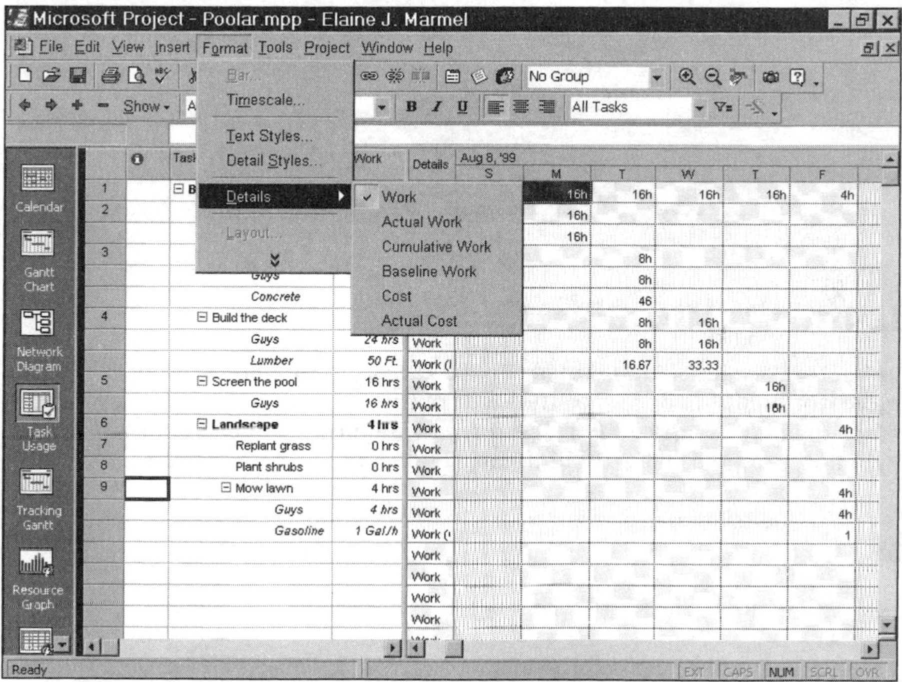


**Figure 6-3:** Change the information that appears in the Details section of the view by selecting from this list.

Project adds rows to the Details section when you make selections from this menu. To remove a row, choose Format ➪ Details and select the item you want to remove.

You can also use the Detail Styles dialog box (choose Format ➪ Detail Styles) in Figure 6-4 to add other information to the Details section.

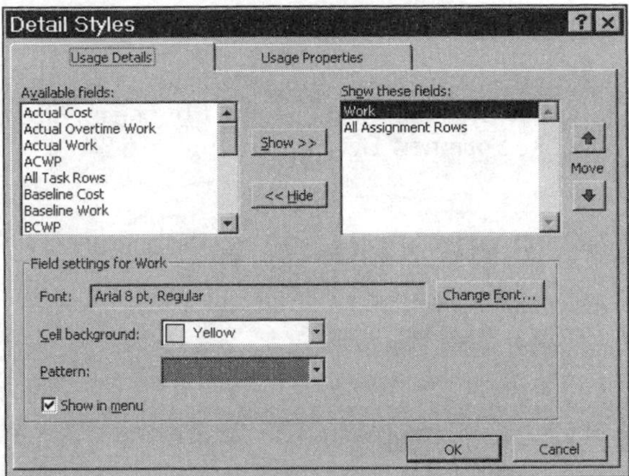


**Figure 6-4:** The Detail Styles dialog box supplies additional choices you can display in the Details section of a view.

# Examining Indicators

Indicators are icons that appear in the Indicator column on table views; the Indicator column appears to the right of the ID column. Indicators represent additional information about the row in which they appear. For example, your own notes appear in this field if you assign a note to a resource.

For more information on assigning notes to resources, refer to Chapter 5.

Different icons represent different types of indicators, as follows:

To identify the purpose of an indicator, point at it. Project tells you what the indicator means or displays additional information to remind you of important details.

✦ **Constraint indicators.** These indicators identify the type of constraint assigned to a task. For example, a task can have a flexible constraint, such as Finish No Later Than, for tasks scheduled from the finish date. Or a task can have an inflexible constraint, such as Must Start On, for tasks scheduled from the start date. Constraint indicators also show that the task hasn't been completed within the time frame of the constraint.

✦ **Task type indicators.** Task type indicators may identify special conditions about a task, such as whether the task is a recurring task or whether the task has been completed. Task type indicators also identify the status of projects inserted in a task.

You can learn more about inserted projects in Chapter 17.

✦ **Workgroup indicators.** Workgroup indicators provide some information about the task and its resources. For example, a workgroup indicator can tell you that a task has been assigned but that the resource hasn't yet confirmed the assignment.

✦ **Contour indicators.** Contour indicators identify the type of contouring used to distribute the work assigned to the task.

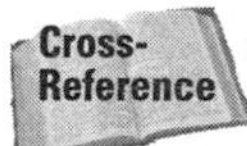


You learn more about contouring in Chapter 10.

✦ **Miscellaneous indicators.** Miscellaneous indicators identify things such as a note or a hyperlink that you created, a calendar that's been assigned to a task, or a resource that needs leveling.

# Admiring the Views

Deciding which of Project's 27 built-in views (or any of your custom views) suits a particular purpose can be a little tricky. As you become more familiar with the features of Project and the way you apply project management concepts and terms to Project, you'll get more comfortable selecting views by name. The View bar lists the eight most frequently used views.

When you initially open the Views window, you'll see only 23 views listed. The four PERT views will not appear in the window until you use them. Once you use them they, too, will appear in the window.

The following sections describe how these views enable you to look at different aspects of your project. Notice the wealth of detail about your project that is available to you.

To display any of these views, choose them from the View bar or right-click the View bar and choose More Views to select them from the More Views dialog box.

## Calendar

The top selection on the View bar is the Calendar view, shown in Figure 6-5. The familiar format of the Calendar view makes it easy to use; a black box surrounds "today." Using a monthly calendar format, the Calendar view indicates the length of a task with a bar running across portions of days, or even weeks. On the Calendar view, nonworking days appear shaded. Although a task bar may extend over nonworking days, such as Saturday and Sunday in this example, the work of the task doesn't actually progress over those days. Don't forget that every project has a calendar (not to be confused with the Calendar view) that tells Project how to handle events, such as 24-hour shifts, weekends, and holidays off, over the life of your project.

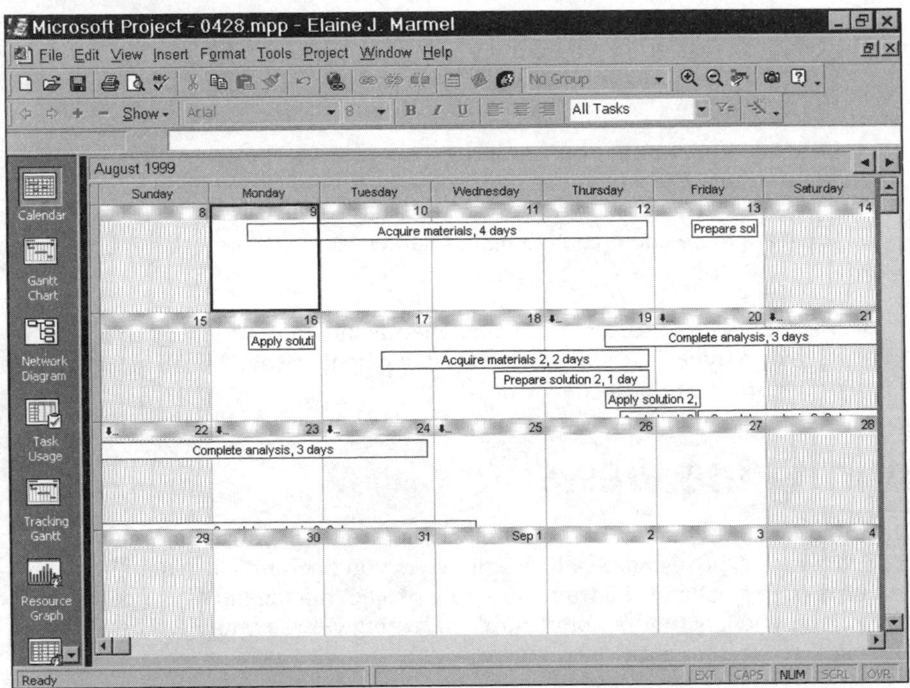


**Figure 6-5:** The Calendar view features a familiar, easy-to-read format.

This view is useful for entering a simple project and for reviewing what needs to be done on a given day. You can move from month to month using the large arrow buttons in the right corner of the view, next to the current month name. Depending on your screen resolution, you can see slightly more than a month at a time onscreen by using the Zoom Out tool on the Standard toolbar while in Calendar view. Zoom Out shrinks the calendar to accommodate about a month and a half of your schedule.

To modify the appearance of the Calendar view—for example, to shade working days and leave nonworking days clear—double-click anywhere on the calendar to open the Timescale dialog box and change the corresponding settings.

## Detail Gantt

The Detail Gantt view shows a list of tasks and related information as well as a chart that displays slack time and *slippage* as thin bars between tasks (see Figure 6-6). Choose this view from the More Views dialog box (choose View ➪ More Views).

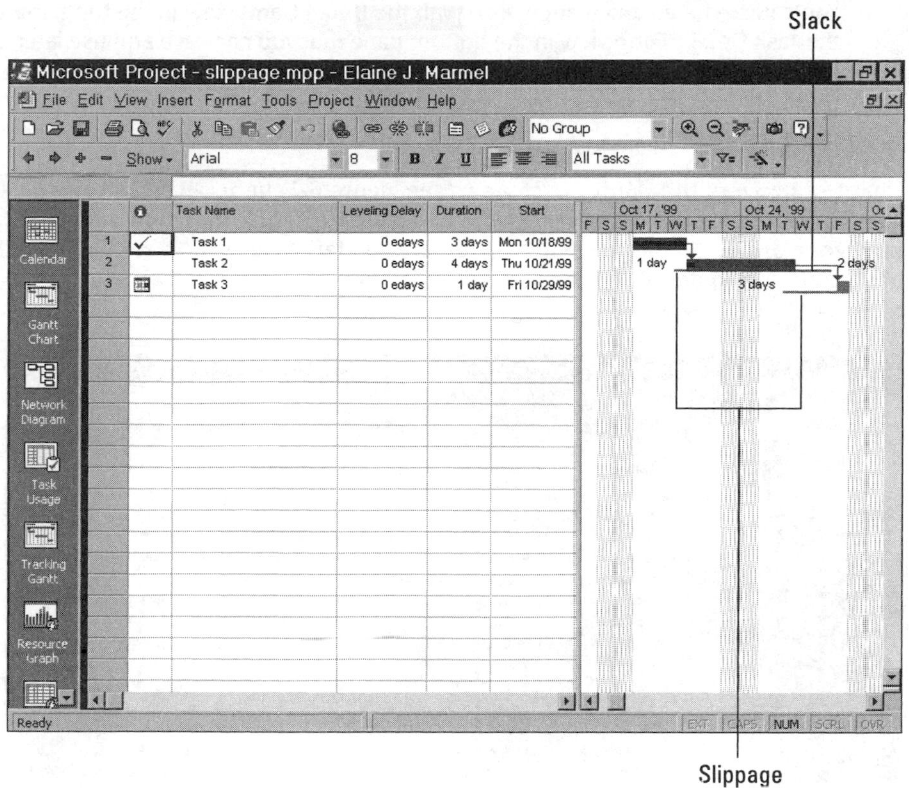


**Figure 6-6:** The Detail Gantt view

The thin bar extending from the right edge of the second task shows slack time between the second and third tasks, and the thin bar that appears at the left edge of the second task represents slippage between the first task and the second task. The number of days appears in both cases. You can think of slack time as flexibility in the schedule. Slippage results when you save a baseline on a project initially, you have started a task but not necessarily completed the task, and the finish date for the task is later than the baseline finish date.

This view is most useful for evaluating slack and slippage. The default table in the Detail Gantt view is the Delay table; use the techniques described earlier in this chapter to change the table.

You may want to incorporate the Task Details Form view in the bottom pane of the Detail Gantt view so that you can look more closely at the tasks associated with slippage or slack. Choose Window ➪ Split, or use the Split Bar to display the Task Details Form view in the bottom pane.

You can create a combination view with the Detail Gantt view in the top pane and the Task Details Form view in the bottom pane that you can save and use later. See Chapter 7 for details.

## Gantt Chart

Chapter 2 covers the Gantt Chart view (see Figure 6-7) in detail. This view makes it easy for you to create a project, link tasks to create sequential dependencies, see how your project is progressing over time, and view tasks graphically while still having access to details.

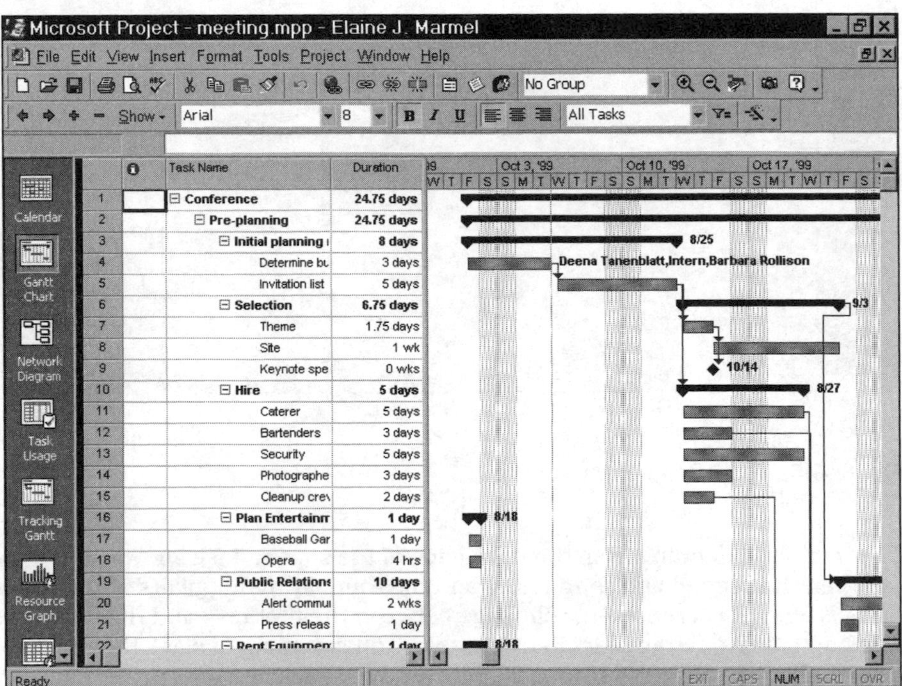


**Figure 6-7:** The Gantt Chart view

## Leveling Gantt

The Leveling Gantt view (see Figure 6-8) focuses on task delays. This view provides a graphic representation of delayed tasks while still providing task detail information. The chart portion of the view shows the effects before and after leveling. The default table that appears in the Leveling Gantt view is the Delay table, but you can change the table using the techniques described earlier in this chapter. You can use the Delay table to add or remove delay time and see the effects of your changes.

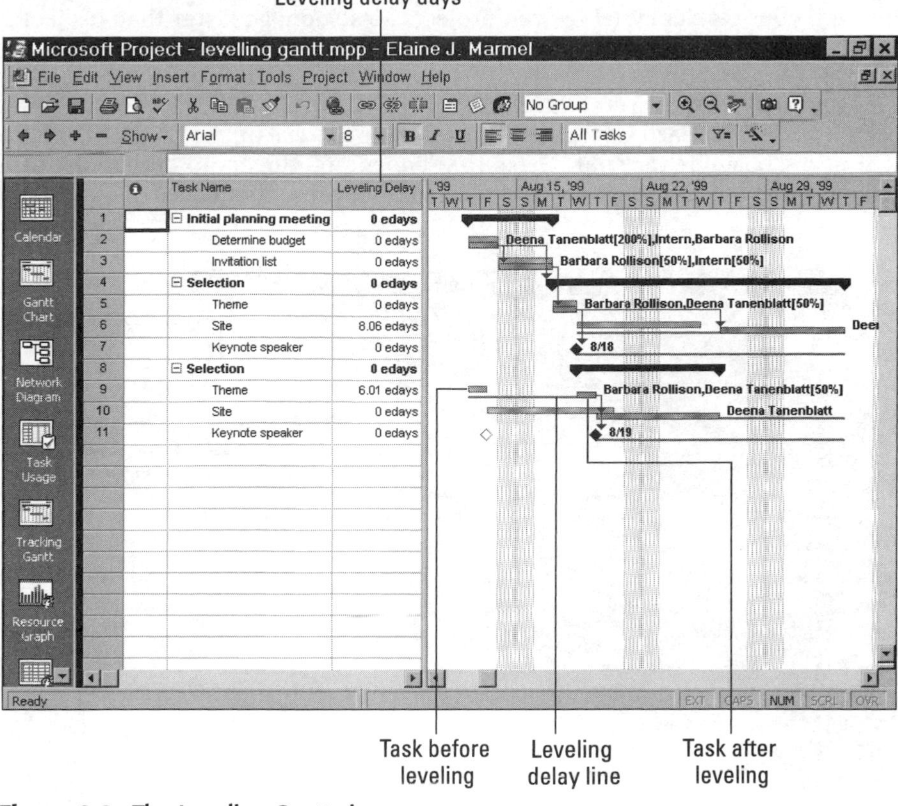


**Figure 6-8:** The Leveling Gantt view

*Leveling* is the process of resolving resource conflicts or overallocations by delaying or splitting certain tasks. You learn more about resource leveling in Chapter 10.

On this chart, you see two tasks showing leveling delays. The bar to the left of these tasks represents delay time, and the table indicates the number of days the leveled tasks are delayed.

# Tracking Gantt

The Tracking Gantt view is also based on the Gantt Chart view. The Tracking Gantt view provides a great visual way to evaluate the progress of individual tasks and the project as a whole. Using the Tracking Gantt view, you can see how your project has shifted from your original estimates and decide how to adjust your plans to accommodate any delays. Theoretically, if a project ever goes faster than you've anticipated, you could also see the amount of extra time you've bought yourself through your efficiency. (However, projects so seldom go faster than projected that I won't show that option here!)

In Figure 6-9, you see a standard Gantt view of a project that has had some activity. The standard Gantt view shows the progress on tasks as a black bar within the baseline task bar. Tasks that depend on the completed tasks have been moved out to reflect any delays in actual work completed.

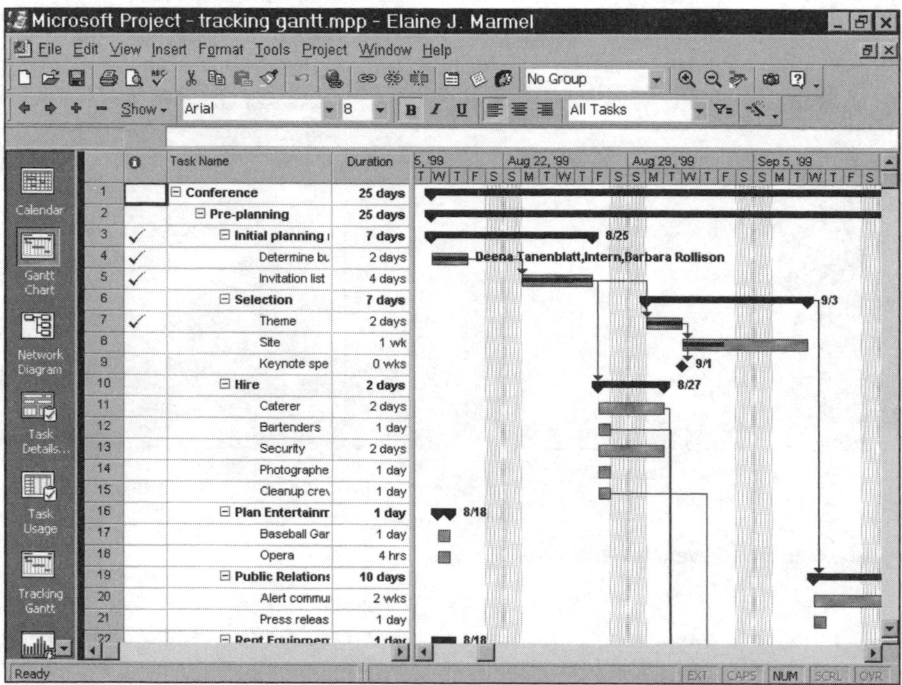


**Figure 6-9:** The standard Gantt view shows you the reality of your project timing at the moment, based on actual work done.

Figure 6-10, on the other hand, shows the same schedule displayed in the Tracking Gantt view. The table portion of the view contains columns that clearly compare planned activity to what has actually occurred. On the chart portion of the view, you see two bars for every task. The bottom bar shows baseline settings. The top bar reflects current scheduled start and finish dates if a task has not yet been started. If a task has been started — that is, if you have supplied some amount of work that has been completed — the top bar represents actual information, while the bottom bar represents baseline information. Project fills in the top bar and makes it solid to represent completed work; a hatching pattern appears in the top bar to represent unstarted work or work in progress. The bottom bars represent baseline task bars, which stay put; only actual work bars push out to reflect delays in timing.

On the Tracking Gantt, you can see that the Determine Budget Invitation list, and Theme tasks have been completed, and the Site task is 40 percent complete. No other tasks have been started, so the top bars on all other tasks represent scheduled start and finish dates, based on progress made so far in the project.

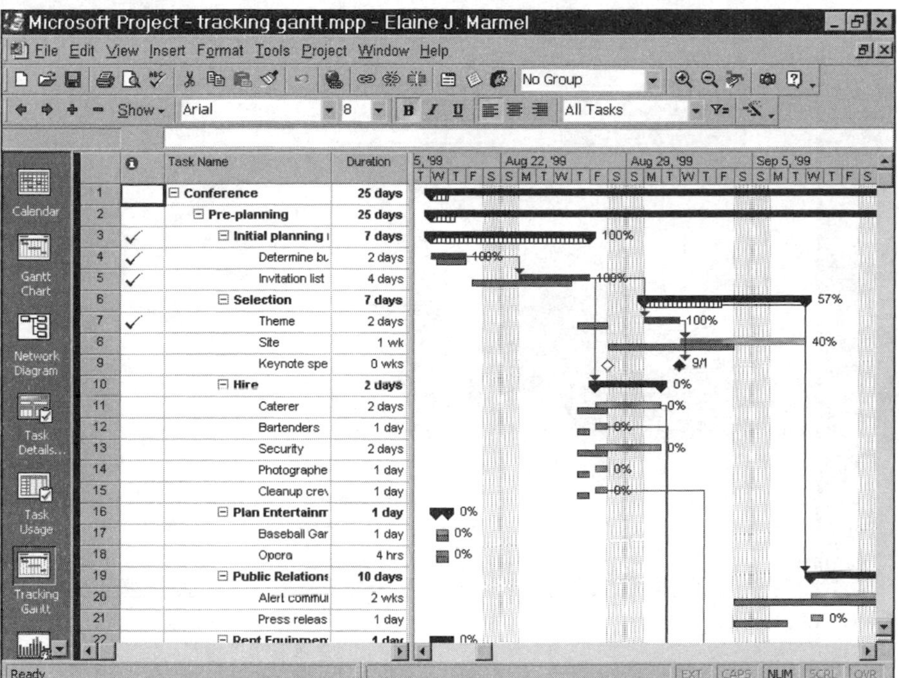


**Figure 6-10:** The Tracking Gantt view shows the discrepancy between your estimates and the real-world activity in your project.

# Network Diagram

The Network Diagram is a new name for the PERT Chart view you found in Project 98.

Project doesn't really produce a PERT chart, but you can use an add-on product, PERT Chart Expert. Try out a sample using the demo on the CD-ROM of this book.

The Network Diagram view shown in Figure 6-11 has less to do with timing than it has to do with the general flow of work and the relationships between tasks in your project. This view makes it easy for you to evaluate the flow of your project and check task dependencies.

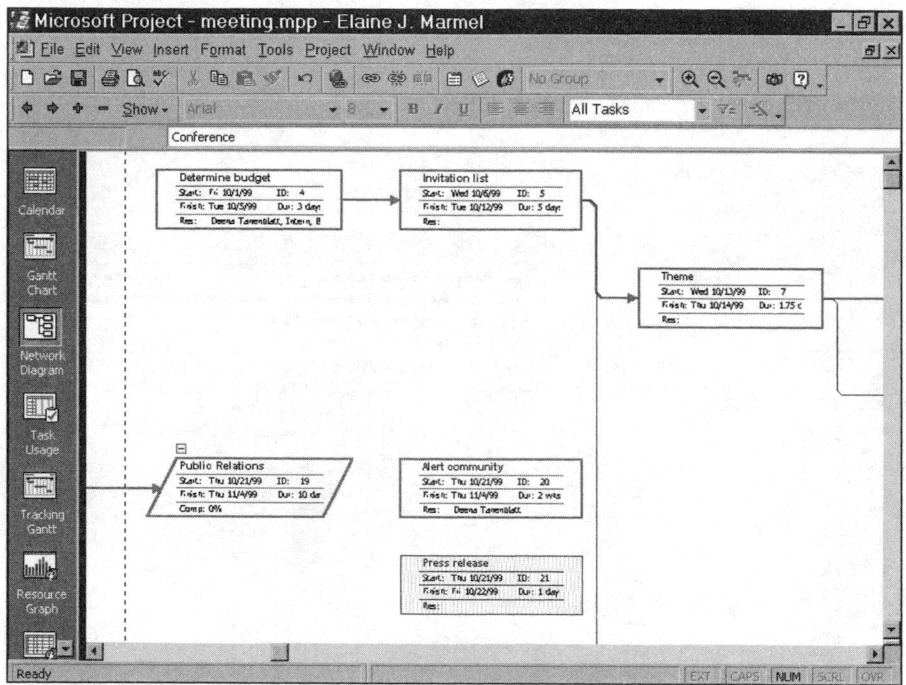


**Figure 6-11:** The Network Diagram view

Each node on the Network Diagram view represents a task in your project. I used Project's Zoom command (View ➪ Zoom) to enlarge a node in Figure 6-12, so that you could see the details. A node contains the task name, duration, task ID number in the sequence of the project outline, start date, end date, and, if assigned, the resource(s). The shape and color of each node represents different types of tasks — that is, critical tasks are red and have pointed sides while noncritical tasks are blue and have more square sides. You can determine — and change — the meaning of node shapes in the Box Styles dialog box (choose Format ➪ Box Styles). The lines that flow between the nodes represent dependencies. A task that must come after another task is complete, called *a successor task,* appears to the right or sometimes below its predecessor.

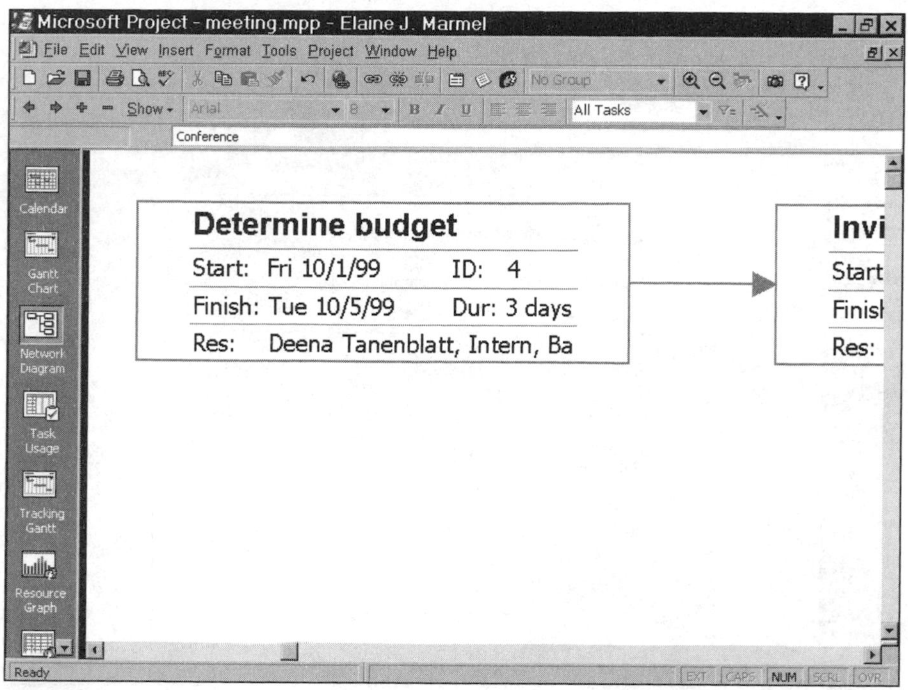


**Figure 6-12:** You can see task details when you examine the nodes of the Network Diagram.

You can now filter tasks in the Network Diagram view; for example, you can show only critical tasks.

You couldn't filter Project 98's PERT Chart view; you can, however, filter the Network Diagram view in Project 2000. While viewing the Network Diagram, choose Project ⇨ Filtered for: and select the filter you want to use.

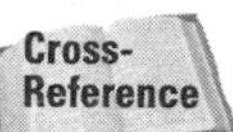


You'll read more about filtering in Chapter 7.

## Descriptive Network Diagram

The Descriptive Network Diagram (see Figure 16-13) is a cousin of the Network Diagram — and so focuses on the general flow of work and the relationships between tasks in your project.

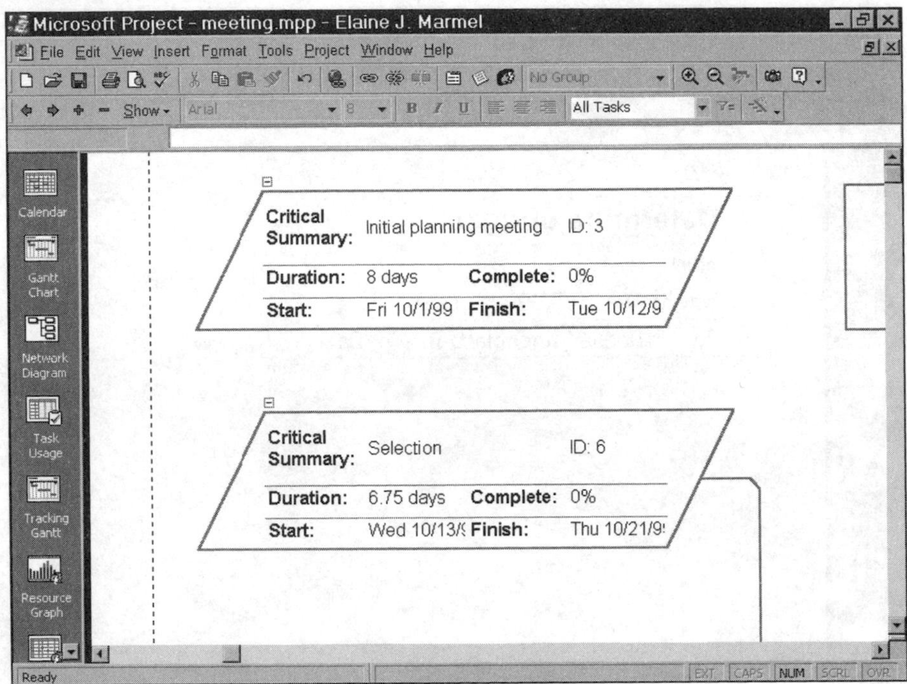


**Figure 6-13:** The Descriptive Network Diagram view

Like its cousin, each node on the Descriptive Network Diagram view represents a task in your project. If you compare Figures 6-12 and 6-13, you'll see more detail in the nodes of the Descriptive Network Diagram than you see in the Network Diagram; the Descriptive Network Diagram includes whether the task is critical and how complete the task is.

You can filter the Descriptive Network Diagram; choose Project ➪ Filtered for: and select the filter you want to use.

## Relationship Diagram

This special version of the Network Diagram view (see Figure 6-14) displays the current task in the center of the pane, with the task's predecessors to the left and successors to the right. When you are working on a large project, this graphic view helps you focus on one task and the tasks linked to it.

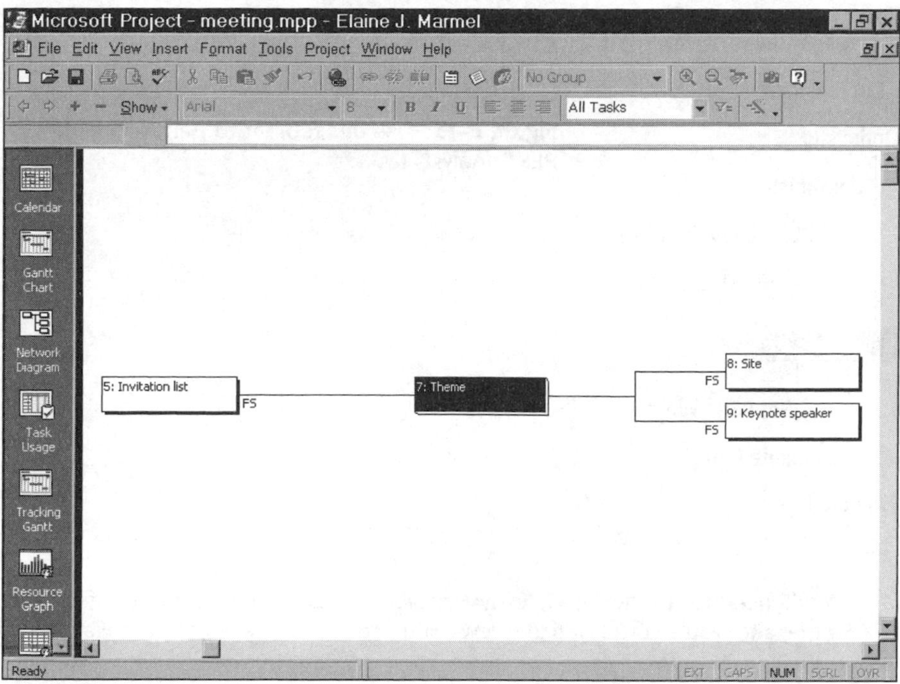


**Figure 6-14:** The Relationship Diagram

## PERT analysis views

PERT analysis is sometimes called what-if analysis, and many project managers use this approach to estimate a probable outcome. The probable outcome you estimate might be the duration of a task, its start date, or its end date. As a function of the estimating process, you specify the optimistic, pessimistic, and expected durations of tasks in your project. Then Microsoft Project calculates a weighted average of the three durations. As you might guess, PERT analysis has little to do with the PERT Chart view that was available in Project 98 and earlier versions. But you can use four PERT analysis views in Project to help you make your estimates:

- ✦ PERT Entry Sheet
- ✦ Optimistic Gantt
- ✦ Expected Gantt
- ✦ Pessimistic Gantt

You can use the PERT Analysis toolbar (see Figure 6-15) to perform PERT analysis. Choose View ➪ Toolbars ➪ PERT Analysis to display the toolbar.

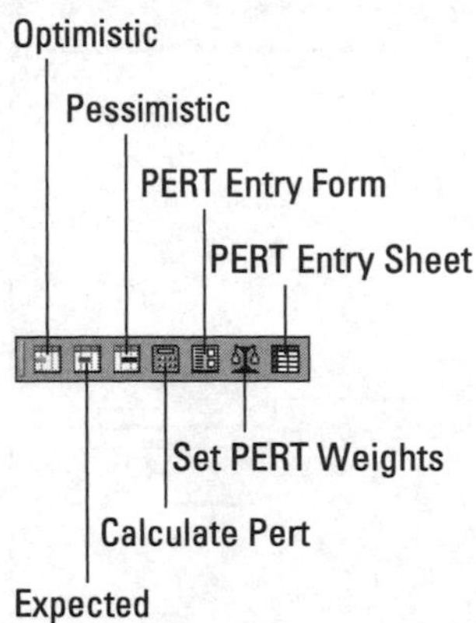


**Figure 6-15:** Use this toolbar to help you with PERT analysis tasks.

You'll need to use the PERT Analysis toolbar to display the four PERT views the first time; after you've displayed the views, you'll see them available in the Views window.

PERT stands for Program Evaluation and Review Technique. The Special Projects Office of the U.S. Navy devised this method of tracking the flow of tasks in the late 1950s.

## PERT Entry Sheet

The PERT Entry Sheet view in Figure 6-16 focuses PERT analysis entirely on durations. Click the PERT Entry Sheet button on the PERT Analysis toolbar to display this sheet.

Using this sheet, you enter optimistic, expected, and pessimistic durations for each task. When you click the Calculate PERT button on the PERT Analysis toolbar, Project uses a weighted average of the numbers you supply and calculates the probable duration of the task. Project displays the result in the Duration column for that task. Notice the duration of 3.75 days for the Invitation task; Project calculated this duration using the weighted average of the numbers in the Optimistic Dur., Expected Dur., and Pessimistic Dur. columns for the task.

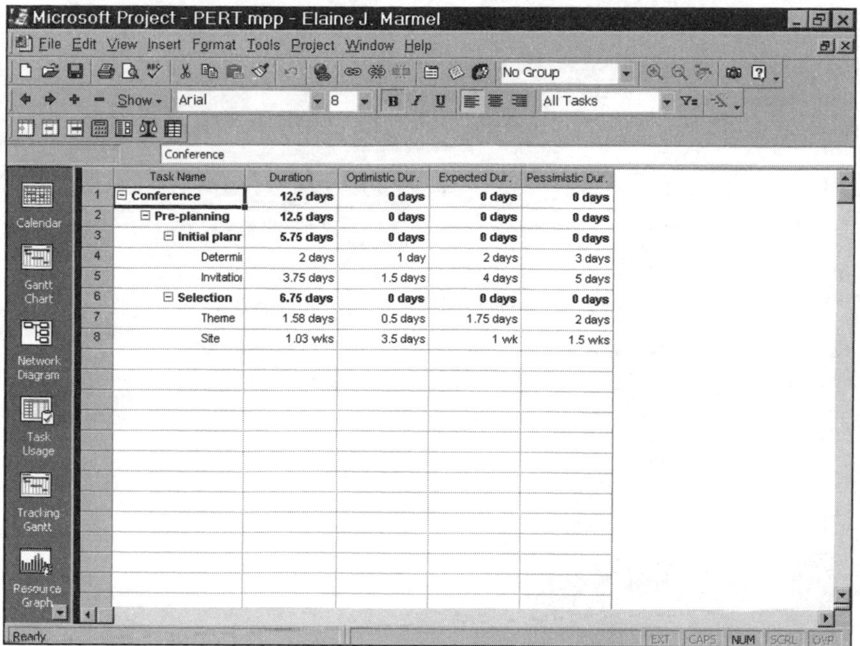

**Figure 6-16:** Use this view to focus on entering estimated durations for PERT analysis.

## Optimistic Gantt

After you have entered optimistic, expected, and pessimistic durations in the PERT Entry Sheet view and calculated, you can view the optimistic results for your entire project in the Optimistic Gantt view. Click the Optimistic Gantt button on the PERT Analysis toolbar to display the Optimistic Gantt view. As its name implies, the Optimistic Gantt view (see Figure 6-17) is a variation of the Gantt Chart view, with the Optimistic Case table on the left side and Gantt bars on the right. You can use this view to enter and evaluate the optimistic scenarios for task durations, start dates, and end dates.

**Note**

Initially, you may not see bars in any of the PERT Gantt views. While displaying any of these views, click the Calculate PERT button on the PERT Analysis toolbar again, and Project displays the bars.

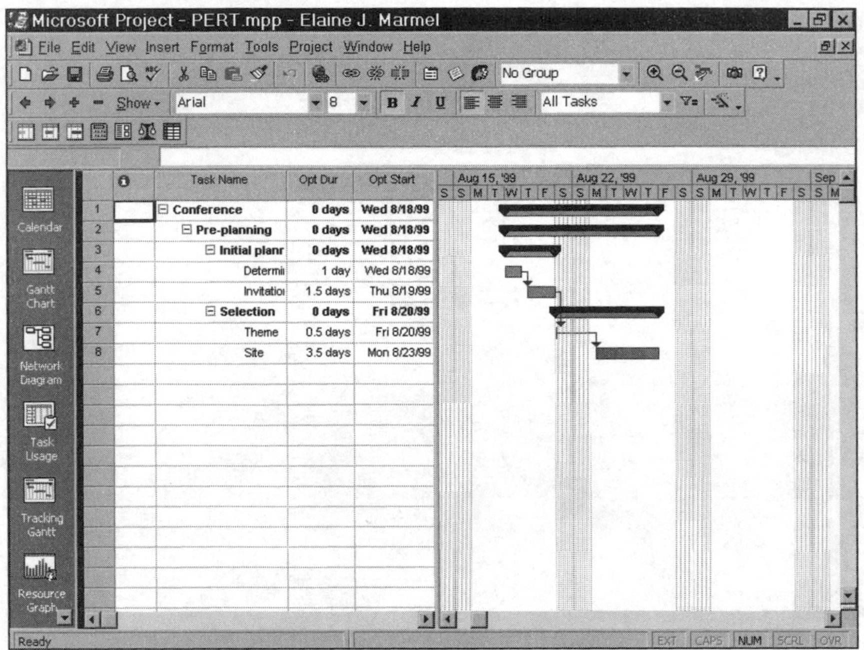

**Figure 6-17:** Use the Optimistic Gantt view to analyze optimistic task durations.

If you prefer to work with start dates and end dates or to focus entirely on optimistic durations while estimating, you can use this view to enter and evaluate the optimistic scenarios for task durations, start dates, and end dates. If you use this approach, you also will need to supply the same type of information in the Expected Gantt view and the Pessimistic Gantt view before you click the Calculate button.

## Expected Gantt

After you have entered optimistic, expected, and pessimistic durations on the PERT Entry Sheet and calculated, you can view the expected results for your entire project on the Expected Gantt view. Click the Expected Gantt button on the PERT Analysis toolbar to display the Expected Gantt view (see Figure 6-18). Like its cousins, the Optimistic and Pessimistic Gantt views, the Expected Gantt view is a variation of the Gantt Chart view. Project displays the Expected Gantt table on the left side and Gantt bars on the right side.

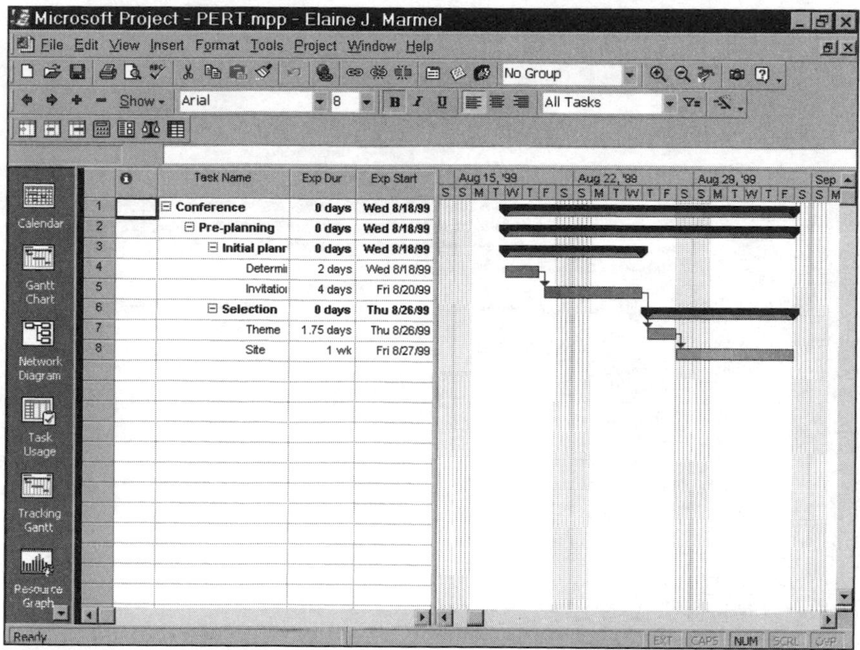


**Figure 6-18:** Use the Expected Gantt view to help create expected task durations.

If you prefer to estimate with start dates and end dates or to focus entirely on expected durations, you can use this view to enter and evaluate the expected scenarios for task durations, start dates, and end dates. If you use this approach, you also need to supply the same types of information on the Optimistic Gantt view and the Pessimistic Gantt view before you click the Calculate button.

## Pessimistic Gantt

After you enter optimistic, expected, and pessimistic durations on the PERT Entry Sheet view and perform the calculations, you can view the pessimistic results for your entire project in the Pessimistic Gantt view. Click the Pessimistic Gantt button on the PERT Analysis toolbar to display the Pessimistic Gantt view (see Figure 6-19). Like its cousins, the Expected Gantt and the Optimistic views, the Pessimistic Gantt view is also a variation of the Gantt Chart view. Project displays the Pessimistic Gantt table on the left and Gantt bars on the right. You can use this view to enter and evaluate the pessimistic scenarios for task durations, start dates, and end dates.

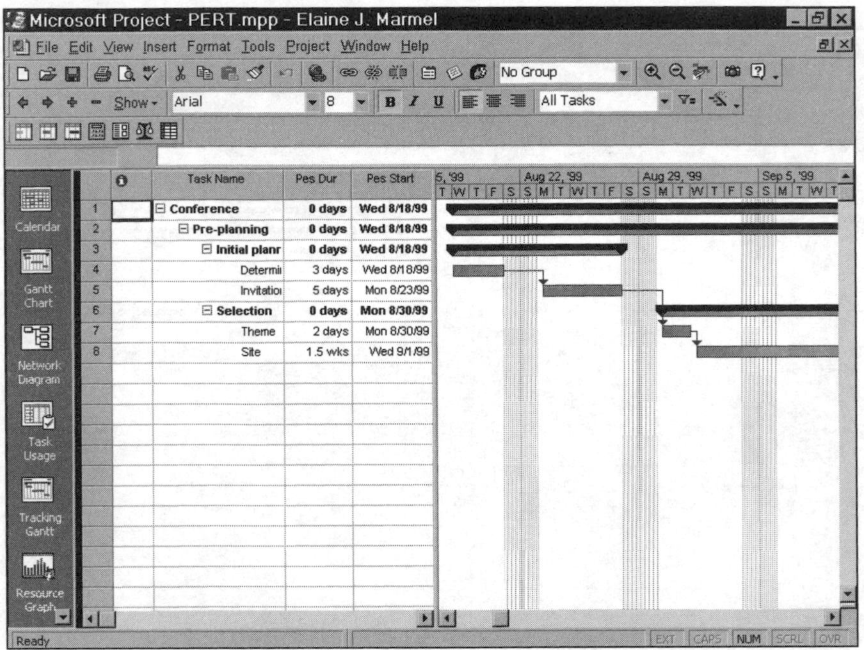


**Figure 6-19:** Use the Pessimistic Gantt view to help create pessimistic task durations.

If you prefer to work with start dates and end dates or to focus entirely on pessimistic durations while estimating, you can use this view to enter and evaluate the pessimistic scenarios for task durations, start dates, and end dates. If you use this approach, you also need to supply start and end dates on the Expected Gantt view and the Optimistic Gantt view before you click the Calculate button.

## PERT Weights

Project calculates a weighted average when you use PERT analysis. You can control the weights Project applies to each scenario from the Set PERT Weights dialog box (see Figure 6-20). Click the PERT Weights button on the PERT Analysis toolbar (second button from the right edge of the toolbar). Note that the values you enter must sum to 6 using the following formula:

```
(optimistic duration) + 4(expected duration) + (pessimistic
duration) ≡ 6
```

You can use different weights to change the emphasis Project applies to its calculation of each scenario.

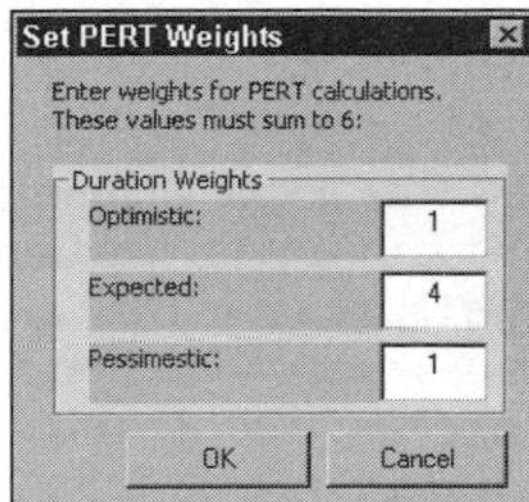


**Figure 6-20:** Use the Set PERT Weights dialog box to adjust the weights Project applies when making PERT calculations.

# Resource Allocation

The Resource Allocation view is a combination view. For example, in Figure 6-21 the Resource Usage view appears in the top pane, and the Leveling Gantt Chart view appears in the bottom pane.

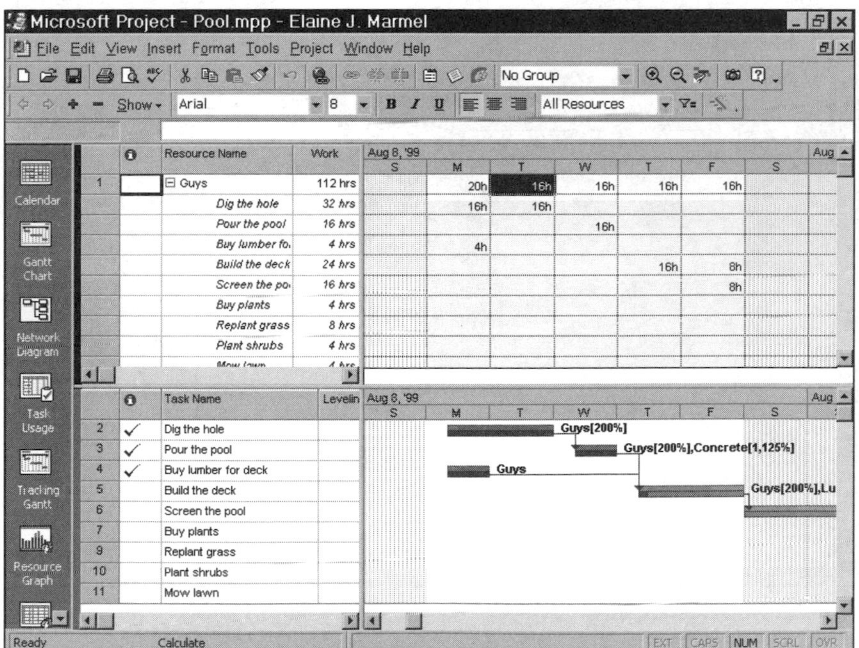


**Figure 6-21:** The Resource Allocation view displays resource allocation relative to the project timing.

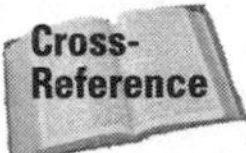


The Resource Usage view is covered later in this chapter, and the Leveling Gantt Chart view was covered earlier in this chapter.

The default table that appears on the Resource Usage view (the upper pane of the combination view) is the Usage table; the default table that appears on the Gantt Chart view (the lower pane of the combination view) is the Entry table. As you scroll the right side of the window, the top and bottom panes move together. You can use the techniques described earlier in this chapter to change either table.

## Resource Form

The Resource Form view displays detailed information about one resource at a time (see Figure 6-22).

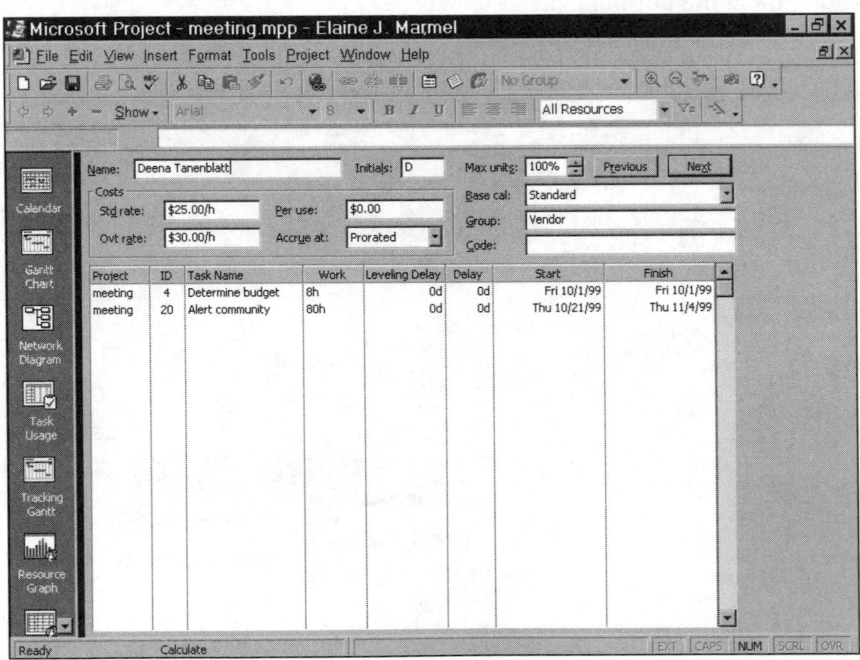


**Figure 6-22:** The Resource Form view

Use the Next and Previous buttons in the upper-right corner of the window to display different resources; if you haven't sorted or filtered resources, Project shows them to you in ID number order.

## Resource Graph

The Resource Graph view shows how a particular resource is being used on a project. You can use the Resource Graph view to spot and correct resources that are inappropriately allocated. Note that the Resource Graph view shows information for one resource at a time. To view a different resource, click the scroll arrows that appear below the left pane in this window. This view works well as part of a combination view.

The Resource Graph view highlights resource conflicts: people, equipment, or other resources that are being overworked or underutilized. Looking at the Resource Graph view as both a single and combination view can show you how assignments on individual tasks are affecting a resource's utilization on a project. Figure 6-23 shows the main Resource Graph view; Figure 6-24 shows the combination view with details at the bottom of the Project window of the tasks being performed. You can create this view by choosing Window ➪ Split.

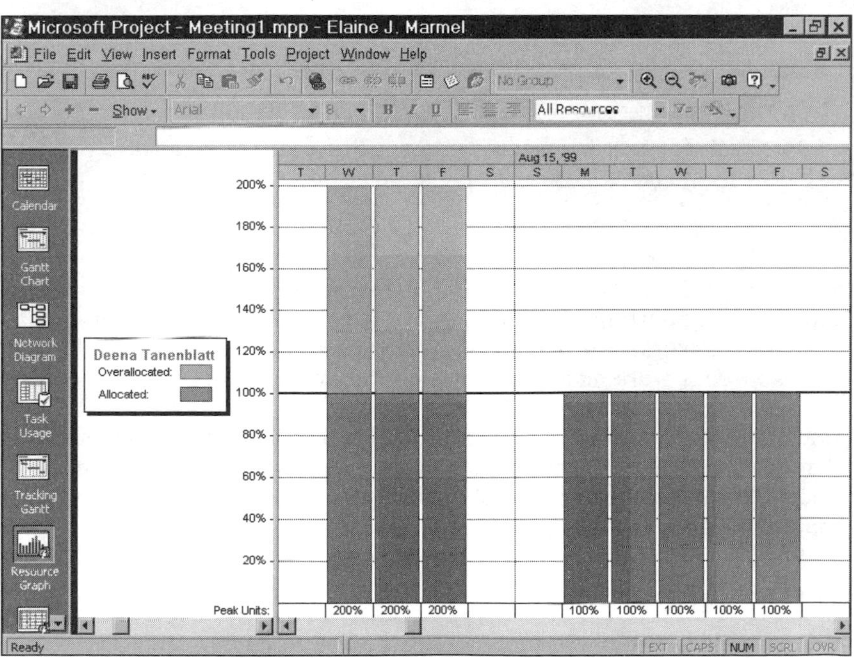


**Figure 6-23:** The percentage of a person's available work time is tracked and displayed as overallocated and underallocated.

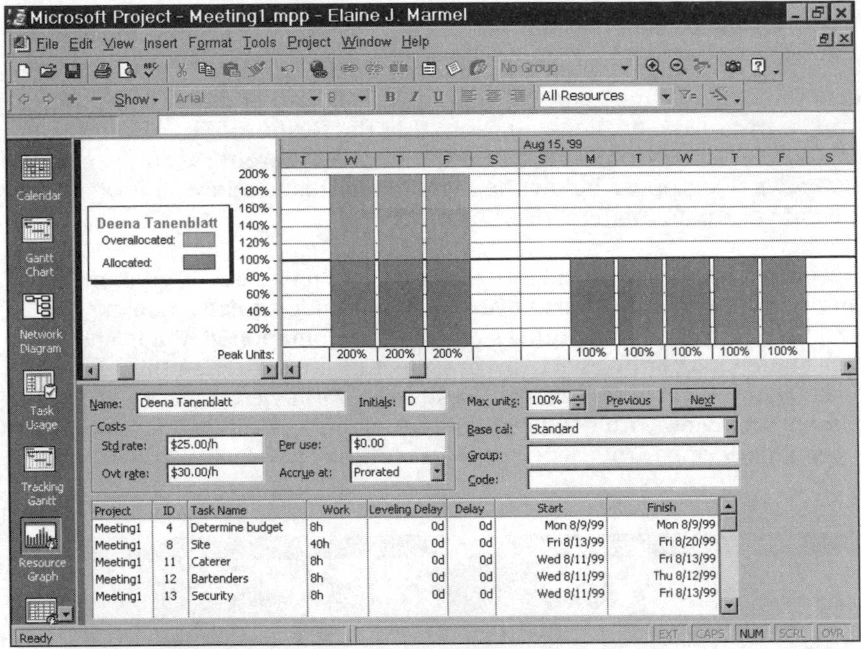


**Figure 6-24:** Displaying task information beneath a Resource Graph can help you see which work assignments are keeping the resource busy.

Project displays a resource's total work hours on any particular day as a bar. A bar that falls short of the 100 percent mark indicates a resource that isn't working full-time and may be underutilized. A bar that extends beyond 100 percent indicates that somebody is working too many hours in a day. The percentage of the workday that the resource is working appears at the bottom of the usage bars.

Underutilization may indicate that a resource is busy with other projects the rest of that day, and overutilization may signal occasional and acceptable overtime. See Chapter 8 for more information about interpreting these bars and Chapter 10 for more about resolving conflicts in resource time.

## Resource Name Form

The Resource Name Form view is a simplified version of the Resource Form view. (Compare Figure 6-25 with Figure 6-22.) None of the cost information appears in this view; nor do you see the resources' maximum units, base calendar, group, or code.

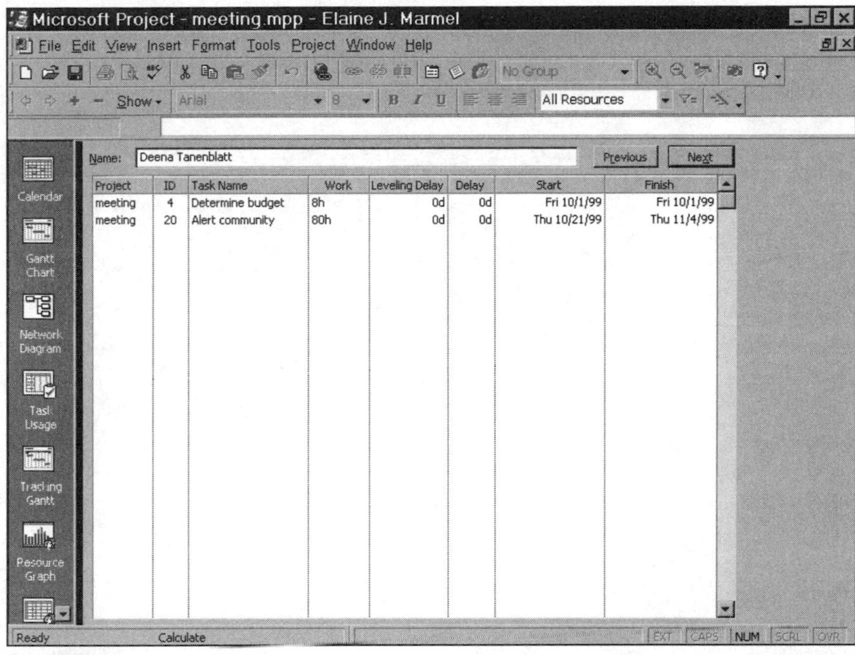


**Figure 6-25:** The Resource Name Form view

You can use this view to set up basic information about resources for a project — which can give you a good idea about a resource's workload. Use the Previous and Next buttons to view different resources.

# Resource Sheet

The Resource Sheet view shown in Figure 6-26 gives you a wealth of information about the resources assigned to your project, including standard and overtime rates, availability for overtime work, and fixed costs.

By assigning group designations to resources such as Marketing, Facilities, or Temporary Help, you can use filters to study resource information for just one or two groups at a time.

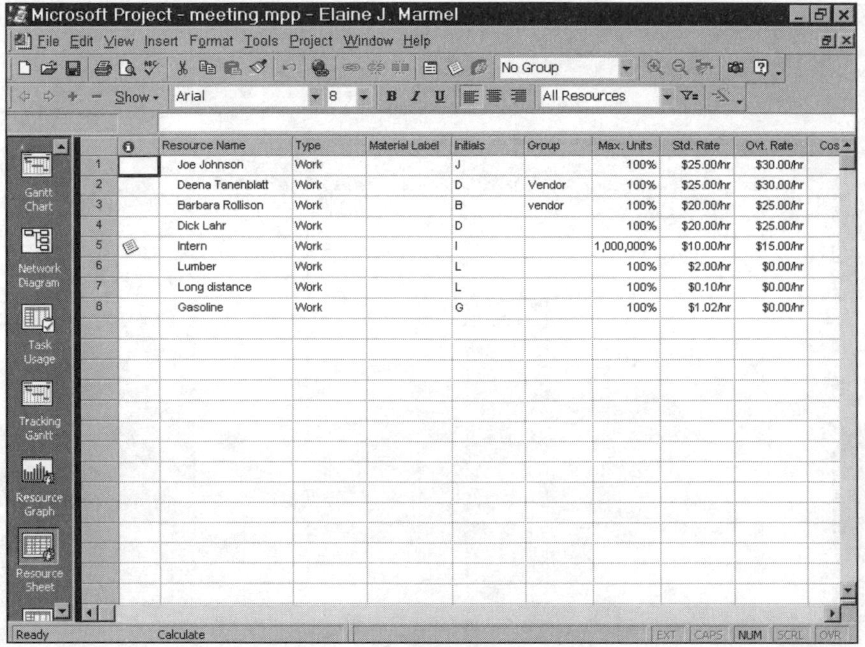


**Figure 6-26:** You can view both standard and overtime rates in the Resource Sheet.

This columnar interface is a great way to prepare to assign resources if, for example, you want to assign lower-cost people to most tasks and higher-cost people to certain mission-critical tasks. This view clearly shows to which group a resource belongs. If overallocations exist, you'll see a warning flag in the Indicator column on the far left of this view. Switch back to the Resource Graph to get details on these problems resource by resource.

The default table that appears on the Resource Sheet view is the Entry table, but you can change the table using the techniques described earlier in this chapter.

# Resource Usage

The Resource Usage view (see Figure 6-27) shows each resource and the tasks assigned to it. You can use the Resource Usage view to enter and edit resource information, and you can assign or reassign tasks to resources on this view by dragging the tasks between resources.

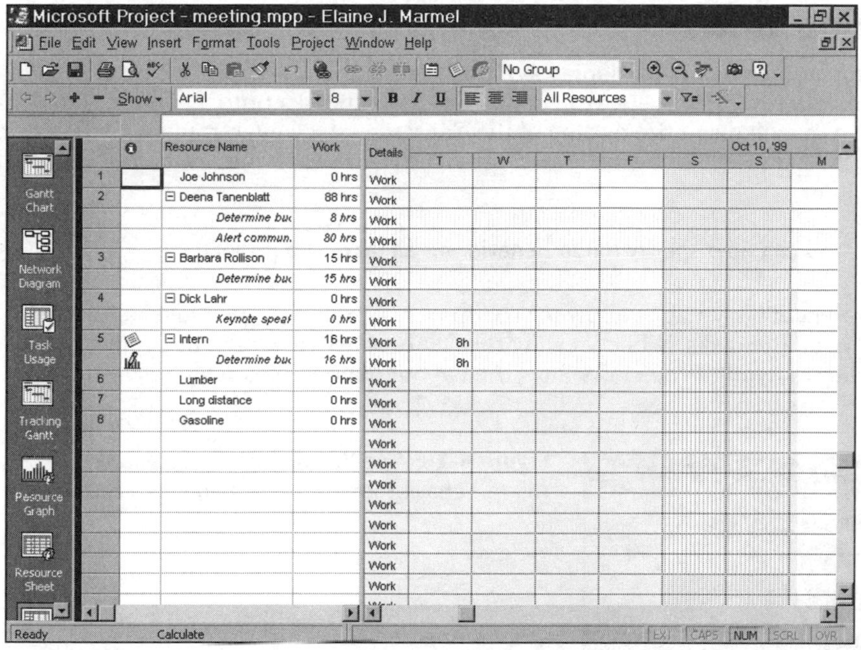


**Figure 6-27:** The Resource view organizes task assignments by resource so that you can easily figure out who's doing what and when in the Resource Usage view.

The Resource Usage view is also useful when you want to:

- ✦ Check resource overallocations
- ✦ Examine the number of hours or the percentage of capacity at which each resource is scheduled to work
- ✦ View a resource's progress or costs
- ✦ Determine how much time a particular resource has for additional work assignments

The default table on the left side of this view is the Usage table. You can use the Table Selection button described earlier to switch to a different table. Similarly, you can use either the Format ➪ Details or the Format ➪ Detail Styles commands to add to or change the information that appears in the Details section. (Work is the default selection.)

## Rollup views

In Project 98, you could display symbols on a summary task bar that represented subtask dates: Effectively, you "rolled up" the subtasks onto a summary task bar when you collapsed the outline of the Gantt view. However, rollup wasn't an easy process in Project 98 because you needed to mark each individual task you wanted to roll up.

You can now specify rollup behavior for all tasks in a project.

In Project 2000, you can allow for rollup behavior at a project level and avoid editing all the tasks. While viewing the Gantt Chart view of your project, choose Format ➪ Layout. Project displays the Layout dialog box shown in Figure 6-28.

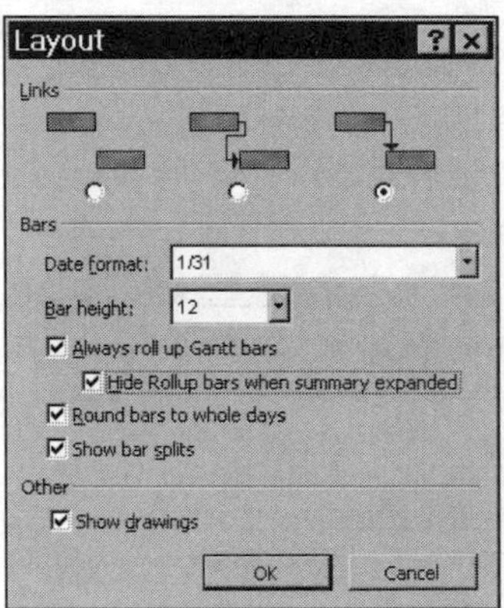


**Figure 6-28:** Use this dialog box to enable rollup behavior for all tasks in your project.

Place a check in the "Always roll up Gantt bars" checkbox; if you don't want see the rollup bars when you expand the project outline to view all tasks, also place a check in the "Hide Rollup bars when summary expanded" checkbox.

### Using the summary task bar

When you enable rollup behavior and collapse the outline, Project displays a summary task bar that contains symbols that represent subtask dates. Compare Figures 6-29, 6-30, and 6-31, which show various effects of collapsing the outline and rollup behavior. In particular, compare Figures 6-29 and 6-30.

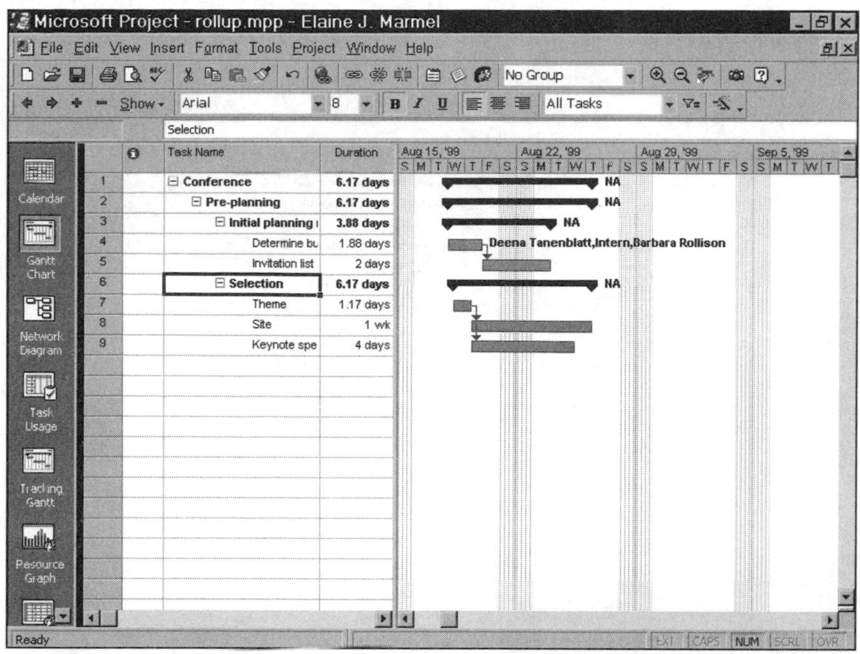

**Figure 6-29:** In this figure, the outline is completely expanded.

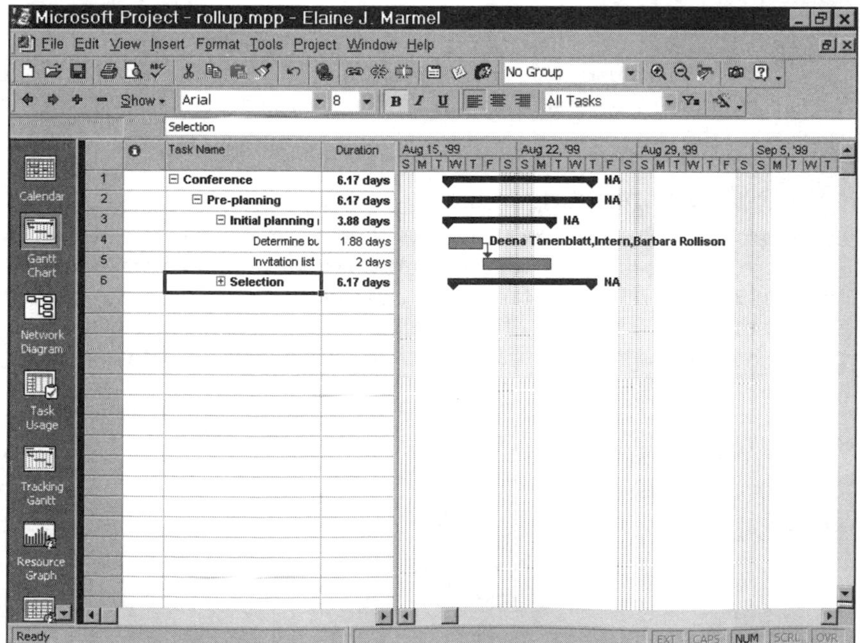

**Figure 6-30:** In this figure, I collapsed the outline for the Selection task, but I didn't enable rollup behavior.

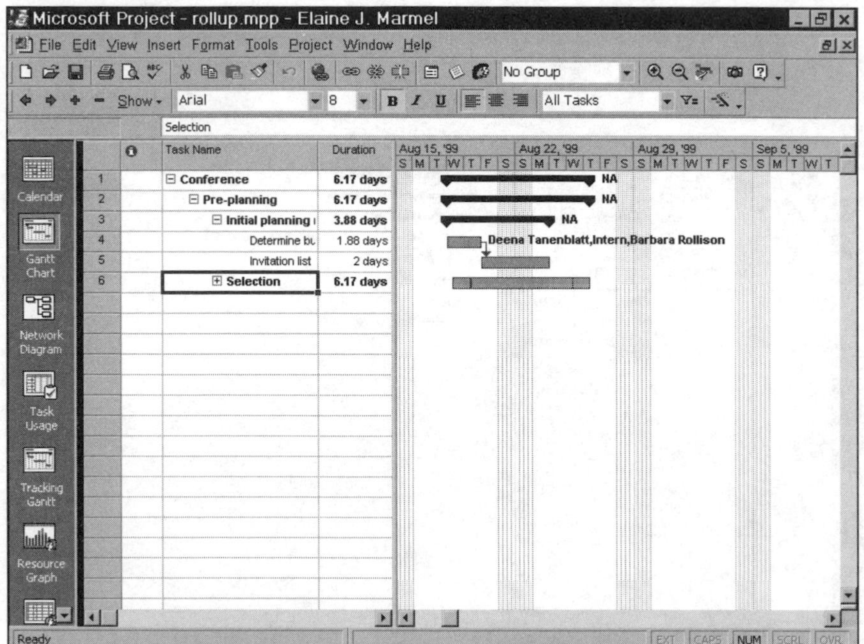


**Figure 6-31:** In this figure, I collapsed the outline for the Selection task and enabled rollup behavior.

You can still specify rollup behavior at the task level so that Project doesn't roll up all tasks to summary bars when you collapse the outline. Remember that changes you make in the Layout dialog box don't affect tasks whose rollup behavior you specified at the task level.

## Using the Rollup_Formatting macro

Project contains a special macro called the Rollup_Formatting macro. When you run this macro, Project displays, on the Gantt Chart view, a summary bar that contains symbols that represent tasks; you can think of these tasks as rolled up onto the summary bar. This type of view helps you create a summarized version of your project and makes important dates visible. Three new views help you see your focus on your project's summary tasks:

- ✦ Bar Rollup
- ✦ Milestone Date Rollup
- ✦ Milestone Rollup

A rollup view displays only the tasks that you format as rollup tasks in the Task Information dialog box. Remember, if you format rollup behavior for tasks in the Task Information dialog box, changing rollup behavior in the Layout dialog box (discussed in the previous section) won't affect the appearance of your Gantt Chart.

This macro won't work unless you first mark tasks on the project as tasks you want to roll up. Follow these steps to mark tasks and run the Rollup Formatting macro:

1. Select tasks in the Gantt Chart view.

You can use Windows selection techniques to select several tasks simultaneously. Click the first task you want to select. Then, to select contiguous tasks, press Shift and click the last task. Or to select noncontiguous tasks, press Ctrl and click each task.

2. Click the Task Information button on the Standard toolbar to open the General tab of the Multiple Task Information dialog box (see Figure 6-32).

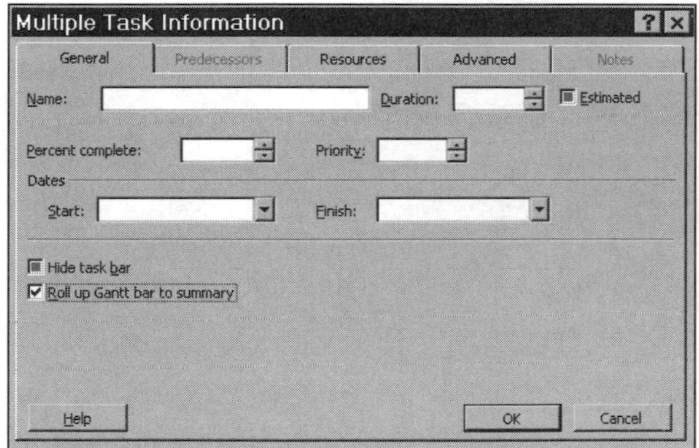


**Figure 6-32:** Use the General tab of the Multiple Task Information dialog box to mark tasks for rollup.

3. Place a check in the "Roll up Gantt bar to summary" checkbox.
4. Click OK.
5. Choose Tools ⇨ Macros. Then choose Macros from the side menu to open the Macros dialog box (see Figure 6-33).
6. Select the Rollup Formatting macro and click Run. Project displays the Rollup Formatting dialog box (see Figure 6-34).

7. Select Bars to display rolled up tasks as bars, or select Milestones to display rolled up tasks as milestones and click OK. Project displays the rolled up version of your project (see Figure 6-35).

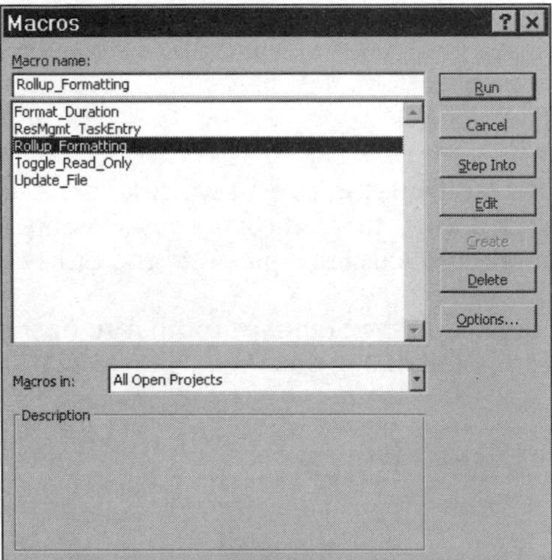


**Figure 6-33:** Run macros from the Macro dialog box.

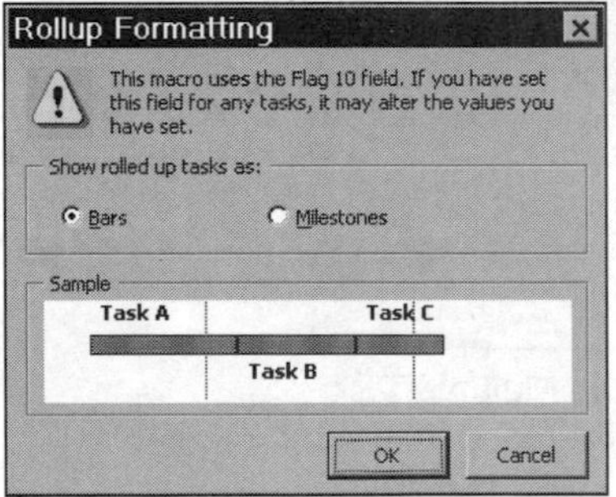


**Figure 6-34:** Choose the style of formatting you want for your rollup.

Using the Rollup Formatting macro can produce unpredictable results if your task start dates are close together. Task names may appear on top of one another—and unreadable.

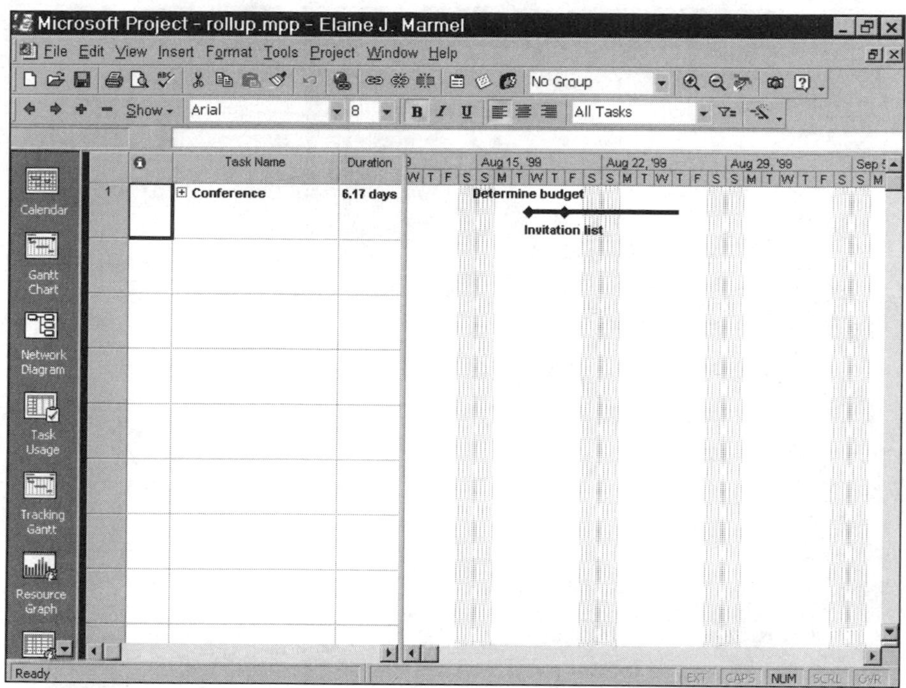


**Figure 6-35:** When you format rollup tasks as milestones, Project displays your project using the Milestone Rollup view.

## Switching rollup views

When you use the Rollup Formatting macro, Project displays only those tasks you formatted for rollup. The table you see in the sheet portion of all of these views is the Rollup table, but you can switch to another table using the techniques explained earlier in the chapter. Figure 6-35 showed the Milestone Rollup view that Project displays if you selected Milestones in Step 7.

If you select Bars in Step 7, Project displays the Bar Rollup view (see Figure 6-36).

To redisplay all subtasks in a typical Gantt Chart view, click the Show button on the Formatting toolbar and choose All Subtasks.

Using the More Views dialog box (click the More Views button on the View bar), you can display the Milestone Date Rollup view (see Figure 6-37).

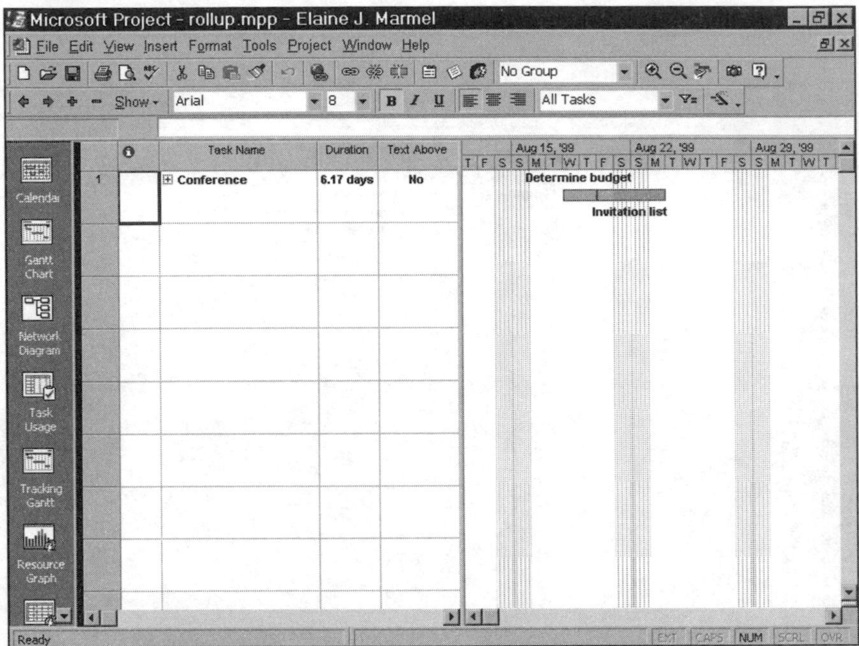

**Figure 6-36:** When you format rollup tasks as bars, Project displays your project using the Bar Rollup view.

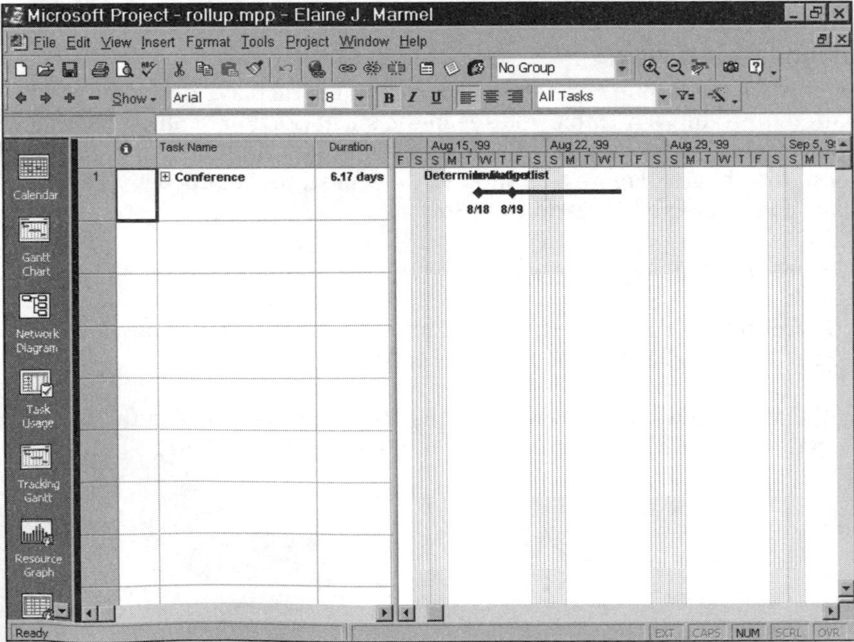

**Figure 6-37:** Use this view to see rollup tasks along with their start dates.

If your start dates are close together, Project overwrites the task names, making them difficult or impossible to read.

## Task Details Form

The Task Details Form view in Figure 6-38 enables you to view and edit tracking information about one task at a time.

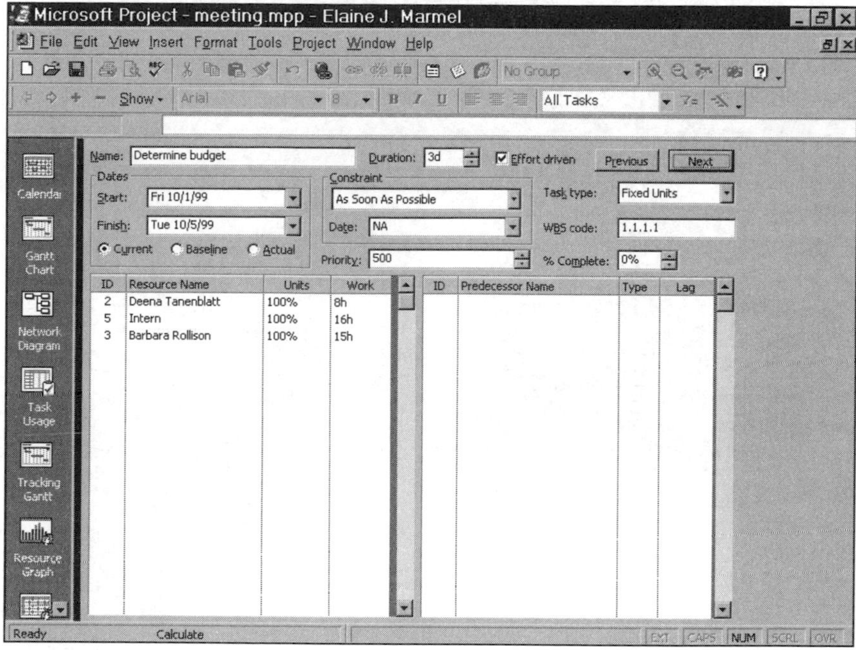


**Figure 6-38:** The Task Details Form view

Use the Previous and Next buttons to switch from task to task. If you haven't sorted or filtered tasks, Project displays them in ID number order. The Task Details Form view is a good choice for part of a combination view.

This view closely resembles the Task Form view and the Task Name Form view.

# Task Entry

The Task Entry view is a combination view. In Figure 6-39 the Gantt Chart view appears in the top pane, and the Task Form view appears in the bottom pane. To see information about a task in the Task Form view, select the task in the Gantt Chart view. You can see this view easily if you select the Gantt view and then choose Window ➪ Split.

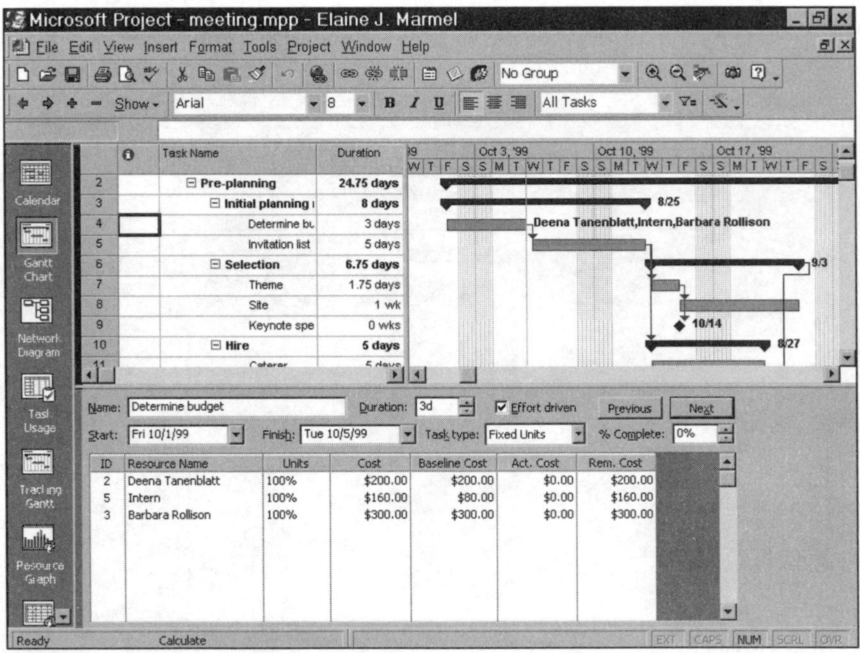


**Figure 6-39:** The Task Entry view

Only the Gantt Chart view in the top pane uses a table. The default table is the Entry table, but you can use the techniques described earlier in this chapter to change the table.

# Task Form

The Task Form view appears on the bottom portion of the Task Entry view, as you saw in Figure 6-39. The Task Form view (see Figure 6-40) closely resembles the Task Details Form view (refer to Figure 6-38).

The Task Form view provides more resource information, such as costs, than the Task Details Form view, and the Task Details Form view provides more task information, such as predecessors, than the Task Form view. Use the Previous and Next buttons to switch tasks. The Task Form view also closely resembles the Task Name Form view (described next).

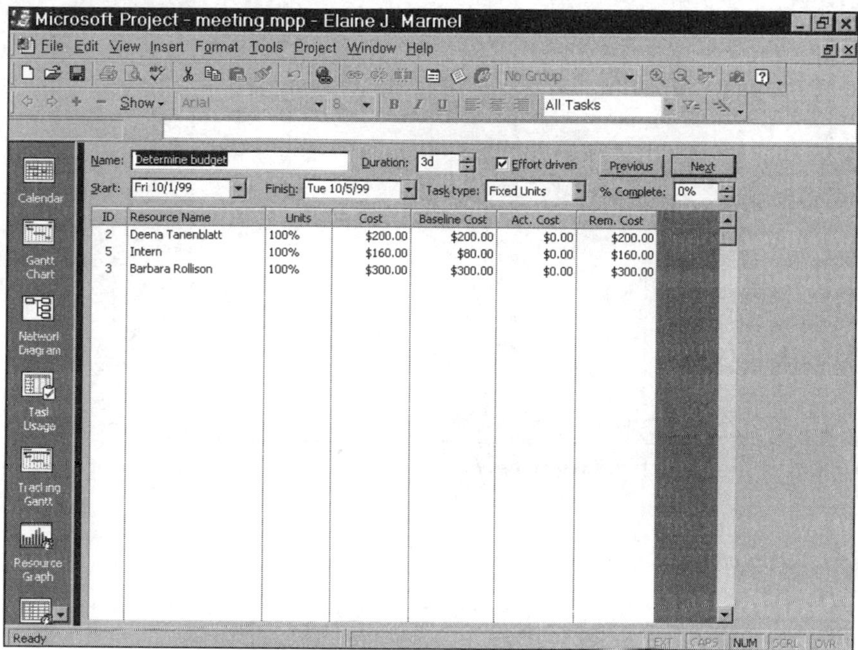


**Figure 6-40:** The Task Form view

## Task Name Form

The Task Name Form view is a cousin to the Task Details Form view and the Task Form view. This simplified version displays the basic characteristics of tasks, one task at a time (see Figure 6-41).

Use the Previous and Next buttons to switch tasks. Again, if you compare Figures 6-38, 6-40, and 6-41, you can see how closely these views resemble each other. The Task Name Form view works well as part of a combination view.

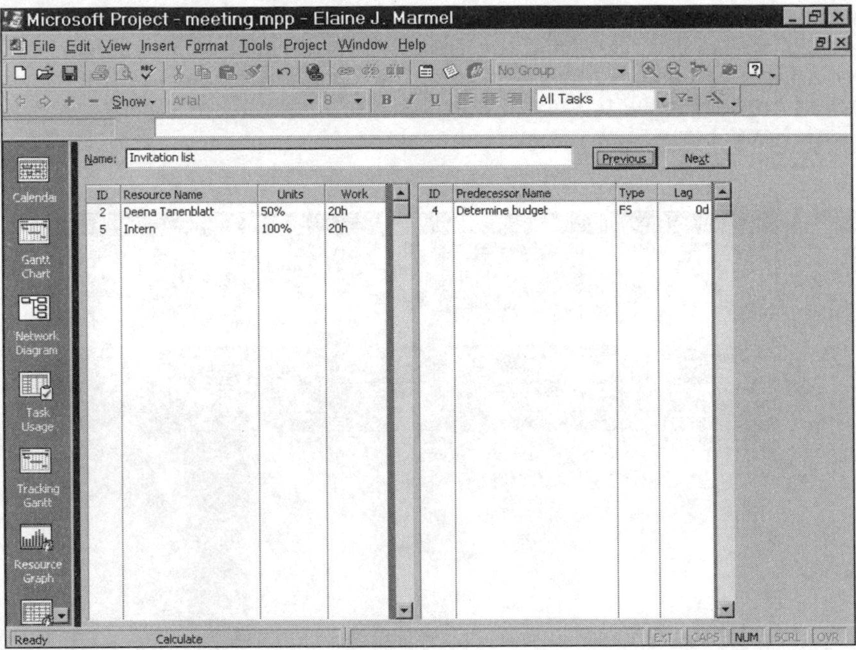


**Figure 6-41:** The Task Name Form view

# Task Sheet

The Task Sheet view is the counterpart of the Resource Sheet view in that the Task Sheet view displays task information in a spreadsheet-like format. In this view you can create tasks, link tasks (establishing dependencies), and even assign resources (see Figure 6-42).

This view closely resembles the left portion of the Gantt Chart view and makes it easy to view tasks in chronological order. The default table that appears on the Task Sheet view is the Entry table, but you can use the techniques described earlier in this chapter to change the table.

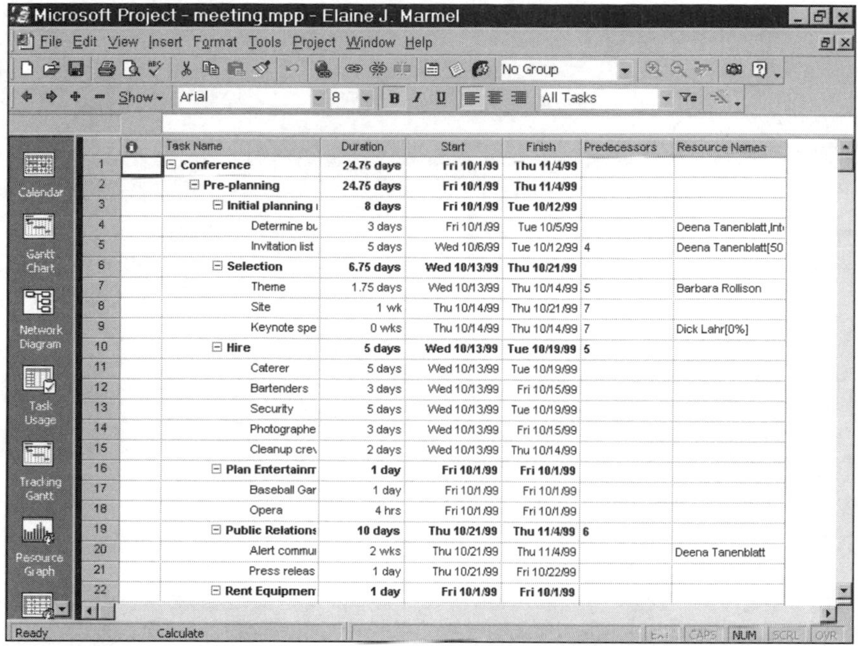

**Figure 6-42:** The Task Sheet view helps you see tasks in chronological order.

## Task Usage

This powerful view (see Figure 6-43) enables you to focus on how resources affect the task by showing resource assignments for each task. Use this view to organize resources by task, evaluate work effort and cost by task, and compare scheduled and actual work and costs.

The default table for the left side of the view, is the Usage table, but you can display other tables by using the Table Selection button, as described earlier in this chapter. Also, by default, Project shows Work in the Details section on the right; again, you can select any item from the Format ➪ Details menu or in the Details Styles dialog box. (Choose Format ➪ Detail Styles.)

**Note** How can you do 15 hours of work in one 8-hour day, as indicated in the sample project shown in Figure 6-43? Remember that this view shows total resource hours: As the figure shows, two people worked seven and eight hours respectively.

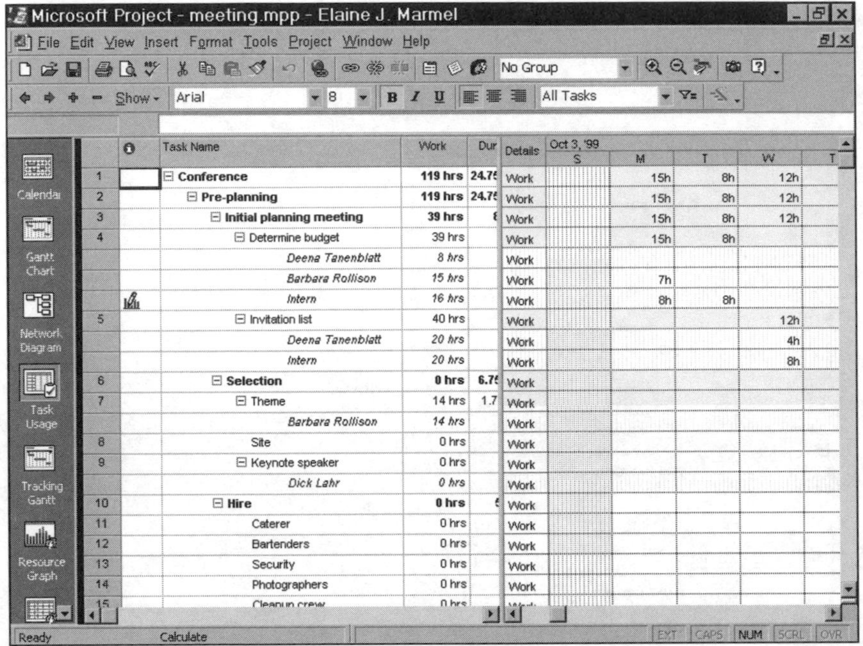


**Figure 6-43:** The Task Usage view shows resources grouped under the tasks to which they are assigned.

# Printing Your Project

When you print a project, you are printing a view. So, before you do anything, select the view you want to print. If you're printing a sheet view, the number of columns you see onscreen determines the number of columns that print. If the printed product requires more than one page, Project prints down and across; that is, the entire left side of your project prints before the right side prints.

Printing in Project is very similar to printing in any other Microsoft product. You can use the Print button on the Standard toolbar to print using default settings. And what are the default settings? They appear in two dialog boxes that you can view if you don't use the Print button.

You can also preview before printing either by clicking the Preview button in the Print dialog box or by clicking the Print Preview button on the Standard toolbar.

Choose File ➪ Print to open the Print dialog box shown in Figure 6-44.

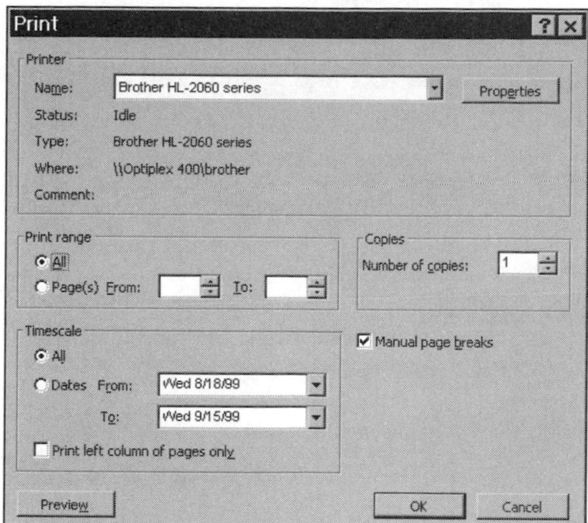


**Figure 6-44:** From the Print dialog box, you can control, for example, the printer to which you print and the number of copies you print.

When you save the project file, Project retains the settings you make in this dialog box for the timescale, including settings for "Print left column of pages only" and manual page breaks.

You cannot open the Page Setup dialog box (see Figure 6-45) from the Print dialog box, but you can open the Page Setup dialog box either by choosing File ⇨ Page Setup or by clicking the Page Setup button that is available in Print Preview. From the Page tab, you can set orientation and scaling. Using scaling, you may be able to fit the printed text onto one page.

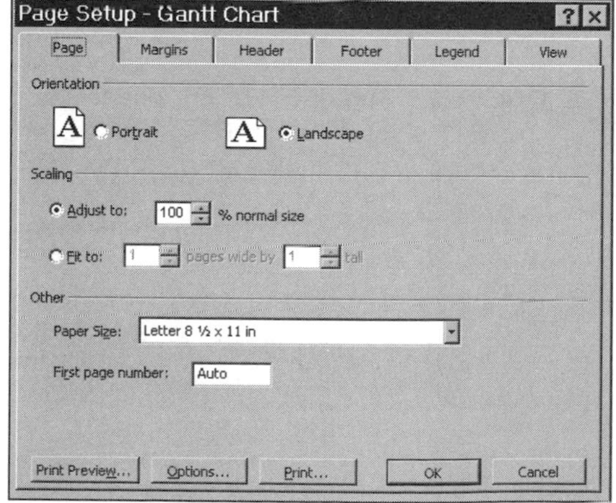


**Figure 6-45:** The Page tab of the Page Setup dialog box

You can set the first page number of the printed product. Suppose, for example, that your project is 10 pages long but you intend to print only pages 5 and 6. Typically, you'd want to number those pages as 1 and 2 – and you can do exactly that by setting the "First page number" box to 1.

From the Margins tab (see Figure 6-46), you can change the margins for your printed text and determine whether a border should appear.

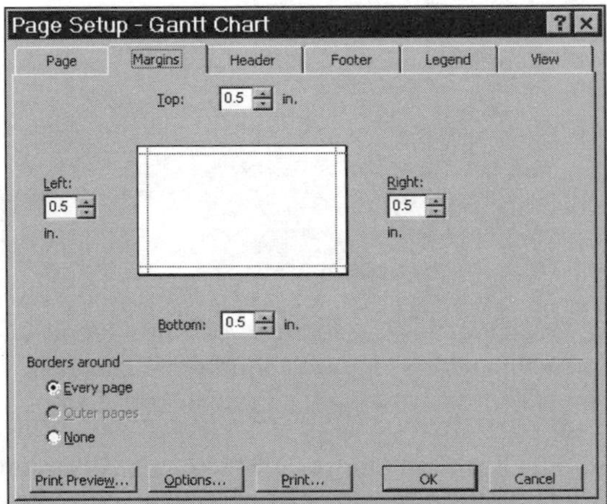


**Figure 6-46:** The Margins tab of the Page Setup dialog box

From the Header tab (see Figure 6-47), you can define and align header information to appear on the top of every page you print. Use either the buttons at the bottom of the box or the list box to add information that you want Project to update automatically, such as page numbers.

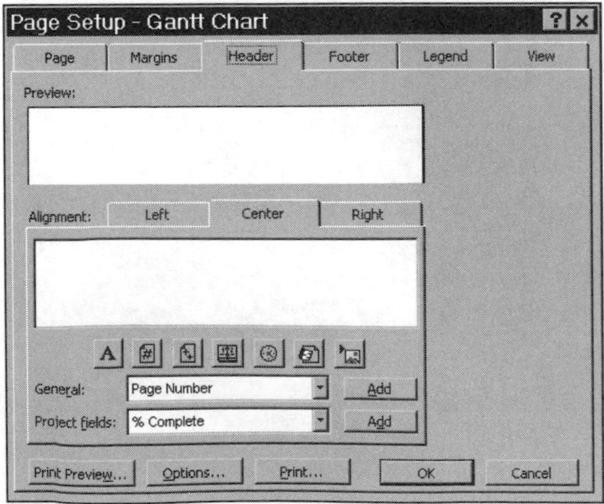


**Figure 6-47:** The Header tab of the Page Setup dialog box

You can include Project level fields in the header, footer, or legend of your printed product. From the appropriate tab of the Page Setup dialog box, use the Project Fields list box to select the field you want to include.

The Footer tab (see Figure 6-48) works just like the Header tab. You can align and include the same kind of updating information in the footer on each page of your printed text.

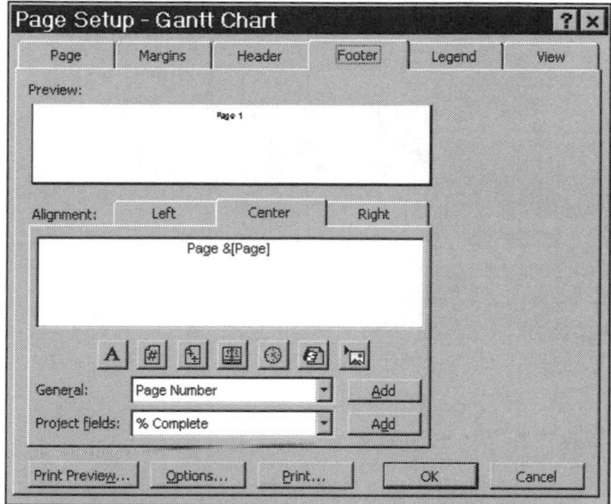


**Figure 6-48:** The Footer tab of the Page Setup dialog box

The Page Setup dialog box changes just slightly, depending on the view you were using when you opened the dialog box. For example, the Legend tab is available only when you're printing a Calendar, Gantt Chart view, or Network Diagram view (see Figure 6-49). The Legend tab works just like the Header and Footer tabs, and you can align and include the same kind of updating information.

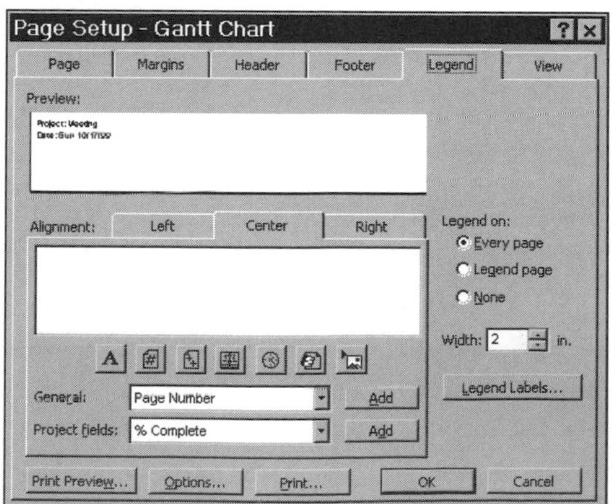


**Figure 6-49:** The Legend tab of the Page Setup dialog box

The View tab enables you to control what Project prints, such as all or only some columns (see Figure 6-50).

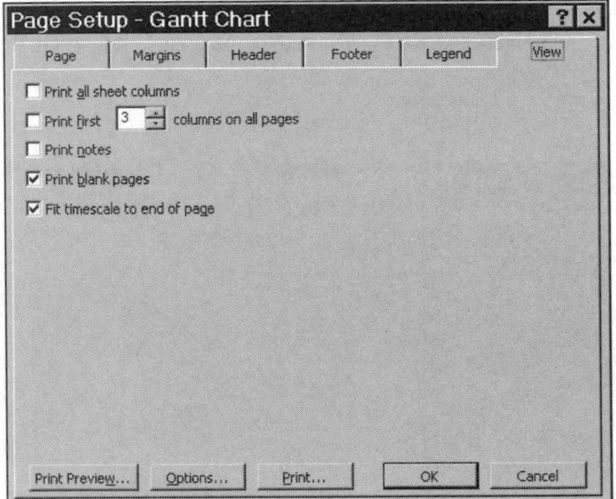


**Figure 6-50:** The View tab of the Page Setup dialog box

# Summary

This chapter covered the standard views available in Project. You:

- ✦ Saw a sample of each view
- ✦ Learned how to print in Project

Chapter 7 takes you beyond the basics in views; you learn how to customize and filter views and show other available information in views.

✦ ✦ ✦

CHAPTER 7

# Using Views to Gain Perspective

✦ ✦ ✦ ✦

**In This Chapter**



✦ ✦ ✦ ✦

In Chapter 6 you saw samples of the built-in views that come with Project; and while you may never need any view other than the ones that come with Project, you're not limited to just those views. The potential for viewing information about your project is almost mind-boggling. In this chapter, you explore ways to make views work for you.

## Customizing Views

You can customize the views in Project so that they show you the information you need. Fiddle with the tables in views that contain tables, or fiddle with the views themselves.

### Changing tables

In views containing tables, you can make changes as simple as modifying the height of the rows or switching to a different table. Or, you can modify the appearance of the default table by moving columns around, hiding columns, or adding columns — and save your changes in a new table.

#### Changing row height

This advantageous feature helps you out whenever information is too wide to fit within a column; when you change the height of a row, the data wraps to fit within the taller row.

The capability to change the height of a row in a table is new to Project 2000.

In Figure 7-1, notice the task names for Tasks 2 and 6 don't fit within the Task Name column. If I increase the height of those rows, both names will wrap so that they will be visible (see Figure 7-2).

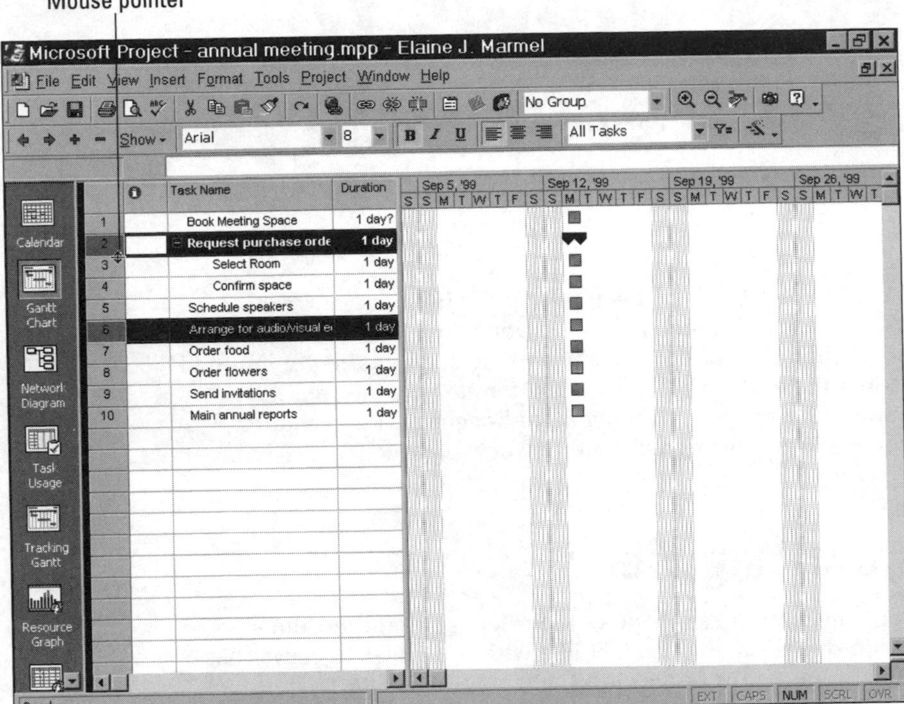


**Figure 7-1:** You can change the height of a row when the mouse pointer looks like a double-headed arrow.

To change the height of more than one row, select each row that you want to change. Use Windows selection techniques to select the rows. For example, to select two noncontiguous rows, click the ID of the first row; then press and hold Ctrl while you click the ID of the second row. When you change multiple rows simultaneously, Project assigns a uniform height to the selected rows.

To change the height of a row, select the row and move the mouse pointer into the Task ID number column at the bottom of the selected row. The mouse pointer changes to a pair of arrows pointing up and down (refer to Figure 7-1). Drag down; when you release the mouse button, Project increases the height of the row and wraps any text in that row that didn't fit within its column.

You can change row heights only in full row increments. That is, you can make a row twice its original size but not one and a half times its original size.

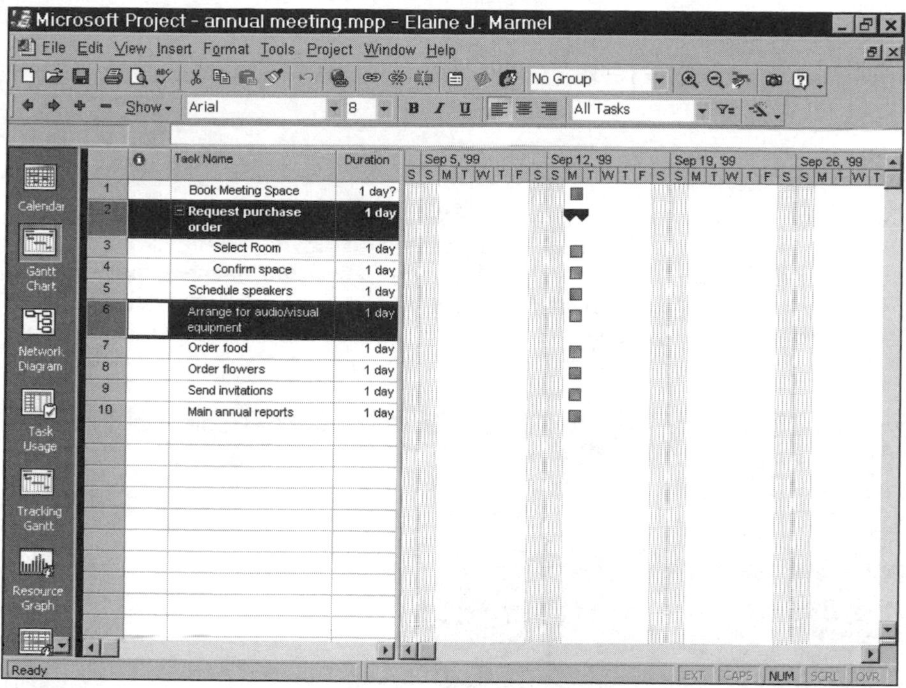


**Figure 7-2:** When you change the height of more than one row at a time, Project assigns a uniform height to all selected rows.

## Hiding and inserting columns

You can temporarily remove a column from a table by hiding it. Right-click the column and choose Hide Column. Note that Project doesn't remove the data in the column from the file; instead, the data is hidden from view. To see the column again (or to add a different column to your table), right-click the column heading you want to appear to the right of the column you're going to insert. Then, choose Insert Column from the shortcut menu that appears. You'll see the Column Definition dialog box shown in Figure 7-3.

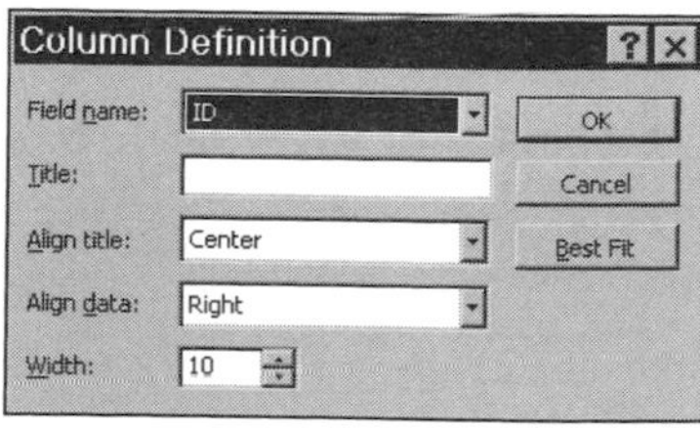


**Figure 7-3:** Use this dialog box to add a column to your table.

Open the Field Name list box and select the name of the column you want to add. You don't need to make any other changes; click Best Fit to make sure Project provides enough space for the column title. Project inserts the column to the left of the selected column.

## Switching tables

Tables don't appear in every view. For example, neither the Network Diagram view nor the Resource Graph view has a table displaying columns of information. However, views that have tables, such as any Gantt view or the Task Usage view shown in Figure 7-4, also have a Select All button. Right-click the Select All button to list the standard tables you can display, as well as the More Tables options.

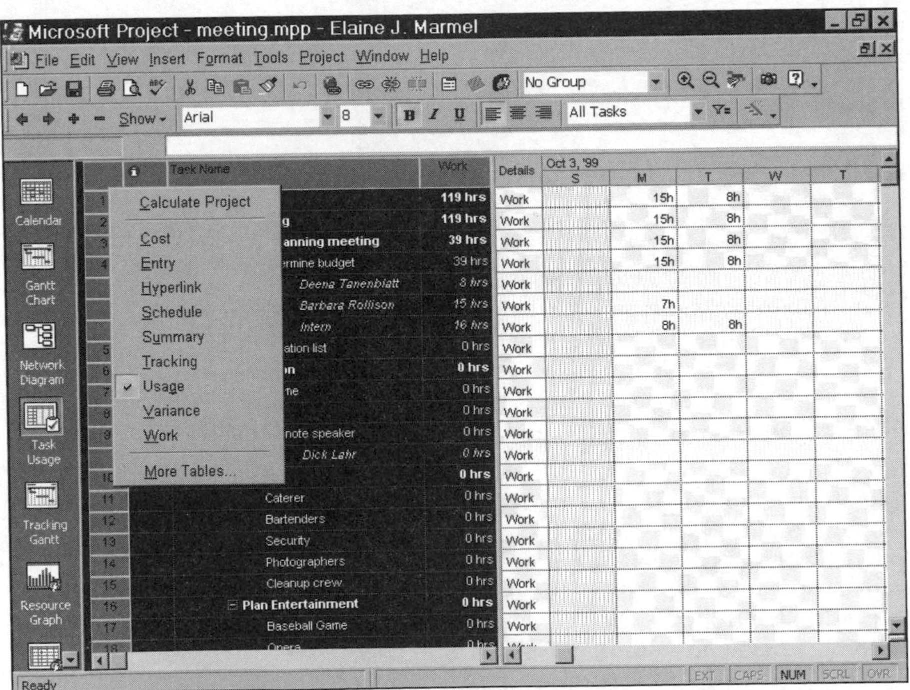


Figure 7-4: Switch to a different table by selecting it from this shortcut menu.

Clicking (instead of right-clicking) the Select All button selects all information in the table portion of the view.

## Creating new tables or editing existing tables

As with views, Project has dozens of tables built in, with a wide variety of information included to help you focus on issues of schedule, resources, tracking, and so on. The More Tables option enables you to switch to tables that don't appear on the shortcut list of tables; you also can use the More Tables dialog box to modify the fields of information displayed in the columns of tables, and even to create new tables. Because of Microsoft's consistency of design, creating new tables in Project is remarkably similar to editing existing tables. You use the same dialog box for both operations.

How do you decide whether to create a new table or modify an existing one? If you can find a predefined table with a similar focus that has several of the fields you want to include, start with a copy of that table. Then delete, rearrange, modify or add fields as needed. If you can't find an appropriate model, you may need to create a new table. I suggest using a copy of the table because someone else using your schedule may expect to find different fields.

Suppose the view would be more meaningful if the columns appeared in a different order than the order in which Project shows them. For example, many tables list baseline information first and then list actual information, resulting in this sequence of columns: Baseline Start, Baseline Finish, Actual Start, Actual Finish. Comparing this information might be easier if you create a table that presents the information in this order: Baseline Start, Actual Start, Baseline Finish, Actual Finish, and so on.

Or perhaps you'd like to add the table to the list of tables on the shortcut menu that appears when you click the Select All button. You may even want to add or delete some fields of information (columns) from the table. You can either edit an existing table or make a copy of it and edit the copy.

The More Tables dialog box does not have a Table reset button; consequently, any changes you make are permanent. I advise you to always make a copy of a table you want to modify, rather than editing the original table. That way the original tables remain intact.

Perform these steps to create a new table or edit an existing table:

1. Choose View ➪ Table ➪ More Tables. Project displays the More Tables dialog box shown in Figure 7-5.

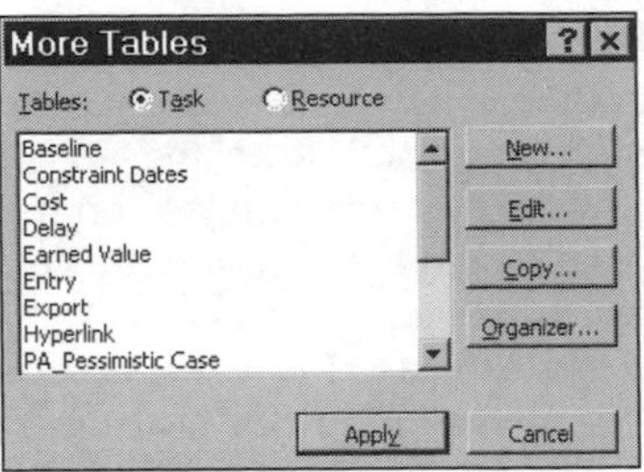


**Figure 7-5:** Select a table to use, edit, or copy from this dialog box.

2. Click the New button to create a new table. Or, select a table you want to edit; you can use the Task or Resource choices at the top of the dialog box to categorize the type of table you need. Then click either the Edit button to edit the original table or the Copy button to edit a copy of the table. The Table Definition dialog box, shown in Figure 7-6, appears.

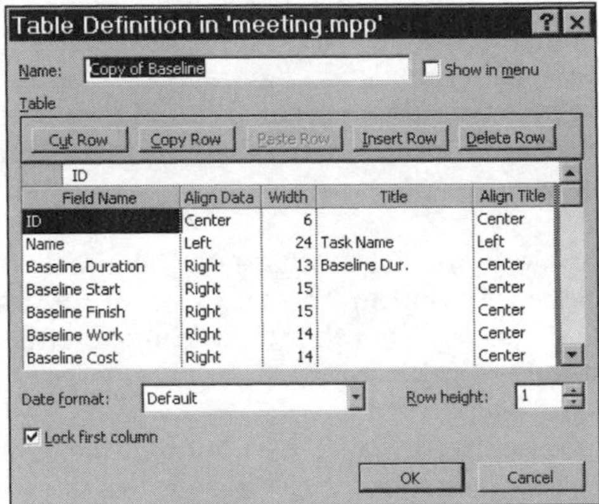


**Figure 7-6:** Use the Table Definition dialog box to make changes to the appearance of a table. When you create a new table, no information appears in the bottom portion of the dialog box.

If you create a copy, you might want to rename it in the Name box instead of using the default "Copy of" name Project supplies.

3. Enter a name for the table in the Name field. If you want to show this table in the shortcut menu that appears when you click the Select All button, select the "Show in menu" checkbox.

4. To add a field to the table, click a blank space in the area under the Field Name column; a cell with an arrow on its right side appears. Click the arrow to display the drop-down list shown in Figure 7-7. Select a field name and then click the Align Data column. Project displays the default settings for alignment of data and title, as well as the width of the column.

5. Click the arrow to the right of the Align Data default; then select Left, Center, or Right alignment for the data in the column.

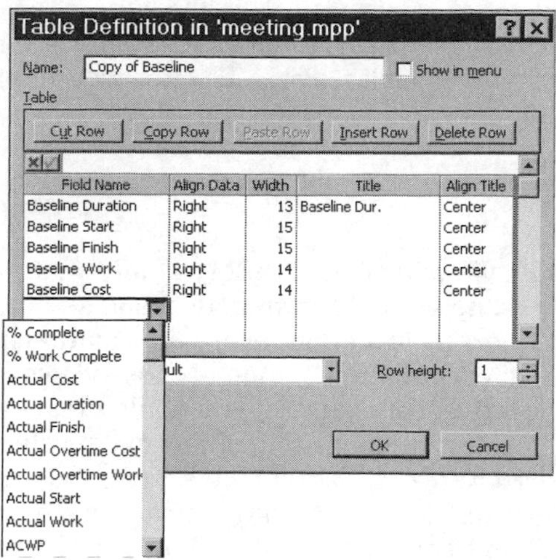

**Figure 7-7:** You can select fields of predefined information to build the columns in your table.

6. Click the Width column and use the spin controls to modify the width of the column to accommodate the type of information you think will typically go there.

Tip

**If you aren't sure about the ideal column width, just accept the default. You can easily adjust column widths when the table is onscreen by clicking the edge of the column heading and dragging to the right or left.**

7. Click the Title field and enter a title for the column if you don't want to use the default field name. Otherwise, skip this step.

8. Click the Align Title column and select a different alignment for the column title if you like.

9. Repeat Steps 4 through 10 to add more fields to your table. To edit your table, use the Cut Row, Copy Row, and Paste Row buttons to reorganize the order of fields in your table. Use the Insert Row and Delete Row buttons to add rows in between existing rows or remove existing rows.

10. If you have included any columns that include dates, such as Start or Finish information, you can modify the date format using the drop-down list of choices in the Date format field. You can also modify the height of all the rows with the Row height setting.

11. If you want the first column of your table to remain onscreen while you scroll across your page, select the "Lock first column" checkbox. Typically, the Task ID column is the column locked in place in a table.

12. Click OK when you are finished. Then click Apply to display the new table on your screen.

By default, changes you make to tables appear only in the current Project file. If you want new or edited tables to be available to other schedules, you must use the Organizer function in the More Tables dialog box to copy them to the Global.mpt file. See Chapter 18 for more information.

## Working with views

As you saw in the previous chapter, views display a variety of information: tables with several fields of data, task bars, network diagram nodes, and so on. Microsoft has provided a plethora of views, meeting just about every information need. Nevertheless, you may want to create a variation on one of those views to look at information from a different perspective. For example, you could create a second Network Diagram view in which you set the nodes to display an entirely different set of information than the standard Network Diagram view. Then, rather than having to modify the nodes in the original Network Diagram view each time to see different information that you call on frequently, you can simply click the new view to display the alternative Network Diagram view. You can base an alternative view on any of the existing views and then change the information that Project displays by default to include only the information you need.

### Adding views

You can select a view from the View bar along the left side of your screen, or you can right-click that bar and choose More Views from the shortcut menu. Project gives you dozens of alternative views to select from (see Figure 7-8). When you create a new view, you can include it on the View bar or make it available in the More Views dialog box only.

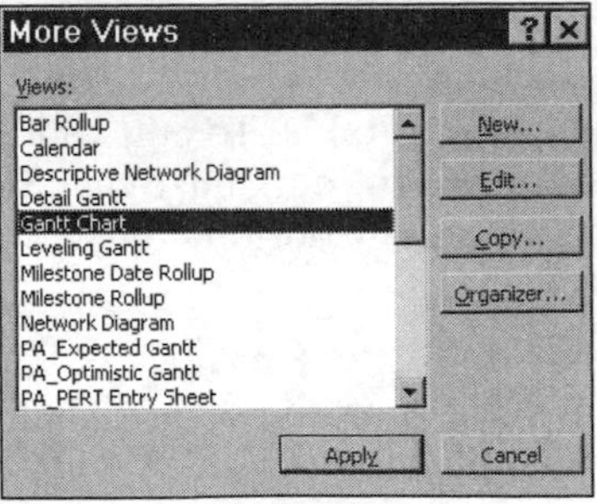


**Figure 7-8:** A wide selection of built-in views meets most informational needs.

You can edit an existing view instead of creating a new view. But, like the More Tables dialog box, the More Views dialog box does not have a View reset button; consequently, any changes you make are permanent. As I suggested earlier, make a copy of a view that you want to modify, rather than editing the original view. That way the original views remain intact.

To add a new view to your copy of Project, perform these steps:

1. Choose View ⇨ More Views (or right-click the View bar and choose More Views from the shortcut menu).
2. Click the New button in the More Views dialog box (refer to Figure 7-8). The Define New View dialog box shown in Figure 7-9 appears.

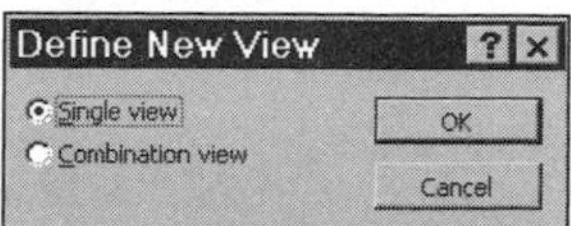


**Figure 7-9:** A simple choice awaits you in the Define New View dialog box: a single or combination view.

If you can, base your new view on a copy of an existing view—you'll have less to do to create the view.

3. Click the radio button for a Single view. The View Definition dialog box shown in Figure 7-10 opens.

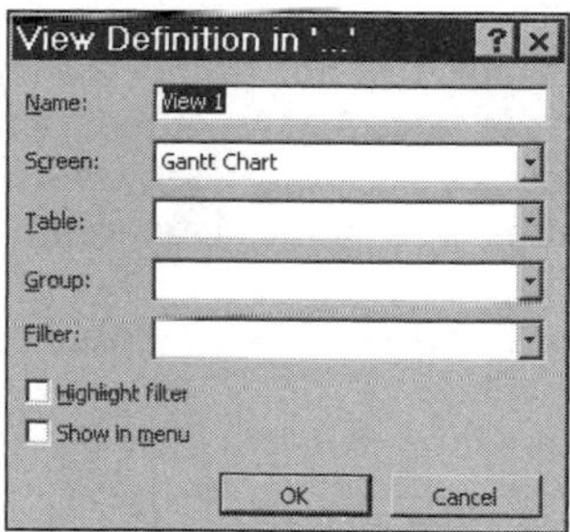


**Figure 7-10:** Use this dialog box to name and describe your new view.

If you click the Combination view option button, the View Definition dialog box requests slightly different information.

4. Enter the Name of the new view. Choose something that describes the information you'll show in the view.
5. Select a current view on which to base the new view by clicking the arrow to open the Screen drop-down list. Then choose a view name.
6. Do one of the following:
   - If the screen you chose in Step 5 gives you the option of selecting a table to include with it, select that table from the Table drop-down list shown in Figure 7-11.

- If the screen you chose in Step 5 does not give you this option, go on to Step 7.

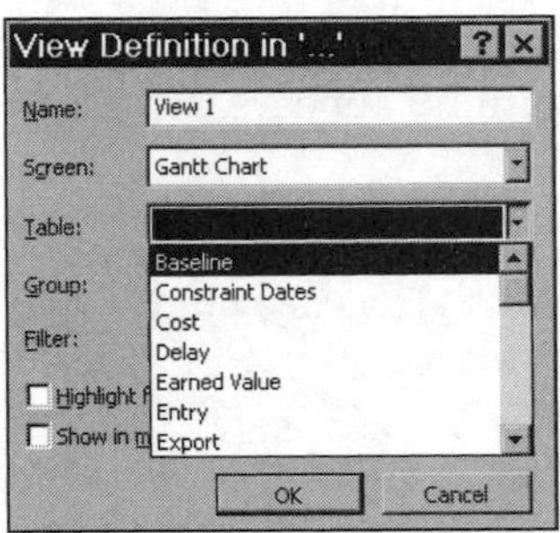


**Figure 7-11:** All the built-in tables and new tables that you have created appear on this list.

7. Open the Filter list box to choose a filter to apply to the view. By default, Project applies the All Tasks filter; therefore, all tasks appear in the view. To apply a selective filter so that Project highlights only filtered tasks, place a check in the Highlight filter checkbox at the bottom of the View Definition dialog box.

You can set filters to remove tasks from the display that don't meet the filtering criteria, or you can set filters to simply highlight the tasks that meet the criteria. If you want to reformat text that Project highlights as meeting filter criteria, choose Format ⇨ Text Styles. You learn more about these techniques later in this chapter.

8. Click the Show in Menu checkbox to make the new view available as a selection in the View bar and on the View menu. If you do not select this option, you must display the view by selecting it from the More Views dialog box.
9. Click OK and then click Apply to save the new view and display it onscreen.

## Creating a combination view

You can manipulate views to see either a single or combination configuration. Combination views display the view you've selected from the View bar as well as a second view, for example, the Task Form view that includes information about the selected task. Figure 7-12 shows the Network Diagram view with a combination of visual and textual information.

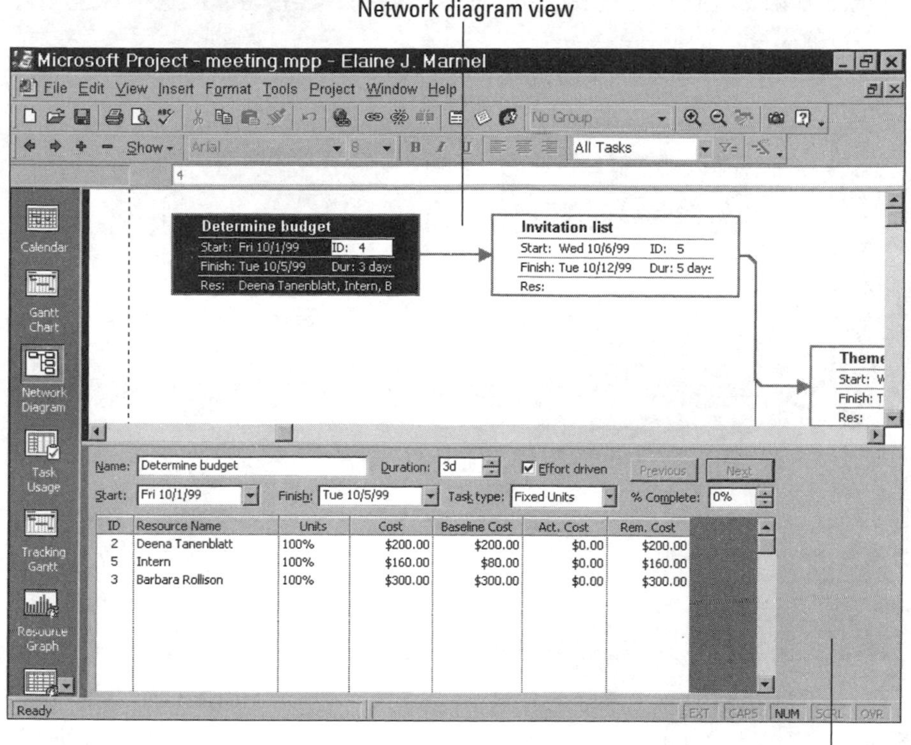


**Figure 7-12:** A combination view displays information for selected tasks.

You can display a combination in any view by moving your pointer to the split bar, shown in Figure 7-13, until the cursor becomes two horizontal lines with arrows; then double-click. You can also click and drag the split bar toward the top of your screen to display the Task Form view, or choose Window ➪ Split. You can return to the simple Network Diagram view by double-clicking the split bar again.

**Tip**

If you are displaying a combination view and you switch views, the new view also appears as a combination view. If you want to display a new view and have it occupy the full screen, hold down the Shift key when you click the view in the View bar. You can always tell which portion of the split view you're in by the active view bar, a dark line that appears along the left edge of the view when you click the upper or lower view.

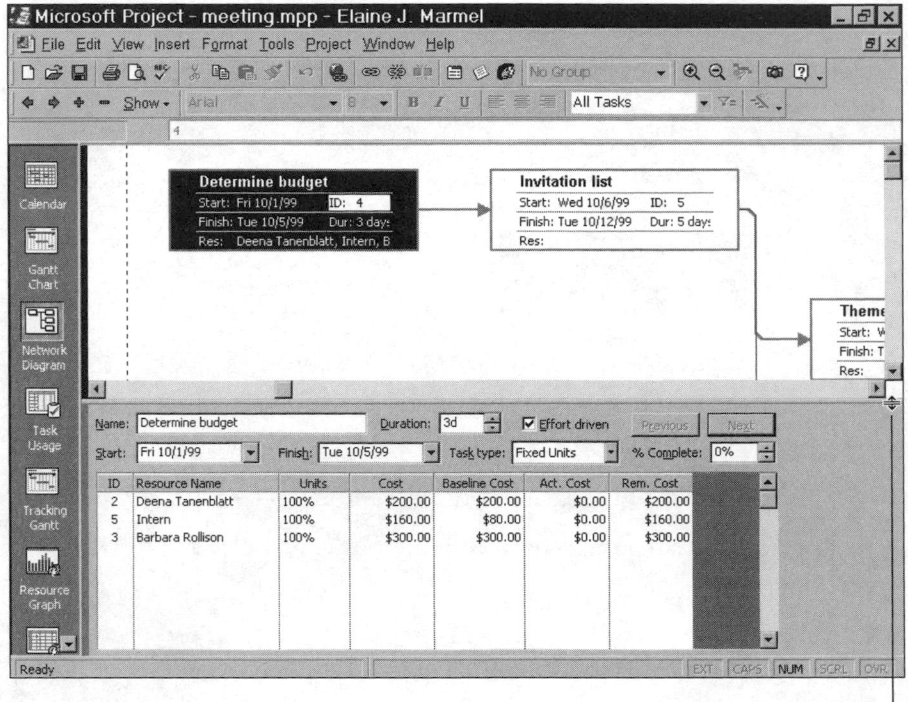


**Figure 7-13:** When the mouse pointer appears in this shape, you can double-click to create a combination view.

Suppose you want to create a combination view that you can display at any time. Create a new combination view that includes the two views you want to see together. Choose View ➪ More Views to display the More Views dialog box. Then, click New to display the Define New View dialog box. In the Define New View dialog box that appears, choose the Combination view option to display the dialog box you see in Figure 7-14.

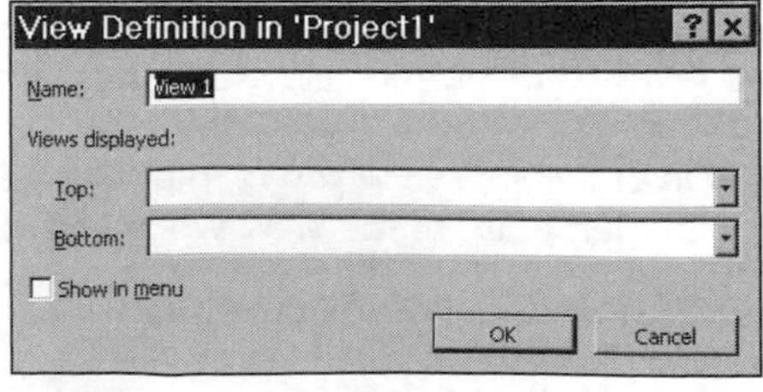


**Figure 7-14:** In the combination view version of the View Definition dialog box, select the two views to place onscreen.

Name the view and designate which view should appear on top of the screen and which view should appear at the bottom. If you want to be able to display the view by choosing it from the View menu, place a check in the Show in Menu checkbox. Click OK when you finish.

# Ordering Tasks in a View

You can think of project management as the attempt to comprehend a large job by breaking the job into progressively smaller pieces — until the job is a collection of tasks. And, of course, you want to organize the tasks so that you can estimate schedules, resource requirements, and costs. You can sort tasks and, new to Project 2000, you can assign WBS codes or outline numbers to help you organize the project.

Project 2000 gives you the capability to assign numbers to tasks in your project.

## Sorting tasks

Sometimes, sorting information in a different way helps you to see things you might not have seen otherwise or even to get a better handle on a problem. In Project, you can sort a project from most views in almost any way that you want.

For example, in the Gantt Chart view, Project automatically sorts tasks by ID (see Figure 7-15). But you may find it easier to view your project information if you sort by Start Date. Choose Project ➪ Sort ➪ by Start Date, and Project reorders the Gantt Chart view so that tasks are ordered by Start Date (see Figure 7-16).

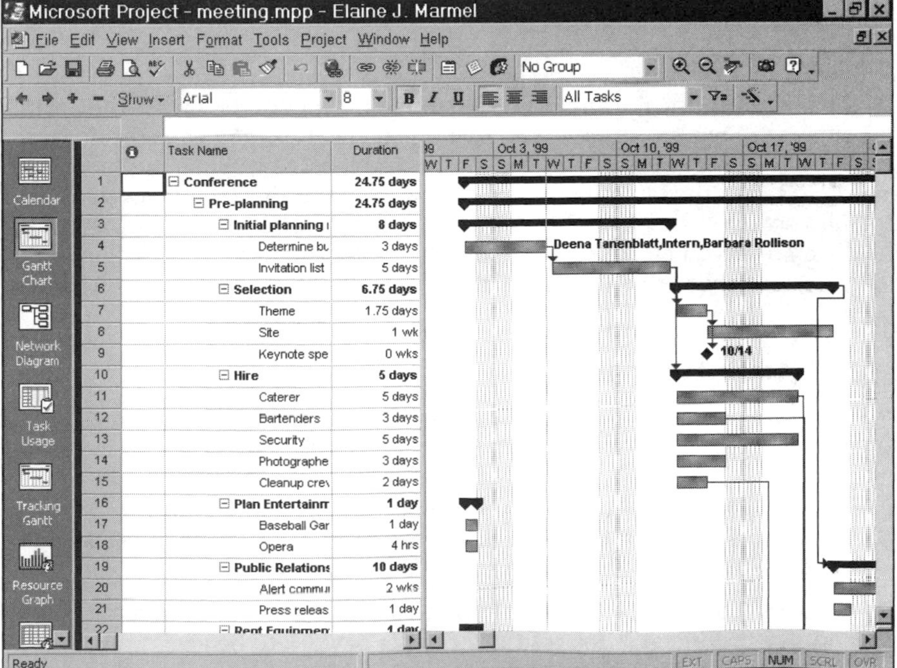


**Figure 7-15:** By default, Project sorts the Gantt view in Task ID order.

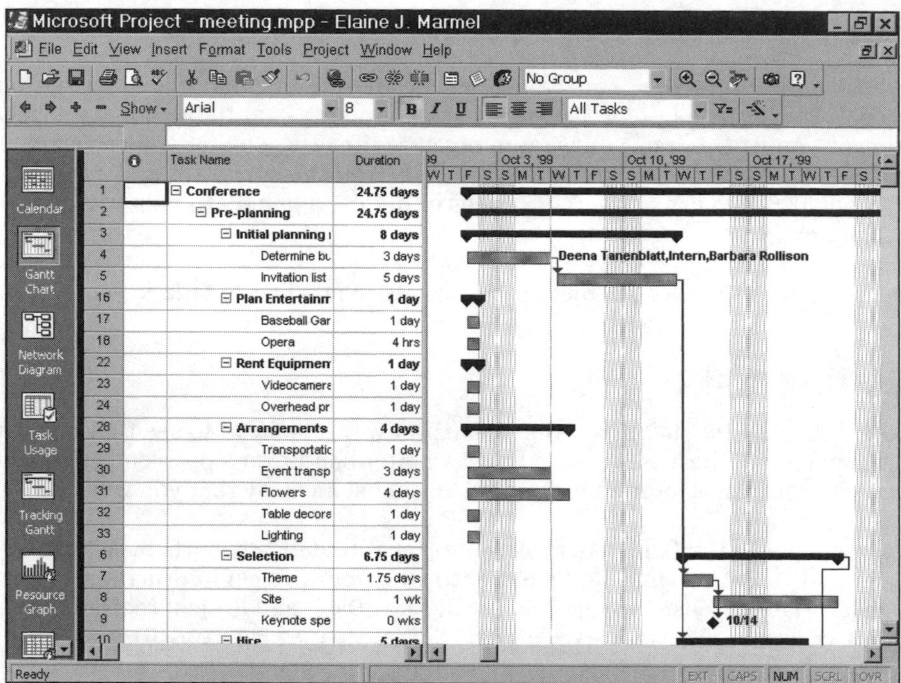


**Figure 7-16:** Using the Sort menu, you can sort a project by Task Start Date.

When you choose Project ➪ Sort, you see five common sort keys (see Figure 7-17), but if you choose the Sort by command at the bottom of the menu, the Sort dialog box shown in Figure 7-18 appears. From this dialog box, you can sort down to three levels. That is, if Project finds a "tie" at the first level, it will use the second sort you specify to break the tie. And, if Project finds a "tie" at the second level, it will use the third sort you specify to break the tie. Using the checkboxes at the bottom of the dialog box, you can make your sort choices permanent by reassigning Task IDs, and you can choose to retain the outline structure of the project.

## Creating WBS codes

The U.S. defense establishment initially developed the work breakdown structure (WBS), and you'll find it described in Section 1.6 of MIL-HDBK-881 (2 January 1998):

- ✦ A product-oriented family tree composed of hardware, software, services, data, and facilities. The family tree structure results from systems engineering efforts during the acquisition of a defense materiel item.
- ✦ A WBS chart displays and defines the product, or products, to be developed and/or produced. It relates the elements of work to be accomplished to each other and to the end product.

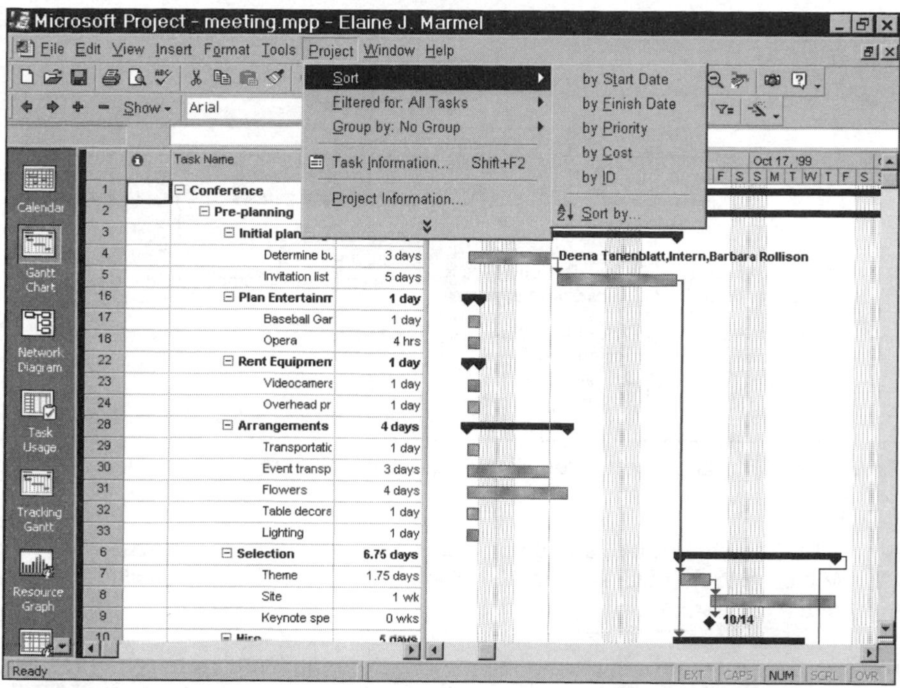


**Figure 7-17:** Choose one of these five common sort keys directly from the Sort menu.

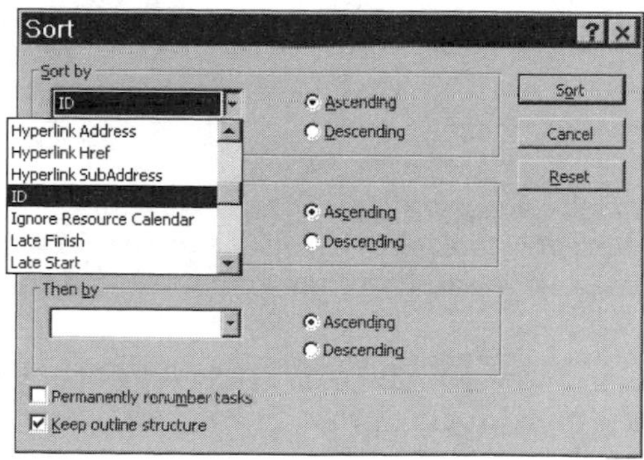


**Figure 7-18:** You can set up a more complex sort structure for Project to use in the Sort dialog box.

More simply put, a WBS chart shows a numbered list of the tasks you must complete to complete a project.

In Project 2000, you still can't produce a WBS graphic representation of your project similar to the one shown in Figure 7-19. You can, however, assign WBS codes to each task; WBS codes can be letters and numbers (or combinations of letters and numbers) that help you identify the relationship between tasks and organize the project.

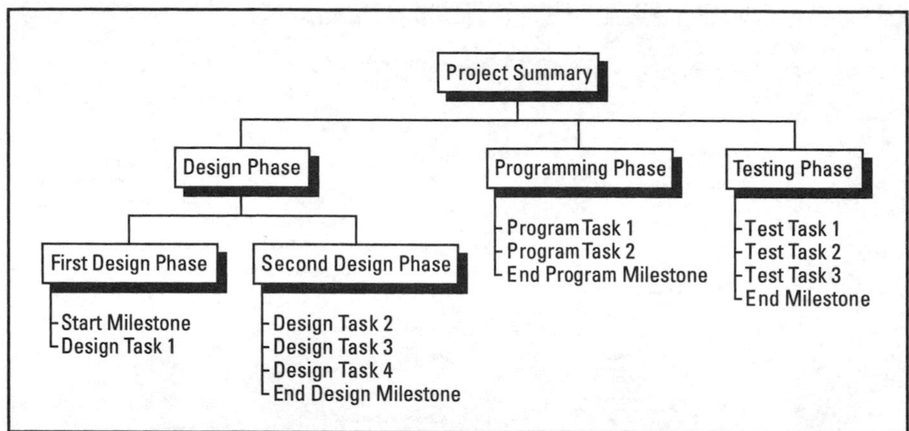


**Figure 7-19:** The WBS chart is reminiscent of a company organization chart.

WBS Chart for Project, an add-on product for Project, creates a WBS chart from a Microsoft Project file. The CD-ROM that accompanies this book includes a sample of the program.

You can use any numbering system you want for your WBS code structure. Suppose you assigned codes to your project similar to the ones shown in Figure 7-20. The task numbered 1.1.2.3 identifies the first box in level 2, the second box in level 3, and the third box on level four of the outline structure of the project. While Project doesn't produce the graphic representation, it assigns the numbers based on the task's level within the project outline.

To assign WBS numbers to a project, follow these steps:

1. Choose Project ➪ WBS ➪ Define Code. Project displays the WBS Code Definition dialog box. The Code preview box shows you the format of the WBS code you're designing as you design it — and therefore remains blank until you make selections in this dialog box.
2. Use the Project Code Prefix box to apply a prefix to *all* WBS codes that you assign. You might want to use the initials of the project name, for example.
3. In the Sequence column at the bottom of the box, select the type of character you want to use for each level of the WBS code. In Figure 7-21, I've selected Numbers (ordered) for both Levels 1 and 2, but you can also include Uppercase or Lowercase letters; if you choose Characters (unordered), Project inserts an asterisk at that position of the WBS code.

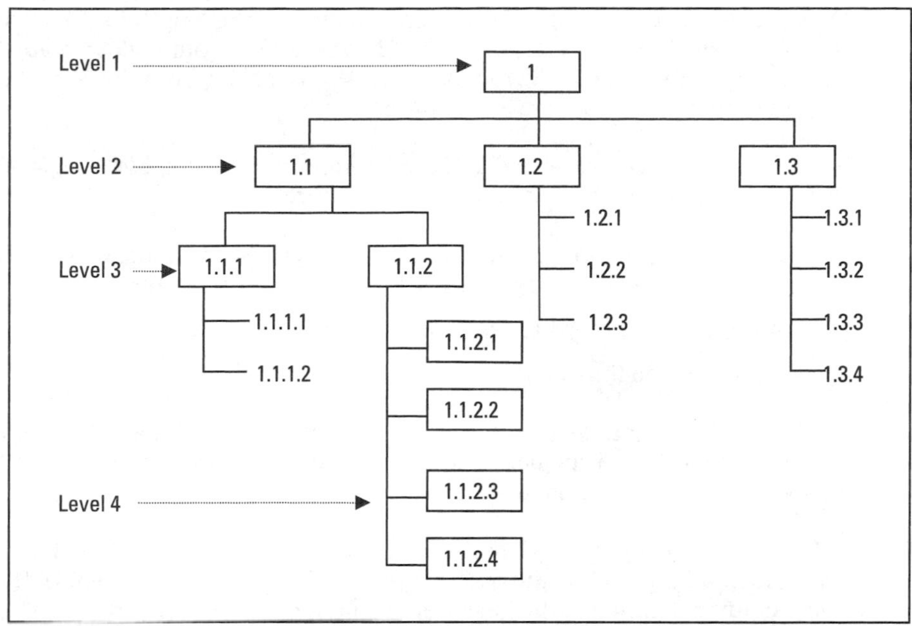


**Figure 7-20:** WBS numbering shows you the hierarchical relationship of tasks in the project.

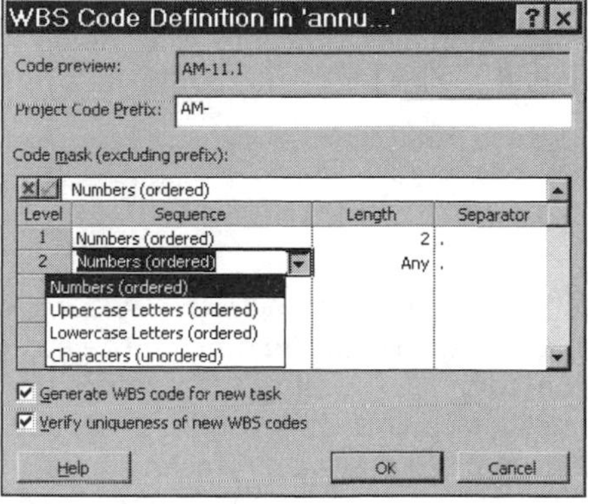


**Figure 7-21:** Use the WBS Code Definition dialog box to define the type of WBS code you want to use.

Using "Character" enables you to enter any characters that you want into that part of the WBS code. For example, suppose you use a mask of Numbers (ordered) Length 1, Numbers (ordered) Length 1, Characters (unordered) Length 3. For any third level task, you can enter any three characters you want for the third part of the WBS. In the example, when you enter a third level task, you'll initially see a WBS of 1.1.***. However, you can change it to something like 1.1.a#3.

4. Open the list box in the Length column and choose the length for the level of the WBS code. In Figure 7-21, I set Level 1 to two digits, but I allowed any number of digits for Level 2; you can choose Any, select from the predefined list of numbers 1–10, or type in any other number.

For the technically curious, I tested 100, and Project accepted it, but using a 100-digit number in a WBS code isn't particularly practical.

5. In the Separator column, use the list box to select period (.), dash (–), plus (+), or slash (/) or type in any value that is not a number or a letter (such as =).
6. Repeat the previous steps for each level you want to define.
7. Click OK when you finish.

You'll probably want to leave both the checkboxes checked at the bottom of the WBS Code Definition dialog box since they ensure that all tasks are assigned WBS codes and that the codes are unique.

The WBS codes don't appear by default on the Gantt Chart view; to view the WBS codes, you must add the WBS column. To add the WBS column to the left of the Task Name column, right-click the Task Name column. Project selects the column and displays a shortcut menu. Choose Insert Column from the shortcut menu, and Project displays the Column Definition dialog box. Open the Field Name list box and select WBS. Alternately, change the alignment of data to Left. Then, click Best Fit to add the column to the worksheet portion of the Gantt Chart view (see Figure 7-22).

If you had added the WBS column *before* defining WBS codes, you would have seen outline numbering that corresponded to the task's position in the project outline.

## Renumbering WBS codes

As you may have noticed from the figures in the preceding sections, WBS codes do *not* automatically renumber themselves in all cases when you change the structure of the project outline. WBS Codes *will* automatically renumber themselves if you change the level of a task within the outline structure of the project. That is, if you drag a Level 1 task to a new Level 1 location or if you drag a subtask to a new location underneath its original parent task, both tasks will retain their original WBS code number. However, if you promote or demote the task, or if you move it so that it appears at a new level in the outline, Project will assign the task a new WBS code. You can test the premise by dragging "Select Room" so that it appears before "Request purchase order." Each subtask retains its original WBS code.

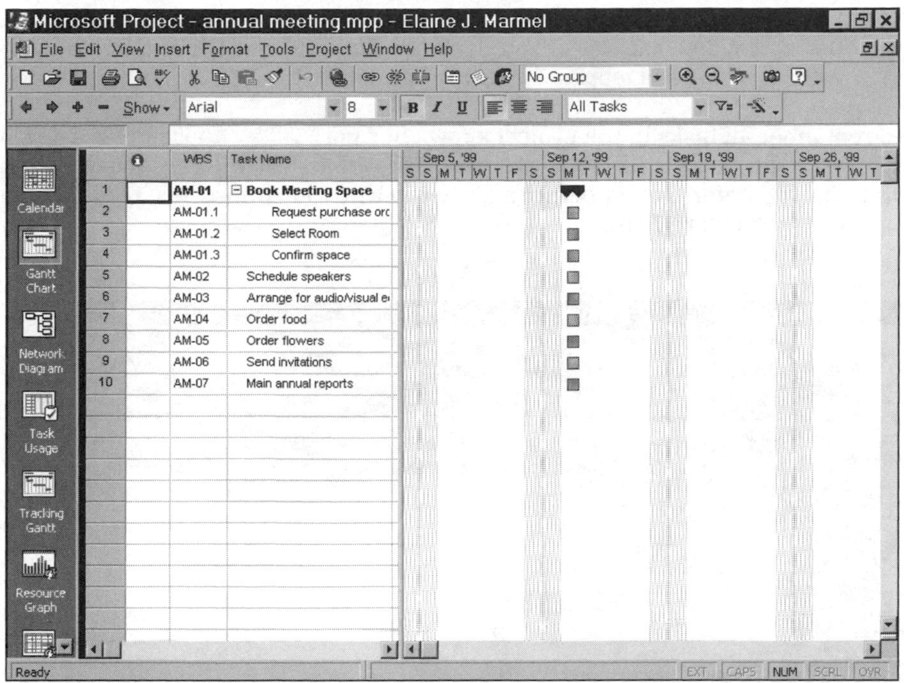

**Figure 7-22:** When you display the WBS column, Project displays the WBS codes for each task in your project.

There is one exception to the preceding rule. If you use the cut and paste method to move a task to a new location *at the same level* in the outline, Project assigns a new WBS code. Why? Because Project views cutting and pasting as the process of deleting one task and adding another task. If you set the options in the WBS Code Definition dialog box to generate new codes for new tasks and verify uniqueness of WBS codes, Project generates a new WBS code for the task you paste instead of reusing the WBS code of the task you cut.

**Note**

If you're working on a government contract for which you and the government have agreed to a numbering scheme and you don't want WBS codes to change even if you move tasks around, use Outline codes, which are completely static. You can assign both an Outline code and a WBS code to a task. (You'll read about Outline codes later in this chapter.)

At times, however, you'll want to renumber the WBS codes, even though Project didn't renumber them automatically—and you can. In fact, you can renumber the entire project or only selected portions of the project. If you choose to renumber selected portions, you must select the tasks before starting the renumbering process.

You can't "undo" renumbering WBS codes so save your project before you start this operation. That way, if you don't like the results, you can close the project without saving and reopen it in its original state before you renumbered.

To renumber all tasks in the project shown in Figure 7-23, choose Project ➪ WBS ➪ Renumber. Project displays the dialog box shown in Figure 7-24. Click OK. Project prompts you before renumbering and then, when you choose Yes, reassigns all WBS numbers (see Figure 7-25).

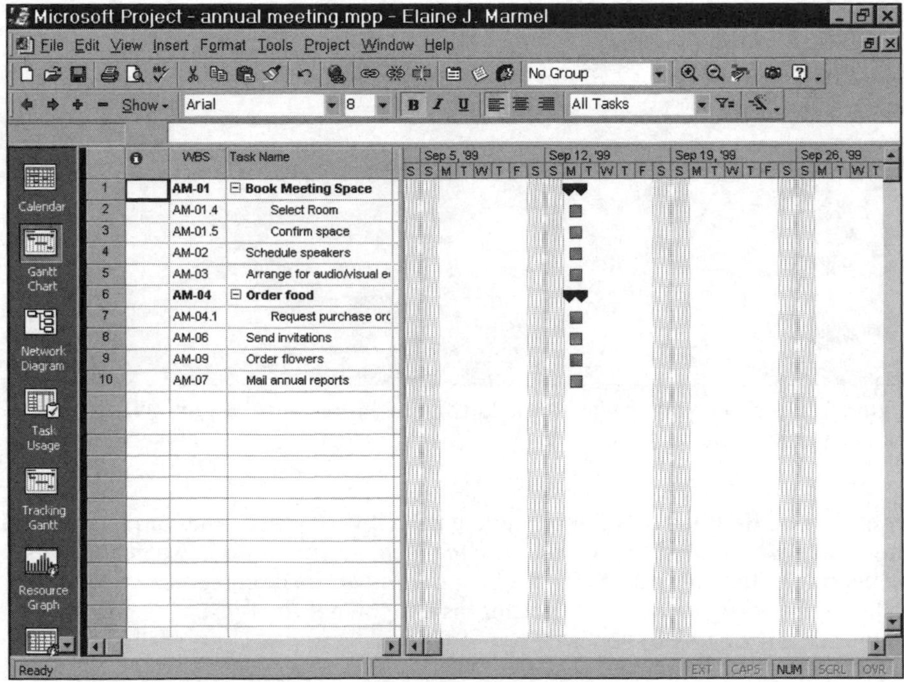


**Figure 7-23:** Because I moved tasks around, the WBS codes are no longer sequential.

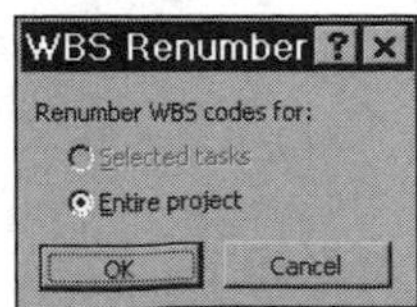


**Figure 7-24:** Use this dialog box to renumber the project.

At this point, I'm going to hide the WBS column to keep the display as clean as possible.

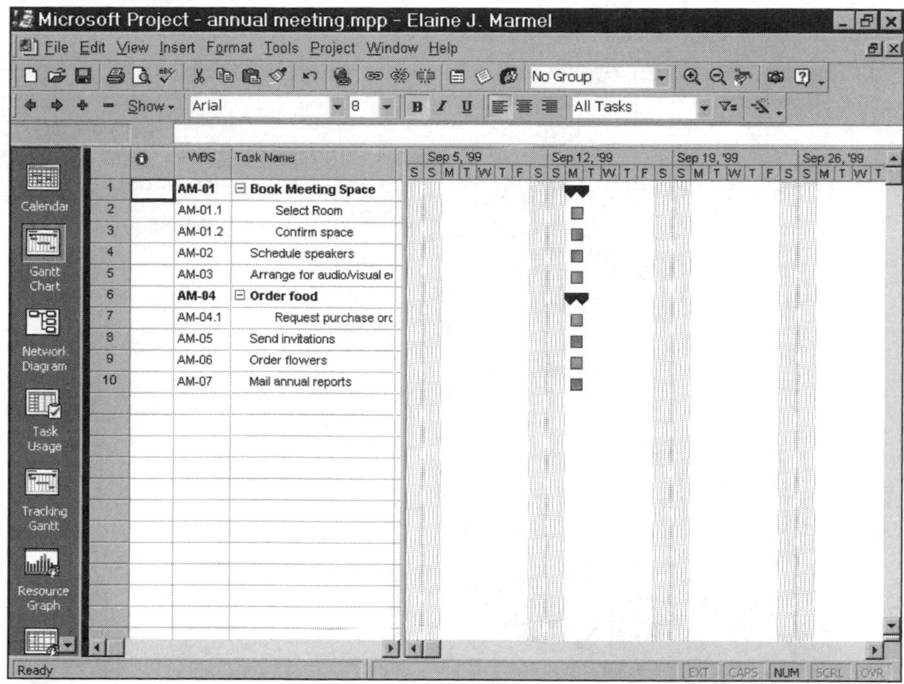

**Figure 7-25:** The WBS codes are again sequential after renumbering.

## Defining outline numbers

In the preceding section, I offered a scenario in which you're working on a government contract, and you and the government have agreed to a numbering scheme. In such a case, you *don't* want WBS codes to change even if you move tasks around. So, don't rely on WBS codes in Project; instead, use Outline codes, which are completely static.

**Note** You can assign both an Outline code and a WBS code to a task.

Outline codes work much the same way WBS codes work; however, outline codes are completely customizable and they are *not* tied to the outline structure of your project. For example, you may want to assign a department code to a task so that you can view the project organized by department. Or, you may want to assign a company cost code to a task so that you can view tasks by cost code. And, you can create a list of valid outline codes for users to enter.

To define outline codes, follow these steps:

1. Choose Tools ➪ Customize ➪ Fields. Project displays the Customize Fields dialog box (see Figure 7-26).

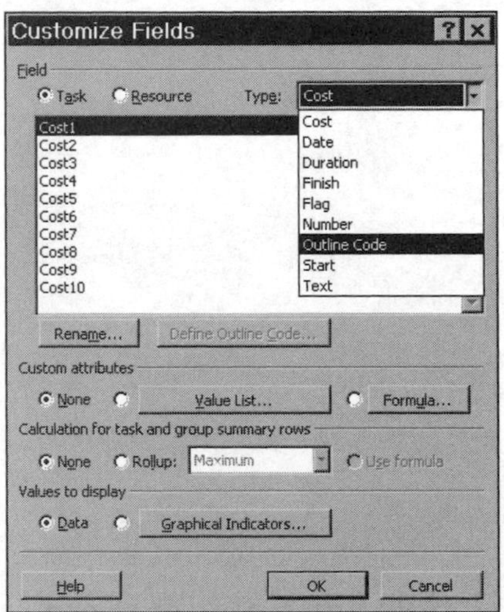


**Figure 7-26:** Select an outline code to customize.

Read more about customizing fields in Chapter 18.

2. Open the Type list box and choose Outline Code.
3. To provide a meaningful name for the code, click the Rename button and type the new name. Then click OK to redisplay the Customize Fields dialog box.
4. Click the Define Outline Code button to display the Outline Code Definition dialog box shown in Figure 7-27.

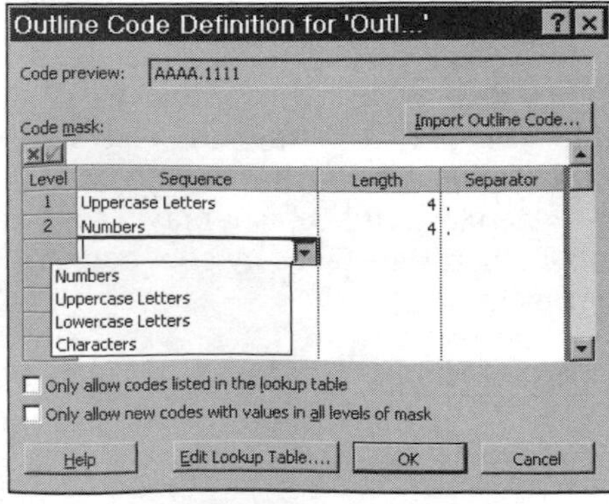


**Figure 7-27:** The Outline Code Definition dialog box looks and operates like the WBS Code Definition dialog box.

5. In the Sequence column in the center of the box, select the type of character you want to use for each level of the outline code.
6. Open the list box in the Length column and choose the length for the level of the outline code.
7. In the Separator column, use the list box to select period (.), dash (–), plus (+), or slash (/) or type in any value that is not a number or a letter (such as =).
8. Repeat the previous steps for each level you want to define.

If you simply want to create a mask for the outline code so that users use the correct format, you can click OK; you may want to place a check in the last checkbox to ensure that users enter outline codes that match the mask.

If you want to restrict the use of outline codes to a specific list of codes, you can click the Edit Lookup Table button in the Outline Code Definition dialog box to display the Edit Lookup Table dialog box shown in Figure 7-28.

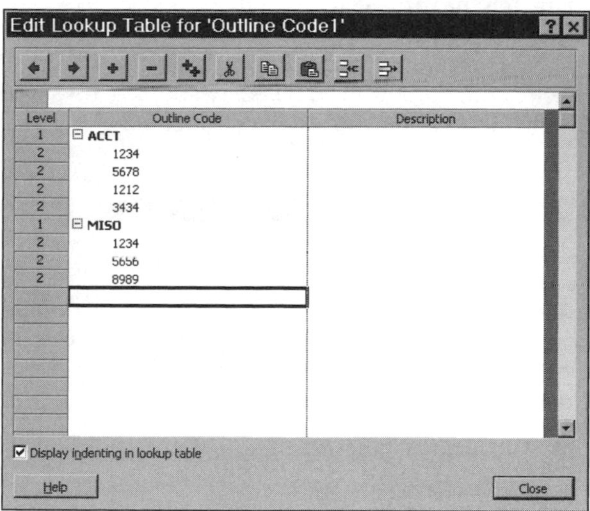


**Figure 7-28:** Use this dialog box to define the allowable lookup codes.

On the first line, type a permissible outline code for Level 1. On the second line, type an outline code for Level 2 that is permissible under the outline code you supplied for Level 1 and click the Indent button at the top of the dialog box. On the third line, type another acceptable Level 2 outline code. If you need a Level 3 outline code under a Level 2 outline code, simply type the code and click the Indent again on a blank line below the Level 2 outline code. To supply another Level 1 code, type the code and click the Outdent button as many times as necessary, depending on the last code you entered.

Repeat the process, filling in the acceptable outline codes. If you forget to include a code, highlight the code you want to appear *below* the code you'll add, and then click the Insert Row button at the top of the dialog box. And, if a code becomes invalid at some later date, reopen this dialog box, highlight the code, and click the Delete Row button.

Click the Close button to redisplay the Outline Code Definition dialog box. If you don't want to allow outline codes that don't appear in the lookup table, place a check in the "Only allow codes listed in the lookup table" checkbox. Then click the OK button to redisplay the Customize Fields dialog box, and click OK again to redisplay your project.

To display a column for an outline code, you follow the same process you used to display the column for the WBS code. Right-click the column you want to appear to the right of the Outline Code column and choose Insert Column. In the Column Definition dialog box, open the Field Name list box and select the outline code that you defined. Click Best Fit, and Project displays the column, but it's empty. Since outline codes don't follow an "ordered" pattern (in other words, alphabetical or numerical), Project has no way of knowing what outline codes to assign to any particular task. If you didn't create list entries, you can simply type the outline codes into the column. Remember—they may need to match the mask you created.

If you did create list entries—and if you told Project to only allow outline codes listed in the lookup table—click in the column. You'll see a list box arrow; when you open it, the entries from the lookup table appear (see Figure 7-29).

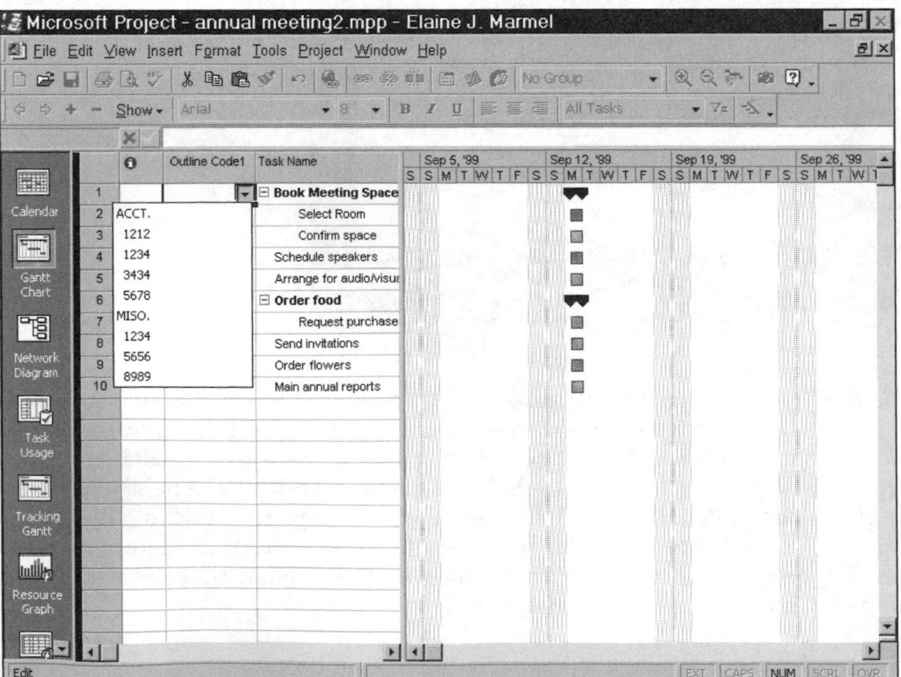


**Figure 7-29:** You can choose outline codes from the entries listed in the lookup table.

# Using Views to Gain Perspective

Filters help you to focus on specific aspects of your project. Suppose, for example, that you want to view the tasks assigned to only certain resources. Or suppose you want to display only the tasks on the critical path of your project. You can apply filters to views to limit the information you see and to help you focus on a particular issue.

Project filters come in two varieties: task filters, which enable you to view specific aspects of tasks, and resource filters, which enable you to view specific aspects of resources. In Table 7-1, you find a description of the default task filters, and in Table 7-2, you find a description of the default resource filters. Many of the filters perform similar functions.

The Tasks with Deadlines filter and the Tasks with Estimated Durations filter (shown in Table 7-1) are both new to Project 2000.

**Table 7-1**
**Default Task Filters**

| *Filter* | *Purpose* |
|---|---|
| All Tasks | Displays all the tasks in your project |
| Completed Tasks | Displays all finished tasks |
| Confirmed | Displays the tasks on which specified resources have agreed to work |
| Cost Greater Than | Displays the tasks that exceed the cost you specify |
| Cost Overbudget | Calculated filter that displays all tasks with a cost that exceeds the baseline cost |
| Created After | Displays all tasks that you created in your project on or after the specified date |
| Critical | Displays all tasks on the critical path |
| Date Range | Interactive filter that prompts you for two dates and then displays all tasks that start after the earlier date and finish before the later date |
| In Progress Tasks | Displays all tasks that have started but haven't finished |

*Continued*

**Table 7-1 (continued)**

| ***Filter*** | ***Purpose*** |
|---|---|
| Incomplete Tasks | Displays all tasks that haven't finished |
| Late/Overbudget Tasks Assigned To | Prompts you to specify a resource. Then, Project displays tasks that meet either of two conditions: the tasks assigned to that resource that exceed the budget you allocated for them, or the tasks that haven't finished yet and will finish after the baseline finish date. Note that completed tasks do not appear when you apply this filter, even if they completed after the baseline finish date. |
| Linked Fields | Displays tasks to which you have linked text from other programs |
| Milestones | Displays only milestones |
| Resource Group | Displays the tasks assigned to resources that belong to the group you specify |
| Should Start By | Prompts you for a date and then displays all tasks not yet begun that should have started by that date |
| Should Start/Finish By | Prompts you for two dates: a start date and a finish date. Then Project uses the filter to display those tasks that haven't started by the start date and those tasks that haven't finished by the finish date. |
| Slipped/Late Progress | Displays two types of tasks: those that have slipped behind their baseline scheduled finish date and those that are not progressing on schedule |
| Slipping Tasks | Displays all tasks that are behind schedule |
| Summary Tasks | Displays all tasks that have subtasks grouped below them |
| Task Range | Shows all tasks that have ID numbers within the range you provide |
| Tasks with Attachments | Displays tasks that have objects attached or a note in the Notes box |
| Tasks with Fixed Dates | Displays all tasks that have an actual start date and tasks to which you assign some constraint other than As Soon As Possible |
| Tasks with Deadlines | Displays all tasks to which you have assigned deadline dates |
| Tasks with Estimated Durations | Displays all tasks to which you have assigned an estimated duration |

| *Filter* | *Purpose* |
|---|---|
| Tasks/Assignments with Overtime | Displays the tasks or assignments that have overtime |
| Top Level Tasks | Displays the highest-level summary tasks |
| Unconfirmed | Displays the tasks on which specified resources have not agreed to work |
| Unstarted Tasks | Displays tasks that haven't started |
| Update Needed | Displays tasks that have changes, such as revised start and finish dates or resource reassignments, and that need to be sent to resources for update or confirmation |
| Using Resource | Displays all tasks that use the resource you specify |
| Using Resource in Date Range | Displays the tasks assigned to a specified resource that start after the first date you specify and finish before the second date you specify |
| Work Overbudget | Displays all tasks with scheduled work greater than baseline work |

**Table 7-2**
**Default Resource Filters**

| *Filter* | *Purpose* |
|---|---|
| All Resources | Displays all the resources in your project |
| Confirmed Assignments | Available only in the Resource Usage view, displays only those tasks for which a resource has confirmed the assignment |
| Cost Greater Than | Displays the resources that exceed the cost you specify |
| Cost Overbudget | Calculated filter that displays all resources with a cost that exceeds the baseline cost |
| Date Range | Interactive filter that prompts you for two dates and then displays all tasks and resources with assignments that start after the earlier date and finish before the later date |
| Group | Prompts you for a group and then displays all resources belonging to that group |
| In Progress Assignments | Displays all tasks that have started but haven't finished |

*Continued*

**Table 7-2 (continued)**

| ***Filter*** | ***Purpose*** |
|---|---|
| Linked Fields | Displays resources to which you have linked text from other programs |
| Overallocated Resources | Displays all resources that are scheduled to do more work than they have the capacity to do |
| Resource Range | Interactive filter that prompts you for a range of ID numbers and then displays all resources within that range |
| Resources with Attachments | Displays resources that have objects attached or a note in the Notes box |
| Resources/Assignments with Overtime | Displays the resources or assignments that have overtime |
| Should Start By | Prompts you for a date and then displays all task and resources with assignments not yet begun that should have started by that date |
| Should Start/Finish By | Prompts you for two dates: a start date and a finish date. Then Project uses the filter to display those tasks or assignments that haven't started by the start date and those tasks or assignments that haven't finished by the finish date. |
| Slipped/Late Progress | Displays two types of resources: those that have slipped behind their baseline scheduled finish date and those that are not progressing on schedule |
| Slipping Assignments | Displays all resources with uncompleted tasks that are behind schedule because the tasks have been delayed from the original baseline plan |
| Unconfirmed Assignments | Displays the assignments for which requested resources have not yet agreed to work |
| Unstarted Assignments | Displays confirmed assignments that have not yet started |
| Work Complete | Displays resources that have completed all of their assigned tasks |
| Work Incomplete | Displays all resources with baseline work greater than scheduled work |
| Work Overbudget | Displays all resources with scheduled work greater than baseline work |

## Applying a filter to a view

By applying a filter to a view, you specify criteria that Project uses to determine what tasks or resources should appear in that view. Project then selects information to display and either highlights the selected information or hides the rest of the information. To apply a filter and hide all other information, follow these steps:

In Project 2000, you can apply a filter to the Network Diagram view.

1. Display the view you want to filter.
2. Choose Project ➪ Filtered for.
3. Choose the filter you want from the Filtered for side menu.

Note

Because Project enables you to apply task filters to task views only and resource filters to resource views only, the Filtered for hierarchical menu shows either All Task or All Resources, depending on the view you displayed before starting these steps.

If you want to apply a filter that doesn't appear on the list, or you want to apply a highlighting filter, follow these steps:

1. Display the view you want to filter.
2. Choose Project ➪ Filtered for ➪ More Filters. Project displays the More Filters dialog box (see Figure 7-30).

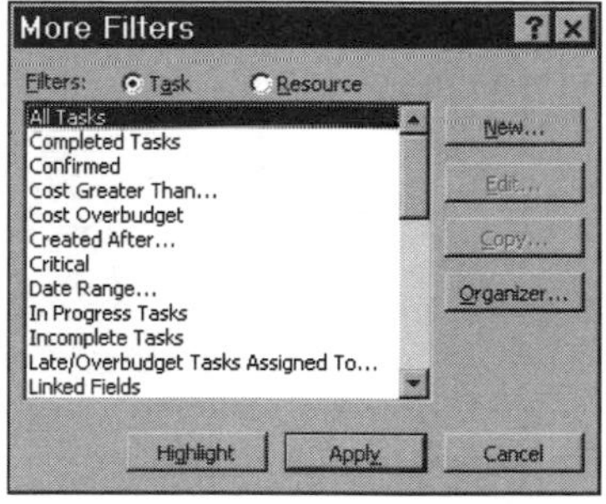


**Figure 7-30:** Use the More Filters dialog box to apply a filter that doesn't appear on the Filtered for list or to apply a highlighting filter.

3. Click the Task option button to select and apply a task filter; select the Resource option button to select and apply a resource filter.

Remember, Project won't let you apply a task filter to a resource view or a resource filter to a task view.

4. Select a filter name in the Filters list.

5. Click Apply to apply the filter or click Highlight to apply a highlighting filter. If the filter you want to apply is an interactive filter, type the requested values.
6. Click OK.

To turn off a filter, choose Project ➪ Filtered for. Then choose All Tasks or All Resources, as appropriate.

## Creating custom filters

If none of Project's default filters meet your needs, you can create a new filter or modify an existing filter by customizing a filter's criteria from the More Filters dialog box. To edit an existing filter, follow these steps:

1. Display the view you want to filter.
2. Choose Project ➪ Filtered for ➪ More Filters to open the More Filters dialog box.
3. Select the option button of the type of filter you want to use: Task or Resource.
4. Highlight the filter you want to modify and then click the Edit button at the bottom of the dialog box. Project displays a Filter Definition dialog box similar to the one in Figure 7-31.

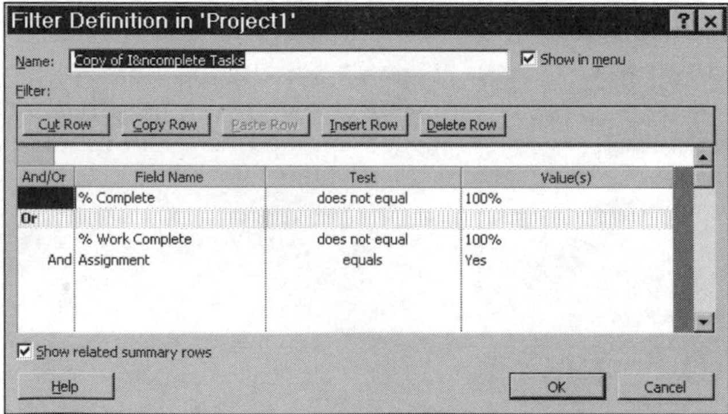


**Figure 7-31:** The Filter Definition dialog box enables you to edit an existing filter.

The More Filters dialog box does not have a Filter reset button; consequently, any changes you make are permanent. I advise you to click the Copy button to make a copy of a filter you want to modify, rather than editing the original filter. That way the original filters remain intact.

5. Click in the Field Name column; Project displays a list box arrow to the right of the field.
6. Select a field from the list.
7. Repeat Steps 5 and 6 for the Test column and supply a comparison operator.
8. Repeat Steps 5 and 6 in the Value(s) column and supply a filtering value.
9. Repeat Steps 5 through 8 for each criterion you want to create; also supply an And/Or operator if you supply additional criteria. Remember, "And" means that the filter displays information only if the task or resource meets all criteria, whereas "Or" means that the filter displays information if a task or resource meets any of the criteria.
10. Click OK to redisplay the More Filters dialog box.
11. Click Apply to apply the filter.

To create a new filter, click the New button in Step 4. In the Filter Definition dialog box, the name "Filter 1" appears in the Name box and no information appears at the bottom of the box. You need to supply a name for the new filter and some filtering criteria. If you want your new filter to appear in the Filtered for list, place a check in the Show in Menu checkbox.

Each line you create in the Filter Definition dialog box is called a statement. If you want to evaluate certain statements together, but separate from other statements in your filter, group the statements into a set of criteria. To group statements, leave a blank line between sets of criteria, and select either operator in the And/Or field for the blank row.

If your filter contains three or more statements within one criteria group, Project evaluates all "And" statements before evaluating "Or" statements. Because versions of Project earlier than 98 did not work this way, using filters you created in versions of Project prior to Project 98 may produce results you don't expect in Project 2000. Also note, however, that across groups, Project evaluates "And" conditions in the order in which they appear.

## Using AutoFilters

AutoFilters are similar to regular Project filters, but you can access them directly on the sheet of any sheet view instead of using a menu or a window. By default, the AutoFilters option is off when you create a project, but you can enable it by clicking the AutoFilter button on the Formatting toolbar.

When you enable AutoFilters, a list box appears at the right edge of every column name in a sheet view. When you open the drop-down list, Project displays filters appropriate to the column (see Figure 7-32).

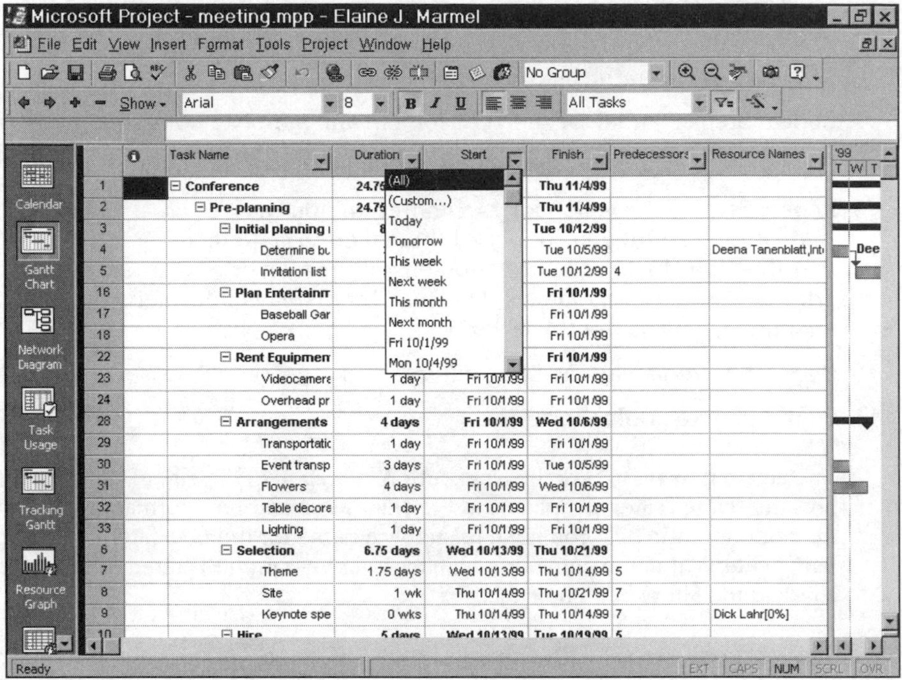


**Figure 7-32:** The Task Sheet view with AutoFilters enabled

Tip

You can turn on AutoFilters automatically for new projects that you create. Choose Tools ➪ Options and click the General tab. Place a check in the "Set AutoFilter on for new projects" checkbox.

## Using grouping

Grouping is another technique you can use to view information about your project. You might be able to solve a problem if you group tasks together by some common denominator. In Figure 7-33, I've grouped tasks by duration to help identify shorter versus longer tasks.

Project contains some predefined groups; to use one of these groups to arrange tasks in a view by the group common denominator, follow these steps:

1. Display the view you want to use to group tasks.
2. Choose Project ➪ Group By.
3. Choose the group you want from the Group By side menu.

Note

Because Project enables you to group tasks only on task views and resources only on resource views, the Group By side menu shows either task groupings or resource groupings, depending on the view you displayed before starting these steps.

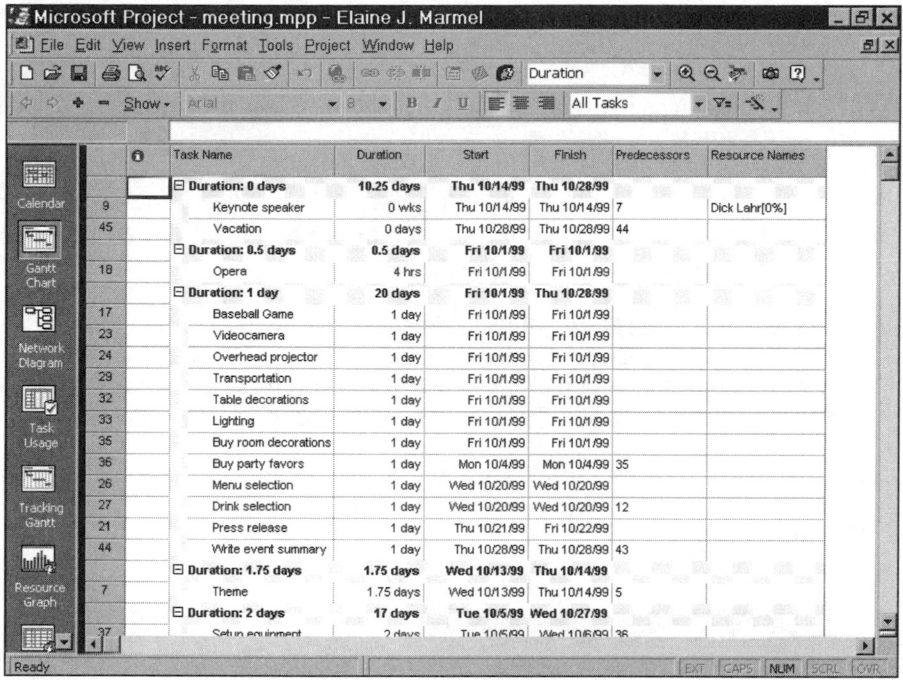


**Figure 7-33:** Group tasks in a view to help you identify information about your project.

You're not limited to using the groups that appear on the Group By menu; you can group by almost any field. If you want to group in a way that doesn't appear on the menu, follow these steps:

1. Display the view you want to use to group tasks.
2. Choose Project ➪ Group by ➪ More Groups. Project displays the More Groups dialog box (see Figure 7-34).

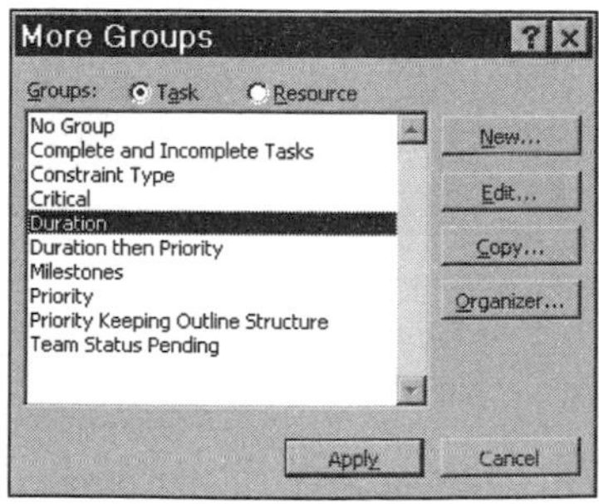


**Figure 7-34:** Use the More Groups dialog box to apply a group that doesn't appear on the Group By list or to create a new group by copying and editing an existing group.

3. Click the Task option button to select and apply a task grouping; select the Resource option button to select and apply a resource grouping.

Remember, Project won't let you apply a task group to a resource view or a resource group to a task view.

4. Select a group name in the Groups list.
5. Click Apply to apply the filter or click Edit or Copy to edit a group or make a copy of a group so that you can edit it.

Like its cousins, the More Groups dialog box does not have a Group reset button; consequently, any changes you make are permanent. As before, I advise you to click the Copy button to make a copy of a group you want to modify, rather than editing the original group. That way the original groups remain intact.

6. If you simply want to apply a group, click OK. If you are creating a new group by copying an existing group, you'll see the Group Definition dialog box shown in Figure 7-35.

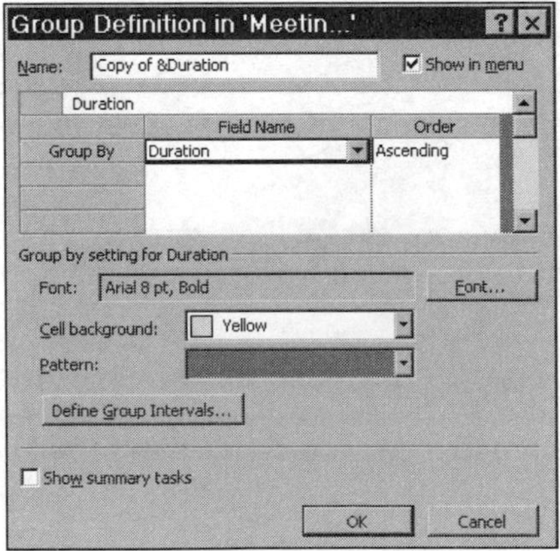


**Figure 7-35:** Use this dialog box to create a custom group based on an existing group.

7. Assign a name to the group you're creating and place a check in the Show in Menu box if you want the group available from the Group By side menu.
8. Open the Field Name list box and select a field on which you want Project to group.
9. In the Order column, choose Ascending or Descending.
10. Optionally, select a font for the grouping title information.
11. Optionally, change the cell background and the pattern that Project displays for the field.

12. Optionally, click the Define Group Intervals button to display the Define Group Interval dialog box shown in Figure 7-36, from which you can control the grouping intervals Project uses.

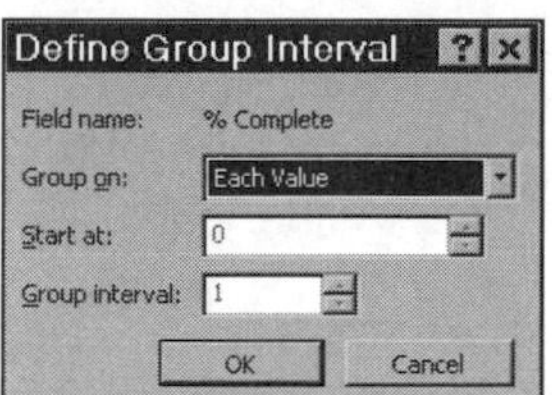


**Figure 7-36:** Use this dialog box to specify the intervals at which you want Project to group the fields.

13. Place a check in the Show summary tasks box to include summary tasks in the grouping.
14. Click OK to save your choices and redisplay the More Groups dialog box.
15. Click Apply to apply the group you just defined.

To turn off grouping, choose Project ⇨ Group By. Then choose No Group.

# Summary

This chapter covered techniques you can use to get more information from Project's views. You learned:

- ✦ How to work with tables
- ✦ How to customize views
- ✦ How to order tasks in a view
- ✦ How to assign WBS codes and outline codes to tasks
- ✦ Methods for filtering information while working
- ✦ Methods for grouping information while working

You can use the skills you've learned here to make Project work in the way that's most comfortable for you.

Chapter 8 explains how to change the appearance of your project by formatting elements and inserting drawings and objects.

✦ ✦ ✦

# Modifying the Appearance of Your Project

✦ ✦ ✦ ✦

**In This Chapter**

Changing Project's looks

Using the GanttChartWizard

Formatting elements one by one

Inserting drawings and objects

✦ ✦ ✦ ✦

After you enter the information for your project, you may want to take the time to format the individual elements of the schedule. After all, you might be working with this project for months or even years. Why not get it to look just right?

Project has dozens of ways to format the appearance of elements from text to task bars, link lines, and network diagram nodes. Some of these changes are practical; others simply provide shapes or styles that might be more pleasing to you. You can use color and insert drawings or pictures into your schedule to make a visual point. You can also copy pictures of your Project file into other Office documents — to include in a report, perhaps. So get ready: This chapter is where you can get creative!

## Changing Project's Looks

Beyond the obvious motivation of making the lines and colors in your schedule more appealing, you might have a practical reason for modifying a schedule's appearance. You might, for example, want to do any of the following to make information about your project more accessible:

- ✦ Display information, such as the start and end dates or resources assigned to the task, in text form alongside task bars. This technique is especially useful in longer schedules in which a task bar may appear on the printed page far to the right of the task name in the Gantt table.
- ✦ Use a bolder color for any tasks on the critical path (tasks that, if delayed, would delay the final completion of the project). This method helps you keep an eye on tasks that are vital to meeting your deadline.

✦ Modify the display of your baseline timing estimate versus actual progress on tasks so that you can more clearly see any divergence.

✦ Display or hide dependency lines between tasks. In a project with many complex dependency relationships, multiple lines can obscure task bar elements or network diagram nodes.

In short, beyond mere cosmetics, paying attention to the format of your schedule elements can help you focus on your project. Keep in mind that these changes pertain only to the currently open schedule, and any changes you make to the format of these elements appear both onscreen and on any corresponding printed versions of the project.

Tip

You can change formats whenever you like and then change them back again without changing the data in your project. For example, you might decide not to display dependency lines to print out a report of resource assignments for your boss because printing the lines can obscure the list of resources next to each task bar. You can always redisplay the dependency lines later.

### Consistency Counts

Displaying an abundance of elements on a schedule can be a mixed blessing. For example, highlighting critical tasks, adding end shapes to task bars, and showing both the baseline and actual lines as well as slack can result in a chart that is confusing. Remember that you're not formatting elements to satisfy your particular penchant for one color or another, but to make project information easier to read.

You'll help everyone in your organization read and understand Project schedules if you make the formatting consistent across your organization. The more your coworkers and management see the same formatting in various schedules, the more quickly they'll learn to read the symbols, and the less likely they are to misread a schedule. Set standards for formatting projects in your workgroup and your division—even across your whole company—and stick to them.

# Using the GanttChartWizard

You can make changes to specific elements in several Project views. However, the Gantt Chart view has its own wizard to help you format the various pieces. Running through the GanttChartWizard highlights some of the options.

Note

A *wizard* is an interactive series of dialog boxes that require you to answer questions or make selections. Project uses your input to create or modify some aspect of your project (in this case, the formatting applied to your Gantt chart). The Microsoft Office family of products uses wizards to automate many functions.

You can use the GanttChartWizard from either the Gantt Chart view or the Tracking Gantt view. Since GanttChartWizard changes apply only to the project file that's open when you run the wizard, start by displaying the project you want to format. Then follow these steps:

1. Click the GanttChartWizard button on the Standard toolbar, or choose Format ➪ GanttChartWizard to start the wizard. The dialog box shown in Figure 8-1 appears.

**Figure 8-1:** Step 1 of the wizard simply greets you and tells you what the wizard does.

The four buttons at the bottom of this dialog box appear at the bottom of each wizard dialog box. You can click Cancel to leave the wizard without saving any settings, Back to move back one step, and Finish to complete the wizard based on the information you've provided to that point.

2. Click Next to move to the next step. In the second wizard dialog box (see Figure 8-2), indicate the category of information you want to display. You can select only one item here. Try clicking each of these choices to see a preview of its style on the left of the dialog box:

   - **Standard.** Shows blue task bars, black summary task bars, and a black line superimposed over the task bars to indicate progress on tasks
   - **Critical path.** The Standard layout with critical path tasks in red
   - **Baseline.** Displays baseline task bars and progress task bars separately, rather than superimposed as with the Standard setup (refer to Figure 8-2)
   - **Other.** Displays a drop-down list that contains several alternative, predefined chart styles for the categories of Standard, Critical Path, Baseline, and Status
   - **Custom Gantt Chart.** The wizard displays several additional screens to enable you to create a highly customized Gantt chart

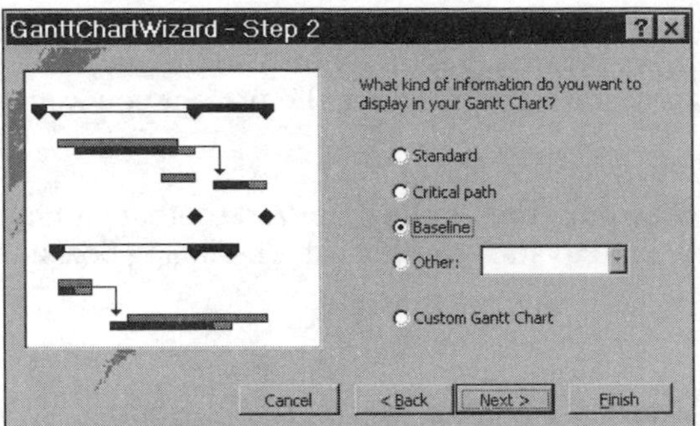


**Figure 8-2:** The preview provides an idea of how each option formats your Gantt chart.

If you select any of the other options in the GanttChartWizard Step 2 dialog box, the remaining wizard dialog boxes deal with the elements you want to display with the task bars, such as resource names, dates, or custom information. You also have an opportunity to designate whether Project should display lines between task bars to indicate dependencies.

3. Click the radio button for Custom Gantt Chart and then click the Next button. The third wizard dialog box appears, as shown in Figure 8-3. In this dialog box, you choose whether to differentiate between critical and noncritical tasks.
4. Leave the default setting of Yes, and click Next to open the Step 4 dialog box, shown in Figure 8-4. Here you can select a color, pattern, and end shape for the critical task bars.

Highlighting critical tasks in a project helps you pay special attention to them when reviewing or tracking progress. If you don't want to format the Gantt chart to treat critical tasks differently, try using a filter to temporarily display only critical tasks, as you learned to do in Chapter 7.

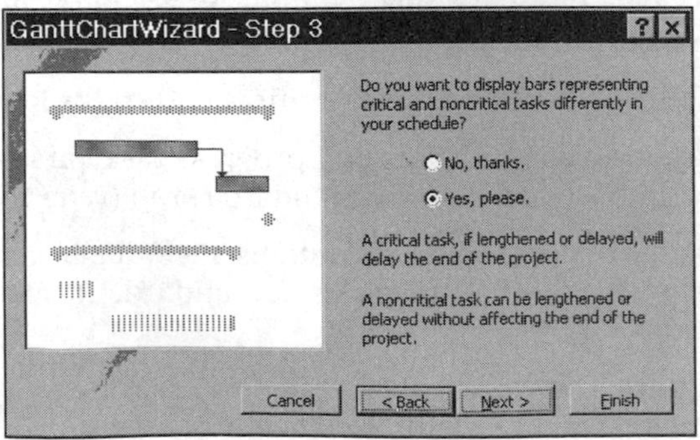


**Figure 8-3:** Formatting critical and noncritical tasks differently can help you spot potential scheduling problems early.

5. Click each drop-down box and select the style options you want. When you're done, click Next. The Step 5 dialog box (not shown) resembles the dialog box in Figure 8-4; in this dialog box, you choose the color, pattern, and end shapes for noncritical task bars.

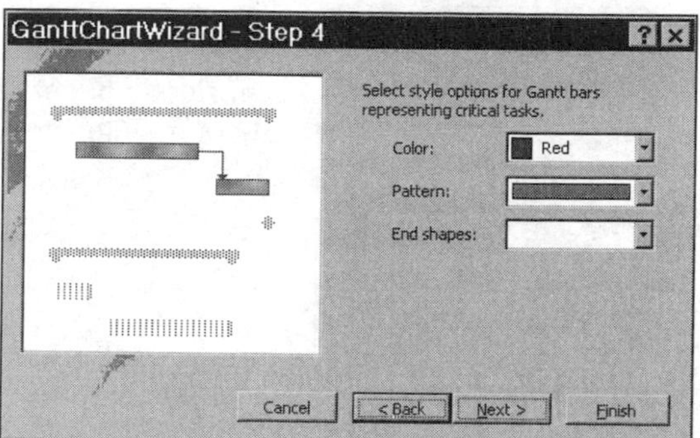


**Figure 8-4:** End shapes delineate the two ends of task bars.

Be careful about selecting a solid pattern for task bars: Superimposed progress lines are typically a solid color (black) and might be hard to see against a solid task bar.

6. Pick a combination that you can differentiate easily from your critical task bar choices and then click Next. Figure 8-5 shows the wizard's Step 6 dialog box, in which you select styles for summary task bars. The additional choice here of Bar style refers to the thickness of the bar.

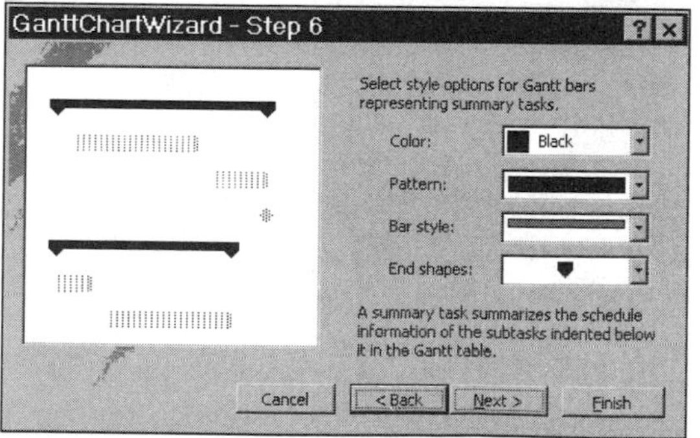


**Figure 8-5:** The thicker bar styles obscure the end shapes. If seeing end shapes is important, use the thinner style shown here.

Be sure to make choices here that differentiate summary task bar styles from the choices you made for normal and critical tasks.

7. Click Next to open the Step 7 dialog box (see Figure 8-6) in which you can select the color, pattern, and shape of milestone symbols. Select a shape for milestones that is different from the end shapes you've chosen for task bars so that the milestones stand out clearly.

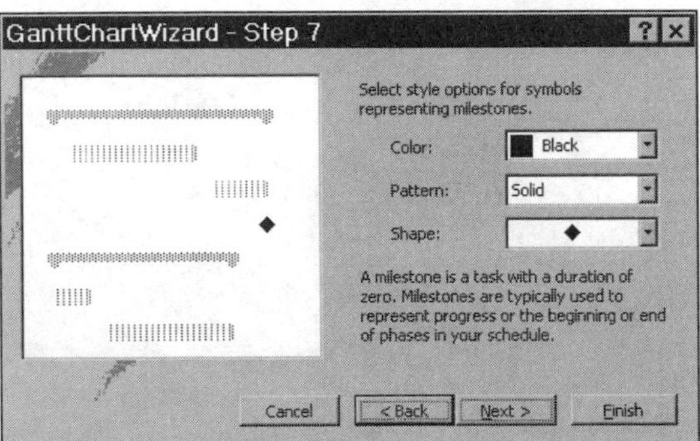


**Figure 8-6:** Solid patterns make a milestone stand out; consider a bright color to make them easy to spot.

8. Click Next to open the Step 8 dialog box (see Figure 8-7) and select the Baseline and slack option to identify the kind of additional Gantt bars to display. Baseline is a picture of the plan before you began tracking actual progress, and slack is any extra time a task can use up before it moves onto the critical path.

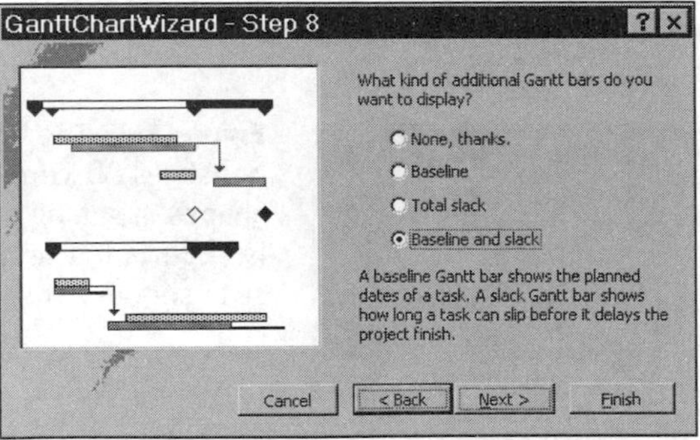


**Figure 8-7:** With this preview, you can begin to see how your choices will look.

9. Click Next to open the Step 9 dialog box in which you can choose the type of task information to display with your Gantt bars: Resources and dates (the end date only), Resources, Dates, None of the choices, or Custom task information. When you choose Dates, as I did in Figure 8-8, Project displays the start date and end date in the task bar area. If you choose this setting, you don't need to

show the corresponding columns for start date and end date in the Gantt table, so this option can help you modify the size of your schedule printout.

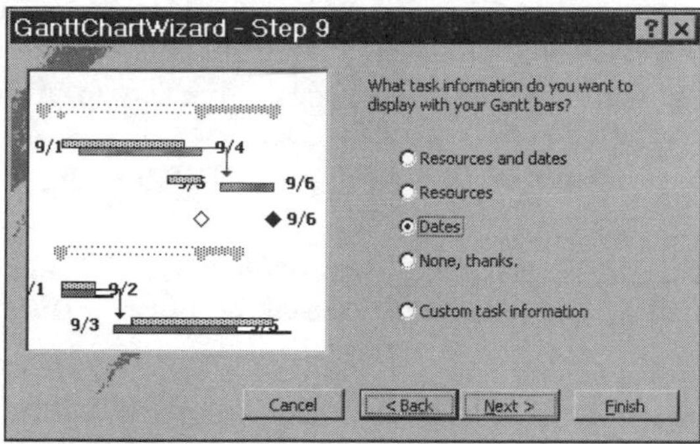


**Figure 8-8:** Placing text alongside task bars can be very useful with larger schedules.

10. Click Next to display the Step 13 dialog box (not shown) in which you specify whether to show link lines between tasks to represent dependency relationships. Leave the default setting — to display the lines.
11. Click Next. The GanttChartWizard Step 14 dialog box (see Figure 8-9) previews your formatting options. You can use the Back button to go back and make changes.

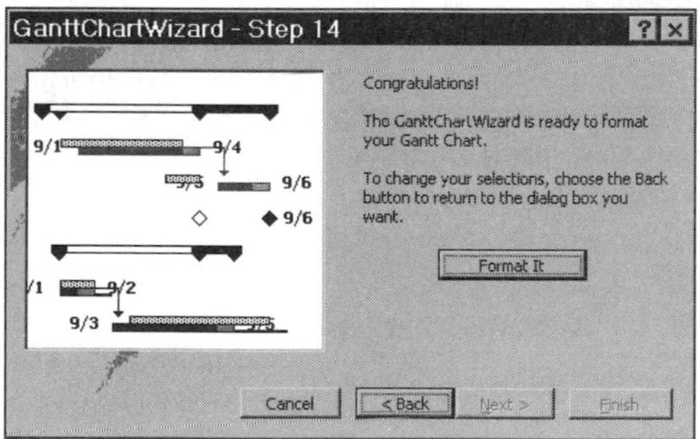


**Figure 8-9:** If you don't like what you see, move back to the dialog box in which you made the original setting, change it, and then move forward to this dialog box again.

12. Click the Format It button to apply your choices. Project displays a final dialog box to tell you that your formatting is complete.
13. Click the Exit Wizard button to close the dialog box and see your changes.

## When Enough Is Too Much

If you select Custom task information in the GanttChartWizard Step 9 dialog box (see Figure 8-9), the wizard opens three consecutive dialog boxes. These three dialog boxes prompt you to display one set of information alongside normal task bars, another set on summary task bars, and a third set next to milestone tasks, respectively. The wizard also prompts you to display one set of data to the left of each task bar, one set to the right, and one inside the task bar itself. You could end up with nine pieces of information in and around your various task bars!

You make your selections from drop-down lists in these three dialog boxes. The information ranges from the task name, duration, and priority to percentage of work complete and types of constraints.

Obviously, if you display nine sets of data in and around task bars, your Gantt chart would become unreadable. However, you might consider this scenario: Put the task name inside both summary and normal task bars, put the start date to the left and the finish date to the right of normal task bars, and put the cost of summary tasks to the right of their bars. (The final element is a total of the cost of all tasks beneath the summary tasks.)

You can also modify the information that is available to someone viewing your schedule by changing the columns displayed in the Gantt table pane of the Gantt Chart view.

# Formatting Elements One by One

The GanttChartWizard enables you to make changes to several common elements, such as summary task bars or dependency lines. But Project also enables you to format each of these elements separately, and to format them with even more options. You can change the style of many other elements in Project, including:

- ✦ Text used in your charts
- ✦ Boxes used in the Network Diagram Chart view
- ✦ Gridlines displayed in various views

## Working with text

You may want to change text to be more readable; some people prefer a larger font, for example, to make views easy to read. Perhaps you want to use boldface for row and column titles or a distinctive font for summary tasks.

You format text the same way for any view. You cannot format fonts in the Calendar view, but you can format categories of text.

You can make all of these changes and more in Project. You can even change all text in a certain category, or simply change the attributes of a single, selected piece of text in any Project table. For example, you may want to apply boldface to the task name of the milestone Grand Opening, but not to all milestone task names.

The Undo function is not available when you make changes to fonts and other formatting features. You must manually return the text to its original settings if you're unhappy with the change.

## Formatting selected text

To format selected text, follow these steps:

1. Move to any view that contains a table of columns (the Gantt chart, Task Usage, or Resource Sheet, for example).
2. Click the cell containing the text you want to format. To format more than one adjacent cell, click the first cell. Then drag your mouse to highlight cells above, below, to the left, or to the right.
3. Choose Format ⇨ Font to open the Font dialog box, shown in Figure 8-10. From the three lists across the top of this dialog box, you can select a new font; select a font style such as Italic or Bold (Regular is normal text that has neither Italic nor bold applied); or change the font size. Click the Underline checkbox to apply underlining to text, or select a color from the Color drop-down palette. A preview of your selections appears in the Sample area.

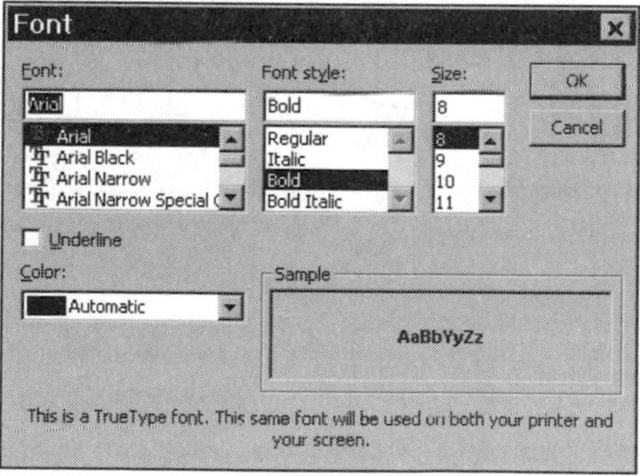


**Figure 8-10:** Project uses the standard Windows Font dialog box, so many settings are probably familiar.

You can also use buttons on the Formatting toolbar to change font and font size or to apply bold, italic, or underline styles.

4. Click OK to save your changes.

You can now preview fonts before you select them, as you can see in Figure 8-11.

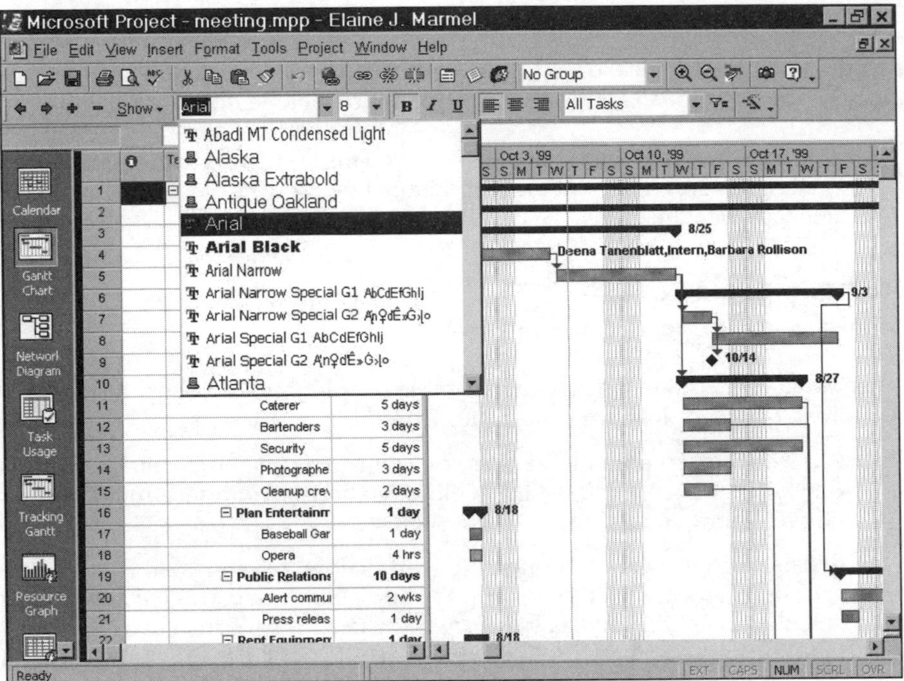


**Figure 8-11:** When you view the fonts in the Font list box, you see a facsimile of the font as it will appear if you choose it.

## Applying formatting to categories of text

You can use text styles to change the format of text for one cell in a table or to apply a unique format to an entire category of information: for example, all task names for milestones. Text styles are identical to the formatting options for text described in the preceding section, but you can apply text styles to specific categories of text.

Follow these steps to use text styles to modify text:

1. Choose Format ➪ Text Styles to open the Text Styles dialog box, shown in Figure 8-12.
2. Click the down arrow next to the Item to Change field to display the options. (This field is the only element that distinguishes the Text Styles dialog box from the Font dialog box you saw earlier.)
3. Use the scroll bar to move down the list. You can format text for categories such as row and column titles, summary tasks, tasks on the critical path, and milestones. Click a category to select it.

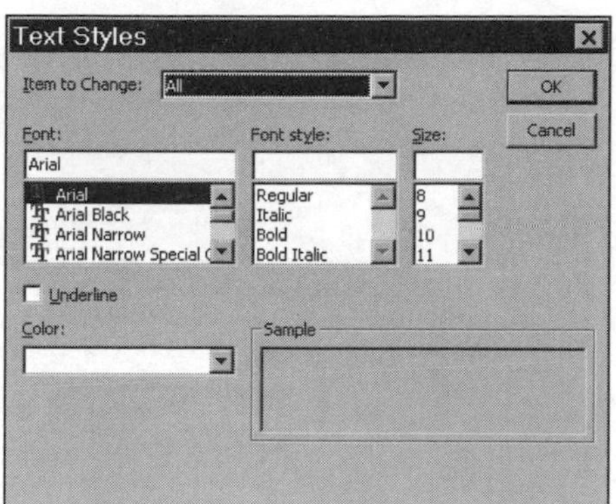


**Figure 8-12:** The default in the Item to Change list box is All (that is, all the text in your project schedule).

4. Select the settings you want for the text, including the font, font size, style, color, and script. When you're done, click OK to apply the formatting.

Using the Items to Change list box, you can format categories of text to add emphasis to certain key items, such as critical tasks and milestones, or to make your schedule more readable by enlarging text or choosing easy-to-read fonts. Figure 8-13 shows a schedule with text styles applied to various elements, such as row and column headings, critical and noncritical tasks, and summary tasks.

Good advice bears repeating: Don't go overboard with multiple fonts on a single schedule. You can actually make a project harder to read by using too many fancy fonts. Avoid using more than one or two fonts in your schedule, and vary the text by using bold or italic or by modifying the font size between categories, rather than using many different fonts. Also, try to set up company standards for formatting so that all your project schedules have a consistent, professional look.

## Changing taskbars

In addition to changing text styles in your schedule, you can modify the look of the task bars. You considered some of these changes when you used the GanttChartWizard. You can make changes to the shape, pattern, and color of bars, as well as to the style of shape that appears on either end of the taskbar.

### Formatting taskbars

Formatting taskbars is similar to formatting text. You can format either an individual taskbar or a category of taskbars, such as milestones or critical tasks. You click a particular task and access the dialog box for formatting just that taskbar by choosing Format ➪ Bar. Alternatively, you can open the dialog box for formatting categories of taskbars by choosing Format ➪ Bar Styles. The actual settings you can modify are the same either way.

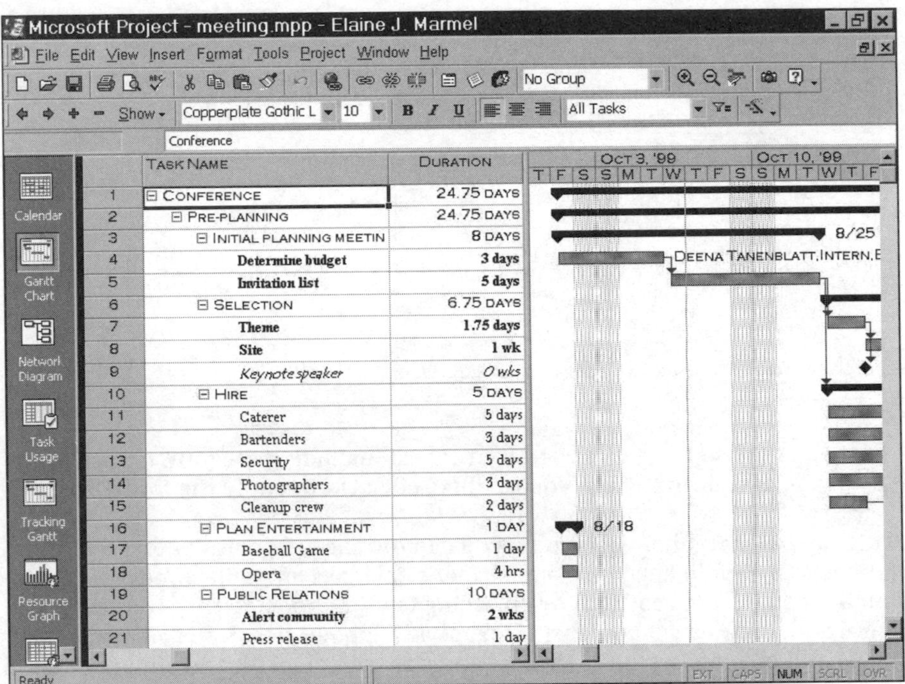


**Figure 8-13:** Italic indicates critical tasks; summary tasks are in boldface.

You can open the Format Bar dialog box by right-clicking the bar you want to modify and choosing Format Bar from the shortcut menu. You can open the Bar Styles dialog box by right-clicking a blank spot in the taskbar area of the Gantt chart and choosing Bar Styles from the shortcut menu that appears.

Figure 8-14 shows the Format Bar dialog box, and Figure 8-15 shows the Bar Styles dialog box. The bottom half of the Bar Styles dialog box has two tabbed sheets called Text and Bars. Counterparts to these tabbed sheets appear in the Format Bar dialog box and are called Bar Shape and Bar Text. The Bar Styles dialog box has a table from which you can designate the category of taskbar that you want to modify and the changes you want to make.

You can use the Bars tab at the bottom of the Bar Styles dialog box to set the shape, type or pattern, and color for the bar and its end shapes, as you did when you used the GanttChartWizard. Use the Text tab to add text to the chart portion of the Gantt Chart view. Follow these steps:

You can place text in more locations around a taskbar from the Bar Styles dialog box than you can by using the GanttChartWizard. This dialog box also enables you to place many more pieces of information near taskbars.

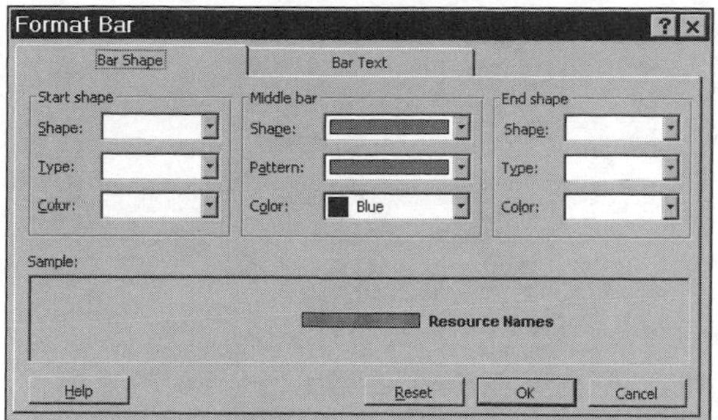


**Figure 8-14:** You can modify the appearance of an individual taskbar to draw attention to it.

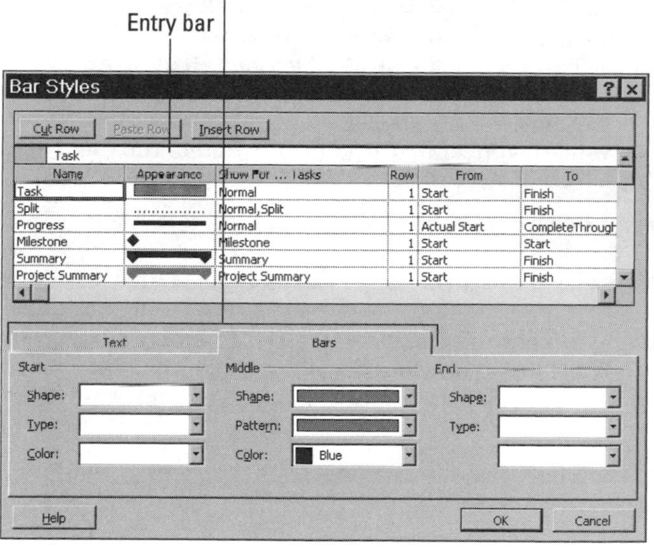


**Figure 8-15:** Use the Bars tab of the Bar Styles dialog box to change the appearance of an entire category of tasks.

1. Click the Text tab to select the information you want to display to the left, right, above, below, or inside the selected category of taskbar (see Figure 8-16).
2. Select the Name of the category of taskbar to which you want to add text. If necessary, make changes to the category in the Bar Styles table at the top of the dialog box. Immediately following these steps is an explanation of the type of information that appears in each column of the table.
3. At the bottom of the dialog box, select the location for the text you want to add. Project displays a list box arrow at the edge of the box.

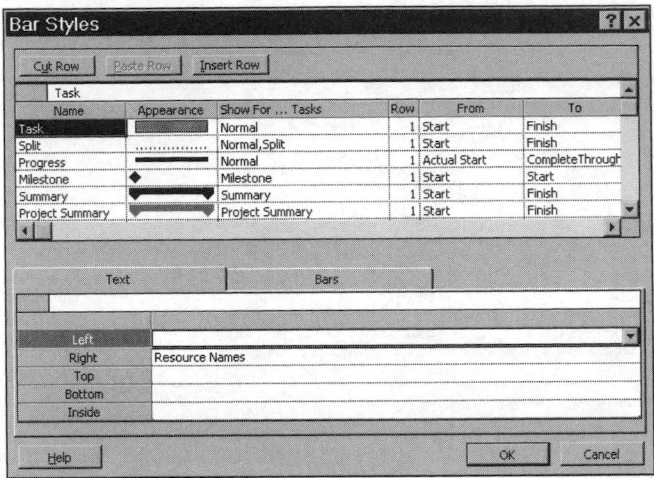


**Figure 8-16:** Be careful not to place too much information around taskbars or you'll create a cluttered, illegible Gantt chart.

4. Select the text you want to appear on the chart portion of the Gantt Chart view for the selected category.
5. Click OK to save your changes.

The columns in the Bar Styles table at the top of the dialog box are as follows:

✦ **Name.** This column specifies the taskbar category. To create a new taskbar category name, click the Insert Row button at the top of the dialog box and type in any name you like. This name appears in a legend for your chart when you print it.

✦ **Appearance.** This column provides a sample of the current formatting settings for the bar.

When you click in any of the next four columns, Project displays a list box arrow at the right edge of the column. Open the list box to identify valid choices for these columns.

✦ **Show For . . . Tasks.** This column defines the types of tasks that the specified formatting affects. You can specify the type of task to affect by selecting the category from a drop-down list or by typing a category name directly in the cell or in the entry bar. If you want to specify more than one category, add a comma (,) after the first type and then select or type a second category. For example, to specify Normal tasks that are critical and in progress as a new category of taskbar style, choose or type: **Normal, Critical, In Progress**.

In Project 2000, you can type directly in a Bar Styles table cell; you don't need to type in the Entry bar.

✦ **Row.** The Row column specifies how many rows of bars (as many as four) you want to display for each task. If you have only one row and you are showing a bar for both the baseline timing and progress, the bars overlap each other. If you want two separate bars, you need two rows. You also can add extra rows to accommodate text above or below taskbars.

If a task fits in several categories, what happens? Project tries to display multiple formatting settings. (For example, if one category is solid blue and the other is a pattern, you get a blue pattern.) If Project can't display the formats together, whichever item is higher in this listing takes over. To modify the formatting precedence, use the Cut Row and Paste Row features to rearrange the rows in the Bar Styles dialog box.

✦ **From and To.** These columns define the time period shown by the bar. The Progress bar, for example, shows the actual date the task started and the amount of task completed through today. Select the time frames from drop-down lists in each of these fields.

Figure 8-17 shows a schedule with expanded rows; the baseline duration is displayed beneath normal taskbars, and the baseline finish date appears to the right of summary taskbars. To display the expanded rows and the baseline duration beneath normal tasks, I used the settings you see in Figure 8-18.

The settings in the Bar Styles dialog box enable you to modify, in great detail, the appearance of your schedule and how Project displays or prints it . If you print a legend along with your schedule, it reflects these changes. However, remember that modifying taskbar colors won't be of much use in black and white printouts of schedules, and creating too many kinds of formatting with too many variables can make your schedule difficult to read. The earlier advice about standardizing these settings across your organization holds for changes you make to task bar formatting as well.

### Changing the layout of the Gantt chart

The layout of a Gantt chart refers to the appearance of link lines, date formats used for information displayed near taskbars, the height of taskbars, and how Project displays certain characteristics of taskbars.

In views other than the Gantt Chart view, layout affects slightly different elements. For example, in the Calendar view, layout affects the order in which Project lists multiple tasks on a singular calendar day and how it splits date bars. And, as you'll read in the next section, layout in the Network Diagram Chart view affects link lines and how Project handles page breaks.

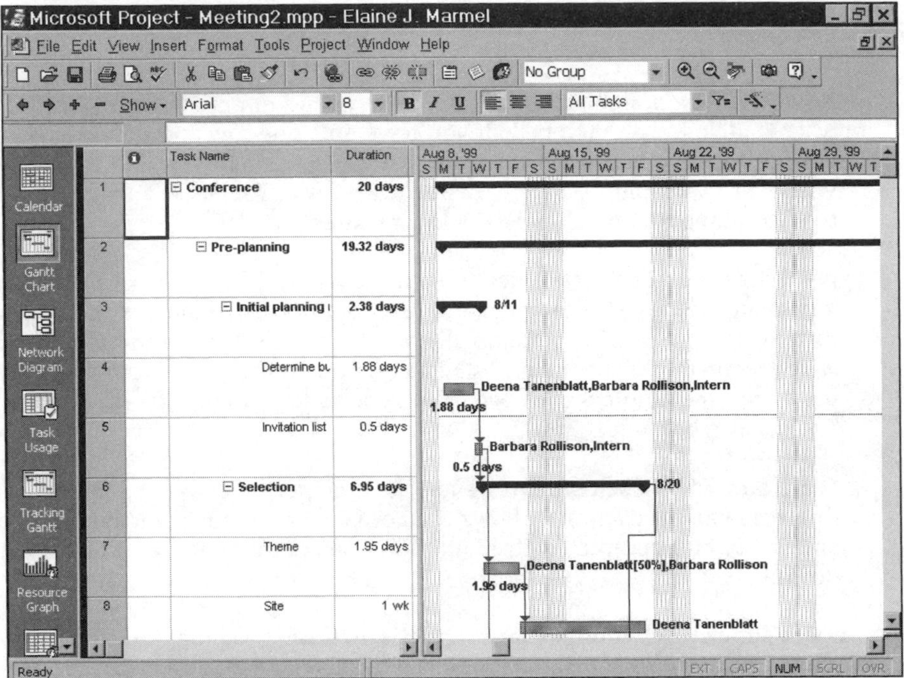


**Figure 8-17:** Adding rows to each task can make your schedule easier to read.

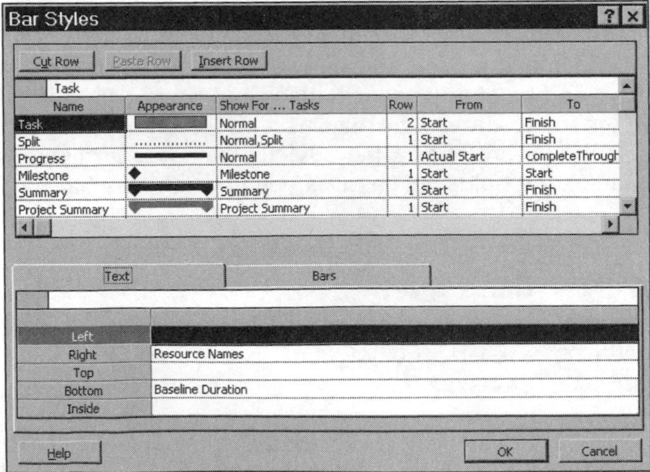


**Figure 8-18:** In the table, I changed the number of rows for normal tasks. At the bottom of the dialog box, I added Baseline Duration to the bottom row of normal tasks.

To modify the layout, choose Format ⇨ Layout. In the Gantt Chart view, the Layout dialog box shown in Figure 8-19 appears.

If you have a short schedule with many tasks running only hours in length, don't round taskbars to whole days.

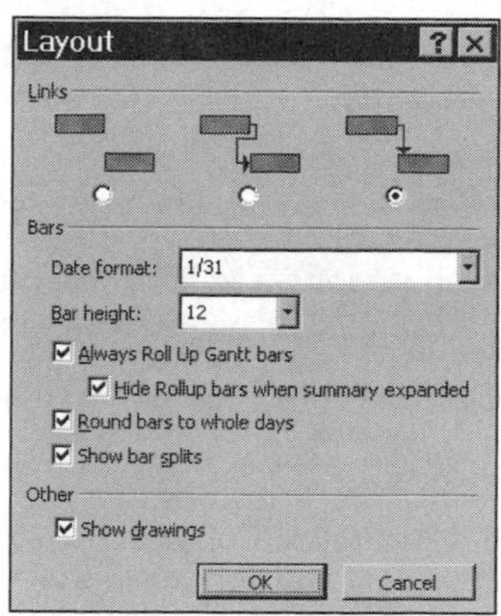


**Figure 8-19:** Because layout affects different elements in different views, the Layout dialog box for the Gantt Chart view is different than the Layout dialog box for the Network Diagram or Calendar views.

Here are the options to set for the Gantt chart layout:

✦ **Links.** Click one of these option buttons to display either no link lines or to use one of the available styles. Remember, link lines graphically display dependency relationships among tasks. If you want to take a quick look at your schedule with no dependency information showing, use the no link lines choice in this dialog box.

✦ **Date format.** Use this drop-down list to select a date or time format. Two interesting date formats include a week number (W5/5 and W5/5/97 12:33 PM) of the year and the day of the week; therefore, W50/3/99 is December 15, 1999 (the third day of the fiftieth full week of the year 1999).

Be aware that your nation or industry may use conventions for numbering weeks that might result in different week numbers than Project 2000 produces.

✦ **Bar height.** Select a height in points for the bars in your Gantt chart.

The first two checkboxes in the Bars section of the Layout dialog box are new to Project 2000.

The checkboxes in the Layout dialog box have the following effects:

✦ **Always Roll Up Gantt bars.** This setting enables you the freedom to display your Gantt schedule by rolling up tasks onto summary bars.

✦ **Hide Rollup bars when summary expanded.** This checkbox works with the preceding checkbox to hide rollup behavior if your schedule is completely expanded.

See Chapter 6 for more on Project's new rollup capabilities.

✦ **Round bars to whole days.** This option works well on longer schedules, but not as well on schedules with tasks that tend to run in hourly or half-day increments.

✦ **Show bar splits.** This option provides graphic representation on the Gantt chart of split tasks.

Split tasks are tasks that start, then stop for a time, and then start again. For example, if you expect to begin hiring employees for the project, but you know that your company imposes a two-week hiring freeze during the last two weeks of the year for accounting purposes, you could create a split task (see Chapter 9). The setting for splits in the Layout dialog box simply enables you to show the split task as separate task bars or one continuous task bar.

✦ **Show drawings**: If you place a check in this checkbox, Project displays drawings that you've inserted on your chart.

Make any choices in the Layout dialog box, and click OK to implement them.

## Changing gridlines

*Gridlines* are those lines in your Gantt chart and the Gantt table that mark off periods of time, rows and columns, pages in your schedule, and regular intervals in the chart. In Figure 8-20, gridlines mark off regular intervals across the chart; this format can help you read across the page on a long schedule. Also, the vertical line that marks the current date appears as a dashed line, rather than as the typical small-dotted line that you've seen in other figures in this chapter.

To modify gridlines, choose Format ➪ Gridlines. The dialog box in Figure 8-21 appears. In the "Line to change" list, the options Gantt Rows, Sheet Rows, and Sheet Columns enable you to set gridlines at regular intervals. For example, the project in Figure 8-21 has the Gantt Rows set to show at an interval of every four rows. You can change the line type and color only — not the interval — for the other choices in the "Line to change" list. To modify these settings, highlight the kind of line you want to change and then select the desired settings from the Type and Color drop-down lists.

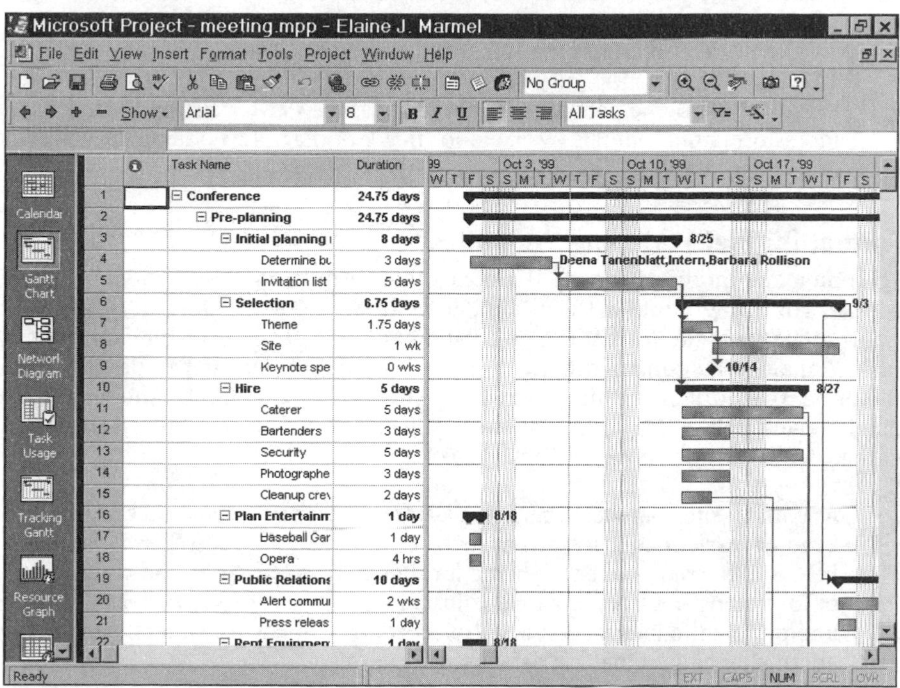


**Figure 8-20:** Displaying additional gridlines can make a schedule easier to read.

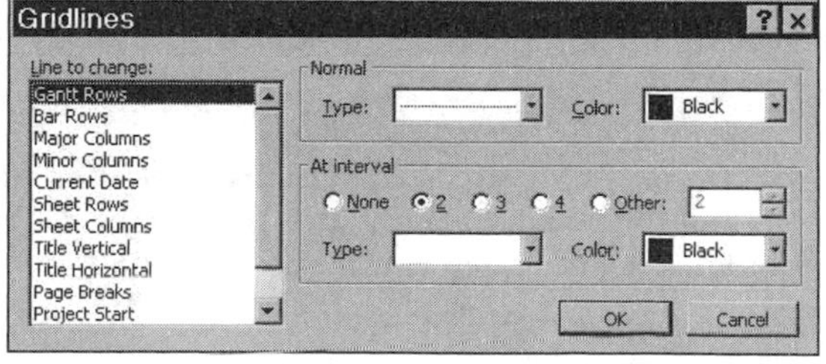


**Figure 8-21:** Only a few types of lines can be set at regular intervals.

If you do make substantial changes in the Gridlines dialog box, consider saving the file as a template for everyone else in your organization to use for their projects. This template not only saves you and your coworkers the effort of repeating the changes but also helps to enforce consistency throughout your organization.

## Changing network diagrams

You can format the nodes in a network diagram, and you can control the layout of the network diagram. You can modify the style of text placed in network diagram boxes and control the number of fields per node. You can control the size and the shape of the node and adjust the thickness and color of the line that defines the box.

In Project 2000, the network diagram replaces the PERT chart, and you have many more formatting options available for network diagram nodes than you had for PERT chart nodes.

### Formatting network diagram nodes

You can make modifications to the boxes that form the various nodes displayed in the Network Diagram Chart view similar to the way you can format taskbars in the Gantt chart. You can format the color and line style of the box itself for each type of task. You also can control the number of fields that appear per node, the shape of the node, the horizontal and vertical alignment of text within the node, and the font used in each cell of the node. Use these settings to draw the reader's attention to categories of nodes you want to emphasize.

As with task text and taskbars in the Gantt Chart view, you should be careful about keeping track of changes you make: The Undo feature doesn't work here. Project has its own color and line scheme for various types of tasks, and you run the risk of formatting one category to look just like another category by mistake. Because interpreting the information in a Project chart is so key to success, be very careful about changing formatting defaults.

#### Modifying node box styles

You can change the formatting of network diagram boxes individually, or you can change the formatting of a particular category of boxes. To change an individual box, select the box in the network diagram and choose Format ➪ Box to display the dialog box you see in Figure 8-22.

Use the Shape box to select one of 10 shapes for the box; similarly, use the Color box to identify the color for the lines of the box and the Width box to specify the width of the box's border. You also can set the Background color and pattern for the node. Make changes and watch the Preview to determine the affects of your changes. When you finish, click OK to save the changes.

To format a category of box, such as all Critical Milestones, use the Box Styles dialog box shown in Figure 8-23. You can display this dialog box by choosing Format ➪ Box Styles.

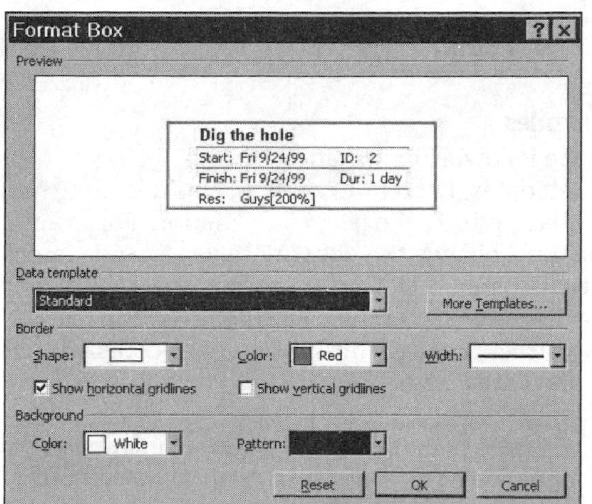


**Figure 8-22:** To modify the appearance of a single box in the network diagram, use this dialog box.

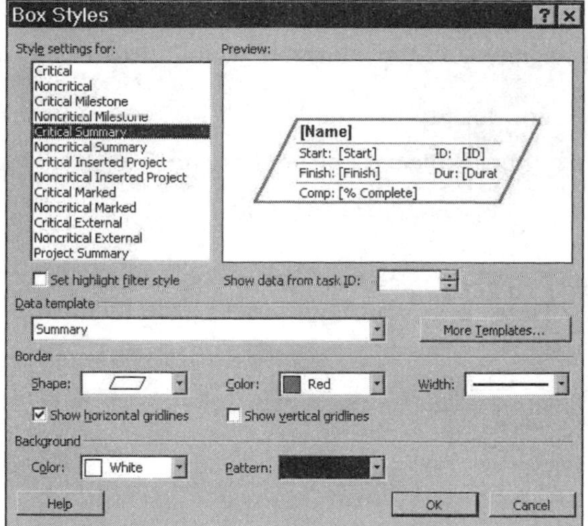


**Figure 8-23:** Use this dialog box to select a category of box to format.

Select the type of box you want to format from the "Style settings for" list. The current settings for the box appear in the Preview. The rest of the options in this dialog box are the same as the options in the Format Box dialog box, except for the Set highlight filter style checkbox. In Project 2000, you can filter information on the network diagram, as you learned in Chapter 7. Placing a check in the Set highlight filter style checkbox enables you to set the color Project uses when filtering tasks on the network diagram.

You should usually make the Name one of the pieces of information you display. Otherwise, the flow of tasks in the network diagram chart is nearly incomprehensible.

### Formatting fields that appear on nodes

Network diagram nodes display the following information by default: Task Name, Duration, ID, Start and Finish dates, Percent Complete, and Resource Name, if assigned. However, you can display up to 16 pieces of information. For example, to focus on costs in today's staff meeting, change the network diagram node information to Task Name, Baseline Cost, Actual Cost, Actual Overtime Cost, and Cost Variance. If your manager wants a network diagram chart report so that he or she can see whether the project schedule is on track, change this information to Task Name, Critical, Free Slack, Early Finish, and Late Finish.

While you can specify up to 16 pieces of information, beware of information overload. Providing too much information on a node will make the network diagram difficult to read and evaluate – and your reader will miss your point.

To modify the appearance of the information in a node in a number of ways: you can change the information included in a node, the font used to display the information, and the horizontal and vertical alignment of the information. Follow these steps:

1. Open either the Format Box or Box Styles dialog box.
2. Click the More Templates button. Project displays the Data Templates dialog box shown in Figure 8-24.

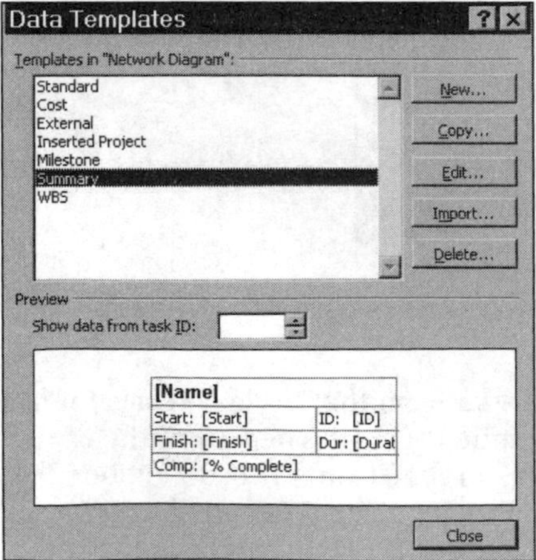


**Figure 8-24:** Select a template to modify or copy, or create a new template.

A template contains previously established node format settings.

3. Highlight the template you want to change and click the Edit button. Alternatively, you can create a new template by clicking the New button, or you can copy an existing template and make changes to the copy by clicking the Copy button. For this exercise, I'll copy the Standard template by clicking the Copy button. Regardless of the button you click, Project displays the Data Template Definition dialog box shown in Figure 8-25.

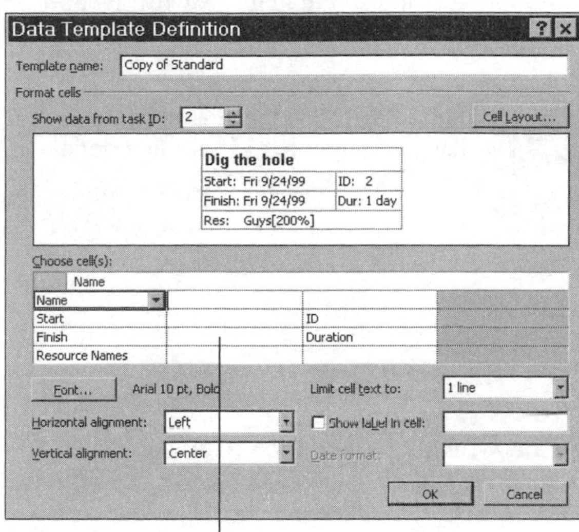


Click here to change the contents of the cells in the node

**Figure 8-25:** Use this dialog box to change the infor-mation you show in all the network diagram nodes.

The picture at the top of the dialog box provides a preview of the current structure of the cell. In the figure, the node contains nine cells—three on each row and three in each column. Blank cells are merged with nonblank cells.

4. To change the contents of a cell of the node, click the corresponding cell in the middle of the dialog box. A list box arrow appears to the right of the cell; open the list box to select a new field for the selected cell.

5. To change the font for a particular cell, select that cell and click the Font button. A dialog box appears, from which you can select a new font, the font size, and font attributes such as boldface or italics.

6. Use the Horizontal and Vertical alignment list boxes to change the alignment of text within its cell.

7. Use the "Limit cell text to" list box to specify the number of lines for each cell; a cell can be as many as three lines.

8. Click the "Show label in cell" checkbox to include an identifier in the cell for the type of information. For example, if you select the cell containing Name and then click the "Show label in cell" checkbox, the title of the task will contain "Name:" followed by the title of the task.

9. To increase or decrease the number of cells in the node, click the Cell Layout button to display the dialog box shown in Figure 8-26. From this dialog box, specify the number of cells for all nodes. After you click OK, Project redisplays the Data Template Definition dialog box with the appropriate number of cells available for formatting.

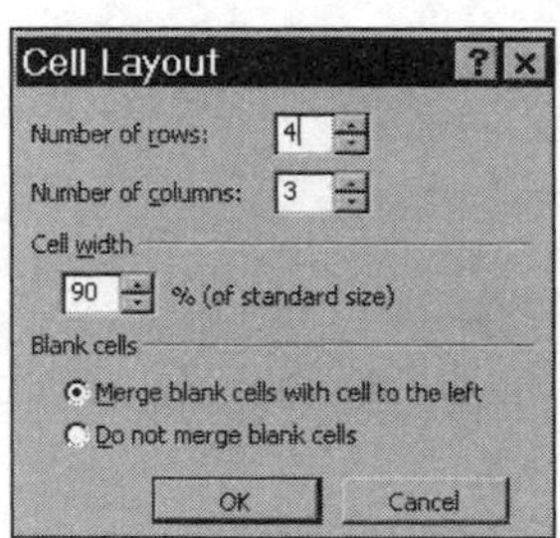


**Figure 8-26:** Use this dialog box to change the number of cells in a node.

10. Click OK to close the Data Template Definition dialog box; click Close to close the Data Templates window, and click OK to close the Box Styles dialog box.

## Changing the layout of the network diagram

The layout controls available for the network diagram in Project 2000 have increased significantly over those previously available for the PERT chart it replaced. As you can see from Figure 8-27, you can control the layout mode, the box arrangement, the link style and color, and several overall options for the network diagram.

By default, Project automatically positions all boxes on the diagram, but you can choose to manually position the boxes.

Using the Arrangement list box, you can change the order in which Project displays the boxes. Choose from Top Down From Left, Top Down By Day, Top Down By Week, Top Down By Month, Top Down — Critical First, Centered From Left, and Centered From Top. The varying arrangements change the number of pages required to print your network diagram.

You also can change the row and column alignment and spacing as well as row height and column width. Using checkboxes in the Box Layout section, you can hide or display summary tasks, keep tasks with their summaries, and adjust for page breaks.

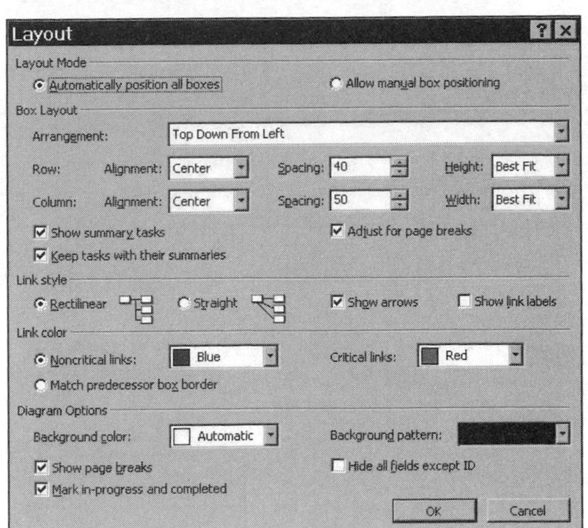


**Figure 8-27:** You can control layout mode, box arrangement, and link style for the network diagram.

You can control the style of the link lines, and you can choose to show arrows and link labels, which, by default, show the type of link dependency that exists between two tasks (Finish-to Start, Finish-to-Finish, and so on). And, you can select different colors for both critical and noncritical links.

For more information on types of links, see Chapter 4.

For the network diagram as a whole—not the individual nodes—you can choose a background color and pattern. You also can mark in-progress tasks with half an *X* and completed tasks with an entire *X*. If you hide all information on the nodes except the ID, Project reduces the size of the nodes on your network diagram and therefore reduces the number of pages that will print. You can also choose to show page breaks, which appear as dotted lines onscreen in the network diagram view. In Figure 8-28, I've included link labels and hidden all task information except the ID. A page break appears at the right side of the diagram.

Remember, creating too many kinds of formatting with too many variables can make your schedule difficult to read. The earlier advice about standardizing these settings across your organization holds for changes that you make to network diagram layouts as well.

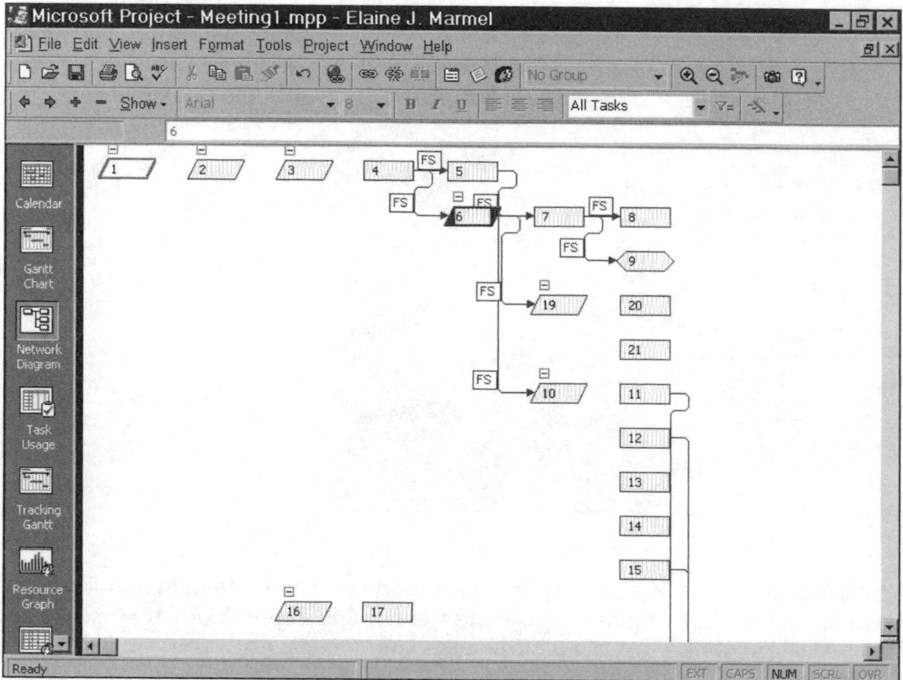


**Figure 8-28:** By adjusting the layout of the network diagram, you can dramatically change its appearance.

# Formatting the Calendar view

As I mentioned earlier in the chapter, you format text in the Calendar view the same way that you format text in any other view. While you cannot format the text of individual items in the Calendar view, you can use the Text Styles dialog box as described earlier in this chapter to format categories of text.

In the Calendar view, you can format bar styles and you can change the layout of the calendar. This section explores those types of changes.

## Formatting the Calendar entries

When you display the Calendar view, by default, entries appear in boxes that Project calls bars. You can, if you prefer, change the style of these bars. For example, you can make all critical tasks appear on the Calendar in red. Choose Format ➪ Bar Styles in the Calendar view to display the dialog box you see in Figure 8-29. Select a type of task from the list on the left. As you make changes in the Bar shape area and the Text area, watch the Sample at the bottom of the box for the effects of your changes.

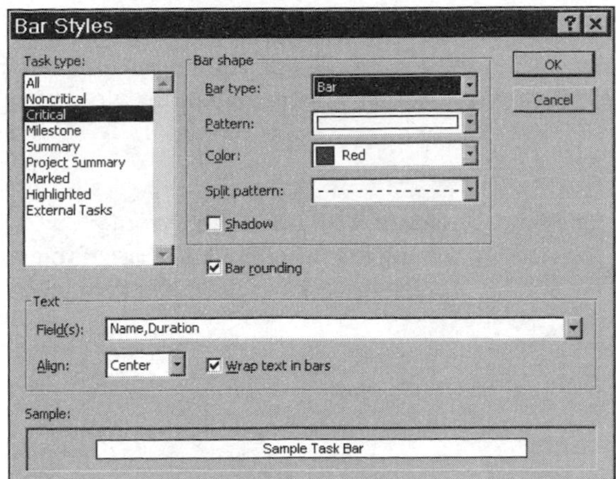


**Figure 8-29:** Use this dialog box to change the appearance of the Calendar view. Add different colors for different task types, or use a line instead of a box to represent the task's duration.

In the Bar shape area, use the Bar type box to change display tasks using a Line, a Bar, or None — choosing None "hides" the selected task type from the Calendar view. If you choose Bar from the Bar type box, open the Pattern list box and select a pattern, which appears inside the box for the task type. If you want, choose a pattern for Project to display between split tasks from the Split pattern box. Place a check in the Shadow box to display a shadow behind a bar (this option is available only if you choose Bar from the Bar type box).

Place a check in the Bar rounding box to tell Project to draw the bar for tasks that take less than one day so that the task's duration is implied. For example, use bar rounding to tell Project to draw a bar that extends three-quarters of the width of the day to represent a task that takes .75 days. If you don't use bar rounding, Project doesn't try to imply the duration of the task by the length of the bar.

In the Text area, you can include Project fields for each task type; to include more than one field, separate fields with a comma, as you see in Figure 8-29. Align the text with the bar or line using the Align list box. If you chose Bar as the Bar type, you can place a check in the Wrap text in bars checkbox; when you place a check in this box, Project wraps text so that it fits within the box. For example, if you show the task name and duration in the box, and the task name is fairly long but the task lasts only one day, Project will wrap the text so that the task takes more than one row when it appears on the calendar. You'll be able to read all displayed information about every task. If you don't place a check in the Wrap text in bars box, Project displays only as much information as it can fit in a box sized to match the task's duration. In the example I just described, you might not see the entire task name, and you certainly won't see the task duration because the box will span only one day.

### Changing the Calendar layout

Use the Layout dialog box, shown in Figure 8-30, to change the layout of tasks on the Calendar view. By default, Project displays tasks in the Calendar view using the current sorted order of tasks.

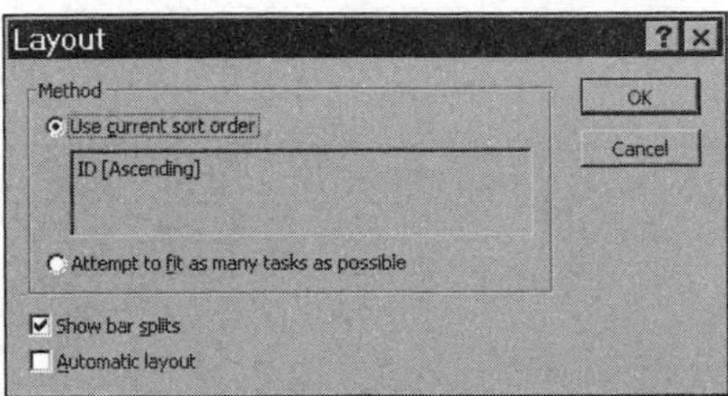


**Figure 8-30:** Use the Layout dialog box to change the way Project presents tasks in the Calendar view.

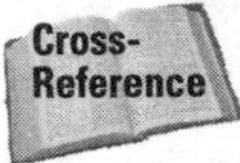


You can read about sorting tasks in Chapter 7.

If you don't want tasks to appear in the Calendar view using the currently sorted order, choose the "Attempt to fit as many tasks as possible" option button. Project sorts tasks by Total Slack and then by Duration to try to fit the maximum number of tasks into the rows for a week without overlapping bars.

Remove the check from the Show bar splits checkbox to hide the designation for split tasks from the Calendar view. Place a check in the Automatic layout checkbox to have Project automatically adjust the Calendar view to accommodate new tasks you add or tasks you delete.

## Inserting Drawings and Objects

We're living in the age of multimedia and MTV. Visual elements have a way of getting a message across that simple text often can't match. In Project, you can insert graphic images (photos, illustrations, or diagrams, for example) in four places:

- ✦ In a Gantt chart, in the taskbar area
- ✦ In notes (task, resource, or assignment)
- ✦ In headers, footers, and chart legends
- ✦ In resource or task forms

You also can copy your Project schedule into other Office products.

## Copying pictures

Suppose you've written a report in Microsoft Word and you would *really* like to include your Gantt chart in the report. You could print it on a separate page, but you could also insert it as a picture in your Word document. Or, suppose you want to post a picture of your Project schedule on the Web. You can easily create a picture for either of these purposes.

Using the Copy Picture command, you can copy your Project schedule to the Windows Clipboard and then paste it into any application as a graphic image. Click the Copy Picture button on the Standard toolbar or choose Edit ⇨ Copy Picture. The dialog box you see in Figure 8-31 appears. To copy the picture to the Clipboard, select the "For screen" option button in the Render image section and click OK. If the image you're copying will fit well into another document, Project simply copies the picture to the Windows Clipboard. But, if the picture you are copying is particularly large, Project warns you and gives you the opportunity to scale the picture before saving or pasting (see Figure 8-32).

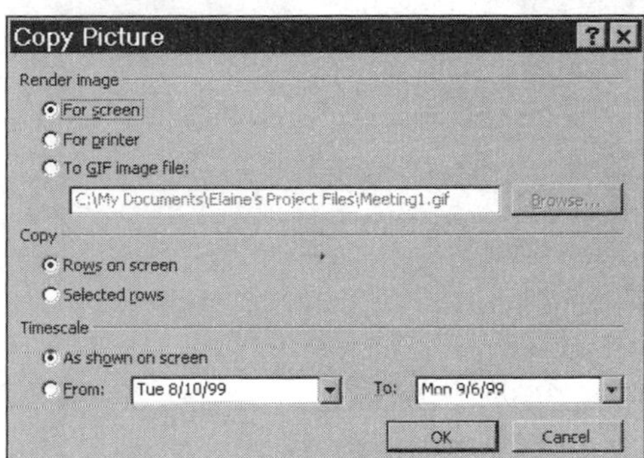


**Figure 8-31:** Choose "For screen" to copy a Project schedule to the Windows Clipboard.

**Figure 8-32:** If the image you're copying is large, Project offers you the opportunity to scale the picture.

Once you've copied the picture, simply switch to the other document in which you want to place the picture and click the Paste button in that document. In Figure 8-33, you see a Gantt chart in Word. When you use the Paste button, you place a graphic in your document; the graphic is not linked to Project in any way, so you cannot:

✦ Edit the chart to make scheduling changes

✦ Double-click the image to open the chart in Project

Even if you choose the Paste Special command, the image you copied from Project is exactly that—an image. It is not a Project file that you can link to from another application.

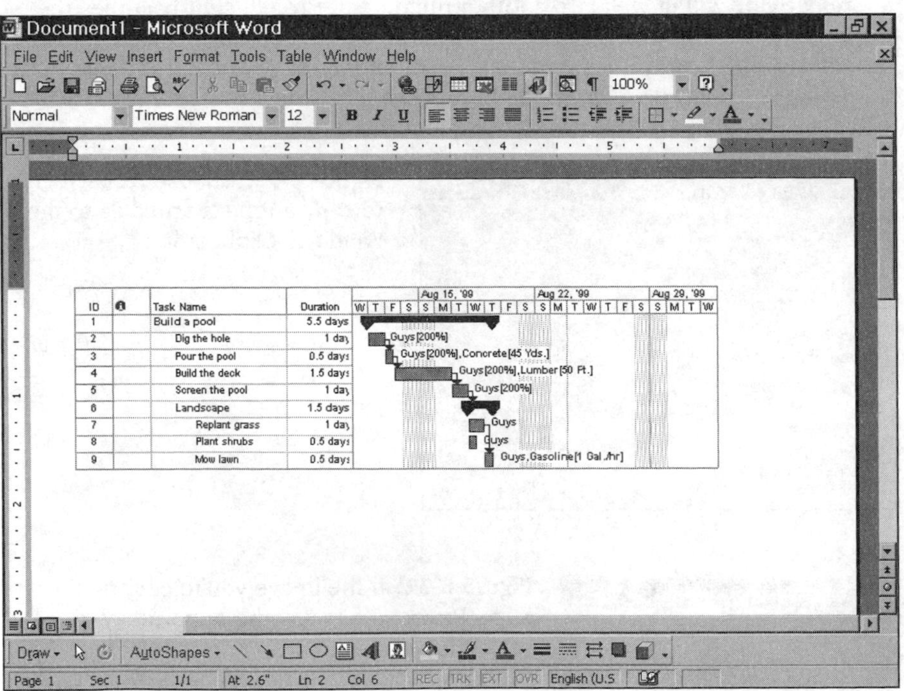


**Figure 8-33:** After you use the Copy Picture command to render an image for the screen, you can paste the image into any document.

To create a graphic image file that you can use on a Web page or in a document, select the To GIF image file option in the Copy Picture dialog box (refer to Figure 8-31). When you choose to render the image for a printer, Project copies the image to the Windows Clipboard but in shades of gray rather than the colors you see onscreen. You can view the image in the Clipboard Viewer applet that comes with Windows (see Figure 8-34) or you can copy it into another application as a "black and white" image.

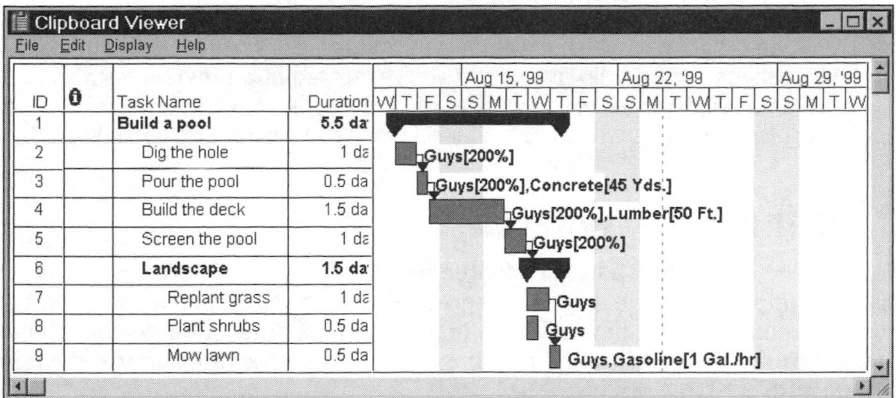


**Figure 8-34:** When you render the picture for a printer, Project places a "black and white" image of your project on the Windows Clipboard.

# Using visuals in schedules

Because project management is often a serious, information-oriented business, you don't want to overdo the visuals. Remember, both the Gantt chart and the network diagram are visuals. And, pictures of bunnies and curly doodads aren't likely to sit well with the head of your engineering division. However, used judiciously, images can reinforce the information about your project and lend a professional look to your reports.

Consider using graphics in the following ways:

✦ Add a company logo to the header of your schedule so it appears at the top of every page.

✦ Add a photograph of each of your key resources in their resource note. The photo helps you get to know all the team members on a large-scale project so that you can address them by name in meetings and in the hallway.

✦ If a particular task involves a schematic or diagram of a product, place a copy of the diagram in the task notes for reference.

Placing graphics in a schedule can take up a big chunk of memory, making your file larger and possibly making calculation time longer; for this reason, use graphics on an as-needed basis.

✦ If your schedule has a key milestone, place a graphic suggesting success or accomplishment next to the milestone in the Gantt chart. Every time you review your schedule with your team, you'll subconsciously focus on that goal and how close you're getting to it, which can boost morale.

Graphic objects come in a variety of file formats, depending on the type of graphic and the program in which it was created. You can use scanned images, photo files, illustrations such as clip art, a chart you've created in a program such as Excel, a Word for Windows table, and even a video clip. Look on the Internet for sources for graphics files, or use the images available to the Microsoft Office family products.

## Inserting visual objects

To insert an object into a header, footer, or legend, choose File ➪ Page Setup and click the appropriate tab. Use the Insert Picture button to open a dialog box that enables you to select a picture file to insert. For task notes, double-click the task to open the Task Information dialog box, select the Notes tab, and use the Insert Object button to insert a file.

You can use the Microsoft Clip Gallery, which comes with Project (and all Microsoft Office family products) to practice placing a graphic in a Project file. Clip art is a collection of line drawings in various styles. These images come in assorted categories, such as Business, Maps, Office, and Transportation.

To insert a piece of clip art from the Microsoft Clip Gallery in the Gantt chart portion of a schedule, with the Gantt Chart view displayed, follow these steps:

If you're using Office 97, you'll see the Clip Gallery 3.0. If you're using Office 2000, you'll see the Clip Gallery 5.0. If you don't use Office, you won't be able to select the Microsoft Clip Gallery.

1. Choose Insert ➪ Object to open the Insert Object dialog box, shown in Figure 8-35.

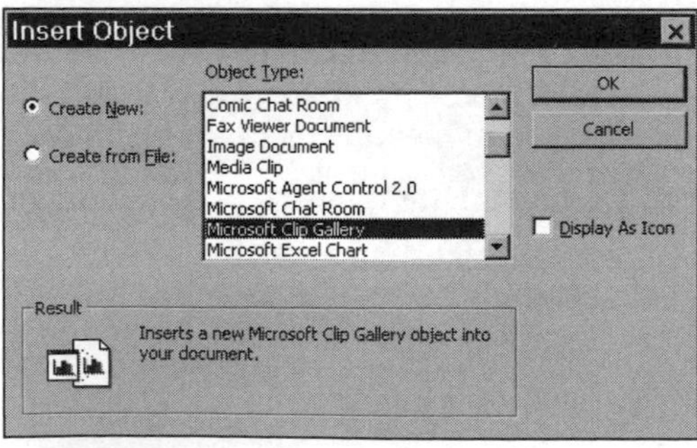


**Figure 8-35:** You can select various types of objects to insert from this list, such as Excel spreadsheets and even video clips.

To insert a graphics file, click the Create from File control button in the Insert Object dialog box. Then click the Browse button and locate your file using the File Open dialog box that appears. You can insert into your schedule any type of file listed in the Insert Object dialog box. With Microsoft products that take advantage of the Object Linking and Embedding (OLE) technology, after you insert an object from another program into Project, you can open the object for editing in the original program from within Project by double-clicking the object.

2. Click Microsoft Clip Gallery in the Object type list and then click OK. The Clip Gallery shown in Figure 8-36 appears.

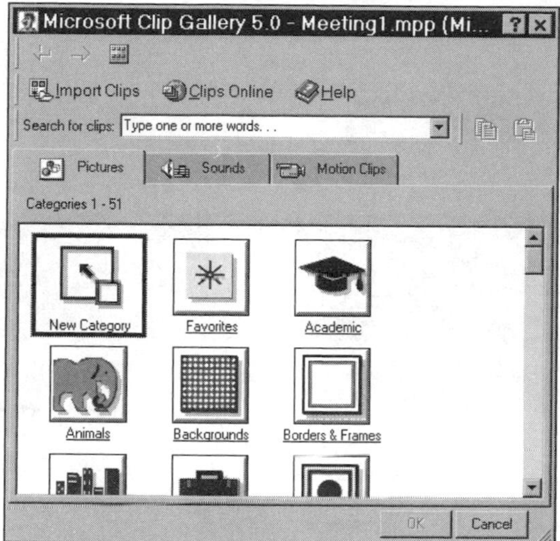


**Figure 8-36:** The various tabs of the Clip Gallery dialog box offer different kinds of media files to insert, although the only tabs with images built in are Clip Art and Pictures.

3. Click a category from the Pictures tab.

By default, Office doesn't install *all* available images because of the space they require. So, you may find some categories initially don't contain any pictures. Using your Office CD-ROM, you can install additional pictures.

4. Use the scroll bar on the right to preview the images in that category.
5. Click the clip you want to insert; a pop-up toolbar appears (see Figure 8-37).
6. Click the top tool on the toolbar to insert the clip; alternatively, you can click the Close button to close the dialog box without placing a picture on your schedule.

The image appears in your Gantt chart area. You will probably have to resize it and move it around, which you will learn to do shortly. For now, look at the image placed in the Gantt chart in Figure 8-38 to see how you can use a piece of clip art to mark a key milestone in a schedule.

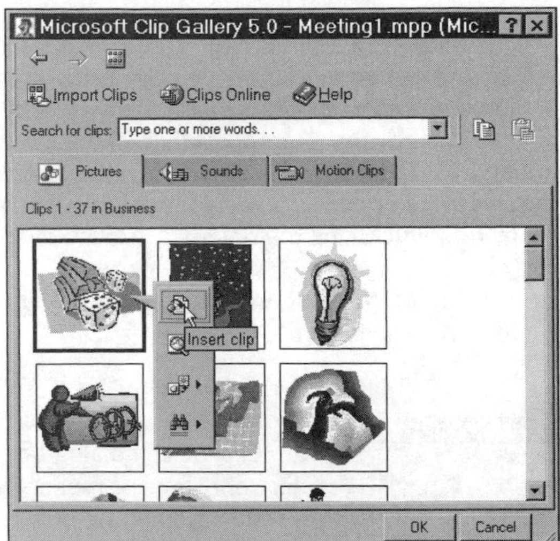


**Figure 8-37:** Use the pop-up toolbar to insert a clip into a schedule.

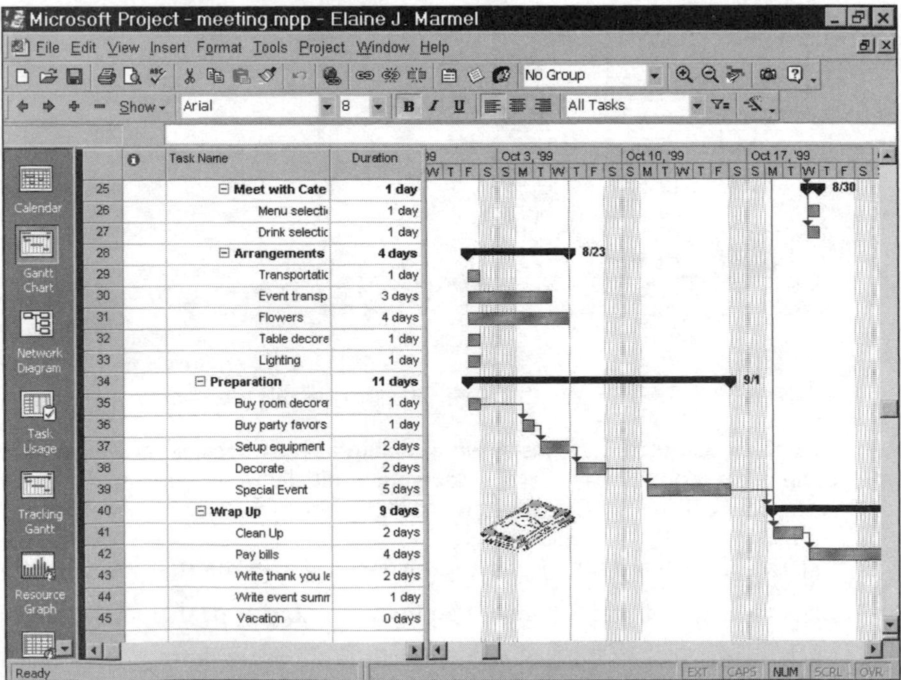


**Figure 8-38:** Hiring a keynote speaker is a key moment in this project, and the small image of money calls attention to it.

## Using the Drawing toolbar

Project also has a drawing feature that you can use to build simple diagrams or add shapes or text boxes to the Gantt chart area of your Project file. For example, you might want to draw a circle around an important taskbar in your schedule to draw attention to it in a presentation. Or, suppose that you want to suggest cutting a task from the project; you might want to draw an X through the task to make your point (see Figure 8-39). The formatting methods you learned earlier in this chapter enable you to create settings so that predefined information appears next to taskbars in your schedule. However, you must use the Drawing Text Box tool to enter your own text.

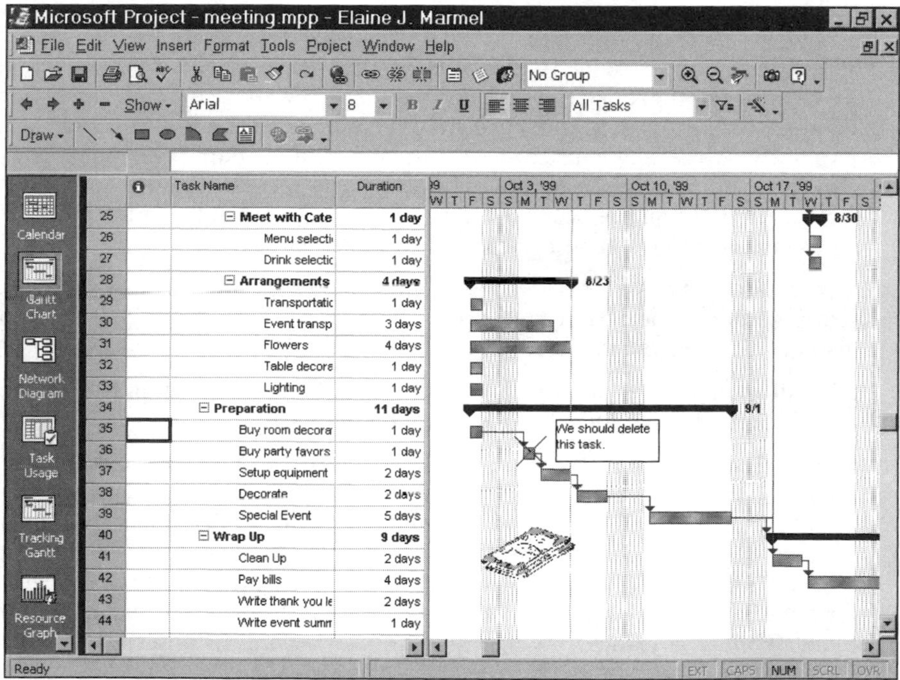


**Figure 8-39:** Consider using this type of drawing to display a project onscreen using an LCD panel, or at a trade show.

To display the Drawing toolbar shown in Figure 8-40, you can choose either View ➪ Toolbars and select the Drawing toolbar for display, or choose Insert ➪ Drawing.

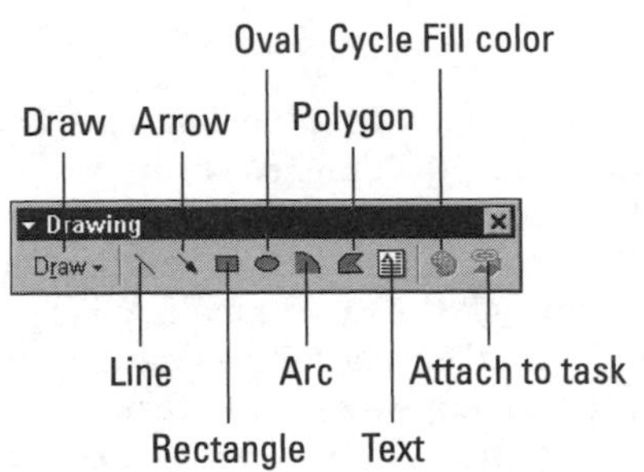


**Figure 8-40:** The Drawing toolbar is a floating toolbar; drag it up near the Formatting toolbar if you want to dock it at the top of your screen, or click the dark blue bar at the top and drag to move it around your screen.

Here's how you can use the tools on the Drawing toolbar:

✦ To draw an object, click the Line, Arrow, Rectangle, Oval, Arc, or Polygon buttons and then click the taskbar area of the Gantt chart. Holding down your mouse button, drag to draw the shape. When using the Polygon tool, you need to draw several segments to define the multisided shape, clicking at the end of each segment. To complete the polygon, double-click at the end of the last segment. With all the other tools, the shape appears automatically when you drag in one direction and release your mouse button.

✦ To create text anywhere around your taskbar, click the Text Box button and drag to draw a box. Your insertion point appears in the box whenever you select the box; you can type any text you like.

✦ To fill an object with color, click the Cycle Fill Color button on the Drawing toolbar repeatedly until you see the color you want.

✦ To anchor a drawing object in the Gantt chart to a particular task bar — so that if you move the task in the schedule the graphic moves with it — select the object and click the Attach to Task button on the Drawing toolbar. Click the Attach to task control button in the Format Drawing dialog box (see Figure 8-41), enter a task ID number, and enter the settings for the point on the taskbar at which you want to attach the object. Then click OK. (You can reach the Format Drawing dialog box at any time by choosing Format ➪ Drawing ➪ Properties.)

You can also use three tools on the Drawing toolbar with other types of graphic objects that you insert. The Draw, Cycle Fill Color, and Attach to Task buttons work with any selected object, such as clip art.

When you no longer need the Drawing toolbar, click the Close button in the upper-right corner to remove it.

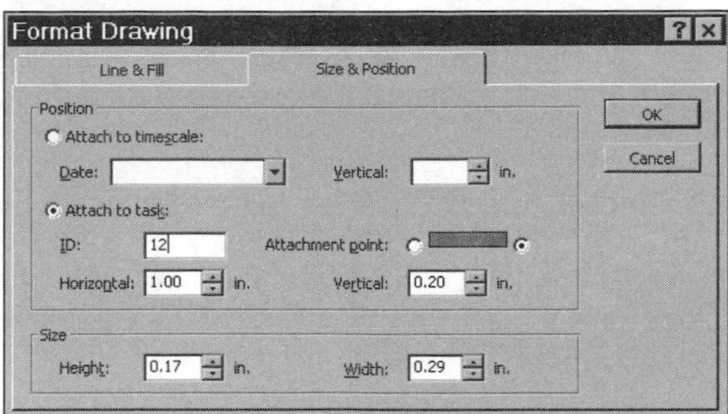


**Figure 8-41:** You could also attach a graphic to a position on the timescale, rather than attaching it to a particular task. Place a graphic at a particular date on the timescale, for example.

## Modifying graphics and drawings

You can also use the Format Drawing dialog box to format graphic object styles. To open this dialog box, right-click any object and choose Properties from the shortcut menu. You'll see the Size & Position tab initially (refer to Figure 8-41). Click the Line & Fill tab to see the choices shown in Figure 8-42.

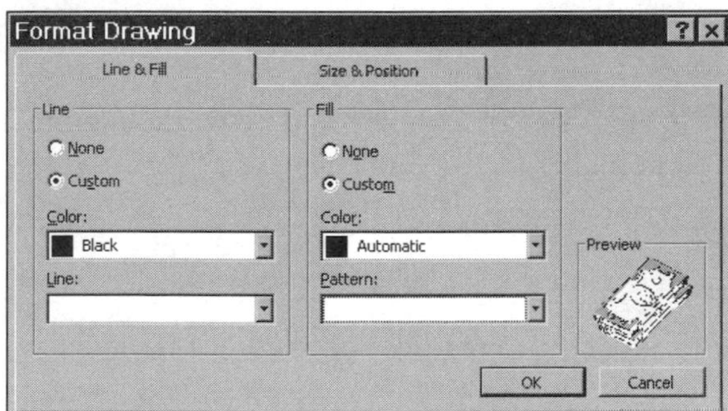


**Figure 8-42:** Rather than cycling through fill colors using the button on the Drawing toolbar, you can select a fill color from a drop-down palette in the Line & Fill tab of the Format Drawing dialog box.

Use the Color and Line drop-down options on the left to assign a style of thickness and color to lines. Use the Fill Color and Pattern options to place a color and pattern, such as solid or thatched lines, inside an object.

Fill color and pattern fill the inside of a drawn object and the background area of a clip art or other predrawn graphic object. The Preview box in Figure 8-42 shows you how a fill pattern surrounds the clip art object, filling the background of the object, rather than filling the object itself.

Resizing and moving drawings and other objects is similar to working with objects in other programs:

- **To resize an object.** Click the object to select it. Click any of the eight selection handles; drag inward to make the object smaller or drag outward to make the object larger.
- **To move an object.** Move your mouse pointer over the object until your cursor changes to four arrows. Click the object, hold down your mouse button, and drag the object anywhere in the Gantt chart area. Release the mouse button to place the object.

# Summary

In this chapter you learned many ways to:

- Format text for individual selections or globally by category of task
- Format taskbars and the information displayed near them
- Format network diagram boxes and change the information that you display in the Network Diagram view
- Change the layout options for Gantt chart taskbars and network diagram nodes
- Add gridlines to the Gantt Chart view
- Insert graphic objects and drawings in the Gantt chart and in notes, or as a header and footer

Chapter 9 explains how to fine-tune timing to resolve scheduling conflicts.

✦ ✦ ✦

# Resolving Scheduling Problems

✦ ✦ ✦ ✦

**In This Chapter**

Understanding why scheduling conflicts occur

Resolving scheduling conflicts

Using the critical path to shorten a project

✦ ✦ ✦ ✦

Scheduling conflicts are the bane of the project manager's existence. Scheduling conflicts typically fall into two categories:

- Your project is taking longer than you had planned.
- Your resources are overassigned.

This chapter considers the first problem and focuses on identifying scheduling problems and resolving them; Chapter 10 focuses on the second problem.

Scheduling conflicts announce themselves in a number of ways. Changing views and filtering information using the techniques described in Chapters 6 and 7 may identify some glaring problem inherent in your original logic. For example, if you filter your project to view only incomplete tasks or slipping tasks, you may spot some problems. More likely, however, you'll unknowingly create a problem by using a task constraint, as explained in the next section.

## Resolving Scheduling Conflicts

Project provides several techniques that you can use to resolve scheduling conflicts. This section covers the following strategies:

- Adding resources
- Using overtime
- Adding time
- Adjusting slack

✦ Changing constraints

✦ Adjusting dependencies

✦ Splitting a task

## Adding resources to tasks

Adding resources to a task can decrease the time necessary to complete the task. On the Advanced tab of the Task Information dialog box (see Figure 9-1), make sure to set the task type to Fixed Units; in this instance, adding resources to the task reduces the duration of the task. Also remember that a check appears by default in the Effort driven checkbox of the Task Information dialog box. When you use the Effort driven option, Project reallocates the work among the assigned resources.

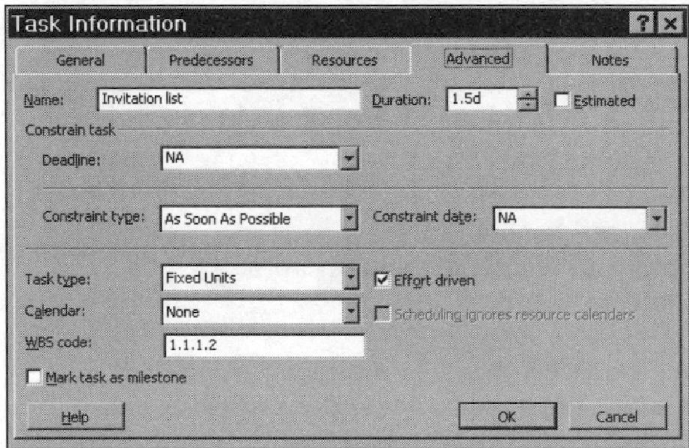


**Figure 9-1:** The Advanced tab of the Task Information dialog box controls the task type and whether the task is effort driven.

## Using overtime

In the best of all possible worlds, you have unlimited resources and you can add resources to resolve scheduling problems. After performing a reality check, however, you'll probably discover that you don't have unlimited resources, and adding resources may not be an option for you. But you might be able to use overtime to shorten a task's duration, which is the next strategy you can use to resolve scheduling problems.

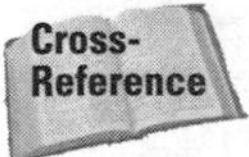


For information on resolving resource conflicts, see Chapter 10.

*Overtime* in Project is the amount of work scheduled beyond an assigned resource's regular working hours. Overtime hours are charged at the resource's overtime rate. Overtime work does *not* represent additional work on a task; instead, it represents the amount of time spent on a task outside regular hours. For example, if you assign 30 hours of work and 12 hours of overtime, the total work is still 30 hours. Of the 30 hours, 18 hours are worked during the regular work schedule (and charged to the project at the regular rate), and 12 hours are worked during off hours (and charged to the project at an overtime rate). Therefore, you can use overtime, to shorten the time a resource takes to complete a task.

To enter overtime, follow these steps:

1. Select the Gantt Chart view from the View bar.
2. Choose Window ➪ Split to reveal the Task Form in the bottom pane.
3. Click the Task Form to make it the active pane.
4. Choose Format ➪ Details ➪ Resource Work. Project adds the Ovt. Work column to the Task form (see Figure 9-2).

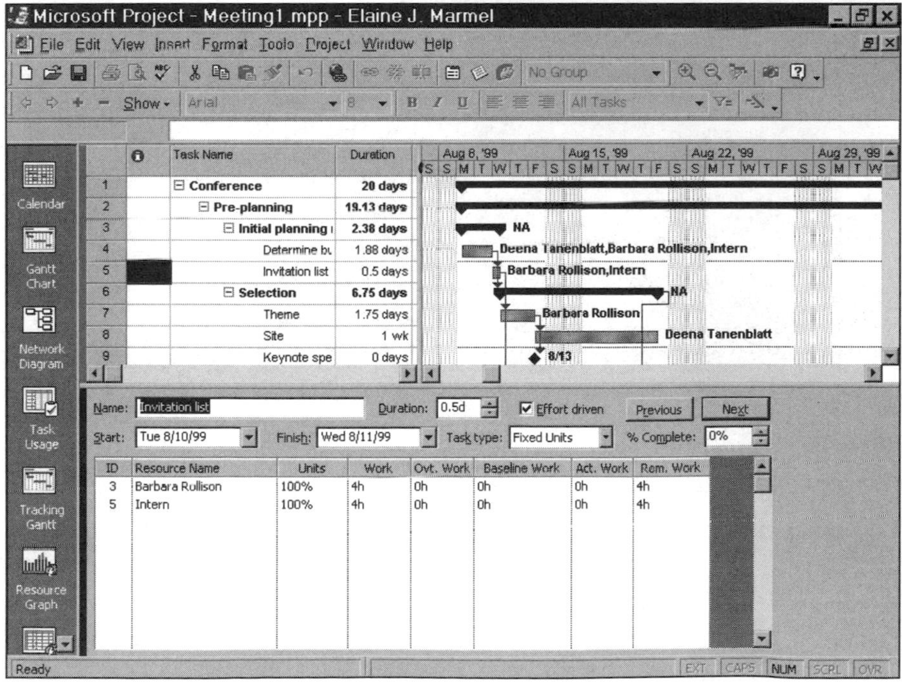


**Figure 9-2:** Use the Task form and display the Overtime column to add overtime.

5. Move to the top pane and select the task to which you want to assign overtime.
6. Move to the bottom pane and fill in the overtime amount for the appropriate resource.

When you finish entering overtime, you can hide the Task form by choosing Window ➪ Remove Split.

## Adding time to tasks

You can also solve scheduling conflicts by increasing the duration of a task. Again, in the best of all possible worlds, you have this luxury. In reality, you may not. But if you can increase the duration of a task, you may find scarce resources available to complete the task given its new timing.

As you know, you can change the duration from several different views, such as the Task Usage view or the Gantt Chart view. Or you can use the Task Information dialog box (see Figure 9-3). To open the Task Information dialog box, double-click the task and use the Duration box to change the duration.

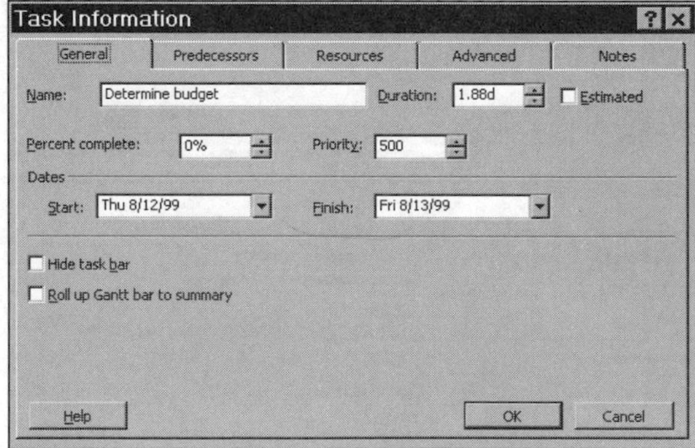


**Figure 9-3:** Change the duration from the Task Information dialog box.

## Adjusting slack

*Slack time* is the amount of time a task can slip before it affects another task's dates or the finish date of the project. *Free slack* is the amount of time a task can be delayed without delaying any other task. Most projects contain noncritical tasks with slack, and these tasks can start late without affecting the schedule. If you have slack in your schedule, you might be able to move tasks around to balance phases of the schedule that have no slack with phases that have too much slack. You can thus use tasks with slack to compensate for tasks that take longer than planned or to help resolve resource overallocations.

**Note**

Slack values can also help you identify inconsistencies in the schedule. For example, you'll see a negative slack value when one task has a finish-to-start dependency with a second task, but the second task has a Must Start On constraint that is earlier than the end of the first task.

Almost by definition, you create slack time if you use the Must Start On constraint when you create your task. As you learned in Chapter 4, you set constraints on the Advanced tab of the Task Information dialog box (see Figure 9-4); to display the Task Information dialog box, double-click the task in your schedule. When the dialog box appears, select the Advanced tab.

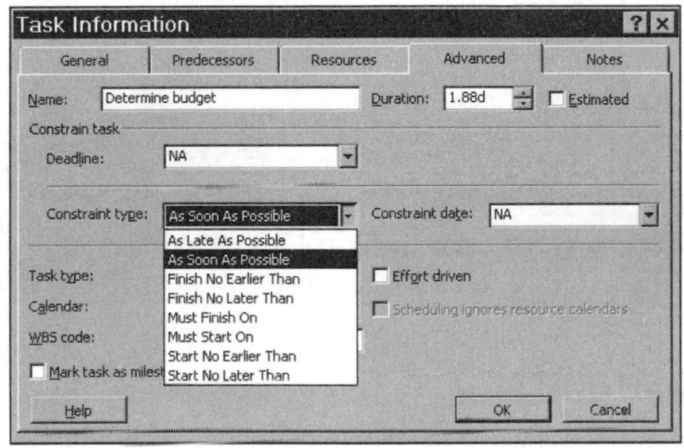


**Figure 9-4:** Constraints can often create slack time.

To avoid creating slack time, use the As Soon As Possible constraint as much as you can. To find tasks with slack time, follow these steps:

1. Choose View ⇨ More Views to open the More Views dialog box.
2. Select Detail Gantt from the list, and then click Apply.

**Tip**

You can identify slack on the Gantt bars. Slack appears as thin lines extending from the regular Gantt bars.

3. Right-click the Select All button and select Schedule from the list of tables.
4. Drag the divider bar to the right to view more of the table. Now you can see the Free Slack and Total Slack fields shown in Figure 9-5.

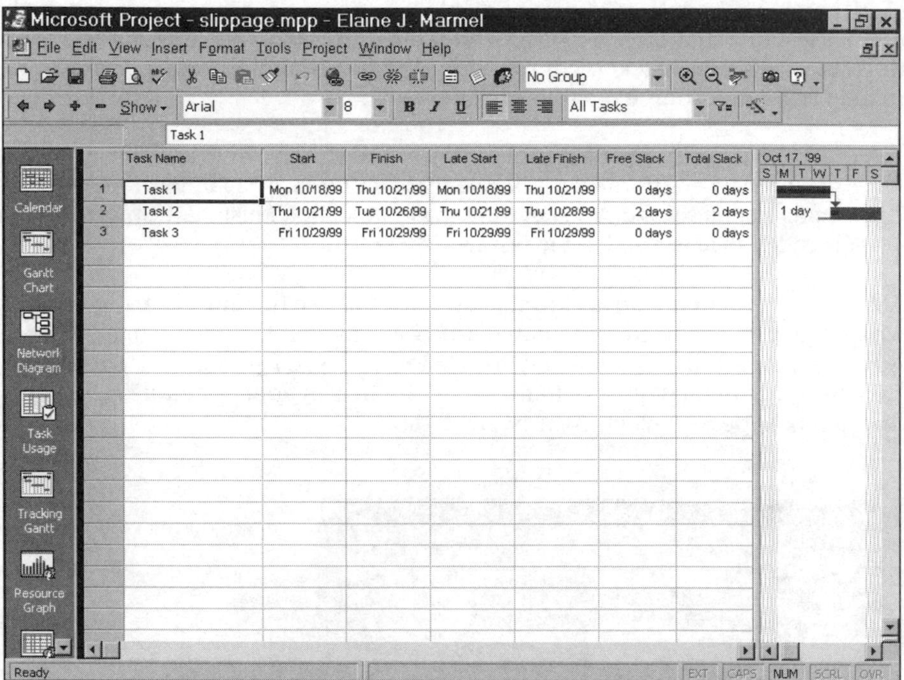


**Figure 9-5:** You can find slack time on tasks using the Detail Gantt view and the Schedule table.

## Changing task constraints

Task constraints are the usual culprits when projects fall behind schedule. By default, Project uses the Planning Wizard to warn you when you are about to take an action that is likely to throw your project off schedule. For example, if you impose a Must Start On task constraint, Project displays the Planning Wizard dialog box shown in Figure 9-6.

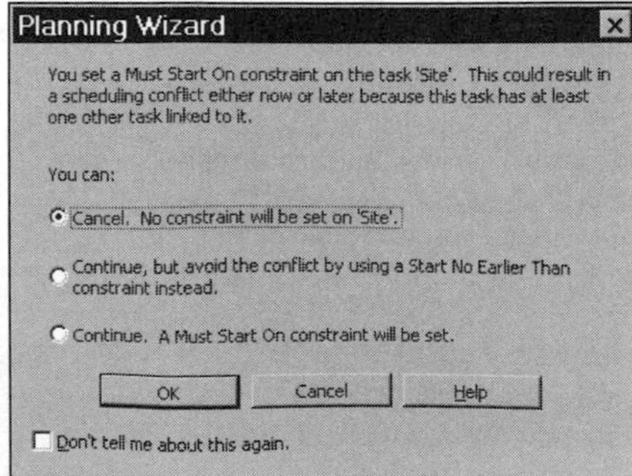


**Figure 9-6:** The Planning Wizard appears by default when you apply a constraint that is likely to lengthen your project schedule.

Similarly, if you impose an illogical start date on a task when recording actual dates, Project displays a Planning Wizard dialog box that resembles the one in Figure 9-7. Suppose, for example, that you accidentally enter a start date for Task 4, and Task 4 is linked to and succeeds Task 3. Further suppose that you have not yet started Task 3 in time for it to complete before the date you set for starting Task 4.

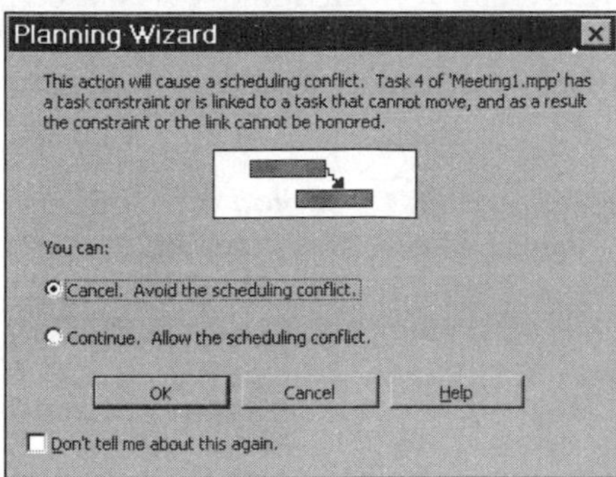


**Figure 9-7:** The Planning Wizard also warns you if you try to record an actual start date that will cause a scheduling conflict.

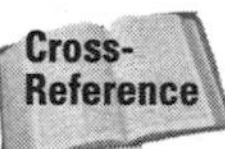


You learn more about entering actual dates in Chapter 12.

Notice that you can turn off the Planning Wizard warnings by placing a check in the Don't Tell Me About This Again checkbox at the bottom of the Planning Wizard dialog box. (Some people just don't like to have Wizards popping up all the time.)

If you turn off the Planning Wizard, Project still warns you if you take actions that cause scheduling problems. Instead of the Planning Wizard, Project displays the more traditional message in Figure 9-8.

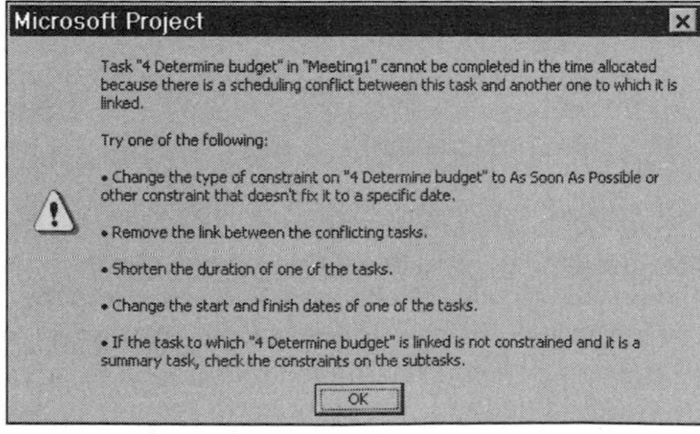


**Figure 9-8:** When you disable the Planning Wizard and take an action that might cause a scheduling problem, Project displays this warning message.

The message in Figure 9-8 refers to the Invitation List task, which is the predecessor task of the Theme task in Figure 9-2. Project makes suggestions concerning actions you can take to avoid the conflict — and the suggestions all refer to the predecessor task. Notice also that, unlike the Planning Wizard, this message box does *not* give you the option of canceling your action.

So, although you may find the Planning Wizard annoying at some levels, it can actually save you effort at other levels. Sorry you turned it off? To turn it on again, choose Tools ➪ Options and click the General tab (see Figure 9-9).

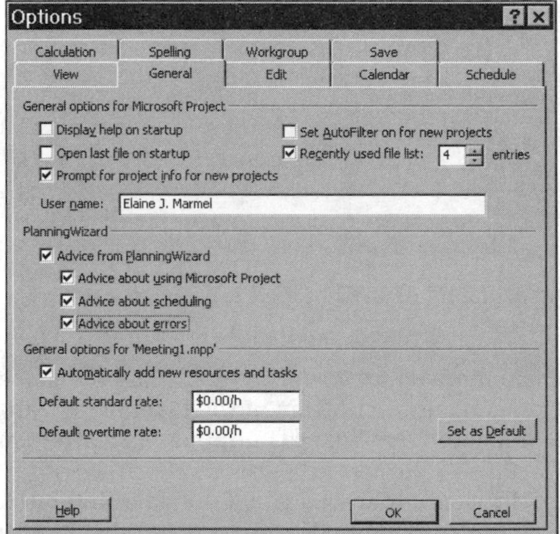


**Figure 9-9:** You can control whether the Planning Wizard appears from the General tab in the Options dialog box.

Place a check in the Advice from Planning Wizard checkbox, and then click the Advice about errors checkbox to place a check in it. (You also can control the other types of advice you receive in the same location.)

# Adjusting dependencies

By changing task dependencies, you can tighten up the schedule and eliminate scheduling conflicts. If you inadvertently link tasks that don't need to be linked, you could create a situation in which you don't have the resources to complete the tasks and the project schedule falls behind. If you discover unnecessary links, you can remove them. When you remove the dependencies, you may find holes in the project schedule where work could be performed but isn't. After you remove unnecessary dependencies, you may be able to move tasks around and fill those holes.

Reviewing dependencies is easiest if you use the Relationship Diagram view in the bottom pane of the Gantt view (see Figure 9-10). The Relationship Diagram view shows you the selected task and its immediate predecessor and successor.

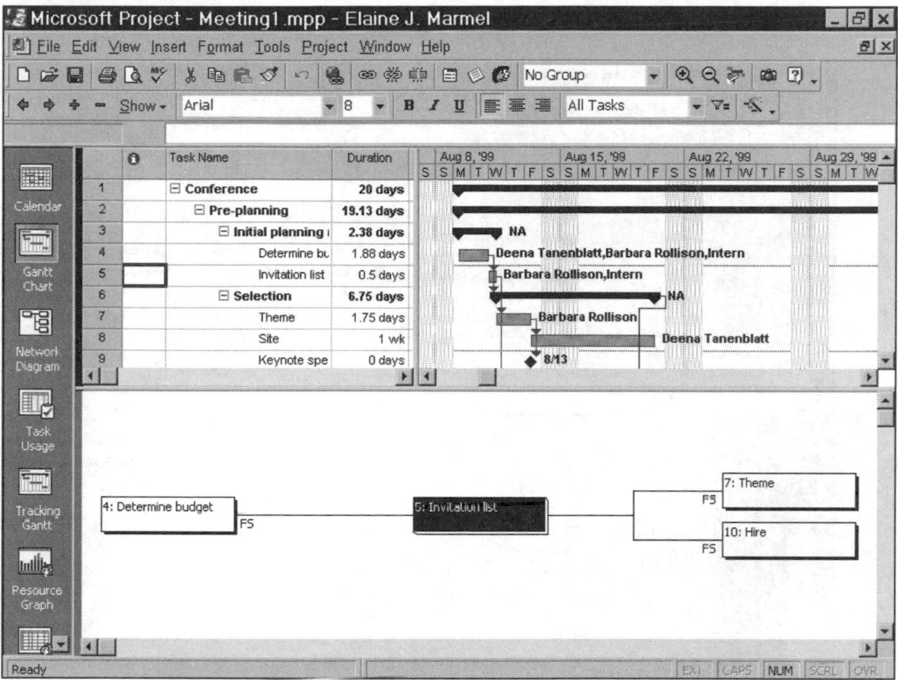


**Figure 9-10:** Use the Relationship Diagram view to review task dependencies.

As you review the tasks, ask yourself these questions: Do I really need to complete *A* before *B* begins? Could I perform them concurrently? Could I do one of them later without harming the project?

# Splitting a task

Splitting a task can sometimes be the best way to resolve a scheduling conflict. You may not be able to complete the task on consecutive days, but you can start the task, stop work on it for a period of time, and then come back to the task. Project enables you to split a task any time you determine you need to make this type of adjustment. Remember that splitting a task creates a gap, which you'll see in the task's Gantt bar. Follow these steps to split a task:

1. Switch to the Gantt Chart view using the View bar.

2. Click the Split Task button on the Standard toolbar. The button appears to be pressed, the mouse pointer changes shape, and a screen tip tells you how to split a task (see Figure 9-11).

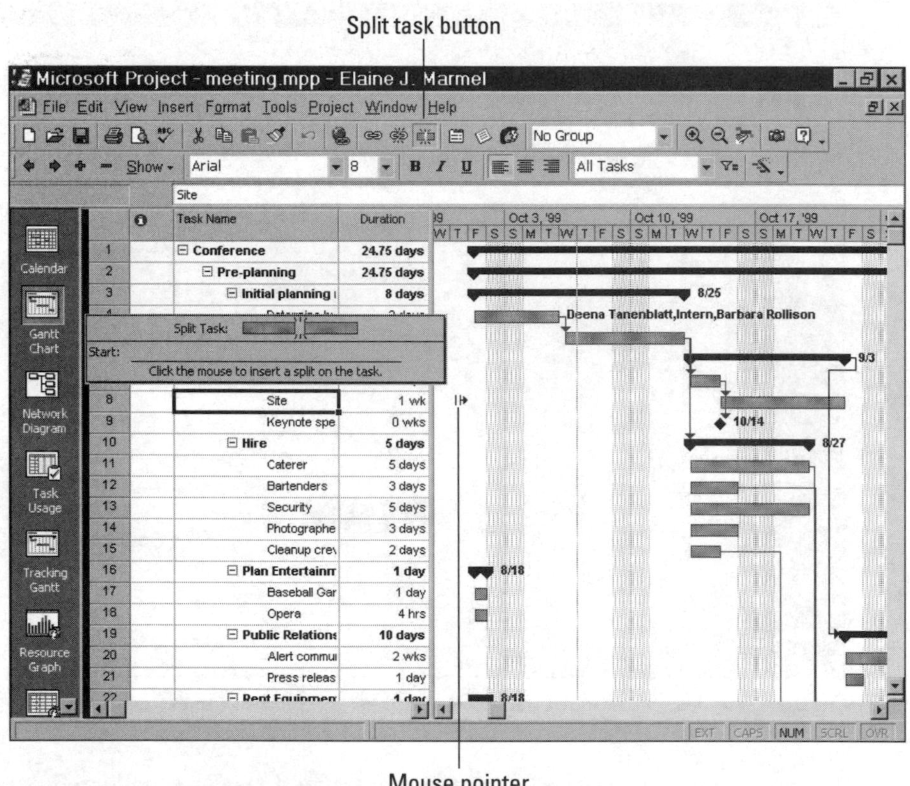


**Figure 9-11:** Use the Split Task button to divide a task.

3. Move the mouse pointer along the bar of the task you want to split. As the mouse pointer moves, dates representing the split date appear in the screen tip.

4. Click when the screen tip shows the date you want to split the task; Project inserts a one-day split.

**If you want the split to last longer than one day, drag to the right instead of clicking.**

After you split a task, it looks like Task 8 in Figure 9-12, with dotted lines appearing between the two portions of the split. If you decide that you want to remove a split, drag the inside portions of the split together so that they touch.

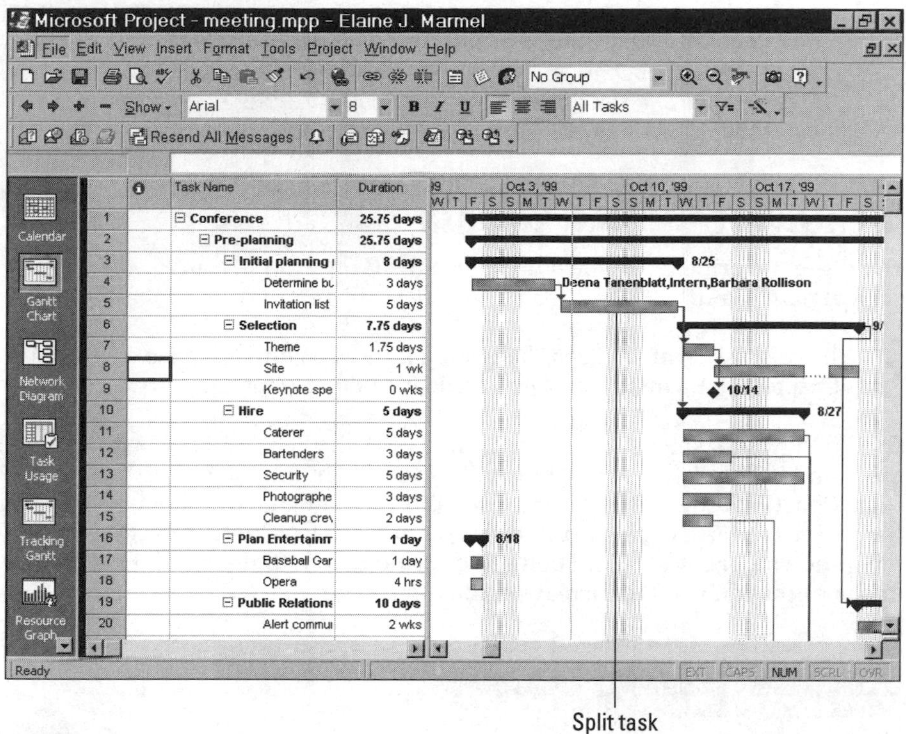


**Figure 9-12:** This Gantt chart shows a split task.

# Using the Critical Path to Shorten a Project

Earlier in this chapter, you examined ways to resolve the scheduling conflicts that develop for one reason or another. But what about being a hero and simply shortening the time frame you originally allotted for the entire project? How would you accomplish that goal? You'd evaluate — and try to shorten — the critical path.

The *critical path* shows the tasks in your project that must be completed on schedule for the entire project to finish on schedule — and these tasks are called *critical tasks.* Most tasks in a project have some slack, and you can delay them some without affecting the project finish date. However, if you delay critical tasks, you affect the project finish date. As you use the techniques described earlier in this chapter to modify tasks to resolve scheduling problems, be aware that changes to critical tasks affect your project finish date.

Noncritical tasks can become critical if they slip too much. You can control how much slack Project allows for a task before defining the task as a critical task. Choose Tools ⇨ Options and then click the Calculation tab. In the box labeled "Tasks are critical if slack is less than or equal to," at the bottom of the tab, enter the number of slack days.

## Identifying the critical path

You'll see the critical path best if you use the GanttChartWizard to display the critical path in red.

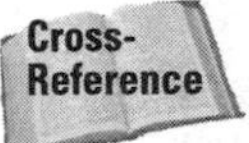

This discussion of the GanttChartWizard focuses on displaying the critical path; see Chapter 8 for a more complete description of that wizard.

On the View bar, select Gantt Chart. Then click the GanttChartWizard button on the Standard toolbar (second button from the right edge) or choose Format ⇨ GanttChartWizard. The first GanttChartWizard dialog box welcomes you to the GanttChartWizard. Click Next to move on to the GanttChartWizard Step 2 dialog box (shown in Figure 9-13). Then select Critical path to describe the kind of information you want to display on the Gantt chart.

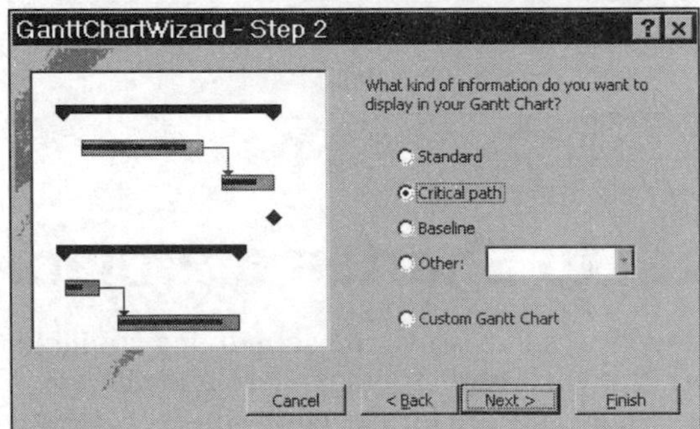


**Figure 9-13:** Select Critical path when you run the GanttChartWizard.

Subsequent dialog boxes in the GanttChartWizard enable you to select other types of information to display, such as resources and dates on Gantt bars and links between dependent tasks. All other choices you make while running the GanttChartWizard are a matter of personal preference, so click Finish and then Format It.

When you view the Gantt chart, all tasks in the project still appear, but tasks on the critical path appear in red.

After you use the GanttChartWizard, you can switch to any view, and critical tasks appear in red. Try the Network Diagram view, for example; the critical tasks appear in red boxes.

You can also use formatting to identify critical tasks. When you apply formatting to critical and noncritical tasks, this formatting appears on all views in which you can see taskbars. The formatting identifies critical tasks with a "Yes" in or near the bar of the tasks and noncritical tasks with a "No."

To apply formatting, follow these steps:

1. Display the Gantt Chart view.
2. Choose Format ➪ Bar Styles. Project displays the Bar Styles dialog box.
3. Select Task from the list at the top of the Bar Styles dialog box to apply formatting to noncritical tasks.
4. Click the Text tab at the bottom of the dialog box.
5. Select a position for the formatting: Left, Right, Top, Bottom, or Inside. When you click a position, a list box arrow appears.
6. Click the list box arrow and scroll to select Critical (see Figure 9-14).

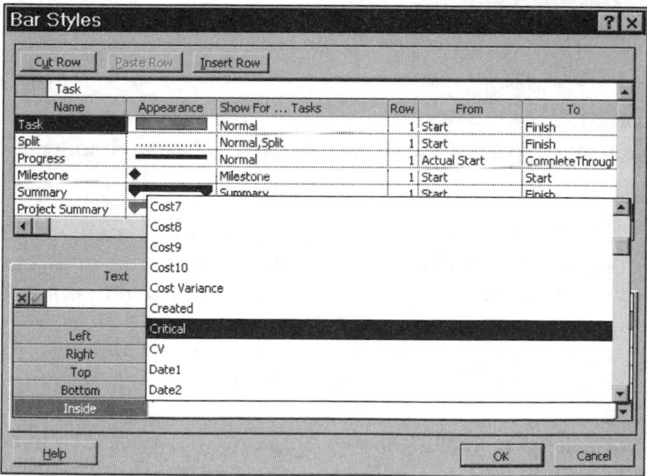


**Figure 9-14:** Use the Text tab of the Bar Styles dialog box to apply formatting that distinguishes critical from noncritical tasks.

7. Click OK.

After you apply the formatting, the Gantt chart shows critical and noncritical tasks and should resemble the Gantt chart in Figure 9-15. "No" appears inside noncritical tasks, while "Yes" appears inside critical tasks.

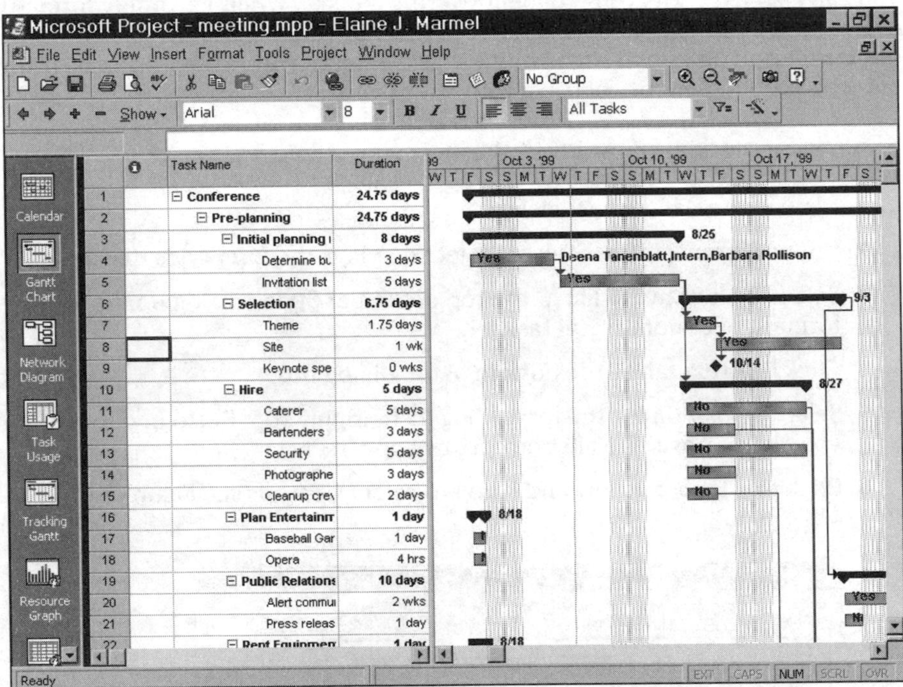


**Figure 9-15:** The formatting in this Gantt chart identifies critical and noncritical tasks.

Even with formatting, this approach to identifying the critical path can be cumbersome if your project contains many tasks. As an alternative, you can identify the critical path by filtering for it. As Chapter 7 explains, you can apply the Critical filter to any task view to display *only* critical tasks (see Figure 9-16). To apply the filter, display the view you want to filter and choose Project ➪ Filtered for ➪ Critical or choose Critical from the Filter list box on the Formatting toolbar.

Filtering is a very effective tool to display only certain aspects of the project, but sometimes you need to view all the tasks in your project and still identify the critical ones. If you use formatting, you can always identify critical and noncritical tasks, even if you are viewing all the tasks in your project.

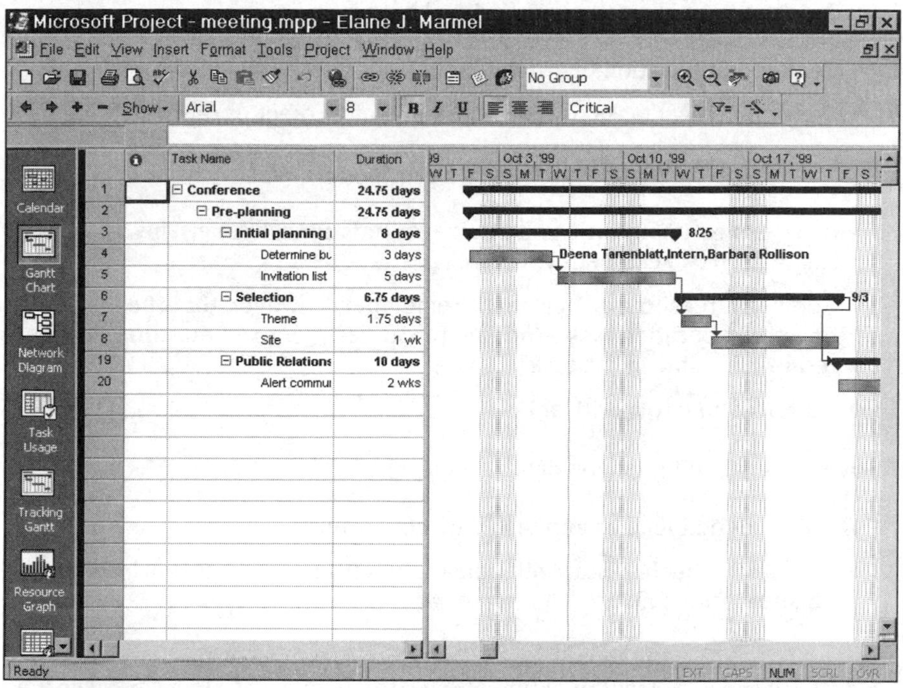

**Figure 9-16:** Filter to display only critical tasks.

# Shortening the critical path

Shortening the time allotted on the critical path shortens your project's duration. The converse is also true; lengthening the time allotted on the critical path lengthens the project. In all probability, you, as project manager, are also responsible, at least to some extent, for the cost of a project — and typically, the longer a project goes on, the more it costs. Therefore, shortening the critical path is often the project manager's goal.

Shortening a project's duration can result in an earlier finish. But it also can mean starting later. Obviously, the second alternative is riskier, particularly if you are not confident in your estimates. If you are new to project management, you probably should not plan to start later; instead, use project management tools to help you evaluate the accuracy of your estimating skills. Over time (and multiple projects), you'll know how accurate your estimates are and then can take the risk of starting a project later than initially planned.

To reduce the time allotted on the critical path, you can:

- ✦ Reduce the duration of critical tasks.
- ✦ Overlap critical tasks to reduce the overall project duration.

To reduce the duration of critical tasks, you can:

- ✦ Reassess estimates and use a more optimistic task time. The Network Diagram Analysis views can help you here.
- ✦ Add resources to a critical task. Remember, however, that the task must not be a fixed-duration task—adding resources to a fixed-duration task does not reduce the time of the task.
- ✦ Add overtime to a critical task.

To overlap critical tasks, you can:

- ✦ Adjust dependencies and task date constraints.
- ✦ Redefine a finish-to-start relationship to either a start-to-start or a finish-to-finish relationship.

Now that you know the techniques you can apply to adjust the critical path, you need to ask the important question: What's the best way to identify tasks you want to change and then make changes? The answer: Select a view and filter it for critical tasks only. The Task Entry view is the best view to use because the top pane displays a graphic representation of your project and the bottom pane displays most of the fields you might want to change (see Figure 9-17).

To add the Task Entry view to the Gantt Chart view, follow these steps:

1. Select the Gantt Chart view.
2. Choose Window ➪ Split and click the bottom pane to select it.
3. Right-click the View bar and choose More Views from the shortcut menu.
4. Select Task Entry from the More Views dialog box and click the Apply button.

To filter for critical tasks, choose Project ➪ Filtered for ➪ Critical. Evaluate each critical task and make changes in the Task Entry form at the bottom of the screen.

You also can sort your critical tasks by duration. That way, the critical tasks are in order from the longest to the shortest, and you can focus on trying to shorten longer tasks.

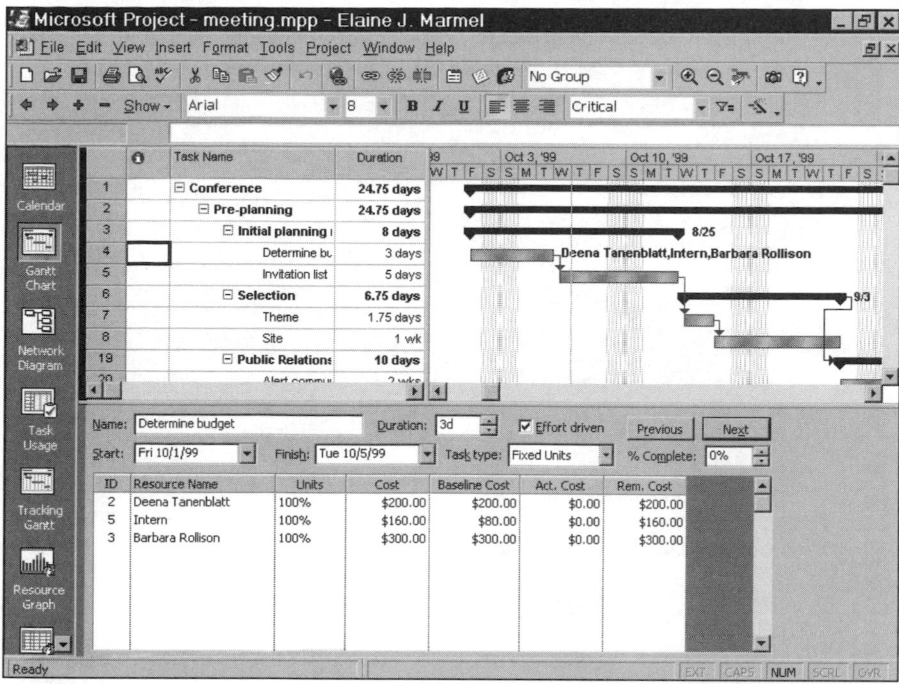


**Figure 9-17:** The Task Entry view, filtered for critical tasks, is probably the easiest view in which to work.

# Summary

This chapter described the following techniques that you can use to resolve scheduling conflicts and shorten the length of your project:

- ✦ Adding resources to tasks
- ✦ Using overtime
- ✦ Adjusting slack
- ✦ Changing task constraints and dependencies

In Chapter 10 you learn how to resolve conflicts that occur with resources.

✦ ✦ ✦

# Resolving Resource Problems

✦ ✦ ✦ ✦

**In This Chapter**

Understanding how resource conflicts occur

Spotting resource conflicts

Resolving conflicts

✦ ✦ ✦ ✦

*Resource allocation* is the process of assigning resources to tasks in a project. Because the potential for resource overallocation always accompanies resource assignment, this chapter explores the causes of resource overallocation and suggests methods to resolve the conflicts.

## Understanding How Resource Conflicts Occur

As you assign resources to tasks, Project checks the resource's calendar to make sure that the resource is working. Note, however, that Project doesn't assess whether the resource is already obligated when you assign the resource to a new task; Project enables you to make the assignment. However, the additional assignment could lead to overallocating the resource. Overallocation occurs when you assign more work to a resource than the resource can accomplish in the time that you've allotted for the work.

For example, if you assign Mary full-time to two tasks that start on the same day, you actually assign Mary to 16 hours of work in an 8-hour day — not possible unless Mary is a *really* dedicated employee who has no life outside work. On the other hand, if you have a group of three mechanics and you assign two mechanics to work on two tasks that start on the same day, you still have one spare mechanic and no overallocation.

Figure 10-1 shows a series of tasks that begin on the same day. By assigning the same resource to all of them, an overallocation is inevitable. And, overallocations can cause lays in the project schedule.

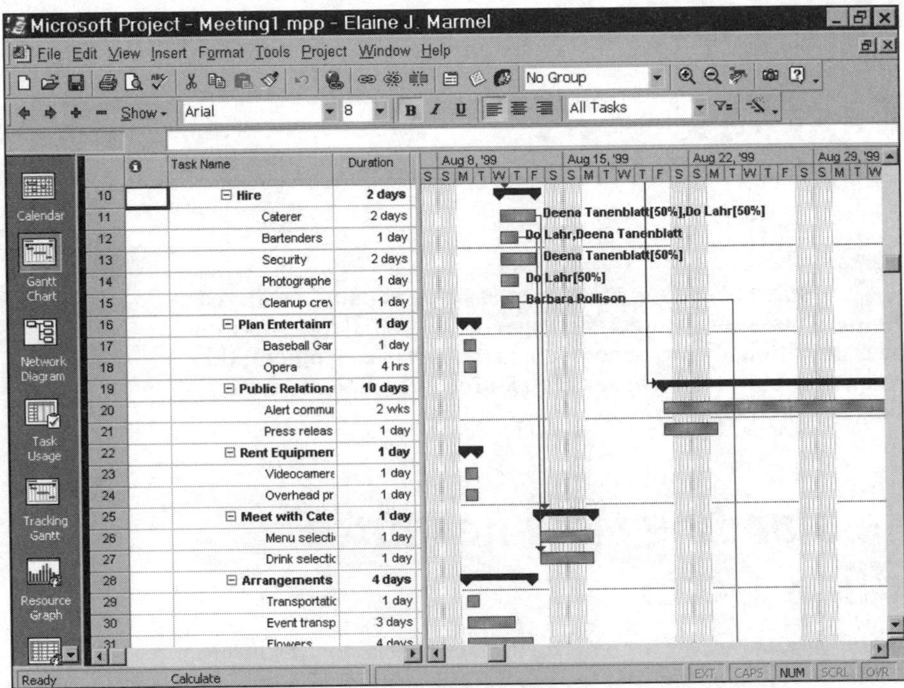


**Figure 10-1:** Assigning the same resource to tasks that run simultaneously causes an overallocation.

To calculate the scheduled start date for a task, Project checks factors such as the task's dependencies and constraints. Then Project checks the resource's calendar to identify the next regular workday and assigns that date as the start date for the task. If you haven't assigned resources to the task, Project uses the project's calendar to calculate the next regular workday. But when it calculates the task start date, Project does not consider other commitments the resource might have.

# Spotting Resource Conflicts

Before you can resolve resource conflicts, you need to spot them. You can use views or filters to help you identify resource overallocation problems.

## Using views to spot resource conflicts

Use a resource view, such as the Resource Sheet view or the Resource Usage view, to find resource conflicts. On these views, overallocated resources appear in red. In addition, a Caution icon appears in the Indicator column to signal an overassigned resource. You can see a message about the overallocation if you point at the icon with the mouse. To display the Resource Usage view shown in Figure 10-2, select Resource age from the View bar.

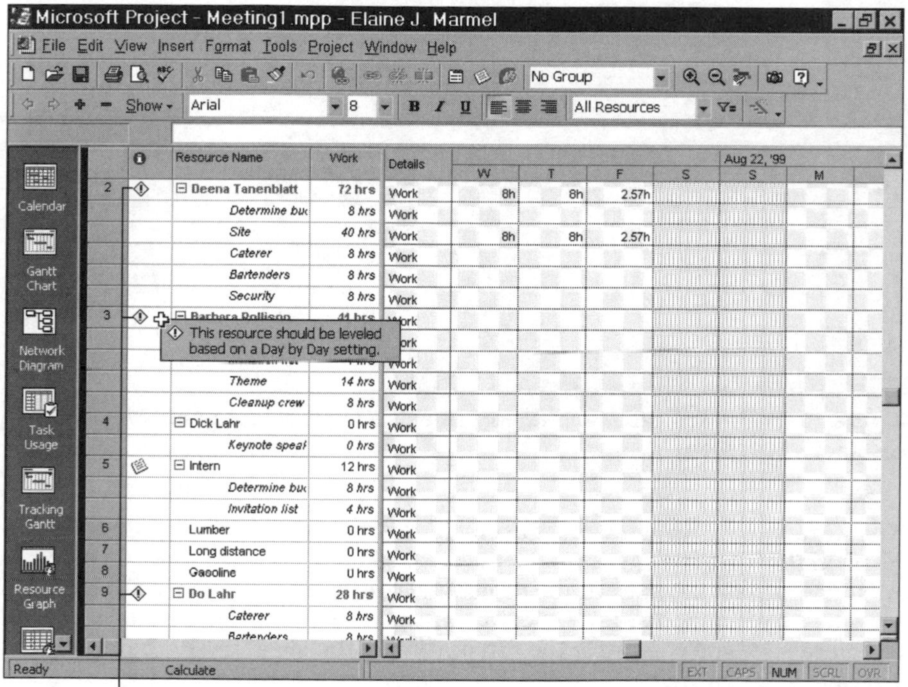

Overallocated resources

**Figure 10-2:** The Resource Usage view displays overallocated resources in red, and an icon appears in the Indicator column.

You also can see a graphic representation of a resource's allocation by switching to the Resource Graph view. To display the view shown in Figure 10-3, select Resource Graph from the View bar.

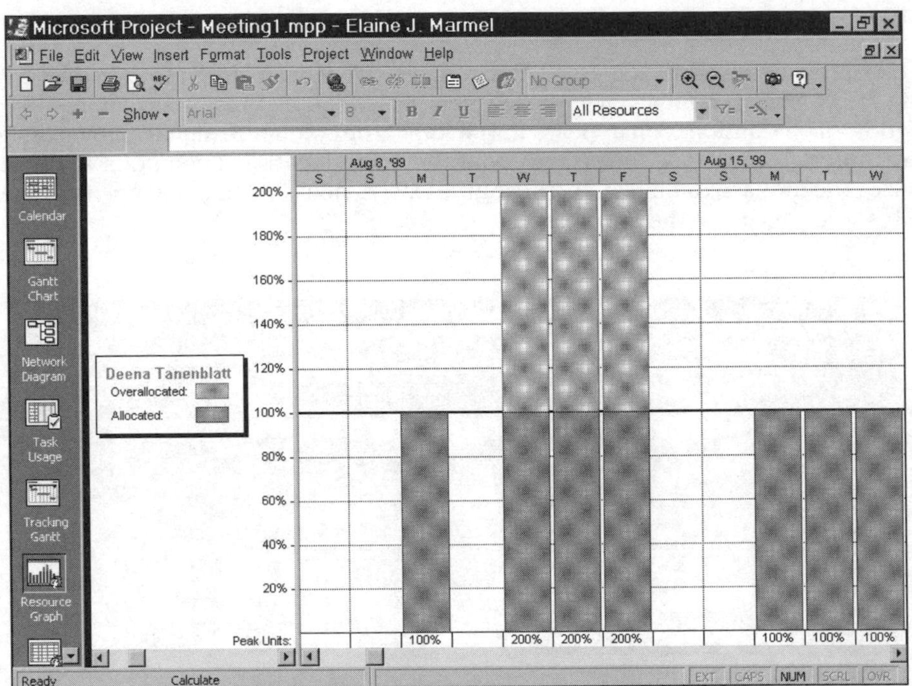


**Figure 10-3:** The Resource Graph view presents a pictorial representation of a resource's allocation.

The Resource Allocation view is useful for working with overallocations — a Gantt chart in the lower pane shows the tasks assigned to the resource you select in the top pane. Tasks that start at the same time overlap in the Gantt chart pane; this view helps you pinpoint the tasks that are causing the resource's overallocation. In Figure 10-4, you can see in the top portion of the view that Barbara Rollison is overallocated on Wednesday and Thursday, August 11 and 12. If you examine Thursday, August 12 more closely, you'll notice that Barbara is scheduled to work 11 hours that day. In the bottom portion of the view, the two tasks to which she's assigned 100 percent of the time are Theme and Cleanup crew — and the Gantt view makes it easy to see the overlap of the two tasks on that Thursday.

To switch to the Resource Allocation view, click the first button on the Resource Management toolbar, which contains several tools to help you adjust resource allocations. You can display the Resource Management toolbar by choosing View ➪ Toolbars. From the list that appears, select Resource Management.

To find the next resource conflict, click the Go To Next Overallocation button on the Resource Management toolbar. It's the third button from the left edge of the toolbar.

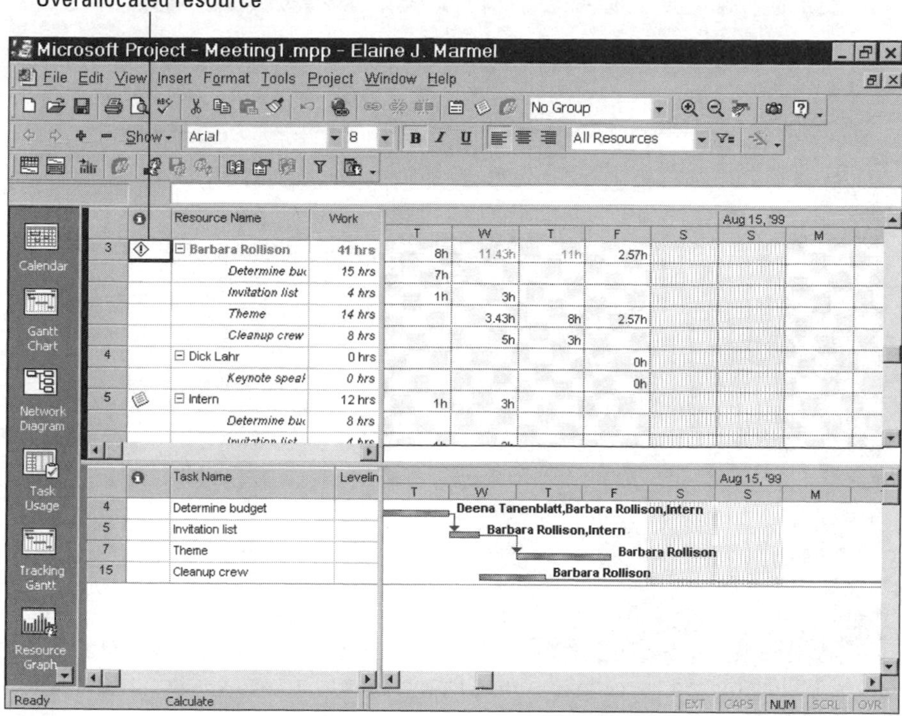


**Figure 10-4:** The Resource Allocation view uses the Gantt chart format to show the tasks assigned to the resource selected in the top pane.

## Using filters to spot resource conflicts

Filtering is another simple technique you can use to help you work on resource conflict problems. If you filter the Resource Usage view (shown in Figure 10-5) to display only overallocated resources, the problems become even more apparent. To filter the view, switch to it first by right-clicking the View bar and choosing Resource Usage. Then open the Filter list box on the Formatting toolbar and choose Overallocated Resources or choose Project ➪ Filtered ➪ Overallocated Resources.

Next add the Overallocation field to the view to identify the extent of the resource's overallocation. Choose Format ➪ Details ➪ Overallocation. As Figure 10-6 shows, Project adds a row to the timescale portion of the view to show you the number of hours you need to eliminate to correct the overallocation.

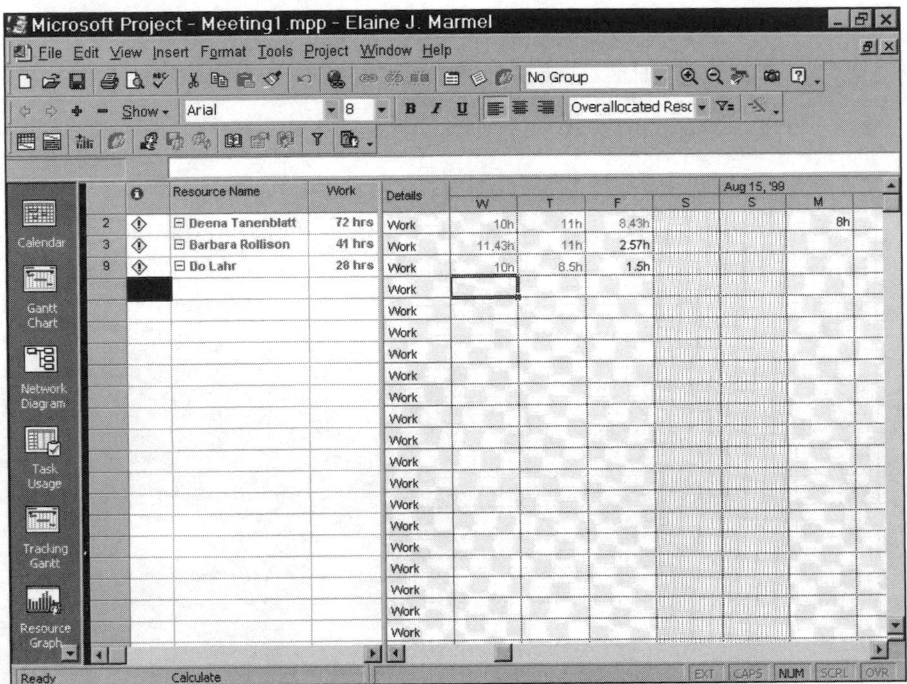


**Figure 10-5:** You can filter the Resource Usage view to show overallocated resources only.

# Resolving Conflicts

Now that you've found the overallocations, you need to resolve the conflicts. Project managers use several methods to resolve conflicts.

## Changing resource allocations

If you play around with resource allocations, you can resolve a resource conflict. Adding a resource is one obvious way to resolve an overallocation. Suppose Task 3 is an effort-driven task that has a resource conflict with Task 4; the two tasks don't run concurrently, but Task 3 is continuing when Task 4 is supposed to start. Further suppose that you need the same resource, Deena Tanenblatt, to work on both tasks. Adding a resource (Do Lahr) to Task 3 reduces the amount of time it takes to finish Task 3, which could eliminate Deena's conflict between Tasks 3 and 4.

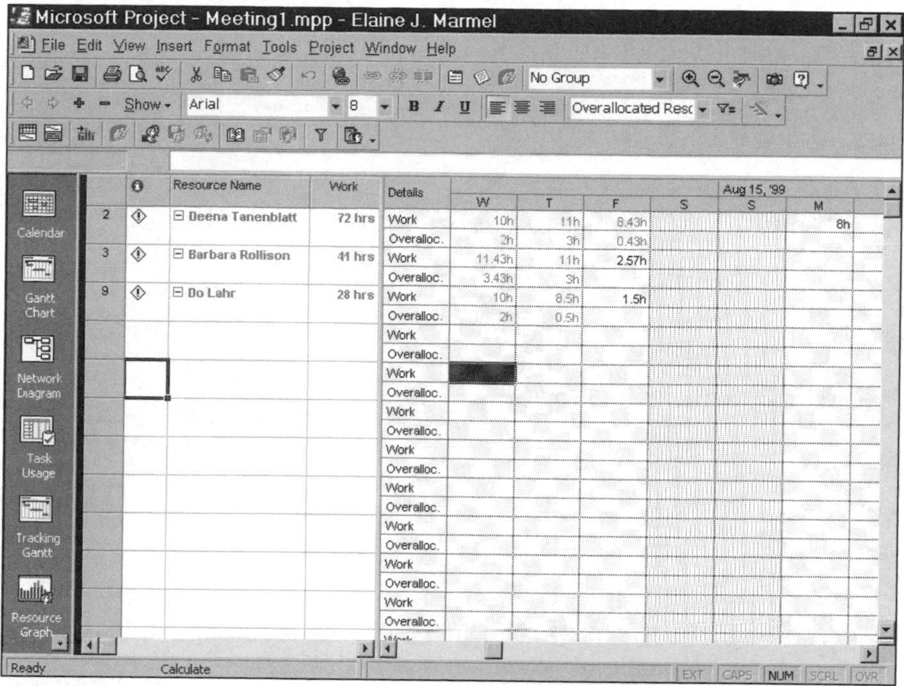


**Figure 10-6:** Add the Overallocation field to the Resource Usage view.

You can add a resource using the techniques described in Chapter 5, or you can add a resource to a task using the Resource Usage view (described later in this chapter).

## Switching resources

You also can resolve resource conflicts by switching resources. You can use this technique when one resource is overallocated, but you have another resource capable of doing the job. You switch resources by adding one and deleting the other from the task in question. When you want to switch resources, work in the Resource Usage view (shown in Figure 10-7) where you can focus on resource conflicts.

First, examine the resource with the conflict and find the task from which you want to remove that resource in the upper pane. Then, click anywhere in the row of the task and press the Del key on your keyboard. Project removes the task from the assigned resource — and, with luck, indicates that the resource no longer has a conflict.

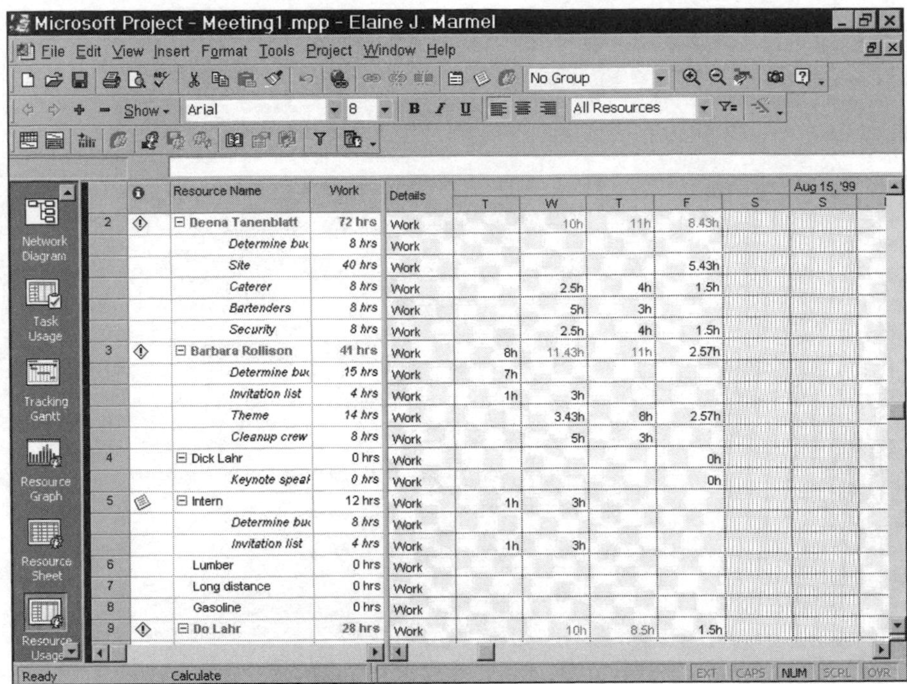

**Figure 10-7:** Use the Resource Usage view to switch resources.

## Adding a task to a resource

To add a task to a resource from the Resource Usage view, follow these steps:

1. Scroll down until you find the resource to which you want to add a task.
2. Click the row of any task to which you have already assigned the resource.
3. Press the Ins key on your keyboard. Project inserts a blank line.
4. Fill in the task name, and Project fills in the default duration for the task.

## Adding or deleting a resource

You can add or delete a resource using a number of techniques. For example, you can work in the Gantt Chart view and then use the split bar to display the Task Entry view. Select a task in the Gantt Chart view and then:

- ✦ **To add a resource.** Select the resource from the list box that appears when you click the Resource Name column of the Task Entry view.
- ✦ **To delete a resource.** Select the resource's ID number in the Task Entry view and press the delete key.
- ✦ **To switch resources.** Use the Replace Resource dialog box (see Chapter 5).

Working in the Gantt Chart view is effective, but the Resource Usage view helps you focus on resource conflicts.

## Scheduling overtime

You also can resolve a resource conflict by scheduling overtime for the resource. Overtime in Project is the amount of work scheduled beyond an assigned resource's regular working hours, and overtime hours are charged at the resource's overtime rate. Overtime work does not represent additional work on a task; instead, it represents the amount of time spent on a task during nonregular hours. By scheduling overtime, the resource may finish the task faster and therefore eliminate the conflict. As you learned in the last chapter, you assign overtime from the Gantt Chart view:

1. Select the Gantt Chart view from the View bar.
2. Choose Window ➪ Split to reveal the Task Form in the bottom pane.
3. Click the Task Form to make it the active pane.
4. Choose Format ➪ Details ➪ Resource Work. Project adds the Ovt. Work column to the Task form. You can see the Ovt. Work column in Figure 10-8. *0h* means that you have not yet assigned overtime.

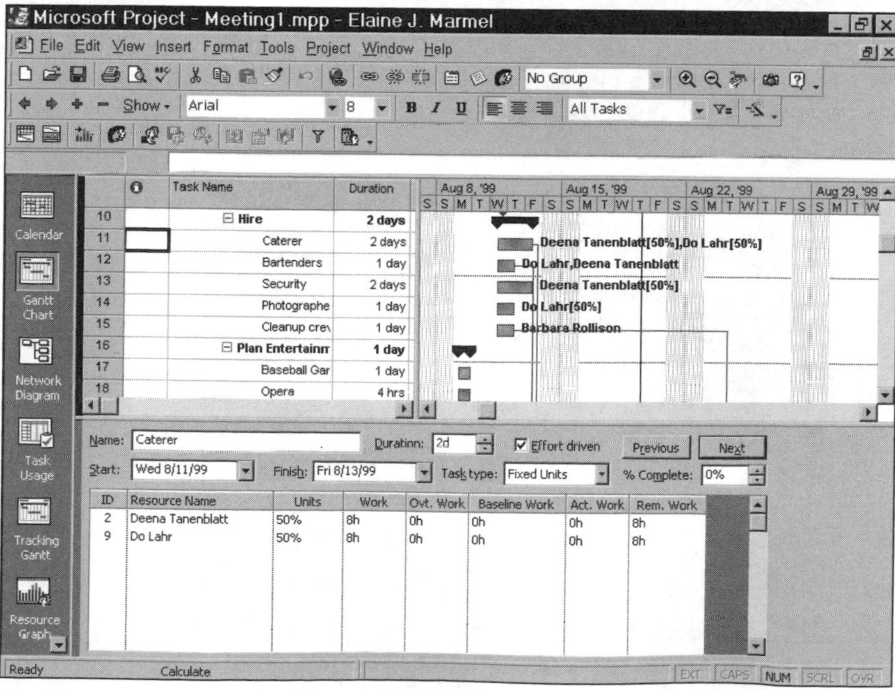


**Figure 10-8:** Use the Task Form and display the Overtime column to add overtime.

5. Select the task in the top pane to which you want to assign overtime.
6. Go to the bottom pane and fill in the overtime amount for the appropriate resource.

When you finish entering overtime, you can hide the Task form by choosing Window ➪ Remove Split.

## Redefining a resource's calendar

If your resource is a salaried resource, you may have the option of redefining a resource's calendar so that hours typically considered nonworking (and therefore charged at an overtime rate if worked) become working hours. If a resource has a conflict and the number of hours in conflict on a given day is low enough, you can eliminate the conflict by increasing the working hours for the resource for that day.

You can make this kind of change to any resource—Project won't stop you. But you need to consider the effects on the cost of your project. If you are paying a resource at an overtime rate for working during nonworking hours, then you don't want to change nonworking hours to working hours in Project. If you do, you will understate the cost of your project.

To change a resource's working calendar, you can start in the Resource Usage view. Identify the resource that has a conflict, and note the number of hours the conflict involves. Double-click the resource that has a conflict to open the Resource Information dialog box for that resource. Click the Working Time tab to view that resource's calendar (see Figure 10-9).

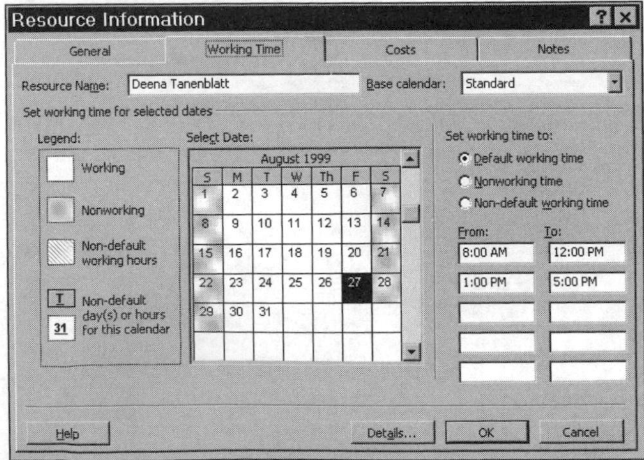


**Figure 10-9:** Use the Working Time tab of the Resource Information dialog box to change the standard working hours for the resource.

To change the standard working hours for a resource, follow these steps:

1. Click the first date on which the resource is overallocated.
2. Click the Default Working Time option button.
3. Use the From and To boxes to set up nonstandard working hours for that day.
4. Repeat this process for each day for which you want to change the work schedule for a particular resource.
5. Click OK when you finish.

## Assigning part-time work

Suppose a resource is assigned to several concurrent tasks and is also overallocated. And further suppose that you don't want to add other resources, switch to a different resource, or add overtime. You could assign the resource to work part-time on each of the tasks to solve the conflict, although the tasks may take longer to complete using this method. Or you may want to use this method in conjunction with additional resources to make sure that you can complete the task on time.

To assign a resource to work part-time, you can change the number of units of the resource that you apply to the task. By default, Project sets task types to Fixed Units; therefore, if you change the amount a resource works on a task, Project changes the duration of the task accordingly.

Note

If you want to retain the duration and assign a resource to work part-time on a task, you should change the task type to Fixed Duration. By making this change, however, you are indicating that the task can be completed by the resource in the allotted amount of time—effectively, you are shortening the amount of time it takes to complete the task because you're applying less effort during the same time frame.

To change the task type to Fixed Duration, follow these steps:

1. Display the Resource Allocation view.
2. Click the task you want to change in the upper pane. Project displays that task in Gantt format in the lower pane.
3. Double-click the task you want to change in the lower pane. Project displays the Task Information dialog box. Click the Advanced tab (see Figure 10-10).
4. Open the Task type list box and select Fixed Duration.
5. Click OK.

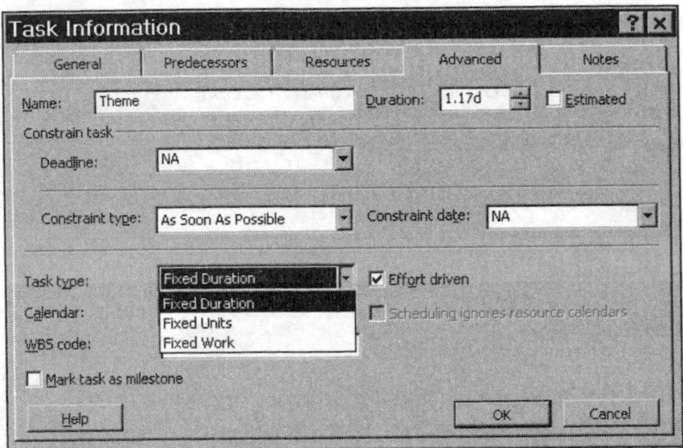


**Figure 10-10:** Use the Advanced tab of the Task Information dialog box to change the task type.

Now you can assign resources to work part-time on this task without changing the task's duration. Follow these steps:

1. In the Resource Allocation view, click a task in the top pane to which the overallocated resource is assigned.
2. Click the Assignment Information button on the Standard toolbar or double-click the task to open the Assignment Information dialog box. You see the General tab in Figure 10-11.

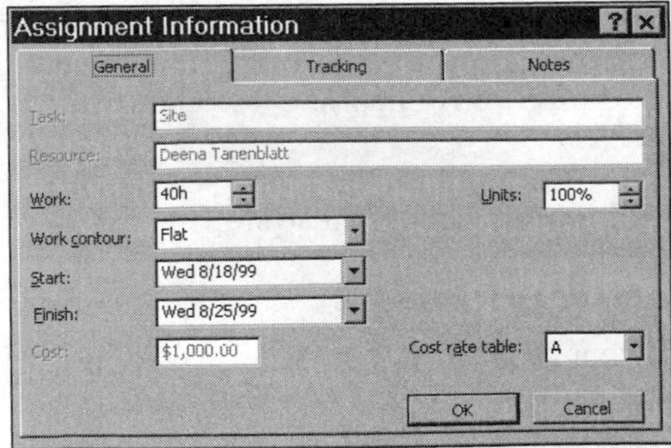


**Figure 10-11:** Use the Assignment Information dialog box to change a resource's workload to part-time.

3. Change the value in the Units box to reflect the percentage of time you want the resource to spend on the task — in this case, the value should be lower than 100%.
4. Click OK.

## Controlling when resources start working on a task

In cases in which you've assigned more than one resource to a task, consider staggering the times the resources start working on the task to resolve resource conflicts. When you delay a resource's start on a task, Project recalculates the start date and time for that resource's work on the task. To stagger start times for resources, work in the Task Usage view and follow these steps:

This technique can extend the duration of the task, which may not be a viable option for you.

1. Click Task Usage on the View bar.
2. Select the resource, whose working time you want to delay, in the Task Name column.
3. Click the Assignment Information button or double-click the resource. Project displays the General tab of the Assignment Information dialog box (see Figure 10-12).

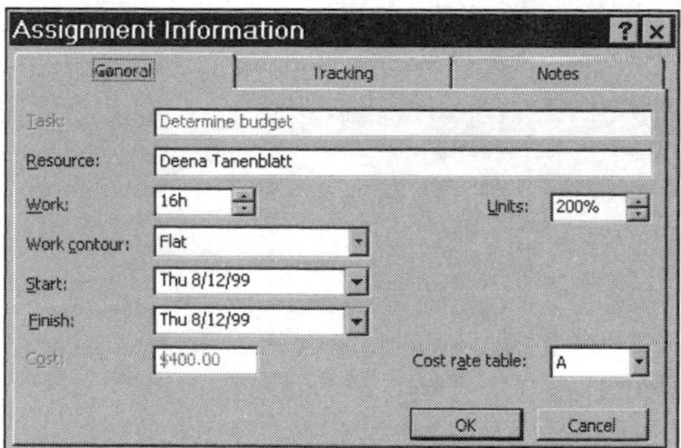


**Figure 10-12:** Use the General tab of the Assignment Information dialog box to delay a resource's start or finish date on a task.

4. Change the dates in the Start or Finish boxes.
5. Click OK.

## Delaying tasks by leveling resource workloads

If you have scheduled several tasks to run concurrently and you now find resource conflicts in your project, you can delay some of these tasks to level or spread out the demands you're making on your resources. You can ask Project to select the tasks to delay or split using its leveling feature, or you can control the process manually by examining the project to identify tasks that you are willing to delay or split. *Leveling* is the process of resolving resource conflicts by delaying or splitting tasks.

## Automatic leveling

When Project does the leveling for you, it redistributes a resource's assignments and reschedules them according to the resource's working capacity, assignment units, and calendar. Project also considers the task's duration and constraints.

Priorities in Project 2000 are no longer 10 words; they are numbers ranging from 1 to 1,000.

In some circumstances, you want Project to level some tasks before it levels others. You can do so by assigning different priority levels to tasks. By default, Project assigns all tasks a priority of 500. The higher the priority level you assign, the longer Project waits before leveling a task. So, before you start to use the automatic-leveling feature, consider how you want to prioritize tasks. To set a priority, follow these steps:

1. Click the Gantt Chart view from the View bar.
2. Double-click the task for which you want to set a priority or click the Task Information button on the Standard toolbar. Project displays the Task Information dialog box.
3. Use the General tab to set a priority (see Figure 10-13).

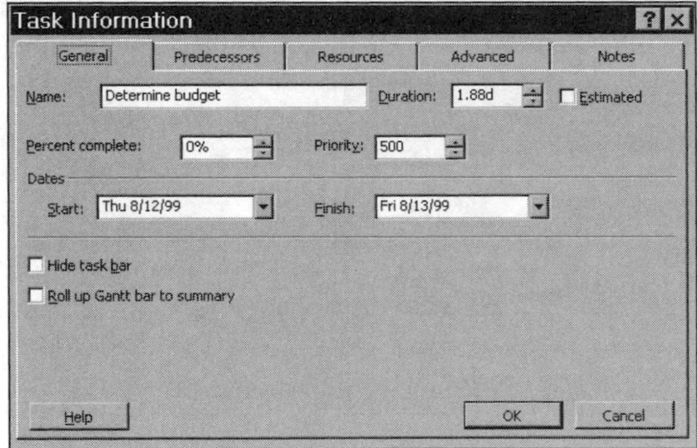


**Figure 10-13:** Set a priority for the task.

After you prioritize tasks but before you level, you can sort tasks by priority to view the tasks that Project is most likely to level.

To level tasks automatically, follow these steps:

1. Choose Tools ➪ Resource Leveling to open the Resource Leveling dialog box, shown in Figure 10-14.
2. Select Automatic to have Project automatically level resources, if necessary, whenever you make a change to your schedule. Select Manual to perform leveling only when you select Level Now from this dialog box.

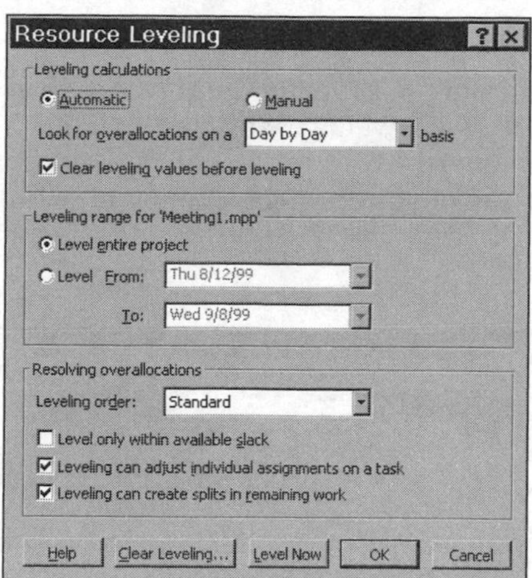


**Figure 10-14:** From the Resource Leveling dialog box, you can set resource leveling options.

3. Use the "Look for overallocations on a . . . basis" list box to select a basis. The basis is a time frame, such as Day by Day or Week by Week. (The Indicator box in the Resource Usage view may contain a note suggesting the appropriate basis.)

The basis you select is the only basis on which Project performs leveling; Project does not change tasks requiring any other basis.

4. Place a check in the "Clear leveling values before leveling" checkbox to make Project 2000 behave like Project 98 when leveling; that is, Project resets all leveling delay values to zero before leveling. If you remove the check from this box, Project 2000 *does not* reset leveling values but builds upon the values. During leveling, the scheduling for previously leveled tasks will probably not change.
5. In the "Leveling range for" area, select either to level the entire project or to level only for specified dates.
6. In the Leveling order drop-down list, select the order you want Project to consider when leveling your project. If you choose ID Only, Project delays or splits the task with the highest ID number. If you choose Standard, Project looks at predecessor dependencies, slack, dates, and priorities when selecting the best task to split or delay. If you choose "Priority, Standard," Project looks first at task priority and then at all the items listed for the Standard leveling order.
7. Place a check next to any of the following options:
   - "Level only within available slack" to avoid changing the end date of your project
   - "Leveling can adjust individual assignments on a task" to have leveling adjust one resource's work schedule on a task independent of other resources working on the same task
   - "Leveling can create splits in remaining work" if you want leveling to split tasks to resolve resource conflicts

8. Click Level Now to apply leveling.

You can review the effects of leveling from the Leveling Gantt Chart view shown in Figure 10-15. Choose Views ➪ More Views ➪ Leveling Gantt and then click Apply. Project adds green bars to your Gantt chart, which represent the duration of tasks before leveling. Depending on the nature of your project, Project may build more slack into your tasks.

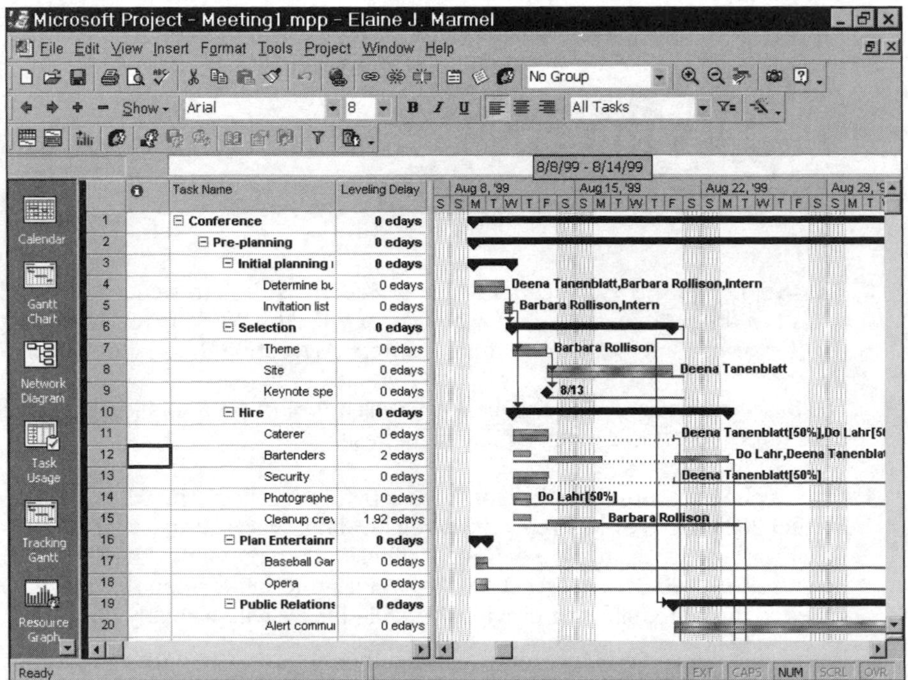

**Figure 10-15:** The Leveling Gantt Chart view shows how leveling affects your project.

To remove the effects of leveling, reopen the Resource Leveling dialog box (choose Tools ➪ Resource Leveling) and click Clear Leveling. A subsequent dialog box enables you to clear leveling for the entire project or for selected tasks only.

**Note** If you are scheduling from a finish date, you still can level to resolve resource conflicts. Project calculates the delay by subtracting it from a task's or assignment's finish date, causing the finish date to occur earlier.

## Manual leveling

Manual leveling is especially handy when automatic leveling doesn't provide acceptable results. Manual leveling is also useful when you have just a few resource conflicts to resolve. To manually level resources in Project, use the Resource Allocation view and follow these steps:

1. Choose View ➪ More Views. From the More Views dialog box, highlight Resource Allocation and click Apply.
2. In the bottom pane, insert the Leveling Delay column to the left of the Duration column. To insert the column, right-click the title of the Duration column and choose Insert Column. The Column Definition dialog box appears; open the Field Name list box and choose Leveling Delay.
3. Highlight the task you want to delay in the top pane.
4. In the bottom pane, enter an amount in the Leveling Delay field. Project delays the task accordingly and reduces the resource's conflict.

Figures 10-16 and 10-17 show before and after pictures for manual leveling of the Theme task. Notice the differences in the two figures between the total scheduled hours on Wednesday (13 hours in Figure 10-16 and 8 hours in Figure 10-17).

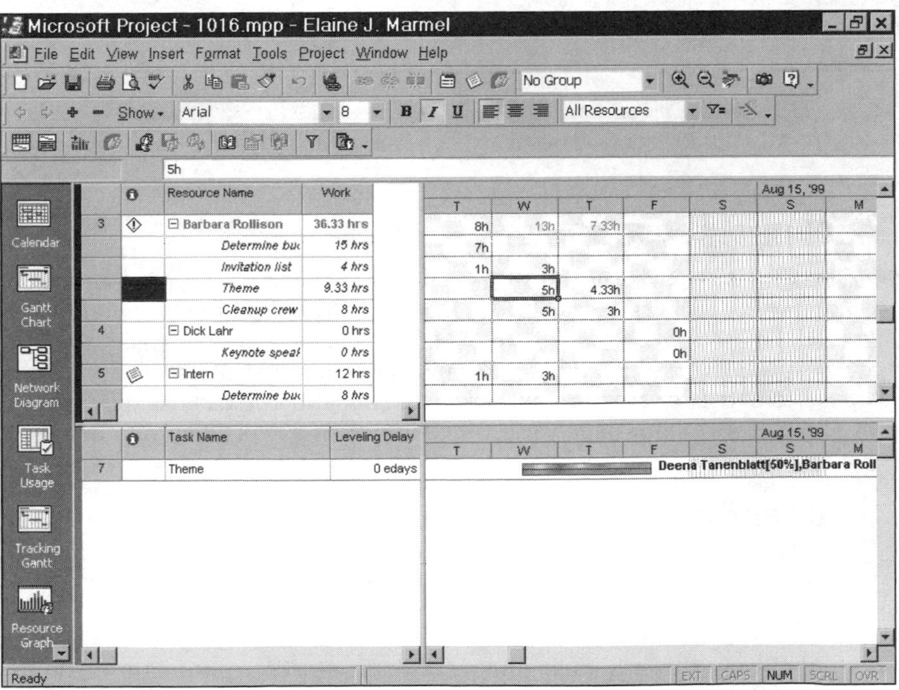


**Figure 10-16:** The Resource Allocation view before manually leveling the Theme task

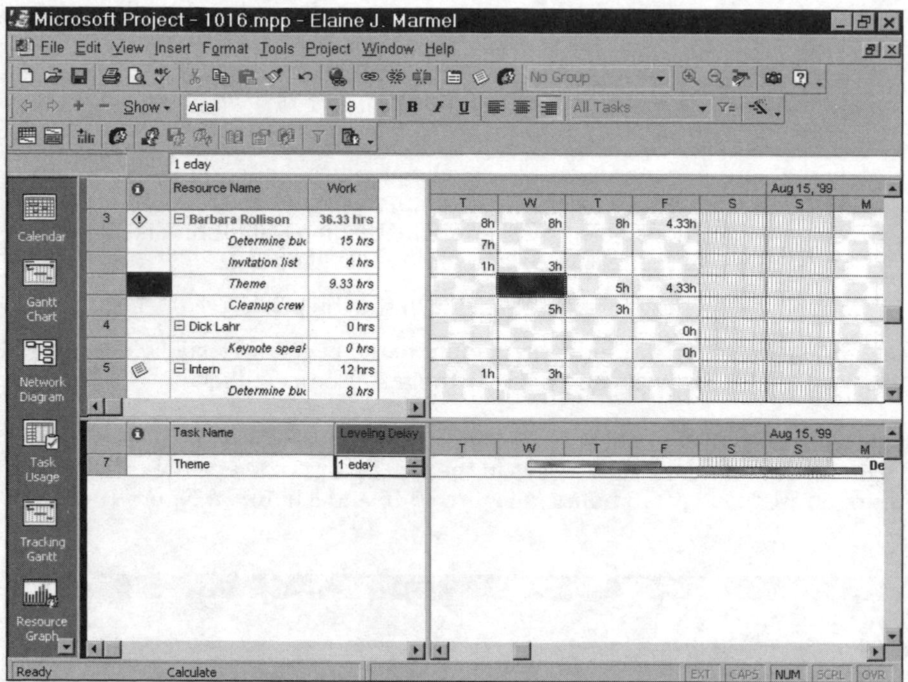

**Figure 10-17:** The Resource Allocation view after manually leveling the Theme task

## Contouring resources

*Contour* is the term Project uses to refer to the shape of a resource's work assignment over time. Contours come in several flavors, the most common being Flat, Back Loaded, Front Loaded, and Bell. The default contour is Flat, which means that a resource works on a task for the maximum number of hours that he or she is assigned to a task for the duration of the assignment. You can use different contours to control how much a resource works on a task at a given time — and possibly resolve a conflict.

Add the Peak Units field to the Resource Usage view to display the maximum effort, as distributed over time, that a resource is expected to work. This field is particularly useful when you have selected a contour other than the default (Flat).

As I just mentioned, Project uses a flat contour by default; this contour assigns a resource to work the maximum number of hours per time period throughout the duration of the task. By changing the contour, you can more accurately reflect the actual work pattern for the resource while working on a task.

When you think of contours, think of dividing each task into 10 equal timeslots. Using the various contours, Project assigns percentages of work to be done in each timeslot. Contours help you assign work to a task based on when the task requires the effort. For example, if a task requires less effort initially, consider using a Back Loaded contour. If a task requires most effort in the middle of the task, consider using a Bell, Turtle, or even an Early Peak contour.

If you start changing contours from the default Flat contour, you could inadvertently create a resource conflict. Therefore, viewing the contours you set can help you resolve resource conflicts.

## Setting a contour pattern

To set a contour pattern, follow these steps:

1. Click the Task Usage view on the View bar. In the sheet portion of the view, Project displays each task in your project with the resources assigned to it listed below the task. The Details portion of the view shows the number of hours per day a resource is assigned to a task.
2. In the Task Name column, double-click the resource for which you want to apply a contour or select the resource and click the Assignment Information button on the Standard toolbar. Then click the General tab of the Assignment Information dialog box (see Figure 10-18).

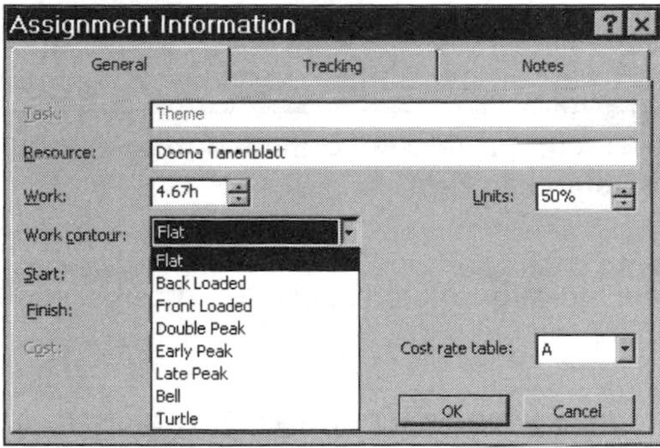


**Figure 10-18:** Use the General tab of the Assignment Information dialog box to select a contour.

3. Open the Work contour list box and select a contour.
4. Click OK.

To change the start and end dates for the resource's work on the task, use the Start and Finish list boxes.

When you select a contour other than Flat, an indicator appears next to the resource in the Indicator column. If you pass the mouse pointer over the indicator, Project identifies the contour applied to the resource (see Figure 10-19).

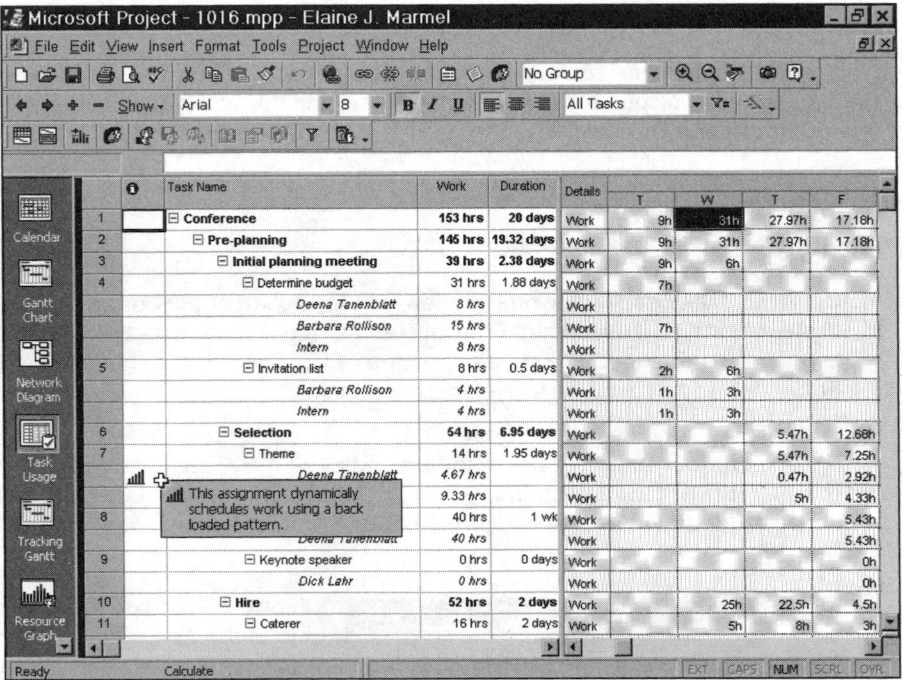


**Figure 10-19:** Project displays an icon in the Indicator column next to a resource for which you have chosen a contour other than Flat.

Tip

The same icon appears in the Indicator column in the Resource Usage view.

Here are a few points to keep in mind when you're working with contours:

✦ Suppose you apply a contour other than the default Flat contour to a task and later you add new total work values to the task. Project automatically reapplies the contour pattern to the task and the resources by first distributing the new task work values across the affected time span and then assigning new work values to the resources working on the task.

✦ If you set a contour and then change the start date of the task or the start date of a resource's work on the task, Project automatically shifts the contour and reapplies it to include the new date, preserving the pattern of the original contour.

✦ If you increase the duration of a task, Project stretches the contour to include the new duration.

✦ Suppose you apply a contour other than the default contour to a task. If you manually edit a work value on the portion of a view displaying the contour, Project no longer applies the contour pattern automatically. However, you can reapply the contour to redistribute the new values.

✦ If you enter actual work and then change the task's total work or total remaining work, Project automatically redistributes the changes to the remaining work values and not to the actual work.

In Project 2000, you can now contour a resource's availability, as described in the following section.

## Contouring a resource's availability

To contour a resource's availability, use the General tab of the Resource Information dialog box (see Figure 10-20). In the Resource Availability box, set Available From and Available To dates for the selected resource. A particular resource may be available to work on your project only part-time for a specified time frame. Or, suppose you have five computer programmers, but only three are available in August and one retires in September. Use the Resource Availability section to specify the availability of your resources, which will influence your project's schedule.

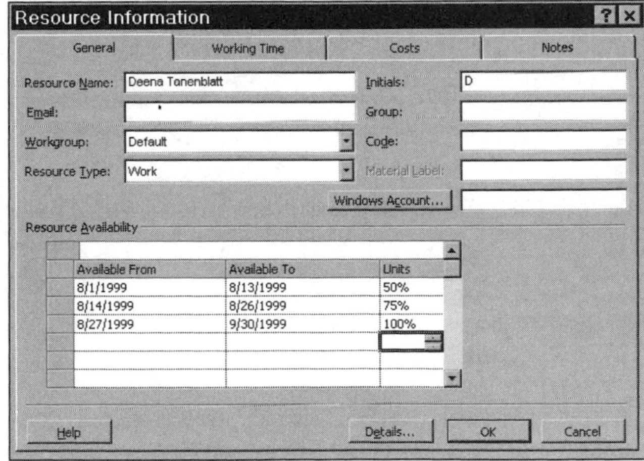


**Figure 10-20:** Set dates that represent the resource's availability so that you can assign the resource to a task using only dates the resource is available.

## Pooling resources

Finally, you can try to solve resource conflicts by using a *resource pool.* A resource pool is a set of resources that are available to any project. You can use resources exclusively on one project, or you can share the resources among several projects.

Typically, resource pooling is useful only if you work with the same resources on multiple projects. Different project managers can share the same resources. Because resource pooling is so closely tied to the topic of managing multiple projects, I'll postpone further discussion until Chapter 17; in that context, you'll better understand the application of resource pooling to resolving resource conflicts.

# Summary

This chapter explained how to identify and resolve resource conflicts that can delay a project. The techniques involve include:

- ✦ Changing resource allocations
- ✦ Scheduling overtime
- ✦ Redefining a resource calendar
- ✦ Assigning part-time work
- ✦ Controlling resource start times
- ✦ Leveling resource workloads
- ✦ Contouring resources

In the next chapter you learn the art of tracking your progress by comparing your project to its baseline.

✦ ✦ ✦

P A R T

# IV

# Tracking Your Progress

✦ ✦ ✦ ✦

**In This Part**



✦ ✦ ✦ ✦

# Understanding Tracking

In This Chapter

Understanding the principles of tracking

Using baselines

Changing the baseline

Viewing progress with the Tracking Gantt

Tracking strategies

This chapter marks something of a turning point in this book and in your use of Project. Up until now you've been in the planning phase: building a project schedule, entering tasks, adding resources, and shifting things around so that resource assignments don't conflict and tasks have the proper relationships to each other. You've even tweaked details such as text formatting and the appearance of taskbars. You now have a workable, good-looking project in hand — and now you are ready to start the project.

*Tracking* is the process of comparing what actually happens during your project to your estimates of what would happen. To track, you need to take a picture of your project schedule at the moment your planning is complete, called a *baseline*. But you also have to understand what steps are involved in tracking and how to set up efficient procedures to handle them.

## Understanding the Principles of Tracking

A good plan is only half the battle. How you execute that plan is key. Think of yourself as the quarterback in a football game. If you run straight down the field toward the goalpost, never swerving to avoid an oncoming opponent, you won't get very far. Project tracking is similar: If you don't swerve and make adjustments for the changes in costs and timing that are virtually inevitable in any human endeavor, you're not playing the game correctly.

Computerized project management greatly enhances your ability to quickly see problems and revise the plan to minimize any damage. Project enables you to compare what you thought would happen to what actually happens over the course of the project.

## Estimates versus actuals

The plan you've been building is an estimate of what could occur; it's your best guess (an educated one, we hope) about how long tasks might take, how one task affects another, how many resources you need to complete the work, and what costs you expect your project to incur. Good project managers keep good records of their estimates and actuals so that they can get to be better project managers. By comparing these two sets of data, you can see where your estimates were off and then use this information to make your next plan more realistic. You can also use data on actual costs and timing to make the changes in your strategy that are necessary to keep you on track and meet your current project's goals.

Tracking in Project consists of entering information about actuals, such as the actual start date, the actual finish date, and the actual duration of a task. You enter actual time worked by resources and actual costs incurred. When you enter information about actuals, Project shows you a revised schedule with projections of how the rest of the schedule is likely to play out, based on your actual activity.

Project managers usually track activity on a regular basis such as once a week or every two weeks. That tracking includes information about tasks in progress, as well as about tasks that have been completed.

This tracking activity also enables you to generate reports that show management where your efforts stand at a given point in time. By showing managers the hard data on your project's status, rather than your best guess, you can make persuasive bids for more time, more resources, or a shift in strategy if things aren't going as you expected. Figure 11-1 shows a Tracking Gantt view using its default table, the Tracking table. The Tracking Gantt view compares baseline estimates with actuals.

Chapter 12 explains the specific steps for updating a project to reflect this kind of progress.

## Making adjustments as you go

Tracking isn't something you leave to the end of the project, or even to the end of individual tasks. Tracking tasks in progress on a regular basis helps you detect any deviation from your estimates. The earlier you spot a delay, the more time you have to make up for it.

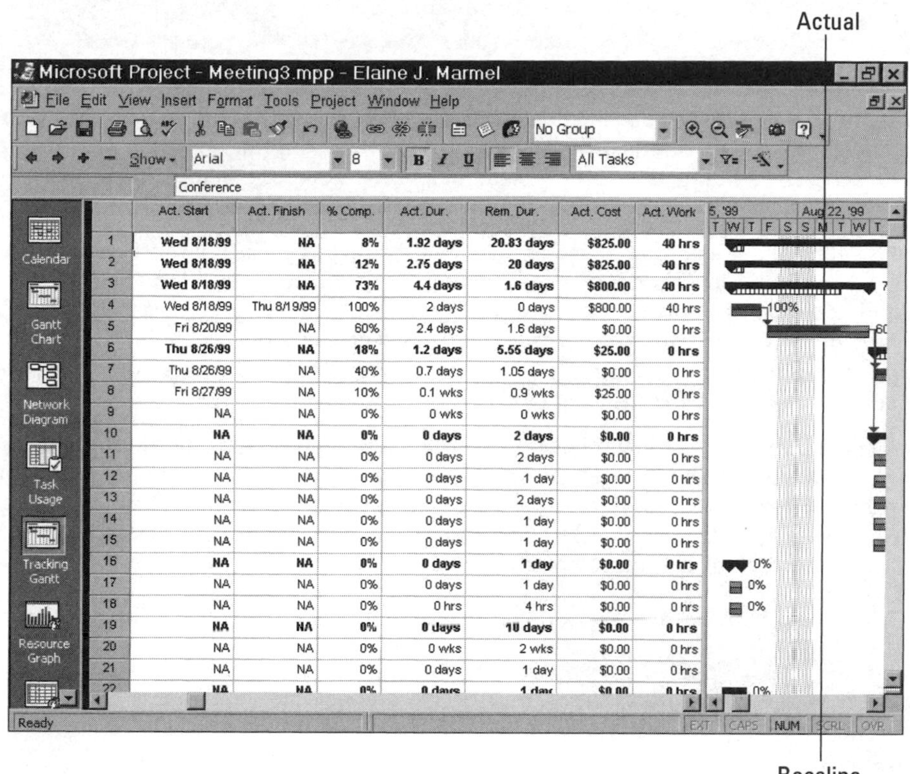


**Figure 11-1:** Use the Tracking Gantt view to display the progress of your project.

For example, suppose that you estimated that a task would take three days. However, you have already put four days of effort into it, and it's still not complete. Project not only tells you that you're running late but also moves future tasks with dependency relationships to this task farther out in the schedule. Project also shows any resource conflicts that result from resources having to put in more work than you estimated in resource views such as Resource Sheet and Resource Graph. Project shows clearly how one delay ripples through your schedule.

Project also shows the effect of unanticipated costs on the total budget. If the costs you track on early tasks are higher than anticipated, Project displays your projected total costs, based on a combination of actual costs and the remaining estimates. Project shows you exactly how much of your budget you have used and how much you have remaining so that you can revise your resource allocations to stay within your overall budget.

## How Much Have You Accomplished?

As explained in Chapter 12, you record activity on a task by entering an estimate of the percentage of the task that's complete, actual resource time spent on the task, or actual costs incurred (such as fees or equipment rentals paid). Estimating the percentage of the task that is complete is not an exact science, and different people use different methods.

With something concrete, such as a building under construction, you can look at the actual building and estimate fairly accurately how far along the project is. But most projects aren't so straightforward. How do you estimate how far along you are in more creative tasks, such as coming up with an advertising concept? You can sit in meetings for five weeks and still not find the right concept. Is your project 50 percent complete? Completion is hard to gauge from other, similar projects—perhaps on the last project you came up with the perfect concept in your very first meeting.

Don't fall into the trap of using money or time spent as a gauge. It's (unfortunately) easy to spend $10,000 on a task estimated to cost $8,000 and still be only 25 percent to completion. You probably have to use the same gut instincts that put you in charge of this project to estimate the progress of individual tasks. Hint: If your project has individual deliverables that you can track, document them and use them consistently when you make your estimate.

# Using Baselines

You complete the planning phase of your project by setting a baseline. You have seen this term in previous chapters, but take a moment to grasp its significance in the tracking process.

## What is a baseline?

A *baseline* is a snapshot of your project when you complete the planning phase, or sometimes at the end of some other critical phase. The baseline is one set of data saved in the same file where you track actual progress data. Project enables you to save an initial baseline and up to ten interim baselines during your project; you can show a wide variety of information about your baseline, or you can choose not to display baseline information at all.

Some projects, particularly shorter ones that run only a few weeks or even a couple of months, may have one baseline set at the outset and proceed close enough to your estimates that they can run their course against that single baseline. Other projects, especially lengthier ones, may require you to set several baselines along the way, particularly if the original estimate is so out of line with what's transpired in the project that the original is no longer useful. You can modify the entire baseline if changes are drastic and occur early in the project, or you can modify the baseline estimates only going forward from a particular point in the project.

For example, if your project is put on hold shortly after you complete the schedule and you actually start work three months later than you had planned, you would be wise to set a new baseline schedule before restarting. If, however, you're six months into your project and it is put on hold for three months, you might want to modify the timing of future tasks and reset the baseline only for tasks going forward to help you retain the ability to accurately assess how well you estimated.

Costs can change a baseline, too. What if you save a baseline set to fit within a $50,000 budget and, before you start work, cost-cutting measures hit your company and your budget is cut to $35,000? You'd be wise to make the changes to your resources and costs and then reset your baseline. Setting interim baselines keeps your projects from varying wildly from your estimates when mitigating circumstances come into play.

## Setting the baseline

You can set the baseline by using either the Planning Wizard or the Tools menu.

In most cases you need to save the project file — without saving the baseline itself — several times during the planning phase. Every time you save the file (File ➪ Save), Project displays the Planning Wizard option that enables you to choose to save the file with or without a baseline. As you're planning, you should select the "Save file without a baseline option." However, after you make your final changes to the project, you can go ahead and save the baseline with the help of the Planning Wizard. Saving the baseline this way replaces any existing baselines and sets the baseline for the entire project. Follow these steps:

1. Choose File ➪ Save. If you haven't saved the file before, the Save As dialog box appears.
2. Select the location to which you want to save the file, enter a filename, and click OK. If you have saved the file before, the Planning Wizard dialog box in Figure 11-2 appears.

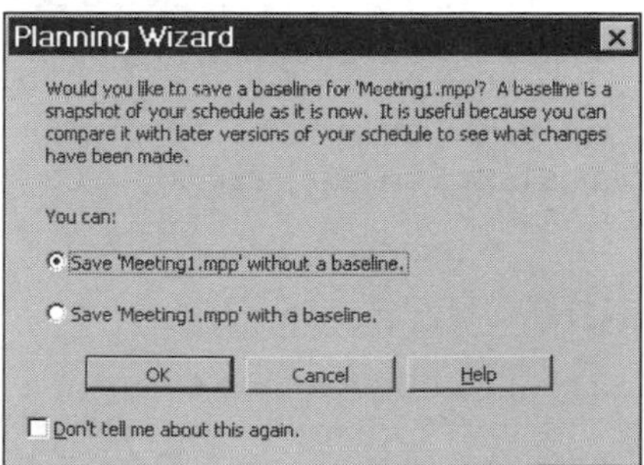


**Figure 11-2:** To save the file before you're ready to set a baseline, click the appropriate control box.

3. Click the "Save file with a baseline" control button and then click OK. Project sets the baseline.

Tip

**If it drives you crazy to have this dialog box appear every time you save a project, click the "Don't tell me about this again" checkbox in the Planning Wizard dialog box and use the method explained in the following steps when you're ready to set a baseline.**

Alternatively, set a baseline by following these steps:

1. Choose Tools ➪ Tracking ➪ Save Baseline to open the Save Baseline dialog box in Figure 11-3.

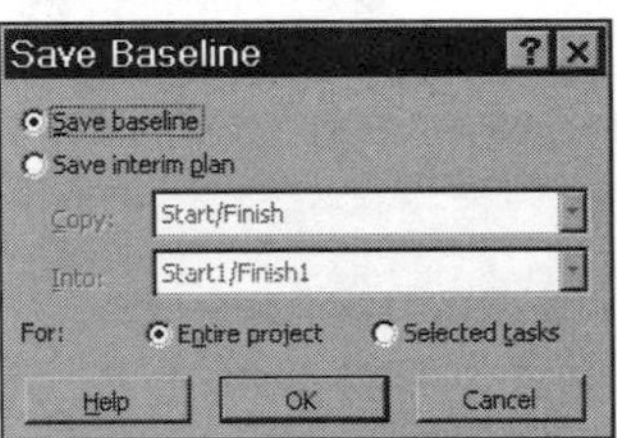


**Figure 11-3:** To save a baseline for the entire project, accept the default selection in the Save Baseline dialog box.

2. Click OK to accept the default—that is, to save the entire project schedule as a baseline.

Project saves the baseline; any changes you make to the project now become part of the record of actual activity performed on the project.

# Changing the Baseline

Most of the time, you *don't* want to make changes to the baseline. It's a moment frozen in time, a record against which you can compare your progress. If you change your original baseline on a regular basis, you are defeating its purpose.

That said, there are strategic times when you will need to modify the baseline and resave it, or to save a second or third baseline to document major shifts in the project. However, if you are overriding the original baseline, you must do so in a thoughtful and efficient way. This section discusses some of the times when changes to the baseline are necessary and explains how you can make those changes.

## Adding a task to a baseline

It is fairly common to set your baseline plan and then realize that you left out a step, or then decide to break one step into two. Perhaps your company institutes a new requirement or process, and you have to modify a task to deal with the change. You don't want to reset your whole project baseline, but you do want to save that one task along with the original baseline. You can make this change shortly after you save the original baseline, or even weeks or months later.

To add a task to your baseline so that you can track its progress, follow these steps:

1. Do one of the following:
   - To add a new task to the schedule and then incorporate it into the baseline, first add the task in the Task Name column on your Gantt chart and then select it.
   - To save modifications to an existing task, first make the changes and then select the task.
2. Choose Tools ➪ Tracking ➪ Save Baseline. The Save Baseline dialog box appears.
3. Click Selected tasks, as in Figure 11-4.

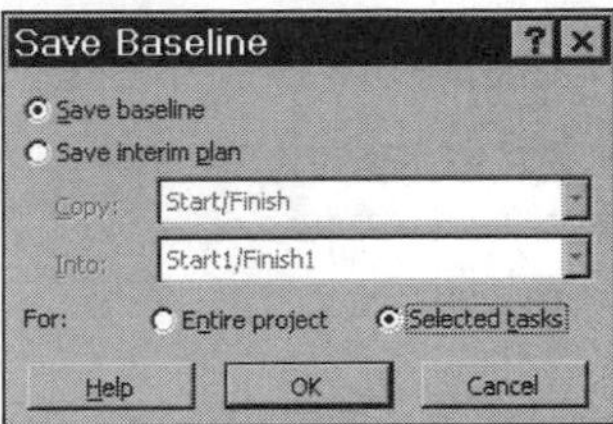


**Figure 11-4:** Make modifications to tasks and save them in an already established baseline.

4. Click OK to save the baseline, which now includes the new task.

You can add tasks to the baseline by entering them in the Gantt table, using columns such as Baseline Duration and Baseline Start or Finish. However, adding baseline data this way does not enable all baseline calculations. For example, adding a task at the end of the project with this method won't effect a change in the baseline finish date.

## Using interim schedules

You can use the baseline in several ways. You can refer to it as your original estimate and compare it with actual results at the end of the project to see how well you guessed and to learn to make better guesses on future projects. But the baseline also has an important practical use during the project: It alerts you to shifts so that you can make changes to accommodate them. The second use may prompt you to save interim baselines.

The initial baseline may quickly take on more historical rather than practical interest. You should not change the initial baseline because that record of your original planning process is important to retain. However, if timing shifts dramatically away from the baseline plan, all the little warning signs Project gives you about being off schedule become useless. A project that starts six months later than expected will show every task as late, every task as critical. To continue generating useful project information, you'll want to revise the schedule to better reflect reality. Only by saving a second, third, or fourth interim baseline can you see how well you're meeting your revised goals.

You can set interim baseline schedules for all the tasks in the project. However, you would usually want to change the baseline only for tasks going forward. For example, if a labor strike pushes out a manufacturing project by two months, you keep the baseline intact for all the tasks that were completed at the time the strike started and change the baseline for all the tasks still to perform when the strike ends.

You can set additional baselines by following these steps:

1. Select various tasks to save a second baseline for specific tasks, rather than for the whole project.
2. Choose Tools ⇨ Tracking ⇨ Save Baseline to open the Save Baseline dialog box.
3. Select "Entire project" to set an interim baseline for the whole project, or select "Selected tasks" to save an interim baseline that retains the original baseline information for any tasks you didn't select but saves new baseline information for the tasks you have selected.
4. Click "Save interim plan." Project makes the Copy and Into fields available.

Be very careful not to leave the "Save baseline" button selected when saving interim schedules. If you do, Project overwrites the original baseline.

5. Click the arrow to the right of the Copy field to display the drop-down list shown in Figure 11-5.
6. Select Start/Finish from the Copy drop-down list to copy current start to finish settings.
7. Open the drop-down list for the Into field and select a numbered item, such as Start1/Finish1, to set an interim baseline.

Don't select Baseline Start/Finish in these drop-down lists. This option copies the information over the original baseline, rather than into any of the ten interim baselines available to you.

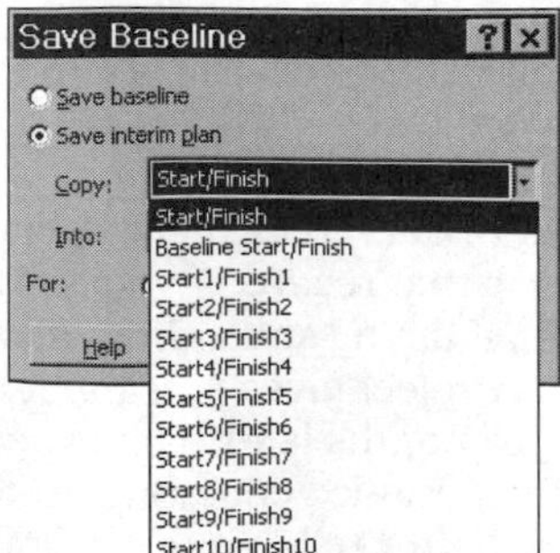


**Figure 11-5:** The choices in the Copy and Into lists enable you to save several versions of your baseline.

8. Click OK to save the interim baseline plan.

Remember that you can use the various numbered Start/Finish items to save up to 10 baselines plus the original, for a total of 11 baselines over the life of your project.

## Clearing the baseline or interim plan

Inevitably, you set a baseline or an interim baseline and then find a reason to clear it. Suppose, for example, that you thought you finished the planning stage of the project. The project hasn't yet started, and you attend a meeting in which you inform everyone that you're "good to go" for next Monday. Naturally, your announcement triggers discussion and, by the time the discussion ends, the scope of the project has expanded (or contracted) considerably. You now need to work again on the planning phase of your schedule—and you really don't want to adjust the baseline. Instead, you want to get rid of it, and, after you make all your changes, you'll set the correct baseline.

Effective in Project 2000, you can clear baselines.

Choose Tools ➪ Tracking ➪ Clear Baseline. Project displays the Clear Baseline dialog box you see in Figure 11-6. In this dialog box, you can choose to clear the baseline plan or an interim plan for the entire project or for selected tasks.

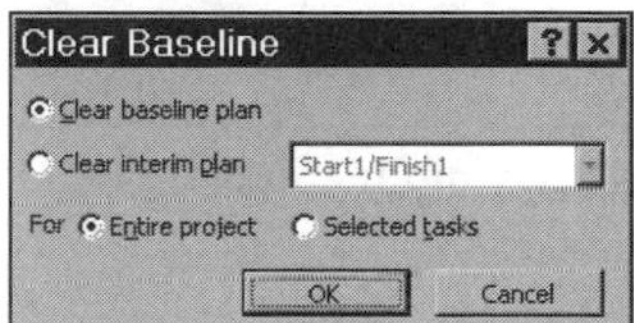


**Figure 11-6:** Set the baseline too soon? Clear it from this dialog box so that you can make adjustments and set the baseline correctly.

# Viewing Progress with the Tracking Gantt

Baselines help you see how your estimates differ from actual activity in the project. Project enables you to see this variance both graphically, with baseline and actual task- bars, and through data displayed in tables in various views. The next section briefly explains how to display a baseline and actual data, and how you can use this feature to understand the status of your project.

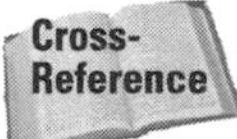


In Chapter 12 you learn how to enter tracking data.

## Interpreting the Tracking Gantt

The Tracking Gantt view is most useful in viewing progress against your baseline estimates. To open the Tracking Gantt view, click its icon in the View bar. This view shows the Tracking table by default. However, you can add or remove fields (columns), or you can display other tables of information. The columns shown in Figure 11-7 include baseline information that I added to the Tracking table.

| | Cost Variance | Baseline Duration | Baseline Cost | Task Name | Act. Start | % Comp. | Act. Dur. | Rem. Dur. | Act. Cost |
|---|---|---|---|---|---|---|---|---|---|
| 1 | **$693.26** | **2.5 days** | **$645.00** | **⊟ Build a pool** | **Thu 8/12/99** | **73%** | **3.59 days** | **1.35 days** | **$990.93** |
| 2 | $240.00 | 1 day | $240.00 | Dig the hole | Thu 8/12/99 | 100% | 2 days | 0 days | $480.00 |
| 3 | $120.00 | 0.5 days | $210.00 | Pour the pool | Mon 8/16/99 | 100% | 1 day | 0 days | $330.00 |
| 4 | ($171.74) | 1.5 days | $460.00 | Build the deck | Tue 8/17/99 | 63% | 0.59 days | 0.35 days | $180.93 |
| 5 | $0.00 | 1 day | $240.00 | Screen the po | NA | 0% | 0 days | 1 day | $0.00 |
| 6 | **$0.00** | **1.5 days** | **$245.00** | **⊟ Landscape** | **NA** | **0%** | **0 days** | **1.5 days** | **$0.00** |
| 7 | $0.00 | 1 day | $120.00 | Replant grass | NA | 0% | 0 days | 1 day | $0.00 |
| 8 | $0.00 | 0.5 days | $60.00 | Plant shrubs | NA | 0% | 0 days | 0.5 days | $0.00 |
| 9 | $0.00 | 0.5 days | $65.00 | Mow lawn | NA | 0% | 0 days | 0.5 days | $0.00 |

**Figure 11-7:** The Tracking Gantt table can display a wealth of information.

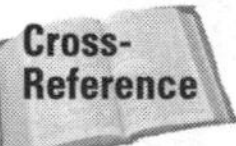


Review Chapter 7 for information on changing and modifying tables.

Notice the Baseline Duration and Baseline Cost, as well as the Actual Duration and the Actual Cost fields, in the Tracking Gantt table. These fields help you compare estimated versus actual timing and costs.

You can modify this table so that the Baseline Duration column is next to the Actual Duration column and Baseline Cost is next to Actual Cost.

The Tracking Gantt table also contains the following information:

✦ **% Complete.** This field shows the progress of various tasks in the schedule. In Figure 11-7 two tasks are complete.

✦ **Cost Variance.** This field tells you the calculated difference between the baseline and actual information. For example, look at the task "Pour the pool" on line 3. The Baseline Cost was $210.00, the Actual Cost was $330.00, and the Cost Variance is $120.00, the difference between the two. Project calculates this amount automatically from baseline and actual data that you enter. You can display other fields that show calculations regarding variances; for example, several fields reflect variance in timing from estimated to actual.

You also can display the taskbars by manipulating the divider between the table and chart areas to get a graphic view of progress on the project. Figure 11-8 uses the Schedule table with the Tracking Gantt and shows the bars of the Tracking Gantt. The various styles of taskbar indicate progress on tasks in the project.

Notice that various graphic representations indicate progress on different types of tasks. Summary tasks may have a white bar with black lines underneath their taskbars. This extra bar indicates the progress (how much is complete) of the summary task. The noncritical tasks are blue and critical tasks are red. The percentage indicator at the edge of a task reflects the percentage complete for that task; the bars of completed tasks are solid in color, while the bars of incomplete tasks are patterned and appear lighter in color. The bars of partially completed tasks are solid on the left and patterned on the right.

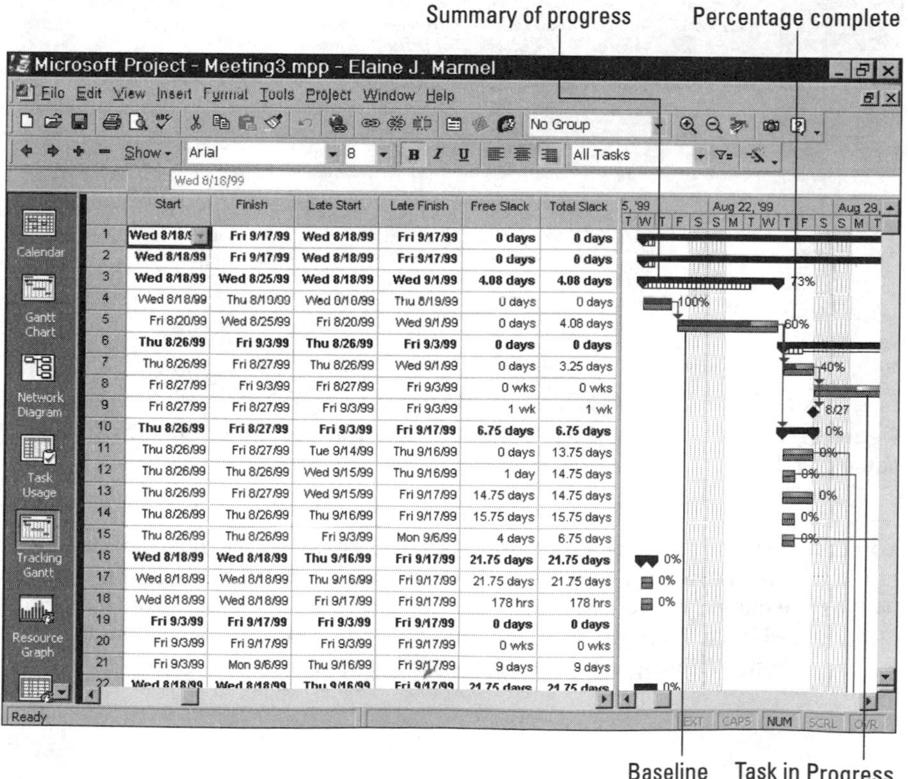


**Figure 11-8:** Various taskbar styles and color codes display the project's progress and variances.

## The Task Variance table

As you change the tables displayed in the Tracking Gantt view, you'll see different information about your progress in the project. The Variance table, for example, highlights the variance in task timing between the baseline and actuals. To display this table, shown in Figure 11-9, right-click the box in the upper-left corner of the table where the row containing column headings and the task number column meet. Select Variance from the list of tables that appears.

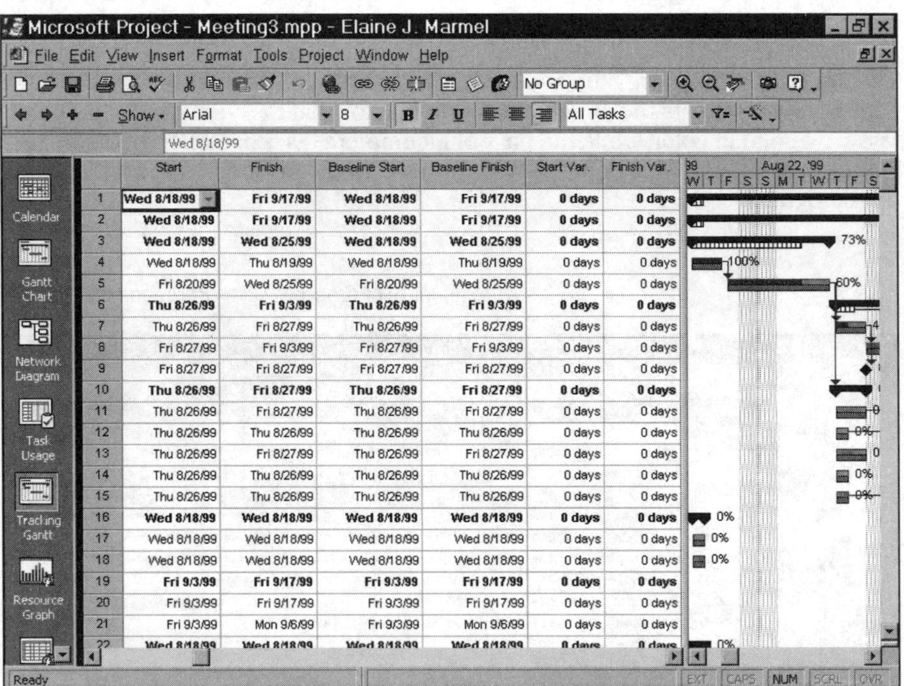


**Figure 11-9:** If you're behind schedule, you can easily see the awful truth in the Variance table.

You can easily compare the Baseline Start and Finish to the actual Start and Finish columns that show actual data for tasks on which you have tracked progress, as well as baseline data for tasks with no progress. This table also contains fields to show you the Start Variance (how many days late or early the task started) and the Finish Variance (how many days late or early the task ended).

## The Task Cost table

The Task Cost table is most useful for pointing out variations in money spent on the project. Figure 11-10 shows a Task Cost table for a project in progress, with some costs incurred and others yet to be expended. At this point the task "Pour the pool" is exceeding its projected cost by $1,120.00. Project takes the following factors into account when calculating cost variations: the actual resource time worked, the estimate of days of resource time still to be expended to complete the task, and actual costs (such as fees and permits) that have been tracked on the task. Compared to a baseline estimate of $210.00, this task is way overbudget.

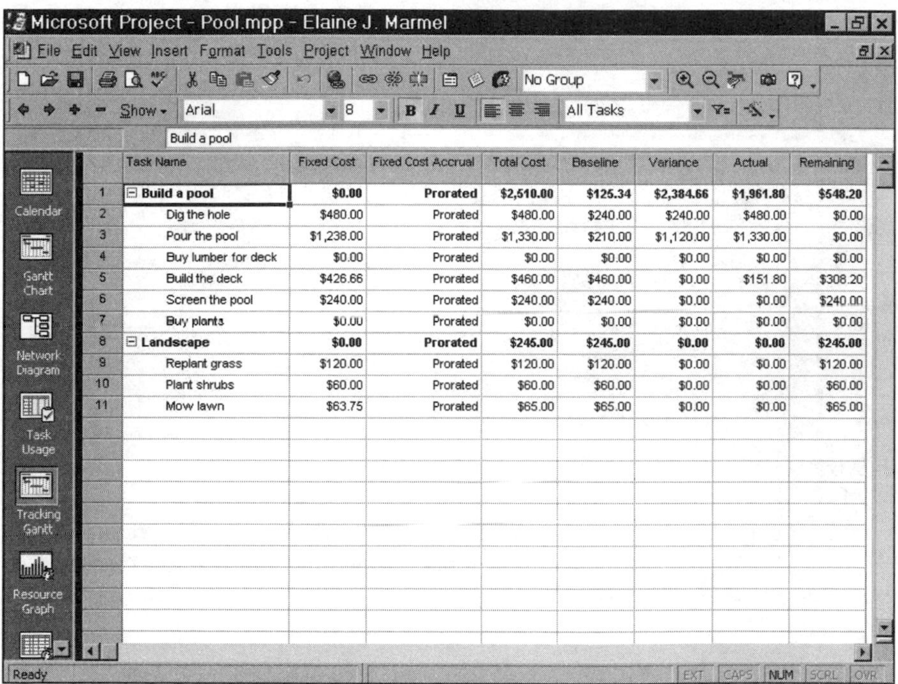

| | Task Name | Fixed Cost | Fixed Cost Accrual | Total Cost | Baseline | Variance | Actual | Remaining |
|---|---|---|---|---|---|---|---|---|
| 1 | **Build a pool** | **$0.00** | **Prorated** | **$2,510.00** | **$125.34** | **$2,384.66** | **$1,961.80** | **$548.20** |
| 2 | Dig the hole | $480.00 | Prorated | $480.00 | $240.00 | $240.00 | $480.00 | $0.00 |
| 3 | Pour the pool | $1,238.00 | Prorated | $1,330.00 | $210.00 | $1,120.00 | $1,330.00 | $0.00 |
| 4 | Buy lumber for deck | $0.00 | Prorated | $0.00 | $0.00 | $0.00 | $0.00 | $0.00 |
| 5 | Build the deck | $426.66 | Prorated | $460.00 | $460.00 | $0.00 | $151.80 | $308.20 |
| 6 | Screen the pool | $240.00 | Prorated | $240.00 | $240.00 | $0.00 | $0.00 | $240.00 |
| 7 | Buy plants | $0.00 | Prorated | $0.00 | $0.00 | $0.00 | $0.00 | $0.00 |
| 8 | **Landscape** | **$0.00** | **Prorated** | **$245.00** | **$245.00** | **$0.00** | **$0.00** | **$245.00** |
| 9 | Replant grass | $120.00 | Prorated | $120.00 | $120.00 | $0.00 | $0.00 | $120.00 |
| 10 | Plant shrubs | $60.00 | Prorated | $60.00 | $60.00 | $0.00 | $0.00 | $60.00 |
| 11 | Mow lawn | $63.75 | Prorated | $65.00 | $65.00 | $0.00 | $0.00 | $65.00 |

**Figure 11-10:** The Task Cost table shows where you've spent too much and where you have a lot more money to spend.

## The Task Work table

The Task Work table of the Tracking Gantt shown in Figure 11-11 focuses on the number of work hours put in by resources working on tasks. For example, the baseline work for the task "Pour the pool" was 8 hours. However, the task is complete and took 24 hours. Therefore, the Variance field (the difference between the baseline hours of work and the actual hours spent) shows a loss of 16 hours. On the other hand, the Baseline estimate for the "Buy lumber for deck" task was 6 hours and the task was completed in 4 hours. The Variance column shows a saving of 2 hours; the negative value indicates fewer hours were used than estimated in the baseline.

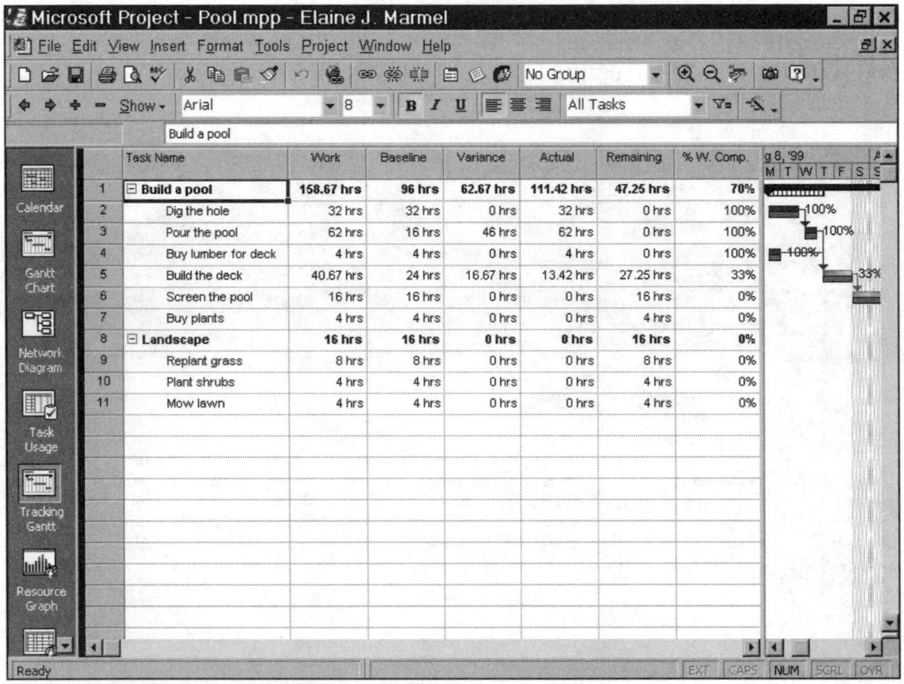
Microsoft Project - Pool.mpp - Elaine J. Marmel
File Edit View Insert Format Tools Project Window Help
No Group
Show
Arial
8
All Tasks
Build a pool
Calendar
Gantt Chart
Network Diagram
Task Usage
Tracking Gantt
Resource Graph
Task Name Work Baseline Variance Actual Remaining % W. Comp.
1 Build a pool 158.67 hrs 96 hrs 62.67 hrs 111.42 hrs 47.25 hrs 70%
2 Dig the hole 32 hrs 32 hrs 0 hrs 32 hrs 0 hrs 100%
3 Pour the pool 62 hrs 16 hrs 46 hrs 62 hrs 0 hrs 100%
4 Buy lumber for deck 4 hrs 4 hrs 0 hrs 4 hrs 0 hrs 100%
5 Build the deck 40.67 hrs 24 hrs 16.67 hrs 13.42 hrs 27.25 hrs 33%
6 Screen the pool 16 hrs 16 hrs 0 hrs 0 hrs 16 hrs 0%
7 Buy plants 4 hrs 4 hrs 0 hrs 0 hrs 4 hrs 0%
8 Landscape 16 hrs 16 hrs 0 hrs 0 hrs 16 hrs 0%
9 Replant grass 8 hrs 8 hrs 0 hrs 0 hrs 8 hrs 0%
10 Plant shrubs 4 hrs 4 hrs 0 hrs 0 hrs 4 hrs 0%
11 Mow lawn 4 hrs 4 hrs 0 hrs 0 hrs 4 hrs 0%
g 8, '99
M T W T F S S
100%
100%
100%
33%
Ready
EXT CAPS NUM SCRL OVR

**Figure 11-11:** To determine whether a task is taking much more effort than you estimated, check the Task Work table.

You'll see many of these tables and more tracking views as you work through the next few chapters. For now, you should have a good idea of the types of information you can get by tracking progress on your project.

# Tracking Strategies

As you use Microsoft Project on real projects, your tracking skills will improve. However, if you follow certain basic principles of tracking from the start, you can save yourself a lot of aggravation in your first few projects.

## Tackling the work of tracking

First, update frequently and at regular intervals. Many people see tracking as a monumental task: All the details of each task's progress and duration, as well as all the resources and costs associated with each task must be entered one by one. You have to gather that data through resource timecards, reports from other project participants, and vendor invoices. You must type in all the information that you gather. I won't kid you: Tracking can be a big piece of work. The more often you track, the less the tracking data will pile up, and the less likely it is to overwhelm you.

Help yourself with the tracking task by assigning pieces of the updating to various people in your project. If a particular resource is in charge of one phase of the project, have him or her track the activity on just that one phase. You can use various methods of compiling those smaller schedules into a master schedule.

Part V of this book provides ideas for compiling several schedules and managing schedules with workgroups.

If you have a resource available, such as an administrative assistant who can handle the tracking details, all the better. Make sure you provide this assistant with appropriate training (and a copy of this book) so that he or she understands the tracking process well enough to be accurate and productive. However, this resource probably does not need to be a Project expert to take on some of the work.

To help you remember to track, enter tracking as a recurring task, occurring once every week or two, within your project file. And don't forget to include required meetings—such as progress meetings and performance reviews—in your schedule.

## Keeping track of tracking

Using task notes to record progress and changes can be another good strategy for effective tracking. If an important change occurs that doesn't merit changing your baseline, use the task notes to record it. When you reach the end of the project, these notes help you document and justify everything from missed deadlines to cost overruns.

Try to set some standards for tracking in your organization. For example, how do you determine when a task is complete? How do you measure costs, and what is the source of information on resource time spent on a task? Project becomes a much more effective management tool if each project manager uses identical methods of gauging progress and expenditures, just as your company's accounting department uses standards in tracking costs.

Setting multiple baselines is useful, but how do you decide when to save each iteration? You might consider setting a different baseline for each major milestone in your project. Even long projects usually have only four or five significant milestones, and they are likely to occur after you have accomplished a sizeable chunk of work.

# Summary

This chapter explored some of the fundamental concepts of tracking activity on a project. You learned the following:

✦ How to set, modify and clear baselines

✦ How to view your baseline estimates against actual progress

Chapter 12 covers the mechanics of tracking, recording the actuals, and streamlining the entry of this data.

✦ ✦ ✦

CHAPTER 12

# Recording Actuals

✦ ✦ ✦ ✦

**In This Chapter**

Organizing the updating process

Updating tasks to reflect actual information

Using actuals and costs

Techniques and tips for updating

Reviewing progress

✦ ✦ ✦ ✦

Actuals represent what has, in fact, occurred during your project. In Microsoft Project you can record actual information about the cost of a task and about the time related to completing the task. By recording actual information, you accomplish several things:

- You let Project automatically reschedule the remainder of your project.
- You provide management with a way to measure how well your project is going.
- You provide yourself with valuable information on your estimating skills — information that you can apply to the remainder of the current project or to your next project.

## Organizing the Updating Process

Before you launch into the mechanics of updating a project, you should take a moment to examine the updating process. Updating a project can become complicated, particularly for large projects with many resources assigned to them. You need to establish efficient manual procedures for collecting information in a timely fashion, and then you need to determine the best ways to enter that information into Microsoft Project.

Individuals working on tasks should answer these questions regularly: Is the task on schedule? How much is done? Is there a revised estimate on the duration of the task? Is there a revised estimate on the work required to complete the task?

You may want to create a form for participants to use for their regular reports. Their reports should provide the information you need to update your project plan in Project. You might be able to use one of the reports in Project — or even customize one of Project's reports — to provide the necessary information.

You also should decide how often you need to receive the collection forms. If you require the reports too frequently, your staff may spend more time reporting than working. If, on the other hand, you don't receive the reports often enough, you won't be able to identify a trouble spot early enough to resolve it before it becomes a major crisis. As the manager, you must decide on the correct frequency for collecting actual information for your project.

You can use the time-phased fields in Project to track actual costs on a daily or weekly basis. Read more about time-phased cost tracking in "Tracking work or costs regularly" later in this chapter.

When you receive the reports, you should evaluate them to identify unfinished tasks for which you need to adjust the planned duration, work, and costs. You'll find these adjustments easiest to make if you make them before you record a task's actual dates or percentage of completion.

Also remember that recording actual information enables you to compare estimates to actuals; this comparison often proves to be quite valuable. If you want to make this comparison, make sure you set a baseline for your project.

# Updating Tasks to Reflect Actual Information

You update a project by filling in fields for each task that track the progress of your project:

- ✦ Actual start date
- ✦ Actual finish date
- ✦ Actual duration
- ✦ Remaining duration
- ✦ Percentage complete

In some cases, when you enter information into one of these fields, Project calculates the values for the other fields. For example, if you enter a percentage complete for a task, Project calculates and supplies a start date, an actual duration, a remaining duration, and an actual work value.

## Setting actual start and finish dates

The Gantt Chart view displays projected start and finish dates for tasks. In this section, I show you how to enter and view actual start and finish dates (and compare current, baseline, and actual dates) in the Task Details view in Figure 12-1.

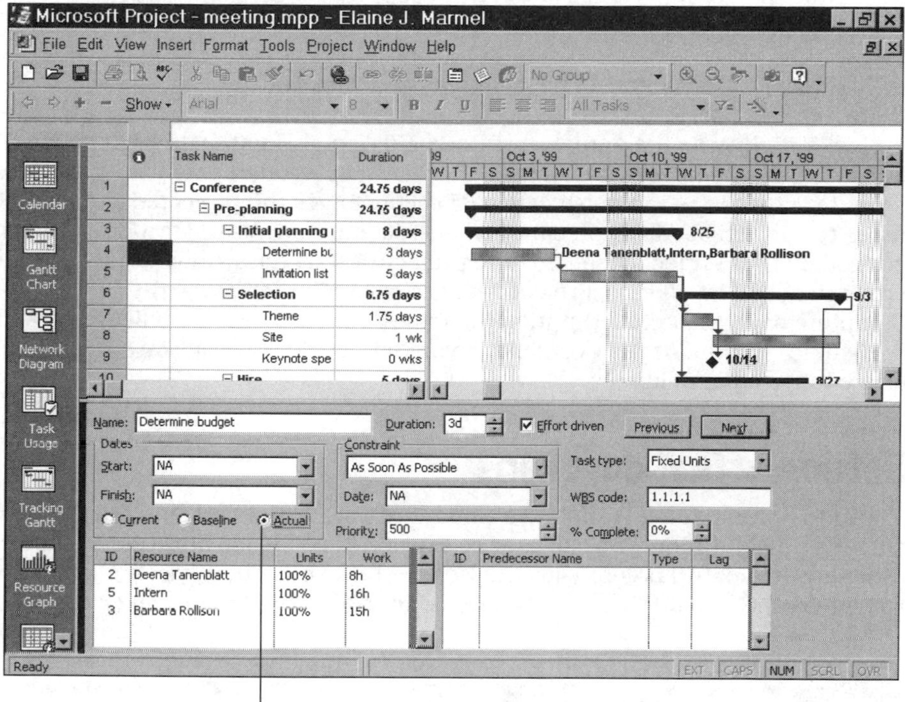


**Figure 12-1:** Use the Task Details form to enter actual information.

Starting from the Gantt Chart view, follow these steps to set up your screen:

1. Choose Window ➪ Split to display the Task Form view.
2. Click the bottom pane and then right-click the View bar to display the shortcut menu.
3. Choose More Views to open the More Views dialog box.
4. Select Task Details Form and click Apply.

5. Select the task (in the top pane of the Task Details form) for which you want to record actuals.

6. Click the Actual option button in the bottom pane to identify the type of dates you want to enter.

The three option buttons — Current, Baseline, and Actual — refer only to the dates you can view and set. That is, you won't see baseline assignments at the bottom of the view if you click Baseline.

7. Record either a Start or a Finish date and click OK.

Project initially sets the Actual Start Date and Actual Finish Date fields to NA to indicate that you have not yet entered a date. When you update your project to provide actual start and finish dates, Project changes the projected start and finish dates to the actual dates you enter. When you enter an actual start date, the only other field that Project changes is the projected start date. However, when you enter an actual finish date, Project changes several other fields: the Percent Complete field, the Actual Duration field, the Remaining Duration field, the Actual Work field, and the Actual Cost field. If you didn't set an actual start date, Project also changes that field.

## Setting actual durations

The actual duration of a task is the amount of time it took to complete the task. To set an actual duration, you can use the Update Tasks dialog box. Choose Tools ⇨ Tracking ⇨ Update Tasks or click the Update Tasks button on the Tracking toolbar to display the Update Tasks dialog box, which appears in Figure 12-2.

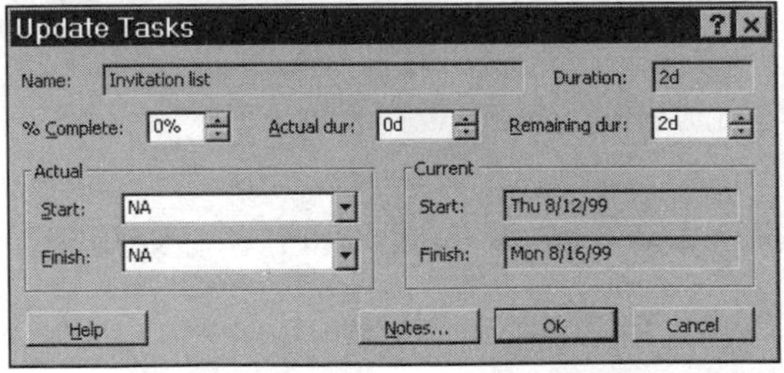


**Figure 12-2:** Use the Update Tasks dialog box to set the actual duration for a task by filling in the Actual dur field.

You can display the Tracking toolbar by choosing View ⇨ Toolbars ⇨ Tracking.

When you set an actual duration that is less than or equal to the planned duration, Project assumes the task is progressing on schedule. Therefore, when you click OK, Project sets the actual start date to the planned start date — unless you previously set the actual start date. In that case Project leaves the actual start date alone. In either case, Project calculates the percentage complete and the remaining duration for the task.

Note

To see the updated remaining duration, reopen the Update Tasks dialog box.

If you set an actual duration that is greater than the planned duration, Project assumes that the task is finished but that it took longer than expected to complete. Project adjusts the planned duration to match the actual duration and changes the Percent Complete field to 100% and the Remaining Duration field to 0%.

You can use the Calculation tab in the Options dialog box (choose Tools ➪ Options) to set Project to update the status of resources when you update a task's status. If you set this option and then supply an actual duration, Project also updates the work and cost figures for the resources. You learn more about this option in "Overriding resource cost valuations" later in this chapter.

Note

Don't change the actual duration of a task if you use effort-driven scheduling. Instead, change the number of resource units assigned or the amount of the resource assignment. Remember that the duration of effort-driven tasks is affected by resource assignments.

## Setting remaining durations

In the two preceding sections, you saw that you can use the Task Form Details view and the Update Tasks dialog box to record and view actual information. The Task Form Details view provides a limited way to update tasks. While the Update Tasks dialog box provides a complete way to enter actual information, I find it easiest to enter all actual information into Project using the Tracking Table view shown in Figure 12-3.

The Rem. Dur. (Remaining Duration) column shows how much more time you need to complete a task. To display the Tracking Table view, start in the Gantt Chart view and follow these steps:

1. Click the top pane of the Gantt chart.
2. Choose Window ➪ Remove Split to display the standard Gantt chart.
3. Right-click the Select All button and choose Tracking. Project displays the Tracking Table view in the left portion of the Gantt Chart view.

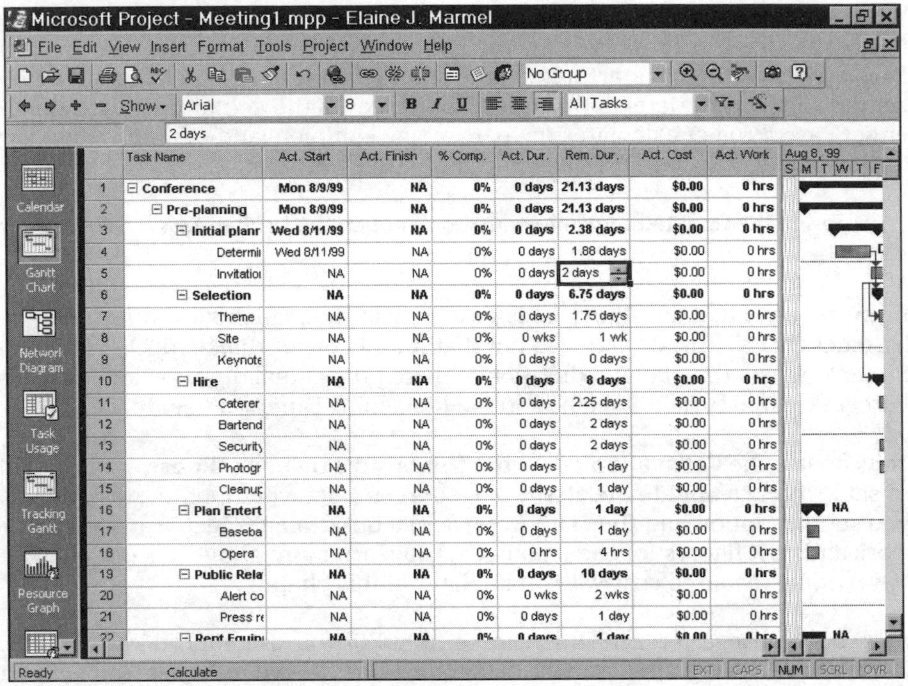

**Figure 12-3:** The Tracking Table view helps you view and enter actual values for tasks.

To see all the columns available on the Tracking Table view, narrow the chart portion of the window.

If you enter a value into the Rem. Dur. (Remaining Duration) column, Project assumes the work has begun on the task and will complete based on the remaining duration value. Therefore, Project sets the Act. Dur. (Actual Duration) and % Comp. (Percent Complete) values based on a combination of the remaining duration value you supplied and the original planned duration. If necessary, Project also sets the actual start date; and, if you set Project's options to update the status of resources when you update a task's status, Project updates the work and cost figures for the resources on the task.

Entering 0 in the Rem. Dur. (Remaining Duration) column is the same as entering 100% in the Percent Complete column. Suppose you change the value in the Remaining Duration column so that it is larger than the existing figure. Project assumes you are changing the planned duration of the task instead of tracking actual progress for the task. In this case, Project adjusts the schedule based on the new planned duration. If the task has already started and you have entered an actual duration when you make the Remaining Duration value larger, Project adds this new estimate to the previously calculated actual duration and adjusts the Percent Complete value.

## Setting Percent Complete

You can establish the progress of work performed on a task by assigning a Percent Complete value to the task. Any value less than 100 indicates that the task is not complete. You can set Percent Complete from the Task Details form, from the Update Tasks dialog box, or from the Tracking Table view. Or you can select the task from any task view and use the percentage buttons on the Tracking toolbar (see Figure 12-4). Right-click on any toolbar and choose Tracking to display the toolbar.

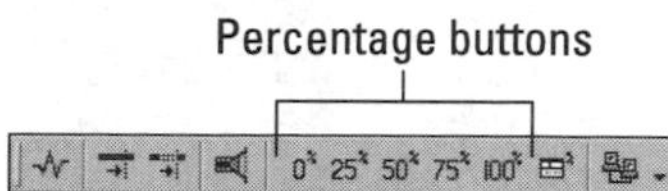


**Figure 12-4:** Use these buttons to set a task's actual progress at 0%, 25%, 50%, 75%, or 100% complete.

A value in the Percent Complete column also affects the Actual Duration and Remaining Duration values. If you make an entry into any of these columns, Project automatically updates the others. When you set the Actual Duration value, Project calculates the value for the Percent Complete column by dividing the Actual Duration value by the original planned duration. If, alternatively, you set the Remaining Duration value, Project recalculates, if necessary, the Actual Duration value and the Percent Complete value.

If you change the Percent Complete value, Project assigns an Actual Start Date (unless you had entered one previously). Project also calculates the Actual Duration and Remaining Duration values. If you set your options to update resources when you update tasks, Project also calculates the Actual Cost and Actual Work values. If you enter 100 into the Percent Complete column, Project assigns the planned finish date to the Actual Finish Date column. If this value is not correct, don't enter a Percent Complete; instead enter an Actual Finish Date.

## Setting work completed

Sometimes, you must schedule tasks based on the availability of certain resources. In these cases tracking progress on a task is easiest if you update the work completed. Updating this value also updates the work that each resource is performing.

In the same way that Project calculates duration information when you fill in a duration field, Project updates the work remaining by subtracting the work performed from the total work scheduled.

Use the Tracking Table view to enter information into the Act. Work column, but start in the Task Usage view so that you can enter actual work performed for specific resources. Click the Task Usage view in the View bar. Then right-click the

Select All button and choose Tracking from the shortcut menu of tables. You'll probably need to drag the divider bar almost completely to the right edge of the screen to reveal the Act. Work column (see Figure 12-5).

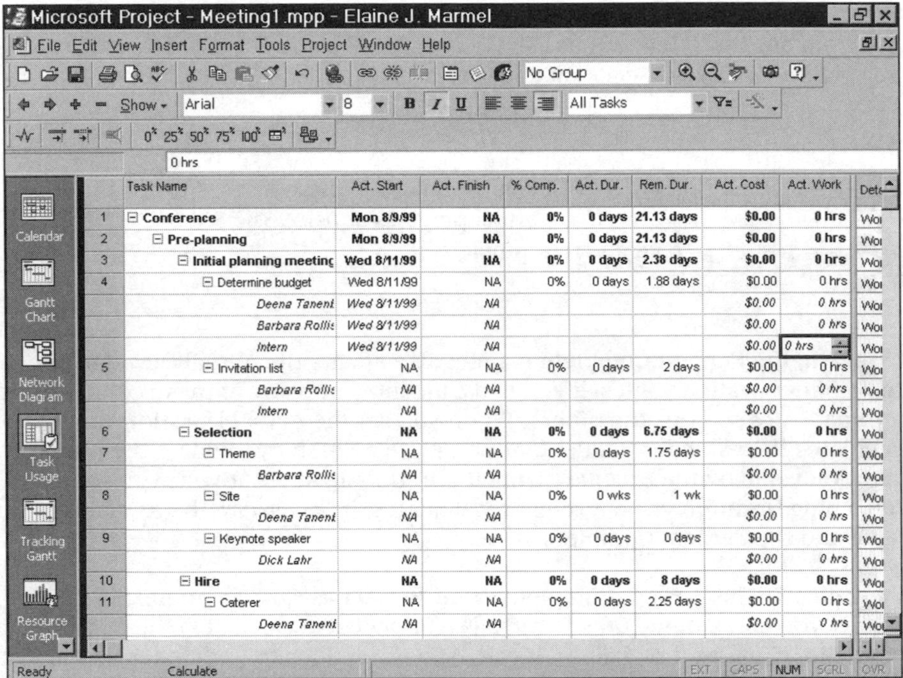


| | Task Name | Act. Start | Act. Finish | % Comp. | Act. Dur. | Rem. Dur. | Act. Cost | Act. Work | Deta |
|---|---|---|---|---|---|---|---|---|---|
| 1 | Conference | Mon 8/9/99 | NA | 0% | 0 days | 21.13 days | $0.00 | 0 hrs | Wo |
| 2 | Pre-planning | Mon 8/9/99 | NA | 0% | 0 days | 21.13 days | $0.00 | 0 hrs | Wo |
| 3 | Initial planning meeting | Wed 8/11/99 | NA | 0% | 0 days | 2.38 days | $0.00 | 0 hrs | Wo |
| 4 | Determine budget | Wed 8/11/99 | NA | 0% | 0 days | 1.88 days | $0.00 | 0 hrs | Wo |
| | Deena Tanent | Wed 8/11/99 | NA | | | | $0.00 | 0 hrs | Wo |
| | Barbara Rollis | Wed 8/11/99 | NA | | | | $0.00 | 0 hrs | Wo |
| | Intern | Wed 8/11/99 | NA | | | | $0.00 | 0 hrs | Wo |
| 5 | Invitation list | NA | NA | 0% | 0 days | 2 days | $0.00 | 0 hrs | Wo |
| | Barbara Rollis | NA | NA | | | | $0.00 | 0 hrs | Wo |
| | Intern | NA | NA | | | | $0.00 | 0 hrs | Wo |
| 6 | Selection | NA | NA | 0% | 0 days | 6.75 days | $0.00 | 0 hrs | Wo |
| 7 | Theme | NA | NA | 0% | 0 days | 1.75 days | $0.00 | 0 hrs | Wo |
| | Barbara Rollis | NA | NA | | | | $0.00 | 0 hrs | Wo |
| 8 | Site | NA | NA | 0% | 0 wks | 1 wk | $0.00 | 0 hrs | Wo |
| | Deena Tanent | NA | NA | | | | $0.00 | 0 hrs | Wo |
| 9 | Keynote speaker | NA | NA | 0% | 0 days | 0 days | $0.00 | 0 hrs | Wo |
| | Dick Lahr | NA | NA | | | | $0.00 | 0 hrs | Wo |
| 10 | Hire | NA | NA | 0% | 0 days | 8 days | $0.00 | 0 hrs | Wo |
| 11 | Caterer | NA | NA | 0% | 0 days | 2.25 days | $0.00 | 0 hrs | Wo |
| | Deena Tanent | NA | NA | | | | $0.00 | 0 hrs | Wo |

**Figure 12-5:** The Tracking Table view with resources displayed

**Tip** If you are scheduling tasks based on the availability of resources in general, instead of availability of specific resources, you can still use this technique to record actual work. However, you need to enter the value on the same row as the task, rather than on the individual rows for the resources. Project divides the actual and remaining work among the resources.

# Using Actuals and Costs

Except for fixed-cost tasks, Project uses the cost of the resources assigned to the task over the duration of the task to calculate a task's cost. Costs are accrued, and total project costs are the sum of all resource and fixed costs. Therefore, if you set up and assigned resources to your tasks, Project has been calculating and accruing the costs for you — all you need to do is review and analyze the costs.

Alternatively, you may have chosen not to assign resources to your tasks, or you may have changed your default options so that Project wouldn't calculate costs. How can you do that? Choose Tools ➪ Options to display the Options dialog box. On the Calculation tab, look at the Calculation options for your project (see Figure 12-6). If you don't see a check in the "Updating task status updates resource status" checkbox, Project has not been calculating your project's costs. Remember, however, that this checkbox contains a check by default, as you see in the figure.

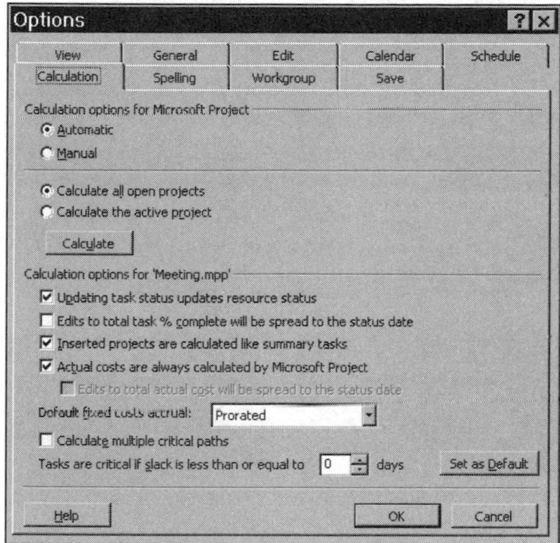


**Figure 12-6:** From the Calculation tab of the Options dialog box, you can tell whether Project has been calculating your project's costs.

If you did not assign resources or you changed the defaults, Project can't calculate the cost of your project unless you provide additional information after the task is completed. You can review and update your project's costs from one of two cost tables: the Cost table for tasks or the Cost table for resources. And you can override the costs Project assigns.

## Using the Cost table for tasks

The Cost table for tasks in Figure 12-7 shows you cost information based on each task in your project. This table shows you the baseline cost (the planned cost), the actual cost, the variance between planned and actual costs, and the remaining cost of the task.

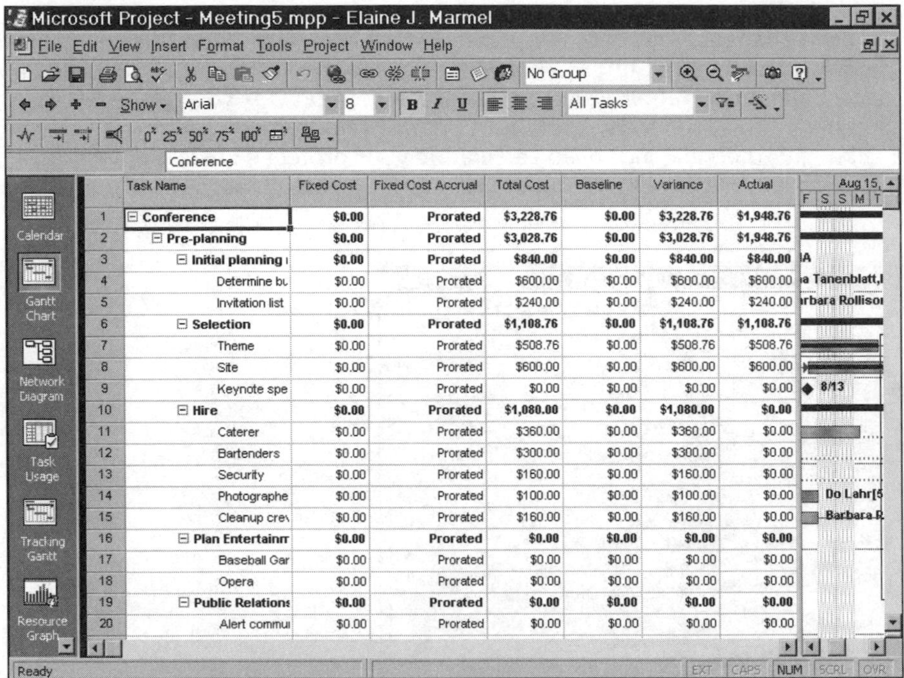

Figure 12-7: The Cost table for tasks

If you assign a fixed cost to a task in this table, Project adds the fixed cost to the calculated cost for the task. To display this table, start in the Gantt Chart view. Then right-click the Select All button to display the shortcut menu of tables, and choose Cost. You may also need to slide the chart pane all the way to the right to see all the fields on the Cost table for tasks.

The Cost table for tasks is most useful if you saved a baseline view of your project because it enables you to compare baseline costs with actual costs.

# Using the Cost table for resources

The Cost table for resources is very similar to the Cost table for tasks, with the breakdown of costs being displayed by resource rather than by task (see Figure 12-8).

To display this table, begin with a resource view such as the Resource Sheet. Then right-click the Select All button and choose Cost from the shortcut menu that appears.

Like the Cost table for tasks, the Cost table for resources is useful if you saved a baseline view of your project because it enables you to compare baseline costs with actual costs.

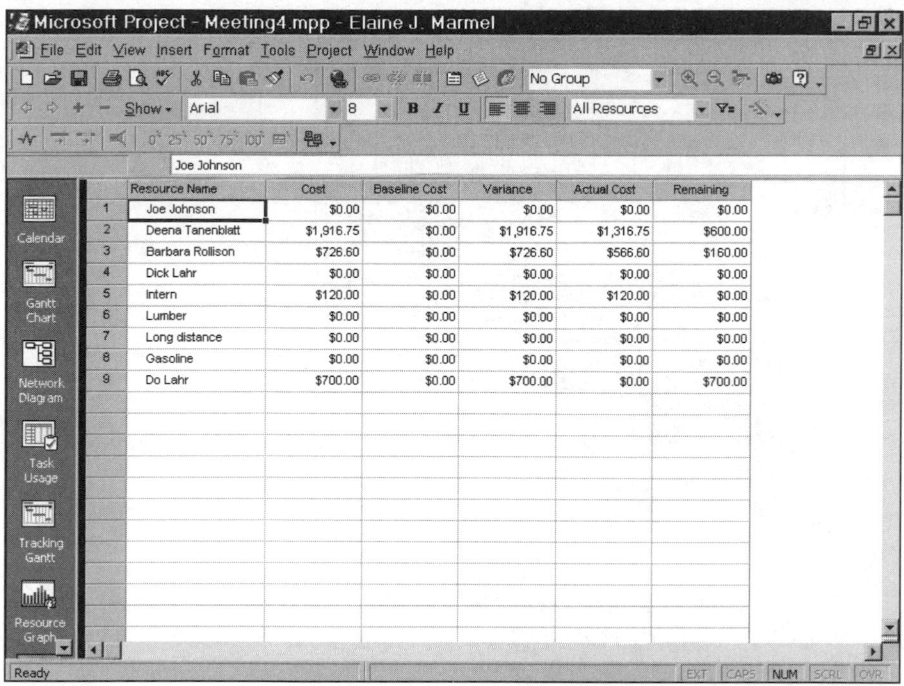

|  | Resource Name | Cost | Baseline Cost | Variance | Actual Cost | Remaining |
|---|---|---|---|---|---|---|
| 1 | Joe Johnson | $0.00 | $0.00 | $0.00 | $0.00 | $0.00 |
| 2 | Deena Tanenblatt | $1,916.75 | $0.00 | $1,916.75 | $1,316.75 | $600.00 |
| 3 | Barbara Rollison | $726.60 | $0.00 | $726.60 | $566.60 | $160.00 |
| 4 | Dick Lahr | $0.00 | $0.00 | $0.00 | $0.00 | $0.00 |
| 5 | Intern | $120.00 | $0.00 | $120.00 | $120.00 | $0.00 |
| 6 | Lumber | $0.00 | $0.00 | $0.00 | $0.00 | $0.00 |
| 7 | Long distance | $0.00 | $0.00 | $0.00 | $0.00 | $0.00 |
| 8 | Gasoline | $0.00 | $0.00 | $0.00 | $0.00 | $0.00 |
| 9 | Do Lahr | $700.00 | $0.00 | $700.00 | $0.00 | $700.00 |

**Figure 12-8:** The Cost table for resources

# Overriding resource cost valuations

Project default settings automatically update costs as you record progress on a task. Project uses the accrual method you selected for the resource when you created the resource.

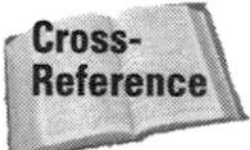


For more information about setting a resource's accrual method, see Chapter 5.

Alternatively, you can enter the actual costs for a resource assignment, or track actual costs separately from the actual work on a task. To do so, after the task is completed, you must enter costs manually to override Project's calculated costs. But before you can override the costs that Project calculated, you must turn off one of the default options. Follow these steps:

1. Choose Tools ➪ Options to display the Options dialog box.
2. Click the Calculation tab.
3. Click the bottom Calculation option "Actual costs are always calculated by Microsoft Project" to clear the checkbox (see Figure 12-9).

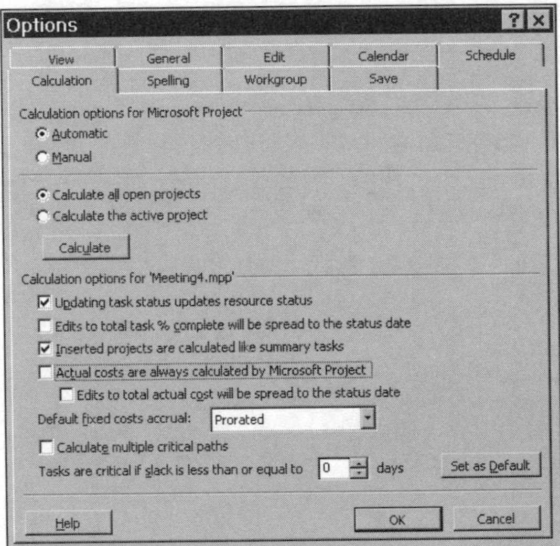


**Figure 12-9:** Revise the default settings to override Project's calculated costs.

The "Edits to total actual cost will be spread to the status date" checkbox becomes available. Place a check in this box if you want Project to distribute the edits you're going to make through the Status Date. If you leave the box unchecked, Project distributes the edits to the end of the actual duration of the task.

4. Click OK.
5. Select the Task Usage view from the View bar.
6. Right-click the Select All button to display the table shortcut menu and choose Tracking. Project displays the Tracking Table view shown in Figure 12-10.
7. Drag the divider bar to the right so that you can see all the columns.
8. Select the task or resource to which you want to assign a cost.
9. Enter the cost in the Act. Cost column.

If you change your mind and want Project to calculate costs as it originally did, repeat Steps 1, 2, and 3 to restore the default calculation method. Project warns you that it will overwrite any manually entered costs when you click OK.

# Techniques and Tips for Updating

Project users can find ways to accelerate the updating process. For example, you can:

- ✦ Use Project's timephased fields to easily update your project on a regular basis

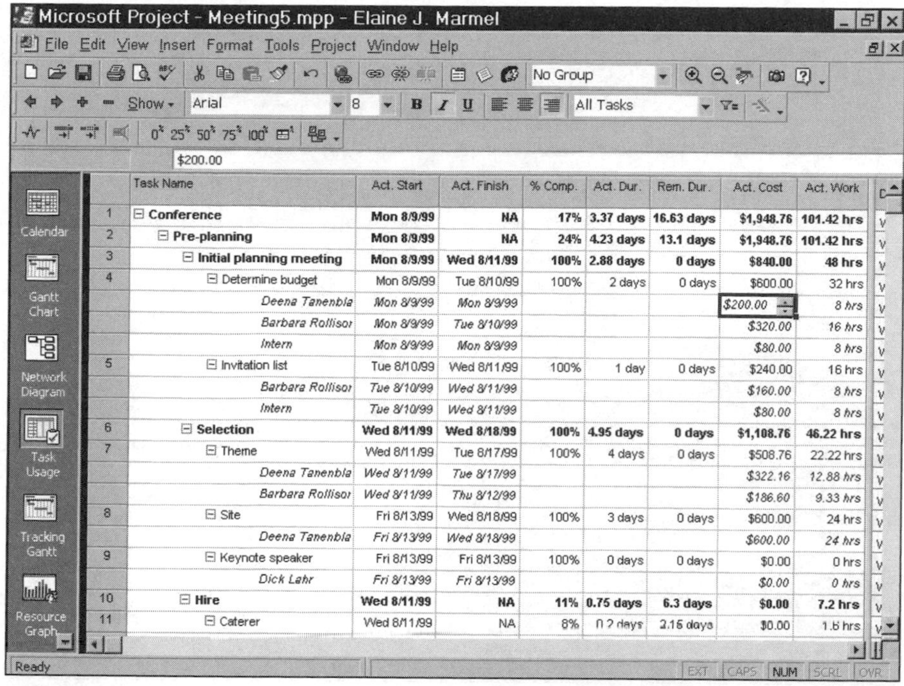

**Figure 12-10:** The Tracking Table view with the Act. Cost (Actual Cost) column visible

- ✦ Update the progress of several tasks simultaneously
- ✦ Reschedule incomplete work so that it starts on the current date

## Tracking work or costs regularly

Project's timephased fields enable you to update the progress on your project on some regular basis, such as daily or weekly. To use timephased fields to record progress information for resources, start by displaying the Resource Usage view (on the View bar, click Resource Usage). Then right-click the Select All button and select Work from the shortcut menu to change the table. Your screen should resemble Figure 12-11.

You're going to want to use most of the right side of the view, but on the left side of the view, you really need only the Actual Work column, which is hidden by the right side of the view. You could slide the divider bar over to the right, but then you'll lose the right side of the view. Or, after sliding the divider bar, you could hide all the columns between the Resource Name column and the Actual Work column — but to redisplay them, you need to insert each of them.

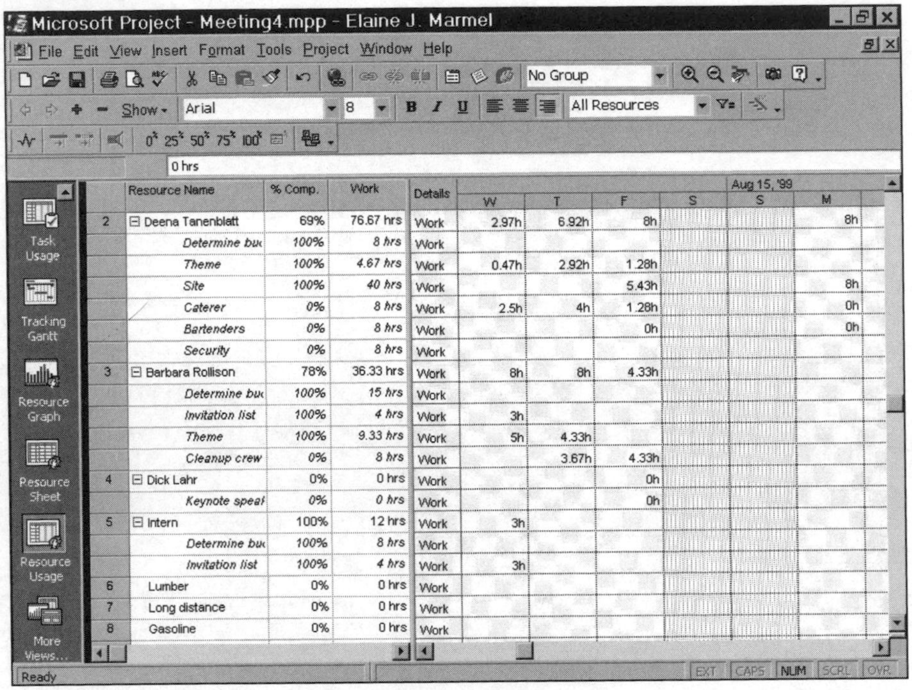

**Figure 12-11:** Setting up to use timephased fields

To set up the left side of the view so that you can see the Actual Work column, add that column between the Resource Name column and the % Comp. (Percent Complete) column. To add the column:

1. Click the title of the Percent Complete column to select the entire column.
2. Choose Insert ➪ Column to open the Column Definition dialog box shown in Figure 12-12.

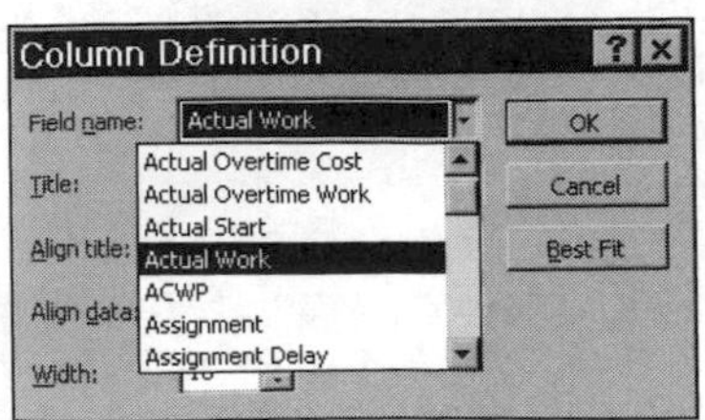


**Figure 12-12:** Add the Actual Work column from the Column Definition dialog box.

3. Open the Field name drop-down list and select Actual Work.
4. Click OK.

Project adds the Actual Work column to the left of the % Comp. column and to the right of the Resource Name column.

Next you should decide how often you want to update your project. If you want to update daily, you don't need to make any changes to the timescale on the right side of the window. But if you want to update weekly (or with some other frequency), you need to change the timescale. To change the timescale, choose Format ⇨ Timescale. Project opens the Timescale dialog box shown in Figure 12-13. This example doesn't require any timescale changes, but if you want to change the timescale to weekly, for example, open the Units list box in the Major scale box and select Months. Then open the Units list box in the Minor scale box and select Weeks.

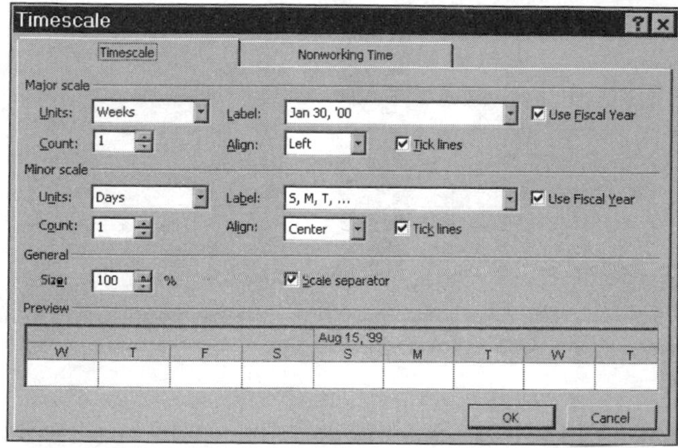


**Figure 12-13:** Use the Timescale dialog box to change the increments that appear on the right side of the Resource Usage view.

**New Feature**

In Project 2000, you can set both the major and minor timescales to use either a calendar or a fiscal year.

When you add a timephased field for Actual Work, you can see the results as you update the schedule. Choose Format ⇨ Details ⇨ Actual Work. Project adds a row for every task on the right side of the view. To enter hours worked for a particular day, click the letter of the column representing that day to select the entire day, as you see in Figure 12-14. Then enter the hours for the correct resource and task in the Actual Work column you added on the left side of the view.

**Note**

Remember, however, that you cannot add costs to override Project's automatically calculated costs unless you open the Options dialog box (choose Tools ⇨ Options), select the Calculation tab, and remove the check from the "Actual costs are always calculated by Microsoft Project" checkbox.

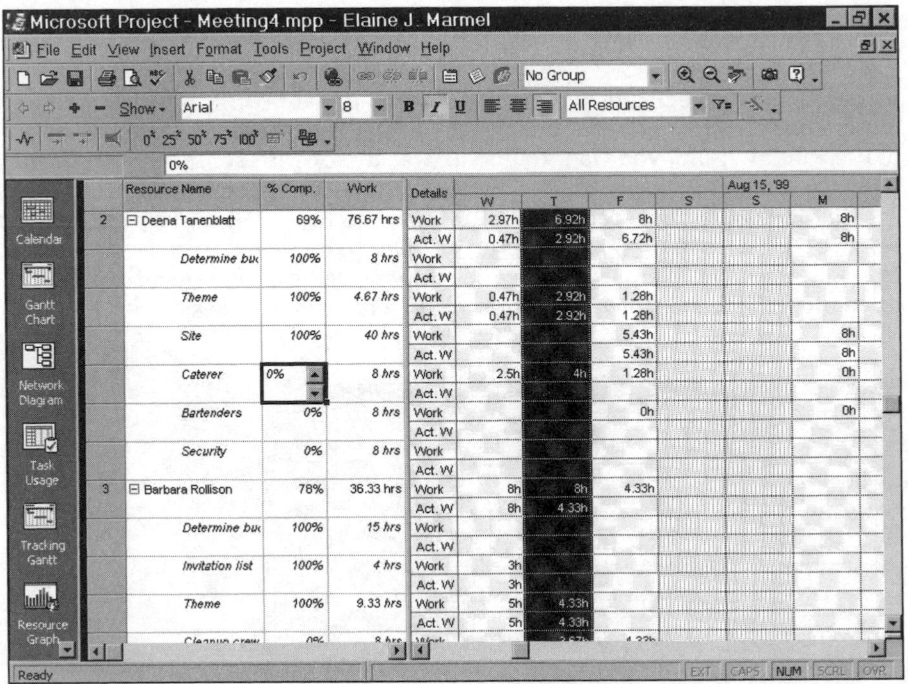


**Figure 12-14:** Add actual work information for a specific day.

This entire process also works if you are updating costs on a daily basis, with two minor changes:

✦ Begin in the Task Usage view instead of the Resource Usage view.

✦ Add the Tracking table instead of the Work table.

Tip

To hide the Actual Work column you added to the left side of the view, select the entire column and then choose Edit ➪ Hide Column. The left side of the view returns to its default appearance. To hide the Actual Work row you added to the right side of the view, choose Format ➪ Details ➪ Actual Work again to remove the checkmark.

# Accelerating the updating process

If you have several tasks that are on schedule or were completed on schedule, you can update these tasks all at once by following these steps:

1. Select the Gantt Chart view from the View bar.

Tip

If you want to update the entire project, don't select any tasks.

2. In the Task Name column, select the tasks you want to update. For example, Figure 12-15 shows three tasks selected for updating.

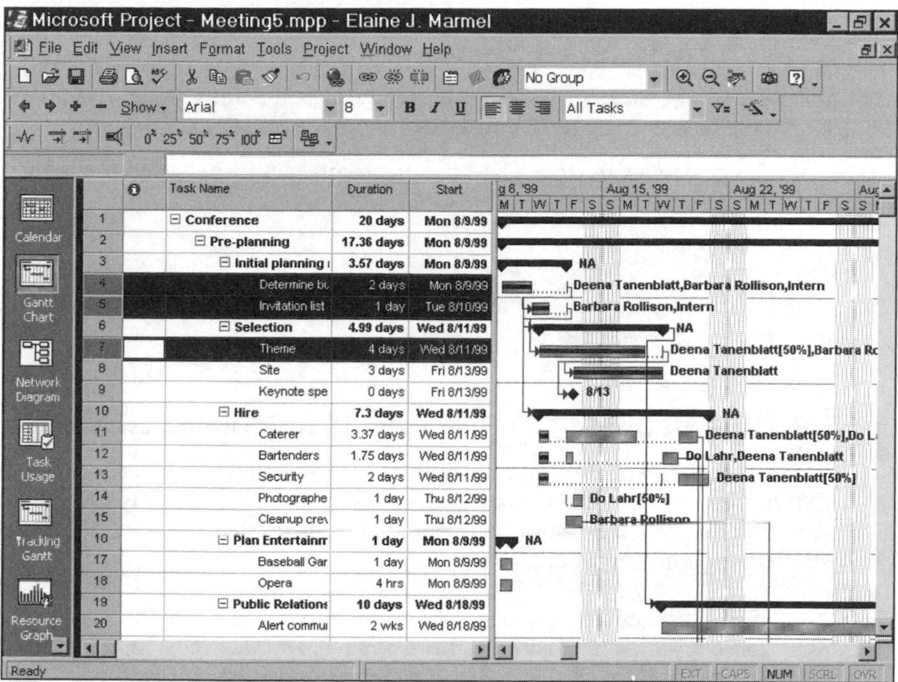

**Figure 12-15:** Selecting tasks to update

You can select tasks using the same techniques you use in Windows Explorer. To select two or more contiguous tasks, click the first task, and then hold down the Shift key and click the last task. To select two or more noncontiguous tasks, hold down the Ctrl key as you click each task that you want to select.

3. Choose Tools ➪ Tracking ➪ Update Project to display the Update Project dialog box shown in Figure 12-16.

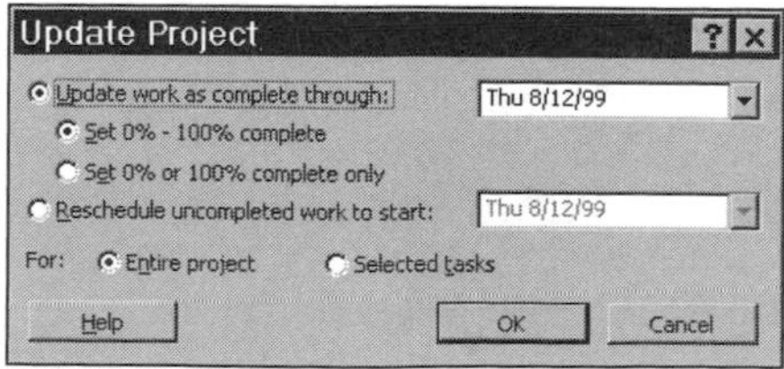


**Figure 12-16:** Use the Update Project dialog box to update your project.

4. Make sure that the correct date appears in the box next to the "Update work as complete through" option button.
5. Select one of the following:
   - "Set 0% – 100% complete" if you want Project to calculate the Percent Complete for each task.
   - "Set 0% or 100% complete only" if you want Project to mark completed tasks with 100% and leave incomplete tasks at 0%.
6. Specify whether to update the entire project or selected tasks by selecting the appropriate option.
7. Click OK.

When you update your project using this method, Project sets the project status date to the date you selected in Step 4.

## Letting Project reschedule uncompleted work

If you updated your project and you had partially completed tasks, you can guarantee that no remaining work is scheduled for dates that have already passed. You can make sure that all remaining work is scheduled for future dates by rescheduling the work to start on the current date.

If you reschedule work using the technique described in this section, Project may remove task constraints you have applied. For example, suppose you reschedule the work of a task that has a Must Finish On constraint, and rescheduling moves the finish date beyond the constraint date. Project does not honor the constraint date; instead, it changes the constraint to As Soon As Possible. If you want to preserve a task's constraints, you should reschedule the remaining work manually.

Follow these steps to tell Project to reschedule remaining work for future dates:

1. Select the Gantt Chart view from the View bar.
2. Go to the Task Name column and select the tasks you want to update.

Tip

See the previous section for techniques you can use to select tasks.

3. Choose Tools ➪ Tracking ➪ Update Project to open the Update Project dialog box shown in Figure 12-17.

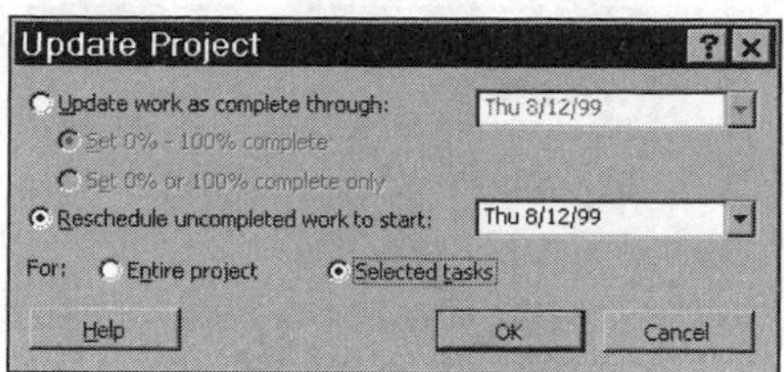


**Figure 12-17:** Use this dialog box to reschedule incomplete work to start today.

4. Click the "Reschedule uncompleted work to start" option button and select the date from which you want to reschedule all unfinished work.
5. Specify whether to update the entire project or selected tasks by selecting the appropriate option button.
6. Click OK.

When you reschedule partially completed tasks using the technique just described, Project automatically splits the task between the completed portion and the remaining portion. Therefore, the Gantt chart may display a split task that has a gap between its two parts because the completed portion may have finished some time before the remaining portion is scheduled to start.

# Reviewing Progress

When you start recording actuals, you're going to want to review the progress of your project — and Project can help you.

## Using the Tracking Gantt view

The Tracking Gantt view in Figure 12-18 probably provides the most effective picture of your project's progress. The bottom bar on the chart portion of the view (black hatching on your screen) represents the baseline dates for each task. The top bar spans either the scheduled start and finish dates or, if a task has been completed, the actual start and finish dates for each task.

If a task is finished, a checkmark appears in the Indicator column on the left side of the view next to the task.

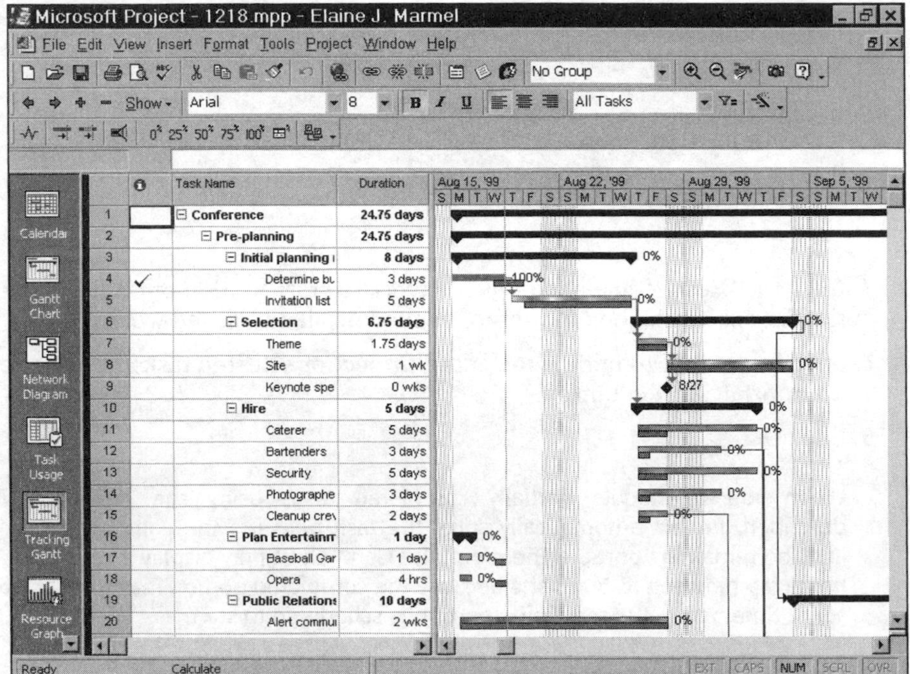


**Figure 12-18:** The Tracking Gantt view helps you understand the progress of your project.

Project formats the taskbar to indicate the task's status:

- ✦ If a task is scheduled, but not yet complete, the top bar appears as blue hatching.
- ✦ If the task is completed, the bar appears solid blue.
- ✦ If a task is partially complete, the completed portion appears as solid blue in the top bar, but the unfinished portion appears as blue hatching.

## Using the Work table for tasks

The Work table for tasks in Figure 12-19 shows the total time required from all resources to complete the task. Work differs from task duration, as follows:

- ✦ Work measures how many person hours are needed to complete a task.
- ✦ Task duration measures the amount of time (number of days) allotted to the task.

If the total work for a task is 16 hours but the task duration is only one day, you'll need to either add another resource (two people could complete the task in one day) or extend the task's duration.

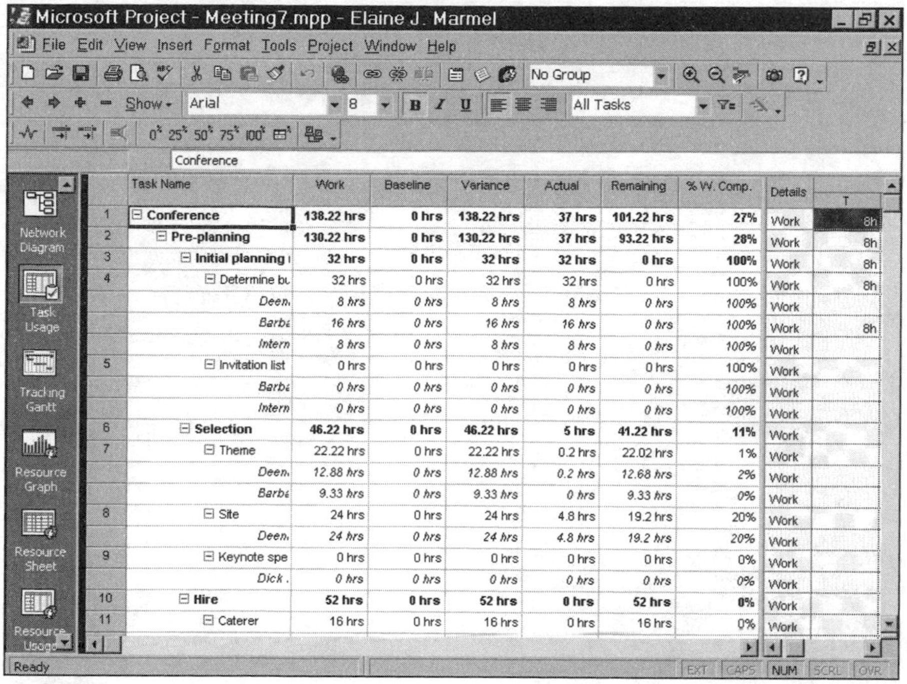

**Figure 12-19:** The Work table for tasks

The Work table for tasks includes baseline information so that you can compare your progress to your original estimate. For this table to be meaningful, therefore, you must have saved a baseline for your project. And as you might have guessed, you can enter information in the Work table for tasks.

You can apply the Work table for tasks to any task sheet view. In Figure 12-19, for example, the Work table for tasks appears on the left side of the Task Usage view. Select the Task Usage view from the View bar; then right-click the Select All button and choose Work.

## Using the Work table for resources

The Work table for resources in Figure 12-20 shows work information for resources. Again, work represents the total time required from all resources to complete the task. The Work table for resources also includes baseline information so that you can compare your progress to your original estimate.

You can apply the Work table for resources to any resource sheet view. In Figure 12-20, for example, the Work table for resources appears on the left side of the Resource Usage view. Select the Resource Usage view from the View bar; then right-click the Select All button and choose Work.

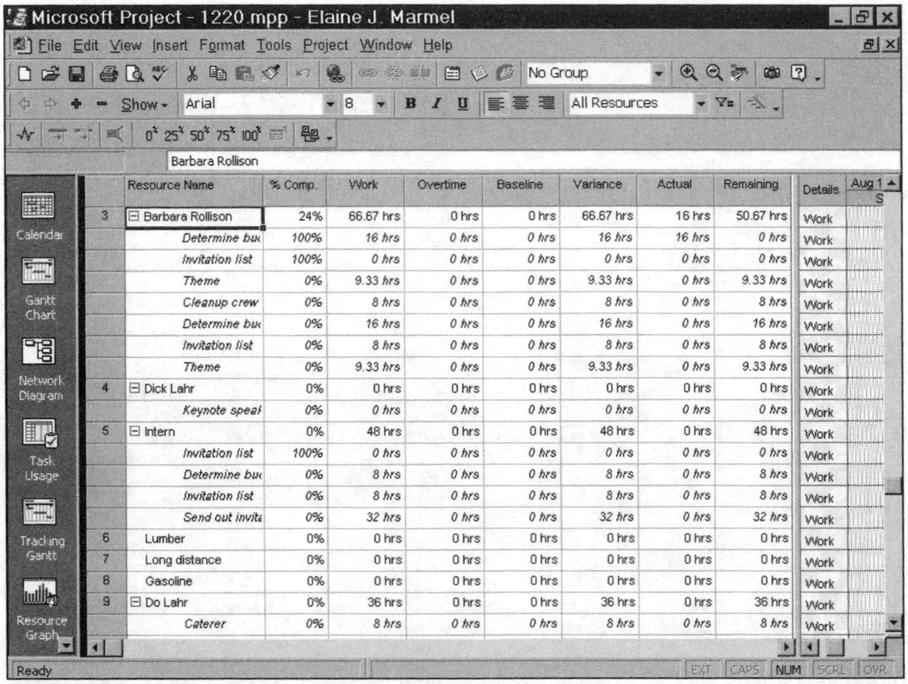


| | Resource Name | % Comp. | Work | Overtime | Baseline | Variance | Actual | Remaining | Details |
|---|---|---|---|---|---|---|---|---|---|
| 3 | ⊟ Barbara Rollison | 24% | 66.67 hrs | 0 hrs | 0 hrs | 66.67 hrs | 16 hrs | 50.67 hrs | Work |
| | *Determine bu* | *100%* | *16 hrs* | *0 hrs* | *0 hrs* | *16 hrs* | *16 hrs* | *0 hrs* | Work |
| | *Invitation list* | *100%* | *0 hrs* | *0 hrs* | *0 hrs* | *0 hrs* | *0 hrs* | *0 hrs* | Work |
| | *Theme* | *0%* | *9.33 hrs* | *0 hrs* | *0 hrs* | *9.33 hrs* | *0 hrs* | *9.33 hrs* | Work |
| | *Cleanup crew* | *0%* | *8 hrs* | *0 hrs* | *0 hrs* | *8 hrs* | *0 hrs* | *8 hrs* | Work |
| | *Determine bu* | *0%* | *16 hrs* | *0 hrs* | *0 hrs* | *16 hrs* | *0 hrs* | *16 hrs* | Work |
| | *Invitation list* | *0%* | *8 hrs* | *0 hrs* | *0 hrs* | *8 hrs* | *0 hrs* | *8 hrs* | Work |
| | *Theme* | *0%* | *9.33 hrs* | *0 hrs* | *0 hrs* | *9.33 hrs* | *0 hrs* | *9.33 hrs* | Work |
| 4 | ⊟ Dick Lahr | 0% | 0 hrs | 0 hrs | 0 hrs | 0 hrs | 0 hrs | 0 hrs | Work |
| | *Keynote speal* | *0%* | *0 hrs* | *0 hrs* | *0 hrs* | *0 hrs* | *0 hrs* | *0 hrs* | Work |
| 5 | ⊟ Intern | 0% | 48 hrs | 0 hrs | 0 hrs | 48 hrs | 0 hrs | 48 hrs | Work |
| | *Invitation list* | *100%* | *0 hrs* | *0 hrs* | *0 hrs* | *0 hrs* | *0 hrs* | *0 hrs* | Work |
| | *Determine bu* | *0%* | *8 hrs* | *0 hrs* | *0 hrs* | *8 hrs* | *0 hrs* | *8 hrs* | Work |
| | *Invitation list* | *0%* | *8 hrs* | *0 hrs* | *0 hrs* | *8 hrs* | *0 hrs* | *8 hrs* | Work |
| | *Send out invit* | *0%* | *32 hrs* | *0 hrs* | *0 hrs* | *32 hrs* | *0 hrs* | *32 hrs* | Work |
| 6 | Lumber | 0% | 0 hrs | 0 hrs | 0 hrs | 0 hrs | 0 hrs | 0 hrs | Work |
| 7 | Long distance | 0% | 0 hrs | 0 hrs | 0 hrs | 0 hrs | 0 hrs | 0 hrs | Work |
| 8 | Gasoline | 0% | 0 hrs | 0 hrs | 0 hrs | 0 hrs | 0 hrs | 0 hrs | Work |
| 9 | ⊟ Do Lahr | 0% | 36 hrs | 0 hrs | 0 hrs | 36 hrs | 0 hrs | 36 hrs | Work |
| | *Caterer* | *0%* | *8 hrs* | *0 hrs* | *0 hrs* | *8 hrs* | *0 hrs* | *8 hrs* | Work |

**Figure 12-20:** The Work table for resources

## Viewing progress lines

Project contains another tool that you can use to show the progress you're making on your project — if you have saved a baseline of your project. If you add progress lines to the Gantt chart of your project, as you see in Figure 12-21, Project draws a line that connects in-progress tasks. The progress line creates a graph of your project, with peaks pointing to the right for work that is ahead of schedule and peaks pointing to the left for work that is behind schedule. The distance between the peaks and the line indicates the degree to which the task is ahead of or behind schedule.

To add a progress line, follow these steps:

1. Click the Gantt Chart view in the View bar.
2. Choose Tools ➪ Tracking ➪ Progress Lines to open the Progress Lines dialog box and display the Dates and Intervals tab.
3. Place a check in the "Display selected progress lines" checkbox to activate the Progress Line Dates drop-down list.

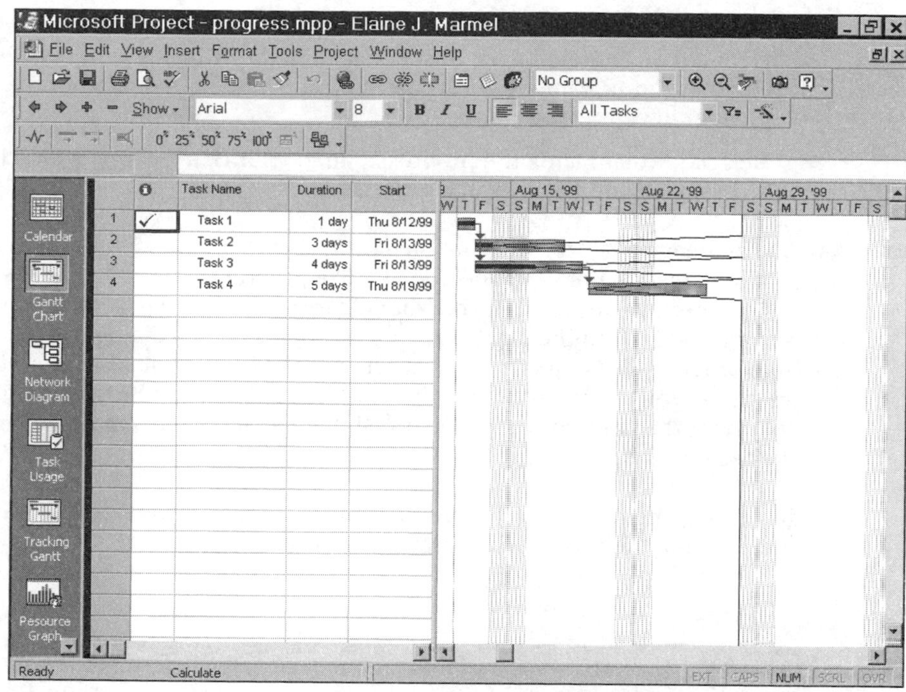

**Figure 12-21:** A Gantt chart with a progress line added

4. Click once on the Progress Line Dates drop-down list. Project displays another list box arrow that you use to set the progress line's date.
5. Click the list box arrow, and a small calendar appears (see Figure 12-22).

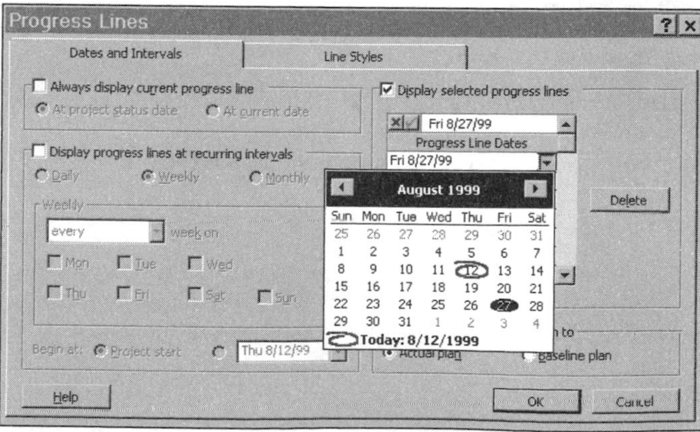

**Figure 12-22:** The Dates and Intervals tab of the Progress Lines dialog box

6. Select a date for the progress line.
7. Select either Actual plan or Baseline plan in the "Display progress lines in relation to" box. These options are partially hidden behind and below the calendar in Figure 12-22.
8. Click OK. Project adds the progress line to your Gantt chart, which looks like the progress line you saw in Figure 12-21.

As you can imagine, a progress line on a project with a large number of tasks could begin to look messy. But if you decide you like progress lines, you can display them at varying intervals, as you can see from Figure 12-22. You can also add specific dates to the list box on the right side of the Progress Lines dialog box to display multiple progress lines on the Gantt chart. If you decide to display more than one progress line, you may want to use the Line Styles tab of the Progress Lines dialog box to format the lines so that you can tell them apart (for example, you can change their colors).

To stop displaying progress lines, reopen the Progress Lines dialog box and remove any checks from the boxes on the Dates and Intervals tab.

# Summary

In this chapter you learned how to record actual information about tasks and resources. For example, you learned how to:

- Set start and finish dates
- Set actual and remaining durations
- Set the percent complete for a task
- Set the work completed for a task
- Use cost tables for tasks and resources
- Review the progress of your project

Chapter 13 shows you how to report on a project's progress.

✦ ✦ ✦

# Reporting on Progress

In This Chapter



As you've seen in Chapters 6 and 7, Project contains various views that help you evaluate the progress of your project, identify areas with problems, and even resolve problems. Although you can print views, sometimes you need to present information in a format that is not available in any view. This chapter examines the use of reports to present your Project information.

## Reporting Commonalities

All reports in Project have certain common characteristics. For example, you can print any report or you can review the report onscreen.

Project organizes reports into categories of reports related to the same subject; that is, all the cost reports fall into the Costs category.

Here's how to display the reports available in a particular category:

1. Choose View ⇨ Reports to open the Reports dialog box (see Figure 13-1).
2. Click the category of report you want.
3. Click Select. Project displays the reports available in that category.
4. Select a report.

As you read through this chapter and see the reports available in each category, you can use the Edit button in the Reports dialog box to change the information that appears on the report. You can also use the Edit button to customize the report, as you learn at the end of this chapter.

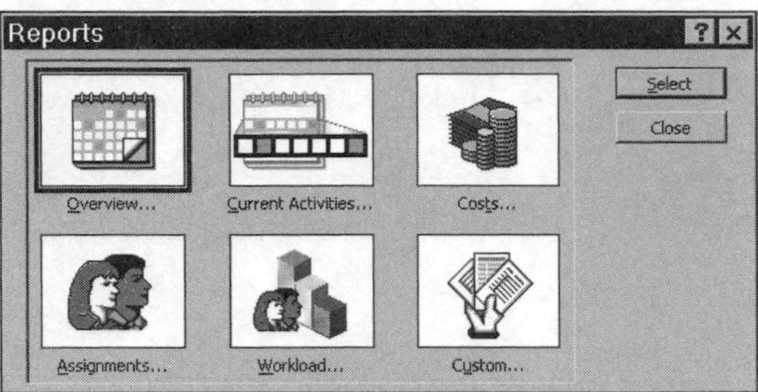


**Figure 13-1:** Select a report category from the Reports dialog box.

5. Click Select. Project displays the report onscreen in Print Preview mode, as you can see in Figure 13-2.

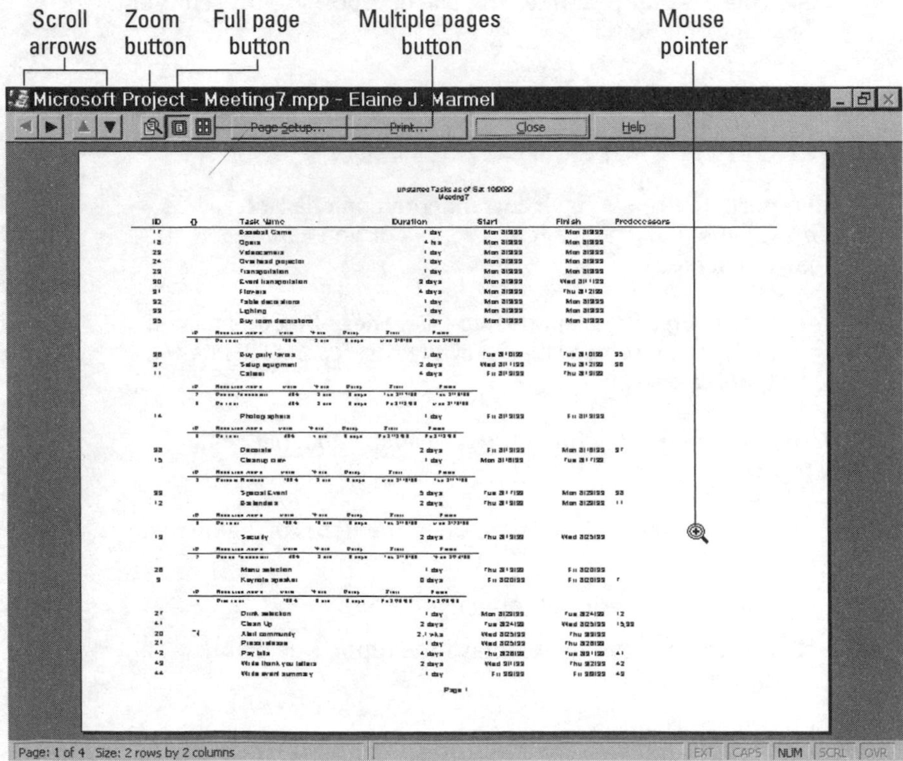


**Figure 13-2:** A report in Print Preview mode

Use the scroll arrows on the toolbar at the top of the screen to move around the report. The Zoom button enlarges the image so that you can read the report's content onscreen. Or if you prefer, click the portion of the report you want to enlarge — the shape of the mouse pointer indicates that it will zoom in on the area you click. To zoom out again, click the Full Page button or click again on the report. To display more than one page at a time, click the Multiple Pages button.

If you decide to print the report, you can review the page settings first. Click the Page Setup button to display the Page Setup dialog box, shown in Figure 13-3.

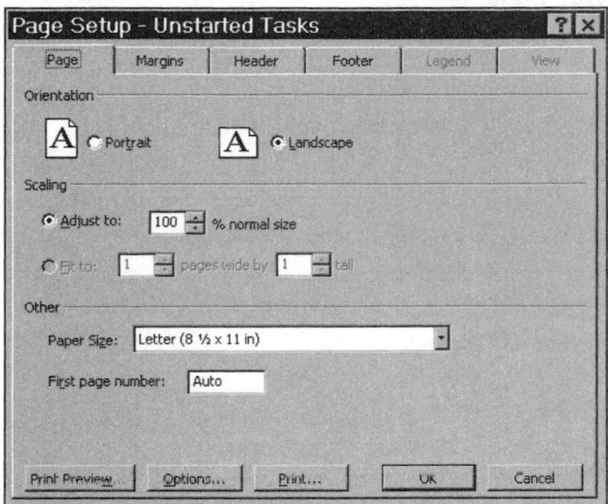


**Figure 13-3:** Use the Page Setup dialog box to set orientation, scaling, margins, and, if appropriate, header and footer information.

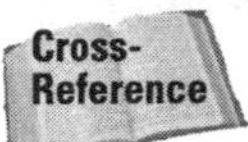


Refer to Chapter 6 for a description of the tabs in the Page Setup dialog box.

To print a report, click the Print button. Project displays the Print dialog box you see in Figure 13-4. Alternatively, you can return to Project by clicking the Close button.

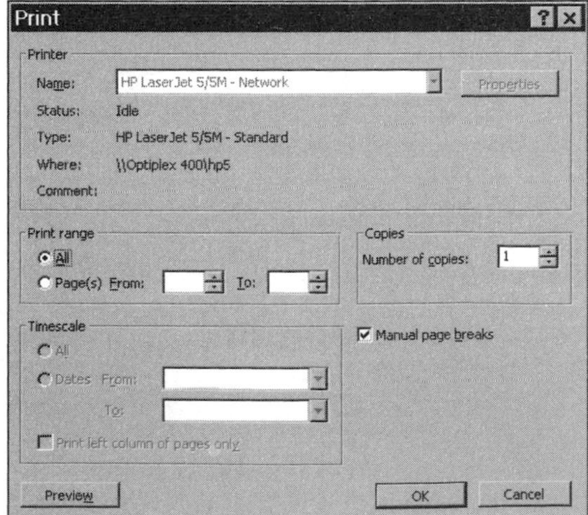


**Figure 13-4:** In the Print dialog box, select a print range for the report.

# Looking at the Big Picture

When you select Overview in the Reports dialog box, Project displays the top-level, summary-type reports (see Figure 13-5).

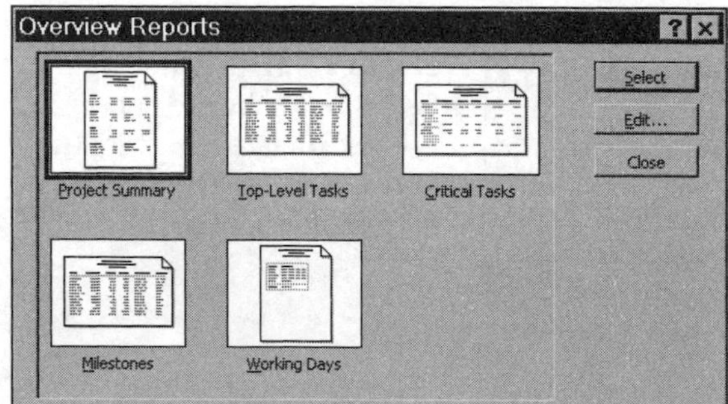


**Figure 13-5:** The reports available in the Overview category

## Project Summary

The Project Summary report (see Figure 13-6) shows top-level information about your project. This report presents summarized information about dates, duration, work, costs, task status, and resource status.

## Top Level Tasks

The Top Level Tasks report (see Figure 13-7) shows, as of today's date, the summary tasks at the highest level in your project. You can see scheduled start and finish dates, the percentage complete for each task, the cost, and the work required to complete the task.

**newres**
**Marmel Enterprises, Inc.**
as of Fri 8/13/99

Dates

| | | | |
|---|---|---|---|
| Start: | Sat 5/15/99 | Finish: | Mon 6/21/99 |
| Baseline Start: | NA | Baseline Finish: | NA |
| Actual Start: | NA | Actual Finish: | NA |
| Start Variance: | 0 days | Finish Variance: | 0 days |

Duration

| | | | |
|---|---|---|---|
| Scheduled: | 26 days | Remaining: | 26 days |
| Baseline: | 0 days | Actual: | 0 days |
| Variance: | 26 days | Percent Complete: | 0% |

Work

| | | | |
|---|---|---|---|
| Scheduled: | 291 hrs | Remaining: | 291 hrs |
| Baseline: | 0 hrs | Actual: | 0 hrs |
| Variance: | 291 hrs | Percent Complete: | 0% |

Costs

| | | | |
|---|---|---|---|
| Scheduled: | $0.00 | Remaining: | $0.00 |
| Baseline: | $0.00 | Actual: | $0.00 |
| Variance: | $0.00 | | |

| Task Status | | Resource Status | |
|---|---|---|---|
| Tasks not yet started: | 21 | Work Resources: | 7 |
| Tasks in progress: | 0 | Overallocated Work Resources: | 1 |
| Tasks completed: | 0 | Material Resources | 0 |
| Total Tasks: | 21 | Total Resources: | 8 |

**Figure 13-6:** The Project Summary report

Top Level Tasks as of Fri 8/13/99
newres

| ID | Task Name | Duration | Start | Finish | % Comp. | Cost | Work |
|---|---|---|---|---|---|---|---|
| 1 | Begin Project | 0 days | Mon 5/17/99 | Mon 5/17/99 | 0% | $0.00 | 0 hrs |
| 2 | **Product Research** | **4 days** | **Mon 5/17/99** | **Thu 5/20/99** | **3%** | **$0.00** | **60 hrs** |
| 7 | **Brochure Design** | **11 days** | **Fri 5/21/99** | **Fri 6/4/99** | **0%** | **$0.00** | **144 hrs** |
| 13 | Write Customer Documentation | 7.25 days | Thu 5/20/99 | Mon 5/31/99 | 0% | $0.00 | 87 hrs |
| 14 | **Press Coverage** | **8.5 days** | **Tue 6/8/99** | **Fri 6/18/99** | **0%** | **$0.00** | **0 hrs** |
| 19 | Print Collateral | 11 days | Mon 6/7/99 | Mon 6/21/99 | 0% | $0.00 | 0 hrs |
| 20 | **Advertising** | **1 day** | **Mon 6/21/99** | **Mon 6/21/99** | **0%** | **$0.00** | **0 hrs** |

**Figure 13-7:** The Top Level Tasks report

## Critical Tasks

The Critical Tasks report (see Figure 13-8) shows the status of the tasks on the critical path of your project—those tasks that make the project late if you don't complete them on time. This report displays each task's planned duration, start and finish dates, the resources assigned to the task, and the predecessors and successors of the task.

Critical Tasks as of Fri 8/13/99
newres

| ID | ⓘ | Task Name | Duration | Start | Finish | Predecessors | Resource Names |
|---|---|---|---|---|---|---|---|
| 1 | | Begin Project | 0 days | Mon 5/17/99 | Mon 5/17/99 | | |

| ID | Successor Name | Type | Lag |
|---|---|---|---|
| 2 | Product Research | FS | 0 days |
| 7 | Brochure Design | FS | 0 days |
| 13 | Write Customer Documentation | FS | 0 days |

| ID | ⓘ | Task Name | Duration | Start | Finish | Predecessors | Resource Names |
|---|---|---|---|---|---|---|---|
| 2 | | Product Research | 4 days | Mon 5/17/99 | Thu 5/20/99 | 1 | |

| ID | Successor Name | Type | Lag |
|---|---|---|---|
| 7 | Brochure Design | FS | 0 days |

| ID | ⓘ | Task Name | Duration | Start | Finish | Predecessors | Resource Names |
|---|---|---|---|---|---|---|---|
| 5 | | Research competition | 4 days | Mon 5/17/99 | Thu 5/20/99 | | Alicia Hon |
| 7 | | Brochure Design | 11 days | Fri 5/21/99 | Fri 6/4/99 | 2,1 | |

| ID | Successor Name | Type | Lag |
|---|---|---|---|
| 19 | Print Collateral | FS | 0 days |

| ID | ⓘ | Task Name | Duration | Start | Finish | Predecessors | Resource Names |
|---|---|---|---|---|---|---|---|
| 8 | | Write copy from overview | 3 days | Fri 5/21/99 | Tue 5/25/99 | | Mick Chen |

| ID | Successor Name | Type | Lag |
|---|---|---|---|
| 9 | Storyboard design | FS | 0 days |

**Figure 13-8:** The Critical Tasks report

## Milestones

The Milestones report (see Figure 13-9) shows information about each milestone in your project. If you marked summary tasks to appear as milestones in the Task Information dialog box, summary tasks also appear on this report as milestones. For each milestone or summary task, Project displays the planned duration, start and finish dates, predecessors, and the resources assigned to the milestone.

Milestones as of Fri 8/13/99
newres

| Task Name | Duration | Start | Finish | Predecessors |
|---|---|---|---|---|
| Begin Project | 0 days | Mon 5/17/99 | Mon 5/17/99 | |
| Press Coverage | 8.5 days | Tue 6/8/99 | Fri 6/18/99 | 10 |
| Press conference | 0 days | Fri 6/18/99 | Fri 6/18/99 | 17 |

**Figure 13-9:** The Milestones report

## Working Days

As you can see from Figure 13-10, the Working Days report shows the base calendar information for your project. You can see the name of the base calendar for the project and the working hours established for each day of the week, along with any exceptions you defined.

| BASE CALENDAR: | Standard |
|---|---|
| Day | Hours |
| Sunday | Nonworking |
| Monday | 8:00 AM - 12:00 PM, 1:00 PM - 5:00 PM |
| Tuesday | 8:00 AM - 12:00 PM, 1:00 PM - 5:00 PM |
| Wednesday | 8:00 AM - 12:00 PM, 1:00 PM - 5:00 PM |
| Thursday | 8:00 AM - 12:00 PM, 1:00 PM - 5:00 PM |
| Friday | 8:00 AM - 12:00 PM, 1:00 PM - 5:00 PM |
| Saturday | Nonworking |
| Exceptions: | None |

**Figure 13-10:** The Working Days report

# Reports on Costs

When you select Costs in the Reports dialog box, Project displays thumbnail sketches of the reports that describe the costs associated with your project (see Figure 13-11).

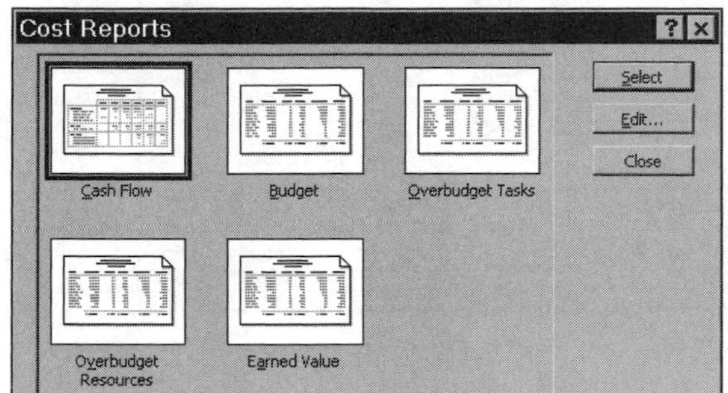


**Figure 13-11:** The reports available in the Cost category

## Cash Flow

The Cash Flow report (see Figure 13-12) is a tabular report that shows, by task, the costs for weekly time increments.

If you click Cash Flow in the Cost Reports dialog box (refer to Figure 13-11) and then select Edit before you choose Select, Project opens the Crosstab Report dialog box, shown in Figure 13-13. On the Definition tab, you can change the time increments.

Cash Flow as of Fri 8/13/99
Space Project Plan

| | 12/28/97 | 1/4/98 | 1/11/98 | 1/18/98 | 1/25/98 | 2/1/98 | 2/8/98 | 2/15/98 |
|---|---|---|---|---|---|---|---|---|
| PROJECT MANAGEMENT | | | | | | | | |
| PLANNING | $536.00 | $2,680.00 | $2,680.00 | $2,680.00 | $2,680.00 | $2,680.00 | $2,680.00 | $2,680.00 |
| SYSTEM ENGINEERING | | | | | | | | |
| REQUIREMENTS | | | | | | | | |
| ANALYSIS | | | | | | | | |
| INTEGRATION | | | | | | | | |
| MISSION OPERATIONS | | | | | | | | |
| SYSTEM TEST PLANNING | | | | | | | | |
| System Engineering Complete | | | | | | | | |
| SPACECRAFT ENGINEERING | | | | | | | | |
| COMMAND AND CONTROL | $536.00 | $2,680.00 | $2,680.00 | $2,680.00 | $2,680.00 | $2,680.00 | $2,680.00 | $2,680.00 |
| ATTITUDE CONTROL | | | | | | | | |
| POWER | | | | | | | | |
| THERMAL | | | | | | | | |
| ORBIT ADJUST PROPULSION | | | | | | | | |
| TANK | $536.00 | $2,680.00 | $2,680.00 | $2,680.00 | $2,144.00 | | | |
| VALVES | | | | | $536.00 | $2,680.00 | $2,680.00 | $2,680.00 |
| THRUSTER | | | | | | | | |
| DESIGN | | | | | | | | |
| FABRICATE | | | | | | | | |
| ASSEMBLE | | | | | | | | |
| TEST | | | | | | | | |
| CONTAINMENT SYSTEM | | | | | | | | |
| Spacecraft Engineering Complete | | | | | | | | |
| AIRBORNE SUPPORT EQUIPMENT | $536.00 | | | | | | | |
| MECHANICAL | $536.00 | $2,680.00 | $2,680.00 | $2,680.00 | $2,680.00 | $2,680.00 | $2,680.00 | $2,680.00 |
| ELECTRICAL | $536.00 | $2,680.00 | $2,680.00 | $2,680.00 | $2,680.00 | $2,680.00 | $2,680.00 | $2,680.00 |
| THERMAL CONTAMINATION | $536.00 | $2,680.00 | $2,680.00 | $2,680.00 | $2,680.00 | $2,680.00 | $2,680.00 | $2,680.00 |
| PRODUCT ASSURANCE | $536.00 | | | | | | | |
| QUALITY ASSURANCE | | | | | | | | |
| RELIABILITY ASSURANCE | $536.00 | $2,680.00 | $2,680.00 | $2,680.00 | $2,680.00 | $2,144.00 | | |
| PARTS CONTROLS | $536.00 | $2,680.00 | $2,680.00 | $2,680.00 | $2,680.00 | $2,680.00 | $2,680.00 | $2,680.00 |
| SYSTEM SAFETY | $536.00 | $2,680.00 | $2,680.00 | $2,680.00 | $2,144.00 | | | |
| MATERIALS & PROCESSES CONTROLS | $536.00 | $2,680.00 | $2,680.00 | $2,680.00 | $2,680.00 | $2,144.00 | | |
| INTEGRATION AND TEST | | | | | | $536.00 | | |
| TEST FACILITIES | | | | | | | $2,680.00 | $2,680.00 |
| TEST SUPPORT | | | | | | | | |
| GSC DESIGN | | | | | | | | |
| POST RETRIEVAL REFURBISHMENT | | | | | | | | |
| DATA REDUCTION | | | | | | | | |
| Assurance and Testing Complete | | | | | | | | |
| LAUNCH SYSTEM INTEGRATION | | | | | | | | |

**Figure 13-12:** The Cash Flow report

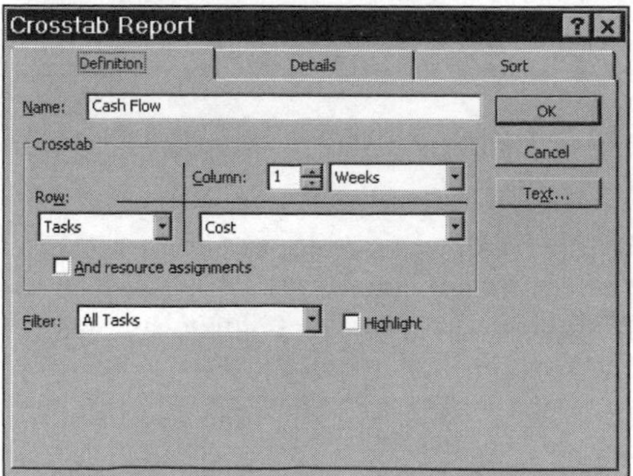


**Figure 13-13:** Use the Crosstab Report dialog box to change the default settings for the report.

See the section "Customizing Reports" at the end of this chapter for more about the Crosstab Report dialog box.

## Earned Value

The Earned Value report (see Figure 13-14) shows you the status of each task's costs when you compare planned to actual costs. Some column headings in the report might seem cryptic; see Table 13-1 for translations.

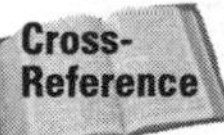

For information on the way Project handles earned value, refer to Chapter 14.

Earned Value as of Fri 8/13/99
Meeting7-98

| ID | Task Name | BCWS | BCWP | ACWP | SV |
|---|---|---|---|---|---|
| 4 | Determine budget | $0.00 | $0.00 | $600.00 | $0.00 |
| 5 | Invitation list | $0.00 | $0.00 | $240.00 | $0.00 |
| 7 | Theme | $0.00 | $0.00 | $321.26 | $0.00 |
| 8 | Site | $0.00 | $0.00 | $35.83 | $0.00 |
| 9 | Keynote speaker | $0.00 | $0.00 | $0.00 | $0.00 |
| 11 | Caterer | $0.00 | $0.00 | $0.00 | $0.00 |
| 12 | Bartenders | $0.00 | $0.00 | $0.00 | $0.00 |
| 13 | Security | $0.00 | $0.00 | $0.00 | $0.00 |
| 14 | Photographers | $0.00 | $0.00 | $0.00 | $0.00 |
| 15 | Cleanup crew | $0.00 | $0.00 | $0.00 | $0.00 |
| 17 | Baseball Game | $0.00 | $0.00 | $0.00 | $0.00 |
| 18 | Opera | $0.00 | $0.00 | $0.00 | $0.00 |
| 20 | Alert community | $0.00 | $0.00 | $0.00 | $0.00 |
| 21 | Press release | $0.00 | $0.00 | $0.00 | $0.00 |
| 23 | Videocamera | $0.00 | $0.00 | $0.00 | $0.00 |
| 24 | Overhead projector | $0.00 | $0.00 | $0.00 | $0.00 |
| 26 | Menu selection | $0.00 | $0.00 | $0.00 | $0.00 |
| 27 | Drink selection | $0.00 | $0.00 | $0.00 | $0.00 |
| 29 | Transportation | $0.00 | $0.00 | $0.00 | $0.00 |
| 30 | Event transportation | $0.00 | $0.00 | $0.00 | $0.00 |
| 31 | Flowers | $0.00 | $0.00 | $0.00 | $0.00 |
| 32 | Table decorations | $0.00 | $0.00 | $0.00 | $0.00 |
| 33 | Lighting | $0.00 | $0.00 | $0.00 | $0.00 |
| 35 | Buy room decorations | $0.00 | $0.00 | $0.00 | $0.00 |
| 36 | Buy party favors | $0.00 | $0.00 | $0.00 | $0.00 |
| 37 | Setup equipment | $0.00 | $0.00 | $0.00 | $0.00 |
| 38 | Decorate | $0.00 | $0.00 | $0.00 | $0.00 |
| 39 | Special Event | $0.00 | $0.00 | $0.00 | $0.00 |
| 41 | Clean Up | $0.00 | $0.00 | $0.00 | $0.00 |
| 42 | Pay bills | $0.00 | $0.00 | $0.00 | $0.00 |
| 43 | Write thank you letters | $0.00 | $0.00 | $0.00 | $0.00 |
| 44 | Write event summary | $0.00 | $0.00 | $0.00 | $0.00 |
| 45 | Vacation | $0.00 | $0.00 | $0.00 | $0.00 |
| | | $0.00 | $0.00 | $1,197.09 | $0.00 |

**Figure 13-14:** The Earned Value report

**Table 13-1**
**Headings in the Earned Value Report**

| *Heading* | *Translation* |
|---|---|
| BCWS | Budgeted Cost of Work Scheduled |
| BCWP | Budgeted Cost of Work Performed |
| ACWP | Actual Cost of Work Performed |
| SV | Schedule Variance |
| CV | Cost Variance |

*Continued*

**Table 13-1 (continued)**

| *Heading* | *Translation* |
|---|---|
| BAC | Budgeted at Completion |
| EAC | Estimate at Completion |
| VAC | Variance at Completion |

Project calculates BCWS, BCWP, ACWP, SV, and CV through the project status date. SV represents the cost difference between current progress and the baseline plan, and Project calculates this value as BCWP minus BCWS. CV represents the cost difference between actual costs and planned costs at the current level of completion, and Project calculates this value as BCWP minus ACWP. EAC shows the planned costs based on costs already incurred plus additional planned costs. VAC represents the variance between the baseline cost and the combination of actual plus planned costs for a task.

## Budget

The Budget report (see Figure 13-15) lists all tasks and shows the budgeted costs as well as the variance between budgeted and actual costs.

Budget Report as of Fri 8/13/99
Meeting7-98

| ID | Task Name | Fixed Cost | Fixed Cost Accrual | Total Cost | Baseline |
|---|---|---|---|---|---|
| 8 | Site | $0.00 | Prorated | $960.00 | $0.00 |
| 4 | Determine budget | $0.00 | Prorated | $600.00 | $0.00 |
| 7 | Theme | $0.00 | Prorated | $508.76 | $0.00 |
| 5 | Invitation list | $0.00 | Prorated | $480.00 | $0.00 |
| 11 | Caterer | $0.00 | Prorated | $400.00 | $0.00 |
| 12 | Bartenders | $0.00 | Prorated | $400.00 | $0.00 |
| 13 | Security | $0.00 | Prorated | $200.00 | $0.00 |
| 35 | Buy room decorations | $0.00 | Prorated | $200.00 | $0.00 |
| 15 | Cleanup crew | $0.00 | Prorated | $160.00 | $0.00 |
| 14 | Photographers | $0.00 | Prorated | $100.00 | $0.00 |
| 9 | Keynote speaker | $0.00 | Prorated | $0.00 | $0.00 |
| 17 | Baseball Game | $0.00 | Prorated | $0.00 | $0.00 |
| 18 | Opera | $0.00 | Prorated | $0.00 | $0.00 |
| 20 | Alert community | $0.00 | Prorated | $0.00 | $0.00 |
| 21 | Press release | $0.00 | Prorated | $0.00 | $0.00 |
| 23 | Videocamera | $0.00 | Prorated | $0.00 | $0.00 |
| 24 | Overhead projector | $0.00 | Prorated | $0.00 | $0.00 |
| 26 | Menu selection | $0.00 | Prorated | $0.00 | $0.00 |
| 27 | Drink selection | $0.00 | Prorated | $0.00 | $0.00 |
| 29 | Transportation | $0.00 | Prorated | $0.00 | $0.00 |
| 30 | Event transportation | $0.00 | Prorated | $0.00 | $0.00 |
| 31 | Flowers | $0.00 | Prorated | $0.00 | $0.00 |
| 32 | Table decorations | $0.00 | Prorated | $0.00 | $0.00 |
| 33 | Lighting | $0.00 | Prorated | $0.00 | $0.00 |
| 36 | Buy party favors | $0.00 | Prorated | $0.00 | $0.00 |
| 37 | Setup equipment | $0.00 | Prorated | $0.00 | $0.00 |
| 38 | Decorate | $0.00 | Prorated | $0.00 | $0.00 |
| 39 | Special Event | $0.00 | Prorated | $0.00 | $0.00 |
| 41 | Clean Up | $0.00 | Prorated | $0.00 | $0.00 |
| 42 | Pay bills | $0.00 | Prorated | $0.00 | $0.00 |
| 43 | Write thank you letters | $0.00 | Prorated | $0.00 | $0.00 |
| 44 | Write event summary | $0.00 | Prorated | $0.00 | $0.00 |
| 45 | Vacation | $0.00 | Prorated | $0.00 | $0.00 |
| | | $0.00 | | $4,008.76 | $0.00 |

**Figure 13-15:** The Budget Report

This report won't have much meaning unless you have saved a baseline of your project; the values in the variance column change from $0.00 as you complete tasks.

## Overbudget reports

Project contains two overbudget reports: one for tasks and one for resources. Neither report prints if you have not yet indicated that some tasks are at least partially completed. Instead, you see the message that appears in Figure 13-16.

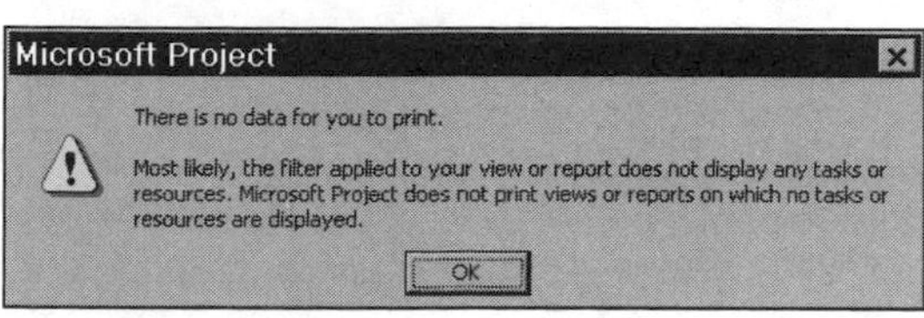


**Figure 13-16:** This message appears when you attempt to print an Overbudget report before you mark any tasks as at least partially complete.

- ✦ **Overbudget Tasks.** This report (see Figure 13-17) shows cost, baseline, variance, and actual information about tasks that exceed their budgeted amounts.
- ✦ **Overbudget Resources.** This report (see Figure 13-18) displays resources whose costs are going to exceed baseline estimates based on the current progress of the project.

Overbudget Tasks as of Fri 8/13/99
Meeting

| ID | Task Name | Fixed Cost | Fixed Cost Accrual | Total Cost | Baseline |
|---|---|---|---|---|---|
| 7 | Theme | $0.00 | Prorated | $1,017.53 | $303.35 |
| 5 | Invitation list | $0.00 | Prorated | $480.00 | $120.00 |
| 8 | Site | $0.00 | Prorated | $1,200.00 | $1,000.00 |
| 4 | Determine budget | $0.00 | Prorated | $600.00 | $580.00 |
| | | $0.00 | | $3,297.53 | $2,003.35 |

**Figure 13-17:** The Overbudget Tasks report

Overbudget Resources as of Fri 8/13/99
Meeting

| ID | Resource Name | Cost | Baseline Cost | Variance |
|---|---|---|---|---|
| 2 | Deena Tanenblatt | $2,444.33 | $1,916.75 | $527.58 |
| 3 | Barbára Rollison | $1,173.20 | $726.60 | $446.60 |
| 9 | Do Lahr | $900.00 | $700.00 | $200.00 |
| 5 | Intern | $240.00 | $120.00 | $120.00 |
| | | $4,757.53 | $3,463.35 | $1,294.18 |

**Figure 13-18:** The Overbudget Resources report

# Reports on Time

Using the Current Activities reporting category, you can produce reports on the timing of your project. Click Current Activities and choose Select to open the Current Activity Reports dialog box (see Figure 13-19) and view the reports available in this category.

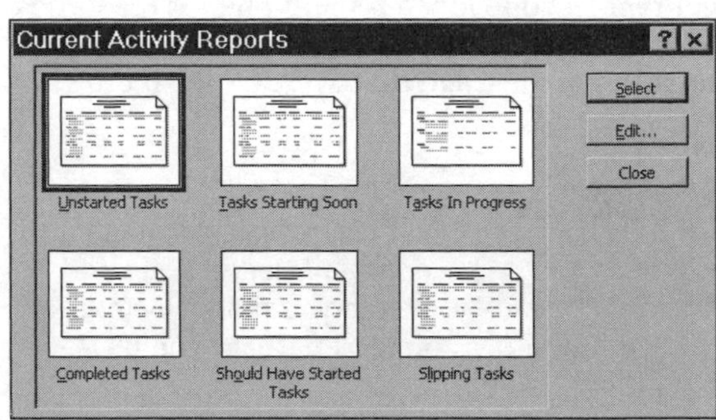


**Figure 13-19:** The reports available in the Current Activity category

## Unstarted Tasks

The Unstarted Tasks report (see Figure 13-20) lists the tasks that have not yet started, sorted by the scheduled start date. For each task, Project displays the duration, predecessor, and resource information if you assigned resources.

Unstarted Tasks as of Fri 8/13/99
Meeting

| ID | | Task Name | Duration | Start | Finish |
|---|---|---|---|---|---|
| 17 | | Baseball Game | 1 day | Mon 8/9/99 | Mon 8/9/99 |
| 18 | | Opera | 4 hrs | Mon 8/9/99 | Mon 8/9/99 |
| 23 | | Videocamera | 1 day | Mon 8/9/99 | Mon 8/9/99 |
| 24 | | Overhead projector | 1 day | Mon 8/9/99 | Mon 8/9/99 |
| 29 | | Transportation | 1 day | Mon 8/9/99 | Mon 8/9/99 |
| 30 | | Event transportation | 3 days | Mon 8/9/99 | Wed 8/11/99 |
| 31 | | Flowers | 4 days | Mon 8/9/99 | Thu 8/12/99 |
| 32 | | Table decorations | 1 day | Mon 8/9/99 | Mon 8/9/99 |
| 33 | | Lighting | 1 day | Mon 8/9/99 | Mon 8/9/99 |
| 35 | | Buy room decorations | 1 day | Mon 8/9/99 | Mon 8/9/99 |

| ID | Resource Name | Units | Work | Delay | Start | Finish |
|---|---|---|---|---|---|---|
| 9 | Do Lahr | 100% | 8 hrs | 0 days | Mon 8/9/99 | Mon 8/9/99 |

| ID | | Task Name | Duration | Start | Finish |
|---|---|---|---|---|---|
| 36 | | Buy party favors | 1 day | Tue 8/10/99 | Tue 8/10/99 |
| 5 | | Invitation list | 1 day | Wed 8/11/99 | Wed 8/11/99 |

| ID | Resource Name | Units | Work | Delay | Start | Finish |
|---|---|---|---|---|---|---|
| 3 | Barbara Rollison | 100% | 8 hrs | 0 days | Wed 8/11/99 | Wed 8/11/99 |
| 5 | Intern | 100% | 8 hrs | 0 days | Wed 8/11/99 | Wed 8/11/99 |

| ID | | Task Name | Duration | Start | Finish |
|---|---|---|---|---|---|
| 37 | | Setup equipment | 2 days | Wed 8/11/99 | Thu 8/12/99 |
| 7 | | Theme | 4 days | Thu 8/12/99 | Tue 8/17/99 |

| ID | Resource Name | Units | Work | Delay | Start | Finish |
|---|---|---|---|---|---|---|
| 2 | Deena Tanenblatt | 50% | 12.88 hrs | 0 days | Thu 8/12/99 | Tue 8/17/99 |
| 3 | Barbara Rollison | 100% | 9.33 hrs | 0 days | Thu 8/12/99 | Fri 8/13/99 |

| ID | | Task Name | Duration | Start | Finish |
|---|---|---|---|---|---|
| 11 | | Caterer | 2 days | Thu 8/12/99 | Fri 8/13/99 |

| ID | Resource Name | Units | Work | Delay | Start | Finish |
|---|---|---|---|---|---|---|
| 2 | Deena Tanenblatt | 50% | 8 hrs | 0 days | Thu 8/12/99 | Fri 8/13/99 |
| 9 | Do Lahr | 50% | 8 hrs | 0 days | Thu 8/12/99 | Fri 8/13/99 |

**Figure 13-20:** The Unstarted Tasks report

## Tasks Starting Soon

When you print the Tasks Starting Soon report (see Figure 13-21), Project displays the Date Range dialog boxes. The information you provide in these two dialog boxes tells Project the date range to use when selecting tasks for this report. In the first dialog box, specify the earlier date and, in the second dialog box, specify the later date. On the report, Project includes tasks that start or finish between the two dates you specify.

Tasks Starting Soon as of Fri 8/13/99
Meeting

| ID | ❶ | Task Name | Duration | Start | Finish |
|---|---|---|---|---|---|
| 5 | | Invitation list | 1 day | Fri 8/13/99 | Fri 8/13/99 |

| ID | Resource Name | Units | Work | Delay | Start | Finish |
|---|---|---|---|---|---|---|
| 3 | Barbara Rollison | 100% | 8 hrs | 0 days | Fri 8/13/99 | Fri 8/13/99 |
| 5 | Intern | 100% | 8 hrs | 0 days | Fri 8/13/99 | Fri 8/13/99 |

| ID | ❶ | Task Name | Duration | Start | Finish |
|---|---|---|---|---|---|
| 7 | | Theme | 4 days | Fri 8/13/99 | Thu 8/19/99 |

| ID | Resource Name | Units | Work | Delay | Start | Finish |
|---|---|---|---|---|---|---|
| 2 | Deena Tanenblatt | 50% | 12.88 hrs | 0 days | Fri 8/13/99 | Thu 8/19/99 |
| 3 | Barbara Rollison | 100% | 9.33 hrs | 0 days | Fri 8/13/99 | Tue 8/17/99 |

| ID | ❶ | Task Name | Duration | Start | Finish |
|---|---|---|---|---|---|
| 8 | | Site | 3 days | Fri 8/13/99 | Mon 8/23/99 |

| ID | Resource Name | Units | Work | Delay | Start | Finish |
|---|---|---|---|---|---|---|
| 2 | Deena Tanenblatt | 100% | 24 hrs | 0 days | Fri 8/13/99 | Mon 8/23/99 |

| ID | ❶ | Task Name | Duration | Start | Finish |
|---|---|---|---|---|---|
| 38 | | Decorate | 2 days | Fri 8/13/99 | Mon 8/16/99 |
| 11 | | Caterer | 2 days | Mon 8/16/99 | Tue 8/17/99 |

| ID | Resource Name | Units | Work | Delay | Start | Finish |
|---|---|---|---|---|---|---|
| 2 | Deena Tanenblatt | 50% | 8 hrs | 0 days | Mon 8/16/99 | Tue 8/17/99 |
| 9 | Do Lahr | 50% | 8 hrs | 0 days | Mon 8/16/99 | Tue 8/17/99 |

**Figure 13-21:** The Tasks Starting Soon report

The information that appears on the report is similar to the information you find on the Unstarted Tasks report: the duration, start and finish dates, predecessors, and resource information, if you assigned resources. Completed tasks also appear on this report; the checkmark that appears in the Indicator column on the report identifies them.

## Tasks in Progress

As you can see from Figure 13-22, the Tasks in Progress report lists tasks that have started but not yet finished. You see the tasks' duration, start and planned finish dates, predecessors, and resource information if you assigned resources.

Tasks in Progress as of Fri 8/13/99
Meeting

| ID | ❶ | Task Name | Duration | Start | Finish |
|---|---|---|---|---|---|
| August 1999 | | | | | |
| 5 | | Invitation list | 1 day | Fri 8/13/99 | Fri 8/13/99 |

| ID | Resource Name | Units | Work | Delay | Start | Finish |
|---|---|---|---|---|---|---|
| 3 | Barbara Rollison | 100% | 8 hrs | 0 days | Fri 8/13/99 | Fri 8/13/99 |
| 5 | Intern | 100% | 8 hrs | 0 days | Fri 8/13/99 | Fri 8/13/99 |

| ID | ❶ | Task Name | Duration | Start | Finish |
|---|---|---|---|---|---|
| 7 | | Theme | 4 days | Fri 8/13/99 | Thu 8/19/99 |

| ID | Resource Name | Units | Work | Delay | Start | Finish |
|---|---|---|---|---|---|---|
| 2 | Deena Tanenblatt | 50% | 12.88 hrs | 0 days | Fri 8/13/99 | Thu 8/19/99 |
| 3 | Barbara Rollison | 100% | 9.33 hrs | 0 days | Fri 8/13/99 | Tue 8/17/99 |

| ID | ❶ | Task Name | Duration | Start | Finish |
|---|---|---|---|---|---|
| 8 | | Site | 3 days | Fri 8/13/99 | Mon 8/23/99 |

| ID | Resource Name | Units | Work | Delay | Start | Finish |
|---|---|---|---|---|---|---|
| 2 | Deena Tanenblatt | 100% | 24 hrs | 0 days | Fri 8/13/99 | Mon 8/23/99 |

**Figure 13-22:** The Tasks in Progress report

## Completed Tasks

The Completed Tasks report (see Figure 13-23) lists tasks that have completed. You can see the actual duration, the actual start and finish dates, the percent complete (always 100 percent — if a task is only partially complete, it won't appear on this report), the cost, and the work hours.

Completed Tasks as of Fri 8/13/99
Meeting

| ID | Task Name | Duration | Start | Finish |
|---|---|---|---|---|
| **August 1999** | | | | |
| 4 | Determine budget | 2 days | Mon 8/9/99 | Tue 8/10/99 |
| 5 | Invitation list | 0 days | Fri 8/13/99 | Fri 8/13/99 |

**Figure 13-23:** The Completed Tasks report

## Should Have Started Tasks

When you print the Should Have Started Tasks report (see Figure 13-24), you must supply a date by which tasks should have started. Project uses this date to determine which tasks appear on the report.

Should Have Started Tasks as of Fri 8/13/99
Meeting

| ID | Task Name | Start | Finish | Baseline Start |
|---|---|---|---|---|
| **1** | **Conference** | **Mon 8/9/99** | **Tue 9/7/99** | **Mon 8/9/99** |
| **2** | **Pre-planning** | **Mon 8/9/99** | **Tue 9/7/99** | **Mon 8/9/99** |
| **16** | **Plan Entertainment** | **Mon 8/9/99** | **Mon 8/9/99** | **Mon 8/9/99** |
| 17 | Baseball Game | Mon 8/9/99 | Mon 8/9/99 | Mon 8/9/99 |
| 18 | Opera | Mon 8/9/99 | Mon 8/9/99 | Mon 8/9/99 |
| **22** | **Rent Equipment** | **Mon 8/9/99** | **Mon 8/9/99** | **Mon 8/9/99** |
| 23 | Videocamera | Mon 8/9/99 | Mon 8/9/99 | Mon 8/9/99 |
| 24 | Overhead projector | Mon 8/9/99 | Mon 8/9/99 | Mon 8/9/99 |
| **28** | **Arrangements** | **Mon 8/9/99** | **Thu 8/12/99** | **Mon 8/9/99** |
| 29 | Transportation | Mon 8/9/99 | Mon 8/9/99 | Mon 8/9/99 |
| 30 | Event transportation | Mon 8/9/99 | Wed 8/11/99 | Mon 8/9/99 |
| 31 | Flowers | Mon 8/9/99 | Thu 8/12/99 | Mon 8/9/99 |
| 32 | Table decorations | Mon 8/9/99 | Mon 8/9/99 | Mon 8/9/99 |
| 33 | Lighting | Mon 8/9/99 | Mon 8/9/99 | Mon 8/9/99 |
| **34** | **Preparation** | **Mon 8/9/99** | **Mon 8/23/99** | **Mon 8/9/99** |
| 35 | Buy room decorations | Mon 8/9/99 | Mon 8/9/99 | Mon 8/9/99 |
| | *ID / Successor Name / Type / Lag* | | | |
| | *36 / Buy party favors / FS / 0 days* | | | |
| 36 | Buy party favors | Tue 8/10/99 | Tue 8/10/99 | Tue 8/10/99 |
| | *ID / Successor Name / Type / Lag* | | | |
| | *37 / Setup equipment / FS / 0 days* | | | |
| 37 | Setup equipment | Wed 8/11/99 | Thu 8/12/99 | Wed 8/11/99 |
| | *ID / Successor Name / Type / Lag* | | | |
| | *38 / Decorate / FS / 0 days* | | | |

**Figure 13-24:** The Should Have Started Tasks report

For each task on the report, Project displays planned start and finish dates, baseline start and finish dates, and variances for start and finish dates. Successor task information appears when a task on the report has a successor defined.

## Slipping Tasks

The Slipping Tasks report (see Figure 13-25) lists the tasks that have been rescheduled from their baseline start dates.

Slipping Tasks as of Fri 8/13/99
Meeting

| ID | Task Name | Start | Finish | Baseline Start | Baseline Finish |
|---|---|---|---|---|---|
| 1 | **Conference** | **Mon 8/9/99** | **Tue 9/7/99** | **Mon 8/9/99** | **Fri 9/3/99** |
| 2 | **Pre-planning** | **Mon 8/9/99** | **Tue 9/7/99** | **Mon 8/9/99** | **Fri 9/3/99** |
| 6 | **Selection** | **Fri 8/13/99** | **Mon 8/23/99** | **Wed 8/11/99** | **Fri 8/20/99** |

| *ID* | *Successor Name* | *Type* | *Lag* |
|---|---|---|---|
| *19* | *Public Relations* | *FS* | *0 days* |

| ID | Task Name | Start | Finish | Baseline Start | Baseline Finish |
|---|---|---|---|---|---|
| 7 | Theme | Fri 8/13/99 | Thu 8/19/99 | Wed 8/11/99 | Fri 8/13/99 |

| *ID* | *Successor Name* | *Type* | *Lag* |
|---|---|---|---|
| *8* | *Site* | *FS* | *0 days* |
| *9* | *Keynote speaker* | *FS* | *0 days* |

| ID | Task Name | Start | Finish | Baseline Start | Baseline Finish |
|---|---|---|---|---|---|
| 8 | Site | Fri 8/13/99 | Mon 8/23/99 | Fri 8/13/99 | Fri 8/20/99 |
| 10 | **Hire** | **Fri 8/13/99** | **Thu 8/19/99** | **Wed 8/11/99** | **Fri 8/13/99** |
| 11 | Caterer | Fri 8/13/99 | Tue 8/17/99 | Wed 8/11/99 | Fri 8/13/99 |

| *ID* | *Successor Name* | *Type* | *Lag* |
|---|---|---|---|
| *12* | *Bartenders* | *FS* | *0 days* |
| *25* | *Meet with Caterer* | *FS* | *0 days* |

**Figure 13-25:** The Slipping Tasks report

This report displays the same information as the information you saw on the Should Have Started Tasks report, but the presentation of the information changes the focus of your attention.

# Reports on Work Assignments

Using the Assignments reporting category, you can produce reports on the resource assignments in your project. Click the Assignments category and choose Select to open the Assignment Reports dialog box (see Figure 13-26) and view the reports available in this category.

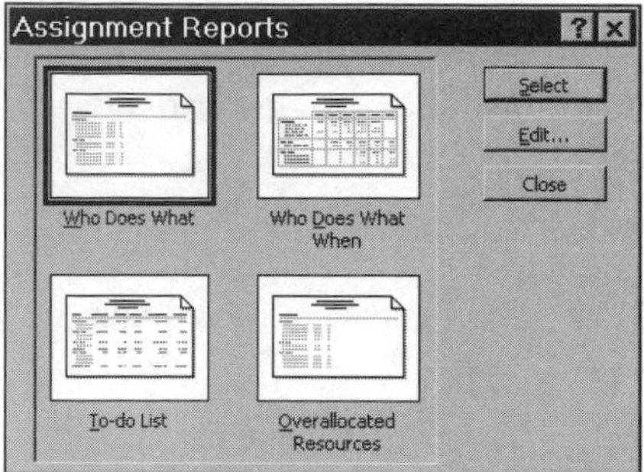


**Figure 13-26:** The reports available in the Assignments category

# Who Does What

The Who Does What report (see Figure 13-27) lists resources and the tasks to which they are assigned, the amount of work planned for each task, the planned start and finish dates, and any resource notes.

| ID | Resource Name | Work |
|---|---|---|
| 1 | Joe Johnson | 0 hrs |
| 2 | Deena Tanenblatt | 60.88 hrs |

| ID | Task Name | Units | Work | Delay | Start | Finish |
|---|---|---|---|---|---|---|
| 4 | Determine budget | 100% | 8 hrs | 0 days | Mon 8/9/99 | Mon 8/9/99 |
| 7 | Theme | 50% | 12.88 hrs | 0 days | Fri 8/13/99 | Thu 8/19/99 |
| 8 | Site | 100% | 24 hrs | 0 days | Fri 8/13/99 | Mon 8/23/99 |
| 11 | Caterer | 50% | 8 hrs | 0 days | Fri 8/13/99 | Tue 8/17/99 |
| 13 | Security | 50% | 8 hrs | 0 days | Tue 8/17/99 | Thu 8/19/99 |

| ID | Resource Name | Work |
|---|---|---|
| 3 | Barbara Rollison | 33.33 hrs |

| ID | Task Name | Units | Work | Delay | Start | Finish |
|---|---|---|---|---|---|---|
| 4 | Determine budget | 100% | 16 hrs | 0 days | Mon 8/9/99 | Tue 8/10/99 |
| 5 | Invitation list | 100% | 0 hrs | 0 days | Fri 8/13/99 | Fri 8/13/99 |
| 7 | Theme | 100% | 9.33 hrs | 0 days | Fri 8/13/99 | Mon 8/16/99 |
| 15 | Cleanup crew | 100% | 8 hrs | 0 days | Fri 8/13/99 | Fri 8/13/99 |

| ID | Resource Name | Work |
|---|---|---|
| 4 | Dick Lahr | 0 hrs |

| ID | Task Name | Units | Work | Delay | Start | Finish |
|---|---|---|---|---|---|---|
| 9 | Keynote speaker | 100% | 0 hrs | 0 days | Thu 8/19/99 | Thu 8/19/99 |

| ID | Resource Name | Work |
|---|---|---|
| 5 | Intern | 8 hrs |

| ID | Task Name | Units | Work | Delay | Start | Finish |
|---|---|---|---|---|---|---|
| 4 | Determine budget | 100% | 8 hrs | 0 days | Mon 8/9/99 | Mon 8/9/99 |
| 5 | Invitation list | 100% | 0 hrs | 0 days | Fri 8/13/99 | Fri 8/13/99 |

| ID | Resource Name | Work |
|---|---|---|
| 9 | Do Lahr | 36 hrs |

| ID | Task Name | Units | Work | Delay | Start | Finish |
|---|---|---|---|---|---|---|
| 11 | Caterer | 50% | 8 hrs | 0 days | Fri 8/13/99 | Mon 8/16/99 |
| 12 | Bartenders | 100% | 16 hrs | 0 days | Tue 8/17/99 | Thu 8/19/99 |
| 14 | Photographers | 50% | 4 hrs | 0 days | Fri 8/13/99 | Fri 8/13/99 |
| 35 | Buy room decorations | 100% | 8 hrs | 0 days | Mon 8/9/99 | Mon 8/9/99 |

**Figure 13-27:** The Who Does What report

# Who Does What When

The Who Does What When report (see Figure 13-28) also lists resources and the tasks to which they are assigned, but this report focuses your attention on the daily work scheduled for each resource on each task.

**Tip** You can use the Edit button in the Assignment Reports dialog box to change the timescale on the report from daily to some other increment, such as weekly. See "Customizing Reports" at the end of this chapter for more information.

Who Does What When as of Fri 8/13/99
Meeting

| | 8/8 | 8/9 | 8/10 | 8/11 | 8/12 | 8/13 | 8/14 | 8/15 | 8/16 | 8/17 | 8/18 | 8/19 | 8/20 | 8/21 |
|---|---|---|---|---|---|---|---|---|---|---|---|---|---|---|
| Joe Johnson | | | | | | | | | | | | | | |
| Deena Tanenblatt | | 8 hrs | | | | ###### | | | ###### | 8 hrs | 8 hrs | ###### | 8 hrs | |
| Determine budget | | 8 hrs | | | | | | | | | | | | |
| Theme | | | | | | ###### | | | ###### | 4 hrs | 4 hrs | 0.2 hrs | | |
| Site | | | | | | 4.8 hrs | | | | | | 7.6 hrs | 8 hrs | |
| Caterer | | | | | | 1.6 hrs | | | 4 hrs | 2.4 hrs | | | | |
| Security | | | | | | | | | | 1.6 hrs | 4 hrs | 2.4 hrs | | |
| Barbara Rollison | | 8 hrs | 8 hrs | | | 16 hrs | | | ###### | | | | | |
| Determine budget | | 8 hrs | 8 hrs | | | | | | | | | | | |
| Invitation list | | | | | | | | | | | | | | |
| Theme | | | | | | 8 hrs | | | ###### | | | | | |
| Cleanup crew | | | | | | 8 hrs | | | | | | | | |
| Dick Lahr | | | | | | | | | | | | | | |
| Keynote speaker | | | | | | | | | | | | | | |
| Intern | | 8 hrs | | | | | | | | | | | | |
| Determine budget | | 8 hrs | | | | | | | | | | | | |
| Invitation list | | | | | | | | | | | | | | |
| Do Lahr | | 8 hrs | | | | 8 hrs | | | 4 hrs | 3.2 hrs | 8 hrs | 4.8 hrs | | |
| Caterer | | | | | | 4 hrs | | | 4 hrs | | | | | |
| Bartenders | | | | | | | | | | 3.2 hrs | 8 hrs | 4.8 hrs | | |
| Photographers | | | | | | 4 hrs | | | | | | | | |
| Buy room decorations | | 8 hrs | | | | | | | | | | | | |

**Figure 13-28:** The Who Does What When report

# To Do List

The To Do List report in Figure 13-29 lists, on a weekly basis, the tasks assigned to a resource you select. When you are ready to print this report, Project first displays the Using Resource dialog box, which contains the Show tasks using list box. When you open the list box, you see a list of your resources. Select a resource and click OK. The To Do List report shows the task ID number, duration, start and finish dates, predecessors, and a list of all of the resources assigned to each task.

To Do List as of Fri 8/13/99
Meeting

| ID | | Task Name | Duration | Start | Finish |
|---|---|---|---|---|---|
| **Week of August 8** | | | | | |
| 4 | ✓ | Determine budget | 2 days | Mon 8/9/99 | Tue 8/10/99 |
| 7 | | Theme | 4.05 days | Fri 8/13/99 | Thu 8/19/99 |
| 8 | | Site | 3 days | Fri 8/13/99 | Mon 8/23/99 |
| 11 | | Caterer | 2.6 days | Fri 8/13/99 | Tue 8/17/99 |
| **Week of August 15** | | | | | |
| 7 | | Theme | 4.05 days | Fri 8/13/99 | Thu 8/19/99 |
| 8 | | Site | 3 days | Fri 8/13/99 | Mon 8/23/99 |
| 11 | | Caterer | 2.6 days | Fri 8/13/99 | Tue 8/17/99 |
| 13 | | Security | 2 days | Tue 8/17/99 | Thu 8/19/99 |
| **Week of August 22** | | | | | |
| 8 | | Site | 3 days | Fri 8/13/99 | Mon 8/23/99 |

**Figure 13-29:** The To Do List report

## Overallocated Resources

The Overallocated Resources report shown in Figure 13-30 shows the overallocated resources, the tasks to which they are assigned, and the total hours of work assigned to them. You can also see the details of each task, such as the allocation, the amount of work, any delay, and the start and finish dates.

Overallocated Resources as of Fri 8/13/99
Meeting

| ID | | Resource Name | Work |
|---|---|---|---|
| 3 | ◈ | Barbara Rollison | 33.33 hrs |

| ID | Task Name | Units | Work | Delay | Start | Finish |
|---|---|---|---|---|---|---|
| 4 | Determine budget | 100% | 16 hrs | 0 days | Mon 8/9/99 | Tue 8/10/99 |
| 5 | Invitation list | 100% | 0 hrs | 0 days | Fri 8/13/99 | Fri 8/13/99 |
| 7 | Theme | 100% | 9.33 hrs | 0 days | Fri 8/13/99 | Mon 8/16/99 |
| 15 | Cleanup crew | 100% | 8 hrs | 0 days | Fri 8/13/99 | Fri 8/13/99 |

| ID | | Resource Name | Work |
|---|---|---|---|
| 2 | ◈ | Deena Tanenblatt | 60.88 hrs |

| ID | Task Name | Units | Work | Delay | Start | Finish |
|---|---|---|---|---|---|---|
| 4 | Determine budget | 100% | 8 hrs | 0 days | Mon 8/9/99 | Mon 8/9/99 |
| 7 | Theme | 50% | 12.88 hrs | 0 days | Fri 8/13/99 | Thu 8/19/99 |
| 8 | Site | 100% | 24 hrs | 0 days | Fri 8/13/99 | Mon 8/23/99 |
| 11 | Caterer | 50% | 8 hrs | 0 days | Fri 8/13/99 | Tue 8/17/99 |
| 13 | Security | 50% | 8 hrs | 0 days | Tue 8/17/99 | Thu 8/19/99 |

94.21 hrs

**Figure 13-30:** The Overallocated Resources report

# Reports on Workloads

You can use the Workload reporting category to produce reports on task and resource usage in your project. Click Workload in the Reports dialog box and choose Select to open the Workload Reports dialog box shown in Figure 13-31.

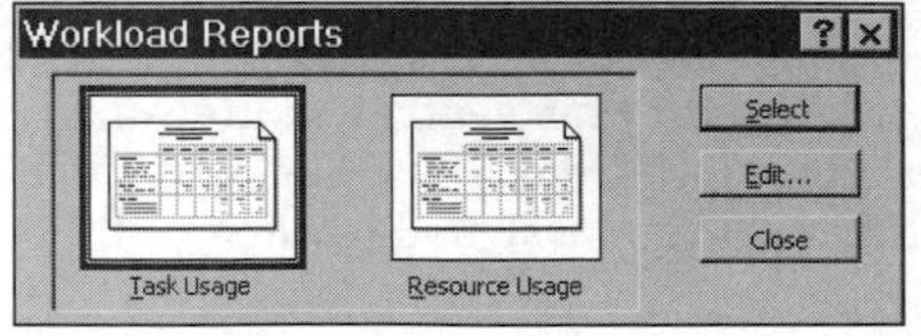


**Figure 13-31:** The Workload Reports dialog box

## Task Usage

The Task Usage report (see Figure 13-32) lists tasks and resources assigned to each task. It also displays the amount of work assigned to each resource in weekly time increments.

You can change the time increment by clicking Edit in the Workload Reports dialog box. See "Customizing Reports" later in this chapter for more information about editing reports.

Task Usage as of Fri 8/13/99
Meeting

| | 8/8/99 | 8/15/99 | 8/22/99 | 8/29/99 | 9/5/99 | Total |
|---|---|---|---|---|---|---|
| Conference | | | | | | |
| Pre-planning | | | | | | |
| Initial planning meeting | | | | | | |
| Determine budget | 32 hrs | | | | | 32 hrs |
| Deena Tanenblatt | 8 hrs | | | | | 8 hrs |
| Barbara Rollison | 16 hrs | | | | | 16 hrs |
| Intern | 8 hrs | | | | | 8 hrs |
| Invitation list | | | | | | |
| Barbara Rollison | | | | | | |
| Intern | | | | | | |
| Selection | | | | | | |
| Theme | 9.12 hrs | 13.1 hrs | | | | 22.22 hrs |
| Deena Tanenblatt | 1.12 hrs | 11.77 hrs | | | | 12.88 hrs |
| Barbara Rollison | 8 hrs | 1.33 hrs | | | | 9.33 hrs |
| Site | 4.8 hrs | 15.6 hrs | 3.6 hrs | | | 24 hrs |
| Deena Tanenblatt | 4.8 hrs | 15.6 hrs | 3.6 hrs | | | 24 hrs |
| Keynote speaker | | | | | | |
| Dick Lahr | | | | | | |
| Hire | | | | | | |
| Caterer | 5.6 hrs | 10.4 hrs | | | | 16 hrs |
| Deena Tanenblatt | 1.6 hrs | 6.4 hrs | | | | 8 hrs |
| Do Lahr | 4 hrs | 4 hrs | | | | 8 hrs |
| Bartenders | | 16 hrs | | | | 16 hrs |
| Do Lahr | | 16 hrs | | | | 16 hrs |
| Security | | 8 hrs | | | | 8 hrs |
| Deena Tanenblatt | | 8 hrs | | | | 8 hrs |
| Photographers | 4 hrs | | | | | 4 hrs |
| Do Lahr | 4 hrs | | | | | 4 hrs |
| Cleanup crew | 8 hrs | | | | | 8 hrs |
| Barbara Rollison | 8 hrs | | | | | 8 hrs |

**Figure 13-32:** The Task Usage report

# Resource Usage

The Resource Usage report (see Figure 13-33) lists resources and the tasks to which they are assigned. Like the Task Usage report, this report shows the amount of work assigned to each resource for each task in weekly time increments, but this report focuses your attention on the resource.

Project 2000 contains two variations on the Resource Usage report—the Resource Usage (material) and Resource Usage (work) reports. Both reports look identical to the Resource Usage report but, as you'd expect, one shows only material resources while the other shows only work resources. Both reports are custom reports; to print them, follow the instructions in the next section.

Resource Usage as of Fri 8/13/99
Meeting

| | 8/8/99 | 8/15/99 | 8/22/99 | 8/29/99 | 9/5/99 | Total |
|---|---|---|---|---|---|---|
| Joe Johnson | | | | | | |
| Deena Tanenblatt | 15.52 hrs | 41.77 hrs | 3.6 hrs | | | 60.88 hrs |
| Determine budget | 8 hrs | | | | | 8 hrs |
| Theme | 1.12 hrs | 11.77 hrs | | | | 12.88 hrs |
| Site | 4.8 hrs | 15.6 hrs | 3.6 hrs | | | 24 hrs |
| Caterer | 1.6 hrs | 6.4 hrs | | | | 8 hrs |
| Security | | 8 hrs | | | | 8 hrs |
| Barbara Rollison | 32 hrs | 1.33 hrs | | | | 33.33 hrs |
| Determine budget | 16 hrs | | | | | 16 hrs |
| Invitation list | | | | | | |
| Theme | 8 hrs | 1.33 hrs | | | | 9.33 hrs |
| Cleanup crew | 8 hrs | | | | | 8 hrs |
| Dick Lahr | | | | | | |
| Keynote speaker | | | | | | |
| Intern | 8 hrs | | | | | 8 hrs |
| Determine budget | 8 hrs | | | | | 8 hrs |
| Invitation list | | | | | | |
| Lumber (Ft.) | | | | | | |
| Long distance (Min.) | | | | | | |
| Gasoline (Gal./hr) | | | | | | |
| Do Lahr | 16 hrs | 20 hrs | | | | 36 hrs |
| Caterer | 4 hrs | 4 hrs | | | | 8 hrs |
| Bartenders | | 16 hrs | | | | 16 hrs |
| Photographers | 4 hrs | | | | | 4 hrs |
| Buy room decorations | 8 hrs | | | | | 8 hrs |
| Total | 71.52 hrs | 63.1 hrs | 3.6 hrs | | | 138.22 hrs |

**Figure 13-33:** The Resource Usage report

# Customizing Reports

Project contains some custom reports; in addition to printing these custom reports, you can customize any of the other reports described in this chapter. Click the Custom category in the Reports dialog box and choose Select to open the Custom Reports dialog box shown in Figure 13-34.

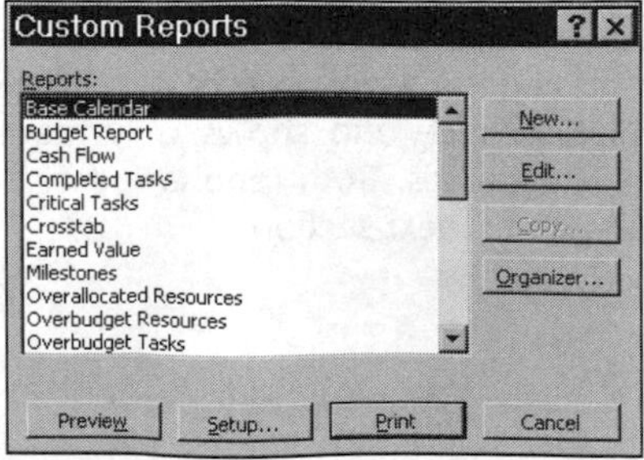


**Figure 13-34:** The Custom Reports dialog box

Not all the reports listed in the Custom Reports dialog box are custom reports. But you can print any of the standard reports either from this dialog box or as described earlier in this chapter. However, you must use this dialog box to print the three custom reports.

**Note**

You can create your own reports by clicking the New button in the Custom Reports dialog box, shown in Figure 13-34. When you define a new custom report, Project offers you four formats. Three formats are based on the reports discussed in this section: the Task report format, the Resource report format, and the Crosstab report format. The fourth format is the Monthly Calendar format, and it functions just like the Working Days report you learned about earlier in this chapter.

# Custom reports

Project contains three custom reports:

- ✦ The Task report
- ✦ The Resource report
- ✦ The Crosstab report

## Task report

The Task report (see Figure 13-35) shows task information such as the ID number, the task name, indicator icons, the task duration, planned start and finish dates, predecessors, and, if resources have been assigned, resource names.

Task as of Fri 8/13/99
Meeting

| ID | ❶ | Task Name | Duration | Start | Finish |
|---|---|---|---|---|---|
| 4 | ✓ | Determine budget | 2 days | Mon 8/9/99 | Tue 8/10/99 |
| 5 | ✓ | Invitation list | 0 days | Fri 8/13/99 | Fri 8/13/99 |
| 7 | | Theme | 4.05 days | Fri 8/13/99 | Thu 8/19/99 |
| 8 | | Site | 3 days | Fri 8/13/99 | Mon 8/23/99 |
| 9 | | Keynote speaker | 0 days | Thu 8/19/99 | Thu 8/19/99 |
| 11 | | Caterer | 2.6 days | Fri 8/13/99 | Tue 8/17/99 |
| 12 | | Bartenders | 2 days | Tue 8/17/99 | Thu 8/19/99 |
| 13 | | Security | 2 days | Tue 8/17/99 | Thu 8/19/99 |
| 14 | | Photographers | 1 day | Fri 8/13/99 | Fri 8/13/99 |
| 15 | | Cleanup crew | 1 day | Fri 8/13/99 | Fri 8/13/99 |
| 17 | | Baseball Game | 1 day | Mon 8/9/99 | Mon 8/9/99 |
| 18 | | Opera | 4 hrs | Mon 8/9/99 | Mon 8/9/99 |
| 20 | ▦ | Alert community | 2.1 wks | Mon 8/23/99 | Tue 9/7/99 |
| 21 | | Press release | 1 day | Mon 8/23/99 | Tue 8/24/99 |
| 23 | | Videocamera | 1 day | Mon 8/9/99 | Mon 8/9/99 |
| 24 | | Overhead projector | 1 day | Mon 8/9/99 | Mon 8/9/99 |
| 26 | | Menu selection | 1 day | Tue 8/17/99 | Wed 8/18/99 |
| 27 | | Drink selection | 1 day | Thu 8/19/99 | Fri 8/20/99 |
| 29 | | Transportation | 1 day | Mon 8/9/99 | Mon 8/9/99 |
| 30 | | Event transportation | 3 days | Mon 8/9/99 | Wed 8/11/99 |
| 31 | | Flowers | 4 days | Mon 8/9/99 | Thu 8/12/99 |
| 32 | | Table decorations | 1 day | Mon 8/9/99 | Mon 8/9/99 |
| 33 | | Lighting | 1 day | Mon 8/9/99 | Mon 8/9/99 |
| 35 | | Buy room decorations | 1 day | Mon 8/9/99 | Mon 8/9/99 |
| 36 | | Buy party favors | 1 day | Tue 8/10/99 | Tue 8/10/99 |
| 37 | | Setup equipment | 2 days | Wed 8/11/99 | Thu 8/12/99 |
| 38 | | Decorate | 2 days | Fri 8/13/99 | Mon 8/16/99 |
| 39 | | Special Event | 5 days | Tue 8/17/99 | Mon 8/23/99 |
| 41 | | Clean Up | 2 days | Tue 8/24/99 | Wed 8/25/99 |
| 42 | | Pay bills | 4 days | Thu 8/26/99 | Tue 8/31/99 |
| 43 | | Write thank you letters | 2 days | Wed 9/1/99 | Thu 9/2/99 |
| 44 | | Write event summary | 1 day | Fri 9/3/99 | Fri 9/3/99 |
| 45 | | Vacation | 0 days | Fri 9/3/99 | Fri 9/3/99 |

**Figure 13-35:** The Task report

## Resource report

As you can see from the report sample shown in Figure 13-36, the Resource report shows resource information: resource ID numbers; indicator icons; resource names, initials, and groups; maximum units; rate information; accrual information; base calendar information; and code information.

Resource as of Fri 8/13/99
Meeting

| ID | | Resource Name | Type | Material Label | Initials | Group | Max. Units |
|---|---|---|---|---|---|---|---|
| 1 | | Joe Johnson | Work | | J | | 100% |
| 2 | | Deena Tanenblatt | Work | | D | | 100% |
| 3 | | Barbara Rollison | Work | | B | | 100% |
| 4 | | Dick Lahr | Work | | D | | 100% |
| 5 | | Intern | Work | | I | | 100% |
| 6 | | Lumber | Material | Ft. | L | | |
| 7 | | Long distance | Material | Min. | L | | |
| 8 | | Gasoline | Material | Gal./hr | G | | |
| 9 | | Do Lahr | Work | | D | | 100% |

**Figure 13-36:** The Resource report

Project 2000 contains two variations on the Resource report—the Resource (material) and Resource (work) reports. Both reports look identical to the Resource report but, as you'd expect, one shows only material resources while the other shows only work resources.

## Crosstab report

The Crosstab report (see Figure 13-37) is a tabular report that shows task and resource information in rows and time increments in columns.

| | 8/8 | 8/15 |
|---|---|---|
| Conference | | |
| Pre-planning | | |
| Initial planning meeting | | |
| Determine budget | $600.00 | |
| Deena Tanenblatt | $200.00 | |
| Barbara Rollison | $320.00 | |
| Intern | $80.00 | |
| Invitation list | $240.00 | |
| Barbara Rollison | $160.00 | |
| Intern | $80.00 | |
| Selection | | |
| Theme | $554.17 | $458.23 |
| Deena Tanenblatt | $207.57 | $431.63 |
| Barbara Rollison | $346.60 | $26.60 |
| Site | $135.83 | $854.17 |
| Deena Tanenblatt | $135.83 | $854.17 |

**Figure 13-37:** The Crosstab report

Much of the information on the Crosstab report also appears on the Task Usage report and the Resource Usage report. These reports give you more formatting options, such as the period covered by the report and the table used in the report.

## Customizing an existing report

You can customize almost every report you've seen in this chapter. For a few reports, such as the Working Days report, the only item you can change is the font information Project uses to print the report. For other reports, however, you can change the table or the task or resource filter to change the content of the report. Click the Edit button when preparing to print the report to make these changes. When you click the Edit button, Project opens the dialog box that relates to the report you selected. For example, if you select the Working Days report and then click Edit in the Overview Reports dialog box, Project opens the Report Text dialog box shown in Figure 13-38.

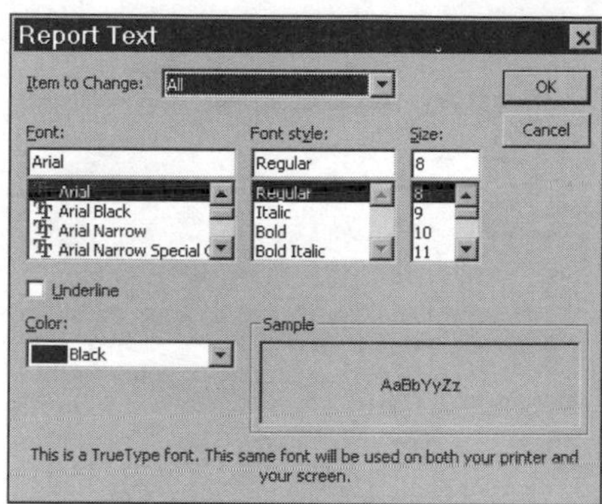


**Figure 13-38:** Use the Report Text dialog box to change the font report items.

Similarly, if you select the Tasks Starting Soon report and then click Edit, Project opens the Definition tab of the Task Report dialog box in Figure 13-39.

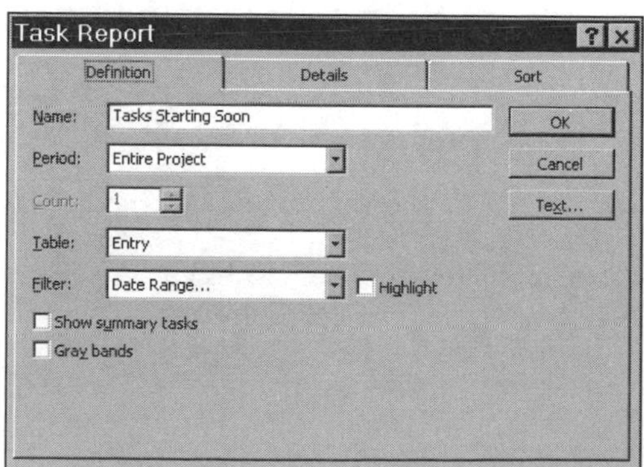


**Figure 13-39:** Use the Definition tab to change the report's filter or table.

From the Details tab (see Figure 13-40), select the information you want included on the report. You might want to display predecessors for tasks or place a gridline between details.

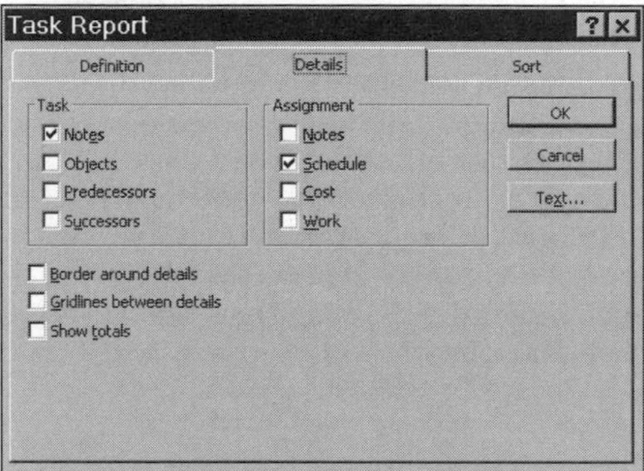


**Figure 13-40:** Use the Details tab to specify the information you want to include on the report.

From the Sort tab shown in Figure 13-41, select the sort orders for the report.

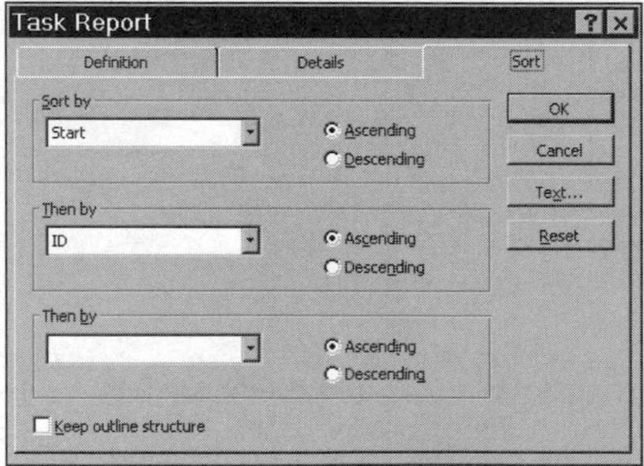


**Figure 13-41:** Select a sort order for the report.

## Editing Reports: The Type Determines the Dialog Box

Remember that the type of report you select initially determines the dialog box you see when you click Edit in the report's category dialog box (for example, the Overview Reports dialog box or the Cost Reports dialog box). In addition to the dialog boxes you've seen here, you may also see the Resource Report dialog box or the Crosstab Report dialog box, both of which contain slightly different options (primarily on the Definitions tab) than the Task Report dialog box.

For example, when you edit the Who Does What report before printing it, Project opens a Resource Report dialog box. On the Definitions tab of this dialog box, you can select filters related to resources, whereas the filters in the Task Report dialog box pertain to tasks. Or, if you edit the Cash Flow report before printing it, Project opens a Crosstab Report dialog box from which you can select the information you want to appear on each row; the default information is Tasks and Cost.

# Summary

In this chapter you learned how to produce reports in Project, and you examined samples of the reports available in each of Project's six report categories:

- Overview
- Current Activities
- Costs
- Assignments
- Workload
- Custom

In addition, you've learned how to customize any standard report in Project. The next chapter shows you how to analyze your project's progress.

✦ ✦ ✦

CHAPTER 14

# Analyzing Financial Progress

✦ ✦ ✦ ✦

**In This Chapter**

Understanding earned value

Evaluating cost information

Making adjustments during the project

✦ ✦ ✦ ✦

When you analyze the progress of your project, you must measure not only the progress of the schedule but also the progress based on the costs you incur. In Microsoft Project you measure the earned value of your project.

## Understanding Earned Value

Earned value is the measure project managers use to evaluate the progress of a project based on the cost of work performed up to the project status date. When Project calculates earned value, it compares your original cost estimates to the actual work performed to show whether your project is on budget. You can think of earned value as a measure that indicates how much of the budget should have been spent when you compare the cost of the work that has been done so far to the baseline cost for the task, resource, or assignment.

To work with and use earned value information effectively, you must first:

- ✦ Save a baseline for your project
- ✦ Assign resources with costs to tasks in your project
- ✦ Complete some work on your project

### Using earned value tables to analyze costs

Project contains a series of earned value fields and two earned value tables that you can use to compare your expected costs with your actual costs. Earned value fields are currency fields that either appear on or can be added to the earned value tables; earned value fields measure various aspects of earned value.

The two earned value tables—Earned Value for Tasks and Earned Value for Resources—help you evaluate the relationship between work and costs. You can use the earned value tables to forecast whether a task will finish within the budget based on the comparison of the actual costs incurred for the task to date and the baseline cost of the task.

## Understanding earned value fields

The fields that appear as headings in the Earned Value report you saw in Chapter 12 also appear on earned value tables. The following table translates the acronyms Project uses to represent the earned value fields.

| *Acronyms* | *Earned Value Fields* |
|---|---|
| BCWS | Budgeted Cost of Work Scheduled |
| BCWP | Budgeted Cost of Work Performed |
| ACWP | Actual Cost of Work Performed |
| SV | Schedule Variance |
| CV | Cost Variance |
| BAC | Budgeted at Completion |
| EAC | Estimate at Completion |
| VAC | Variance at Completion |

BCWS, BCWP, ACWP, SV, and CV are all calculated through today or through the project status date. SV represents the cost difference between current progress and the baseline plan, and Project calculates this value as BCWP minus BCWS. CV represents the cost difference between actual costs and planned costs at the current level of completion, and Project calculates this value as BCWP minus ACWP. EAC shows the planned costs based on costs already incurred plus additional planned costs. VAC represents the variance between the baseline cost and the combination of actual plus planned costs for a task.

Project uses BCWS, BCWP, ACWP, SV, and CV as task fields, resource fields, and assignment fields; Project also uses timephased versions of each field. BAC, EAC, and VAC, however, are task fields only.

## Using the Earned Value table for tasks

When you use the Earned Value table for tasks, you can compare the relationship between work and costs for tasks. This table helps you evaluate your budget to estimate future budget needs and prepare an accounting statement of your project. You can use the information in the table to determine whether sufficient work is getting done for the money you're paying or whether tasks need more money, less money, or perhaps should be cut. That is, the information in the Earned Value table helps you assess whether the money you're spending on a task is enough money, too much money, too little money, or perhaps wasted money.

To display the Earned Value table for tasks, start in any view that contains a table. You can get to the table in Figure 14-1, for example, by starting with the Task Usage view. Right-click the Select All button and choose More Tables from the shortcut menu. In the More Tables dialog box, select Earned Value and click Apply.

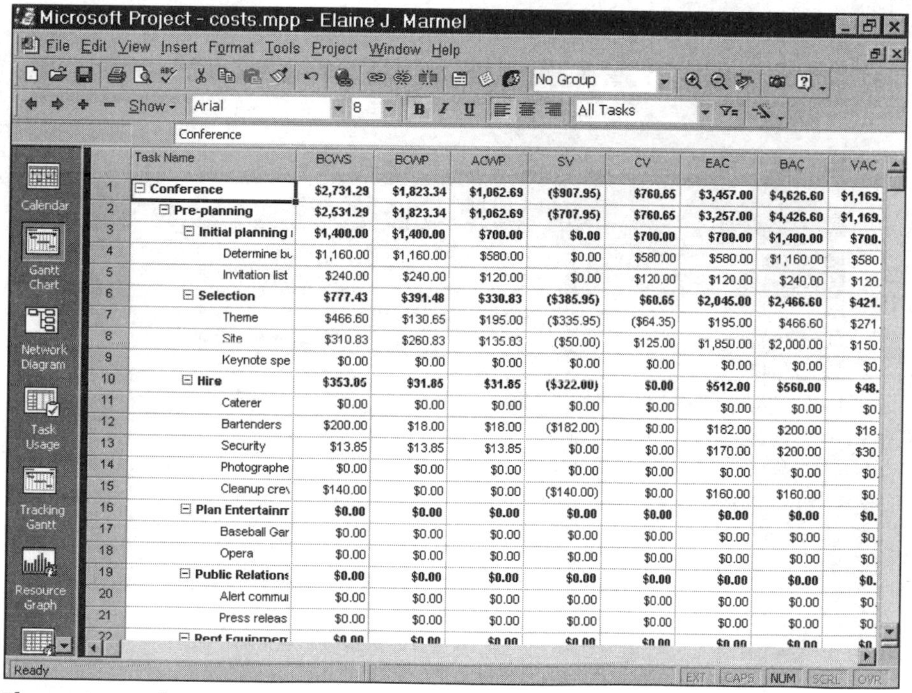

| | Task Name | BCWS | BCWP | ACWP | SV | CV | EAC | BAC | VAC |
|---|---|---|---|---|---|---|---|---|---|
| 1 | **Conference** | **$2,731.29** | **$1,823.34** | **$1,062.69** | **($907.95)** | **$760.65** | **$3,457.00** | **$4,626.60** | **$1,169.** |
| 2 | **Pre-planning** | **$2,531.29** | **$1,823.34** | **$1,062.69** | **($707.95)** | **$760.65** | **$3,257.00** | **$4,426.60** | **$1,169.** |
| 3 | **Initial planning** | **$1,400.00** | **$1,400.00** | **$700.00** | **$0.00** | **$700.00** | **$700.00** | **$1,400.00** | **$700.** |
| 4 | Determine bu | $1,160.00 | $1,160.00 | $580.00 | $0.00 | $580.00 | $580.00 | $1,160.00 | $580. |
| 5 | Invitation list | $240.00 | $240.00 | $120.00 | $0.00 | $120.00 | $120.00 | $240.00 | $120. |
| 6 | **Selection** | **$777.43** | **$391.48** | **$330.83** | **($385.95)** | **$60.65** | **$2,045.00** | **$2,466.60** | **$421.** |
| 7 | Theme | $466.60 | $130.65 | $195.00 | ($335.95) | ($64.35) | $195.00 | $466.60 | $271. |
| 8 | Site | $310.83 | $260.83 | $135.83 | ($50.00) | $125.00 | $1,850.00 | $2,000.00 | $150. |
| 9 | Keynote spe | $0.00 | $0.00 | $0.00 | $0.00 | $0.00 | $0.00 | $0.00 | $0. |
| 10 | **Hire** | **$353.85** | **$31.85** | **$31.85** | **($322.00)** | **$0.00** | **$512.00** | **$560.00** | **$48.** |
| 11 | Caterer | $0.00 | $0.00 | $0.00 | $0.00 | $0.00 | $0.00 | $0.00 | $0. |
| 12 | Bartenders | $200.00 | $18.00 | $18.00 | ($182.00) | $0.00 | $182.00 | $200.00 | $18. |
| 13 | Security | $13.85 | $13.85 | $13.85 | $0.00 | $0.00 | $170.00 | $200.00 | $30. |
| 14 | Photographe | $0.00 | $0.00 | $0.00 | $0.00 | $0.00 | $0.00 | $0.00 | $0. |
| 15 | Cleanup crev | $140.00 | $0.00 | $0.00 | ($140.00) | $0.00 | $160.00 | $160.00 | $0. |
| 16 | **Plan Entertainm** | **$0.00** | **$0.00** | **$0.00** | **$0.00** | **$0.00** | **$0.00** | **$0.00** | **$0.** |
| 17 | Baseball Gar | $0.00 | $0.00 | $0.00 | $0.00 | $0.00 | $0.00 | $0.00 | $0. |
| 18 | Opera | $0.00 | $0.00 | $0.00 | $0.00 | $0.00 | $0.00 | $0.00 | $0. |
| 19 | **Public Relations** | **$0.00** | **$0.00** | **$0.00** | **$0.00** | **$0.00** | **$0.00** | **$0.00** | **$0.** |
| 20 | Alert commu | $0.00 | $0.00 | $0.00 | $0.00 | $0.00 | $0.00 | $0.00 | $0. |
| 21 | Press releas | $0.00 | $0.00 | $0.00 | $0.00 | $0.00 | $0.00 | $0.00 | $0. |
| 22 | **Rent Equipmen** | **$0.00** | **$0.00** | **$0.00** | **$0.00** | **$0.00** | **$0.00** | **$0.00** | **$0.** |

**Figure 14-1:** The Earned Value table for tasks

All the fields on this sheet are calculated except EAC and BAC. You can type values in those fields to change information in the table.

## Using the Earned Value table for resources

When you use the Earned Value table for resources, you can compare the relationship between work and costs for resources. This table also helps you evaluate your budget to estimate future budget needs and prepare an accounting statement of your project. You can use the information in the table to determine whether the work is getting done for the money you're paying or whether you need more or less of a particular resource.

To display the Earned Value table for resources, follow these steps:

1. Start in any resource view, such as the Resource Sheet view.
2. Right-click the Select All button and choose More Tables from the shortcut menu that appears.
3. Select Earned Value in the More Tables dialog box, and click Apply. Your screen will look similar to the one you see in Figure 14-2.

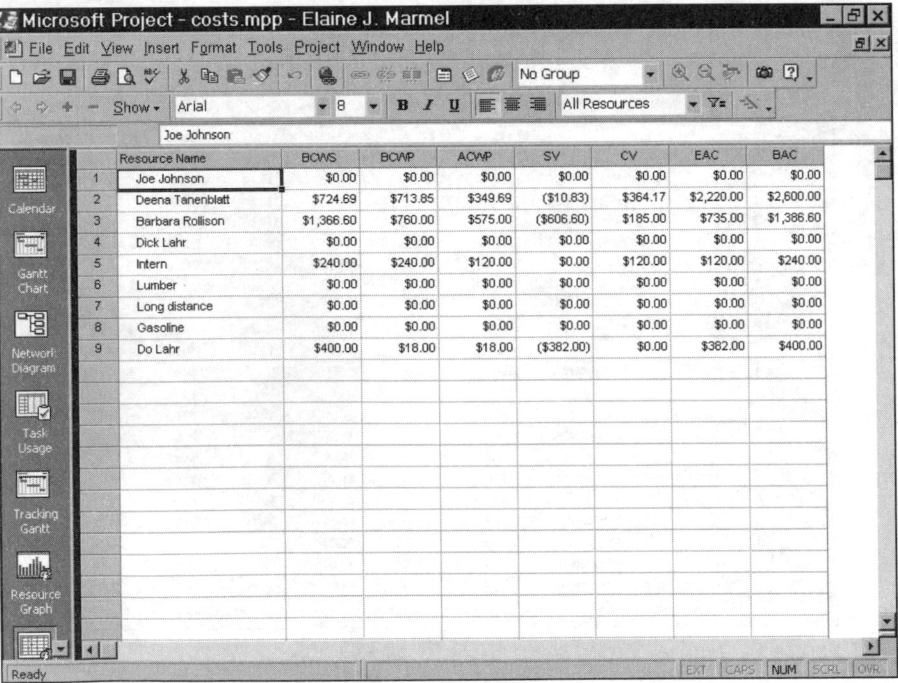


| | Resource Name | BCWS | BCWP | ACWP | SV | CV | EAC | BAC |
|---|---|---|---|---|---|---|---|---|
| 1 | Joe Johnson | $0.00 | $0.00 | $0.00 | $0.00 | $0.00 | $0.00 | $0.00 |
| 2 | Deena Tanenblatt | $724.69 | $713.85 | $349.69 | ($10.83) | $364.17 | $2,220.00 | $2,600.00 |
| 3 | Barbara Rollison | $1,366.60 | $760.00 | $575.00 | ($606.60) | $185.00 | $735.00 | $1,386.60 |
| 4 | Dick Lahr | $0.00 | $0.00 | $0.00 | $0.00 | $0.00 | $0.00 | $0.00 |
| 5 | Intern | $240.00 | $240.00 | $120.00 | $0.00 | $120.00 | $120.00 | $240.00 |
| 6 | Lumber | $0.00 | $0.00 | $0.00 | $0.00 | $0.00 | $0.00 | $0.00 |
| 7 | Long distance | $0.00 | $0.00 | $0.00 | $0.00 | $0.00 | $0.00 | $0.00 |
| 8 | Gasoline | $0.00 | $0.00 | $0.00 | $0.00 | $0.00 | $0.00 | $0.00 |
| 9 | Do Lahr | $400.00 | $18.00 | $18.00 | ($382.00) | $0.00 | $382.00 | $400.00 |

**Figure 14-2:** The Earned Value table for resources

All the fields on this sheet are calculated except BAC: You can type values in this field to change information in the table.

## Setting the date for earned value calculations

By default, Project uses today's date to calculate earned value information. But you can set a project status date for Project to use instead of today's date when it calculates earned value. From any view, choose Project ⇨ Project Information to open the Project Information dialog box (see Figure 14-3).

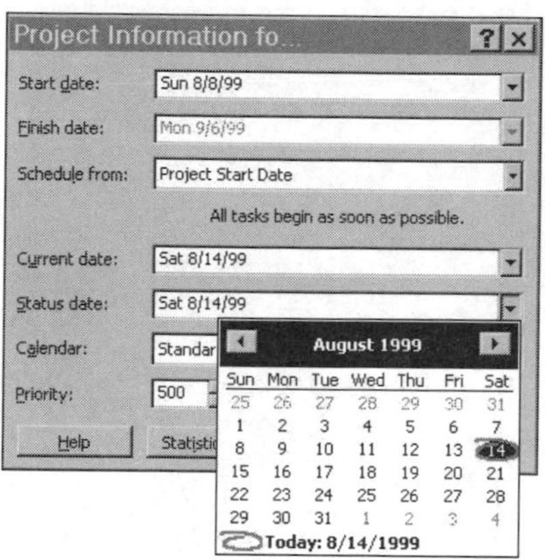


**Figure 14-3:** Use this dialog box to set a date for Project to use when calculating earned value.

Open the Status date list box, select the date you want Project to use when it calculates earned value, and click OK.

# Evaluating Cost Information

If you own Microsoft Excel, you can use it to help you evaluate cost information. By exporting information to Excel, you can chart earned value, analyze timescaled information, or create pivot tables.

## Charting earned value

The saying goes: A picture is worth a thousand words. And when looking at earned value information, you might find it easier to understand the information if you use a picture rather than study Project's Earned Value tables. You can export the earned value information to Microsoft Excel (you must be using Excel version 5.0 or later) and then use Excel's ChartWizard to create charts of earned value information.

To learn more about Project's capabilities to export and import data, see Chapter 20.

When you export earned values from Project to Excel, you create an Excel workbook that contains each task ID, name, and the various earned values for each task (see Figure 14-4).

Microsoft Excel - Meeting Costs.xls

| ID | Name | BCWS | BCWP | ACWP | SV | CV | EAC | BAC | VAC |
|---|---|---|---|---|---|---|---|---|---|
| 1 | Conference | $2,731.29 | $1,823.34 | $1,062.69 | ($907.95) | $760.65 | $3,457.00 | $4,626.60 | $1,169.60 |
| 2 | Pre-planning | $2,531.29 | $1,823.34 | $1,062.69 | ($707.95) | $760.65 | $3,257.00 | $4,426.60 | $1,169.60 |
| 3 | Initial planning meeting | $1,400.00 | $1,400.00 | $700.00 | $0.00 | $700.00 | $700.00 | $1,400.00 | $700.00 |
| 4 | Determine budget | $1,160.00 | $1,160.00 | $580.00 | $0.00 | $580.00 | $580.00 | $1,160.00 | $580.00 |
| 5 | Invitation list | $240.00 | $240.00 | $120.00 | $0.00 | $120.00 | $120.00 | $240.00 | $120.00 |
| 6 | Selection | $777.43 | $391.48 | $330.83 | ($385.95) | $60.65 | $2,045.00 | $2,466.60 | $421.60 |
| 7 | Theme | $466.60 | $130.65 | $195.00 | ($335.95) | ($64.35) | $195.00 | $466.60 | $271.60 |
| 8 | Site | $310.83 | $260.83 | $135.83 | ($50.00) | $125.00 | $1,850.00 | $2,000.00 | $150.00 |
| 9 | Keynote speaker | $0.00 | $0.00 | $0.00 | $0.00 | $0.00 | $0.00 | $0.00 | $0.00 |
| 10 | Hire | $353.85 | $31.85 | $31.85 | ($322.00) | ($0.00) | $512.00 | $560.00 | $48.00 |
| 11 | Caterer | $0.00 | $0.00 | $0.00 | $0.00 | $0.00 | $0.00 | $0.00 | $0.00 |
| 12 | Bartenders | $200.00 | $18.00 | $18.00 | ($182.00) | ($0.00) | $182.00 | $200.00 | $18.00 |
| 13 | Security | $13.85 | $13.85 | $13.85 | $0.00 | ($0.00) | $170.00 | $200.00 | $30.00 |
| 14 | Photographers | $0.00 | $0.00 | $0.00 | $0.00 | $0.00 | $0.00 | $0.00 | $0.00 |
| 15 | Cleanup crew | $140.00 | $0.00 | $0.00 | ($140.00) | $0.00 | $160.00 | $160.00 | $0.00 |
| 16 | Plan Entertainment | $0.00 | $0.00 | $0.00 | $0.00 | $0.00 | $0.00 | $0.00 | $0.00 |
| 17 | Baseball Game | $0.00 | $0.00 | $0.00 | $0.00 | $0.00 | $0.00 | $0.00 | $0.00 |
| 18 | Opera | $0.00 | $0.00 | $0.00 | $0.00 | $0.00 | $0.00 | $0.00 | $0.00 |
| 19 | Public Relations | $0.00 | $0.00 | $0.00 | $0.00 | $0.00 | $0.00 | $0.00 | $0.00 |
| 20 | Alert community | $0.00 | $0.00 | $0.00 | $0.00 | $0.00 | $0.00 | $0.00 | $0.00 |
| 21 | Press release | $0.00 | $0.00 | $0.00 | $0.00 | $0.00 | $0.00 | $0.00 | $0.00 |
| 22 | Rent Equipment | $0.00 | $0.00 | $0.00 | $0.00 | $0.00 | $0.00 | $0.00 | $0.00 |
| 23 | Videocamera | $0.00 | $0.00 | $0.00 | $0.00 | $0.00 | $0.00 | $0.00 | $0.00 |
| 24 | Overhead projector | $0.00 | $0.00 | $0.00 | $0.00 | $0.00 | $0.00 | $0.00 | $0.00 |
| 25 | Meet with Caterer | $0.00 | $0.00 | $0.00 | $0.00 | $0.00 | $0.00 | $0.00 | $0.00 |
| 26 | Menu selection | $0.00 | $0.00 | $0.00 | $0.00 | $0.00 | $0.00 | $0.00 | $0.00 |

Earned Value

**Figure 14-4:** An Excel workbook created by exporting earned value information from Project to Excel.

To create an Excel workbook like the one you see in Figure 14-4, follow these steps:

1. Choose File ➪ Save As to open the File Save dialog box.
2. Type a name for the Excel workbook in the File Name list box. Don't worry about the extension; Project supplies it.
3. Open the Save as type list box and select Microsoft Excel Workbook. The file Save As dialog box should resemble Figure 14-5.

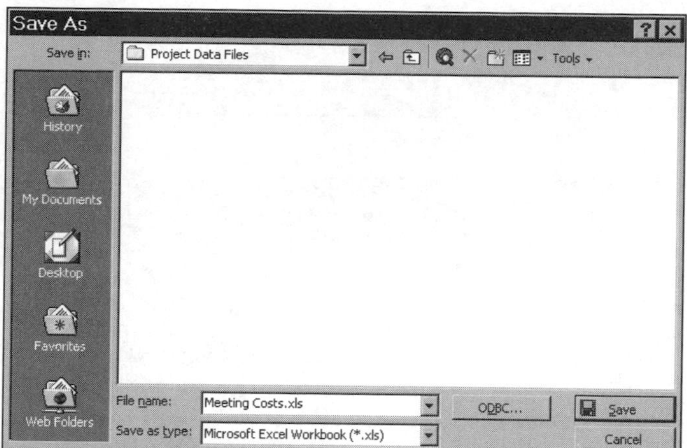


**Figure 14-5:** The file Save As dialog box after you choose to save an Excel workbook file.

4. Click Save to open the Export Mapping dialog box you see in Figure 14-6.

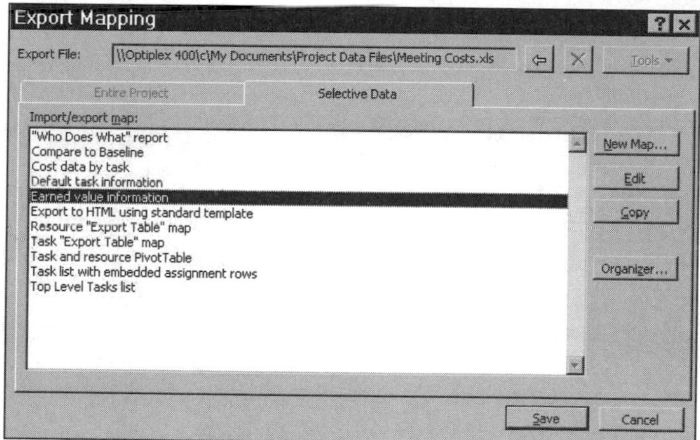


**Figure 14-6:** The Export Mapping dialog box

5. Select "Earned value information" as the map to use for exporting.
6. Click Save. Project saves your workbook in the folder you specified.

Open Microsoft Excel and then choose File ⇨ Open to open the workbook you just created. You can use Excel's ChartWizard to create as many charts from this data as you want. For example, the chart in Figure 14-7 shows all earned values for one task, and the chart in Figure 14-8 shows one earned value for selected tasks.

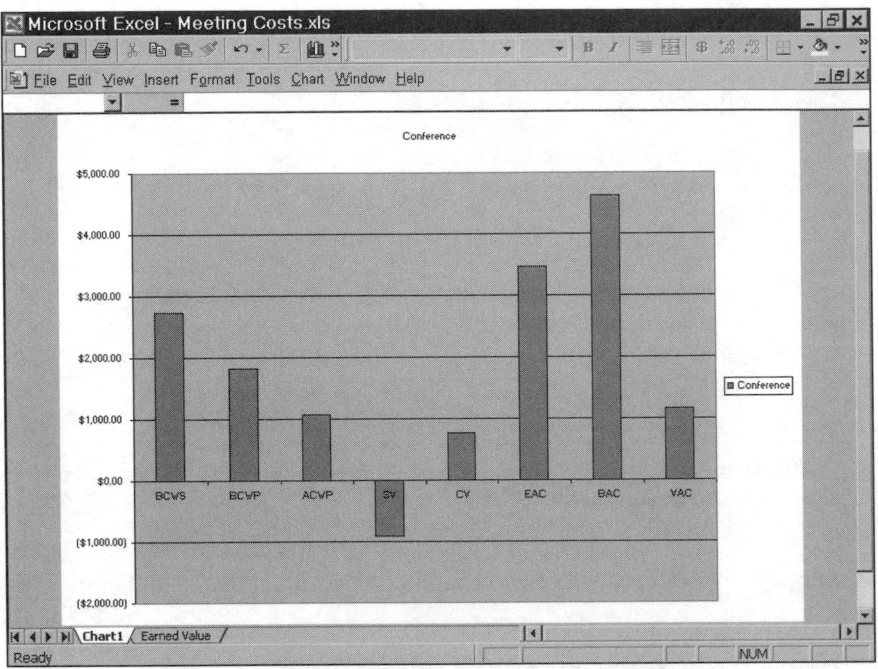


**Figure 14-7:** An Excel chart of all earned values for one task

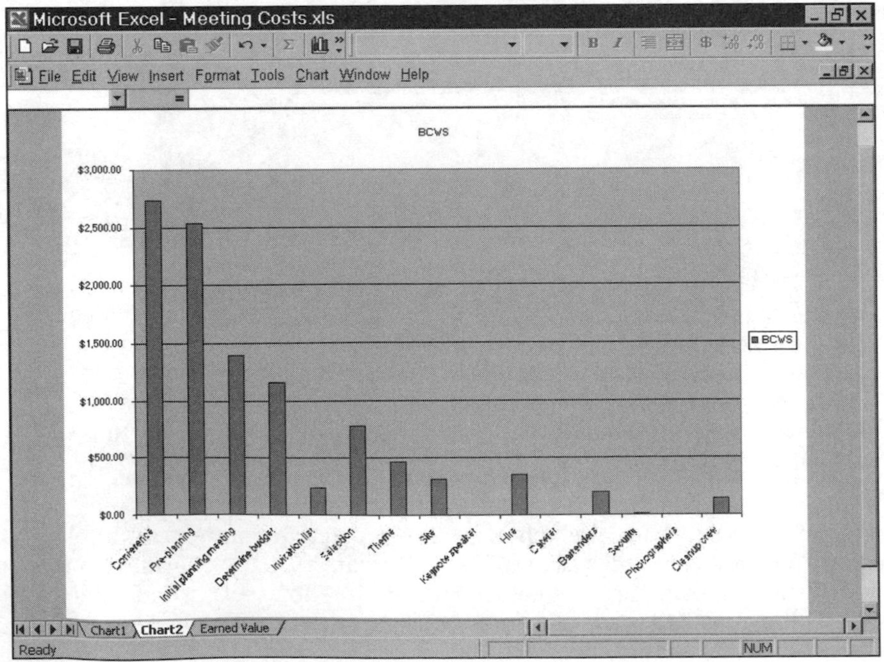


**Figure 14-8:** An Excel chart of one earned value for selected tasks

If your project is small, you might be able to chart one earned value for all tasks, but if your project is large, Excel might display an error message if you try to chart one earned value for all tasks.

To create a chart like the one in Figure 14-7 in Excel, follow these steps:

1. Click the ChartWizard button on the Standard toolbar to start the ChartWizard. In the first ChartWizard dialog box, select the type of chart you want to create.
2. Click Next to open the second ChartWizard dialog box (see Figure 14-9). In this dialog box, select Rows for the "Series in" option.

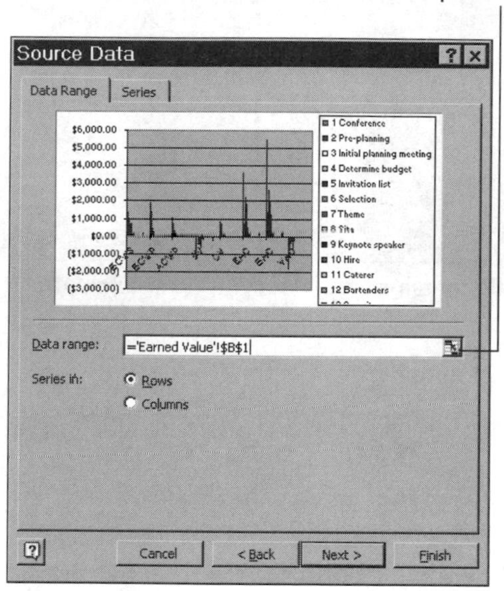


**Figure 14-9:** Chart the data by rows.

3. Click the Collapse Dialog button at the right edge of the Data Range box (refer to Figure 14-9) to hide the ChartWizard so that you can select the task you want to chart from the worksheet.
4. Highlight (by dragging) the cells in the row containing the information you want to chart. Note that I've excluded the ID in Column A in Figure 14-10.

Tip

Your chart will be more meaningful if you omit Column A, which contains the task ID number.

5. Click the Collapse Dialog button to redisplay the ChartWizard.
6. Click the Series tab.

Microsoft Excel - Meeting Costs.xls

Source Data - Data range:

='Earned Value'!$B$2:$J$2

| ID | Name | BCWS | BCWP | ACWP | SV | CV | EAC | BAC | VAC |
|---|---|---|---|---|---|---|---|---|---|
| 1 | Conference | $2,731.29 | $1,823.34 | $1,062.69 | ($907.95) | $760.65 | $3,457.00 | $4,626.60 | $1,169.60 |
| 2 | Pre-planning | $2,531.29 | $1,823.34 | $1,062.69 | ($707.95) | $760.65 | $3,257.00 | $4,426.60 | $1,169.60 |
| 3 | Initial planning meeting | $1,400.00 | $1,400.00 | $700.00 | $0.00 | $700.00 | $700.00 | $1,400.00 | $700.00 |
| 4 | Determine budget | $1,160.00 | $1,160.00 | $580.00 | $0.00 | $580.00 | $580.00 | $1,160.00 | $580.00 |
| 5 | Invitation list | $240.00 | $240.00 | $120.00 | $0.00 | $120.00 | $120.00 | $240.00 | $120.00 |
| 6 | Selection | $777.43 | $391.48 | $330.83 | ($385.95) | $60.65 | $2,045.00 | $2,466.60 | $421.60 |
| 7 | Theme | $466.60 | $130.65 | $195.00 | ($335.95) | ($64.35) | $195.00 | $466.60 | $271.60 |
| 8 | Site | $310.83 | $260.83 | $135.83 | ($50.00) | $125.00 | $1,850.00 | $2,000.00 | $150.00 |
| 9 | Keynote speaker | $0.00 | $0.00 | $0.00 | $0.00 | $0.00 | $0.00 | $0.00 | $0.00 |
| 10 | Hire | $353.85 | $31.85 | $31.85 | ($322.00) | ($0.00) | $512.00 | $560.00 | $48.00 |
| 11 | Caterer | $0.00 | $0.00 | $0.00 | $0.00 | $0.00 | $0.00 | $0.00 | $0.00 |
| 12 | Bartenders | $200.00 | $18.00 | $18.00 | ($182.00) | ($0.00) | $182.00 | $200.00 | $18.00 |
| 13 | Security | $13.85 | $13.85 | $13.85 | $0.00 | ($0.00) | $170.00 | $200.00 | $30.00 |
| 14 | Photographers | $0.00 | $0.00 | $0.00 | $0.00 | $0.00 | $0.00 | $0.00 | $0.00 |
| 15 | Cleanup crew | $140.00 | $0.00 | $0.00 | ($140.00) | $0.00 | $160.00 | $160.00 | $0.00 |
| 16 | Plan Entertainment | $0.00 | $0.00 | $0.00 | $0.00 | $0.00 | $0.00 | $0.00 | $0.00 |
| 17 | Baseball Game | $0.00 | $0.00 | $0.00 | $0.00 | $0.00 | $0.00 | $0.00 | $0.00 |
| 18 | Opera | $0.00 | $0.00 | $0.00 | $0.00 | $0.00 | $0.00 | $0.00 | $0.00 |
| 19 | Public Relations | $0.00 | $0.00 | $0.00 | $0.00 | $0.00 | $0.00 | $0.00 | $0.00 |
| 20 | Alert community | $0.00 | $0.00 | $0.00 | $0.00 | $0.00 | $0.00 | $0.00 | $0.00 |
| 21 | Press release | $0.00 | $0.00 | $0.00 | $0.00 | $0.00 | $0.00 | $0.00 | $0.00 |
| 22 | Rent Equipment | $0.00 | $0.00 | $0.00 | $0.00 | $0.00 | $0.00 | $0.00 | $0.00 |
| 23 | Videocamera | $0.00 | $0.00 | $0.00 | $0.00 | $0.00 | $0.00 | $0.00 | $0.00 |
| 24 | Overhead projector | $0.00 | $0.00 | $0.00 | $0.00 | $0.00 | $0.00 | $0.00 | $0.00 |
| 25 | Meet with Caterer | $0.00 | $0.00 | $0.00 | $0.00 | $0.00 | $0.00 | $0.00 | $0.00 |
| 26 | Menu selection | $0.00 | $0.00 | $0.00 | $0.00 | $0.00 | $0.00 | $0.00 | $0.00 |

Earned Value

**Figure 14-10:** Select the cells containing the data you want to chart.

7. Click the Collapse Dialog button to the right of the "Category (X) axis labels" box.
8. Select the headings in Row 1 that contain the labels for the earned value fields. Your selection will probably include cells C1 through J1.
9. Click the Collapse Dialog button to redisplay the ChartWizard. The Series tab should look similar to the one in Figure 14-11.
10. Click Next and fill in the other dialog boxes for the ChartWizard.

When you finish, your chart should resemble the chart in Figure 14-7, which displays all earned values for one task.

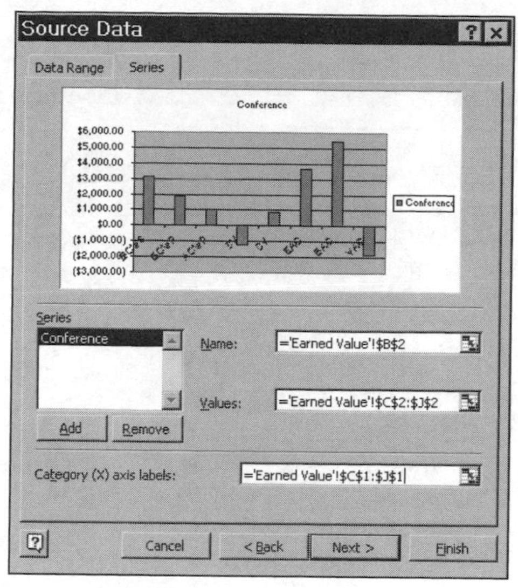


**Figure 14-11:** The Series tab after selecting X-axis labels

To create the chart in Figure 14-8, use the ChartWizard again and, in the second ChartWizard dialog box, use the following settings:

✦ **On the Data Range tab.** Select the "Columns for the Series in" option. For the Data Range, select the cells containing the earned value information you want to chart.

✦ **On the Series tab.** Remove, from the Series list, all series except one (otherwise your chart will be *very* messy). Select the cells containing the task names (cells in Column B in the pictured worksheet) in the "Category (X) axis labels" box.

## Analyzing timescaled information

Project contains a wizard that helps you chart timescaled earned value data. You can use the Analyze Timescaled Data Wizard to automatically create a chart in Microsoft Excel of earned value information for the entire project. The chart you get when you complete the wizard looks similar to the one in Figure 14-12.

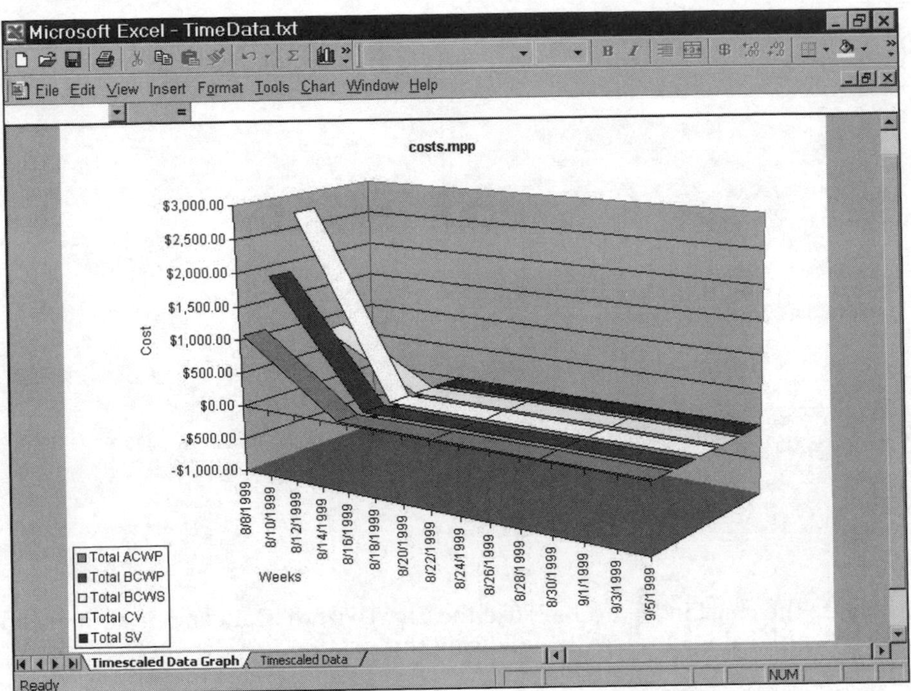


**Figure 14-12:** A chart of earned values created in Excel by using the Analyze Timescaled Data Wizard in Project

To use the Timescaled Data Wizard in Project, follow these steps:

1. Click the Gantt chart icon in the View bar.

**Tip** If you want to chart data for selected tasks, select them now.

2. Choose View ➪ Toolbars ➪ Analysis. Project displays the Analysis toolbar (see Figure 14-13).

**Figure 14-13:** The Analysis toolbar

3. Click the Analyze Timescaled Data in Excel button. Project opens the first of five Analyze Timescaled Data Wizard dialog boxes (see Figure 14-14).

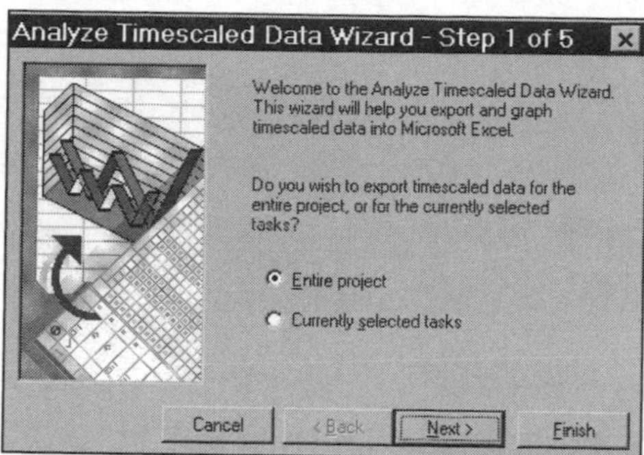


**Figure 14-14:** The first dialog box of the Analyze Timescaled Data Wizard

4. Select either “Entire Project” or “Currently selected tasks” and then click Next to open the Step 2 dialog box.
5. Select the appropriate earned value fields from the Available fields list; click Add to move the fields to the Fields to export list. Highlight the Work field in the Fields to export list, and click the Remove button (see Figure 14-15). Click Next.

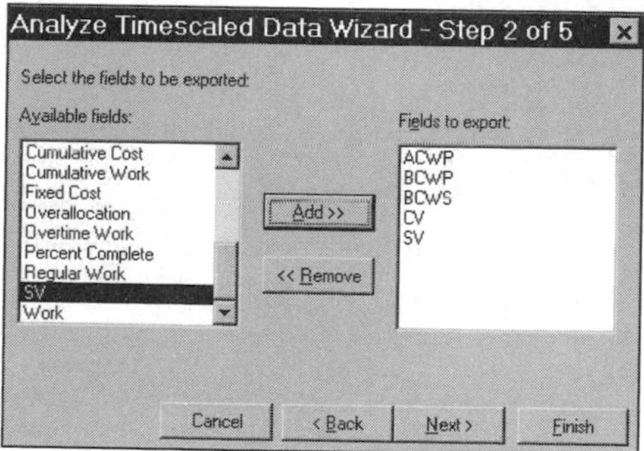


**Figure 14-15:** Select fields to export to Excel.

6. Select the date range and time increments you want to use. The default time increment is days, but in Figure 14-16, I selected Weeks. Click Next to open Step 4.

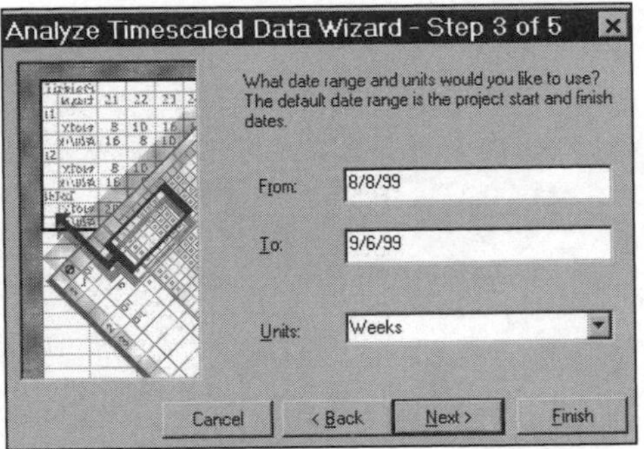


**Figure 14-16:** Select the date range and time increments for which you want to export data.

7. Select "Yes, please" if you want to graph the data. Otherwise, select "No, thanks" (see Figure 14-17). Click Next to open the wizard's final dialog box.

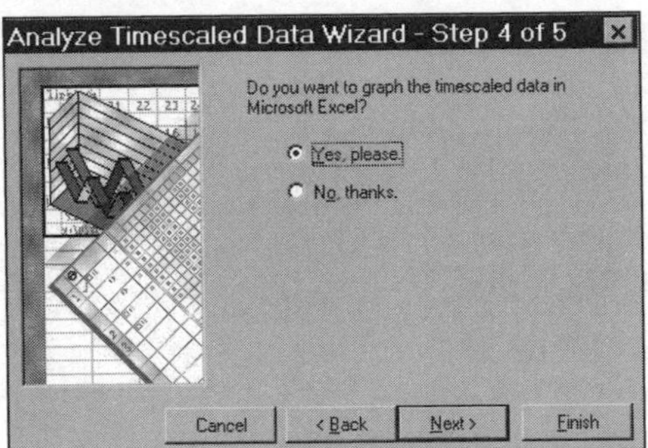


**Figure 14-17:** Tell Project whether or not to graph the data.

8. Click Export Data to export the Project data into Microsoft Excel (see Figure 14-18).

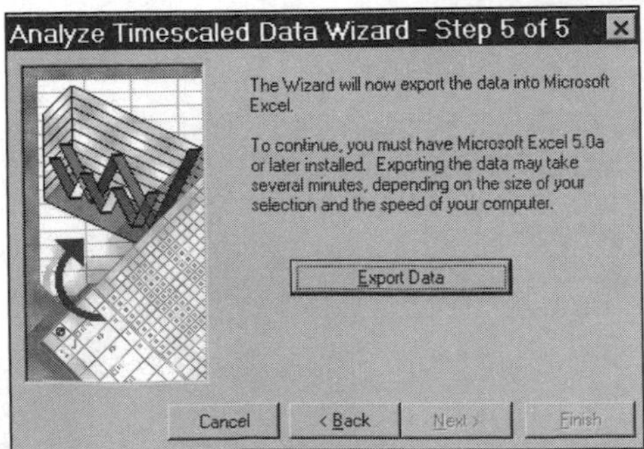


**Figure 14-18:** Finish the process by exporting your data to Excel.

Excel starts up, processes your data, and then displays a chart similar to the one in Figure 14-12 at the beginning of this section. Excel also creates a worksheet in the workbook that you can view by clicking the Timescaled Data tab (see Figure 14-19). The worksheet contains the earned value information that Excel used to create the chart in Figure 14-12.

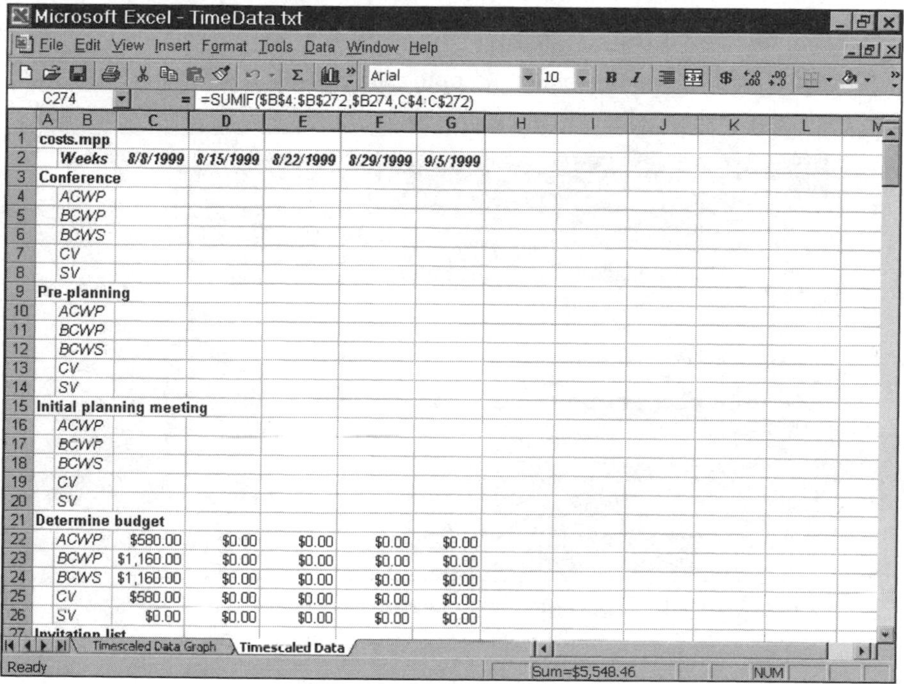


**Figure 14-19:** The worksheet Excel uses to create the chart

# Using PivotTables for analysis

Excel PivotTables can be interesting and useful when you want to analyze Project earned value data. The PivotTable is an interactive table that summarizes large amounts of data in a cross-tabular format. When you use Project to create a PivotTable in Excel, you get two PivotTables in the same workbook: a Task PivotTable and a Resource PivotTable. The Task PivotTable shows resources, tasks to which the resources are assigned, and costs for the resource per task. The Resource PivotTable summarizes resources by showing work assigned to each resource and the total cost of each resource. In addition to the PivotTable worksheets, the same Excel workbook also includes two worksheets that Excel uses to create these two PivotTables; their names are Tasks and Resources.

To export Project information to create PivotTables in Excel, follow these steps:

1. Start in any view of your project.
2. Choose File ➪ Save As to open the File Save dialog box.
3. Type a name for the Excel workbook you want to create in the File name box. Don't worry about the extension; Project supplies it.
4. Select Microsoft Excel PivotTable from the Save as type list box.
5. Click Save to open the Export Mapping dialog box (see Figure 14-20).

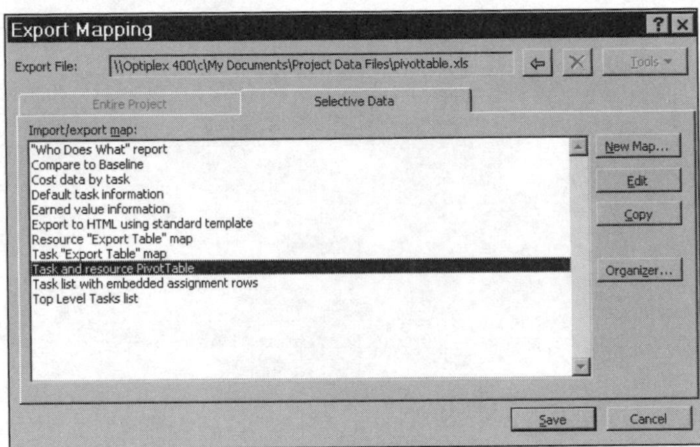


**Figure 14-20:** The Export Mapping dialog box

6. Select "Task and resource PivotTable" and click Save.

You'll see the hourglass icon for the mouse pointer, indicating you should wait while action takes place. You'll also hear action on your hard disk. To view the PivotTables and their source data, start Excel and open the file you just created. The workbook contains four sheets that should resemble the sheets in Figures 14-21, 14-22, 14-23, and 14-24.

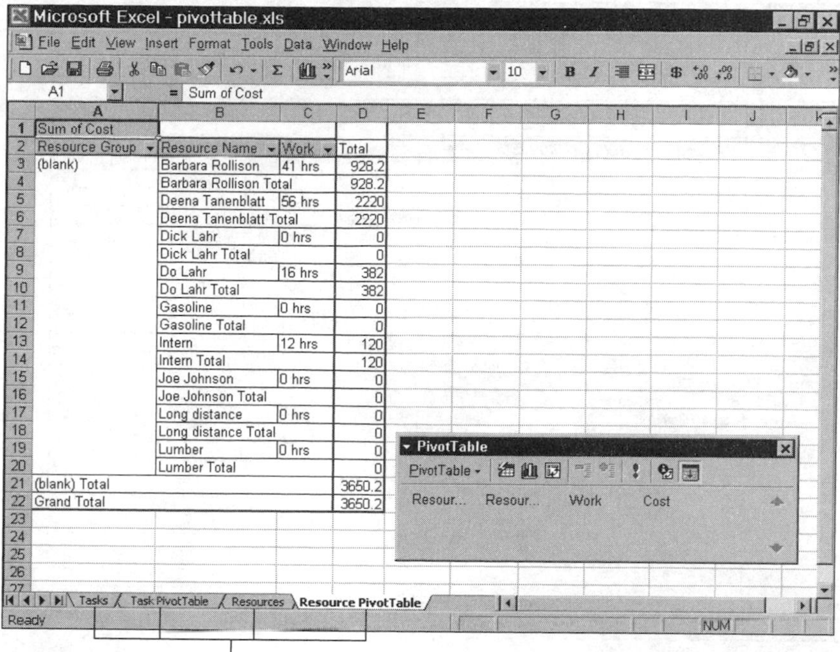

| Sum of Cost | | | |
|---|---|---|---|
| Resource Group | Resource Name | Work | Total |
| (blank) | Barbara Rollison | 41 hrs | 928.2 |
| | Barbara Rollison Total | | 928.2 |
| | Deena Tanenblatt | 56 hrs | 2220 |
| | Deena Tanenblatt Total | | 2220 |
| | Dick Lahr | 0 hrs | 0 |
| | Dick Lahr Total | | 0 |
| | Do Lahr | 16 hrs | 382 |
| | Do Lahr Total | | 382 |
| | Gasoline | 0 hrs | 0 |
| | Gasoline Total | | 0 |
| | Intern | 12 hrs | 120 |
| | Intern Total | | 120 |
| | Joe Johnson | 0 hrs | 0 |
| | Joe Johnson Total | | 0 |
| | Long distance | 0 hrs | 0 |
| | Long distance Total | | 0 |
| | Lumber | 0 hrs | 0 |
| | Lumber Total | | 0 |
| (blank) Total | | | 3650.2 |
| Grand Total | | | 3650.2 |



Click the sheet tabs to switch sheets.

**Figure 14-21:** The Resource PivotTable

Microsoft Excel - pivottable.xls

| Resource Group | Resource Name | Work | Cost |
|---|---|---|---|
| | Joe Johnson | 0 hrs | $0.00 |
| | Deena Tanenblatt | 56 hrs | $2,220.00 |
| | Barbara Rollison | 41 hrs | $928.20 |
| | Dick Lahr | 0 hrs | $0.00 |
| | Intern | 12 hrs | $120.00 |
| | Lumber | 0 hrs | $0.00 |
| | Long distance | 0 hrs | $0.00 |
| | Gasoline | 0 hrs | $0.00 |
| | Do Lahr | 16 hrs | $382.00 |

Tasks / Task PivotTable / Resources / Resource PivotTable

**Figure 14-22:** The Resources sheet that Excel used to create the Resource PivotTable

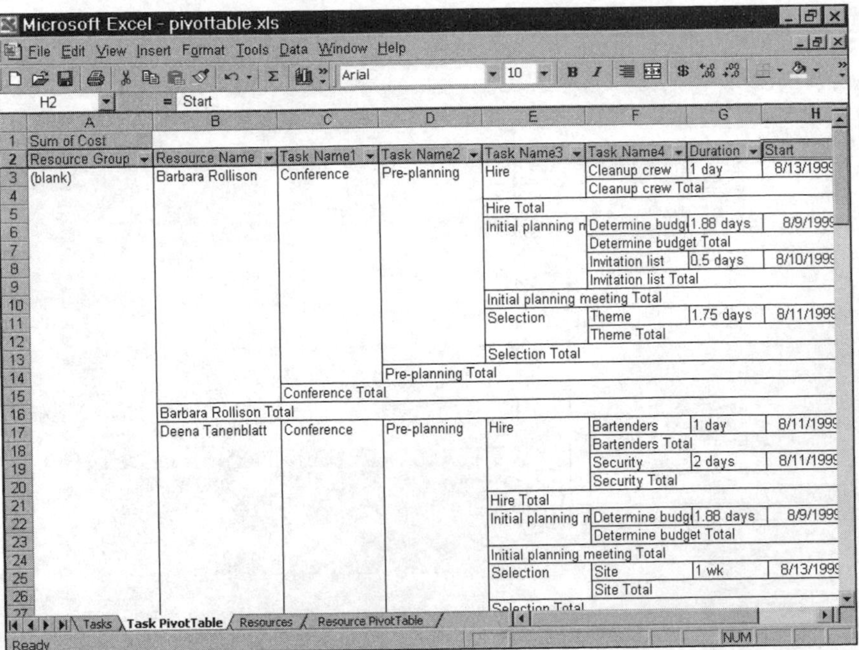


**Figure 14-23:** The Task PivotTable

| | A | B | C | D | E | F | G | H |
|---|---|---|---|---|---|---|---|---|
| 1 | Resource Group | Resource Name | Task Name1 | Task Name2 | Task Name3 | Task Name4 | Duration | Start |
| 2 | | Deena Tanenblatt | Conference | Pre-planning | Initial planning meeting | Determine budget | 1.88 days | 8/9/19 |
| 3 | | Barbara Rollison | Conference | Pre-planning | Initial planning meeting | Determine budget | 1.88 days | 8/9/19 |
| 4 | | Intern | Conference | Pre-planning | Initial planning meeting | Determine budget | 1.88 days | 8/9/19 |
| 5 | | Barbara Rollison | Conference | Pre-planning | Initial planning meeting | Invitation list | 0.5 days | 8/10/19 |
| 6 | | Intern | Conference | Pre-planning | Initial planning meeting | Invitation list | 0.5 days | 8/10/19 |
| 7 | | Barbara Rollison | Conference | Pre-planning | Selection | Theme | 1.75 days | 8/11/19 |
| 8 | | Deena Tanenblatt | Conference | Pre-planning | Selection | Site | 1 wk | 8/13/19 |
| 9 | | Dick Lahr | Conference | Pre-planning | Selection | Keynote speaker | 0 days | 8/13/19 |
| 10 | | | Conference | Pre-planning | Hire | Caterer | 1.71 days | 8/11/199 |
| 11 | | Do Lahr | Conference | Pre-planning | Hire | Bartenders | 1 day | 8/11/19 |
| 12 | | Deena Tanenblatt | Conference | Pre-planning | Hire | Bartenders | 1 day | 8/11/19 |
| 13 | | Deena Tanenblatt | Conference | Pre-planning | Hire | Security | 2 days | 8/11/19 |
| 14 | | Do Lahr | Conference | Pre-planning | Hire | Photographers | 0 days | 8/11/199 |
| 15 | | Barbara Rollison | Conference | Pre-planning | Hire | Cleanup crew | 1 day | 8/13/19 |
| 16 | | | Conference | Pre-planning | Plan Entertainment | Baseball Game | 1 day | 8/9/19 |
| 17 | | | Conference | Pre-planning | Plan Entertainment | Opera | 4 hrs | 8/9/19 |
| 18 | | | Conference | Pre-planning | Public Relations | Alert community | 2 wks | 8/23/199 |
| 19 | | | Conference | Pre-planning | Public Relations | Press release | 1 day | 8/23/199 |
| 20 | | | Conference | Pre-planning | Rent Equipment | Videocamera | 1 day | 8/9/19 |
| 21 | | | Conference | Pre-planning | Rent Equipment | Overhead projector | 1 day | 8/9/19 |
| 22 | | | Conference | Pre-planning | Meet with Caterer | Menu selection | 1 day | 8/13/19 |
| 23 | | | Conference | Pre-planning | Meet with Caterer | Drink selection | 1 day | 8/13/19 |
| 24 | | | Conference | Pre-planning | Arrangements | Transportation | 1 day | 8/9/19 |
| 25 | | | Conference | Pre-planning | Arrangements | Event transportation | 3 days | 8/9/19 |
| 26 | | | Conference | Pre-planning | Arrangements | Flowers | 4 days | 8/9/19 |
| 27 | | | Conference | Pre-planning | Arrangements | Table decorations | 1 day | 8/9/19 |

**Figure 14-24:** The Tasks sheet that Excel used to create the Task PivotTable

You may need to widen columns in Excel to see all the data. Double-click the right border of the column letter.

# Making Adjustments During the Project

Now that you've seen the various ways you can collect and analyze financial data about your project, you need to use that information to make improvements to your project. You can use many of the techniques you used to implement changes to your project because of scheduling problems or resource conflicts.

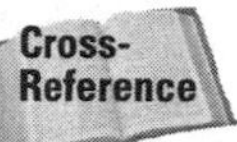

Learn how to deal with scheduling problems using techniques discussed in Chapter 9. You'll find help resolving resource problems in Chapter 10.

## Changing the schedule

After evaluating earned value information, you might want to change the schedule. For example, you might want to:

- ✦ Add resources to tasks
- ✦ Use overtime
- ✦ Increase task duration
- ✦ Adjust slack
- ✦ Change task constraints
- ✦ Adjust dependencies
- ✦ Split tasks
- ✦ Adjust the critical path

You might also need to make changes to the baseline project you saved.

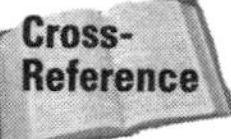

For more information on adjusting the baseline, see Chapter 11.

## Modifying resource assignments

Your evaluation of earned value information may prompt you to make changes to resource assignments on your project. For example, you might need to:

- ✦ Change resource allocations
- ✦ Schedule overtime
- ✦ Redefine a resource's calendar

✦ Assign part-time work

✦ Control when resources start working on a task

✦ Level workloads

✦ Contour resources

✦ Pool resources

When you're working with an unusually large project, you may find it easier to break your project into smaller, more manageable portions called subprojects. In Project, you can create subprojects and then consolidate them into the larger project to see the bigger picture (see Chapter 17).

# Summary

This chapter explained how to analyze the costs in your project. In this chapter, you:

✦ Learned how to use Project's Earned Value tables

✦ Learned to chart earned value information, to analyze timescaled information, and to use Microsoft Excel PivotTables

✦ Reviewed how to make adjustments to your project

In Chapters 15 through 17, you'll learn how Project helps you work in groups.

✦ ✦ ✦

# Working in Groups

P A R T

# V

✦ ✦ ✦ ✦

**In This Part**



✦ ✦ ✦ ✦

CHAPTER 15

# Using Project in an E-mail Workgroup

In This Chapter

Setting up an e-mail workgroup

Building a resource list

Communicating via e-mail

Customizing your workgroup

Establishing management procedures

Sending notes and routing files

To paraphrase John Donne, no project manager is an island. Most projects involve you and at least one other person. The people involved in your project constitute your workgroup, and the project manager is the workgroup manager. Workgroups can vary in their structure: On one project you might manage a project, coordinating activities of all its resources; on another project you might be a member of a workgroup team that someone else is managing. In either case you'll be interacting with many people over the days, weeks, or months that it takes to reach your goal — and you need tools to make that interaction a success.

Project has many workgroup features to help you manage and work with other members of a project team, and Project permits you to communicate using either e-mail or the Internet. This chapter explores workgroup tools that you can use when communicating via e-mail:

- For communication
- To make task assignments
- To keep your schedule up-to-date

In Chapter 16, you learn about using Project Central, Project's New Internet project management tool, to update and manage projects.

If you've used earlier versions of Project, you'll notice a significant change in Microsoft's strategy for handling project management for workgroups via e-mail and project management for workgroups using the Web. In Project 98, Project combined techniques for workgroup project management; that is, you basically used the same techniques whether you used e-mail or the Web. In Project 2000, Microsoft has completely separated the Web-based strategy from the e-mail strategy—and the techniques have changed completely. This chapter focuses on using e-mail to manage projects in workgroups from the perspective of people using Microsoft Exchange Server and Microsoft Outlook as their tools.

# Setting Up an E-mail Workgroup

To use an e-mail based workgroup, the manager and workgroup members must have access to a Messaging Application Programming Interface (MAPI) compliant, 32-bit e-mail setup. MAPI is a standard e-mail interface that Microsoft supports with products such as Outlook, Microsoft Exchange, and Microsoft Mail, but it is common to other major e-mail products as well.

With Project you set up a workgroup by establishing a workgroup manager and the members of the workgroup. You can then exchange workgroup messages through e-mail. The exchange of information enables the workgroup manager to alert workgroup members to task assignments through Project's TeamAssign feature. Workgroup members can return information to the workgroup manager, which he or she can use for tracking progress during the life of the project, using Project's TeamStatus feature. Finally, managers can use the TeamUpdate feature to notify workgroup members about shifts in the schedule or other project parameters.

The workgroup manager is the person who builds and maintains the project schedule and makes task assignments. The "boss" creates the schedule, makes assignments, and uses communications from workgroup members to track their activities.

The workgroup manager must first install and set up Project to enable workgroup management on his or her computer. Although workgroup members can also install Project on their computers, this step isn't absolutely necessary. On the workgroup manager's computer, complete the following steps to set up a particular project to exchange information via e-mail:

1. Choose Tools ⇨ Options.
2. Click the Workgroup tab to select it (see Figure 15-1).
3. Select the default workgroup messaging method from the Default workgroup messaging for resources drop-down list. For e-mail only, select the E-mail option.

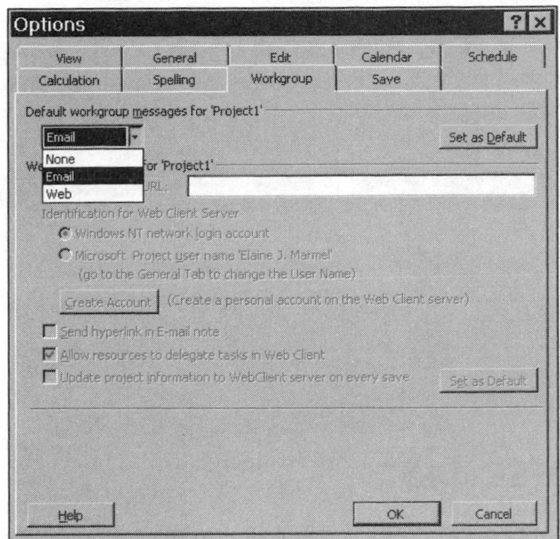


**Figure 15-1:** To use e-mail for workgroup management, set the default messaging method to E-mail.

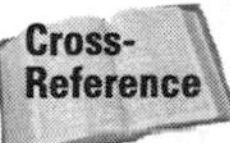


See Chapter 16 for information on setting up Project for workgroup management using your company's intranet or the World Wide Web.

4. Click OK to save your settings.

In addition, to use e-mail for workgroups, *all* workgroup members, including the workgroup manager, must run an executable file called Wgsetup.exe from the Project CD-ROM so they'll be able to send and receive messages.

It's possible that some members of your team will *not* have Project on their computers, and that's okay. By running Wgsetup.exe, they will have everything they need to communicate via e-mail.

To run Wgsetup.exe, follow these steps:

1. At each workgroup member's computer, insert the Project CD-ROM.

2. Choose Install MAPI Workgroup Message Handler. Project displays the Workgroup Message Handler Setup dialog box shown in Figure 15-2 and asks each user to confirm the location for the file.

When a user confirms that location, Project automatically completes the installation.

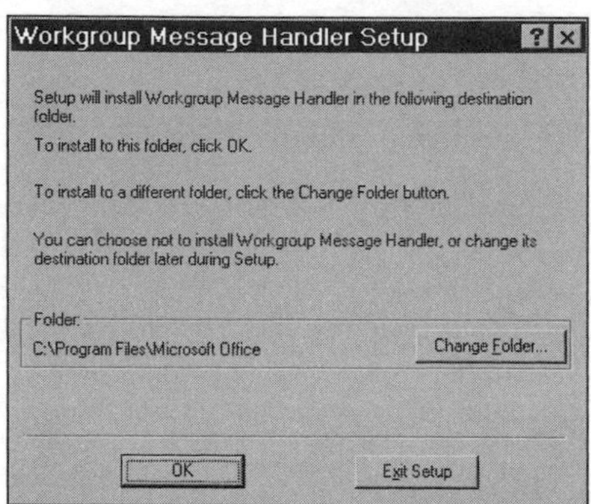


**Figure 15-2:** You can either accept the default location for the workgroup setup file or create a specially named folder for it.

# Building a Resource List

To use Project's workgroup communication features, you must assign resources to your project and designate them as being in your group. When you create these resources, you enter an online address so Project can communicate with them. Follow these steps to create a resource group:

1. Display the Resource Sheet view by clicking it in the View bar.
2. Enter a resource name and any other pertinent information about the resource in the columns of the Resource Sheet.
3. Double-click the resource name to open the Resource Information dialog box shown in Figure 15-3.

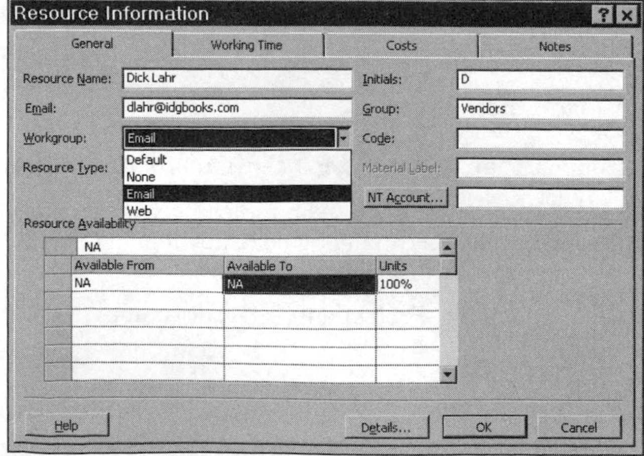


**Figure 15-3:** Enter a group name and e-mail address for every resource you want in your workgroup communications circle.

4. Enter an e-mail address in the E-mail field.
5. Enter a group name in the Group field; this entry is required to use the workgroup features with this resource.
6. Select a workgroup from the Workgroup drop-down list. This choice should match the messaging method you chose when you set up the workgroup manager's connection.
7. Click OK to save the resource, who is now part of the workgroup and is set up for workgroup communications.

# Communicating via E-mail

After a manager sets up a workgroup, both the manager and the workgroup members can use Project's workgroup communication features. You'll find workgroup commands by choosing Tools ➪ Workgroup; the commands are not available when you're viewing any resource view, but you'll see them when you view any other type of view. You also can use the Workgroup toolbar by choosing View ➪ Toolbars ➪ Workgroup. The labels in Figure 15-4 identify the Workgroup toolbar tools.

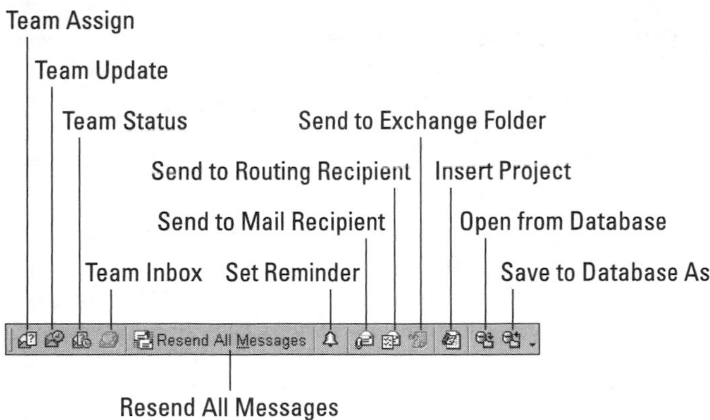


**Figure 15-4:** Use the Workgroup toolbar to access workgroup features that help you communicate with your team.

Here are some of the useful actions you can perform from the Workgroup toolbar:

✦ **Set Reminder.** Opens a dialog box that uses Microsoft Outlook's features to set reminders related to a task you selected in your schedule. For example, you can ask Project to remind you 15 minutes before a task involving a meeting or phone conference.

- **Send to Mail Recipient as Attachment.** Sends an e-mail message to anyone you want, attaching a graphic image of a Resource Sheet description.
- **Send to Routing Recipient.** Enables you to create a routing slip to pass a message and the Project file to any group of people you like — but usually your project team.
- **Send to Exchange Folder.** Opens a new Microsoft Exchange message box, with the file already included as an attachment. Simply enter a recipient's address and any accompanying message, and send the e-mail through your e-mail system.
- **Insert Project.** Places another project file into the currently open file.

You also can use the first three tools to create any of the team message types: TeamAssign, TeamUpdate, and TeamStatus.

## TeamAssign

After you establish a workgroup, you can automatically generate messages notifying resources of assignments from any view that shows tasks — even the Calendar view — and clicking the TeamAssign tool to open the Workgroup Mail dialog box shown in Figure 15-5.

**Figure 15-5:** In the Workgroup Mail dialog box, you specify assignments by a single task or for all tasks in the project.

When you complete your schedule, you might want to send information about all tasks involving the resource to that resource; you can use the Task Usage view and select the tasks to which you've assigned a particular resource. After the project begins and you periodically add the resource to a task or two, you can notify the resource about selected tasks only. You can use the Workgroup Mail dialog box to specify that you want to send a message to a team member for the currently selected task only or for all tasks in the project. Select one of the options and click OK. Project displays the TeamAssign dialog box shown in Figure 15-6. You use this message form to enter specifics for messages concerning team assignments.

The recipient listed in the To space at the top of the TeamAssign dialog box is the first resource assigned to the task (either the selected task, or the first task in your schedule if you selected to send a message for all tasks). The default Subject is TeamAssign, but you can modify that if you wish.

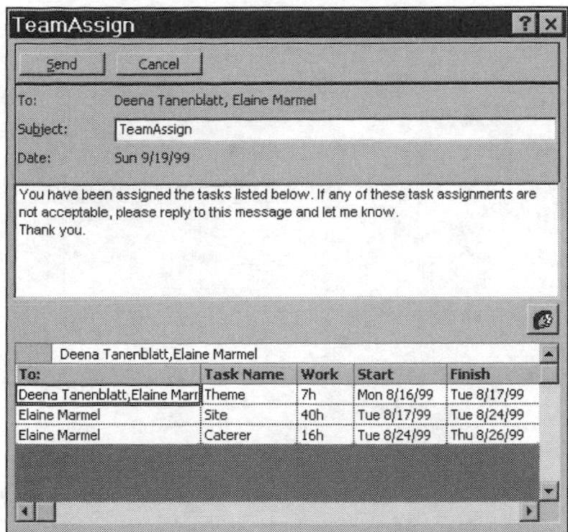


**Figure 15-6:** In this message, all tasks in the project are being forwarded to team members.

Project automatically generates a message that asks the recipient to indicate his or her acceptance of the assignment. You can either send this generic message or enter a message of your own.

Project lists the task or tasks to which the resource is assigned in a table below your message, indicating:

- ✦ The name of the task
- ✦ The amount of work time you expect from the resource on the task
- ✦ The task start and finish dates
- ✦ Any comments you entered into the Comments column of the Gantt table

You can modify the information in this table, as explained in "Customizing Your Workgroup" later in this chapter.

When the information in the TeamAssign dialog box is correct, click the Send button at the top to send the message. Project places indicator icons next to the tasks included in the TeamAssign message (see Figure 15-7). Project also places messages that you'll need to send in your e-mail client's Outbox.

The message a team member receives in his or her e-mail client Inbox looks something like the message shown in Figure 15-8. When you double-click the message, you'll see the TeamAssign reply window (see Figure 15-9). Project displays a slightly revised version of the TeamAssign window, from which the recipient can review the assignment(s) and reply to accept or decline the assignment.

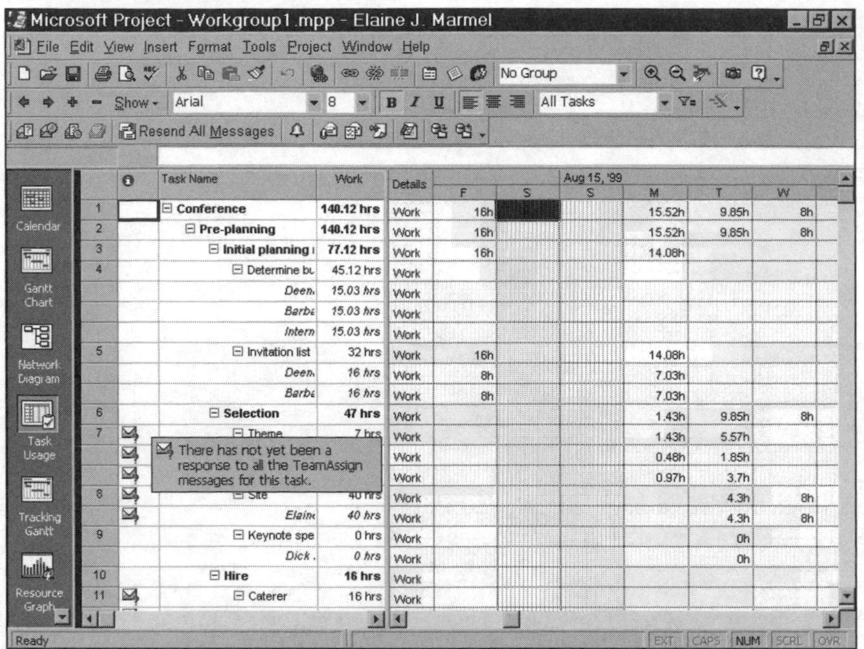

**Figure 15-7:** To remind you that you've sent TeamAssign requests, Project inserts indicator icons next to the affected tasks.

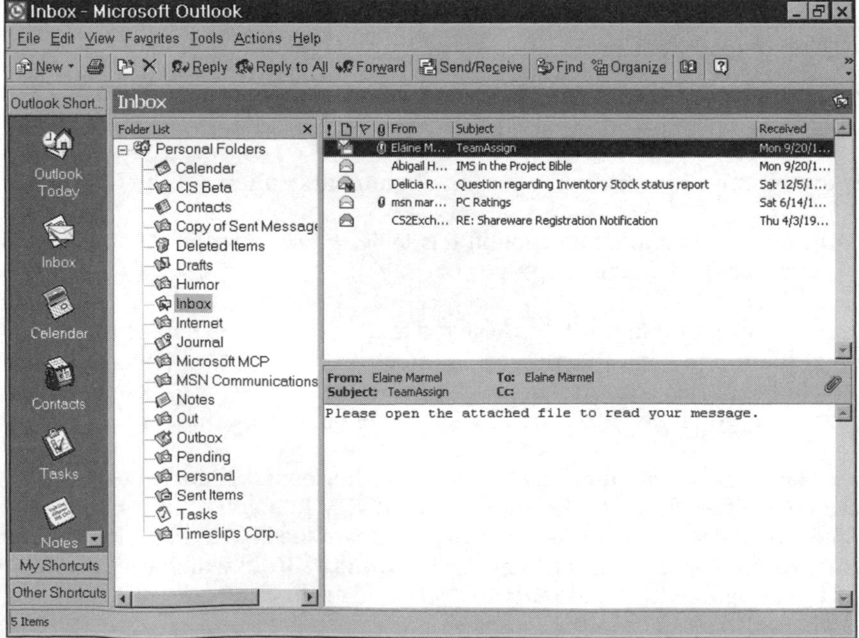

**Figure 15-8:** The recipient of a TeamAssign request gets an e-mail that looks like this.

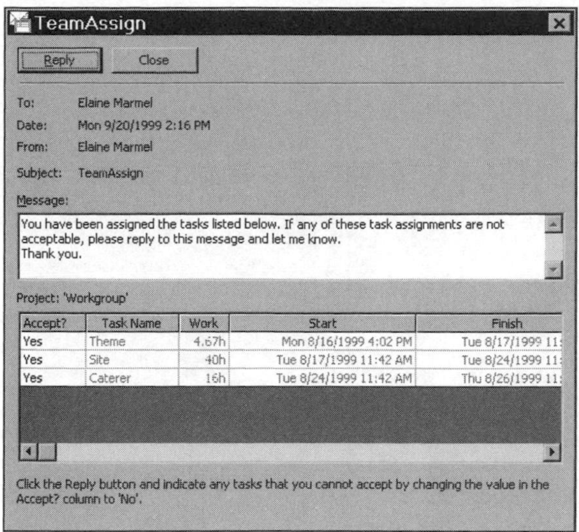


**Figure 15-9:** This message clearly asks the workgroup member to accept or decline the assignment.

To accept an assignment received through e-mail, the team member leaves the Yes in the Accept? column. To decline the assignment, the recipient double-clicks in the Accept? column to change Yes to No, or the recipient can type an *N* in the Accept? column. If appropriate, the recipient can enter a message and click Reply. When you send your reply, the TeamAssign message disappears from the e-mail client Inbox, and Project places a team member's response in the workgroup manager's e-mail Inbox. When the workgroup manager double-clicks the message, a window like the one in Figure 15-10 appears. Notice the Update Project button; the workgroup manager can click this button to transfer the changes to the project schedule. Project opens and applies the changes. As you can see from Figure 15-11, the icons in the Indicator column change to reflect the receipt of a reply to the TeamAssign message — and Project suggests that the workgroup manager send out a TeamUpdate message, which you'll read about in the next section.

Do not try to read a TeamAssign message while Project is open. You'll "hang" your e-mail client.

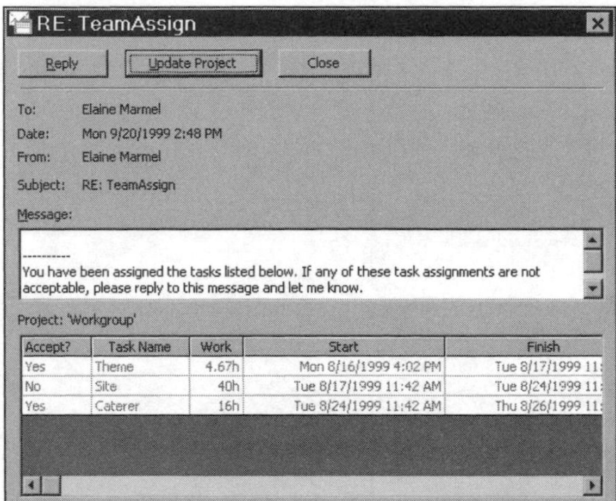


**Figure 15-10:** The reply to a TeamAssign message contains a button the workgroup manager can use to automatically update Project.

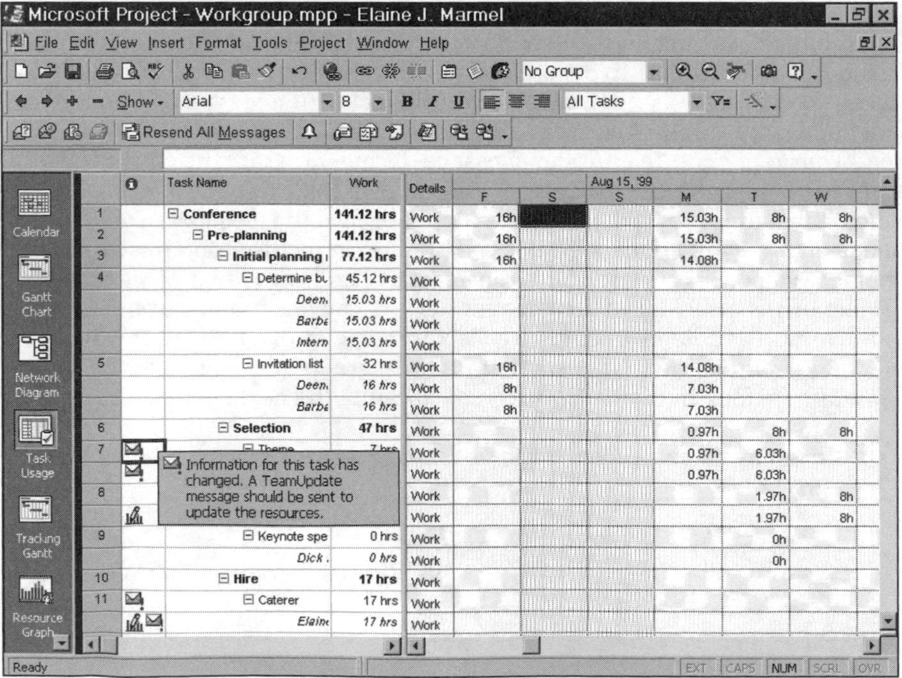


**Figure 15-11:** After receiving a reply to a TeamAssign message and allowing the reply to update the project schedule, the icons in the Indicator column prompt the workgroup manager to send out a TeamUpdate message.

## TeamUpdate

A TeamUpdate message is similar to a TeamAssign message, but you use this message to convey a change to the start or finish date of a task or tasks. You must exchange TeamAssign messages before you can send a TeamUpdate message because you will be updating team members on changes to task timing that have occurred since a resource accepted the assignment.

When you click the TeamUpdate button, Project opens the TeamUpdate dialog box shown in Figure 15-12. Type in a subject, type your message, and then click Send to send a list of updated tasks.

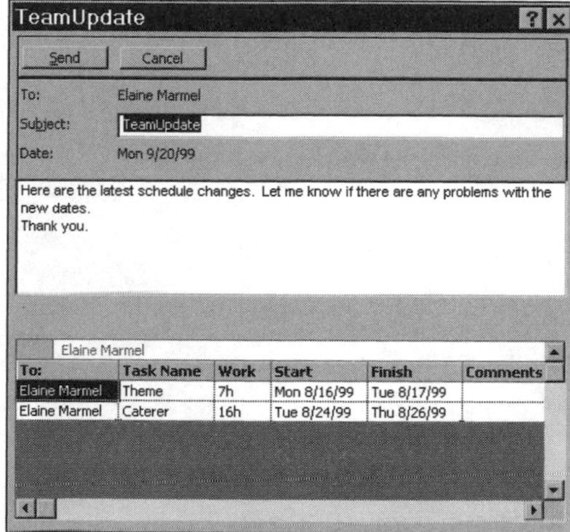


**Figure 15-12:** The table of information in this message notifies someone working on your project of a change in task timing.

Only tasks that involve the recipient (that resource) and that have changed appear in this list. The message appears either in a workgroup member's e-mail inbox or TeamInbox, depending on how you have set up the workgroup. To respond to a TeamUpdate message, click Reply, type a message, and then click Send.

## TeamStatus

The third standard message type, TeamStatus, works similarly, but it goes beyond simple communication. You can use responses to your TeamStatus requests to automatically update your project. This feature saves you hours of time tracking and entering progress information manually.

When you send a TeamStatus message to team members, you ask them to update the workgroup manager as to the status of tasks. When you click the TeamStatus button on the Workgroup toolbar, Project asks if this message is for All tasks or just the Selected tasks. Make your choice and click OK. The dialog box in Figure 15-13 then appears.

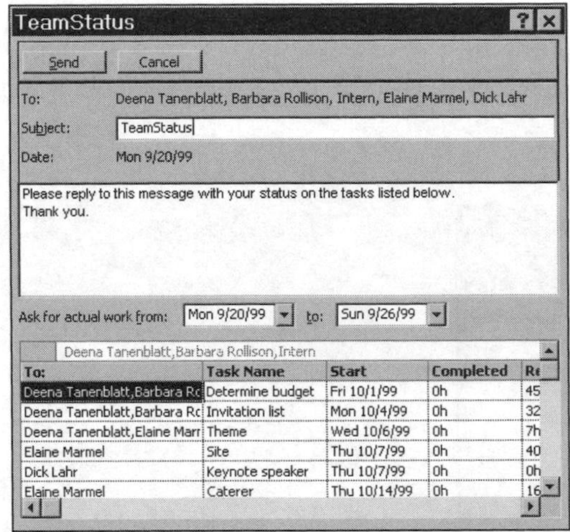


**Figure 15-13:** Similar to the TeamAssign dialog box, TeamStatus requests that the workgroup team member inform you of progress on tasks.

Follow these steps to complete a TeamStatus request:

1. Type another subject into the Subject line if desired.
2. Keep the default message, or delete it and enter one of your own.
3. Set a date range of the work period for which you want the recipient to respond.
4. Click the Send button.

The team member receives a message that looks like the TeamStatus message in Figure 15-14.

Team members can edit the task information fields for Start, Remaining Work, and the days of the week. The team member enters information in the Remaining Work field reflecting actual work progress, optionally adds a return message about the status of the tasks, and then clicks Send to return the message to the workgroup manager. When the manager receives the response and clicks the Update Project button at the top of the message, Project uses the team member's entries to update the tasks in the actual schedule — automatically.

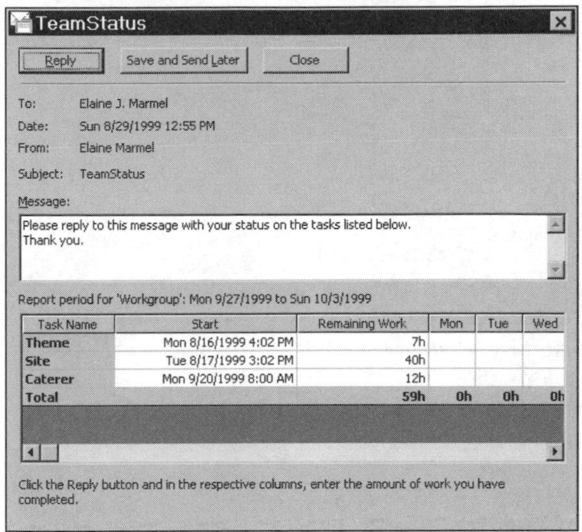


**Figure 15-14:** To respond to the TeamStatus request, the recipient clicks the Reply button – and Outlook changes the Reply button to the Send button.

# Customizing Your Workgroup

You can modify the task information that appears in your workgroup messages by using the customizing feature of Project. This feature enables you to add or delete items that appear in the task information fields, rearrange the fields, or request more detailed breakdowns of task timing.

In Project 2000, you'll find more fields that you can include in your workgroup messages, increasing your customization options.

Follow these steps to customize your messages:

1. Choose Tools ➪ Customize ➪ Workgroup to open the Customize Workgroup dialog box in Figure 15-15.

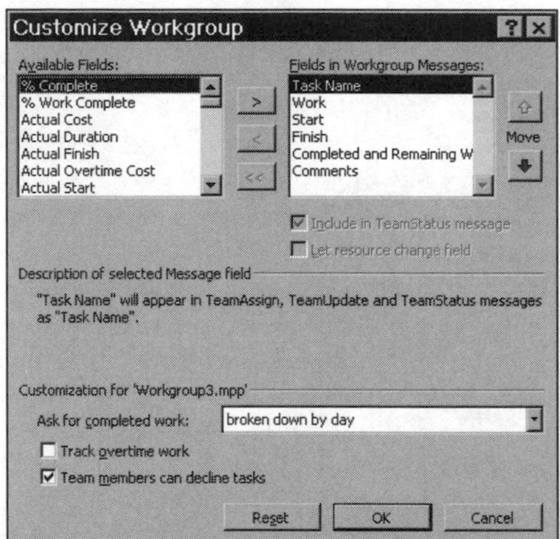


**Figure 15-15:** Use the Customize Workgroup dialog box to include the information most relevant to your project in your workgroup messages.

2. Make any of the following changes:
   - **Add a field.** Highlight the field in the Available Fields list on the left side of the dialog box and click the button containing the arrow button pointing to the right. The new field appears above whatever field was highlighted when you clicked the Add button.
   - **Delete a field.** Click the name of the field you want to delete in the Fields in Workgroup Messages list on the right side of the dialog box and then click the arrow button pointing to the left. Note that you cannot delete the Task Name field.
   - **Change the order of fields.** Use the Move Up and Move Down buttons to change the order of fields in the table of information.
   - **Designate the breakdown of status information.** You can see status information by day, by week, or for the entire time for which you are requesting information by making the appropriate selection in the "Ask for completed work" drop-down list.

If you have made several changes and want to return to Project's standard settings for workgroup messaging, click the Reset button in the Customize Workgroup dialog box.

3. Click OK to save the new settings.

# Establishing Management Procedures

If you are responsible for managing a workgroup, your job involves more than just setting up your group to send and receive workgroup messages. You also need to orchestrate those communications and manage project files efficiently to get the most out of the workgroup structure. Use these suggestions to guide you:

- Make sure all workgroup members understand how Project's workgroup features work. You (the workgroup manager) could well be the only person in the workgroup to have a copy of Project on your computer. Help your team to understand not only how to use the workgroup features that are available to them but also why these features are important to using Project effectively.
- Set up a communication schedule with your workgroup. Make assignments and status requests on a regular basis, perhaps allowing a week or two of activity to occur before you perform updates. If workgroup members know they will receive requests for updates and status reports every Friday, for example, and that they must respond by end of day Tuesday, they can establish a routine to deliver the information in a timely way.
- Check your mailbox on a regular basis. If you aren't being responsive to your workgroup's input, they'll stop being responsive to your requests.

# Sending Notes and Routing Files

Project has two other tools that are most helpful in communicating with various resources assigned to a project, whether they are part of your designated workgroup or not. First, you can send a project schedule note to selected resources assigned to the project. Second, you can route a project file from one resource to another. The ability to route notes and files can be useful if you want each resource to add information to the file or note and then forward it to the next person for his or her comments.

## Sending Project notes

You can send a copy of your Project file, and perhaps a note to all resources or a subset of resources on a project, even if they are *not* part of your regular workgroup. Before beginning this procedure, select a specific task if you want to send a note concerning the resources assigned to that task only. Otherwise, don't have any specific task selected. To send a message through your MAPI-compliant e-mail system, follow these steps:

1. Choose Tools ➪ Workgroup ➪ Send Schedule Note.

2. Select the people to whom you want to send the note in the Address message to field in the Send Schedule Note dialog box shown in Figure 15-16. Your choices include the Project manager, Resources for the selected task or entire project, or contacts. Then select the appropriate options:

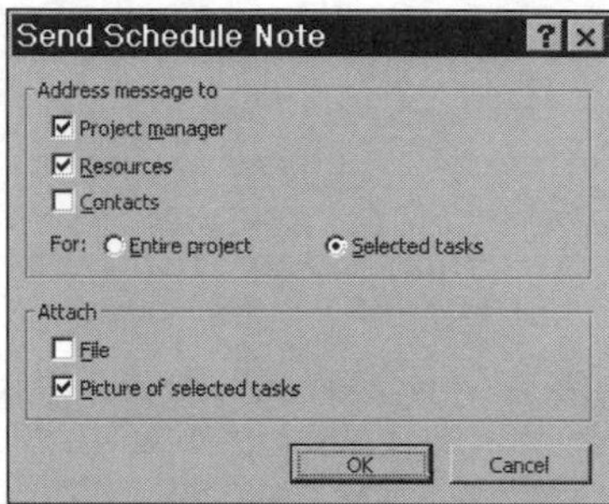


**Figure 15-16:** This dialog box gives you some flexibility for designating who should get this note: resources, the project manager, or various contacts for the project such as a vendor.

- **Address message to.** If you want everyone on the project to get this message, choose Entire project. If you want only the resources assigned to the task you selected before opening this dialog box, choose Selected tasks.
- **Attach.** If you want to attach the currently open Project file to your message, place a check in the File checkbox.

3. Click OK. A new e-mail message form, like the one shown in Figure 15-17, appears, with a copy of the Project file attached.

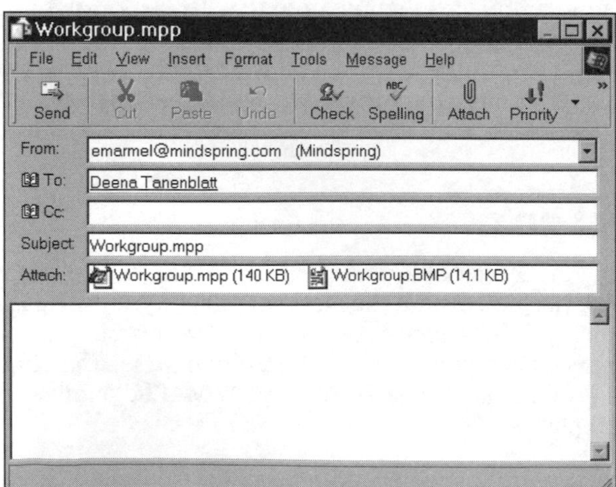


**Figure 15-17:** The e-mail form in your system may look different from this one, but you'll see some kind of blank message form.

4. Type your message in the large, blank message area.
5. Use your e-mail addressing method (for example, in the figure shown, you would click the To: button to access saved lists of addresses in this e-mail software) to send the message to anyone other than the designated resources assigned to tasks who were automatically addressed when you created the message.
6. Send the message.

## Routing a Project file

Routing a Project file to a group of people is another good way to keep workgroup members informed and involved in the project. Each person can add information that the next person on the route can build or comment on. Routing a file is a simple process. Follow these steps:

1. Choose File ➪ Sent To ➪ Routing Recipient, or click the Send to Routing Recipient button on the Workgroup toolbar to open the Routing Slip dialog box in Figure 15-18.

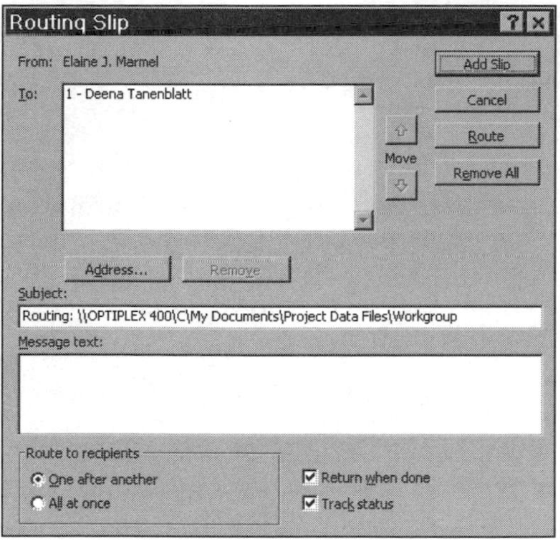


**Figure 15-18:** The Routing Slip dialog box enables you to track your message as it moves along its route by clicking the Track status checkbox.

2. Click the Address button to display the address book for your e-mail software program. Select as many addressees as you wish using this method and then click OK to return to the Routing Slip dialog box.
3. Enter information for the Subject of the message.
4. Type your message in the Message text box.

5. Select one of the option buttons in the Route to recipients box, choosing to route sequentially or all at once.
6. Place a check in the Return when done checkbox if you want Project to return the file to you at the end of the route.
7. Place a check in the Track status checkbox if you want Project to notify you each time the file moves to the next person on the routing list.
8. Click Route to send the message.

If you're the last recipient of the routing, you can remove the routing slip from the Project file. Click the Remove All button in the Routing Slip dialog box.

# Summary

Because most projects are team efforts and successful teams communicate effectively, establishing good workgroup procedures in your projects is key. In this chapter, you learned how to:

- ✦ Set up the workgroup manager and workgroup members to send and receive project information via e-mail
- ✦ Use TeamAssign, TeamStatus, and TeamUpdate to keep members informed and update the project file
- ✦ Route messages and files among team members

In addition to knowing how to use these features, you must know how to set up effective, consistent procedures for their use among your workgroup members.

Chapter 16 covers how to use Project Central to manage projects on your company's intranet or on the World Wide Web.

✦ ✦ ✦

# Project Management and the Web

✦ ✦ ✦ ✦

**In This Chapter**

Project and the World Wide Web

Using the Web toolbar

Working with hyperlinks

Managing projects on the Web

Administering Project Central

✦ ✦ ✦ ✦

By now you realize that the world of project management has moved beyond the traditional pencil-and-ruler war room and into the world of technology. Nowhere is this shift more evident than in the many ways project managers can take advantage of the Internet to communicate with others, present information, and gather data.

The Internet is a large network of computers you can use to send and retrieve information, images, and messages around the globe. The World Wide Web is perhaps the biggest success story on the Internet: This graphical Internet service enables you to move around the Web using a programming language called Hypertext Markup Language (HTML). With HTML you can jump between Web locations by clicking images or text linked to a specific online address. These links are *hyperlinks.*

## Project and the World Wide Web

Connectivity helps you manage projects more effectively, and Project includes a few useful tools that help you access and use the World Wide Web:

- ✦ You can insert hyperlinks to Internet addresses within your project file. That way, you or someone using your schedule can move instantly to an area on the Web that contains related information or images. For example, if your project has to do with the design of a network for your company, you can insert a hyperlink in your schedule to the network software vendor's home page so that you can find answers to technical questions or order software.

✦ You can use Project's Web capabilities to navigate around the Internet using the Web toolbar. Rather than embedding a link to a site in your schedule, you can save lists of your favorite Web locations and go quickly to a site on that list using the Web toolbar. Your favorite sites might include your company's Web page, a newsgroup related to your industry, or a data source, such as a university library, that you search often for information related to your project.

✦ Using Project Central, a manager can use Project on his or her computer to manage projects that rely on people who don't have Project on their computers. That is, you don't need everyone in the workgroup to have a copy of Project. Those people who don't have Project can use Project Central to view the tasks they need to accomplish, update the schedule with work done, and even enter new tasks that may arise. Project Central lets both the project manager and the "worker bees" communicate with each other—without everyone using Project.

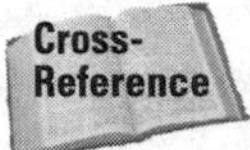


You can also use the Internet to communicate with your workgroup via e-mail. Chapter 15 covers this feature in more detail.

# Using the Web Toolbar

Project has a special set of tools specifically designed for navigating around the World Wide Web. You can display this toolbar by right-clicking anyplace on the Standard Toolbar and choosing Web from the shortcut menu that appears; or, you can choose View ⇨ Toolbars ⇨ Web. Figure 16-1 shows you the tools that are available.

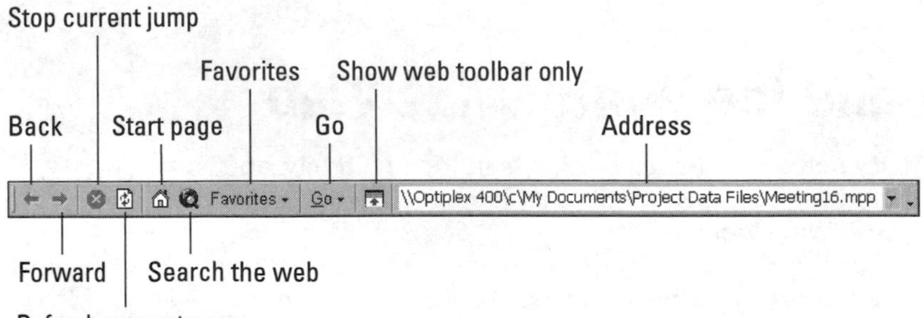


**Figure 16-1:** The Web toolbar appears just below the Formatting toolbar, though you can drag it away to be a floating toolbar if you prefer.

The tools here work with your Web browser to help you to navigate around either an organizational intranet or the Web. Table 16-1 briefly describes each tool.

Table 16-1
**The Project Web Toolbar**

| *Tool* | *Function* |
|---|---|
| Back | Takes you back to the last site visited during the current online session. |
| Forward | Moves you one site ahead in the list of sites visited during the current online session. |
| Stop Current Jump | Becomes active if you initiate a jump to a site; clicking this button when it's active stops the hyperlink jump that's in progress. |
| Refresh Current Page | Refreshes or updates the contents of a currently displayed page, incorporating any changes made by the author as you're reading the page. |
| Start Page | Takes you to the home page that you have set your Web browser to access. |
| Search the Web | Takes you to whatever search page you have set your Web browser to use. |
| Favorites | Opens a list of favorite sites that you have saved into a Favorites folder. Click any site name in this list to go directly to that site. |
| Go | Displays a menu of common Web navigation commands. |
| Show Web Toolbar Only | Hides any other currently displayed toolbars, leaving only the Web toolbar visible onscreen. |
| Address | Shows the address of the current site and, when opened by clicking the arrow on the right, displays a drop-down list of recently visited sites. |

To use these tools, you need an Internet connection and a Web browser. When all the elements are in place and you click, for example, the Search tool button, Project connects with the Internet and opens the search page you have set up in your browser. When you are connected, you can use the Back and Forward buttons to move through the Web pages. You can use your browser's Favorites feature to save addresses of sites you like to visit often; Project also saves these addresses in its own Favorites list.

Note

Microsoft provides the latest version of its Internet Explorer browser with Project. You can install the browser from your Project CD-ROM. You can also download Internet Explorer from the Microsoft Web site at `www.microsoft.com/ie/default.asp`.

# Working with Hyperlinks

A hyperlink is a mechanism that enables you to jump from the currently displayed document to another document on your hard drive or on a computer network, or to an Internet address (referred to as a *Uniform Resource Locator,* or URL).

Suppose your company is planning to move into a new manufacturing facility, and Finance has placed the budget for the move in an Excel spreadsheet on your company's network. You, on the other hand, must manage the move and have created a project schedule that deals with moving all equipment into your new manufacturing facility. You can place a hyperlink in the project schedule that connects to the Excel file that contains the budget for the move to the new facility. The hyperlink appears as an icon in the Indicator field of the Gantt chart. When you open the project file and click that hyperlink, the Excel file appears so that you can check on the budgeted dollars for each aspect of the move.

You can also insert a hyperlink to an Internet address, for example, to link a research task to the Internet site where most of the research is performed.

## Inserting a hyperlink

To insert a hyperlink in your project, complete the following steps:

1. Select the task for which you want to create a hyperlink. (When you finish inserting the hyperlink, a link icon appears in the Indicator column for the selected task.)
2. Choose Insert ➪ Hyperlink or click the Insert Hyperlink button on the Standard toolbar. The Insert Hyperlink dialog box shown in Figure 16-2 appears.

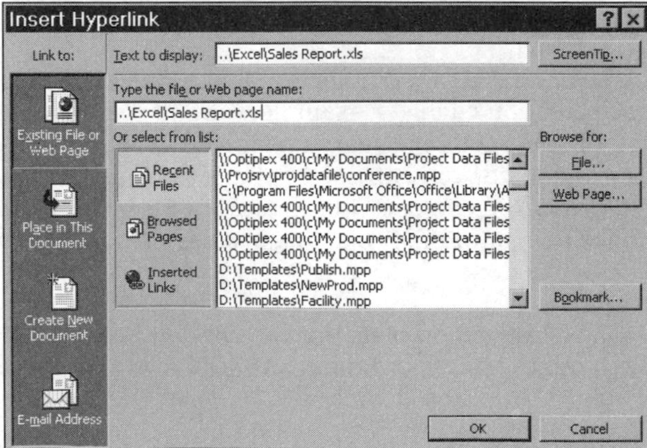


**Figure 16-2:** Enter a file path and name, or a URL, to set up the hyperlink.

3. In the "Type the file or Web page name" box, do any of the following:
   - To link to an Internet address, type the URL (for example, `http://www.microsoft.com`) or browse for a URL by clicking the Web Page button.
   - To link to a file on your hard drive or a network, type the path or browse for the file by clicking the File button.
4. In the Text to display box, type the text you want to appear in your Project schedule to represent the hyperlink.
5. Click OK to insert the hyperlink. A hyperlink icon, like the one shown in Figure 16-3, appears in the Indicator field to the left of the selected task.

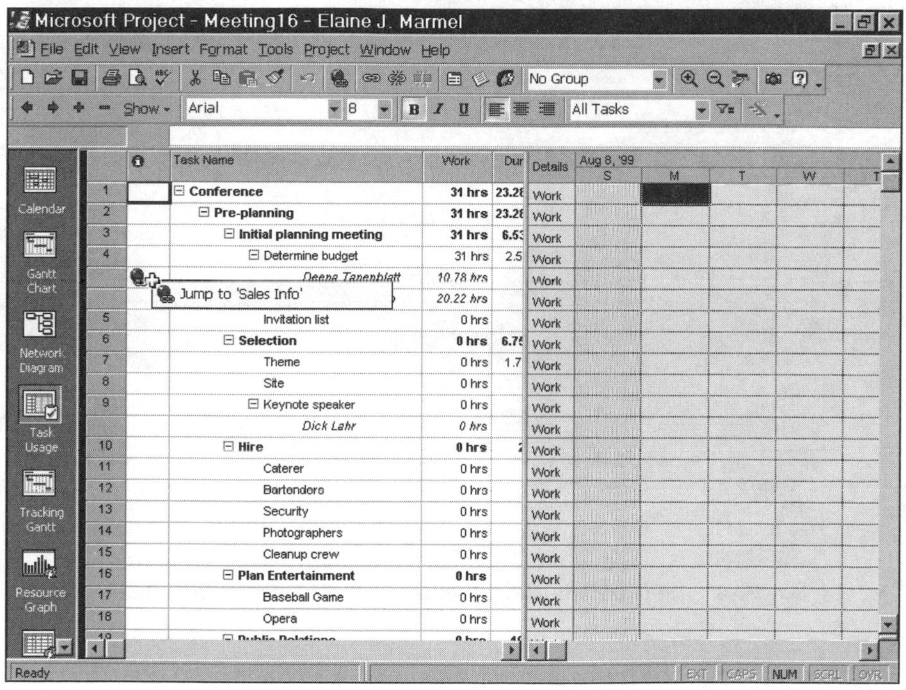


**Figure 16-3:** To go to a URL or file, click the hyperlink icon.

To remove a hyperlink, right-click the task for which you created the link and then choose Hyperlink ⇨ Remove Hyperlink. No warning appears; Project simply removes the hyperlink.

## Editing hyperlinks

If you create a lot of hyperlinks, identifying them can be tedious if you reply on the ScreenTip you see when you point at each link. You can, however, display the links in one of Project's built-in tables. Start in any view that includes a table, such as the Task Usage view. Choose View ⇨ Table ⇨ Hyperlink. The hyperlink table in Figure 16-4 shows columns of information relevant to any links you've created for your project.

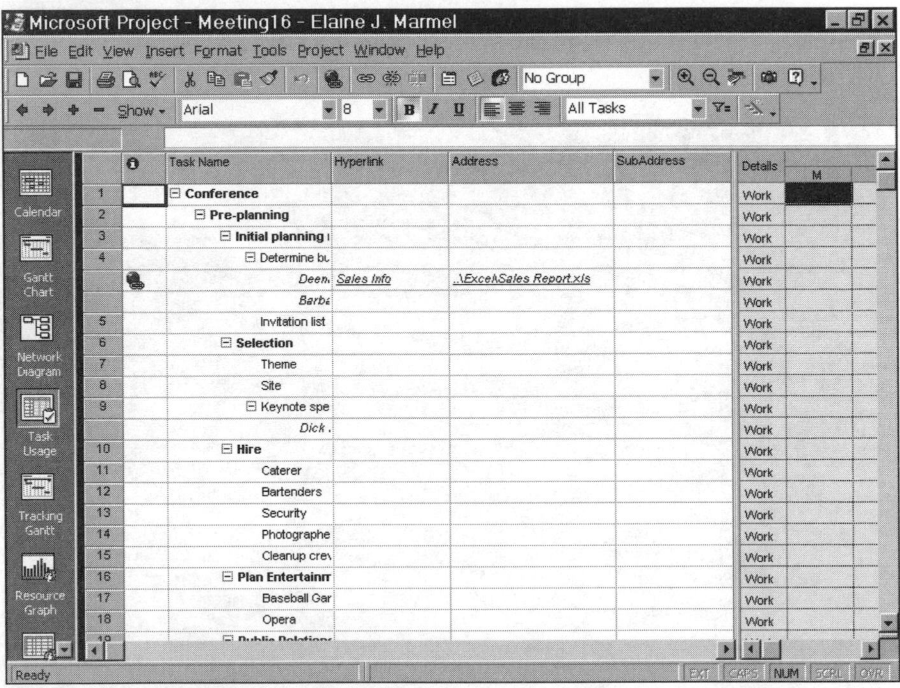

**Figure 16-4:** The hyperlink address and representation are two fields available here.

To edit either the hyperlink or its address or sub-address, click the task name of the task for which you created the hyperlink. Then, use the right-arrow key to move to the cell you want to edit and make the changes you want to make. If you prefer to work in the Hyperlink dialog box, right-click the link and choose Hyperlink ⇨ Edit Hyperlink to reopen the dialog box and make changes.

Because the cells in this table contain hypertext, clicking the field itself activates the link.

## When Hyperlinks Don't Work

After you establish a hyperlink, some things can happen to cause the link to not work. This condition usually involves a change in the location of the linked file. On a network or hard drive, a file could simply have been moved to another directory or deleted. Similarly, a Web site could have been moved to a new URL, or perhaps it no longer exists.

Or, you may have mapped your hyperlink to a file on a network that is in a location to which you don't have access. Or perhaps you gave a copy of your schedule to a coworker, and she doesn't have access to that location from her computer.

The best way to work around this problem is to use relative addressing whenever possible when you create the hyperlink. For example, `f:\budget.xls` is an absolute address. If your server changes from `f:`, the link won't work. However, if you use `\\server\share\budget.xls`, a relative address, your server can change from `f:` to `g:`, and the relative address to your server would still work. For more help with hyperlink problems, check out the hyperlink troubleshooting topic in Project's Help feature.

### Moving or copying hyperlinks

You can also use the hyperlink table to move or copy a hyperlink. Follow these steps to do so:

1. Select the hyperlink cell by clicking its task name and then by using the right-arrow key to move to the hyperlink cell.
2. Press the Shift key and the right-arrow key to also select the address of the hyperlink.
3. Do one of the following:
   - To move the link, click the Cut button on the Standard toolbar, click the hyperlink cell next to the task where you want to move the link, and click the Paste button.
   - To copy the link, select the link, click the Copy button, click the hyperlink cell next to the task where you want to place a copy of the link, and click the Paste button.

# Managing Projects on the Web

Project Central enables you to manage projects on your company's intranet or on the Internet—and only the manager must actually install and use Project. All other resources on the project use Project Central, which accesses a Web-based database that contains your project data. Without using Microsoft Project, resources can:

✦ View a project's Gantt chart

- Receive, refuse, and delegate work assignments
- Update assignments with progress and completion information
- Send status reports to the project manager

The project manager alerts team members to task assignments through Project's TeamAssign feature, and the manager can use the TeamUpdate feature to notify team members about shifts in the schedule, changes in assignments, or other project parameters. Team members use Project Central to update work assignments and send status reports to the project manager. Work assignments appear in the Microsoft Project Central Inbox.

The network administrator installs Project Central Server on a Web server or the company's server. The project manager creates a project in Microsoft Project and sets up the project so that it is "Web-based." Once the project manager sends assignments to resources, the resources will be able to log on to Project Central, view the project, review assignments, and so on.

## Setting up a Web-based project

Setting up a Web-based project involves the following:

- A network administrator installing Project Central Server on a Web server or on your company's server
- The project manager creating a project in Microsoft Project, including the resources the project will need and attaching the project to the Web-based database
- Resources and the project manager using Project Central (the client side) to update the project

The project manager uses both Project and Project Central, but other project resources use only Project Central.

### Setting up Project Central Server and Project Central

You'll need a network administrator-type to set up Project Central Server on a Web server or on the company's server. That machine should have Windows NT Server 4.0 with Service Pack 4 or 5 and Option Pack 4 (which includes Microsoft Internet Information Server, also called IIS). You'll also need Oracle, SQL Server, or Microsoft Database Engine (MSDE). MSDE is a scaled down version of SQL server.

Note

In Microsoft Project 98, you could use Personal Web Server supplied by Microsoft. This product will no longer suffice if you intend to use Web-based project management for groups.

When you install Project Central Server, it installs and sets up a connection between your database engine and IIS.

On the client side, the project manager needs Project, but other resources need only Internet Explorer 4.01 or higher. Microsoft includes the latest shipping version of Internet Explorer on the Project CD-ROM. If you don't want to use IE 4.01, you can install, on client machines, the browser module for Microsoft Project Central (a 32-bit Windows client) that you'll find on your Microsoft Project CD-ROM.

The browser you use must natively support ActiveX controls in the way Project expects; therefore, you must use either Internet Explorer or the 32-bit Windows client you'll find on the Project CD-ROM.

In addition, each person in the workgroup must be able to access either your organization's network or a TCP/IP network.

## Creating a Web-based project

The workgroup manager is the person who builds and maintains the project schedule and makes task assignments. The "boss" uses Project to create the schedule and make assignments to workgroup members to track their activities.

The workgroup manager must set up the project schedule to enable Web-based communications on his or her computer. Although workgroup members can also install Project on their computers, this step isn't necessary. Follow these steps to set up a project schedule to use Web communications on the workgroup manager's computer:

1. Choose Tools ➪ Options.
2. Click the Workgroup tab to select it (see Figure 16-5).

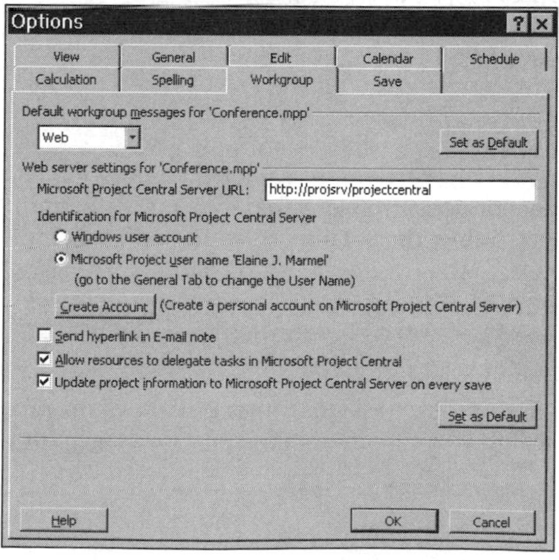


**Figure 16-5:** To use the Web for workgroup management, set the default messaging method to Web.

3. Select the default workgroup messaging method from the "Default workgroup messaging for" drop-down list. Select Web for a Web server setup, including an intranet or the World Wide Web.

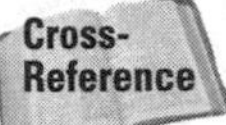


See Chapter 15 for information on setting up a project schedule to use e-mail for workgroup management.

4. In the Microsoft Project Central Server URL box, enter the URL that resources should use to display Project Central, along with the folder that contains the Web database. This Internet address points to a Web server or your organizational server and a folder that contains the Web database.
5. For the method of identification, you can allow one of two methods:
   - Resources can use their Windows NT login information by choosing Windows user account.
   - Resources can use their Microsoft Project user name, which you can set on the General tab of the Options dialog box.
6. As the project manager, you may not be assigning yourself any tasks. However, you'll need access to Project Central on the Web to interact with your team members electronically. To provide access for yourself to Project Central, click the Create Account button.
7. Use the checkboxes to set up Project to send a hyperlink that provides the URL for the Web database to resources in e-mail messages. You also can control whether resources can delegate tasks in Project Central, and you can update the Web database each time you save your project in Project.

You can manually update the Web database whenever you want by choosing Tools ➪ Workgroup ➪ Update Project to Web Server.

8. Click OK to save your settings.

## Making assignments

The project manager assigns work to resources. To notify the resources of the work assignments, the project manager uses Project's TeamAssign command. After making assignments in Project, follow these steps to send work assignments to resources:

1. (Optional) Select the tasks about which you wish to notify resources of work assignments.
2. Choose Tools ➪ Workgroup ➪ TeamAssign. Project displays the Workgroup Mail dialog box, from which you can choose to send messages for all tasks or selected tasks.

3. Choose All tasks or Selected task and click OK. Project displays the TeamAssign window shown in Figure 16-6.

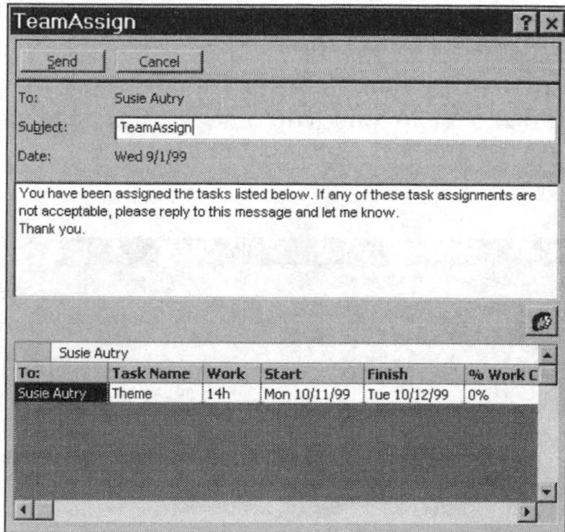


**Figure 16-6:** Use this window to send notice of a work assignment to a resource.

Project displays a message prior to displaying the TeamAssign window. The message tells you how you can send messages to resources using their Windows user accounts.

4. If you want, edit the message or the subject line. Then, click Send. Project sends the message to the resource(s) listed in the To line of the message.

Sending a TeamAssign message to a resource also tells Project to add that resource's name to the Log On list for Project Central. That is, a resource won't be able to log onto Project Central until he or she receives a TeamAssign message from the project manager.

## Logging on to Project Central

To log onto Project Central, a resource needs to know the URL for the Web database. The project manager may have sent the URL in an e-mail or the resource may have received notification in some other fashion. Open Internet Explorer or the 32-bit Windows client that you installed from the Project CD-ROM to use Project Central. In the Address box, type the URL of the Web database.

Save the URL in your Favorites list or, if you use Project Central more than any other Web page, set it up as your home page when you open Internet Explorer. To set Project Central as your home page, type the address into the Address box. Then, choose Tools ➪ Internet Options. On the first page, click the Use Current button in the Home Page section, and click OK.

The window you see next depends on the logon method you're using for Project Central. If you are *not* using Windows NT logons, you'll see a Web page similar to the one shown in Figure 16-7.

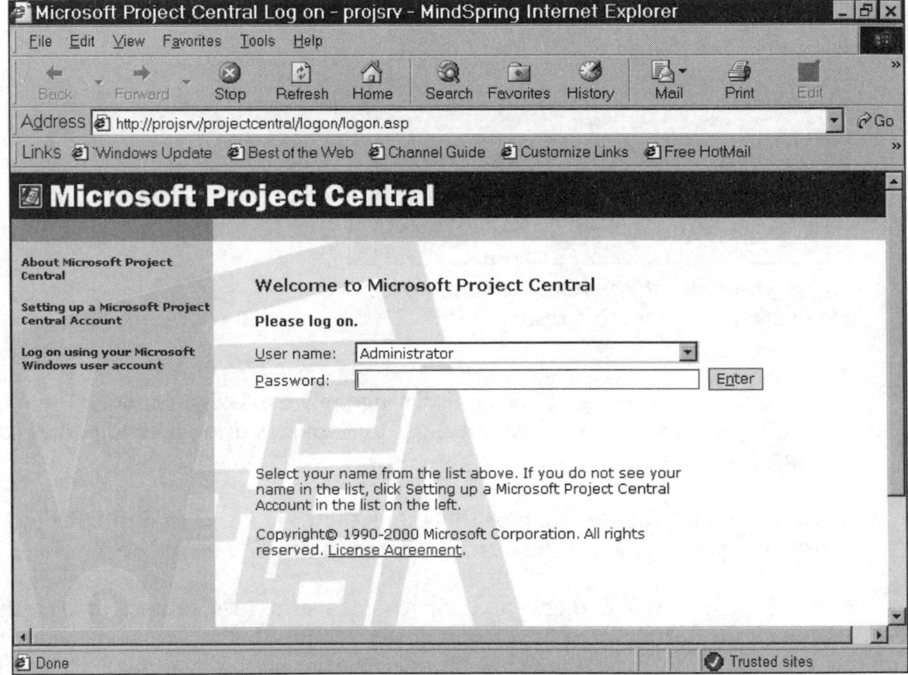


**Figure 16-7:** The opening page of Project Central for users who don't use Windows NT logon information

If you're using Windows NT logons, you won't see the Logon page; instead, you'll bypass this page and see your home page, which is discussed in the next section.

Select your name from the User name list. If you're not using Windows NT logons, then initially your password is blank so you don't need to enter anything in the Password box. Simply click Enter.

If you set a password using the techniques described later in this chapter, you'll need to supply that password in the Password box if you see the Logon page of Project Central.

## Reviewing the Home page

After you've selected yourself from the User Name list and clicked Enter (or, after you've entered the URL for Project Central if you're using Windows NT logon information), you'll see your Project Central Home page. It looks similar to the page you see in Figure 16-8.

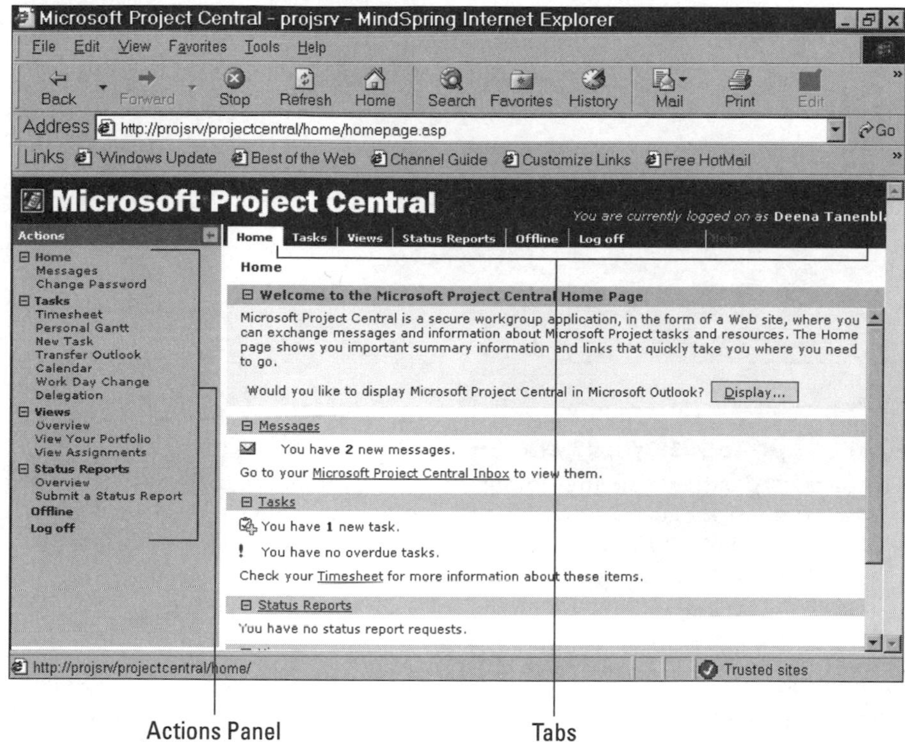


**Figure 16-8:** A typical Project Central Home page, from which you can navigate to other areas of Project Central

The Project Central Home page serves the same function as most home pages on the Web; it introduces you to Project Central, displays summary information such as the number of new messages you have, and provides you with links to navigate to other areas of Project Central. The tabs (Home, Tasks, Views, Status Reports, Offline, Logoff, and Help) across the top of Project Central remain visible at all times and, if you point at them, a drop-down menu appears, providing you with choices. The Actions pane on the left side remains visible as long as you're viewing the Home page, your Inbox, or the Change Password page. To navigate in Project Central, you click a link or point at a tab and click a choice from the drop-down menu.

## Implementing security

When you begin to pass around plans for a project, you may run into issues of security. For example, you might have resource rate information you don't want every Tom, Dick, and Mary to see. Maybe you want messages you receive on project status to be for your eyes only. You can protect the contents of your Microsoft Project Central Inbox by assigning a password to it.

If you aren't using Windows NT logon information, your password is initially blank. As long as your password remains blank, Project Central will prompt you to change your password each time you use Project Central. You'll see a dialog box similar to the one shown in Figure 16-9.

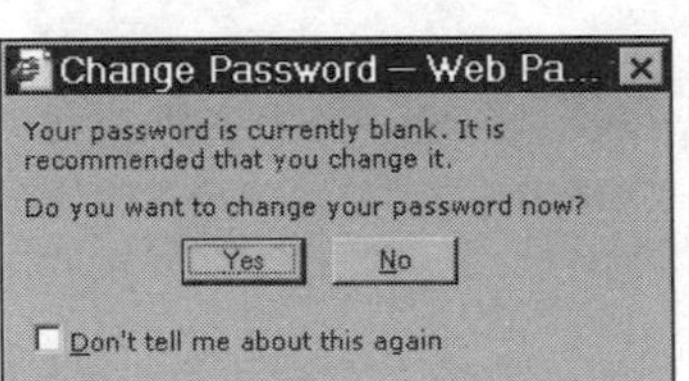


**Figure 16-9:** As long as your password remains blank, Project Central prompts you to create a password.

### A word about passwords and security

The password is the basic method of protecting project data. However, setting a password does not guarantee safety; the procedures you use to devise an effective password and keep it from being discovered are vital to project security.

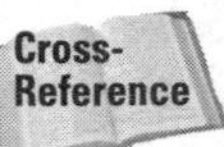


For information on setting passwords for individual files in Project, see Chapter 2.

Whether for serious motives, like industrial espionage, or simple workplace curiosity, people may try to peek at your project information. The computer world has spawned a whole subculture of people, known as hackers, who have made an art out of breaking into supposedly secure files.

Here are some guidelines for working with passwords:

✦ Don't use an easy-to-guess password. A clever hacker can find out your spouse's name, your middle name, your phone extension, and your date of birth in no time flat.

✦ Use the longest password that Project allows (up to 17 characters); the longer the password, the harder it is to crack.

✦ Don't give your password to anybody. If you have to give it out, for example, if you are away from the office and someone else must access data to keep the project going, be sure to change your password as soon as you return.

✦ Create a password that is a random combination of letters and numbers. For example, T2J773N is a good password; MyFile isn't.

✦ Change your password on a regular basis, even if you never give it to anyone. Hackers break passwords by trying out different options and combinations; it may take them a few sessions to break your code. The more often you change your password, the more times someone else will have to start from scratch to break it.

## Setting your password

When you haven't set a password, Project Central prompts to set one each time you log in (refer to Figure 16-9). If you click Yes, you'll see the page shown in Figure 16-10, where you enter a password and confirm it.

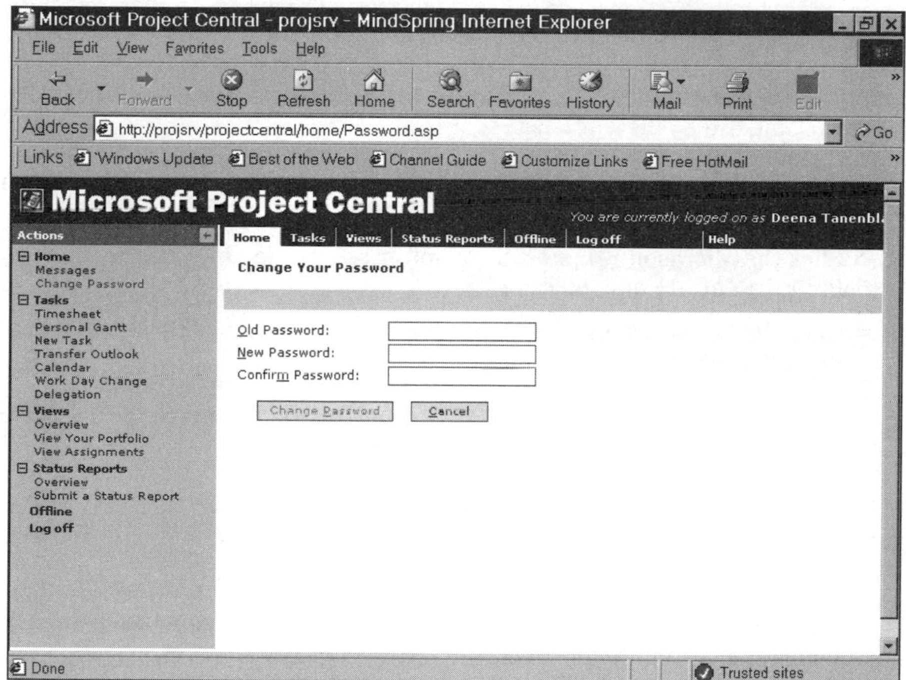


**Figure 16-10:** After you set a password, you must enter it in the Password box to enter Project Central.

You can display this page at any time by clicking the Change Password link on the left side of Project Central.

If you had no password at all, leave the Old Password box blank. Type your new password twice — first in the New Password box and then in the Confirm Password box. If you make a mistake, Project asks you to enter the password again. Click Change Password to save the password; the next time you log on to Project Central, you'll need to supply this password.

Note: You can change your password at any time by clicking Change Password in the column of links on the left side of the page. If you previously assigned a password, type it in the Old password field.

## Checking the messages in your Inbox

When a project manager sends a message to his or her team, that message appears in Project Central in each recipient's Microsoft Project Central Inbox. When team members respond to a message, Project places that response in the project manager's Microsoft Project Central Inbox.

Team members and the project manager can check their Microsoft Project Central Inboxes using three different links:

- ✦ Click the Messages link that serves as a heading for the Messages section of your Project Central Home page,
- ✦ Click the Microsoft Project Central Inbox link in the Messages section of your Project Central Home page, or
- ✦ Click the Messages link that appears in the Action pane on the left side of Project Central.

The project manager can choose Tools ⇨ Workgroup ⇨ TeamInbox, and Project displays the manager's opening page in Project Central.

In Figure 16-11, you see a typical Microsoft Project Central Inbox, which lists each message with information about the sender, project, subject, and date and time the message was received.

Managers send various types of messages to team members, and the team members respond. Both team members and managers see the messages in their Microsoft Project Central Inboxes. Managers use the following commands, found on the Tools ⇨ Workgroup menu in Project, to:

- ✦ Make assignments (TeamAssign)
- ✦ Communicate about changes in dates (TeamUpdate)

In Project Central, you open a message by clicking the subject; if you prefer, you can click at the left edge of the message to select it and then click the Open Message command above the list of messages (refer to Figure 16-11). An open message looks similar to the one you see in Figure 16-12.

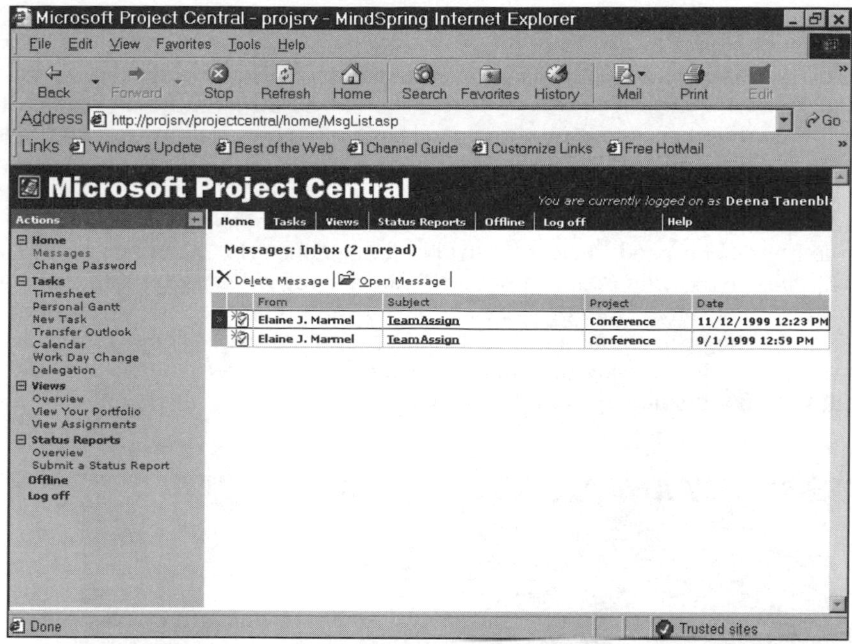


**Figure 16-11:** You can use the Microsoft Project Central Inbox to keep track of and manage messages from your workgroup.

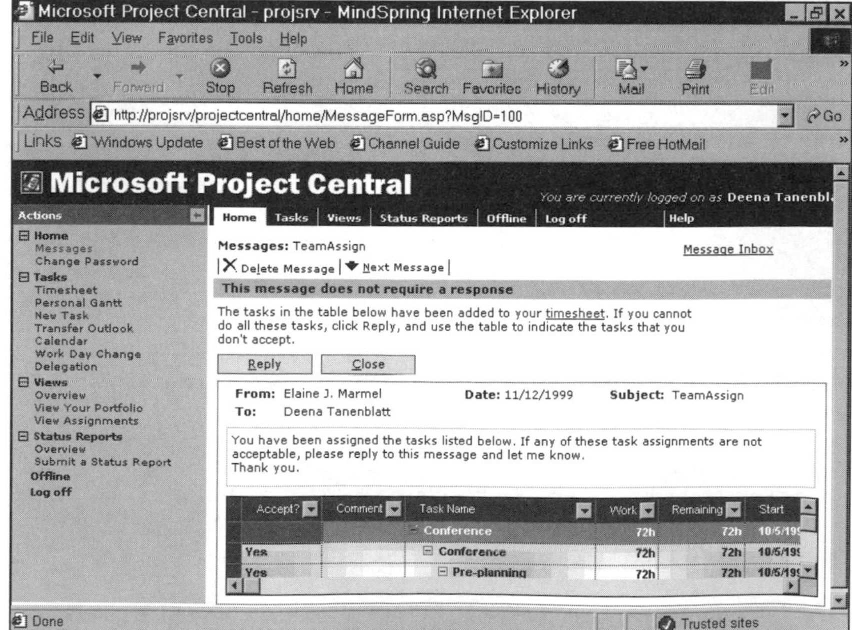


**Figure 16-12:** After reading (and responding to) an open message, you can view the next message.

If you need to reply, you can click the Reply button; Project Central presents a blank, preaddressed message. To review the next message in the Microsoft Project Central Inbox, click the Next Message link at the top of the message. If you're finished reviewing messages, you can click the Close button in the message (Project Central redisplays the Inbox) or you can click a link in the Action pane on the left side or a tab at the top of Project Central.

The project manager's Microsoft Project Central Inbox looks a little different than a team member's Microsoft Project Central Inbox because the manager has the ability to set up *messaging rules* (see Figure 16-13). Messaging rules permit the manager to set up rules to automatically process messages and update the project schedule. For example, the project manager may want to automatically accept new tasks that come from a particular team member. Using a rule, the project manager can do that without reading the message and taking action.

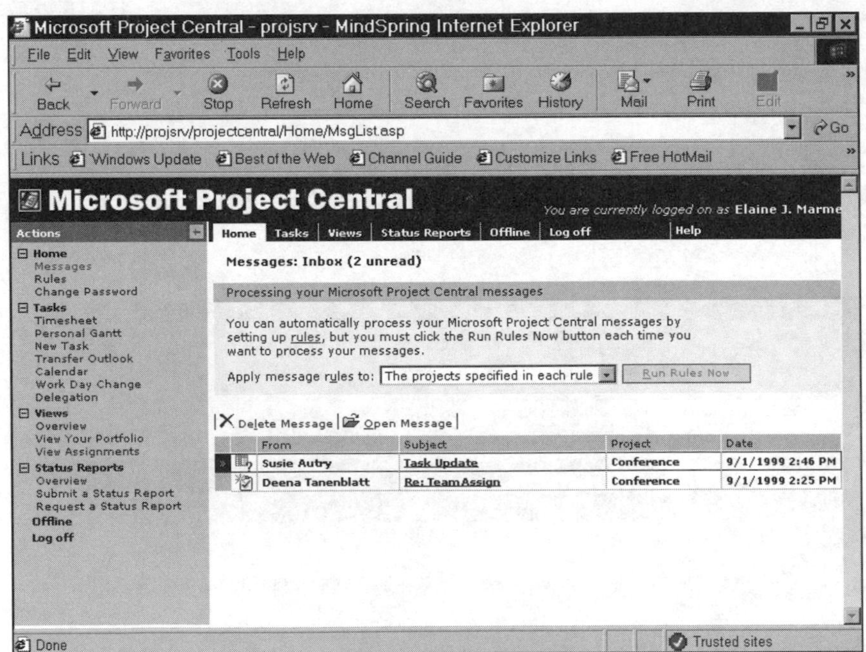


**Figure 16-13:** The project manager's Microsoft Project Central inbox

To set up rules, click the Rules link in the text at the top of the page. Project Central displays a page of your current rules; click the New Rule command on that page to run a wizard that walks you through creating a rule. The first page of the wizard looks similar to the page you see in Figure 16-14.

Select the type of messages you want to automatically accept and click Next. Project Central displays the page you see in Figure 16-15.

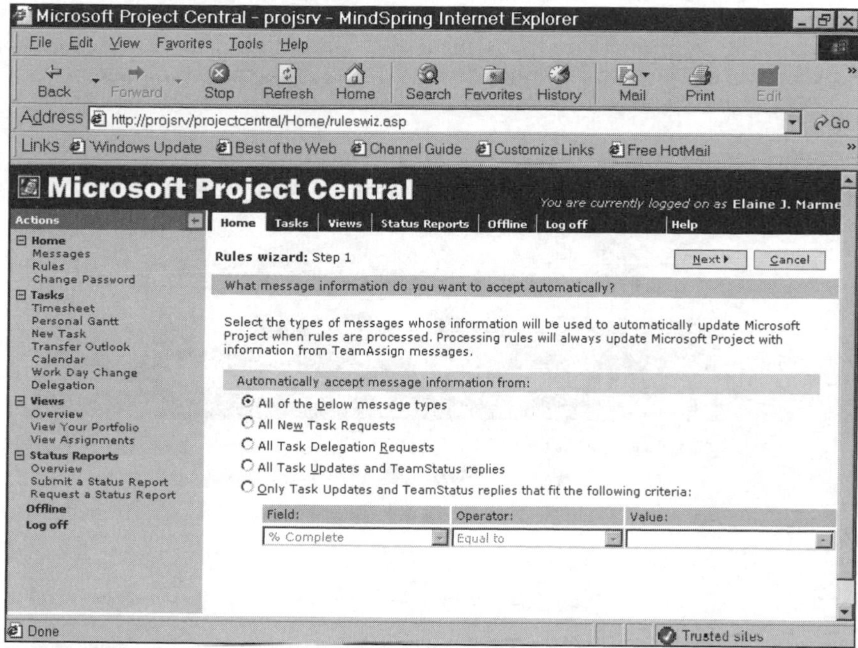


**Figure 16-14:** On the first page of the wizard, choose the type of messages you want to automatically accept.

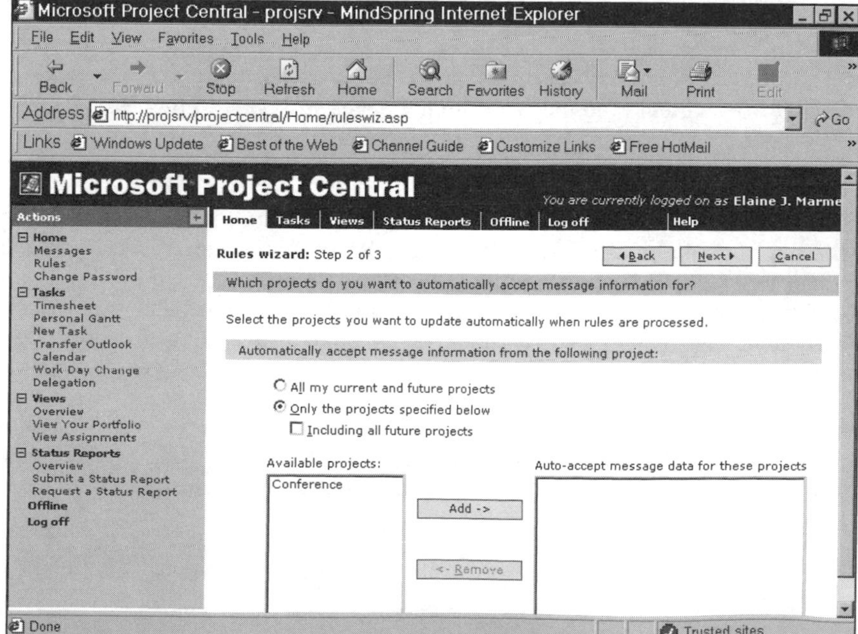


**Figure 16-15:** Select the projects to which you want to apply the rules.

To automatically accept messages for particular projects, select the project from the list of available projects on the left and click the Add button. Click Next when you finish selecting projects. Project Central displays the page you see in Figure 16-16.

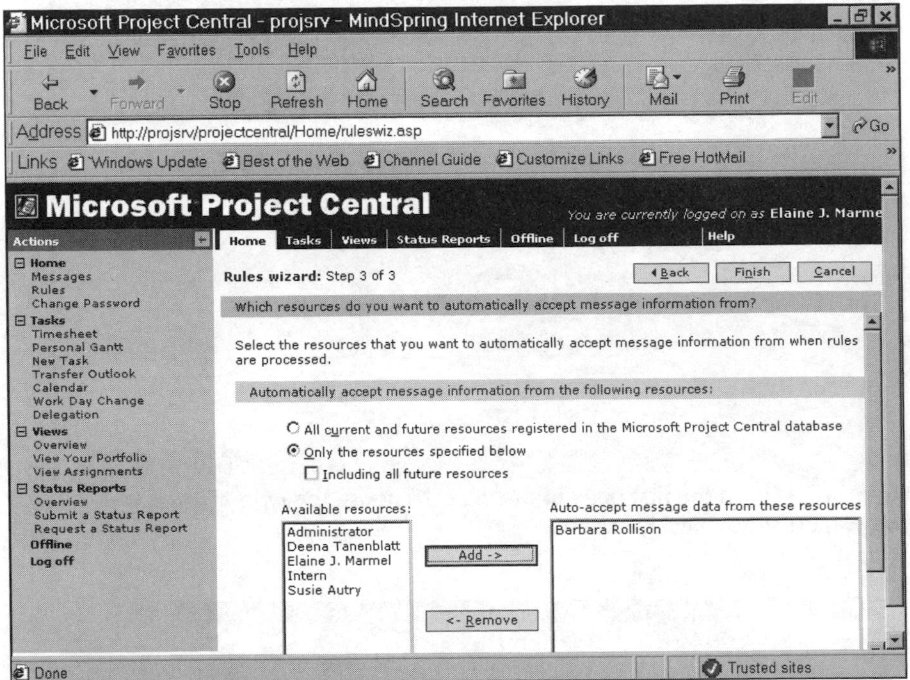


**Figure 16-16:** Select team members whose messages you want to process automatically.

Select the team members from whom you want to automatically process messages from the list of available resources on the left. When you finish, click the Finish button. Project Central displays a message telling you that the rule will only apply to future messages and that you'll need to manually handle any existing messages. After you click OK, Project Central displays the page showing your current list of rules (see Figure 16-17).

To use the rules you establish, work from your Microsoft Project Central Inbox page (refer to Figure 16-13). Click Run Rules Now to have Project Central process messages in your Microsoft Project Central Inbox based on the rules you established.

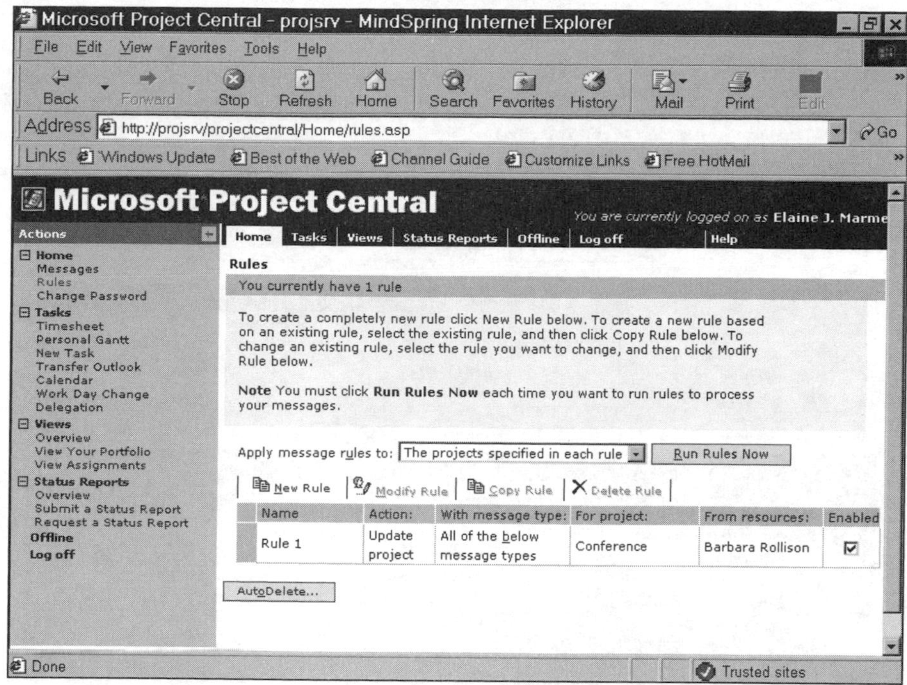


**Figure 16-17:** The project manager's current list of rules

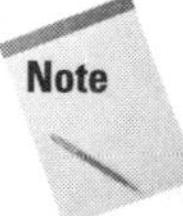


Notice the AutoDelete button in Figure 16-17. If you click the button, you can specify message types to automatically delete after running rules.

## Working with your timesheet

In Project Central, you have a timesheet that you can use to record and report work you've performed. In Figure 16-18, you see the View Options tab of the Timesheet page; when you click either the Filter and Grouping tab or the Delegation tab, the Timesheet page redisplays with different options appearing above the tasks. For example, using the Filter and Grouping tab, you can change the order in which tasks appear from the default — by project name — to start date, work, or task name. From the Delegation tab, you can choose to show only delegated tasks, only your own tasks, or both; you also can delegate tasks from this tab.

Note that you can display tasks stored in Outlook along with tasks assigned to you in Project.

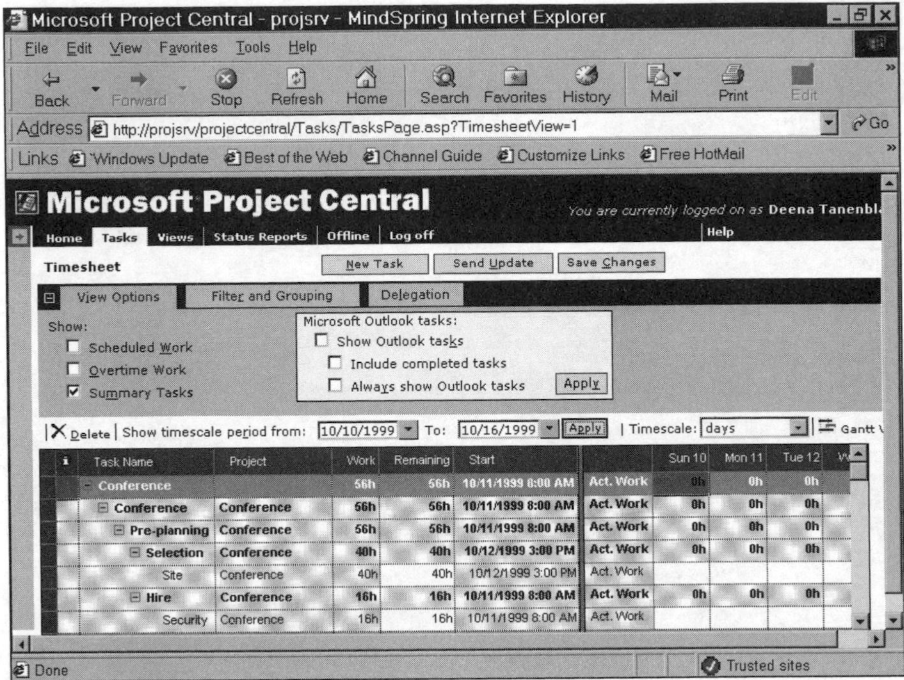


**Figure 16-18:** The Timesheet page of Project Central

## Entering time on tasks

The Timesheet works like a spreadsheet; you click in the cell you want to update, and then you type. Use the timescale period list boxes to display the time frame you want to update. Then, click in the cell that represents the intersection of the day you worked and the task on which you worked, type the number of hours you worked, and click the Save Changes button at the top of the Project Central page.

The information that you save updates the Web database, but it doesn't automatically update the manager's information stored in the Project file. To let your manager know that you've completed some work, click the Send Update button. Project Central sends a message to your manager.

The manager will find the message in the Microsoft Project Central Inbox; either log onto Project Central or, from inside Project, choose Tools ➪ Workgroup ➪ TeamInbox. Project Central opens; log on if necessary and then view the Microsoft Project Central Inbox. Find and open the Task Update message. You'll see a page similar to the one shown in Figure 16-19.

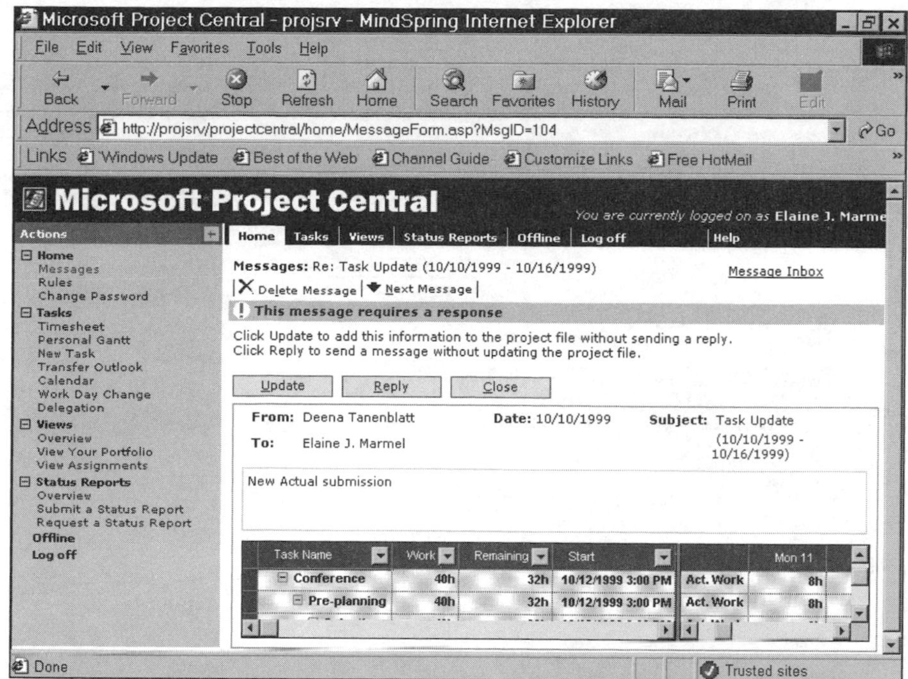


**Figure 16-19:** Modify the Project file with updates received from team members.

As the manager, you can choose to update the Project file without replying to the team member (click the Update button), or you can send a reply without updating the Project file (click the Reply button). When you update, Project Central updates the Project file.

The Project file can be open when you update, but make sure that you're viewing the Gantt view. Otherwise, you'll see a message that tells you to switch to the Gantt view.

## Adding tasks

As a team member, you may realize that what you're doing will require more work than the manager anticipated — and may even call for tasks that the manager didn't assign to you. You can enter the tasks in Project Central and notify your manager about the additional work.

To create a new task, point the mouse pointer at the Tasks tab to see a drop-down menu; then choose New Task. Project Central displays a page similar to the one you see in Figure 16-20.

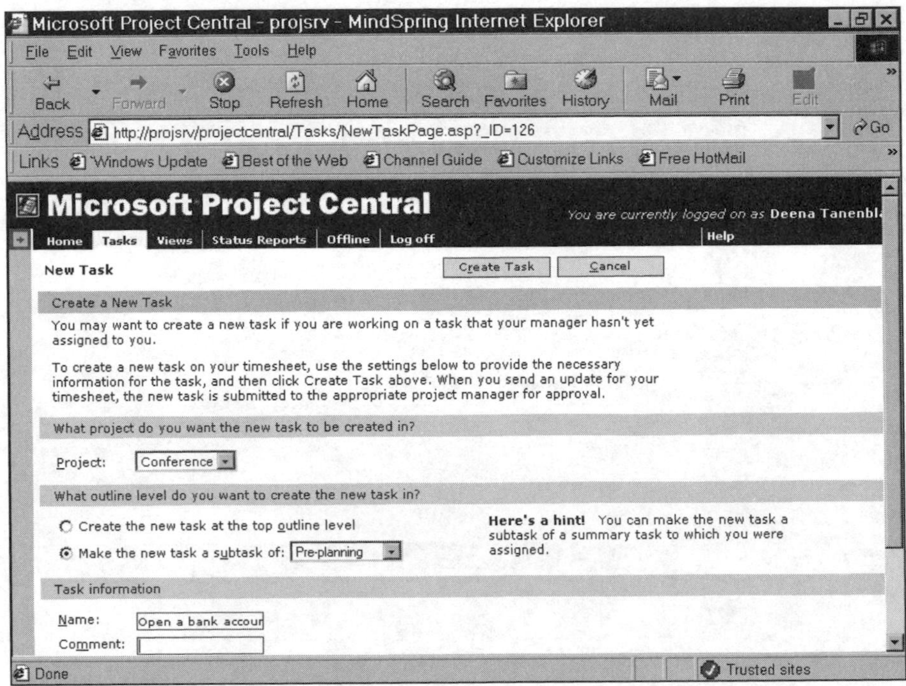


**Figure 16-20:** Add tasks to the project from this page.

Select the project to which you need to add the task from the Project drop-down list and then select the task's level in the outline. For the Task Information, supply a task name, an optional comment about the task, a start date, and the amount of work that you estimate the task will require. Click the Create Task button, and Project Central adds the task to your Timesheet. You'll see an icon in the Remarks column on your Timesheet (see Figure 16-21).

To notify your manager of the new task, click the Send Update button on your Timesheet. Project Central sends the notice of the new task to the manager and changes the icon to reflect the task's new status — that you've notified your manager, but your manager hasn't yet updated the project.

As a manager, you have the option to add the task to the project or to reject the task — and you can choose to reply to the team member about the new task. If you accept the task, be sure to close Project or display the Gantt view of the project you're updating.

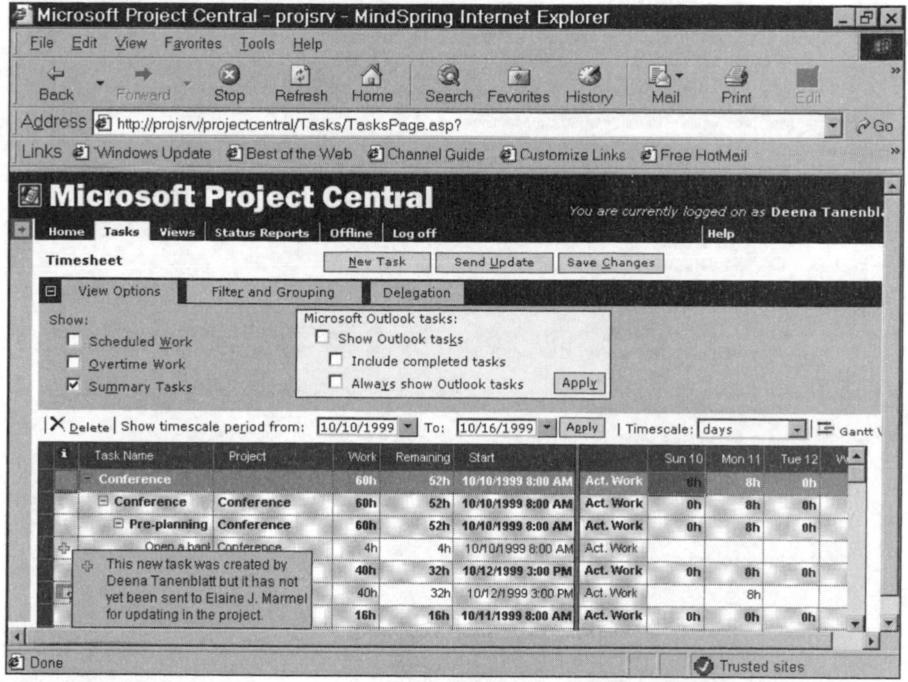


**Figure 16-21:** After you create a new task, Project Central reminds you that you haven't notified your manager about the task.

## Transferring information from Microsoft Outlook

Do you use Outlook? Would you like to be able to get a better handle on *all* the things you need to do by viewing them all in one place? Transfer nonworking time from your Outlook Calendar into Project Central so that you can view your entire schedule in one place.

If you want Project Central to display in Outlook, then you need Outlook 2000. If you want to transfer Outlook information into Project Central, then you can use Outlook 98 or above.

Point the mouse pointer at the Tasks tab and choose Transfer Calendar Entries from Outlook from the drop-down list that appears. Project Central displays the page you see in Figure 16-22. Click the Next button to enable a wizard to walk you through the process.

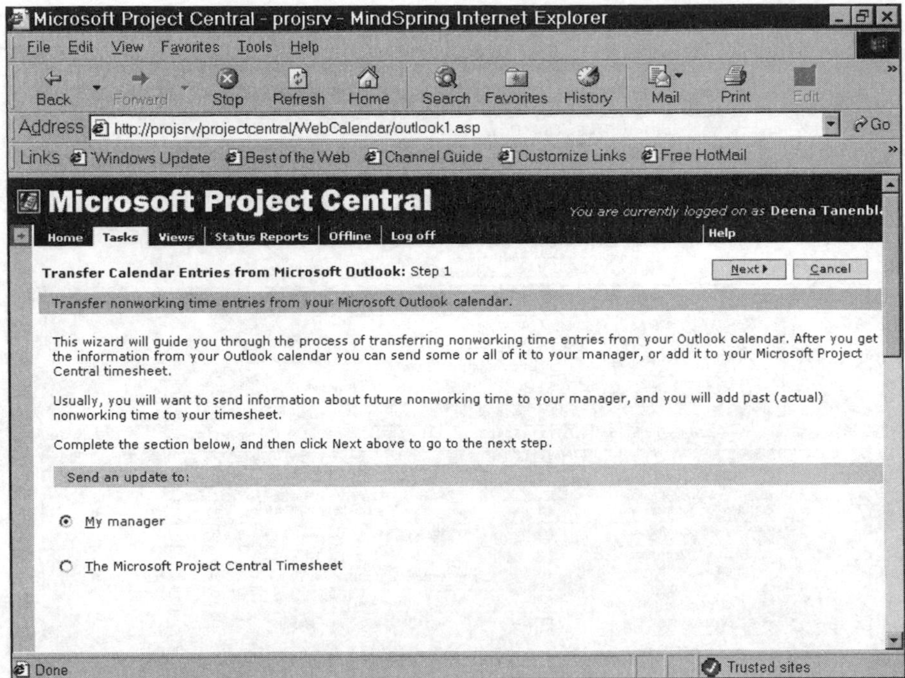


**Figure 16-22:** Use this wizard to walk you through the process of transferring nonworking time entries from your Outlook Calendar to your Project Central Timesheet.

## Notifying managers of workday changes

You were just selected for jury duty. And, of course, you're scheduled to work on a project at the same time. It happens: Something comes up and you are not available to work time you had previously been scheduled to work. Or, you are now available to work when you thought you wouldn't be available: The case you were hearing wrapped up earlier than expected and the jury's been dismissed.

You can use a wizard in Project Central to notify your manager of changes to your workday from Project Central. Point the mouse pointer at the Tasks tab and choose "Notify your manager of a work day change" from the drop-down list. Project Central displays the page you see in Figure 16-23. Click Next to enable the wizard to walk you through the process.

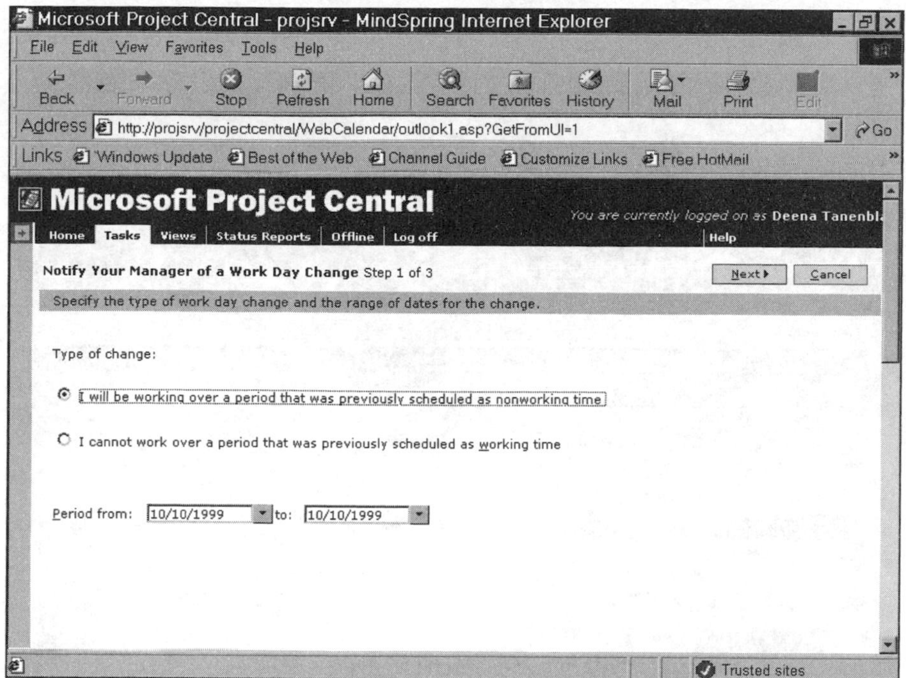


**Figure 16-23:** Enable this wizard to walk you through the process of notifying your manager about a change in your work schedule.

## Delegating a task

You're overloaded with work and can't possibly complete everything to which you've been assigned. But, lucky for you, they just approved your request to hire an intern to help you. Now you need to delegate some tasks — and keep your project manager informed of the change in assignment.

To delegate tasks, you use the Delegation tab of the Timesheet to identify the tasks you want to delegate to other team members. You can display the Delegation tab by clicking it while viewing the Timesheet, or you can point the mouse pointer at the Tasks tab and choose Delegation from the drop-down menu that appears. Project Central displays a page that looks like the one you see in Figure 16-24.

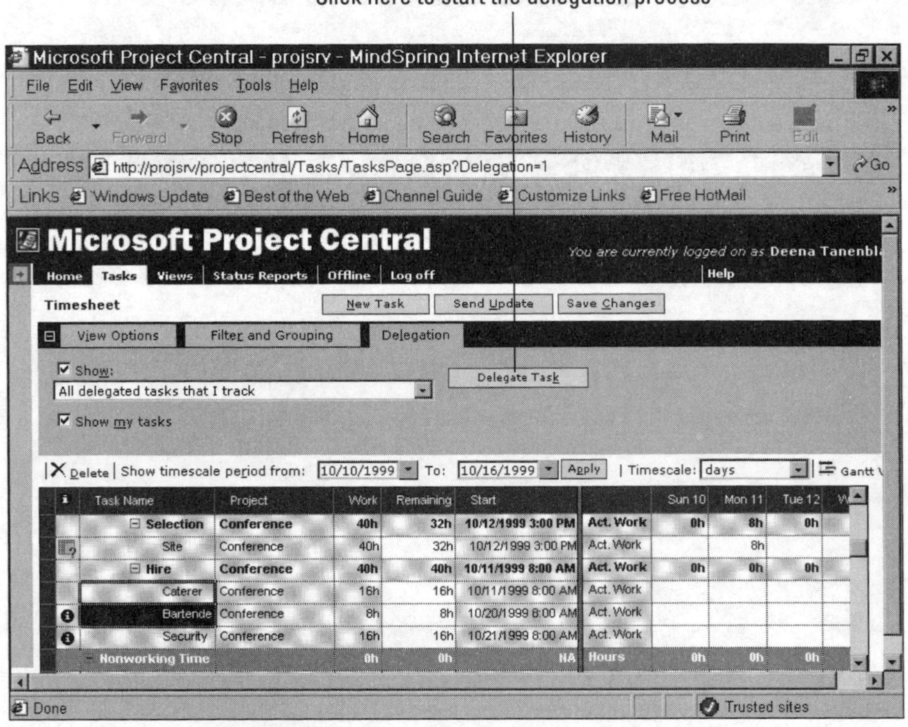


**Figure 16-24:** Identify the tasks you want to delegate.

Select the tasks you want to delegate and click the Delegate Task button. A new page appears — and a wizard walks you through the delegation process (see Figure 16-25). Click Next after you fill in the information for Step 1.

If the resource to whom you want to delegate the task doesn't appear in the drop-down list, click the Create a New Resource link and Project Central will place the resource in the list for you. You'll need to know if the resource will use Windows NT logon information or Project Web Server logon information. If the resource uses Windows NT logon information, you'll need to know the name of the Windows NT domain.

In Step 2 of the wizard, you send a message to the delegate and to your project manager to notify them of the action (see Figure 16-26).

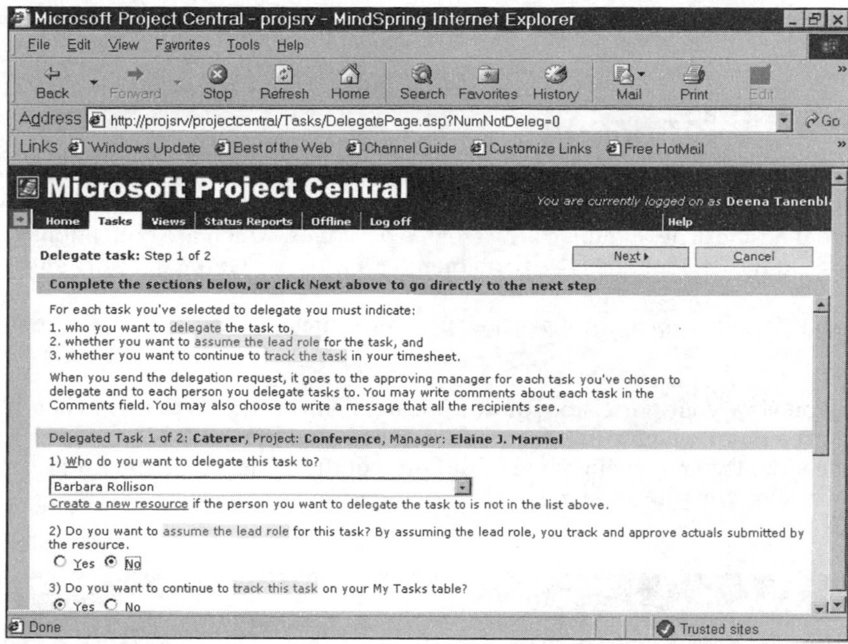


**Figure 16-25:** Identify to whom you want to delegate the tasks and what role you want to continue to play.

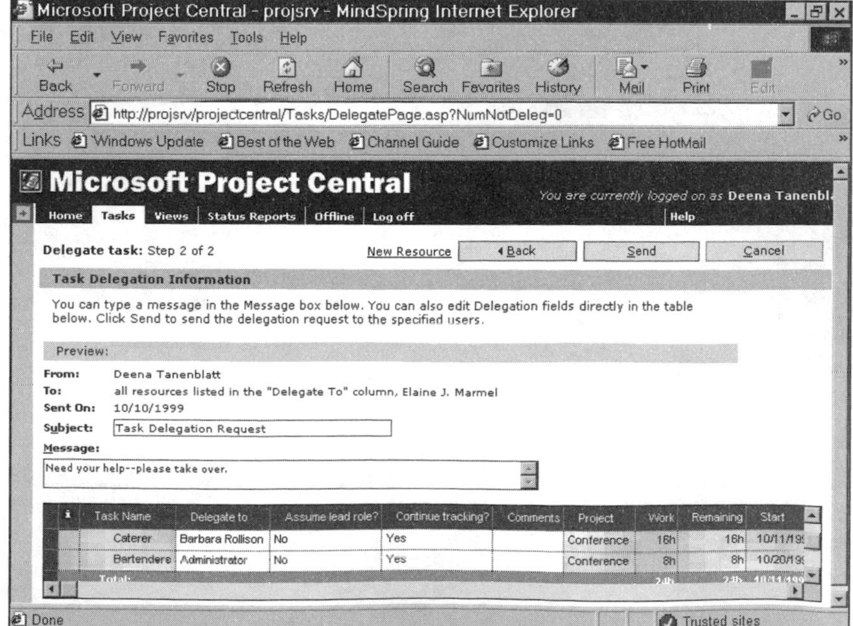


**Figure 16-26:** To complete the delegation process, you notify everyone affected of the delegation.

Click Send to complete the process; messages will appear in the Microsoft Project Central Inbox of each recipient — and the delegate can refuse the assignment.

## Viewing information

As life would have it, you may not work on only one project at a time. To help you manage your time, Project Central enables you to view tasks from more than one project at a time. The administrator creates *portfolios*, which are collections of projects, and then identifies the team members who can view each portfolio.

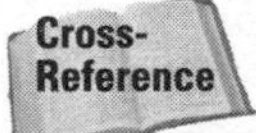


Later in this chapter, you'll see how the administrator creates a portfolio view.

When you view your portfolio, you see line item entries that represent each Web-based project for which you have work assigned (see Figure 16-27). On each line, you see a Gantt bar showing you the duration of the project and any progress that's been made on the project so far.

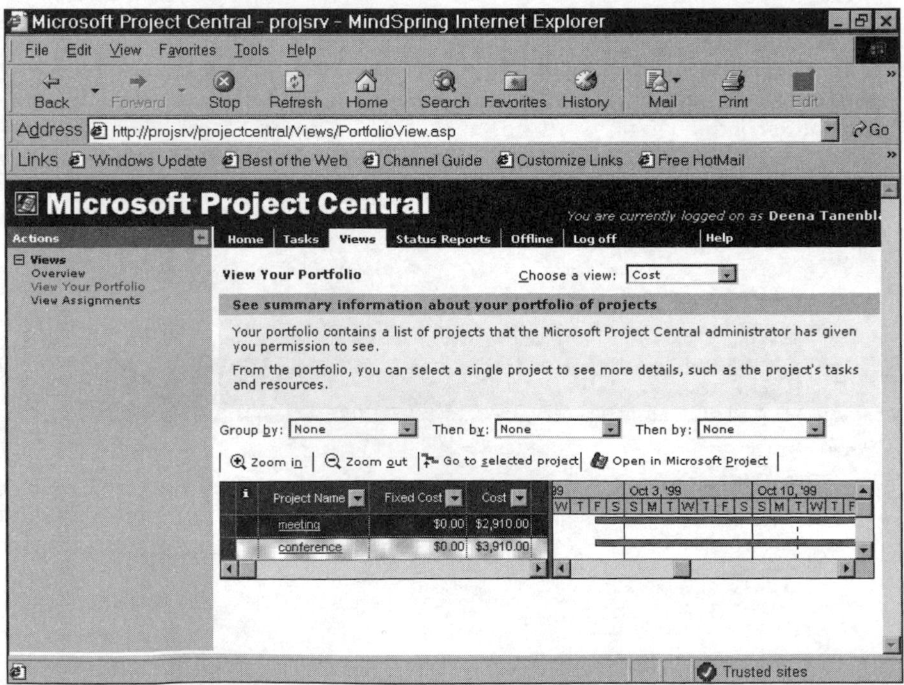


**Figure 16-27:** Your portfolio contains a list of Web-based projects for which you have assignments.

You can group your portfolio using the list boxes that appear above the list of projects, and you can open a particular project in Project Central by clicking the link that appears in the Project Name column.

When you open a project, you choose a view; in Figure 16-28, you see the Task Tracking view. Again, you can group the tasks in the project; or you can zoom in or out or go to a particular task. If the Administrator has defined multiple views for you, you can change the view using the Choose a view list box at the top of the page.

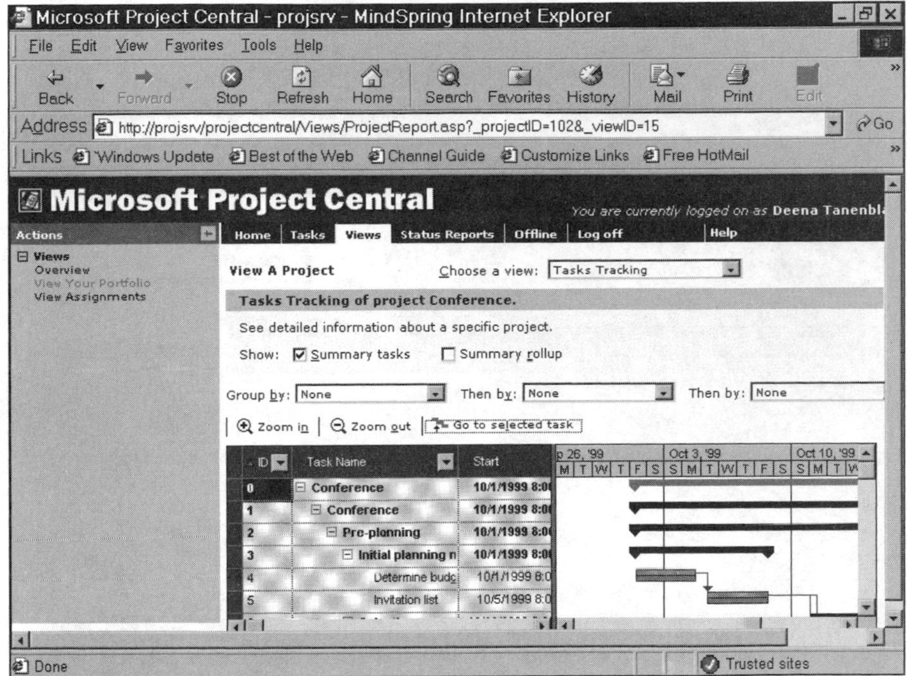


**Figure 16-28:** When you open a project, you see a more detailed Gantt chart of that project.

You can also view your assignments from the View Assignments page (see Figure 16-29). You'll be able to see the assignments the Administrator has defined in the view available to you; for example, in the figure, Deena Tanenblatt can see only her own assignments.

Perhaps you'd prefer a more personal Gantt view of your tasks: Use the Personal Gantt view. Point at the Tasks tab and choose Personal Gantt; Project Central displays the Gantt view you see in Figure 16-30.

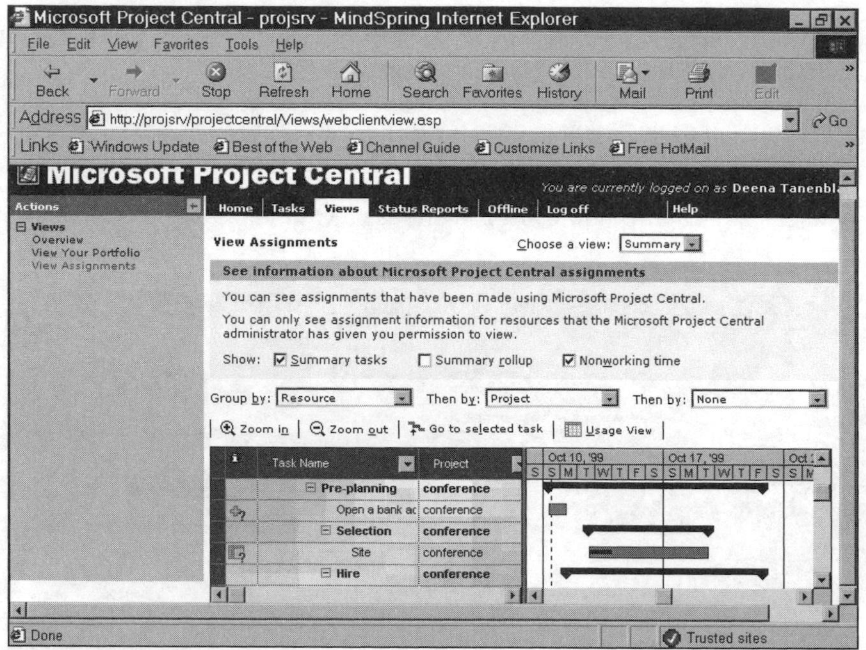

**Figure 16-29:** Viewing your assignments

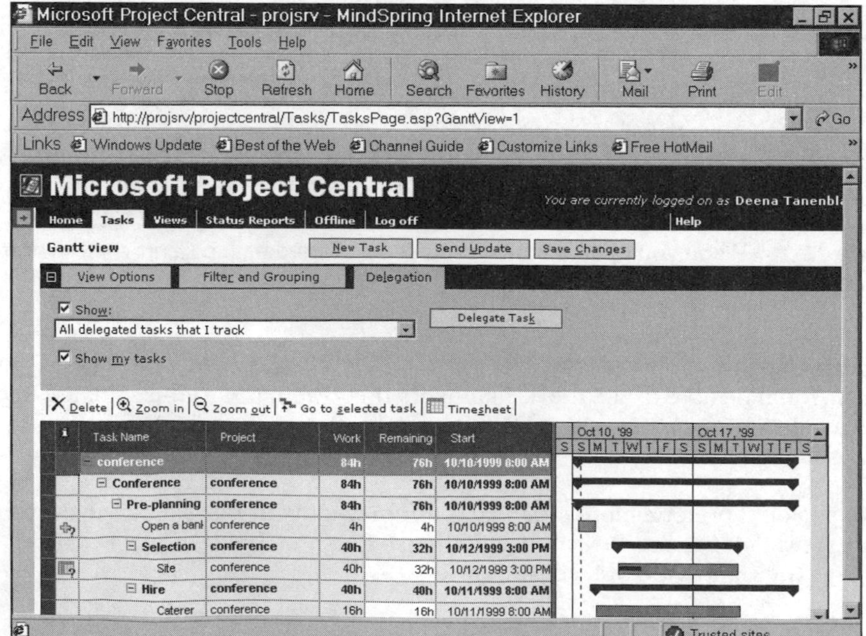

**Figure 16-30:** A typical Personal Gantt view in Project Central shows only your task assignments in Gantt chart format.

## Reporting the status of things

You've already seen how Project Central enables you to send updates from the Timesheet view. But you also can send both solicited and unsolicited status reports to your project manager. Point at the Status Reports tab and click Submit a Status Report. You'll see a link in the Actions pane that permits you to create a status report. If your project manager has not requested a status report, you'll see a page like the one in Figure 16-31; if your project manager has set up status reports due on certain dates, you'll see a page like the one in Figure 16-32.

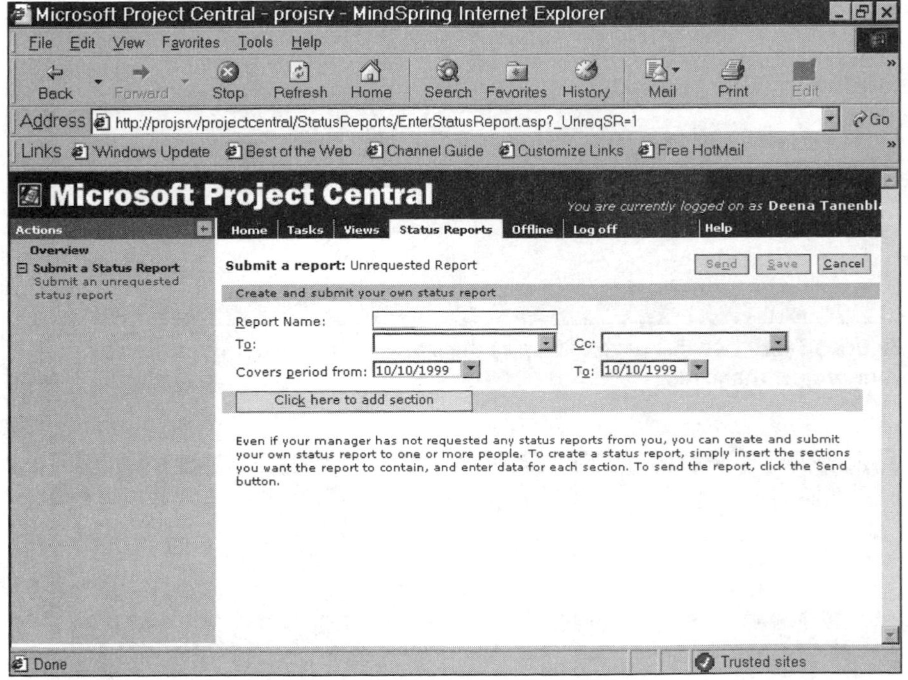


**Figure 16-31:** Use this page to submit an unsolicited status report or simply communicate with other members of your team.

When you click the link to create your status report, you see a page similar to the one in Figure 16-33. The actual page you see depends on the status report your manager sets up. Fill in the report and click the Send button.

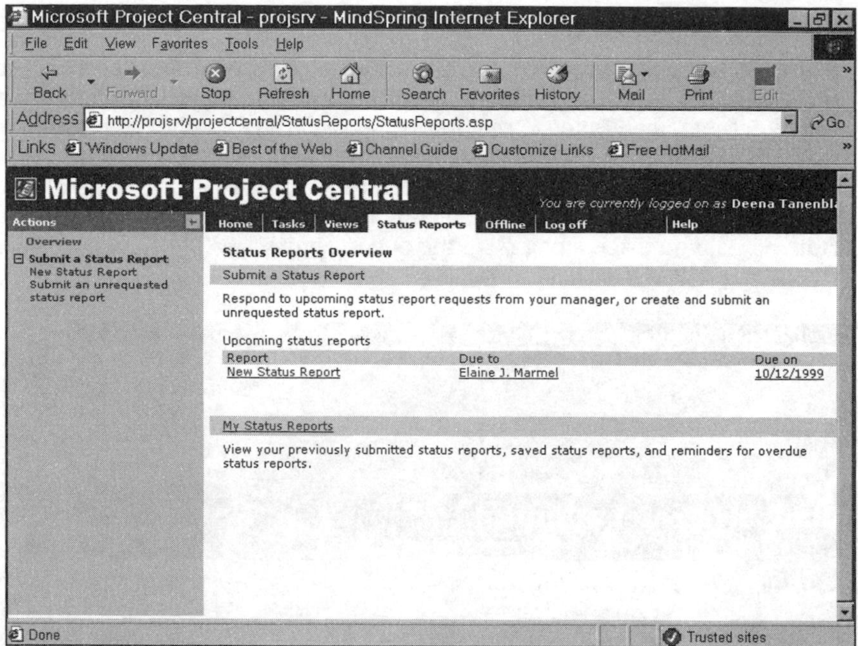

**Figure 16-32:** Use this page to display the status report layout requested by your project manager.

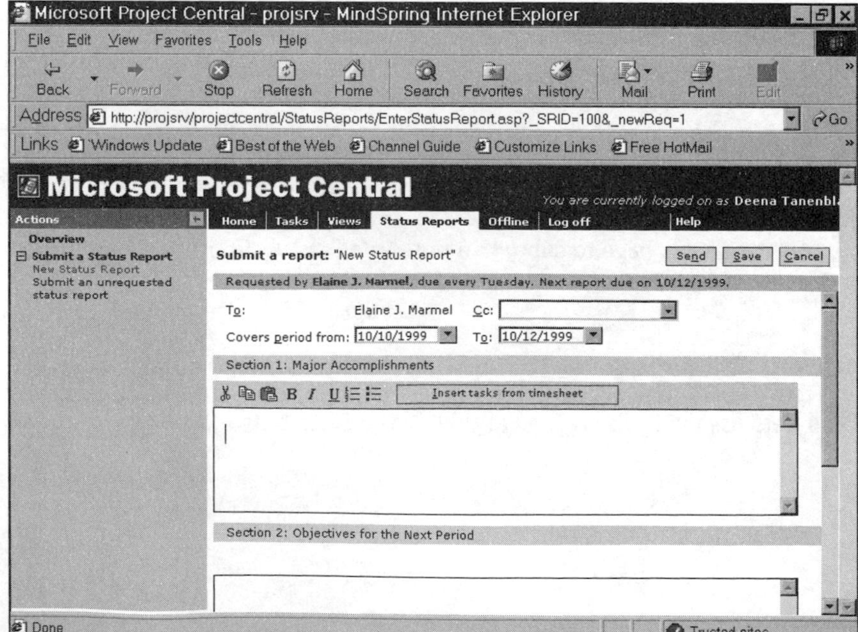

**Figure 16-33:** A typical status report page

As a manager, you can create the layout for the status report you want to see from your team members — and you can specify how often you want status reports.

The project manager's status report page looks a little bit different than the team member's page (see Figure 16-34).

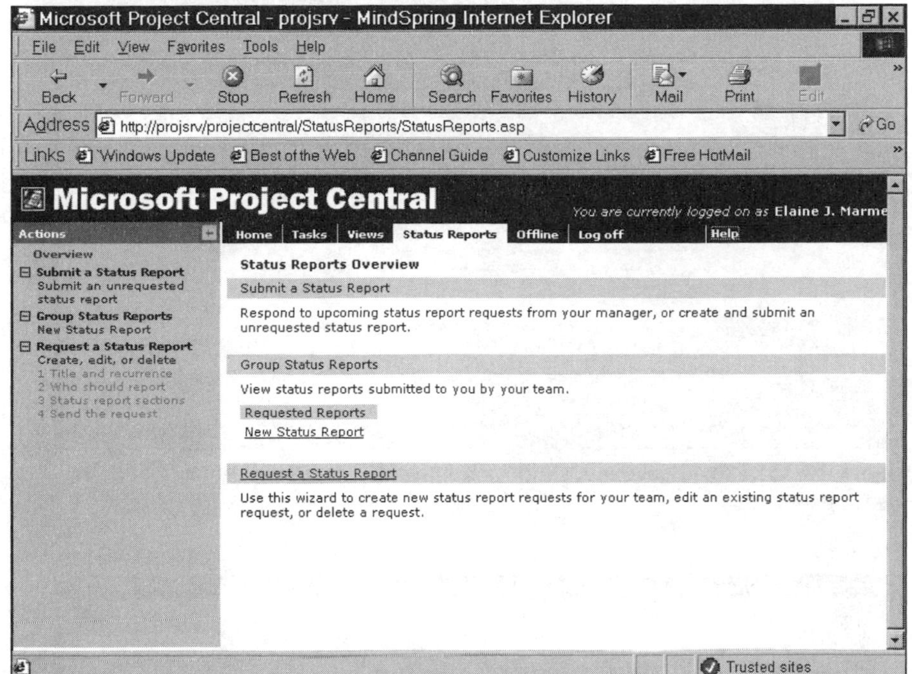


**Figure 16-34:** The project manager can create a status report format for use by the team.

Using the Group Status Reports feature, managers can combine the status reports of team members into one overall status report.

To create a standard layout for a status report, click the Request a Status Report link in the Actions pane to start a wizard that walks you through the process. Project Central displays a page similar to the one shown in Figure 16-35.

Fill in the page and click Next. You'll see a page like the one in Figure 16-36.

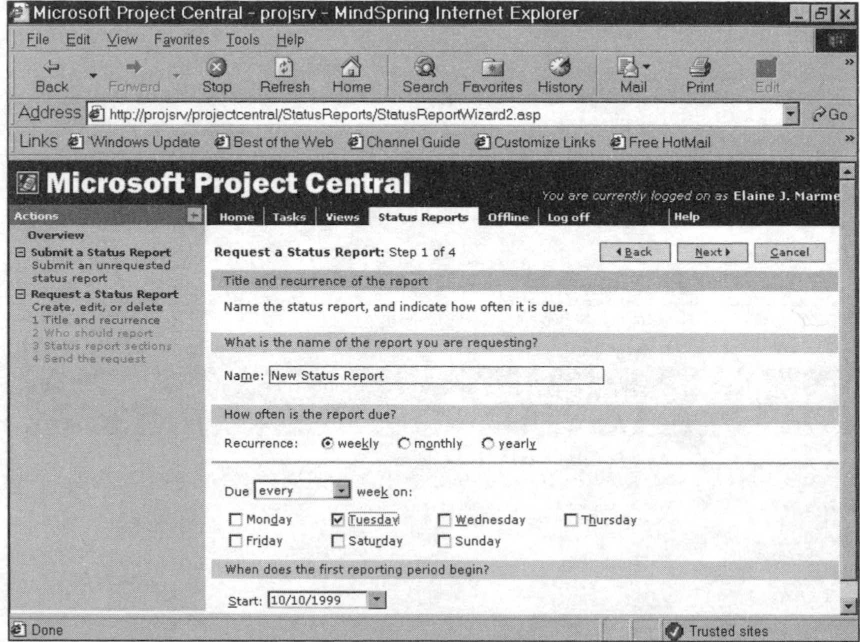


**Figure 16-35:** Provide overview information for the status report layout you're creating.

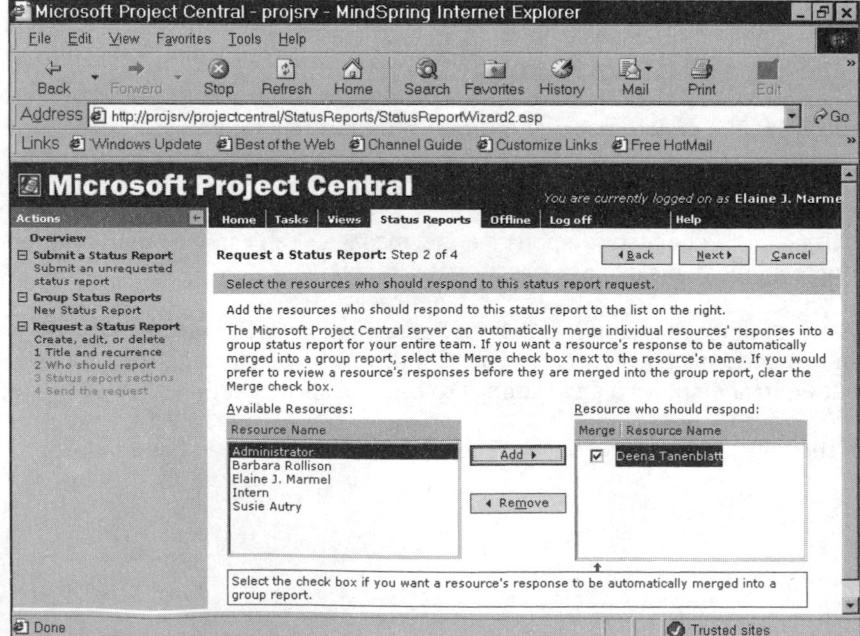


**Figure 16-36:** Select resources to submit status reports.

Decide who should submit status reports using this layout and click Next. Project displays a page like the one shown in Figure 16-37, where you can identify the topics you want covered in the status report and click Next.

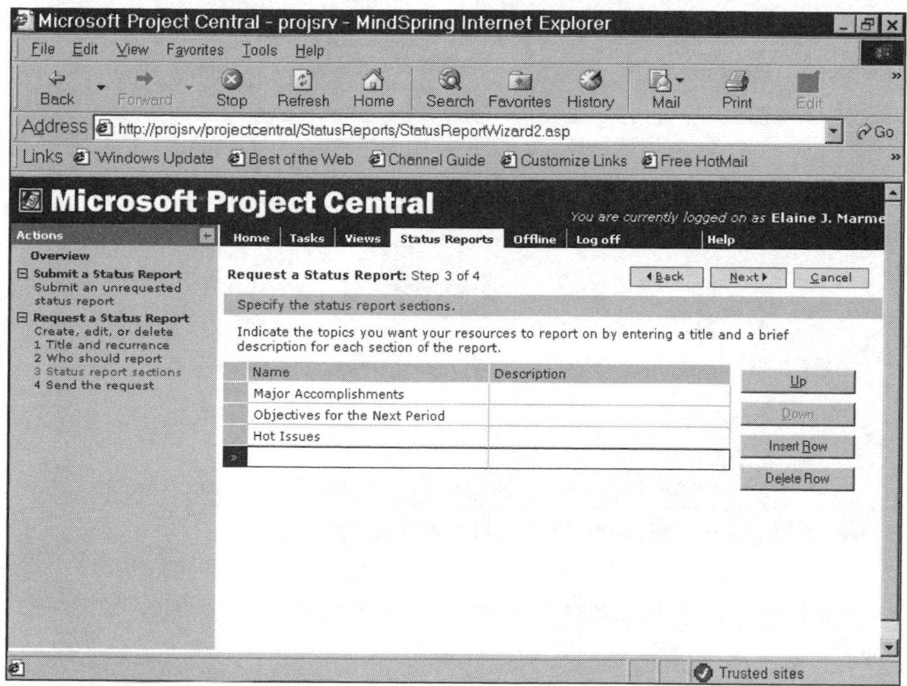

**Figure 16-37:** List the topics you want included in the status report.

On the last page of the wizard (see Figure 16-38), click the Send button to send the status report layout to the selected team members.

## Working offline

You can work offline in Project Central; suppose you use Project Central from a notebook computer and need to travel; while you're gone, you want to keep track of the time you work and perhaps even prepare status reports. If you use Project Central offline, you can do those things. You *can't* send updates from your Timesheet, send your status report, or view messages.

Note: The only dates available to you in your Timesheet will be for the time period you select before you go offline.

Use the Offline page (see Figure 16-39) to go offline.

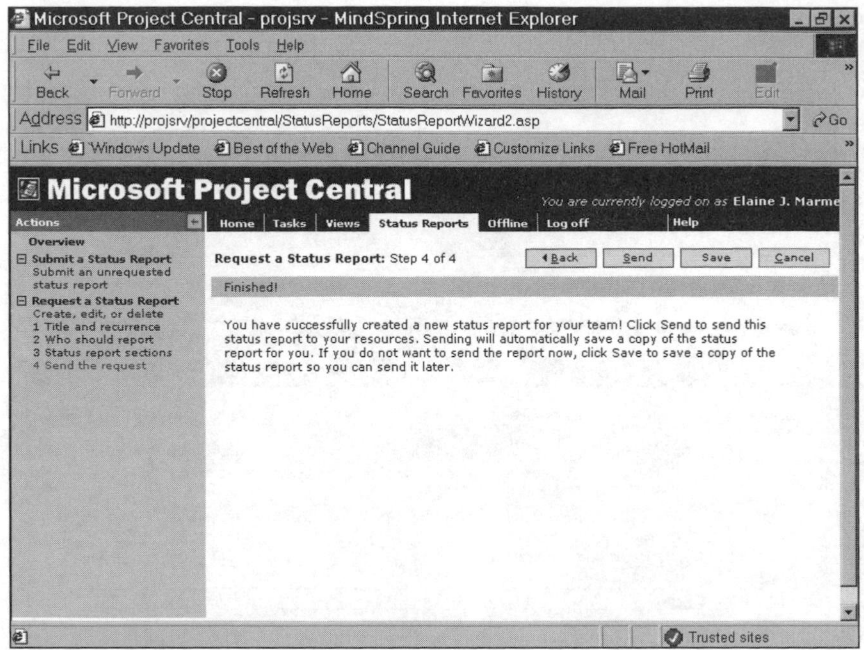


**Figure 16-38:** Send the layout to the selected team members.

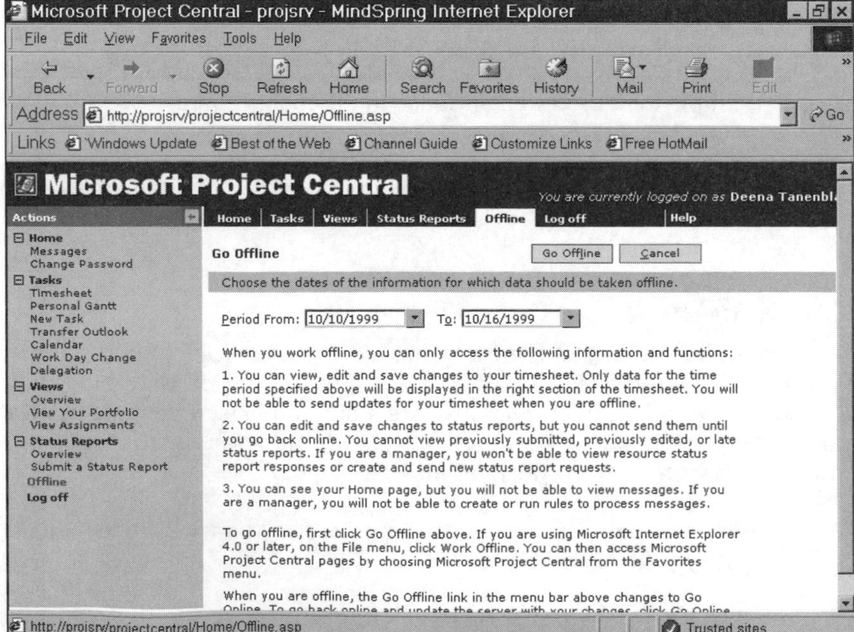


**Figure 16-39:** Set Project Central to work offline.

After you click the Go Offline button, in Internet Explorer, choose File ⇨ Work Offline. To access Project Central, type the Web URL in the Address box or choose it from your Favorites list.

When you return from your trip, reconnect by opening Project Central and returning to the Offline page. The Go Offline button will become the Go Online button.

## Logging off

When you finish working in Project Central, click the Logoff tab to complete your session.

# Administering Project Central

So far, you've seen how team members and the project manager use Project Central. But there's an administrator role involved in Project Central. The Administrator manages the information in the Web-based database and can customize Project Central in a variety of ways.

## Reviewing the Home page

Like any other user, the administrator needs to launch Internet Explorer or the 32-bit Web client shipped on the Project CD-ROM and enter the URL for the Web database. If necessary, the administrator selects Administrator and clicks Enter. The administrator sees the Project Central Home page for the administrator, which looks very similar to the page you see in Figure 16-40.

The Actions pane contains additional links on the administrator's Home page — links that enable the administrator to manage and customize the Web-based database and Project Central.

The administrator's Project Central Home page serves the same function as the Home page seen by team members and the project manager. It introduces you to Project Central, displays summary information such as the number of new messages you have, and provides you with links to navigate to other areas of Project Central. It contains the same tabs that team members and the Project Manager saw, with one exception: It also contains the Admin tab (see Figure 16-41).

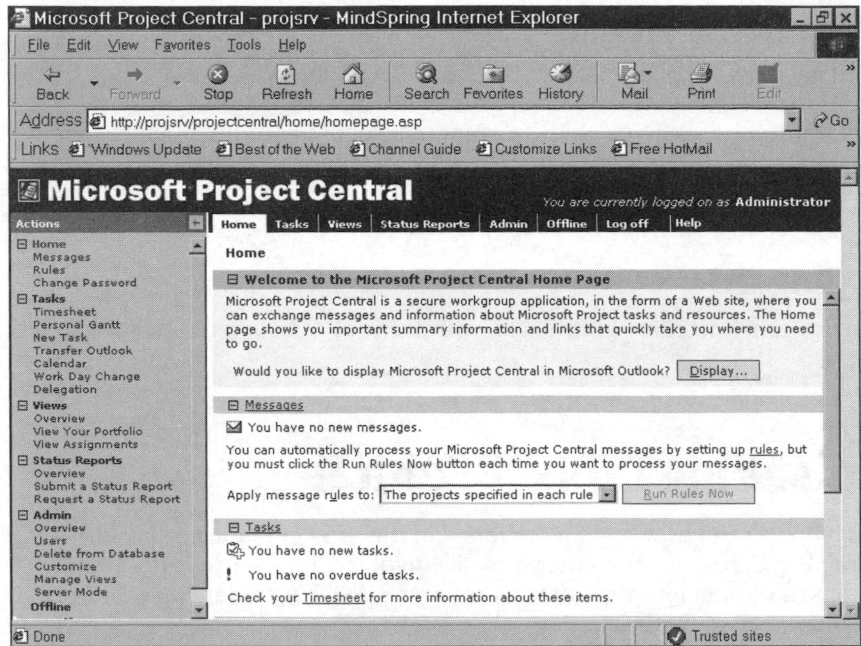

**Figure 16-40:** The administrator's Project Central Home page closely resembles the Home page that team members and the project manager see.

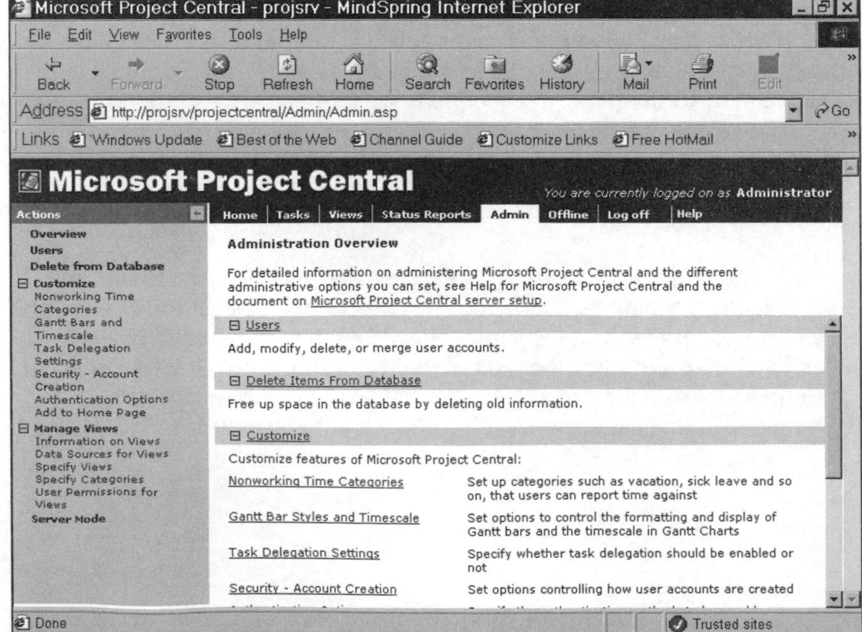

**Figure 16-41:** The administrator uses the Admin tab to perform most duties.

# Customizing Project Central

The administrator manages the Web-based database by making changes to user accounts and deleting information from the database. The administrator can customize Project Central in a number of ways:

- Set up nonworking time categories
- Control the formatting of Gantt bar styles and the timescale
- Enable or disable task delegation
- Set security and authentication options
- Add links to the Home page
- Control data sources for views
- Create views and categories and set rights to views

## Modifying users

From the Users page (see Figure 16-42), the administrator can add, modify, or delete users from the Web-based database; in addition, the administrator can merge two user names into one account if a user appears twice in the Log On list under two different names.

When you modify a user, you supply the same type of information for the user that you saw on the Web tab of the Options dialog box in Project. You can specify the type of authentication to use (Windows NT or Project Central server), the user's e-mail address, role (resource, manager, or administrator) and account status (active or inactive). You provide the same information if you choose to add a new user.

## Setting the server mode

The Server Mode link that appears at the bottom of the Actions pane on the Admin tab displays the Server Mode page (see Figure 16-43), from which the administrator can obtain exclusive use of the database, locking out any other users. The administrator requires exclusive use so he or she can take certain actions, such as deleting information from the Web database.

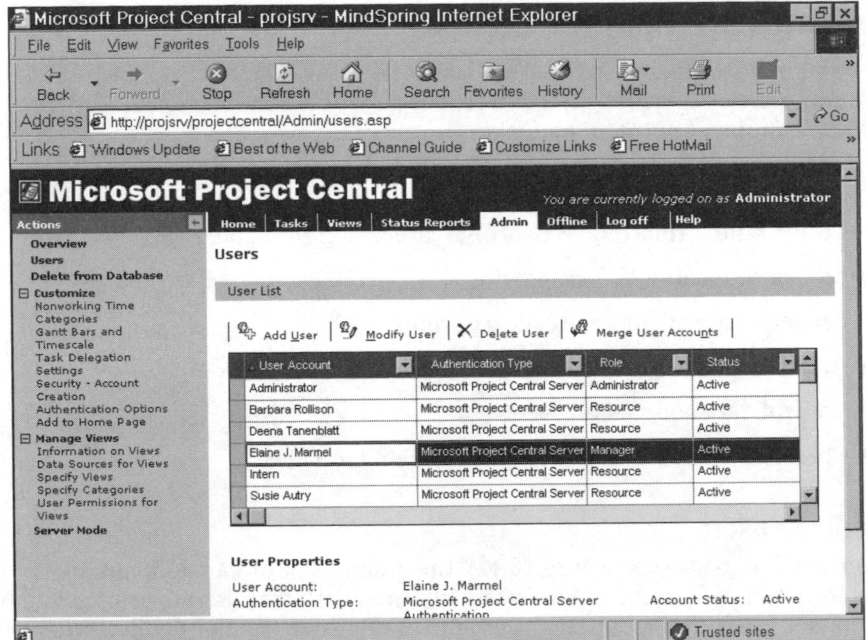


**Figure 16-42:** Use the Users page to make changes to user accounts in Project Central.

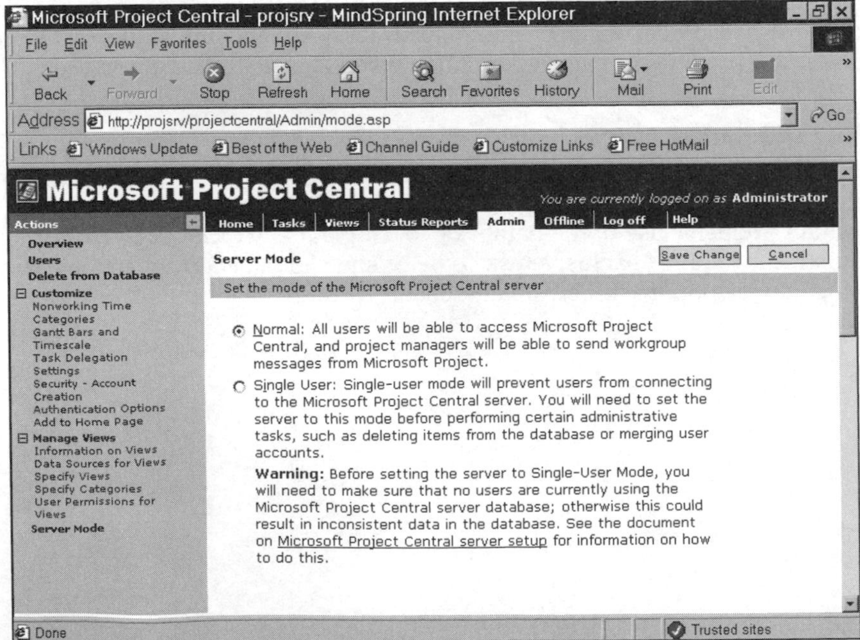


**Figure 16-43:** Use the options on this page to use the database exclusively.

Choose the Single User option button and click Save Changes to lock other users out of the database.

Before you can switch to Single User mode, you must make all other users stop using the database.

When you finish making changes, you use this page to change the mode to Normal so that others can again access the database.

## Deleting information from the database

The administrator manages the information in the database and controls the size of the database. The administrator can—and should—periodically delete old information from the database because response time from the database will slow down as the database grows in size. To help maintain some semblance of speed for team members when they use the database, the administrator can delete old, unnecessary information using the Delete Items from Database page (see Figure 16-44).

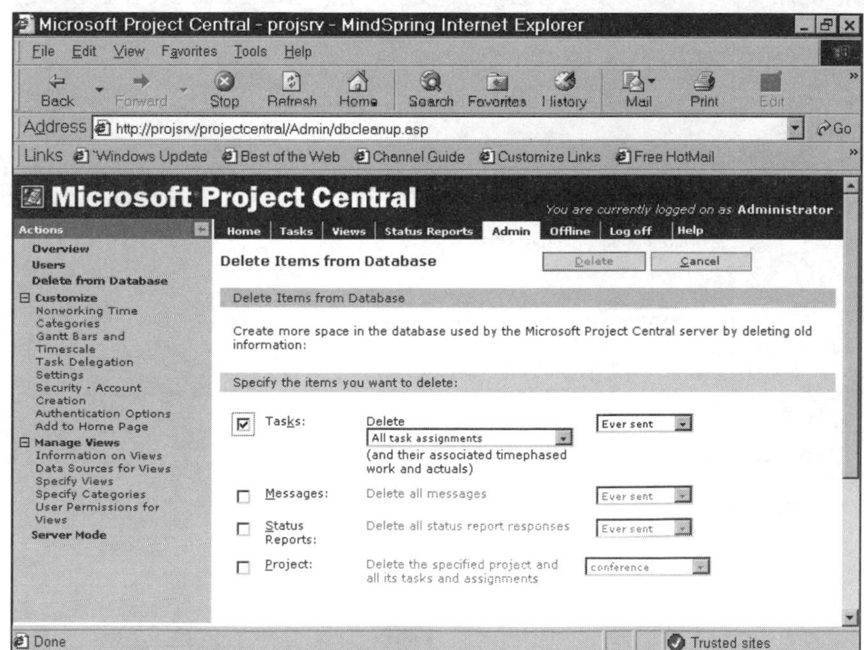


**Figure 16-44:** Use this page to reduce the size of the database and speed up the processing in the database.

You must place the database in Single User mode to delete information.

Place checks in the boxes next to the items you want to delete. Note that you can "selectively delete" information. And, although you can't see these options in Figure 16-44, from the bottom of the Delete Items from Database page, you can delete task, message, and status report information for specified users. After setting up the page, click the Delete button.

## Setting up nonworking time categories

By default, Project Central contains categories that team members can use to record time spent on work other than projects. By letting users record nonproject time, you can use Project Central to account for all time a user spends working. This nonproject time appears in the Timesheet view, where users can record the time spent on tasks outside projects.

From the Nonworking Time Categories page (see Figure 16-45), the administrator can change the default categories, add new categories, or delete old categories.

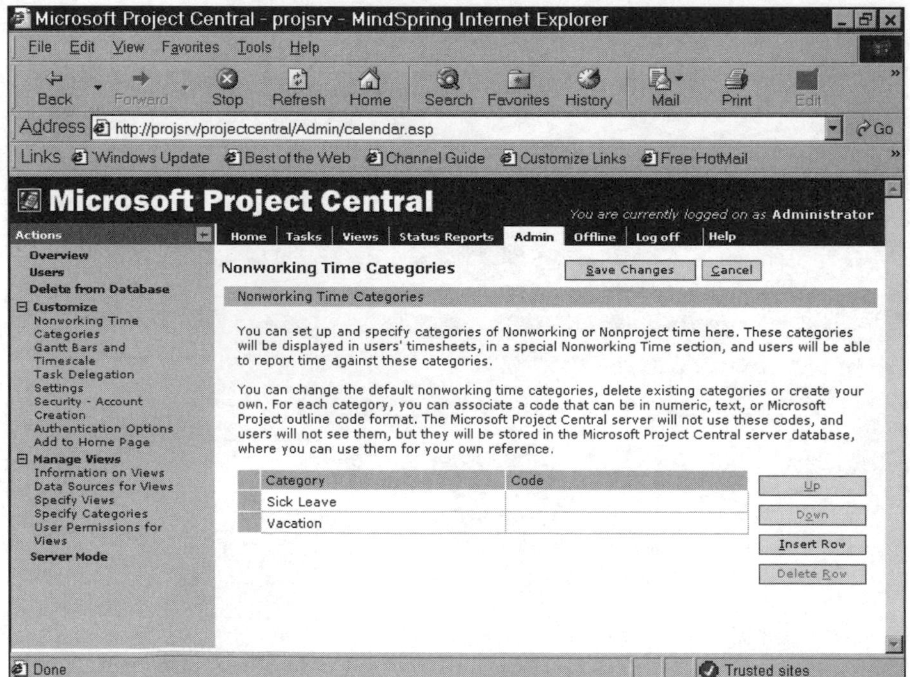


**Figure 16-45:** Establish or modify nonworking time categories.

You must place the database in Single User mode to work with nonworking time categories.

## Selecting the Gantt bar styles and timescales

Using the Gantt Bar Styles and Timescale page (see Figure 16-46), the administrator can control the appearance of Gantt bars and the timescale on Gantt charts for some or all Gantt charts that team members and managers view in Project Central. To select specific Gantt charts to change, use the Gantt Chart list box on the page.

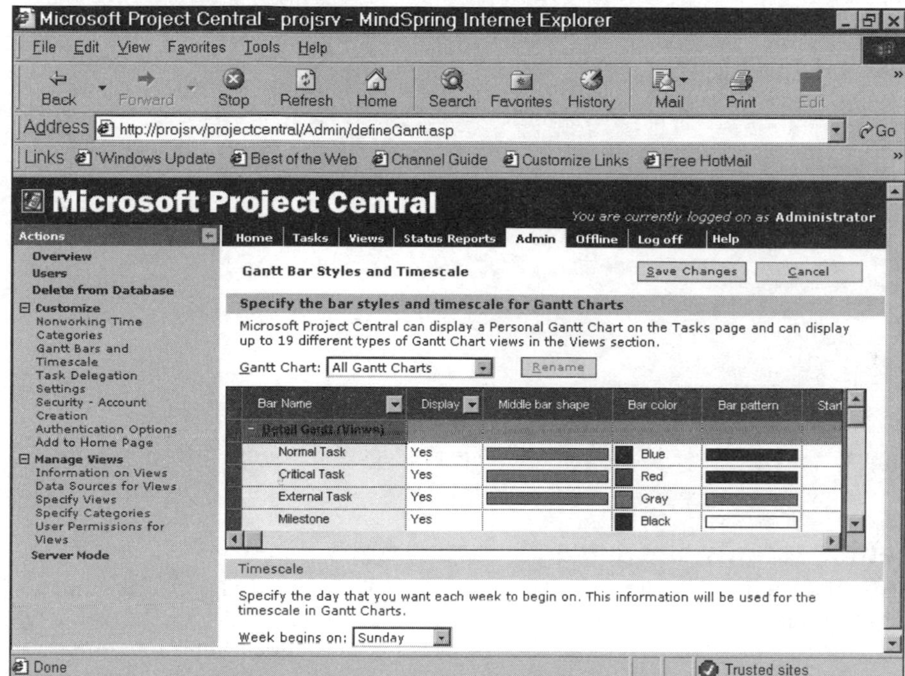


**Figure 16-46:** The administrator can modify the appearance of Gantt bars and timescales in Project Central.

## Controlling task delegation

From the Task Delegation Settings page (see Figure 16-47), the administrator controls whether team members or the manager can delegate tasks to other team members. This is an "on/off" switch; either you allow delegation or you don't. You can't selectively allow delegation. That is, you can't turn on delegation for some team members while turning it off for other team members.

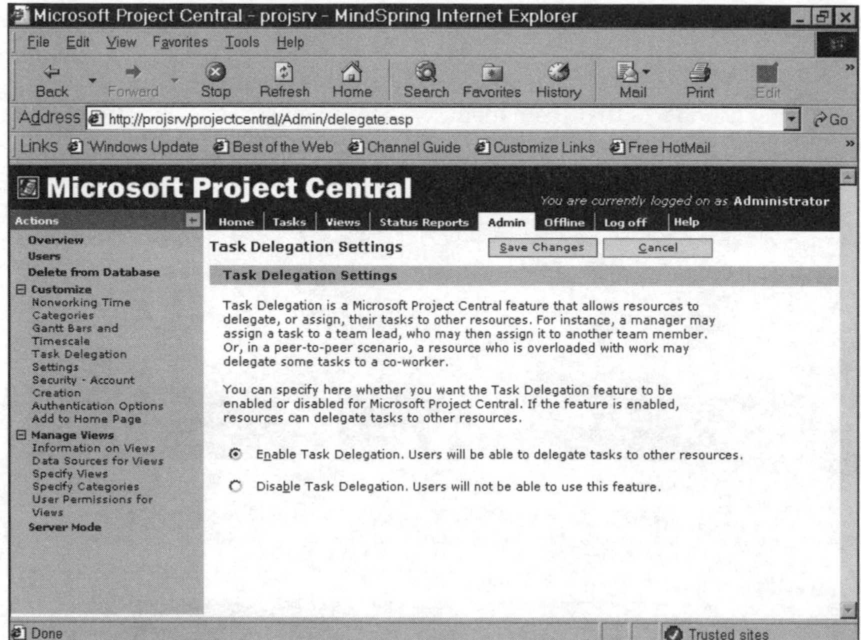

**Figure 16-47:** Choose to enable or disable task delegation from this page.

## Setting security and authentication options

From the Security Options page (see Figure 16-48), the administrator controls whether managers and resources can create accounts in Project Central. If allowed, managers can create accounts when they send messages to team members or request status reports. If allowed, resources can create accounts when delegating tasks.

From the Authentication Options page (see Figure 16-49), the administrator decides how the Project Central server should authenticate users who try to log onto Project Central. In addition, from this page, the administrator can determine the minimum length to which users must set their passwords.

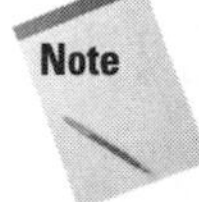


You must place the database in Single User mode to work with authentication options.

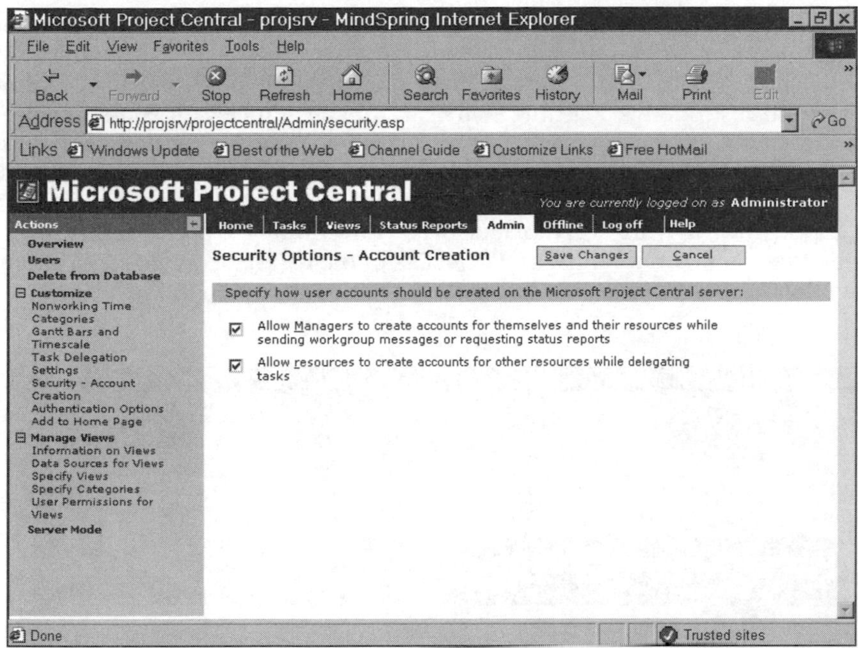


**Figure 16-48:** The administrator decides who creates accounts in Project Central.

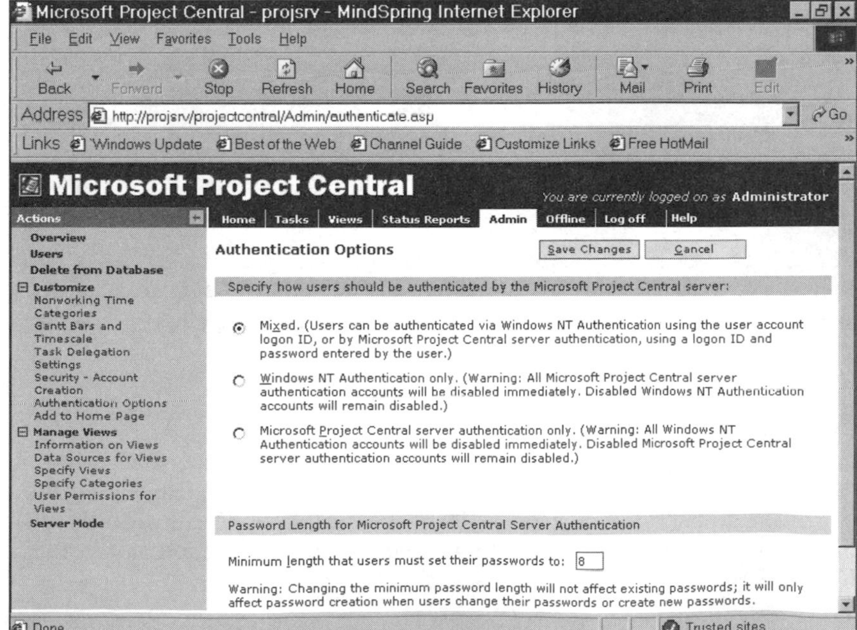


**Figure 16-49:** Control authentication and password issues from this page.

### Adding information to the Project Central Home page

The administrator can use the Add to Home Page page (see Figure 16-50) to modify the appearance of the Home page each team member sees when he or she logs onto Project Central. From this page, the administrator can add links or content to the Home page. Links may jump team members to other places on the company server or on the Internet. Content might be important information or an announcement that you want users of Project Central to see when they log on. For links, the administrator must supply the URL (the full path, including "http" or the file prefix) for the link. For content, the administrator must provide a link to the file that contains the content and specify the height, in pixels, that the content should take up on the Home page.

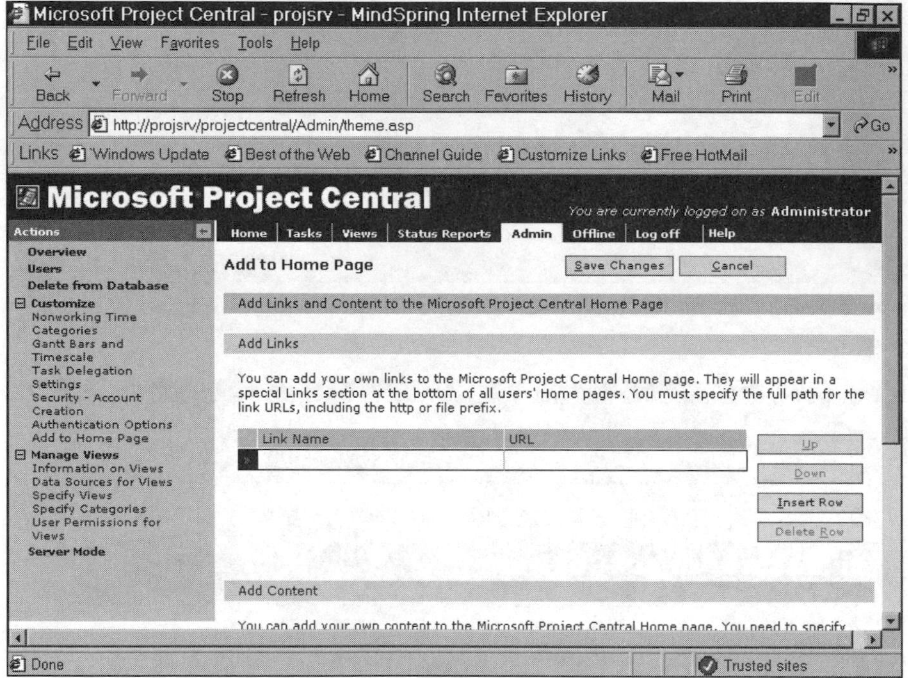


**Figure 16-50:** Use this page to add information to the Home page in Project Central.

## Working with Views

Through views, the administrator controls what you see in Project Central. The administrator can establish links to databases external to the Project Central Web database so users can access projects in other databases. In addition, the administrator establishes views that enable users to look at project information in different ways.

## Controlling data sources for views

Using the Data Sources for Views page (see Figure 16-51), the administrator can establish connections to external databases that contain project information. Suppose, for example, that project information isn't stored in a Microsoft Project file. In this case, the administrator can establish a "shortcut" that defines the location of the source of the project information, enabling team members to access that information from Project Central.

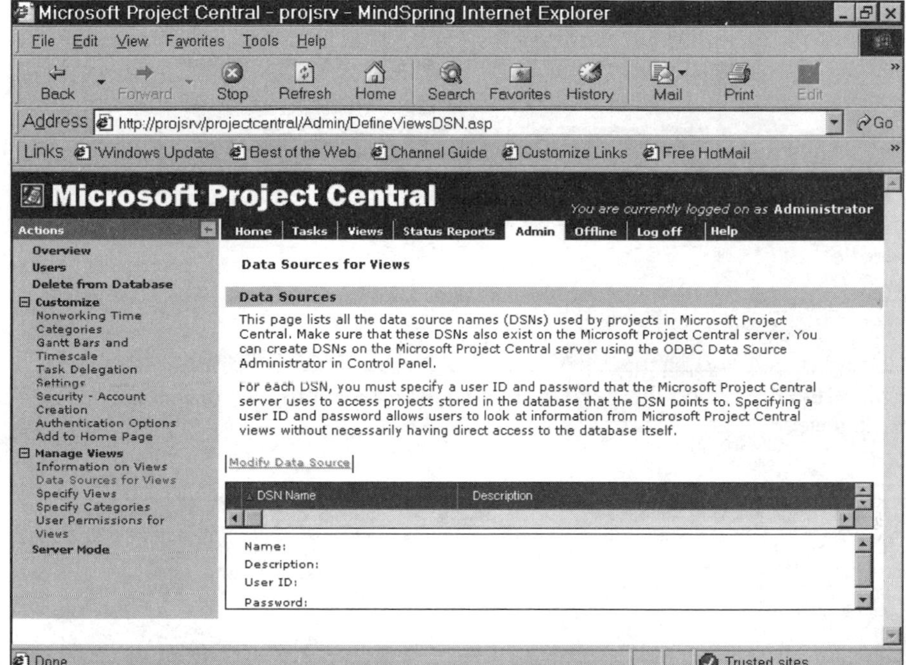


**Figure 16-51:** Use this page to establish data sources for projects that aren't stored in an MPP file.

## Creating a view

Earlier in this chapter, I mentioned that the administrator creates a portfolio view so team members can see projects on which they work. The administrator uses the Specify Views page (see Figure 16-52) to create new views or modify or delete existing views. A view contains a set of fields and filters that Project Central uses when displaying project information.

When you create a new view, you determine whether the view is a project view, a portfolio view, or an assignment view; in Figure 16-53, I'm creating a portfolio view. A project view shows information only in one project, while a portfolio view can include more than one project. As you would expect, an assignment view focuses on assignments.

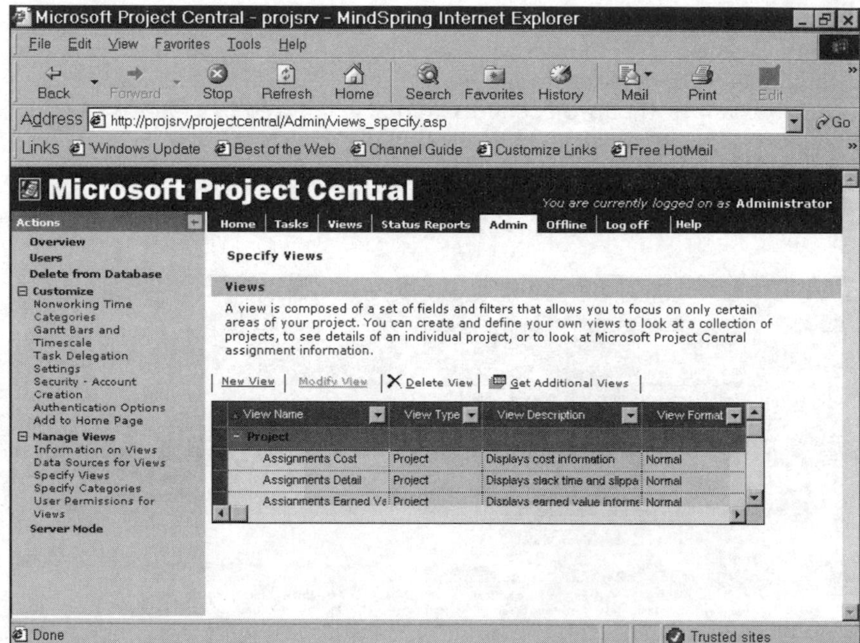

**Figure 16-52:** Start on this page to create a new view or modify or delete an existing view.

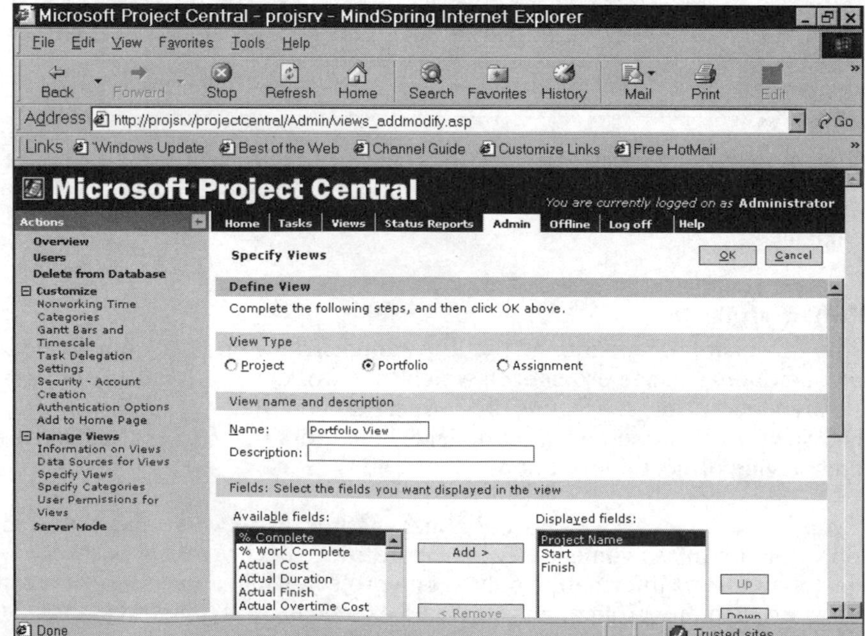

**Figure 16-53:** Creating a portfolio view

You also specify the fields that should appear in the view; for example, in a project view, you'd specify tasks you want to include, while in a portfolio view, you'd specify project names. At the bottom of the page when creating a portfolio view, you select the Gantt chart format (Gantt, Detail Gantt, Leveling Gantt, Tracking Gantt, and so on) and the categories to which this view belongs. In the next section, I'll discuss categories. Click OK to save the view.

## Working with categories

Categories enable you to map users to projects and views; that is, in a category, you identify the users, projects, project views, portfolio views, and assignment views to include in the category.

To create a new category, start on the Specify Categories page shown in Figure 16-54 and click New Category. Project Central displays the page you see in Figure 16-55.

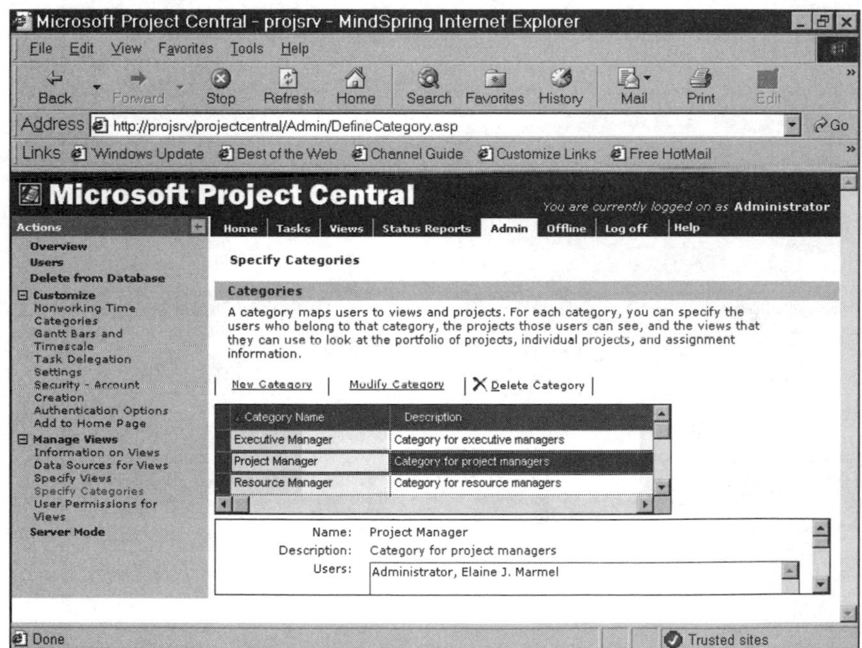


**Figure 16-54:** Use this page to create a new category or modify or delete an existing category.

At the top of the page, provide a name and, optionally, a description for the category. Select the users you want to include in this category. In the next section of the page (see Figure 16-56), specify the projects you want to include in the category.

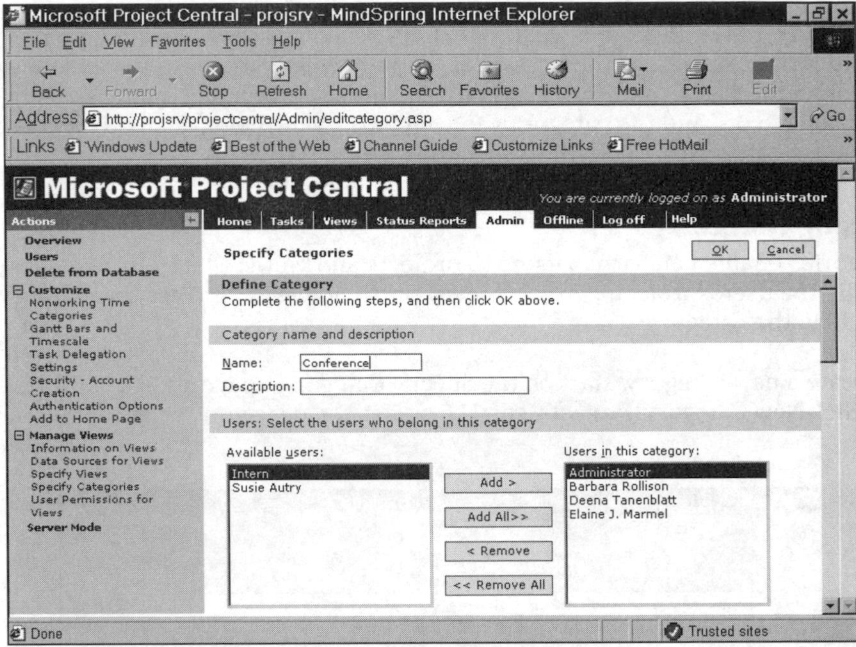


**Figure 16-55:** Use this page to define the users that you want to include in the category.

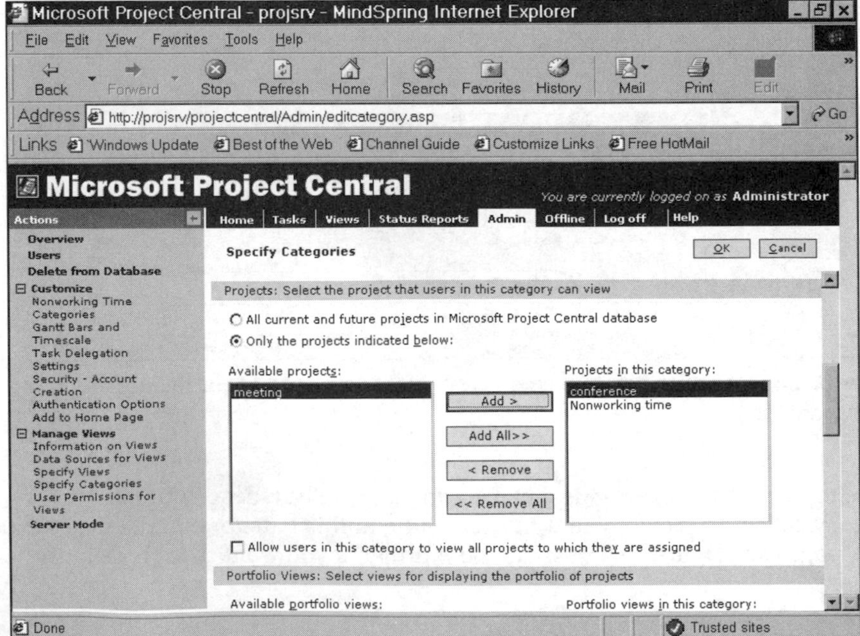


**Figure 16-56:** Specify the projects you want to include in the category.

In the next section of the page (see Figure 16-57), add the portfolio views that you want to include in the category.

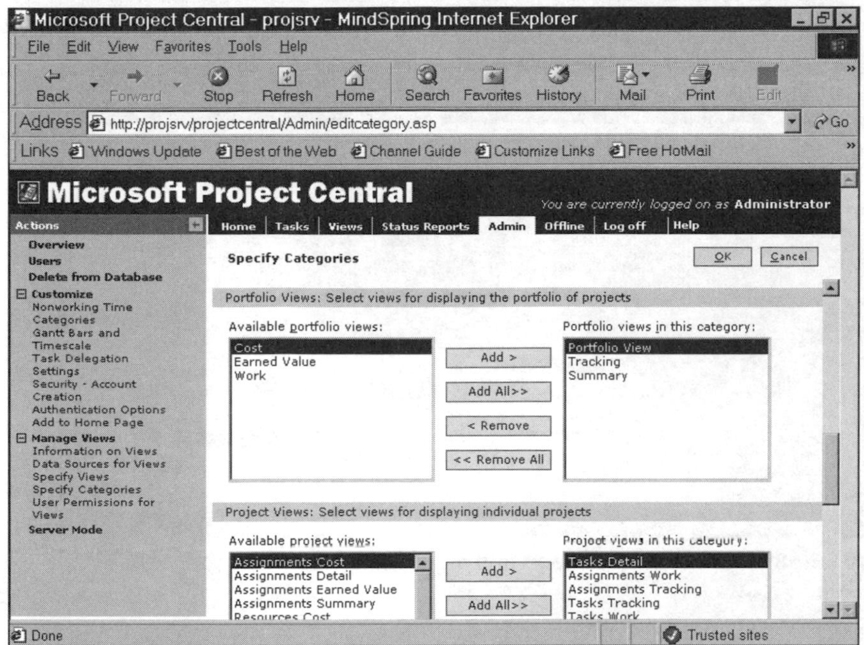


**Figure 16-57:** Add the portfolio views you want to include in the category.

In the last portion of the page (see Figure 16-58), add the project views and assignment views that you want to include in the category.

Click OK to save the category.

If necessary, return to the Specify Views page that you saw in the last section, select a view, and modify it to assign a category to it.

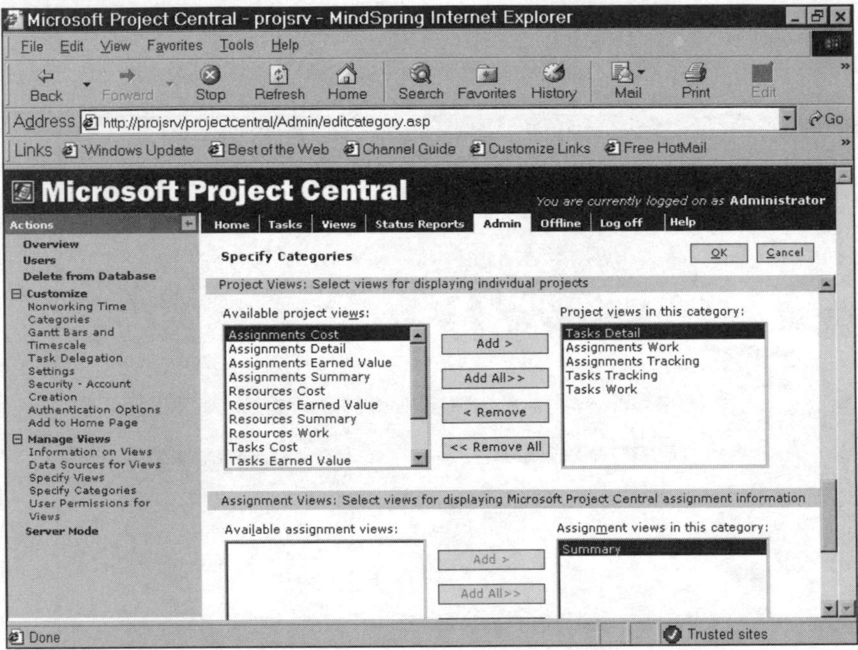


**Figure 16-58:** Add the project views and assignment views that you want to include in the category.

## Setting rights to a view

You need to specify rights to views to control what users see; this action is particularly important for assignment views because you may not want a team member to see any information other than information pertaining to him or her.

To specify rights, click the User Permissions for Views link in the Actions pane to display the page you see in Figure 16-59.

Select the user whose permissions you wish to modify and click Modify User Permissions. Project Central displays a page where you can modify the categories to which a user belongs and the assignments a user can view. At the top of the page, you can modify the categories to which a user belongs. In the section of the page shown in Figure 16-60, you see the assignments the user can view.

You also can use this page to decide whether the user can see assignments of the team members to whom he or she has sent messages.

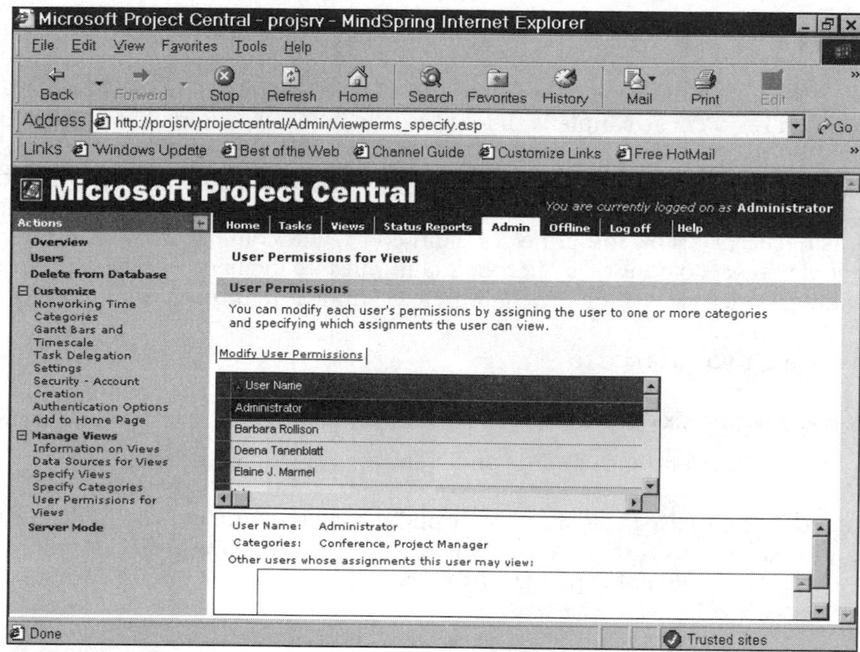


**Figure 16-59:** Start on this page to modify user permissions.

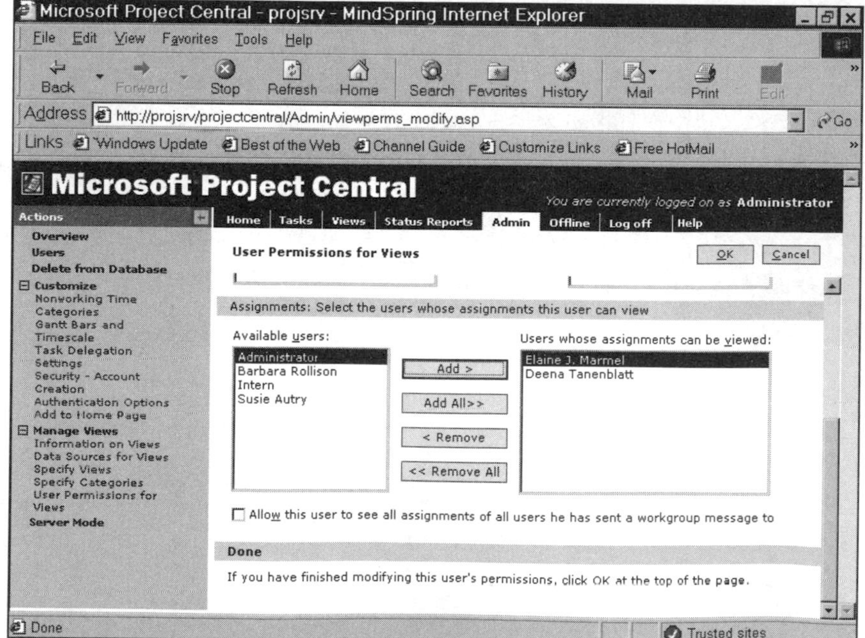


**Figure 16-60:** Set user permissions on this page.

# Summary

Project's Web capabilities enable you to link files or to create links from a file to an Internet address. These simple Web features can help you communicate project information to coworkers or clients in an effective, high-tech way. With Project Central, resources don't need a copy of Project to update a project. Using Project Central, users can receive work assignments, report work accomplished, add new tasks as necessary, view the project's Gantt chart, and communicate with the project manager. No doubt, as Microsoft continues its focus on online support and communication, new Web-specific features will appear in future versions of Project.

In this chapter you learned to

- ✦ Insert hyperlinks
- ✦ Use Project Central to update and manage projects on the Web

As you continue to use Project to create and manage schedules, you'll discover more about all the features described in this book. After a few projects, you'll be taking full advantage of this powerful software.

✦ ✦ ✦

CHAPTER 17

# Coordinating Multiple Projects

✦ ✦ ✦ ✦

**In This Chapter**

Consolidating projects

Consolidated projects and dependencies

Viewing multiple projects

Using multiple critical paths

Sharing resources among projects

✦ ✦ ✦ ✦

Large projects are the most difficult to manage. Organization is a cornerstone to good project management, and in a large project, the sheer number of tasks makes the job more difficult than usual. In Microsoft Project you can use the concept of consolidated projects to break projects down into smaller "bite-sized" pieces and then combine the smaller projects to view the bigger picture.

When this book went to press, consolidating projects on a computer on which you've installed both Project 98 and Project 2000 could have unexpected results.

## Consolidating Projects

When you're faced with a complex problem, finding the solution typically becomes easier if you can simplify the problem. Similarly, when you need to manage a complex project with many tasks, you may find it easier to organize the process if you deal with a limited number of tasks at one time.

Microsoft Project makes it easy for you to take this approach to planning large complex projects. Using Project's consolidation features, you create subprojects, which you can think of as the tasks that constitute one portion of your large project. When you create a subproject, you save it as a separate project file. You can assign resources and set up each subproject with links and constraints as if it were the entire project. When you need to view the bigger picture, you consolidate the subprojects into one large project. When you consolidate, you actually insert one project into another project; therefore, subprojects are also called *inserted projects.*

## Consolidation Concepts

Consolidation changed from Project 95 to Project 98. In Project 95, many project tools, such as copying and pasting, didn't work in consolidated projects. Project 95 used two techniques to work with multiple projects: one called *consolidation* and the other called *master projects* and *subprojects.* With the second technique, you created a link between a placeholder task in the master project and the subproject.

In Project 98, you no longer needed to think about master projects versus subprojects. Subprojects still existed as separate projects, but you included them in a consolidated project. In addition, Project 98 provided much greater flexibility in the consolidated project. Project 2000 handles consolidation in the same way as Project 98. You can think of the consolidated project as the host project into which you insert subprojects.

When you work in a consolidated project, you can focus on just the portion of the project that you need. Subprojects appear as summary tasks in the consolidated project, and you can use Project's outlining tools to hide all tasks associated with any subproject.

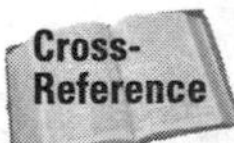


See Chapter 3 for more information on outlining.

From the consolidated project, you can view, print, and change information for any subproject just as if you were working with a single project.

# Setting up to use consolidation

Consolidation can help you achieve several objectives. For example:

- ✦ Tasks in projects managed by different people may be interdependent. Through consolidation, you can create the correct dependencies to accurately display the project's schedule and necessary resources.
- ✦ A project may be so large that breaking it into smaller pieces can help you organize it. You can use consolidation to combine the smaller pieces and then view the big picture.
- ✦ You may be pooling the resources of several projects and find you need to level the resources; consolidating enables you to link the projects sharing the resources so that you can level the resources.

When should you decide to use consolidation? It doesn't really matter. You may realize right away that the project is too large, or you may discover that the project is bigger than you originally thought while you are working on it. Suppose, for example, that the marketing department of a software company decides midway through the development cycle to bundle together various products under development. This introduces dependencies where none originally existed and provides an interesting opportunity for using consolidation.

If you decide to use consolidation before you start your project, simply create separate Microsoft Project files for various portions of the project. These files act as subprojects when you consolidate. You need to set up each subproject file so that it is complete by itself, and you need to create links as needed within each subproject file. This chapter explains techniques for consolidating the subprojects and linking them.

If you start a project and then decide that you want to use consolidation, you can create subprojects by following these steps:

1. Save your large project file.
2. Select all the tasks you want to save in your first subproject file and click the Copy button.
3. Click the New button to start a new project and use the Project Information dialog box that appears in Figure 17-1 to set basic Project information, such as the project's start date and scheduling method.

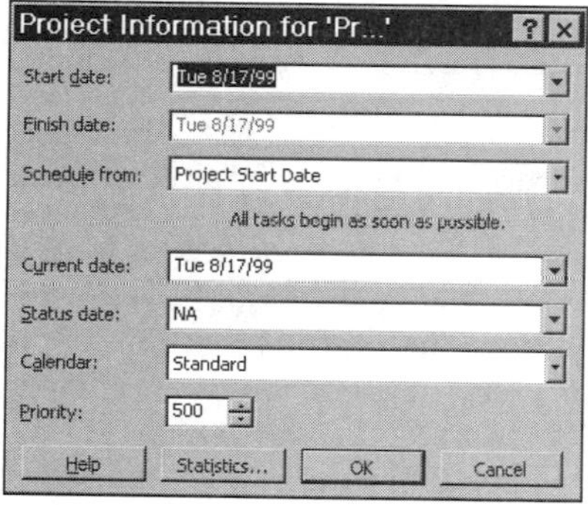


**Figure 17-1:** Use the Project Information dialog box to set basic project information such as the project's start date.

4. Click the Paste button.
5. Save the subproject and close it.
6. Select all the tasks you want to save in your second subproject file and click the Copy button.
7. Repeat Steps 3 through 7 until you have saved several separate files that contain portions of your larger project.

Edit each subproject file you create to make it a complete project by itself. Then you can use the following techniques to consolidate the subprojects and link them.

## Inserting a project

To consolidate project files into one large project, you insert projects into a host project file we refer to as the *consolidated project file*. Each project you insert appears as a summary task in the consolidated project file, and Project calculates inserted projects like summary tasks. As you can see from Figure 17-2, an icon in the Indicator field identifies an inserted project.

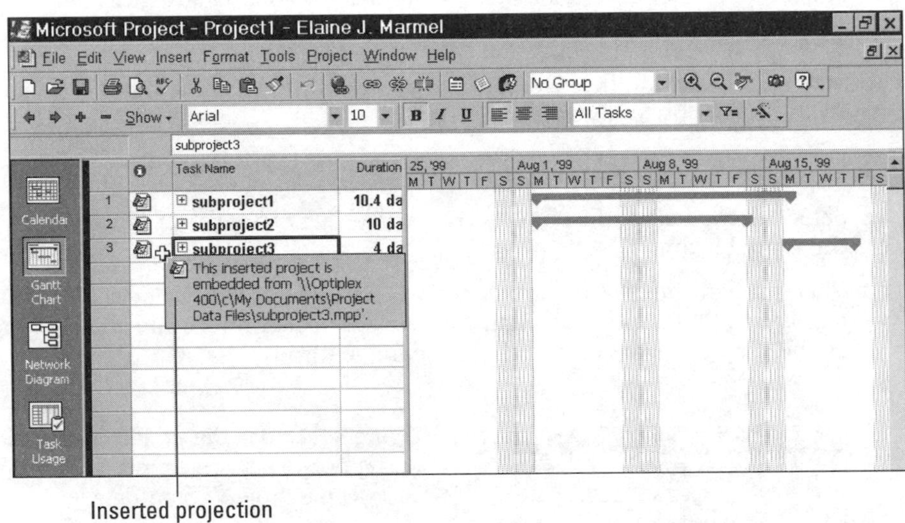


**Figure 17-2:** A special icon in the Indicator column identifies inserted projects.

You can insert projects at any outline level. The level at which an inserted project appears depends on the outline level that appears at the location where you intend to insert a project. To insert a project, you select the task you want to appear below the inserted project; Project inserts the project above the selected task. Typically, an inserted project appears at the same level as the selected task. However, if the task above the selected task is indented further than the selected task, the inserted project will appear at the same level as that indented task. Or, if the task above the selected task is at the same level or outdented further than the selected task, the inserted project will appear in the outline at the same level as the selected task. Compare Figures 17-3, 17-4, and 17-5.

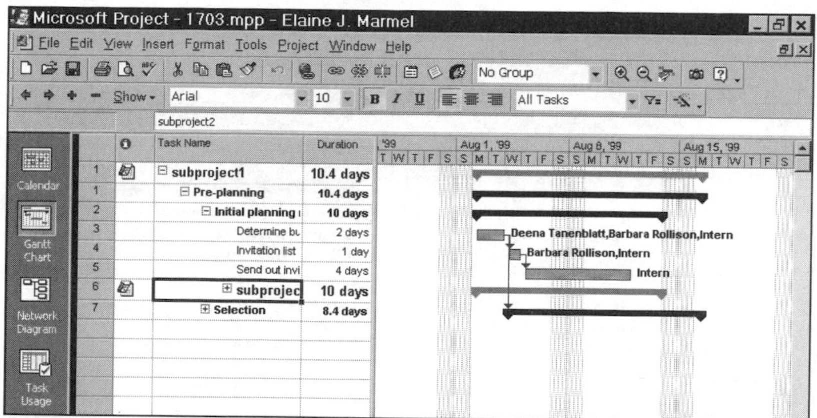


**Figure 17-3:** I expanded the Initial planning meeting task and then chose the Selection task when I inserted subproject2; it appears at the same outline level as the Invitation list task above it.

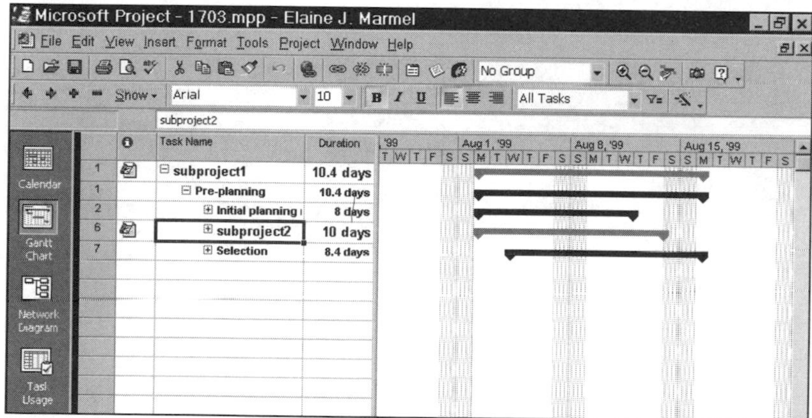


**Figure 17-4:** I collapsed the Initial planning meeting task and then chose the Selection task when I inserted subproject2; it appears at the same outline level as the Initial planning meeting task.

To produce a consolidated project in which the inserted projects line up at the highest outline level as they do in Figure 17-6, make sure that you collapse the preceding inserted project so that you cannot see its tasks when you insert the next subproject.

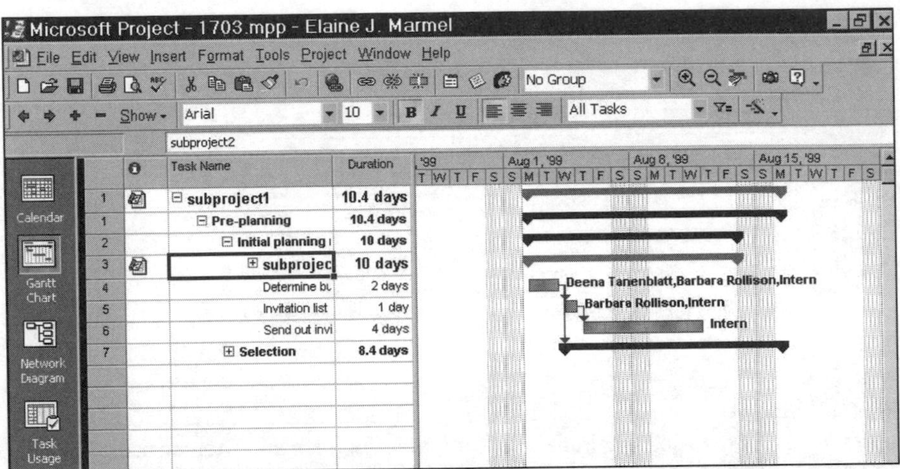


**Figure 17-5:** I selected the Determine budget task and then inserted subproject2; it appears at the same outline level as Determine budget because the task above – Initial planning meeting – is outdented further than Determine budget (the selected task).

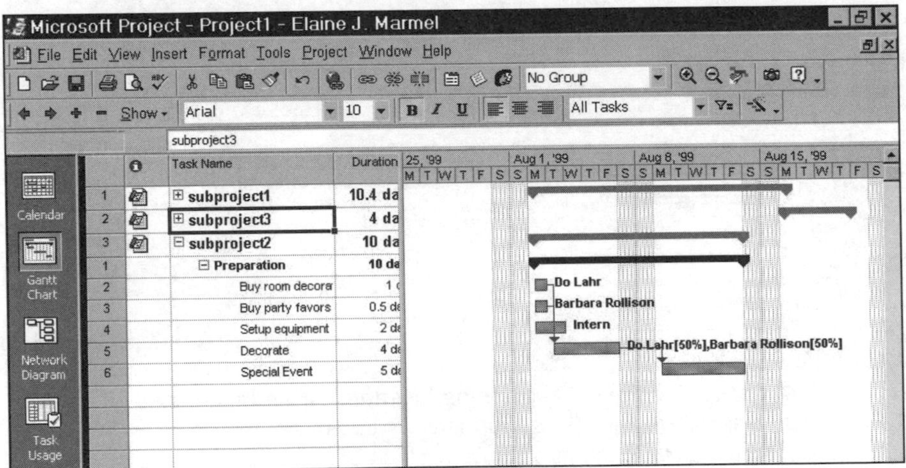


**Figure 17-6:** When subproject3 was inserted, subproject2 was selected and its subordinate tasks were visible, but the subordinate tasks of subproject1 were not visible.

You can hide or show tasks after you insert the project by clicking the summary task's outline symbol – the plus or minus sign next to the task name.

To insert a project, follow these steps:

1. Open the project in which you want to store the consolidated project.

2. Click the Gantt Chart icon in the View bar.
3. Click the Task Name column on the row where you want the inserted project to begin.

When you insert a project, Project places the project immediately above the selected row. Therefore, if your consolidated project already contains tasks, click the task in the Task Name column that you want to appear below the subproject.

4. Choose Insert ➪ Project to open the Insert Project dialog box you see in Figure 17-7.

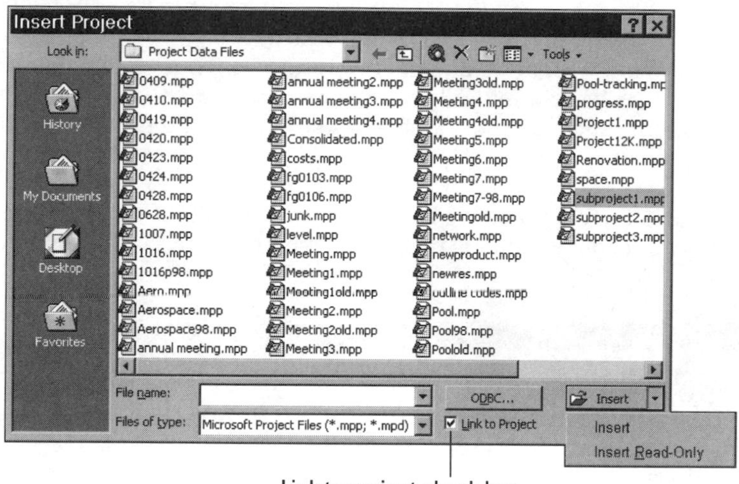


**Figure 17-7:** The Insert Project dialog box works like the Open dialog box.

5. Use the Look in list to navigate to the folder that contains the project you want to insert.
6. Highlight the file you want to insert.
7. Change any insert project options:
   - If you remove the check from the Link to Project checkbox, the inserted project won't be linked to its source project.
   - If you choose Insert Read-Only from the Insert dropdown menu, Project does not change the source project when you change the inserted project.
8. Click Insert (or Insert Read-Only). Project inserts the selected file into the open project. The inserted file appears as a summary task, with its subordinate tasks hidden.

## Using inserted projects and their source files

As you saw in Figure 17-7, you can link an inserted project to its source file. If you do not want to link an inserted project to its source file, any changes you make to the inserted project in the consolidated project file do not affect the source file. Similarly, any changes you make to the source file do not affect the consolidated project file containing the subproject. Why wouldn't you want to link the files? You may want to create a consolidated file just so that you can generate a report quickly.

Under many circumstances, linking the files makes updating easier. Linking ensures that any changes you make in either the consolidated project or the subproject file affect the other file. When you insert a project and link it to its source file, you are creating a link between two files; that link works like any link you create between two files in the Windows environment. For example, if you rename the subproject file or move it to a different folder than the one in which you originally saved it, you need to update the link to the consolidated project; otherwise, the link does not work.

If you do move a file that you have linked, you can update the link on the Advanced tab of the Task Information dialog box for the inserted project (see Figure 17-8).

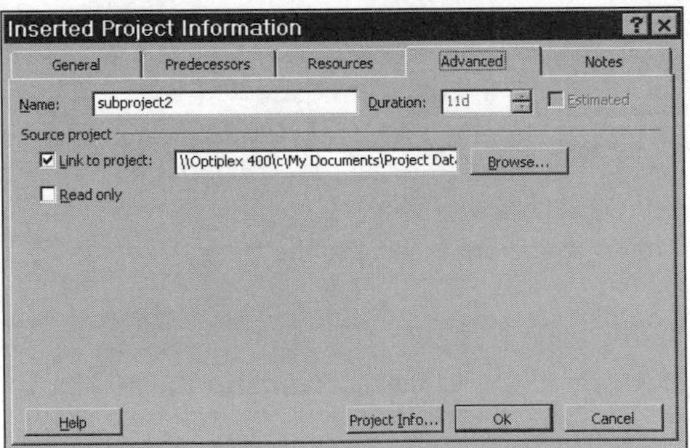


**Figure 17-8:** The Advanced tab of the Inserted Project Information dialog box

You can also unlink subprojects from their source files using the Advanced tab of the Inserted Project Information dialog box. Remove the check from the Link to project checkbox.

Or, you can simply attempt to expand the inserted project; when you click the plus sign next to the subproject, Project automatically displays a dialog box that looks like the Open dialog box. Use it to navigate to the new location of the file and click OK when you finish.

## Consolidating all open projects: A shortcut

Follow these steps to consolidate several subprojects at the same time:

1. Open all the subprojects that you want to consolidate.
2. Choose Window ⇨ New Window to open the New Window dialog box that appears in Figure 17-9.

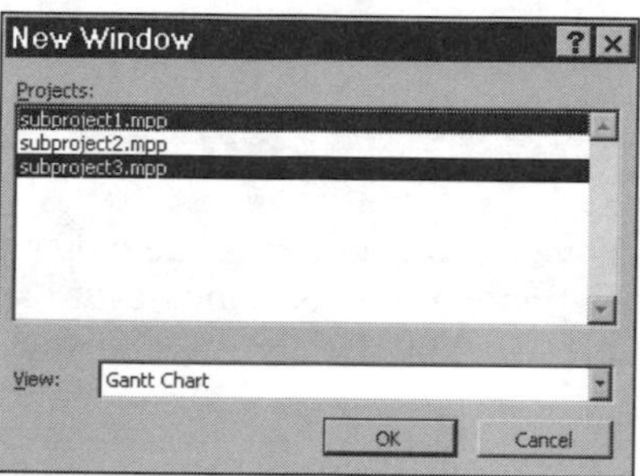


**Figure 17-9:** Use the New Window dialog box to quickly consolidate open projects.

3. Hold down the Ctrl key and click each project you want to consolidate.
4. Click OK.

Project creates a new consolidated project that contains the projects you selected in the New Window dialog box. Project inserts the subprojects into the consolidated project in the order in which the subprojects appear in the New Window dialog box.

## Moving subprojects within a consolidated project

You can move subprojects around in the consolidated project by cutting a subproject row to delete it and then pasting the row where you want it to appear. When you select a summary row representing a subproject and click the Cut button on the Standard toolbar, Project opens the Planning Wizard dialog box in Figure 17-10.

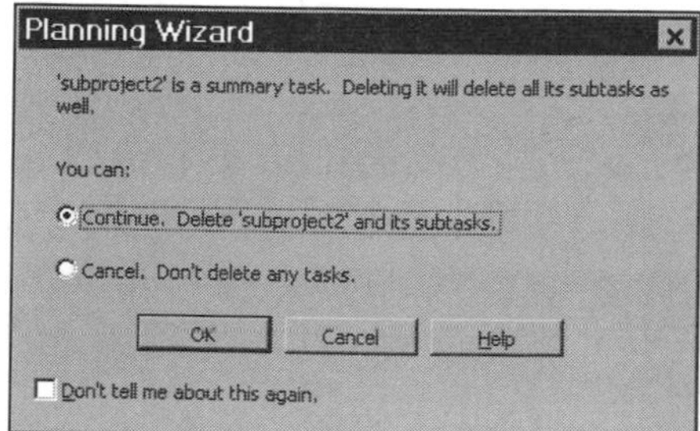


**Figure 17-10:** The Planning Wizard appears when you try to delete a summary task.

Select the Continue option button and click OK. The summary task representing the subproject and all its subordinate tasks disappears. When you paste the subproject, Project places the subproject immediately above the selected row. Therefore, in the Task Name column, you must click the task you want to appear below the subproject. Then click the Paste button on the Standard toolbar. Project reinserts the subproject at its new location.

If you're going to be moving a lot of tasks, you might want to place a check in the "Don't tell me about this again" box to avoid viewing it.

# Consolidated Projects and Dependencies

In a consolidated project you typically have tasks — either in the consolidated project or in one subproject — that are dependent on tasks in another subproject. You can create links between projects in a consolidated file and, if necessary, you can change the links you create.

## Linking tasks across projects

You can create four different types of dependencies: finish-to-start, start-to-start, finish-to-finish, and start-to finish. In addition, these types support lead and lag time. The process of linking tasks with dependencies across projects is much the same as the process of creating dependencies for tasks within the same project because you create the dependency in a consolidated project. Starting in the consolidated project file, follow these steps:

1. Click the Gantt Chart on the View bar.
2. Select the tasks you want to link.

To select noncontiguous tasks, hold down the Ctrl key as you click each task name.

3. Click the Link Tasks button on the Standard toolbar. Project creates a finish-to-start link between the two tasks.

You can create the link in the consolidated project file by dragging from the Gantt bar of the predecessor task to the Gantt bar of the successor task.

You also can link tasks by typing in the Predecessor field, using the format project name\ID#. Project name should include the path to the location of the file as well as the filename, and ID# should be the ID number of the task in that file. In Figure 17-11 the Buy room decorations task is linked to the Site task, which is Task 8 in a Project file called SUBPROJECT1.MPP. You can see the complete path name of a linked task in the Entry bar (just below the toolbars) when you highlight the task.

| | Task Name | Duration | Start | Finish | Predecessors | Resource Names |
|---|---|---|---|---|---|---|
| 1 | subproject1 | 10.4 days | Mon 8/2/99 | Mon 8/16/99 | | |
| 1 | Pre-planning | 10.4 days | Mon 8/2/99 | Mon 8/16/99 | | |
| 2 | Initial planning meeting | 9.17 days | Mon 8/2/99 | Fri 8/13/99 | | |
| 3 | Determine budget | 2 days | Mon 8/2/99 | Tue 8/3/99 | | Deena Tanenblatt,Ba |
| 4 | Invitation list | 2 days | Wed 8/4/99 | Fri 8/6/99 | 3 | Barbara Rollison,Inte |
| 5 | Send out invitations | 4 days | Fri 8/6/99 | Fri 8/13/99 | 4 | Intern |
| 6 | Selection | 8.4 days | Wed 8/4/99 | Mon 8/16/99 | 3 | |
| 7 | Theme | 4 days | Wed 8/4/99 | Mon 8/9/99 | | Deena Tanenblatt[50 |
| 8 | Site | 3 days | Tue 8/10/99 | Mon 8/16/99 | 7 | Deena Tanenblatt |
| 2 | subproject2 | 20.4 days | Mon 8/2/99 | Mon 8/30/99 | | |
| 1 | Preparation | 20.4 days | Mon 8/2/99 | Mon 8/30/99 | | |
| 3 | Buy room decorations | 1 day | Mon 8/16/99 | Tue 8/17/99 | \\Optiplex 400\c\M | Do Lahr |
| 4 | Buy party favors | 0.5 days | Mon 8/2/99 | Mon 8/2/99 | | Barbara Rollison |
| 5 | Setup equipment | 2 days | Mon 8/2/99 | Tue 8/3/99 | | Intern |
| 6 | Decorate | 4 days | Tue 8/17/99 | Mon 8/23/99 | 3,4 | Do Lahr[50%],Barbai |
| 7 | Special Event | 5 days | Mon 8/23/99 | Mon 8/30/99 | 6 | |
| 3 | subproject3 | 9 days | Mon 8/30/99 | Fri 9/10/99 | | |
| 1 | Wrap Up | 9 days | Mon 8/30/99 | Fri 9/10/99 | | |
| 2 | Clean Up | 2 days | Mon 8/30/99 | Wed 9/1/99 | | Intern |
| 3 | Pay bills | 4 days | Wed 9/1/99 | Tue 9/7/99 | 2 | Do Lahr |
| 4 | Write thank you letters | 2 days | Tue 9/7/99 | Thu 9/9/99 | 3 | Barbara Rollison |

**Figure 17-11:** You can type in the Predecessor field to create a link between tasks across Project files.

When you link tasks between projects, the task links look like standard links in the consolidated project. However, as Figure 17-12 shows, when you open either of the subproject files, you'll see that Project has inserted an external link. The name and the Gantt Chart bar of each externally linked task appear gray. If you point at the Gantt Chart bar, Project displays information about the task, including that it is an external task.

If you double-click the task name of the external task, Project opens the subproject containing the task to which the external task is linked.

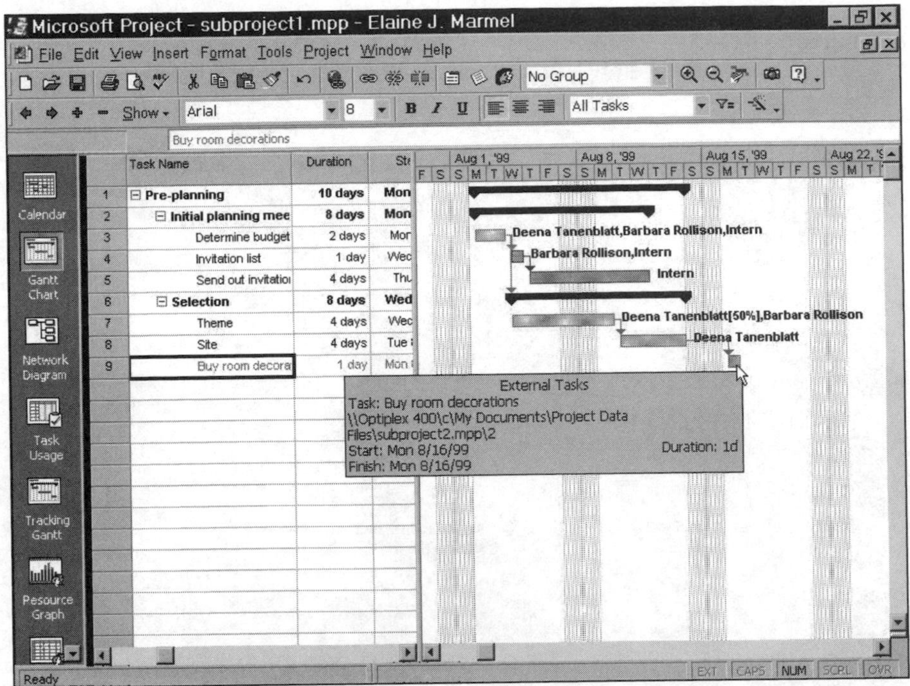


**Figure 17-12:** When you link tasks across files, Project inserts an external link in the subproject file.

# Changing links across projects

After you link tasks across projects, you may need to change information about the link. For example, you may want to change the type of dependency from the default finish-to-start link, or you may want to create lag time.

You can modify a link between tasks in different subprojects from either the subproject or from the consolidated project. In the subproject, double-click the line that links an internal task to the external task (see Figure 17-13). In the consolidated project, double-click the line that links the two tasks (see Figure 17-14). Project displays the Task Dependency dialog box.

The two versions of the dialog boxes differ slightly. If you work from within the subproject, you can update the path of the link and use the Type box to change the type of link and the Lag box to change the amount of lag time between the linked tasks. If you work from within the consolidated project, you cannot update the path of the link, but you can change the type of link and the amount of lag time.

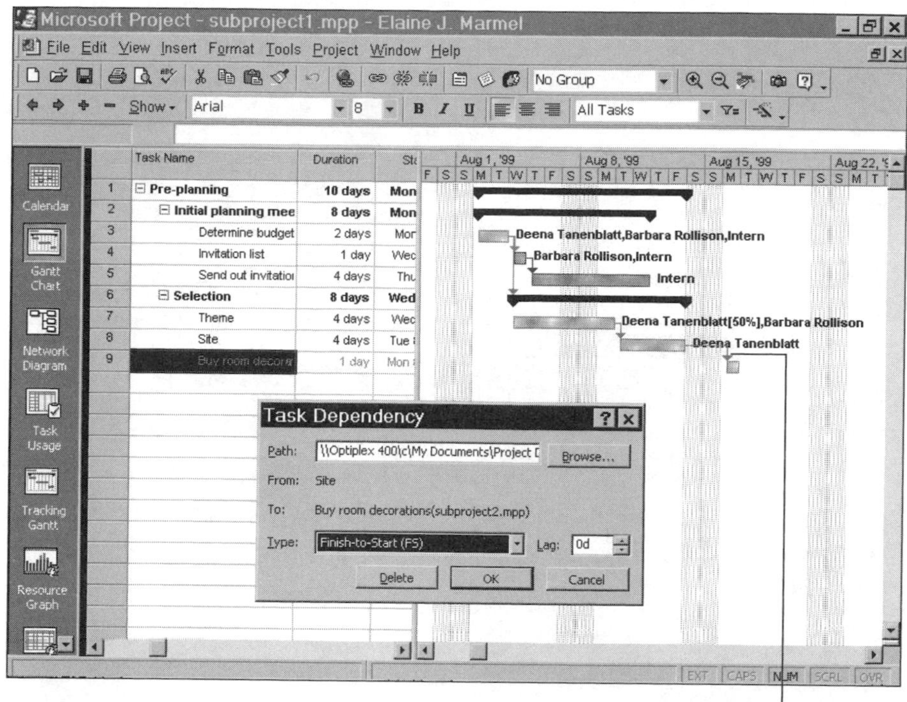


**Figure 17-13:** In a subproject, double-click the link line between the internal task and the external task to display the Task Dependency dialog box.

## Consolidated projects – to save or not to save

You don't need to save consolidated project files unless you want them. You can create the consolidated project file using either the Window ➪ New Window method or the Insert ➪ Project method described in this chapter. You can use the consolidated project to create links and maybe even reports, and then close the consolidated project file without saving it. Suppose you created the consolidated project by inserting projects and the inserted projects are not open. When you close the consolidated project, Project first asks if you want to save the consolidated project; your answer does not affect changes you made to inserted projects (see Figure 17-15).

If you created the consolidated project using Window ➪ New Window, Project asks you whether you want to save changes to the subprojects as you close them.

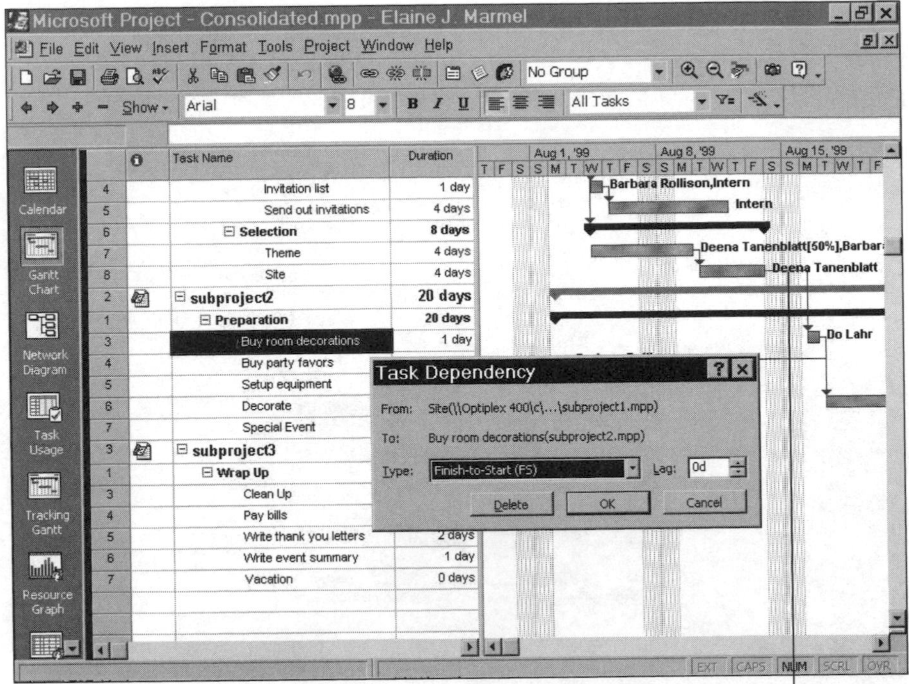


**Figure 17-14:** In a consolidated project, double-click the line that links the tasks to display the Task Dependency dialog box and change the dependency information about tasks linked across projects.

If you save the changes to the subprojects, even if you don't save the consolidated project, external tasks such as the one you saw in Figure 17-12 appear in the subproject files when you open them.

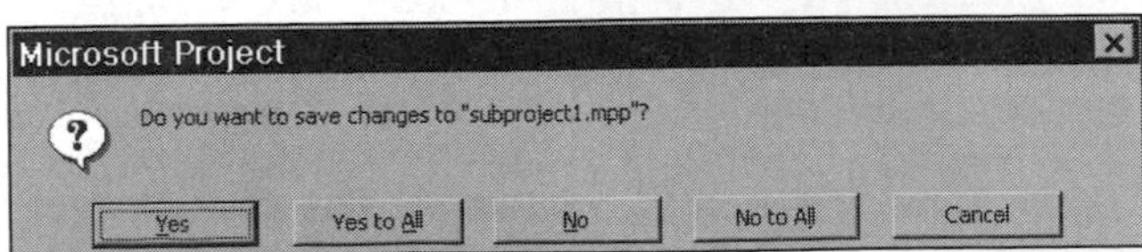


**Figure 17-15:** When you close a consolidated project you created by inserting projects, Project asks if you want to save changes, including links, you made to each subproject.

# Viewing Multiple Projects

Creating a consolidated project makes your work easier because you can display and hide selected portions of your project.

The consolidated project in Figure 17-16 contains three inserted projects. As you can tell from the outline symbols, you can't see all the tasks in this consolidated project in the figure; the tasks for subproject3 are hidden.

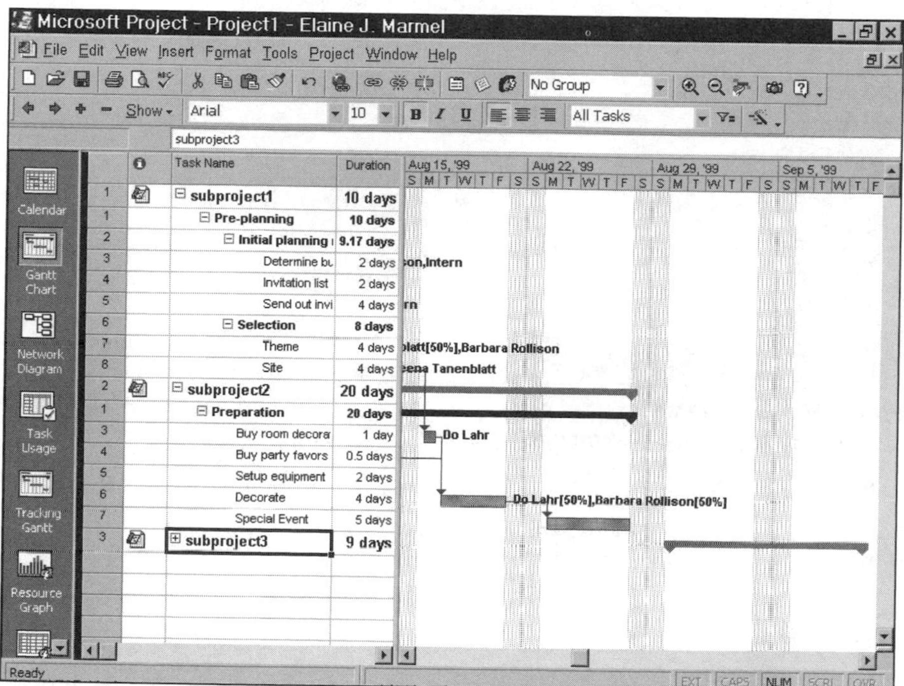


**Figure 17-16:** This consolidated project contains three inserted projects.

Suppose you need to focus on the middle portion of the project. As you can see in Figure 17-17, you can easily focus on the portion of the project that currently needs your attention by clicking the outline symbols to the left of each summary task to expand only the portion of the project you want to view.

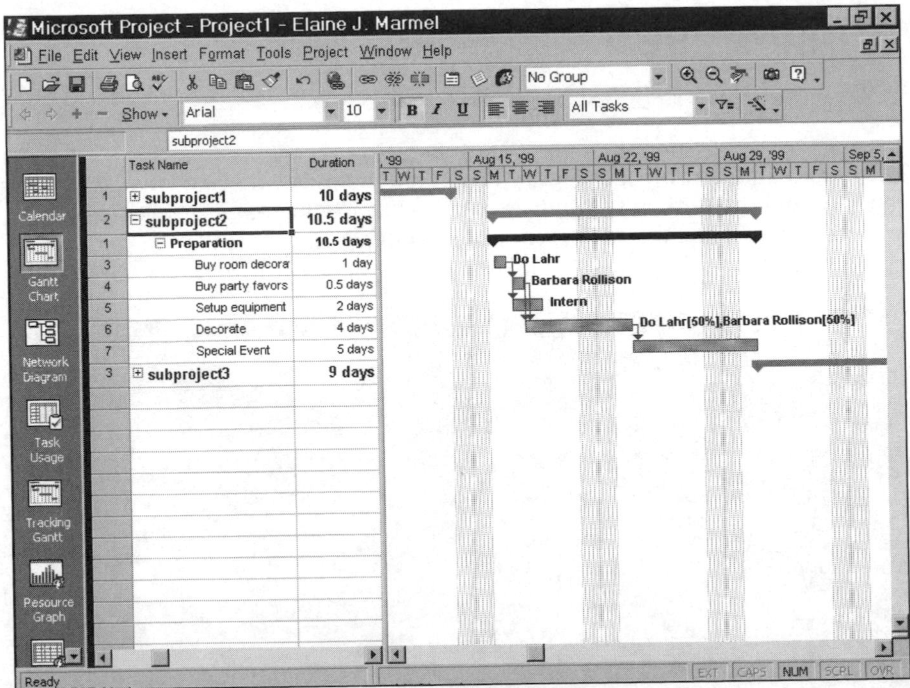


**Figure 17-17:** Close up inserted projects so that just their summary tasks appear when you want to focus on a portion of a consolidated project.

# Using Multiple Critical Paths

Multiple critical paths can help you consolidate projects. By displaying multiple critical paths, you can see a critical path for each inserted project.

By default, Project displays only one critical path, but you can change this default. Choose Tools ➪ Options and click the Calculation tab to display the dialog box you see in Figure 17-18. Place a check in the "Calculate multiple critical paths" checkbox and click OK.

When you view your project in a view that displays critical paths, such as the Tracking Gantt view, you can see critical paths for each independent set of tasks. Project sets the late finish date of any task without a successor to the task's early finish date, giving the task no slack and making it critical. Figure 17-19 uses the Tracking Gantt to show three critical paths; in the figure, you can distinguish critical path tasks from noncritical path tasks by their striped hatching pattern. If you could see them onscreen in color, you would easily identify the critical paths because the critical tasks appear striped and in red.

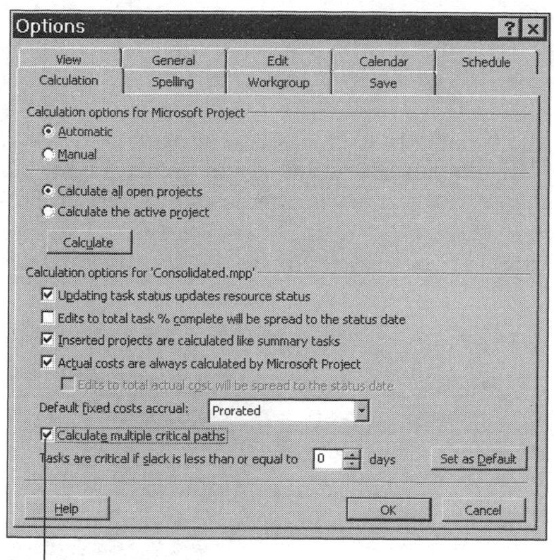


**Figure 17-18:** The Calculation tab of the Options dialog box

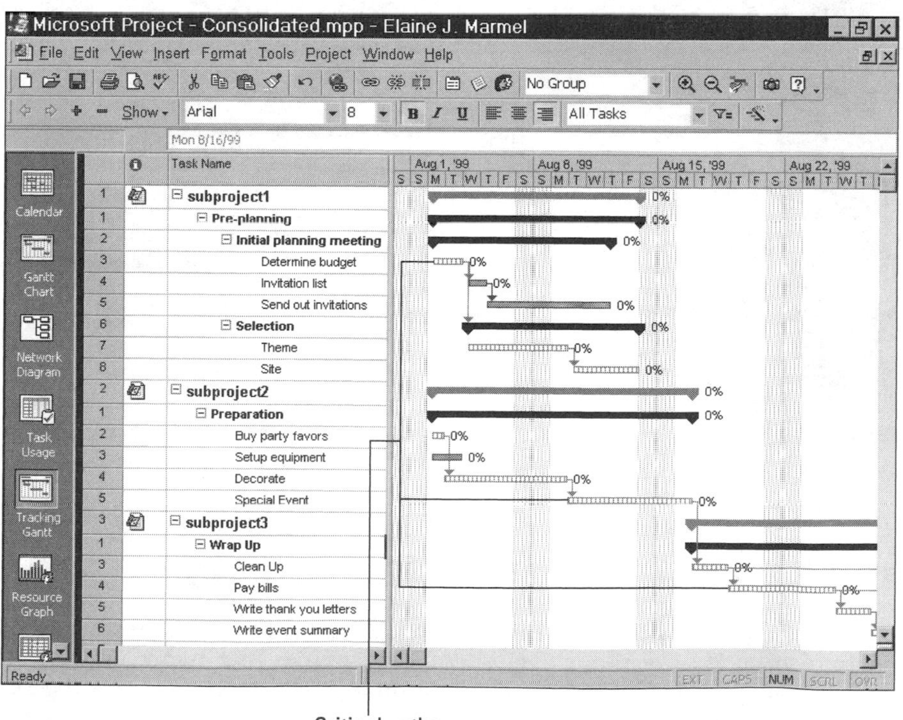


**Figure 17-19:** You can display multiple critical paths, which can be particularly effective when you work in a consolidated project.

With the release of Project 2000, you can now display one critical path for an entire consolidated project because Project treats inserted projects like summary tasks and calculates late finishes across all inserted projects.

Displaying multiple critical paths can be effective, but seeing one critical path for a consolidated project (by leaving the checkbox unchecked in Figure 17-18) can be enlightening. For example, the first inserted project in the consolidated project shown in Figure 17-19 plays no part in the critical path. In Figure 17-20, I've used the Tracking Gantt, which adds vertical stripes to the bars that represent tasks on the critical path.

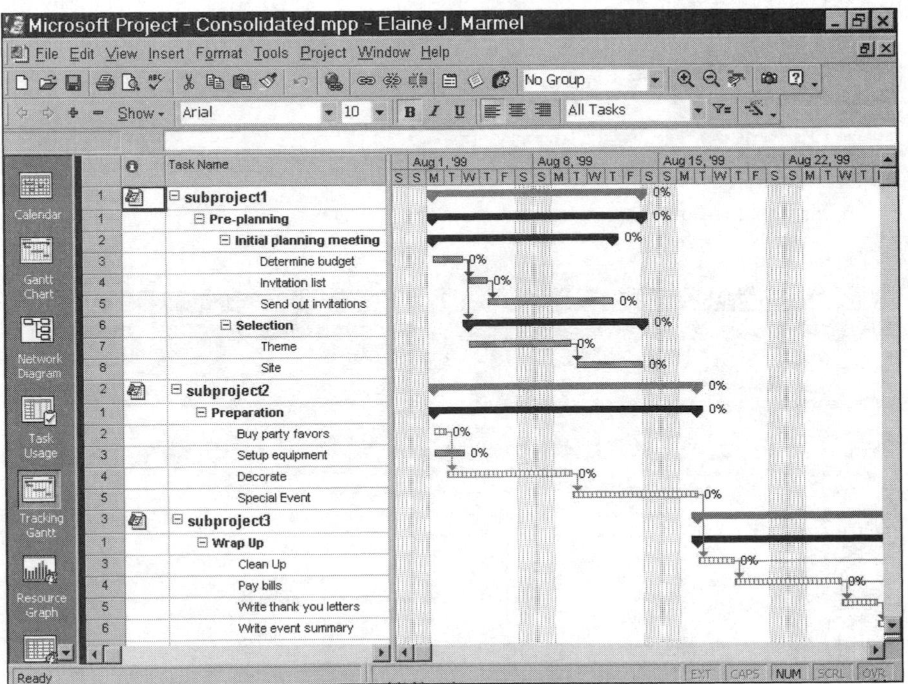


**Figure 17-20:** Because the consolidated project calculates the late finish date across all inserted projects, you can display one critical path for the consolidated project.

# Sharing Resources Among Projects

Creating a resource pool can be useful if you work with the same resources on multiple projects. A resource pool is a set of resources that are available to any project. You can use resources exclusively on one project, or you can share the resources among several projects.

If you work in an environment in which several project managers use the same set of resources on various projects, consider using a resource pool. Setting up a resource pool in Project can be a good way to schedule resources and resolve resource conflicts.

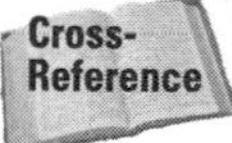


See Chapter 10 for more information on other techniques you can employ to resolve resource conflicts.

## Creating a resource pool and sharing the resources

Setting up a resource pool in Project can facilitate resource management, especially for resources shared on several projects. To create a resource pool, you simply set up a project file that contains only resource information.

If you already have a project set up that contains all the resources available, you can use that project as a model. After you identify a project that can serve as the resource pool, you designate it as the resource pool project as follows:

Note

You don't need to delete all of the tasks in the project that will serve as the model for of the resource pool. You just need the resource information in the file.

1. Open the project that contains the resources and that will serve as the resource pool file.
2. Open the project that is to use the resource pool (that is, the project on which you want to work).
3. Choose Tools ➪ Resources ➪ Share Resources. Project displays the Share Resources dialog box (see Figure 17-21).

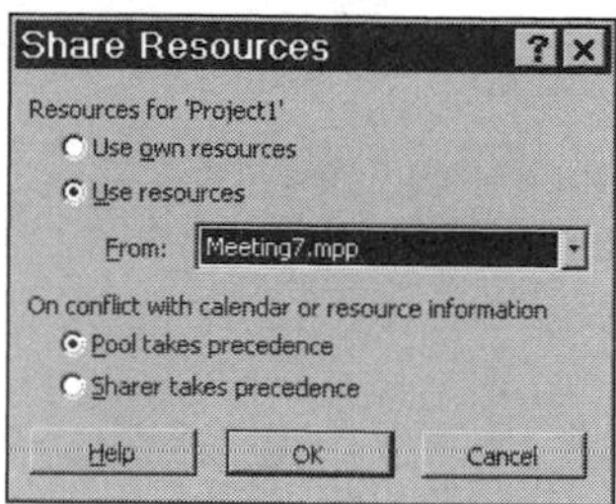


**Figure 17-21:** The Share Resources dialog box

4. Click the Use resources option button; then use the From list box to select the resource pool project to indicate you want to use the resources defined in that project.

If you open only the project on which you want to work, the "Use own resources" option button is the only choice available and you won't be able to share resources with the resource pool. The first time you want to enable resource sharing, you must open both the project on which you want to work and the project you determined would be the resource pool. In addition, if you have any other projects open, they appear as candidates for the resource pool project when you open the From list box because Project enables you to select from any open project when you identify the resource pool.

5. Tell Project how to handle calendar conflicts. If you select "Pool takes precedence," the resource calendars in the resource pool file will take precedence when conflicts arise. If, however, you select "Sharer takes precedence," the resource calendars in the file you're updating will take precedence over the resource calendars in the resource pool file when conflicts arise.
6. Click OK.

If you switch to the Resource Sheet view of the file you want to update, Project displays all the resources contained in the resource pool file along with any resources you may have set up in your project file.

You can now continue working in your project, or you can save your project and close it. You can also close the resource pool file.

## Opening a project that uses a resource pool

At some point you will save and close your file and then come back to work on it a second time. You don't need to open the resource pool file at that time. Instead, when you open your file after you have set it up to share resources, you see the dialog box that appears in Figure 17-22.

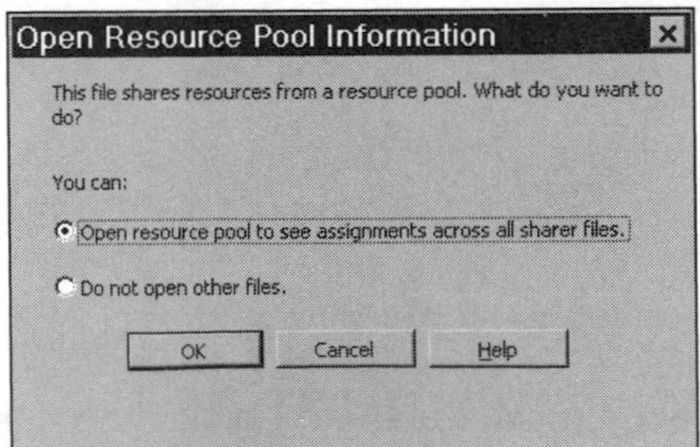


**Figure 17-22:** The Open Resource Pool Information dialog box

When you select the first option, Project opens your file, the resource pool, and all other files that are using the resource pool. If you select the second option, Project opens only your file; Project does not transfer any changes you make to the resources in your file to the resource pool because the resource pool file won't be open.

When you select the first option, Project automatically opens the resource pool file as a read-only file. This action enables you to make changes to your project without tying up the resource pool file and, therefore, allows multiple users to simultaneously use the resource pool.

## Updating information in the resource pool

If you make any changes to resource information while you're working on your project, you must update the resource pool file so that others using the resource pool have the most up-to-date information. To update the resource pool, make sure the resource pool file is open, even in read-only mode. Then choose Tools ➪ Resources ➪ Update Resource Pool (see Figure 17-23).

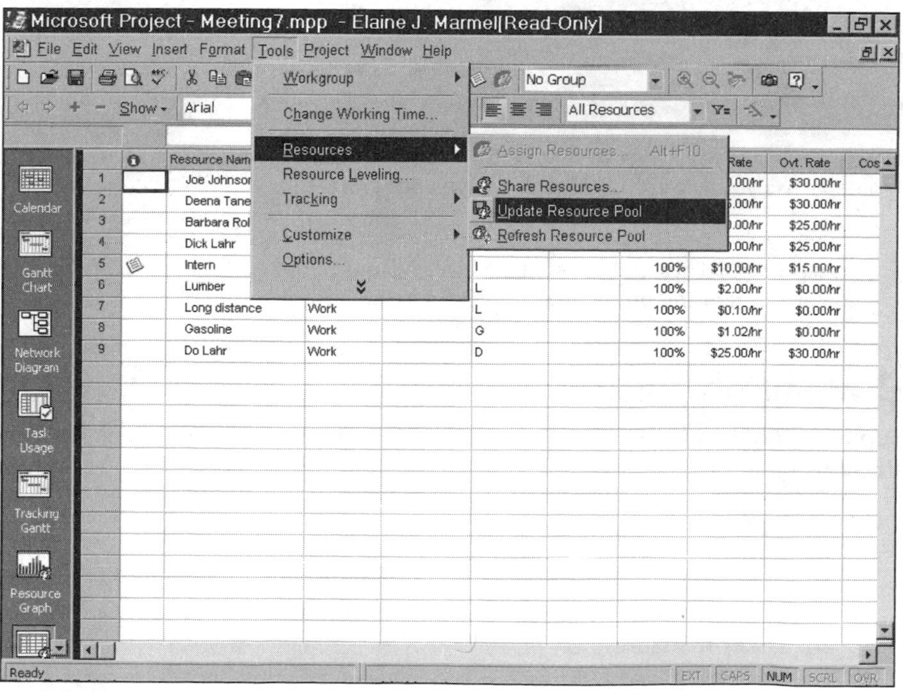


**Figure 17-23:** The Update Resource Pool command is available if you set up resource sharing and you make a change in your project while the resource pool file is open.

If you opened only your project and made changes to the resources, this command is not available while working in your project. Further, if you opened only your project, saved and closed your project, and then opened the resource pool file, this command still is not available. To ensure that Project incorporates the changes you make to resources in your project in the resource pool, be sure to open the resource pool file when you open your file.

Tip: To ensure consistency and avoid arguments in the workplace, it's best to make one group or person responsible for updating the resource pool.

If you forget to update the resource pool after you make a change in your project that affects the resource pool, Project displays the message you see in Figure 17-24 when you close your project and save it.

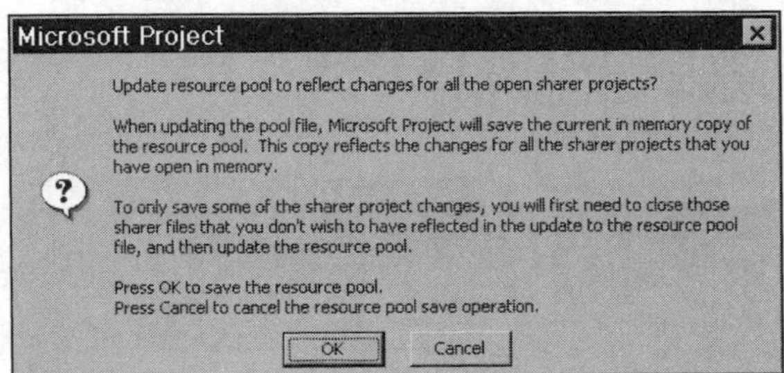


**Figure 17-24:** If you forget to update the resource pool, Project alerts you when you close and save your project.

New Feature: Project 2000 stores the relative path to projects linked to resource pools; if you move one or the other, Project will still be able to open the files.

## Quit sharing resources

Suppose you decide that you no longer want to use the resource pool file. Follow these steps to disable the resource pool for a specific project:

1. Open that project.
2. Choose Tools ➪ Resources ➪ Share Resources.
3. Select the "Use own resources" option button in the Share Resources dialog box (refer to Figure 17-21).

But what if you decide that you want to disable the resource pool in general for all files sharing the resources of one resource pool. Do you need to open each file and disable resource sharing? No. Follow these steps to disable the resource pool file in general:

1. Open the resource pool file in read-write mode using the Open dialog box— the same way you'd open any file. Project displays the dialog box you see in Figure 17-25. Choose the middle option or the last option—either will enable you to disable the pool because both open the file as a read-write file.

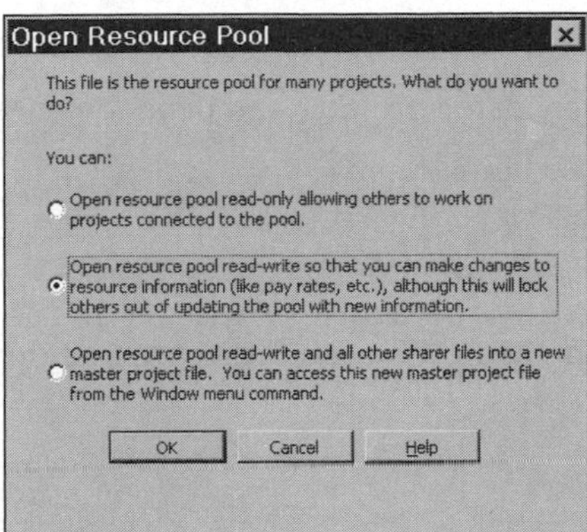


**Figure 17-25:** Use this dialog box to determine whether you open the resource pool file as a read-only file or a read-write file.

2. Choose Tools ➪ Resources ➪ Share Resources. Project displays the Share Resources dialog box you see in Figure 17-26.

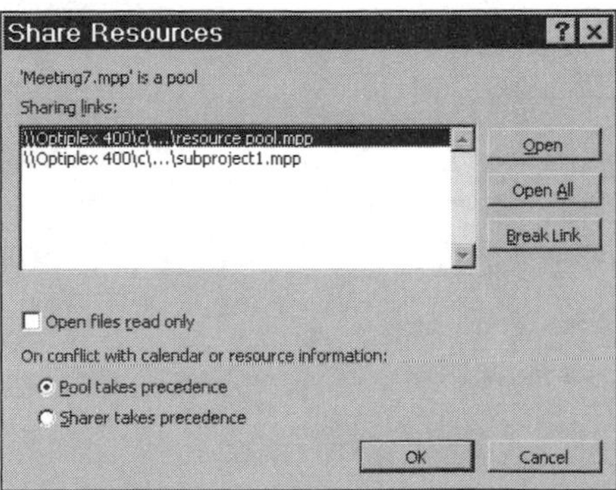


**Figure 17-26:** The Share Resources dialog box

3. Select the project(s) you want to exclude from the resource pool. You can select multiple noncontiguous projects by holding the Ctrl key when you click the mouse or contiguous projects by holding the Shift key when you click.
4. Click Break Link.

# Summary

This chapter described how to consolidate projects and pool resources. You learned how to:

- Insert projects
- Understand and work with consolidated projects and dependencies
- Manage the view of a consolidated project
- Display multiple critical paths
- Share resources

In Chapter 18, you'll read about customizing Microsoft Project to suit the way you work.

✦ ✦ ✦

# Advanced Microsoft Project

P A R T

# VI

✦ ✦ ✦ ✦

**In This Part**



✦ ✦ ✦ ✦

CHAPTER 18

# Customizing Microsoft Project

✦ ✦ ✦ ✦

**In This Chapter**

Using custom fields

Customizing the interface

✦ ✦ ✦ ✦

You can customize the Project working environment in several ways. For example, you can use custom fields to store and manipulate custom data in a project file. And you can change the way various elements appear onscreen and how you use Project's tools and commands. Suppose that you use a particular command for sharing resources all the time—you could perform that action quickly if you could access it from a tool on the standard toolbar. Or maybe you never use the Task Note tool and prefer to get it off the toolbar and place its command on a menu. Perhaps none of Project's built-in views or tables contains quite the combination of information you use most often.

Microsoft Project enables you to customize most of its elements. This chapter shows you how to create and use custom fields, make changes to the behavior of the Project interface, and create and modify toolbars and menus to make Project work the way that's best for you.

## Using Custom Fields

In Chapter 7, you read about Outline codes. Outline codes in Project are custom fields, and, in the past, you've had the ability to store custom data in a project file. However, you haven't been able to manipulate that data. Custom fields in Project 2000 enable you to create pick lists to use to ensure accurate data entry, create formulas to perform calculations on custom data, and insert icons that indicate graphically that a field contains custom data.

## Customizing data entry

Suppose your boss wants your best guess about whether you'll keep to the schedule on a task-by-task basis. You could set up a custom field and provide the information on any sheet view of Project. I'll show you this process in two phases. In the first phase, I'll create the custom field and, in the second phase, I'll show you how to use it.

To create a custom field, follow these steps:

1. Choose Tools ➪ Customize ➪ Fields. Project displays the Customize Fields dialog box (see Figure 18-1).

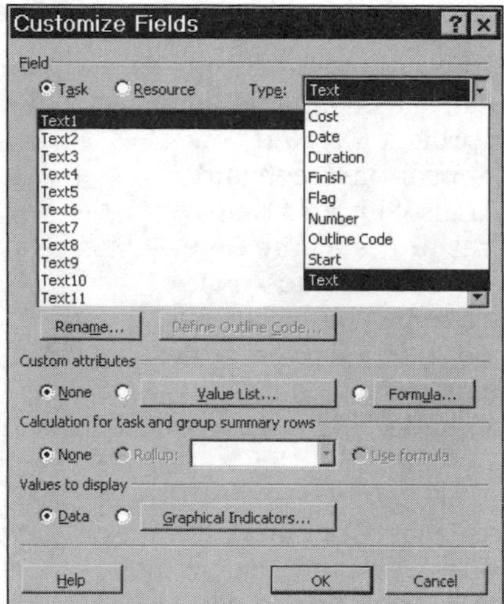


**Figure 18-1:** Select a custom field type.

2. Select either Task or Resource and then open the Type list box and choose the type of field you want to customize. The type you choose determines the values you can include in the pick list. Choose Text to include only in the pick list. If you choose Date, Start, or Finish, you must include date-formatted numbers in the pick list. If you choose Number or Cost, you can include only numbers in the pick list. If you choose Flag, you can include only Yes or No in the Value List. For the example, I chose Text because I want to set up a value list that contains Yes, No, and Maybe.
3. To provide a meaningful name for the code, click the Rename button and type the new name. You can't use any name that Project already uses. In the example, I named the field Best Guess. Then, click OK to redisplay the Customize Fields dialog box.

4. Click the Value List button to display the value list for Field Name dialog box shown in Figure 18-2.

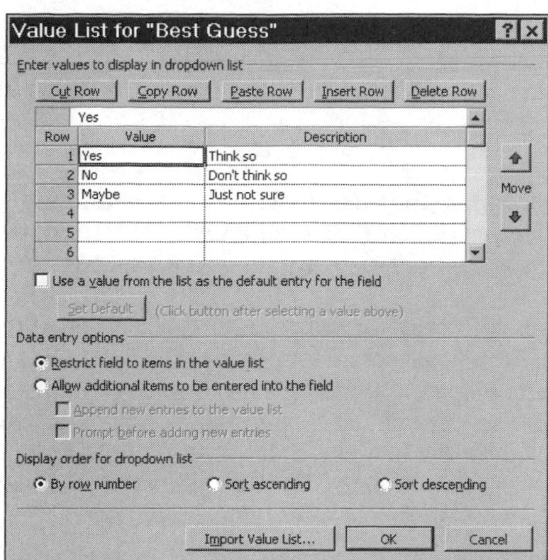


**Figure 18-2:** Use this dialog box to define the values you want Project to display in the pick list during data entry.

5. In the Value column, type the first value you want to appear in the list. The values Project lets you include in the value list depend on the field type you chose in Step 2. If you chose Text, you can include only combinations of letters and numbers. If you chose Date, Start, or Finish, you must include date-formatted entries. If you chose Number or Cost, you can include only numbers in the value list. If you chose Flag, you can include only Yes or No in the value list.

If you chose Flag, you'll need to substitute Yes or No for such standard flag choices as True and False or On and Off.

6. Optionally, in the Description column, provide a description of the value.
7. Repeat Steps 5 and 6 for each level you want to define.
8. If you want, you can set a default value to appear as the entry for the field by placing a check in the "Use a value from the list as the default entry for the field" box. If you choose this option, highlight a value in the light and click the Set Default button to select the value as the default.

9. In the Data Entry options section of the dialog box, you can restrict data entry so that the user can enter only values in the value list, or you can permit the user to enter values other than those in the list — and add those values to the value list.
10. You can specify the order for the value list in the last section of the dialog box.
11. Click OK to save the value list and redisplay the Customize Fields dialog box.
12. Click OK again to redisplay your project.

That was Phase 1. In Phase 2, you use the custom field that you defined. To use it, you need to display it on a sheet view. If you defined a task field, then use any task sheet view; if you defined a resource field, use any resource sheet view.

To display the column, right-click the title of the column that you want to appear to the left of the custom field. Project selects the column and displays a shortcut menu from which you can choose Insert Column. In the Column Definition dialog box (see Figure 18-3), open the Field Name list box and select the custom field you defined, using the name you supplied when you defined the field. Optionally, change the rest of the information in the dialog box and click OK. The custom field appears onscreen.

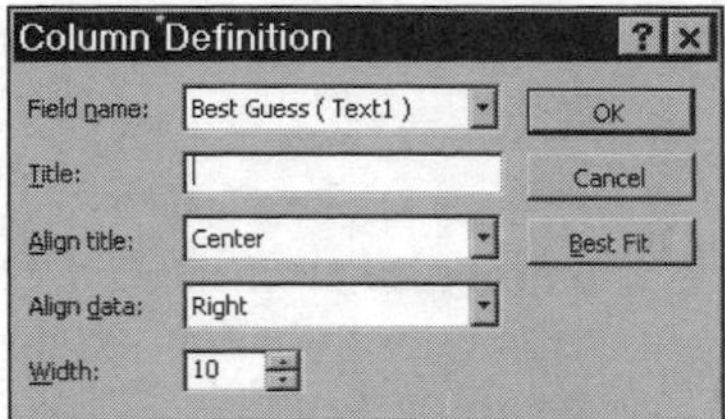


**Figure 18-3:** Select the custom field you created.

When you click in the field, a list box arrow appears; when you open the list box, you see the value list you established (see Figure 18-4). Select values from the list or simply type them; in my example, if you try to enter a value that doesn't exist in the list, Project displays an error message instructing you to use a value from the list.

You can't use custom fields to create value lists for regular Project fields. Suppose, for example, that you've decided that you don't want to use all 1,000 of Project's priorities; in fact, you want your people to use only five possible priorities:100, 200, 300, 400, and 500, with 100 being the lowest priority and 500 being the highest priority. You could create a Number custom field (called, for example, Priority Lvl) that only allows the entry of these five values on a sheet view. However, users could open the Task Information dialog box and assign *any* priority value in the Priority field – and Project would permit the assignment. The custom field Priority Lvl is *not* substituting for the actual field Priority, and users could circumvent the custom value list.

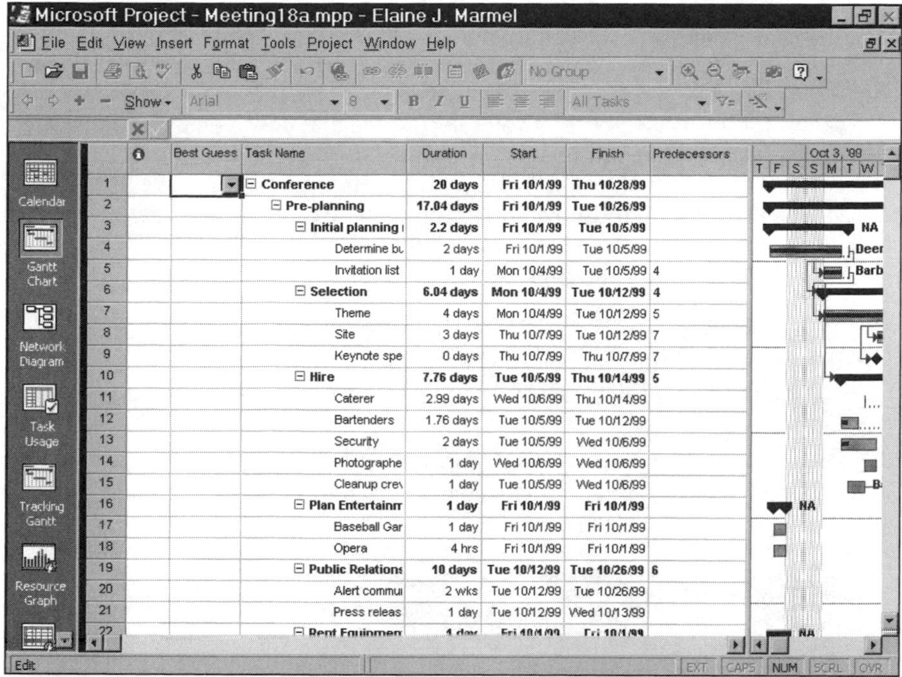


**Figure 18-4:** As you fill in the field, select from the pick list.

# Using formulas in custom fields

Suppose that your manager tells you that part of your evaluation in project management will depend on the accuracy of your cost estimates. Under these circumstances, you might want to monitor the tasks for which actual cost exceeds baseline cost. You can set up a custom field to help you easily identify those tasks.

1. Choose Tools ➪ Customize ➪ Fields. Project displays the Customize Fields dialog box (refer to Figure 18-1).
2. Select either Task or Resource and then open the Type list box and choose the type of field you want to customize. In this example, I'll choose Cost because I want to compare cost values.

The type of field you select from the Type list doesn't matter as much when you're creating a formula as it does when you're creating a value list. If you select the wrong type when creating a value list, you won't be able to set up the appropriate values for the list. However, if you select a type that doesn't match what you're trying to calculate in a formula, Project simply displays "ERROR" in the custom field column on the sheet. For example, suppose that you want to calculate a cost and you select Date from the Type list. Project still permits you to create the formula but, because the formula really doesn't make sense, you'll see "ERROR" when you display the custom field column.

3. To provide a meaningful name for the code, click the Rename button and type the new name. You can't use any name that Project already uses; in the example, I named the field Difference. Then, click OK to redisplay the Customize Fields dialog box.
4. Click the Formula button to display the "Formula for" dialog box. In Figure 18-5, I've already set up the formula for this example.

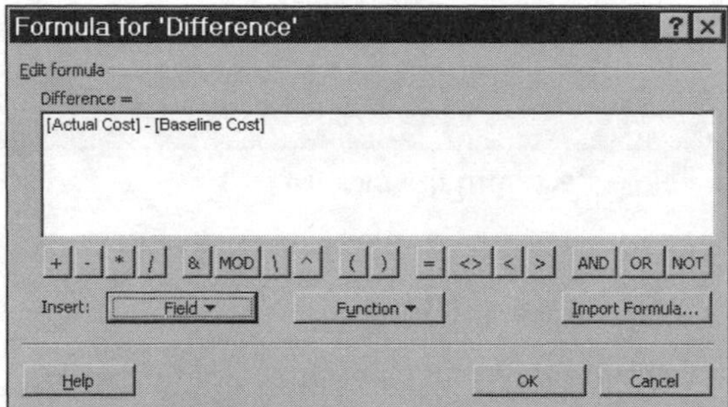


**Figure 18-5:** This dialog box lets you define the values you want Project to display in the pick list during data entry.

5. Create a formula in the text box by selecting fields or functions. To select a field, click the Field button; Project displays a list of field categories. Select the appropriate field category, and Project displays a list of the available fields (see Figure 18-6). To select a function, follow the same process, clicking the Function button.

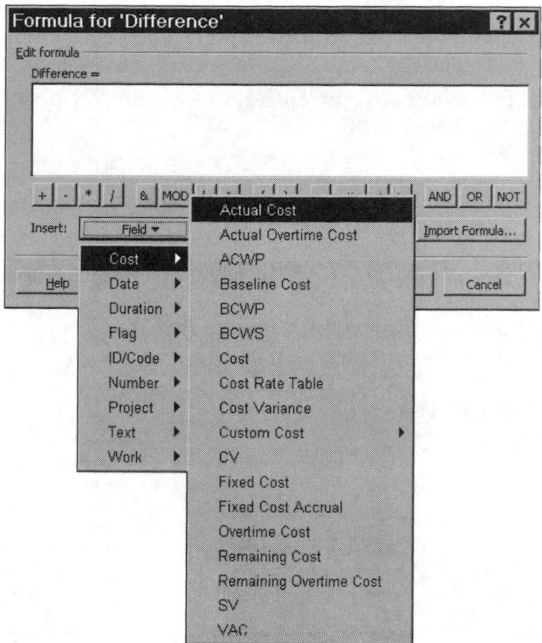


**Figure 18-6:** Select a field or a function to include in the formula.

In Appendix C, you'll find three tables. Table C-1 contains a list of all available Task fields, and Table C-2 contains the same information for Resource fields. Table C-3 lists the functions you can include in a formula as well as a description of each function's purpose.

6. To make a calculation, use the operators that appear above the Field and Function buttons.

If you've created this formula in another project, you can import the formula. You can import the formula from the Global template (assuming you save the formula in the Global template), or you can open the project that contains the formula before you create the formula in the new project. When you click the Import Formula button, Project displays a list of available templates or open Project files. Select the appropriate location, field type, and field name. Then click OK.

7. Click OK. Project warns that it will discard any information previously stored in the custom field and replace the information with the calculated values based on the formula.
8. Click OK to save the formula and redisplay the Customize Fields dialog box.
9. Optionally, assign the formula to summary rows.

If you click OK at this point, Project calculates a value for the formula. You can see the value if you display the column for the custom field, as I've done in Figure 18-7. Based on the formula I created, positive values represent tasks where Actual Cost exceeded Baseline Cost — and technically, my Difference column is nothing more than the Variance column of the Cost table.

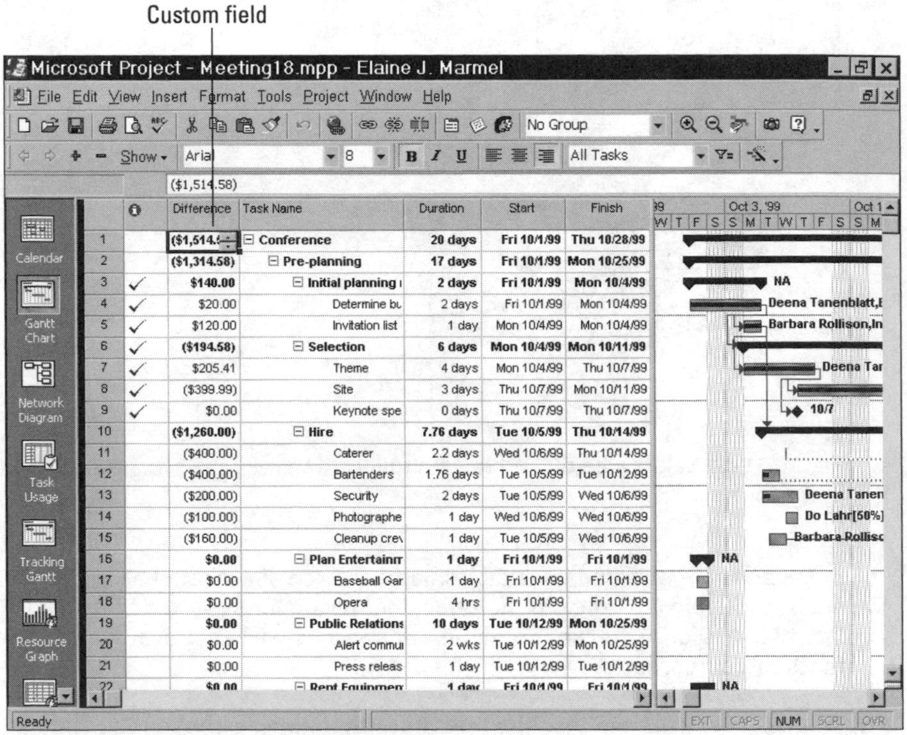

Custom field

**Figure 18-7:** When you display the column for the custom field, you see the result of the formula.

But suppose that you don't want to eyeball figures to find the problem tasks. You can insert icons to represent positive and negative values — and make the job of identifying the problem tasks much easier — by following these steps:

1. In the Custom Fields dialog box, highlight the custom field you created and click the Graphical Indicators button (see Figure 18-8).

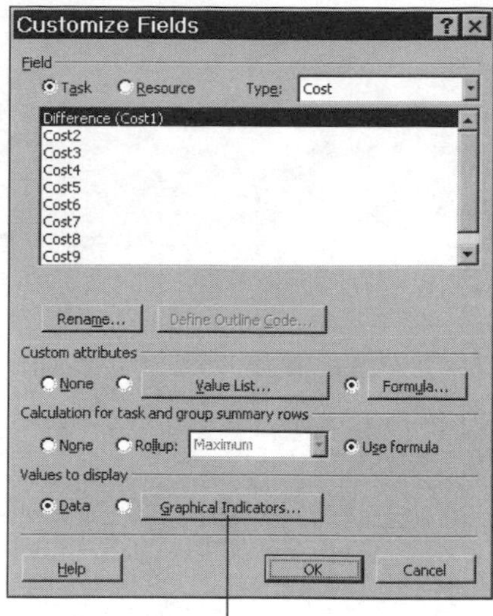


**Figure 18-8:** Click this button to assign icons to custom fields.

2. Choose the type of row to which you want to assign an indicator: Nonsummary, Summary, or Project summary.

3. In the Test for section, set up the test Project should use. In each column, you can choose from lists; in the Value(s) column, you can compare the formula result to the value of another field or to a numeric value, as I do in Figure 18-9. In my example, if the result of the formula is greater than zero, I want to see a red flag, because the actual cost of the task exceeds the baseline cost. If, however, the actual cost is less than or equal to the baseline cost, things are fine, so I want to see a happy face (you'll find other indicator choices in the Image list).

Tip

If you've set up graphical indicators in another project, you can import the criteria from either the Global template (assuming you saved the formula in the Global template) or from another open project. When you click the Import Graphical Indicator Criteria button, Project displays a list of available templates or open Project files. Select the appropriate location, field type, and field name. Then click OK.

4. If you want to see the mathematical results of the formula in a ToolTip when you point the mouse at the indicator, place a check in the "Show data values in ToolTips" checkbox.

5. Click OK to redisplay the Customize Fields dialog box.

6. Click OK again to redisplay your project.

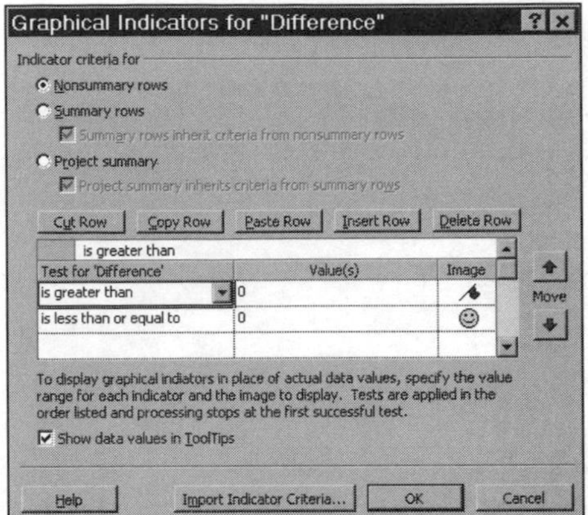


**Figure 18-9:** Set up the test Project should perform on the formula's result and the indicator to display, based on the test results.

If necessary, display the column for the custom field; right-click the column you want to appear to the right of the custom field, and choose Insert Column. Then, select the custom field. When Project displays the column, it will contain an indicator (see Figure 18-10). If you placed a check in the "Show data values in ToolTips" checkbox, you can point the mouse at an indicator to see the results of the formula.

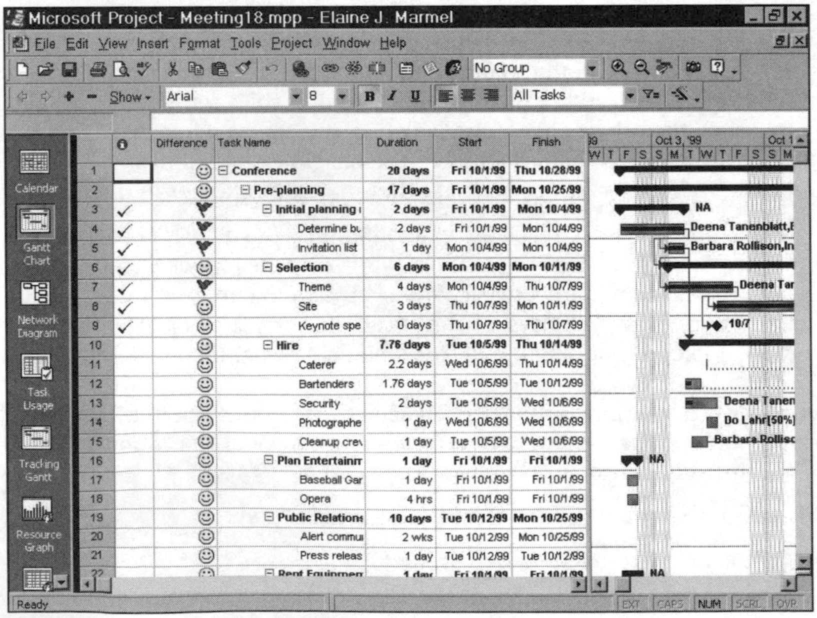

**Figure 18-10:** The custom field column contains an indicator.

# Customizing the Interface

In addition to using custom fields to customize data entry and make calculations, you can customize Project's interface. For example, you can control the number of icons that appear in the Windows taskbar when you open multiple projects. Project 2000 contains some new options you can take advantage of when saving files. Use Project's Organizer to move tables and views between project files. And, modify toolbars and customize menus to make them work the way you work.

## Windows taskbar icons

In Project 98 and earlier versions of Project, you saw only one icon on the Windows task- bar while Project was open, regardless of the number of Project files you opened. In Project 2000, by default you see an icon on the Windows taskbar for every open Project file (see Figure 18-11).

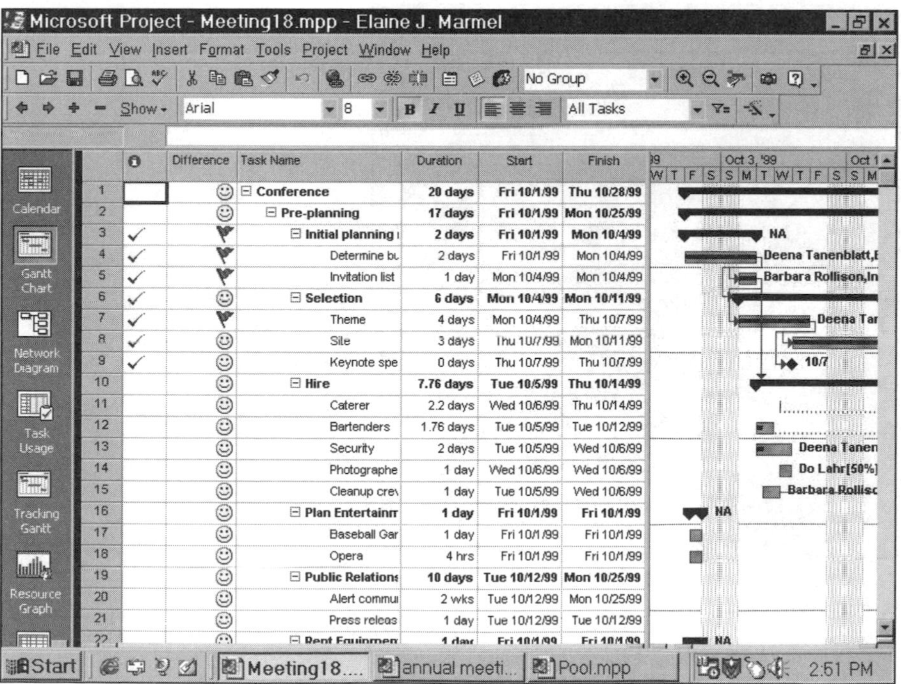


**Figure 18-11:** By default, you'll see multiple icons for Project on the Windows taskbar when you open multiple projects.

Starting with Office 2000 products, users have the ability to see individual icons in the Windows taskbar for each open Office file. Project 2000, as part of the Office family, also contains this feature.

While you can't necessarily identify the file from the icon on the Windows taskbar, you can see a few letters of the filename on the icon; in addition, if you point the mouse at the icon, you'll see a ToolTip showing the entire path and filename.

Suppose you belong to the school of users who don't *want* individual icons on the Windows taskbar for each open file — you believe that makes working harder, not easier. You can reinstate the behavior of earlier versions of Project by removing the check from the Windows in taskbar box on the View tab of the Options dialog box (see Figure 18-12).

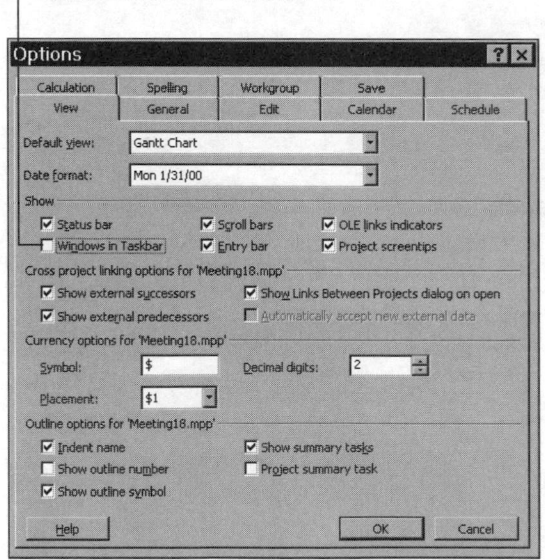


**Figure 18-12:** To reintroduce the behavior of earlier versions of Project, remove the check from the Windows in Taskbar checkbox.

Regardless of the behavior you choose, all open Project files will appear at the bottom of the Windows menu, and you can switch between Project files using the Windows menu in Project or the Windows taskbar.

## Saving Project files

Using the Save tab of the Options dialog box (see Figure 18-13), you can set several defaults.

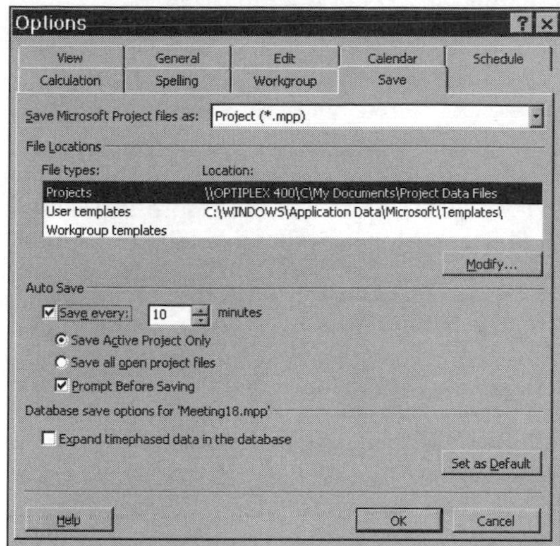


**Figure 18-13:** Project has several new features associated with saving files.

The Save tab in the Options dialog box is new to Project 2000.

✦ Using the "Save Microsoft Project files as" list box, you can specify the file format for each new Project file that you save. For example, you can save all Project 2000 files in Project 98 format if you regularly share files with someone who uses Project 98.

If you save files you create in Project 2000 in the format of an earlier version of Project, you may lose information. For example, WBS and outline codes don't exist in any version of Project prior to Project 2000. If you use them in a file and then save the file in Project 98 format, you'll lose them.

✦ You can set a default file location to save all files, user templates, and workgroup templates. By setting this location, you won't need to navigate to the correct folder each time you want to save a new file.

✦ Use Project 2000's Auto Save feature to save project files on a regular basis. The Auto Save feature is particularly valuable to people who tend to work extensively and forget to save regularly — and become victims of power failures. If you use Auto Save, you'll be able to open your file as of the last automatic save.

✦ You can choose to expand timephased data in the database.

# Using the Organizer

Project uses the Organizer to help you share views, tables, forms, reports, and more between projects. To display the Organizer dialog box, choose View ➪ More Views. Project displays the More Views dialog box shown in Figure 18-14. Click the Organizer button to display the Organizer dialog box shown in Figure 18-15.

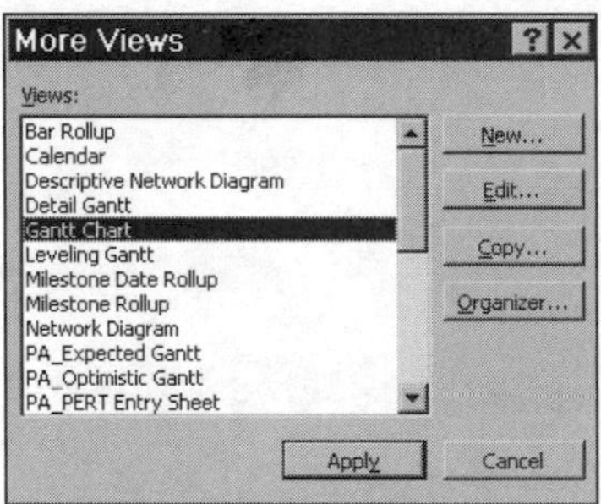


**Figure 18-14:** You display the Organizer by clicking the Organizer button in the More Views dialog box.

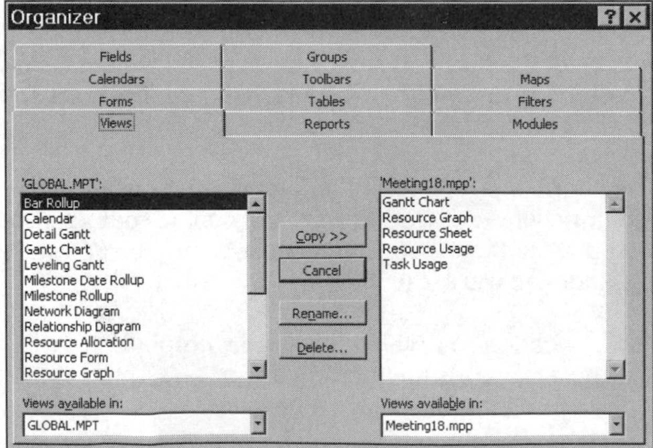


**Figure 18-15:** All views in the Global template (Global.mpt) file are available to every file based on the Global.mpt file.

Use the various tabs in the Organizer dialog box to copy elements from the Global template (Global.mpt) to the current project. You also can copy elements from the current project to the Global template or simply between projects. Use the views available in list boxes at the bottom of the Organizer to select files to use when copying elements.

Note

When you copy an element to the Global template, that element becomes available to all files created with your copy of Project.

## Making changes to toolbars

Toolbars are to Windows software what remote controls are to television: effortless, hi-tech ways to take action. Toolbars are easy to use and always right at hand. However, you and Microsoft might not agree on which tools you use most often.

You can easily modify the arrangement of tools in Project. You can add or remove tools from a toolbar, change the function of a tool, create your own set of tools, or even edit the look of tools.

You can make changes to your Project environment effective for your copy of Project alone, for those in a group, or across your company. Project saves your changes to a file named Global.mpt and opens new projects based on the Global file by default; consequently, your changes remain intact. You can use the Organizer to make the changed Global file available to others.

### Combining or separating toolbars

Throughout this book, you've seen the Standard toolbar on a separate row from the Formatting toolbar — much like they appeared in Project 98 and earlier versions. If screen real estate is vital to you, consider placing the toolbars on the same row, as you see in Figure 18-16. When you use this feature, Project initially displays the tools that Microsoft thinks users use most often. If you need a tool that you don't see, you click the More Buttons tool to display a hidden palette of additional available buttons (see Figure 18-17). Once you select a tool from the hidden palette, that tool appears on the toolbar, replacing the least used tool if necessary. As you work, the toolbars become personalized to your work habits, displaying the tools you use most often.

In Project 2000, the Standard and Formatting toolbars can share the same row onscreen, increasing the screen "real estate" available for your project information. Also, menus can show only the most recently used commands.

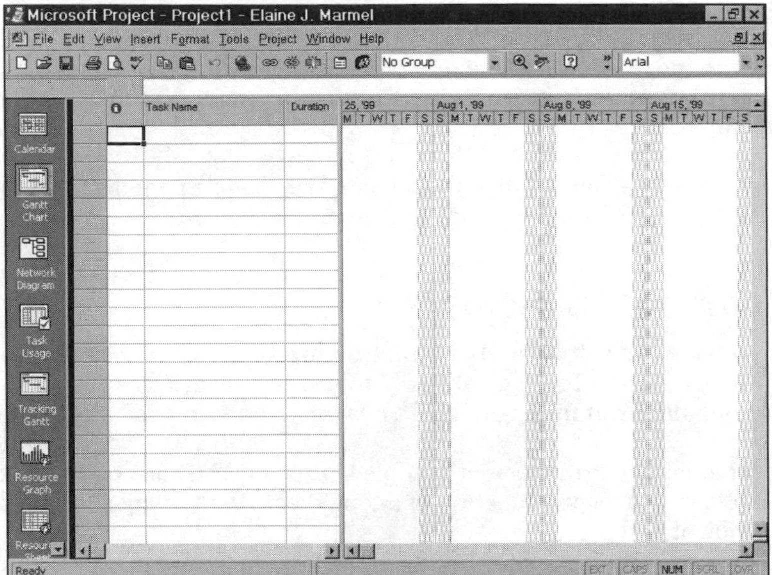


**Figure 18-16:** You can make the Standard and Formatting toolbars share a row onscreen.

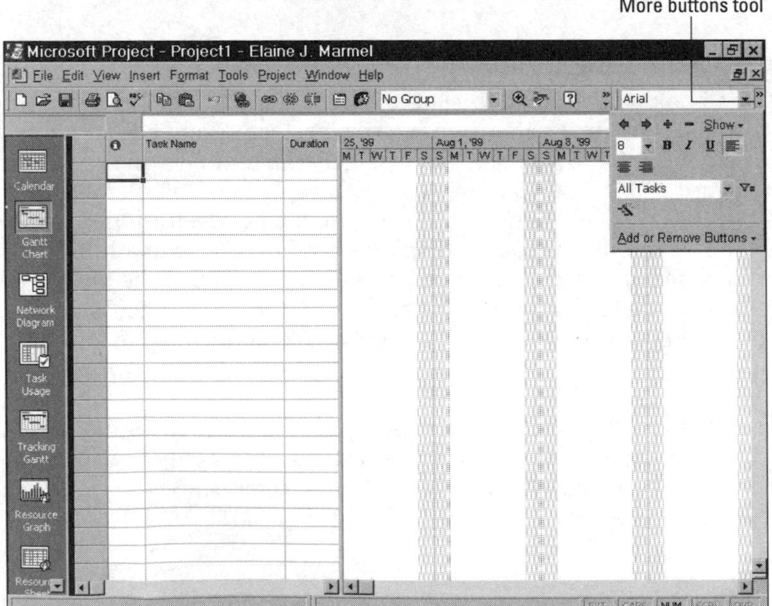


**Figure 18-17:** You can select a button you don't see initially by opening the hidden palette.

In a similar fashion, you can personalize the menus in Project to display the commands you use most frequently. When you enable this behavior and open a menu, you see a limited set of commands. At the bottom of the menu, you see the Expand arrows pointing down (see Figure 18-18). When you click the Expand arrows, the rest of the commands on the menu appear. The hidden commands appear on a lighter background than the more frequently used commands (see Figure 18-19). Like the tools on the toolbars, if you select a "hidden" command, it becomes a "frequently used" command and appears on the abbreviated menu the next time that you open the menu.

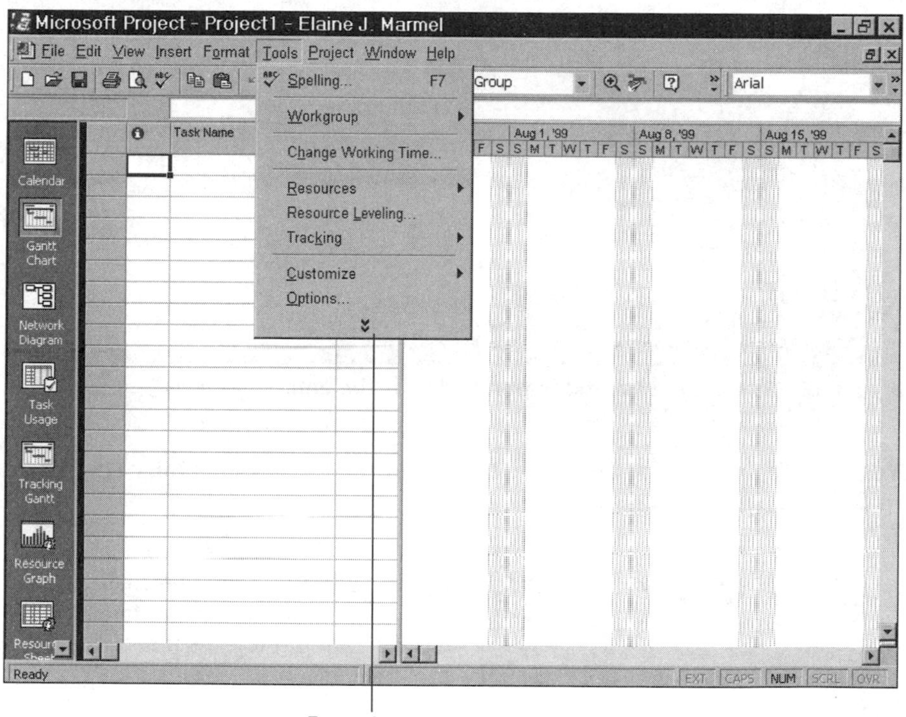


**Figure 18-18:** Initially, only some commands appear on the menu.

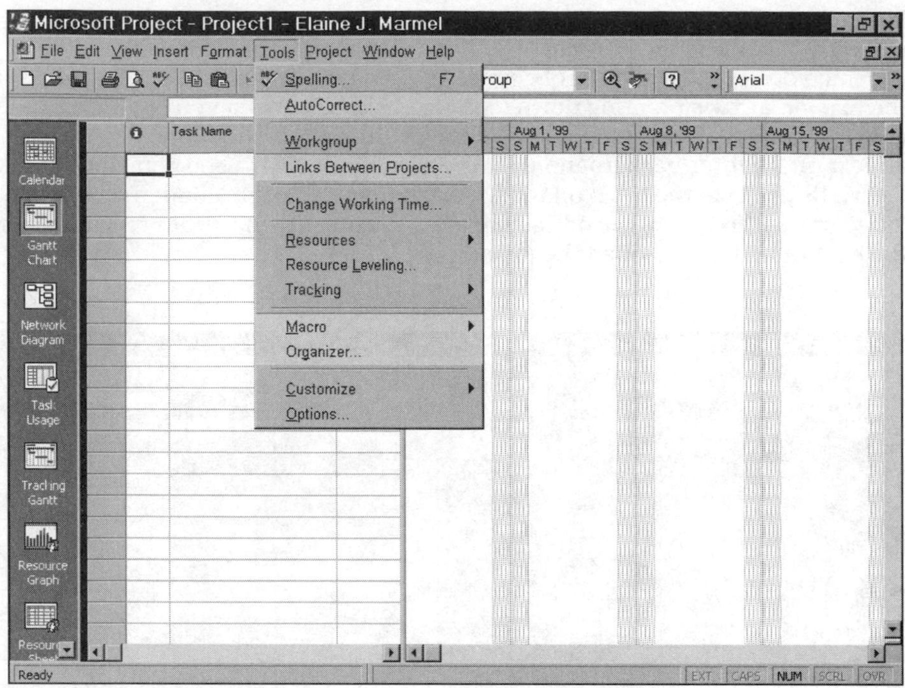

**Figure 18-19:** Click the Expand button to display the entire menu.

You control this toolbar and menu behavior from the Options tab of the Customize dialog box (see Figure 18-20).

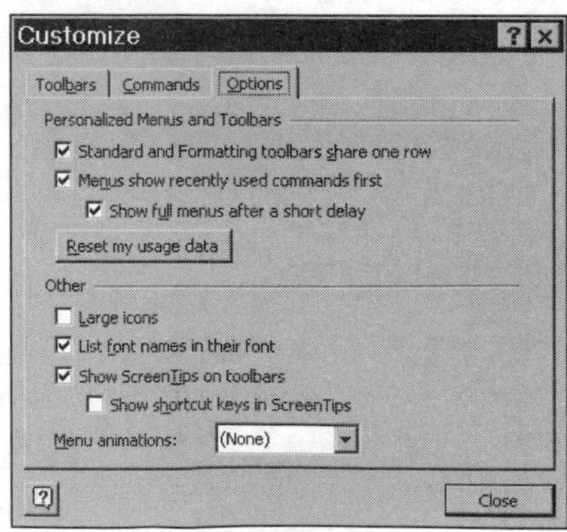

**Figure 18-20:** Use the Personalized Menus and Toolbars section to control the behavior of Project's menus and toolbars.

## Adding and deleting tools from a toolbar

Although toolbars include many commonly used functions, they aren't all-inclusive. For example, the Formatting toolbar includes commands to change the font and font size; apply bold, italic, and underline effects; and align tasks. But it doesn't include tools for modifying the timescale, gridlines, or bar styles. If you use those features often, you might want to add them. Alternatively, you might prefer to have a tool that appears on one toolbar by default appear on the Standard toolbar instead.

To add tools to any toolbar, locate the tool in the appropriate category and then drag it onto the toolbar where you want it to appear. Follow these steps to add a tool to a toolbar:

1. Choose View ⇨ Toolbars ⇨ Customize to open the Customize dialog box shown in Figure 18-21 and click the Toolbars tab.

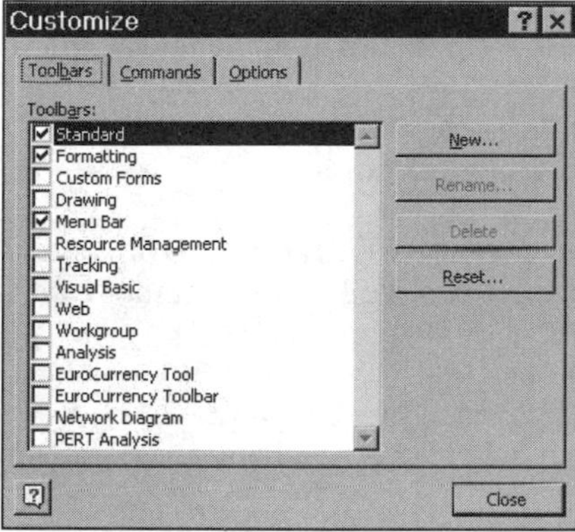


**Figure 18-21:** The toolbars that have a checkmark here are currently displayed onscreen.

2. Click the checkbox for the toolbar on which you want to place the tool so that Project displays that toolbar. For example, if you want to add the Paste as Hyperlink button to the Web toolbar, make sure the Web toolbar is displayed.
3. Click the Commands tab, shown in Figure 18-22.
4. Click the category of command that contains the tool you want to add to a toolbar. For example, the Paste as Hyperlink tool appears in the Edit category because that category is where cutting, copying, and pasting tools typically reside.

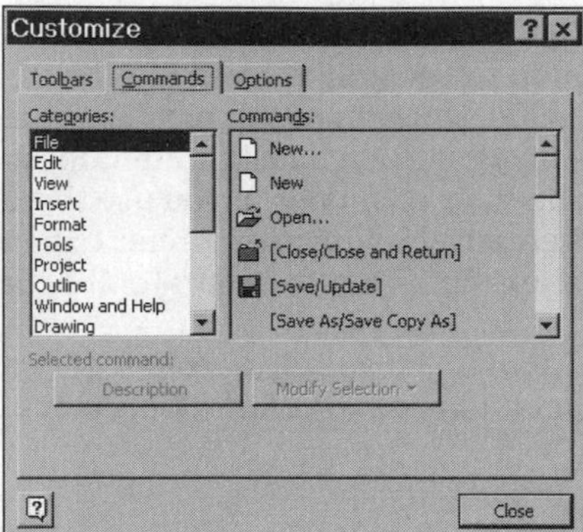


**Figure 18-22:** These categories of commands contain all the possible tools built into Project.

Tip

If you don't know the category to which a tool command belongs, use the scroll bar in the Categories list and select All Commands at the bottom of the list. The Commands list displays every available command in alphabetical order.

5. Click the item in the Commands list, drag it from the dialog box onto your screen, and place it on the toolbar of your choice.

You also can easily remove a tool from a toolbar. With the Customize dialog box open, display the toolbar that contains the tool you want to remove and drag the tool off the toolbar.

Note

To restore a toolbar's original settings, open the Customize dialog box, select the Toolbars tab, click the toolbar name in the list of toolbars, and click Reset. Project restores the default tools.

## Creating custom toolbars

Rather than modifying some of Project's toolbars, you might prefer to create a custom toolbar that contains all the tools you use most often. You create custom toolbars from the Customize dialog box by following these steps:

1. Display the Toolbars tab of the Customize dialog box.
2. Click the New button. The New Toolbar dialog box shown in Figure 18-23 appears.

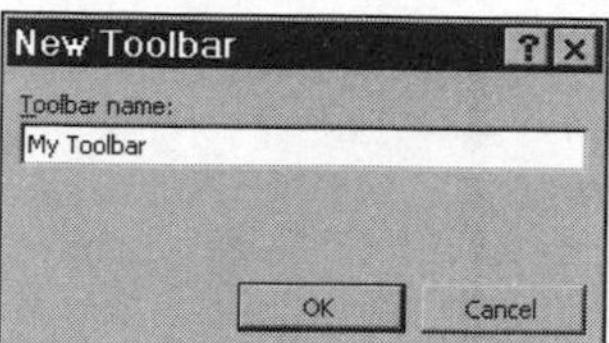


**Figure 18-23:** Name your toolbar anything you like—perhaps after your spouse, your pet, or your favorite movie star.

3. Type a toolbar name and click OK. A small toolbar, devoid of tools at the moment, appears. You can drag this floating toolbar to any location on the screen that's convenient for you.
4. Click the Commands tab to select it.
5. Click tools in any category and then drag them onto the new toolbar. The new toolbar resembles the toolbar in Figure 18-24.

**Figure 18-24:** Place these tools in any order you like. If you want to move a tool, drag it off the toolbar and place it again.

6. Add dividers (thin gray lines) to separate groups of tools on your new toolbar. Select the tool that you want to place to the right of the divider and click the Modify Selection button on the Commands tab. The menu shown in Figure 18-25 appears.

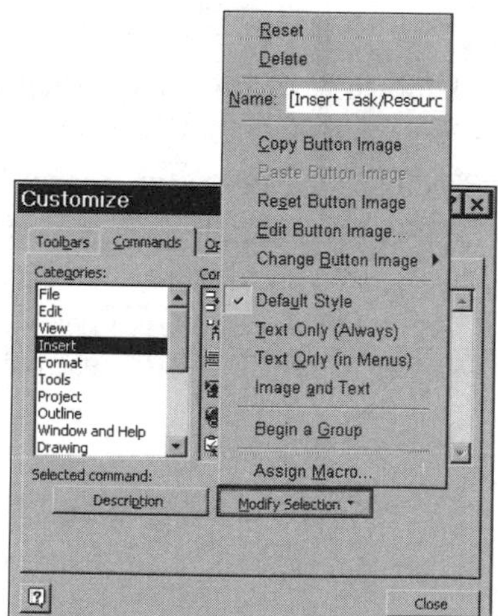


**Figure 18-25:** This menu offers options to work with button images, as well as options to modify other toolbar features.

7. Select the Begin a Group command from this menu to insert a divider in your toolbar, as shown in Figure 18-26.

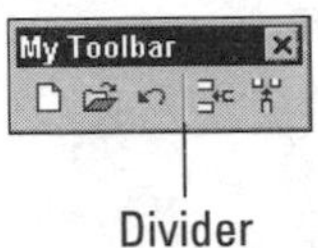


**Figure 18-26:** Place a divider on a toolbar to make logical groupings of tools that perform certain types of functions.

To delete a divider, select the tool to its right and, using the Modify Selection pop-up menu, select Begin a Group again to deselect that command.

## Changing and editing button images

Don't like the little pictures Microsoft assigned to its tools? Feeling creative? Project enables you to select from a whole set of other button designs, from smiling faces to musical notes, or to edit a button image yourself with picture and color tools.

If anyone else uses your copy of Project, be cautious about changing tool images. Someone accustomed to Project's standard tool images might press a button and, unaware of its true function, do damage or simply not be able to function with your copy of Project. And you aren't immune from forgetting the changes you made.

To change the images that appear on tools, follow these steps:

1. Choose Views ➪ Toolbars ➪ Customize to open the Customize dialog box.
2. Click the Commands tab to select it.
3. Click a tool on any toolbar you have displayed. (If you need to display a toolbar, you can select it on the Toolbars tab of this dialog box.)
4. Click the Modify Selection button and select Change Button Image. The pop-up palette of images shown in Figure 18-27 appears.

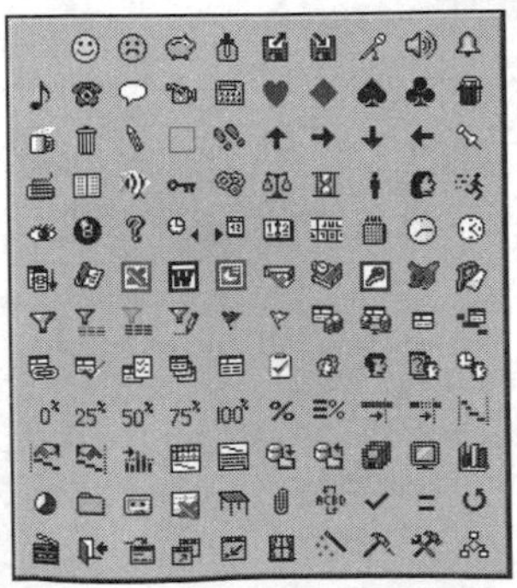

**Figure 18-27:** From an hourglass to an eight ball, these images are both clever and descriptive.

5. Click an image you want to use.

To return an image to its original setting, choose Modify Selection ➪ Reset Button Image.

6. Click Close to close the Customize dialog box when you finish.

ToolTips still work with modified buttons and are a great help in remembering what function a button performs. Just pass your mouse pointer over any tool, and its original name appears.

If you prefer, rather than replacing the button image with a predefined picture, you can edit the existing picture by modifying the pattern and colors on it. For example, if two tools seem similar to you, help yourself differentiate them by applying a bright red color to either one. Button images comprise many tiny squares called pixels. By coloring in the pixels, you can form an image. You can use a color palette and the individual pixels to modify button images or even draw an entirely new image.

To edit a button image, follow these steps, starting from the Customize dialog box Commands tab:

1. Click a tool on any displayed toolbar and then click Modify Selection.
2. Select the Edit Button Image command to open the Button Editor dialog box in Figure 18-28.

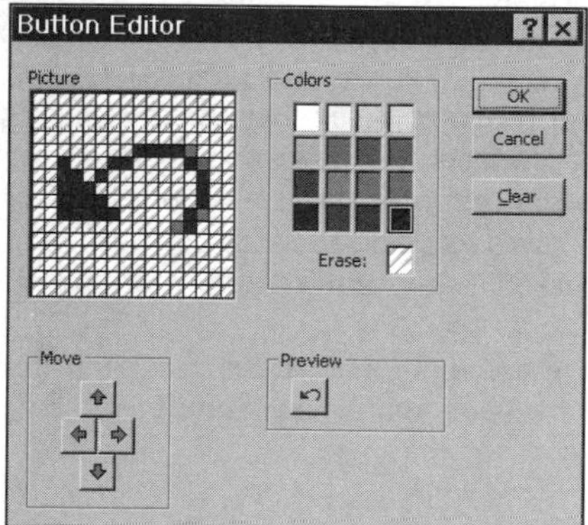


**Figure 18-28:** The small Preview helps you see how changes to individual picture pixels will appear on the button image.

3. Try the following techniques:

   - To make changes to an image, click a color block in the Colors palette and then click an individual pixel.
   - To remove color from a pixel, click the Erase block in the Colors palette and then click the pixel.

To color in or erase a large area of pixels, click a color in the palette or the Erase block, then click a pixel, and then drag your cursor in any direction to color or erase multiple pixels in one motion. Release your cursor to stop painting or erasing the pixels.

   - To see more of a large button that doesn't fit in the Picture box, use the Move arrows to move from side to side or up and down to display the image's edges.

4. Click OK to save your changes and to return to the Customize dialog box. Click Close to return to your Project screen.

## Customizing project menus

Toolbars aren't the only way to get things done in Project, and they aren't the only elements in Project that you can customize. You also can create new menus and modify existing menus to your heart's content. For example, you could add a command to the File menu that changes the current view to the Network Diagram view and prints a report. You can add these functions because menu commands are actually *macros,* that is, recorded series of keystrokes or programming commands.

Macros are really a form of computer program. Visual Basic is the macro-programming language you use in Microsoft products. In a macro, you save a string of commands that instruct the software to perform one or more actions. Project provides an easy method for selecting commands to associate with a macro and for saving the macro as a custom menu command. See Chapter 19 for more on macros.

When you select a menu command, you are really running a macro, telling Project to repeat the sequence of events that copies a selected piece of text, causes a dialog box to appear, and so on.

You can use your own macros and Project's built-in commands to customize Project by building new menus and changing the function of existing commands. Or, you can delete menus or commands on menus that you don't need.

## Adding menus

To add a new menu to your Project menu bar, you follow a process similar to that used to add a new toolbar. First you drag a new, blank menu to the menu bar, then you assign it a name, and finally you drag commands onto it.

Note

As with toolbars, Project adds new menus to your Global file, the default file on which all project files are based. Therefore, changes you make to menus or the menu bar are, in effect, for all files you create with this copy of Project.

Follow these steps to add a new menu to Project:

1. Choose View ⇨ Toolbars ⇨ Customize to open the Customize dialog box.
2. Make sure the menu bar is showing on your screen; if it's not, click the menu bar item on the Toolbars tab of the Customize dialog box.
3. Click the Commands tab to select it.
4. Scroll to the bottom of the list of Categories and click the category named "New Menu." The single selection, New Menu, appears in the list of Commands, as in Figure 18-29.

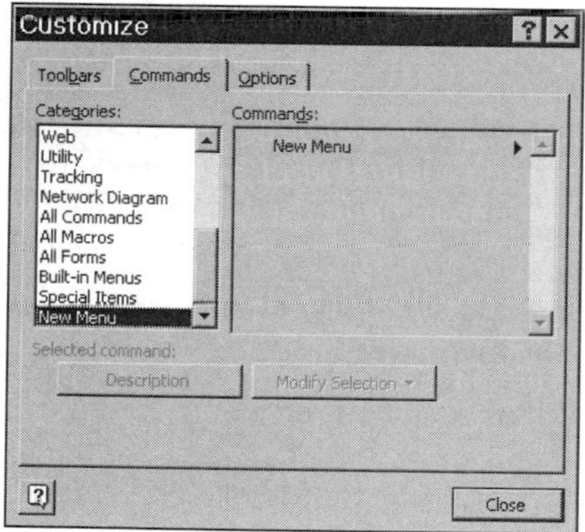


**Figure 18-29:** The New Menu category has only one command in it.

5. Click the New Menu item in the Commands list and drag it up to the menu bar. When the dark vertical line of your mouse pointer appears where you want to place the new menu, release the mouse button. Project places a New Menu item on the menu bar.
6. Select the New Menu and click Modify Selection. From the new pop-up menu (see Figure 18-30), highlight New Menu and type a specific menu name. Then click outside the Modify Selection menu to close it.

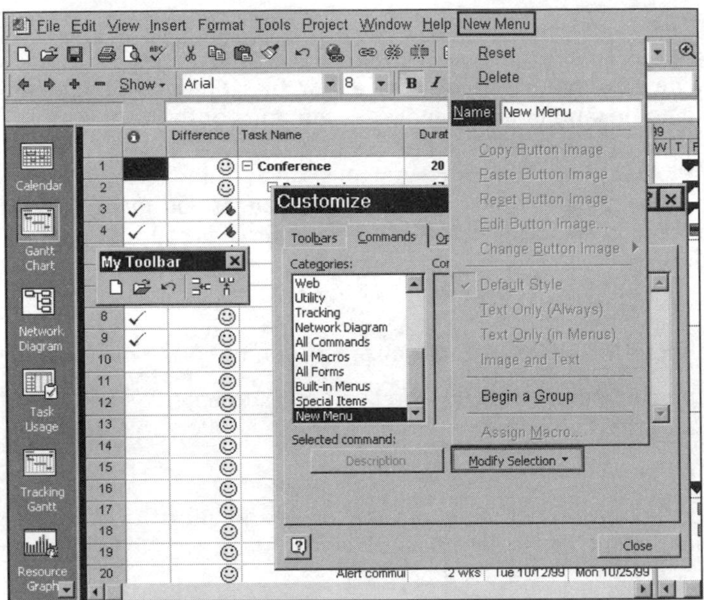


**Figure 18-30:** The menu name should help you remember what kinds of commands it contains.

7. Select a category of command that you want to place on the new menu. If you have created a macro and want to place it on the menu, select the category All Macros, which includes standard menu command macros as well as macros you've created.

8. Drag an item in the Commands list up to the New Menu on the menu bar. A small, blank box appears under the menu heading.

9. Place the mouse pointer in that blank area and release the mouse button to place the command on the menu.

10. Click Close to close the Customize dialog box.

You can repeat Steps 7 through 9 to build the new menu. To divide the menu into groups of commands, you can use Modify Selection ➪ Begin a Group to add dividing lines.

## Assigning new commands

You might also want to modify the function of an existing menu command. For example, if you create a macro that invokes the Print command and accepts all the Print dialog box defaults for you, you could assign that macro to the Print command. That way you don't have the extra step of clicking OK to accept print defaults every time you print. As always, be careful about replacing the function of one command with another if other people will be using your copy of Project.

You can reinstate all the menu defaults by opening the Toolbars tab in the Customize dialog box, clicking the Menu Bar item, and clicking Reset.

To change the macro associated with a command, follow these steps:

1. Display the Customize dialog box (View ➪ Toolbars ➪ Customize).
2. Open the menu on which you want to edit a command.
3. Right-click the command you want to change; the menu in Figure 18-31 appears.

**Figure 18-31:** You can use this menu to add a button image next to a menu command.

4. Select the Assign Macro command from this menu to open the Customize Tool dialog box shown in Figure 18-32.

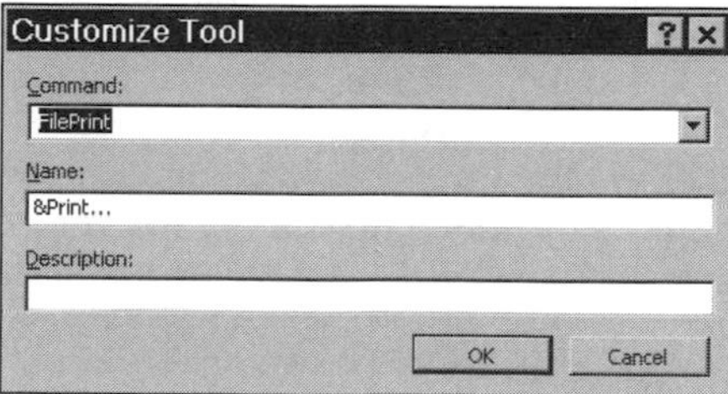


**Figure 18-32:** The Name entry in the Customize Tool dialog box is the name of the macro it invokes.

5. Click the Command drop-down list and select the command you want to associate with the menu item.
6. Type a Description of what this command does (optional).
7. Click OK to return to the Customize dialog box and then click Close to save the new command with the menu item.

### Deleting commands and menus

Is your screen getting cluttered with custom commands and menus? To remove a particular command or a whole menu without resetting all the menu changes you've made, follow these steps:

1. Open the Customize dialog box.
2. Click a menu name, or open the menu and click a particular command.
3. Drag the item off the menu bar and close the Customize dialog box.

That's all there is to it!

## Summary

In this chapter you've learned how to:

- ✦ Work with custom fields to create data entry value lists and formulas
- ✦ Modify Project's behavior to display only one icon on the Windows taskbar or to display an icon for each open project
- ✦ Take advantage of the new features for saving your projects
- ✦ Display the Standard and Formatting toolbars on the same row or on separate rows
- ✦ Customize the features (toolbars and menus) you use to get things done

In the next chapter you learn details about creating your own macros, which can form the basis for new tools and menus and streamline the repetitive tasks you perform to create and track a schedule.

✦ ✦ ✦

CHAPTER 19

# Using Macros to Speed Your Work

✦ ✦ ✦ ✦

**In This Chapter**

Why use macros?

Recording macros

Running macros

Using shortcuts to run macros

✦ ✦ ✦ ✦

Macros are small programs that carry out repetitive tasks you perform frequently. You may have used macros in a word processing program; macros work the same way in Project as they do in your word processor.

Don't let the word "program" in the preceding paragraph deter you from learning about macros. Although you can actually work with the macro programming code, Project provides an easier way for you to write a macro, as you learn in this chapter.

## Why Use Macros?

Macros are most useful when you need to perform any repetitive task. In particular, you can use Project macros to:

- ✦ Display or hide frequently used toolbars
- ✦ Display frequently used tables
- ✦ Display frequently used views
- ✦ Switch to a custom view
- ✦ Generate standard reports

As you learn to use Project, you'll identify the steps you take over and over again; these tasks are excellent candidates for macros.

# Recording Macros

Project stores macros in the Visual Basic for Applications programming language. And if you're adept at programming, you can write your macro directly in the Visual Basic for Applications programming language. A sample of the instructions stored in a macro in Visual Basic appears in Figure 19-1.

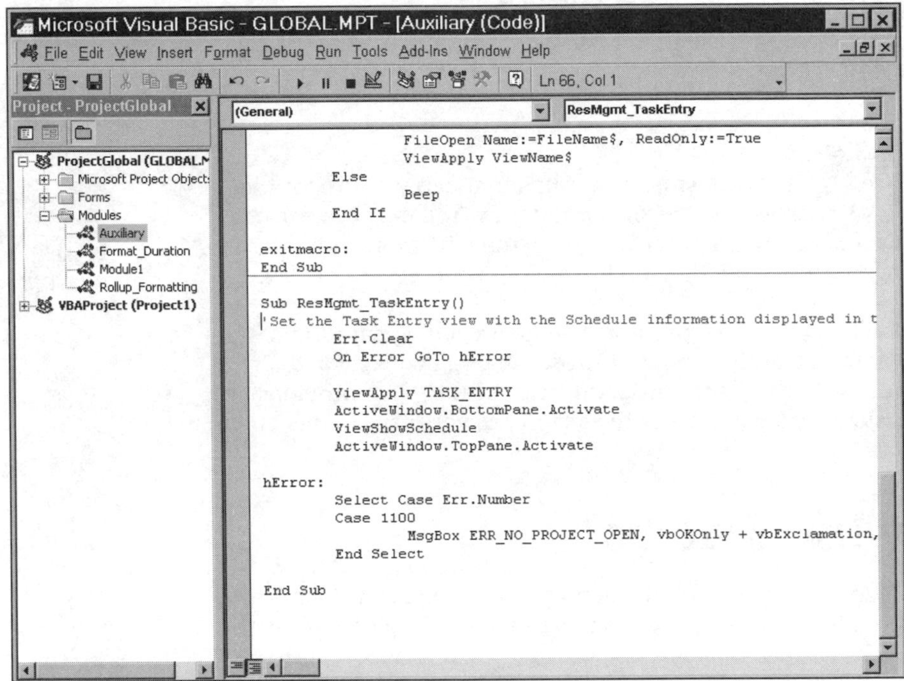


**Figure 19-1:** A sample set of instructions stored in a macro

Most people prefer to record a macro. When you record a macro, you have Project memorize the steps you want to take and store those steps. That is, you do whatever it is you want Project to do; Project converts those actions into Visual Basic statements and stores the statements in a macro. Later, when you want to take that action again, you run your macro, which you learn how to do in the next section.

Before you record a macro, you should run through the steps that you want to take. You might even want to write down the steps. That way, you are less likely to make (and record) mistakes.

Suppose you want to create a macro that displays the Task Details Form in the bottom pane when you display the Gantt Chart view. Here are the steps you need to record for this macro:

1. Click Gantt Chart in the View bar.

By selecting the view first, you force Project to start your macro from the Gantt Chart view, regardless of the view you were using before you ran your macro.

2. Use the split bar (or choose Window ➪ Split) to open the bottom pane that shows, by default, the Task Form view.
3. Click the bottom pane and choose View ➪ More Views to open the More Views dialog box.
4. Select the Task Details Form.
5. Click Apply.

Now that you know what you're going to record, use the following steps to record the macro:

1. Choose Tools ➪ Macro ➪ Record New Macro to open the Record Macro dialog box you see in Figure 19-2.

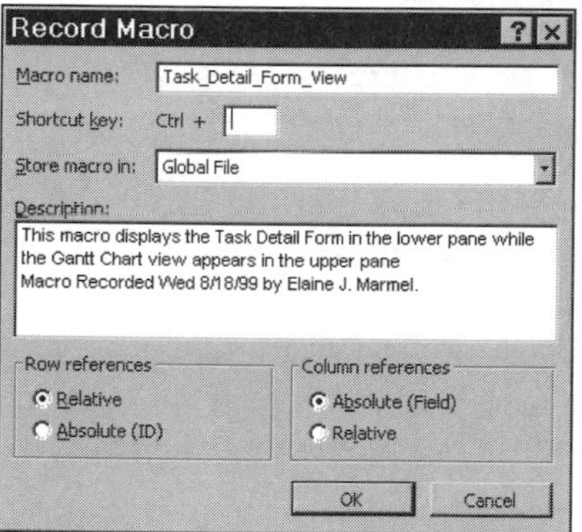


**Figure 19-2:** The Record Macro dialog box

2. Enter a name for the macro in the Macro name box.

The first character of the macro name must be a letter, but the other characters can be letters, numbers, or underscore characters. You cannot include a space in a macro name, so try using an underscore character as a word separator or capitalize the first letter of each word.

3. (Optional) To assign the macro to a keyboard shortcut, type a letter in the Shortcut key box. The letter you assign can be any letter key on your keyboard, but it cannot be a number or a special character. You also cannot assign a key combination that is already used by Microsoft Project; if you select a reserved letter, Project displays the warning message shown in Figure 19-3 when you click OK.

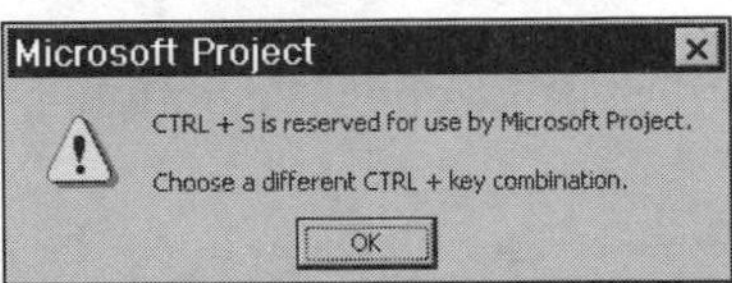


**Figure 19-3:** Project displays this warning message if you select a keyboard shortcut already in use.

Keyboard shortcuts are only one way you can run a macro. Later in this chapter you learn the other methods to play back a macro as well as how to assign a keyboard shortcut after you've recorded and stored your macro.

4. Open the "Store macro in" box and click the location where you want to store the macro. You can store the macro in the Global File or in the current project. To make a macro available to all projects, select Global File.

The Global File is also called the Global template, and it acts like the Normal template in Word or the Book1 template in Excel. Any customized features, such as macros, toolbars, or menus, that you store in the Global File are available to any project file. On the other hand, customized features you store in an individual project file are available only to that file.

5. Type a description of the purpose of the macro or the function it performs in the Description box. This description appears whenever you run the macro from the Macro dialog box.

6. Use the options in the Row references and Column references boxes to control the way the macro selects rows and columns if you select cells while running a macro. For rows, the macro always selects rows regardless of the position of the active cell because it records relative references to rows. If you want a macro to always select the same row, regardless of which cell is first selected, select Absolute (ID).

For columns, the macro always selects the same column each time it is run, regardless of which cell is first selected, because it records absolute references to columns. If you want a macro to select columns regardless of the position of the active cell when you run the macro, select Relative.

7. Click OK. Project redisplays your project, and you won't notice any differences, but Project is now recording each action you take.
8. Take all the actions you want to record.
9. Choose Tools ➪ Macro ➪ Stop Recorder (see Figure 19-4) to stop recording.

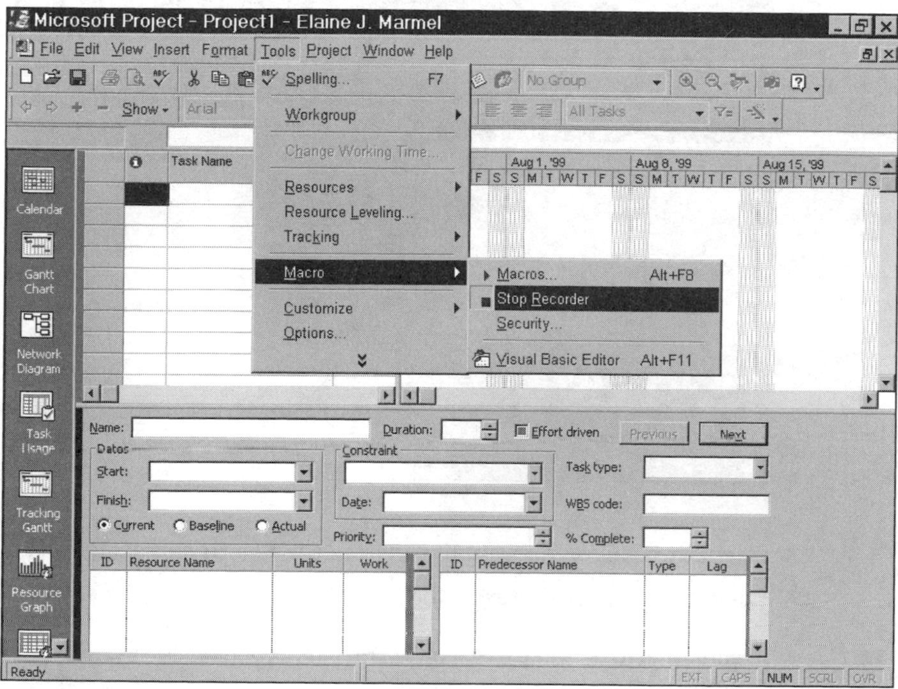

**Figure 19-4:** When you're recording a macro, the Stop Recorder command is available.

# Running Macros

To use a macro that you have recorded, you run the macro. Some people refer to this action as "playing back" the macro because they associate recording and playing back with the process of recording a TV program on a VCR and then playing back the recording.

If your macro makes substantial changes to your project, you should save the project before you run the macro. You can't undo the effects of a macro easily. To run a macro, follow these steps:

1. Open the project that contains the macro; if you stored the macro in the Global file, you can open any project.
2. Choose Tools ➪ Macro ➪ Macros to open the Macros dialog box you see in Figure 19-5.

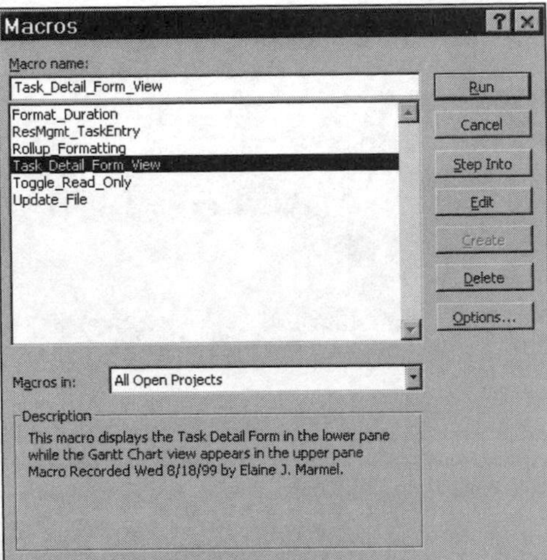


**Figure 19-5:** The Macros dialog box

3. Select the macro you want to run from the Macro name list.
4. Click Run. Project performs the steps you recorded in the macro.

If your macro is long and you want to stop it while it's still running, press Ctrl+Break. If your macro is short, it will probably finish before you can stop it.

# Using Shortcuts to Run Macros

Although you can run macros by selecting them from the Macro dialog box, if you use a macro on a regular basis, you might want to shorten the method for running the macro. You can create one of the following:

- ✦ A toolbar button that runs the macro
- ✦ A menu command that runs the macro
- ✦ A keyboard shortcut that runs the macro

## Assigning a macro to a toolbar button

Suppose you're a fan of toolbar buttons, and you create a macro that you use a lot. You find yourself wishing for a toolbar button that you could click to make your macro run. Well, you can get your wish by adding a button to a toolbar and assigning your macro to that button.

Adding buttons to the toolbars that come with Project isn't always a good idea. If you add a toolbar button to one of the toolbars that comes with Project and you reset that toolbar, the button you added disappears.

The following steps explain how to add a button assigned to a macro to the Standard toolbar, but you can also add toolbar buttons for macros to a custom toolbar you create.

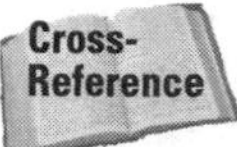


Chapter 18 explains how to create a custom toolbar.

1. Check to see whether the toolbar to which you want to add a button appears on screen. If it does, go to Step 2. Otherwise, display the toolbar by right-clicking any toolbar button and choosing the toolbar from the shortcut menu that appears.
2. Choose View ➪ Toolbars ➪ Customize to open the Customize dialog box.

You can also open the Customize dialog box by choosing Tools ➪ Customize ➪ Toolbars.

3. Choose Commands to display the Commands tab shown in Figure 19-6.

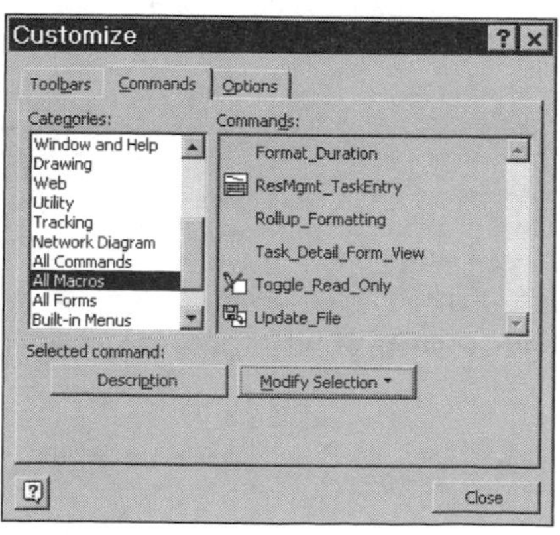


**Figure 19-6:** From the Commands tab of the Customize dialog box, you can add macros as buttons to toolbars.

4. Scroll down the Categories list and select All Macros. Project displays a list of macros in the Commands list on the right side of the dialog box.
5. Drag the macro you want to add onto the desired toolbar (see Figure 19-7). As you drag, the mouse pointer image changes to include a small button and a plus sign. As you move the mouse pointer over a toolbar, a large insertion point marks the location where the button appears when you release the mouse button.
6. Release the mouse button and a new button appears on the toolbar, as shown in Figure 19-8. The name of the button is so long that Project wrapped the Standard toolbar onto a second row.

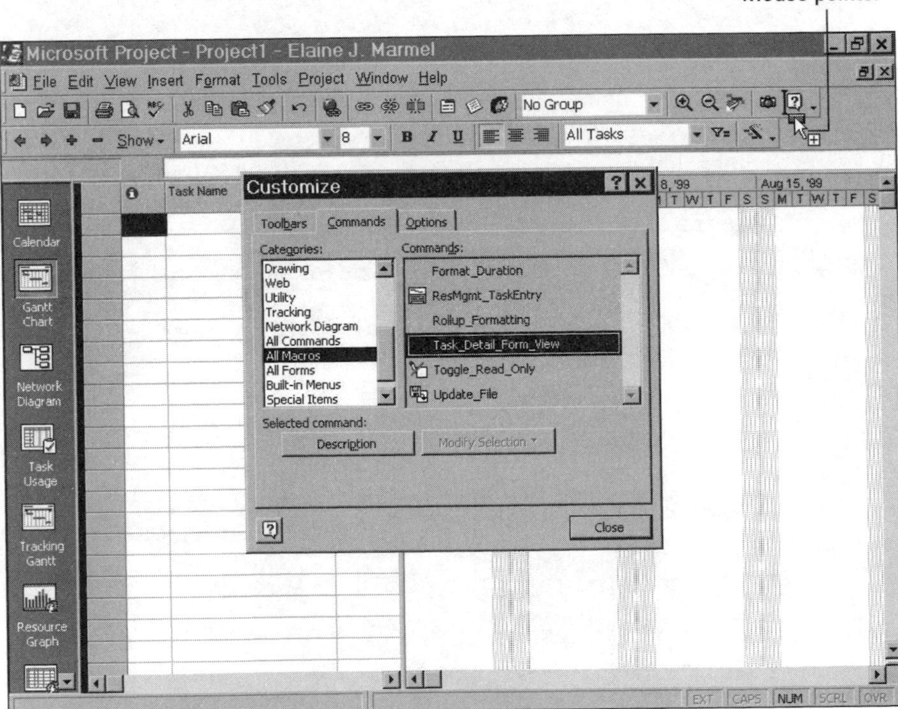


**Figure 19-7:** The image of the mouse pointer icon changes as you drag a macro onto the Standard toolbar.

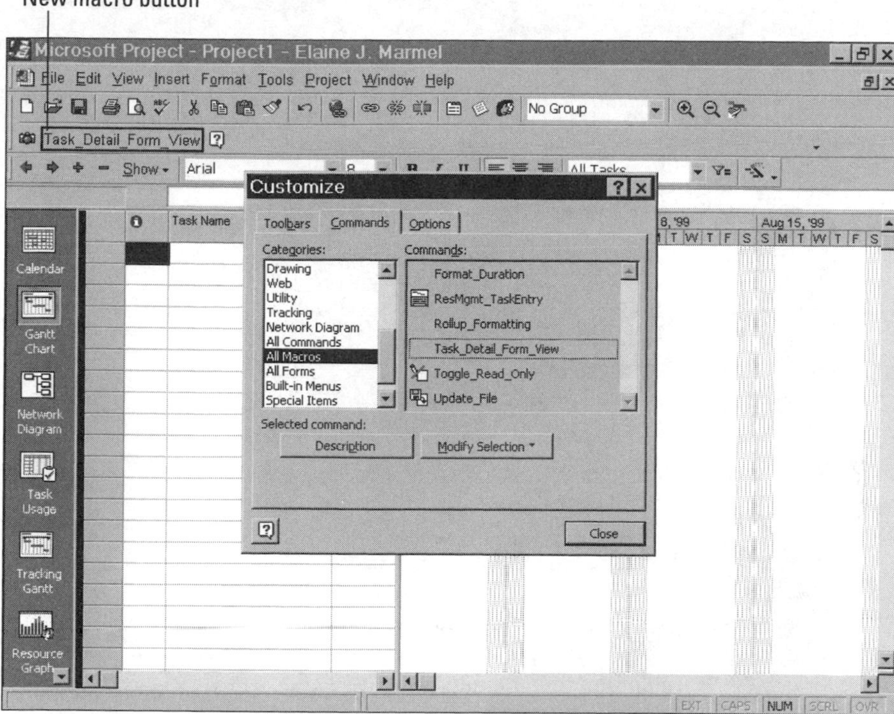


**Figure 19-8:** The new button after dropping it on the toolbar

If you're concerned about using excessive screen real estate, you may want to take advantage of the new feature in Project 2000 that permits the Standard toolbar and the Formatting toolbar to share the same row. Buttons not used frequently reside on a hidden palette. See Chapter 18 for more information on interface changes and Project 2000.

7. To change the name on the toolbar button, click Modify Selection in the Customize dialog box to open the pop-up menu shown in Figure 19-9.
8. Type the name, exactly as you want it to appear on the toolbar button, into the Name box. You can include spaces.

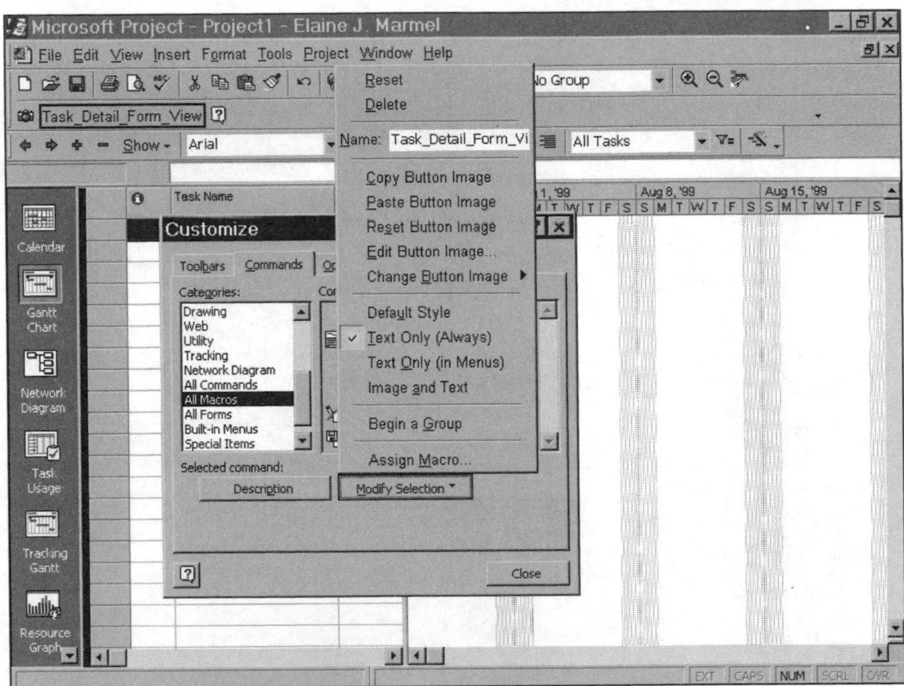


**Figure 19-9:** The menu that appears when you click the Modify Selection button to change a macro button's name

9. Press Enter. The pop-up menu disappears, and Project renames the macro toolbar button, as shown in Figure 19-10.

10. Close the Customize dialog box.

When you add a toolbar button to an existing toolbar, Microsoft Project saves it in your Global file. Any other project files you open on your computer using that Global file contain the new toolbar button.

If you change your mind and don't want the button on the toolbar, you can remove it by opening the Customize dialog box and then simply dragging the button off the toolbar and dropping it anywhere on your project. The button disappears, but the macro is still available.

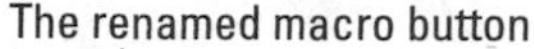


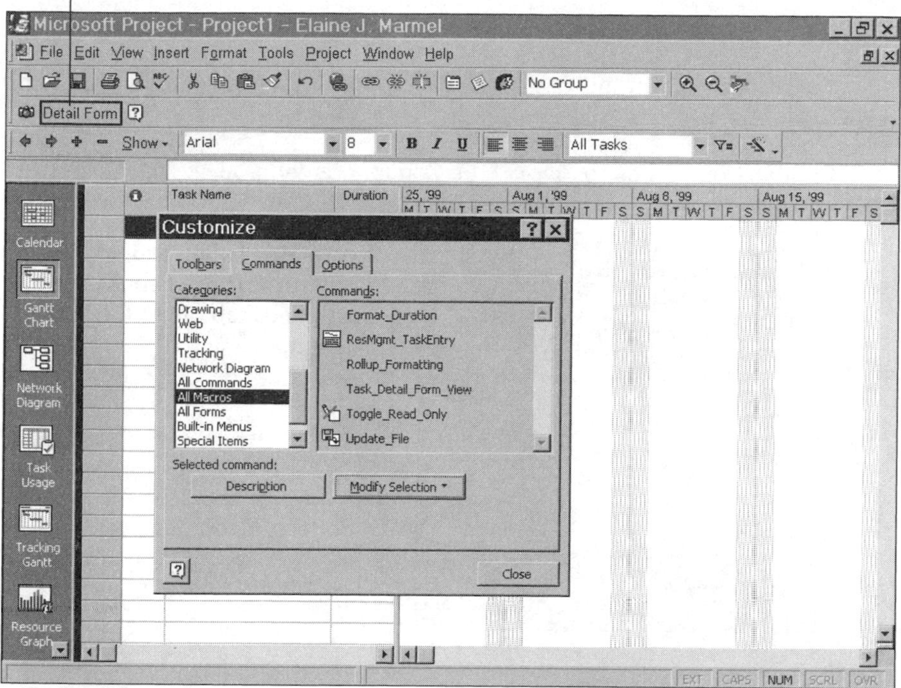


**Figure 19-10:** The toolbar button after renaming it

# Assigning a macro to a menu command

Maybe you're not a toolbar person, or maybe you just prefer to use menu commands. This section shows you how to add a command assigned to a macro to the Tools menu.

As with toolbars, be aware that adding commands to the menus that come with Project isn't always a good idea. If you add a command to one of the standard menus and you reset that menu, the command you added will disappear.

You can also add commands for macros to custom menus you create, and if you don't want your custom menu to appear all the time, you can create a custom toolbar and drag menus onto it. Then you can hide or display the toolbar as needed.

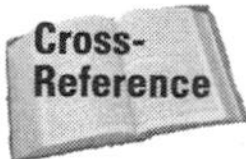


See Chapter 18 for information on creating custom menus and toolbars.

Follow these steps to add a command that runs your macro from a menu:

1. Choose View ➪ Toolbars ➪ Customize to open the Customize dialog box.

Tip

You also can open the Customize dialog box by choosing Tools ➪ Customize ➪ Toolbars.

2. Choose Commands to display the Commands tab you see in Figure 19-11.

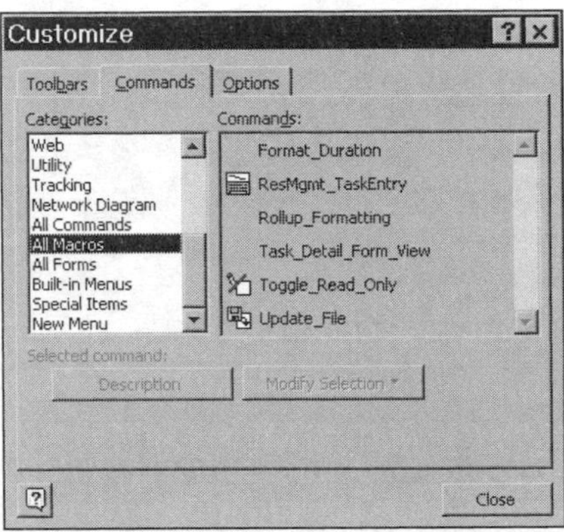


**Figure 19-11:** You can add macros as commands on menus using the Commands tab of the Customize dialog box.

3. Scroll down the Categories list and select All Macros. Project displays a list of macros in the Commands list on the right.
4. Drag the macro you want to add to the desired menu (see Figure 19-12). As you drag, the mouse pointer image changes to include a small button and a plus sign. As you move the mouse pointer over a menu, the menu opens; a large horizontal insertion point marks the location where the button appears when you release the mouse button.
5. Release the mouse button. The macro appears on the menu (see Figure 19-13).
6. To change the name on the menu, click Modify Selection in the Customize dialog box to open the pop-up menu shown in Figure 19-14.
7. Type the name (including spaces) in the Name box exactly as you want it to appear on the toolbar button.

Note

To provide a hotkey for your macro name, place an ampersand (&) immediately before the character you want to be the hot key—as I did before the D of Detail. Make sure that the letter you select is not already in use by some other command on the same menu. When the command appears on the menu, the hotkey letter will be underscored, enabling you to choose it from the menu using the hotkey letter. For example, I could choose the Detail Form command by pressing Alt+T+D.

8. Press Enter. The pop-up menu disappears, and Project renames the menu command. As Figure 19-15 shows, the command includes your hotkey if you added an ampersand.

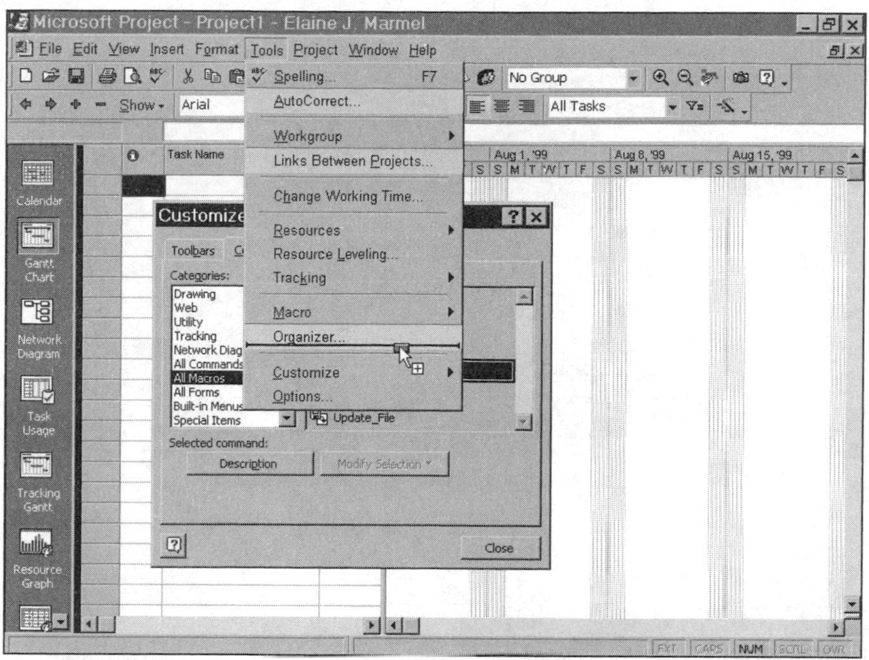


**Figure 19-12:** The image of the mouse pointer icon changes as you drag a macro onto a menu.

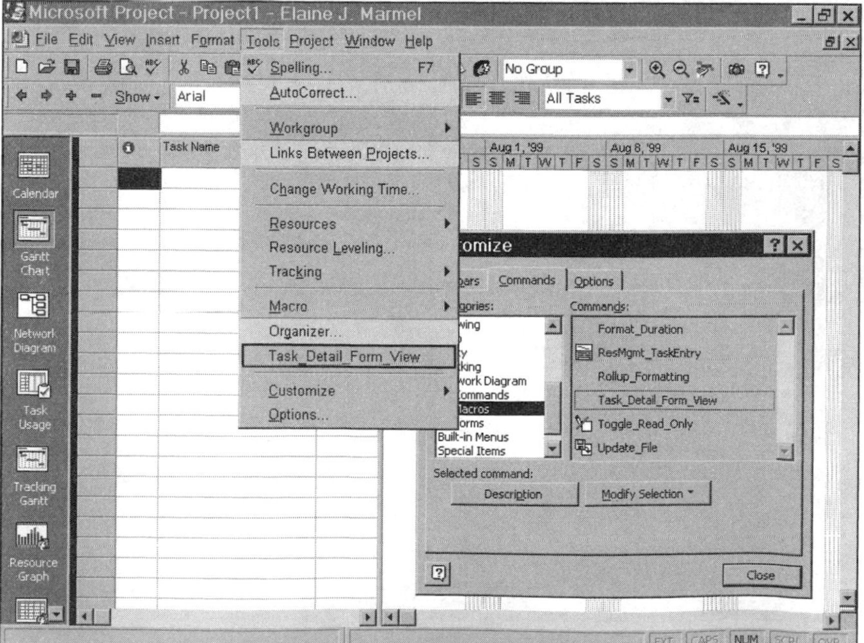


**Figure 19-13:** A macro placed on the Tools menu

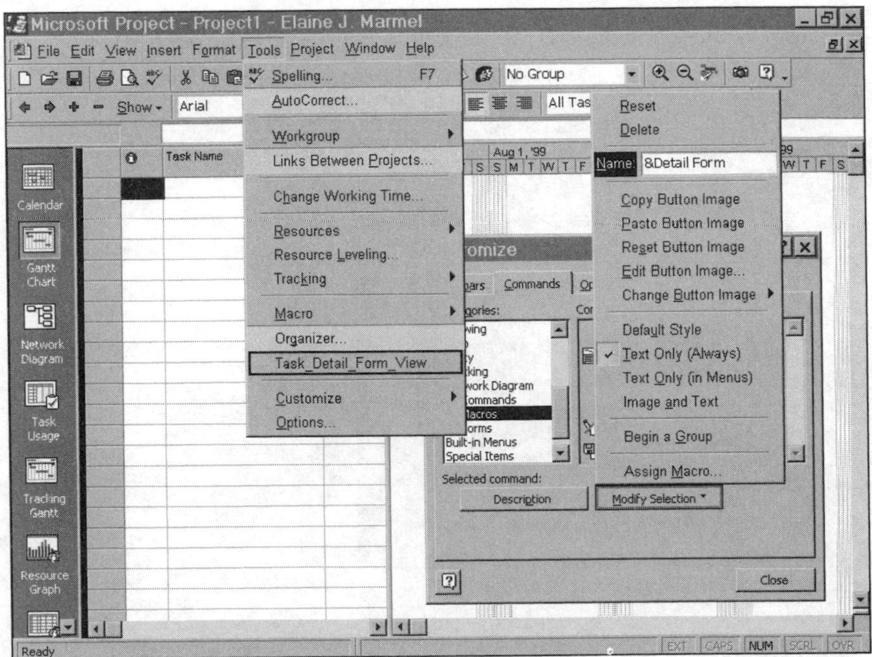


**Figure 19-14:** Modifying the command name on the menu

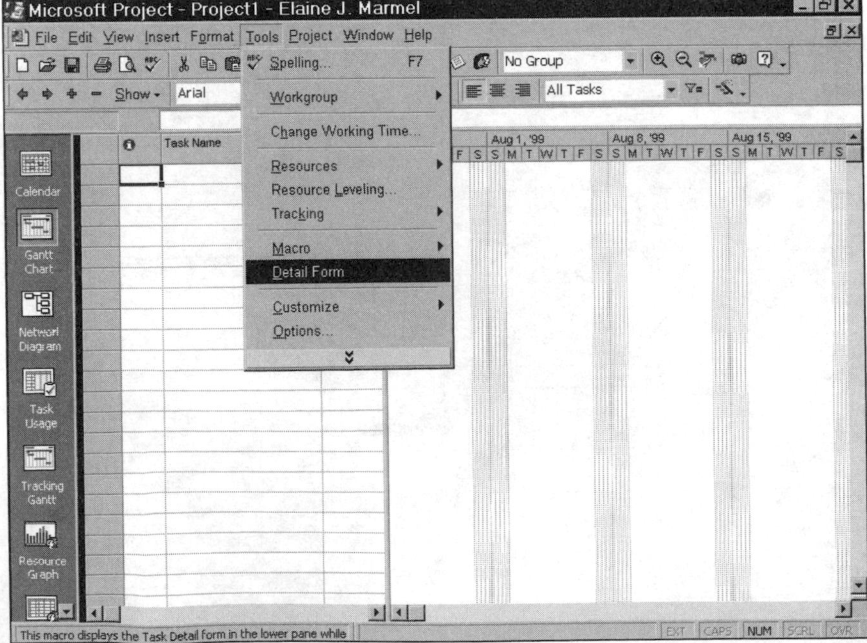


**Figure 19-15:** The command after renaming it and assigning a hotkey

9. Close the Customize dialog box.

When you add a command to one of the default menus, Microsoft Project saves the command and the menu in your Global file. Any other project file you open on your computer using that Global file contains the new menu command.

If you change your mind and don't want the command on the menu, you can remove it by opening the Customize dialog box and then simply dragging the command off the menu and dropping it anywhere on your project or even the Customize dialog box. The command disappears, but the macro is still available.

## Assigning a keyboard shortcut to a macro

So, suppose after you experiment, you decide that you really want to run your macro from a keyboard shortcut. Further suppose that you didn't set a shortcut when you created the macro. Follow these steps to add a keyboard shortcut to the macro after you create it:

1. Open the project containing the macro.
2. Choose Tools ➪ Macro ➪ Macros to open the Macros dialog box shown in Figure 19-16.

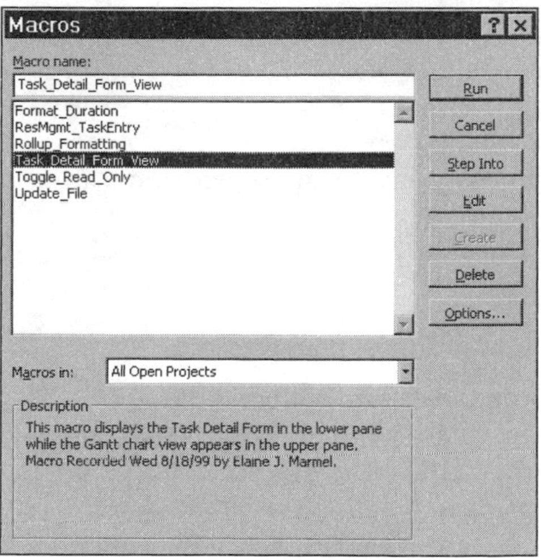


**Figure 19-16:** The Macros dialog box

Tip

You can also press Alt+F8 to display the Macros dialog box.

3. Highlight the macro to which you want to add a keyboard shortcut.
4. Click Options to open the Macro Options dialog box that appears in Figure 19-17.

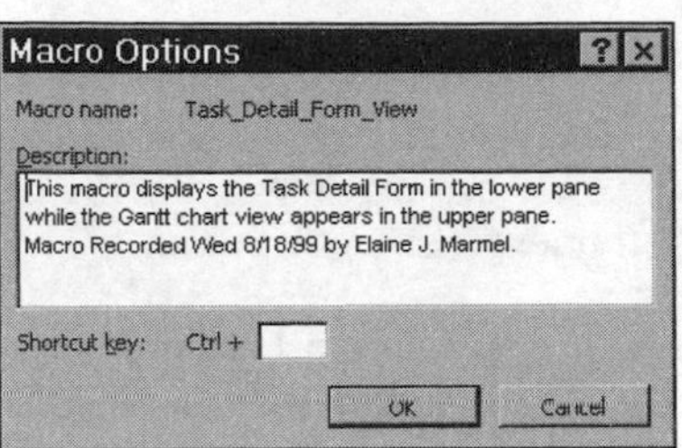


**Figure 19-17:** Set a keyboard shortcut for a macro from the Macro Options dialog box.

5. Place the insertion point in the Shortcut key box and type a letter.
6. Click OK. If the combination you selected (Ctrl plus the letter you typed) is not in use by Project, Project displays the Macros dialog box again. If Project is using the combination you selected, even for another macro, Project asks you to try a different combination.
7. Close the Macros dialog box.

To run your macro, press the keyboard combination you assigned. If you decide that you don't want to run your macro using this keyboard combination, you can change the combination using the preceding steps, or you can remove the keyboard combination you assigned completely by reopening the Macro Options dialog box and deleting the letter from the Shortcut key box.

# Summary

In this chapter you learned about using macros in Project. You learned how to:

✦ Create macros

✦ Use macros

✦ Assign shortcuts to macros to make them easy to run

Chapter 20 explains how to import and export Project data.

✦ ✦ ✦

# Importing and Exporting Project Information

✦ ✦ ✦ ✦

**In This Chapter**

Creating and editing import/export maps

Exporting information

Importing information

Troubleshooting

✦ ✦ ✦ ✦

Sometimes you need to move information in and out of Project. While you can move information into and out of Project by copying and pasting the information, you'll find that you make these moves primarily using Project's import and export functions. You can import and export information using various file formats; for example, you can export a Project schedule as a graphic image to use in a graphics program, on a Web page, or to print on a plotter.

## Creating and Editing Import/Export Maps

When you import information into Project or export information from Project to another program, you usually use an import/export map. Project comes with a series of useful import/export maps that you can edit if necessary, or you can create a custom map.

An import/export map defines the information you want to import or export and enables you to describe how to match the information in the Project file with the information in the other program's file. For example, when you charted earned value in Excel in Chapter 14, you selected the Earned Value Information export map to send the data to Excel. This mapping information told Project what data to send to Excel for charting and how to identify the information in Excel.

## Preliminary steps for mapping

To view, copy, or edit any of the predefined import/export maps, or to create your own map, you must simulate importing or exporting a file. In the following steps, you simulate exporting a file to an Excel workbook:

1. Open any Project file.
2. Choose File ➪ Save As to open the File Save dialog box.
3. Type a name in the File name list box for the file you want to simulate exporting.
4. Open the Save as type list box and select Microsoft Excel Workbook. Or you can select any file type other than Microsoft Project.
5. Click Save. Project opens the Export Mapping dialog box shown in Figure 20-1.

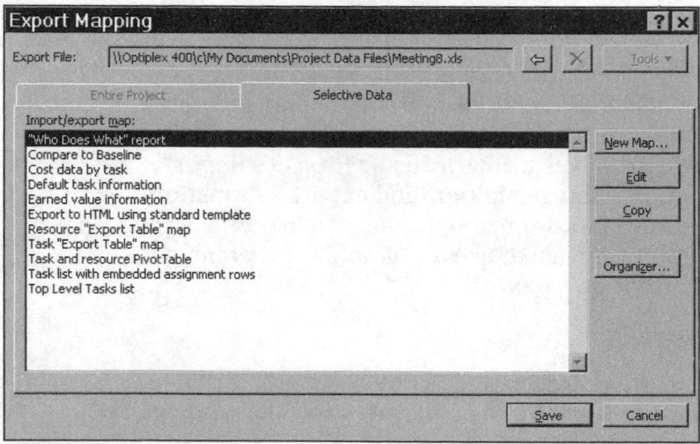


**Figure 20-1:** The Export Mapping dialog box

You can now create your own map by selecting New Map. Or you can edit or copy an existing map by highlighting the map you want to use and then selecting Edit or Copy. If you simply want to view a map, select Edit and don't save any changes you might make while looking at the map. If you select Copy, Project creates a copy of the highlighted map, so if you make changes and save them, you won't affect any of Project's default maps.

## Creating a new map

When you select New Map, the Options tab of the Define Import/Export Map dialog box appears. Provide a name for the new map in the "Import/Export map name" text box. This name appears in the list in the Export Format dialog box.

Although this section talks about defining a new map for Excel, the concepts and steps are almost identical for defining a new map for another program. You simply wouldn't have some of the Excel-specific options, such as the Destination Worksheet Name on the Task Mapping tab or the Microsoft Excel checkboxes on the Options tab.

As you can see in Figure 20-2, you can use the Options tab to select the type of data to import or export. The boxes you check determine which mapping tabs become available.

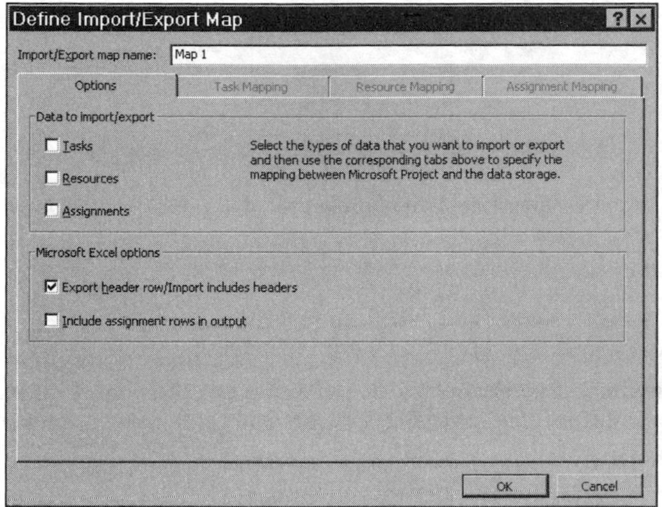


**Figure 20-2:** The Options tab of the Define Import/Export Map dialog box for an Excel file type

If you want your Excel workbook to contain assignments listed under tasks or resources, similar to the Task Usage or Resource Usage views, place a check in the "Include assignment rows in output" checkbox.

After you select the type of data to import or export on the Options tab, some or all of the mapping tabs become available. All three mapping tabs in this dialog box work the same way. In Figure 20-3, you see the Task Mapping tab, which functions as follows:

The titles in the Define Import/Export Map dialog box refer to exporting because you simulated the export process to open this dialog box. If you had simulated importing, the titles in the box would refer to importing.

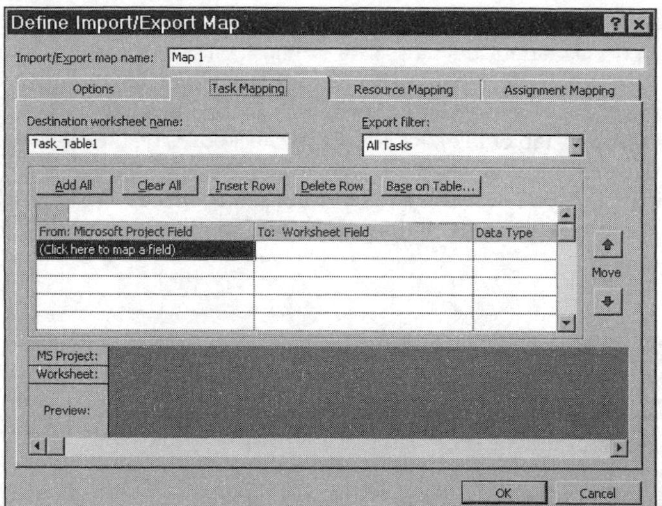


**Figure 20-3:** The Task Mapping tab where you identify the task fields you want to import or export

✦ **Destination worksheet name.** This box contains the name Excel will assign to the sheet in the workbook. You can change this name.

✦ **Export filter.** Use this list box to select the tasks you want to export. By default, Project assumes you want to export all tasks, but you can export, for example, just completed tasks.

✦ **From: Microsoft Project Field.** Under this column, click "(Click here to map a phrase)" to add fields to export one at a time. After you click, you can use the list box arrow to view a list of fields available for exporting and to select a field.

✦ **To: Worksheet Field.** Select a field to export and click the column next to the field you added. Project suggests a column heading for the field in the Excel worksheet; you can change this heading.

✦ **Data Type.** You cannot, however, change the data type for the field in the destination program, which appears in this column.

✦ **Add All.** To quickly add all the fields in the Project file, click the Add All button.

✦ **Base on Table.** To add all the fields in a particular Project table, such as the Entry table or the Cost table, click the Base on Table button. Project displays the Select Base Table for Field Mapping dialog box, from which you can select a table. When you click OK, Project adds all fields contained in that table to the list of fields you want to export. As you add fields, the Preview section at the bottom of the dialog box shows you how the Excel worksheet will appear (see Figure 20-4).

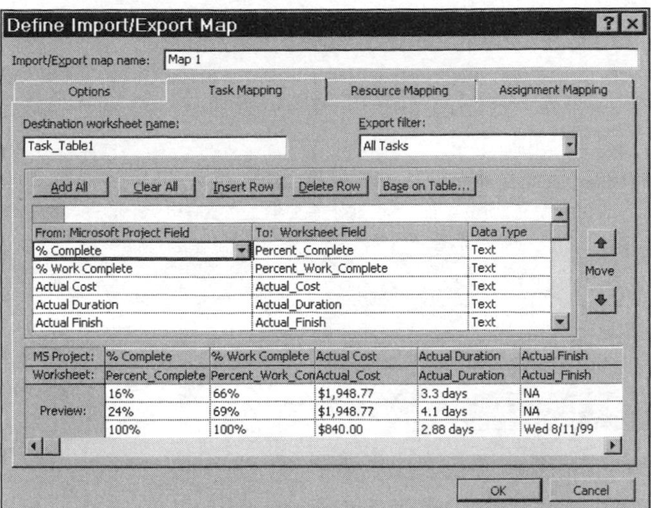


**Figure 20-4:** As you add fields, a preview of the Excel worksheet you're creating appears at the bottom of the Define Import/Export Map dialog box.

✦ **Insert Row.** If you decide to add a field between two existing fields, click the row you want to appear below the new field. Then click the Insert Row button, and Project inserts a blank row above the selected row.

✦ **Move.** You can use the Move buttons on the right side of the dialog box to reorder fields. Click the field you want to move and then click either the Move up arrow or the Move down arrow.

✦ **Delete Row.** To delete a field, click anywhere in the row containing the field and click the Delete Row button.

✦ **Clear All.** To remove all the fields you added, click the Clear All button.

When you click OK to save your map, Project redisplays the Export Format dialog box. Your map appears in the Selective data list box.

If you don't want to export information at this time, click Close. Project retains the map you created but cancels the export operation.

## Viewing, copying, or editing import/export maps

You must simulate the process of exporting or importing to view, copy, or edit an import/export map. The process for creating a new map and viewing, copying, or editing an existing map are essentially the same; the slight differences in the Define Import/Export Map dialog box depend on the action you select.

For example, if you highlight an existing map and select Copy in the Export Format dialog box, you still see the Define Import/Export Map dialog box. However, the name of the map indicates that it's a copy, and when you view the map (task, resource, or assignment), the fields are already inserted, as shown in Figure 20-5.

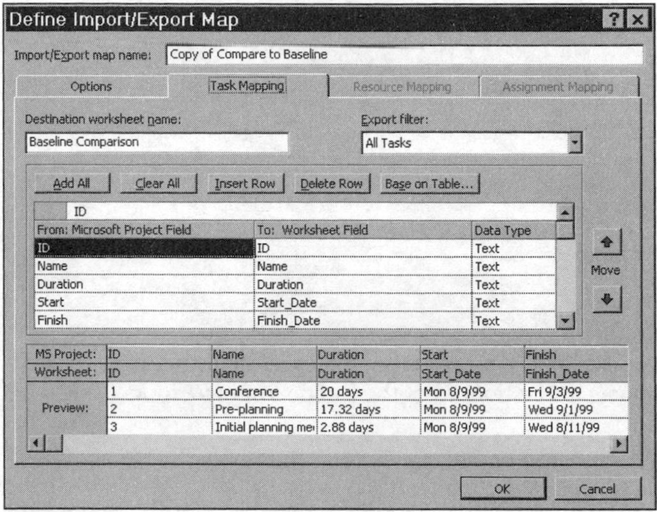

**Figure 20-5:** When you copy an existing map, the word "Copy" appears in its default name, and Project fills in the fields for you.

You can use the Edit button to view an existing map or to make changes to the map. If you highlight an existing map and select Edit in the Export Format dialog box, you still see the Define Import/Export Map dialog box with the title of the map you selected. As you would expect, when you view the map (task, resource, or assignment), you see fields already inserted (see Figure 20-6).

**Tip** Although you can edit an existing map, I suggest that you make a copy of the map and edit the copy; that way, you'll still have the original version installed with Project.

# Exporting Information

When you import, you bring information into a Project file from another program; when you export, you send information from Project to another program. You can export information to Microsoft Office products such as Excel workbooks, Access databases, or Word documents. You also can export some Project information to graphic images that you can use in any graphics program or as an image on a Web page. And you can export information to any program that can read text (TXT) files or comma-separated value (CSV) files.

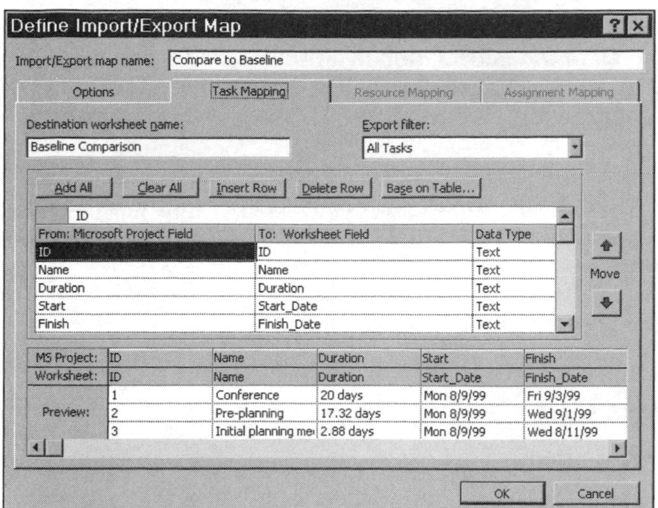


**Figure 20-6:** When you edit a map, the dialog box looks the same as when you copy an existing map except for the map name.

# Exporting to Office files

You can use import/export maps to export information to Excel workbooks or to Access databases. You also can include Project information in Word, but you won't use the import process.

## Sending Project data to Excel

In Chapter 14 you learned how to export information to Excel when you learned about analyzing cost information. And earlier in this chapter you saw how to create or edit a map to export Project information to Excel. Rather than repeat this information, consider the overview of the process:

1. Open the Project file containing the information you want to export.
2. Save the file as either an Excel workbook or an Excel PivotTable.

When you create an Excel PivotTable file, Project creates two sheets in the workbook for each type of data you export. One sheet contains the data used in the PivotTable, and the other sheet contains the PivotTable. Project uses the last field in each map as the default field for the PivotTable, and all the other fields appear as rows in the PivotTable.

3. Select a map or create a new map from the Export Format dialog box.
4. Click Save. Project exports the data specified in the map to the Excel workbook you specified.

## Sending Project data to an Access database

You can export some or all of the information in a Project file to an Access 97 or later database file using an import/export map. If none of the existing maps can export data into the proper fields in your Access database, you might need to create a new map.

When you export to any database format, Project makes the following changes to the names of some fields in the database to ensure compatibility with database field naming conventions:

- ✦ Underscores replace spaces and forward slashes (/).
- ✦ The string "Percent" replaces the percent sign (%).
- ✦ Periods are deleted.
- ✦ Start changes to Start_Date.
- ✦ Finish changes to Finish_Date.
- ✦ Group changes to Group_Name.
- ✦ Work changes to Scheduled_Work.

You can append Project information to an existing Access database. However, you should make sure you have a backup copy of the database, just in case the information doesn't appear the way it should in Access. You may even want to create a test copy of your database and use the copy to ensure that Project information appears in the correct fields.

Follow these steps to export Project information to a file in Microsoft Access database format:

1. Open the Project file containing the data you want to export.
2. Choose File ➪ Save As to open the File Save dialog box.
3. Open the Save as type list box and select Microsoft Access Databases.
4. Type a name in the File name box for the file you are exporting.
5. Click Save. If you selected an existing Access database, Project displays the message that appears in Figure 20-7.
6. To add information to the database, click Append. To replace the existing database, click Overwrite. To select a different file, click Cancel. Project opens the Save to Database dialog box shown in Figure 20-8.

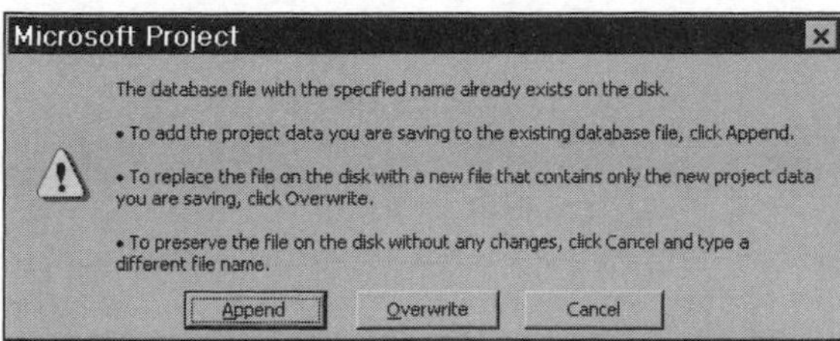


**Figure 20-7:** The message that appears when you select an existing Access database as the export file.

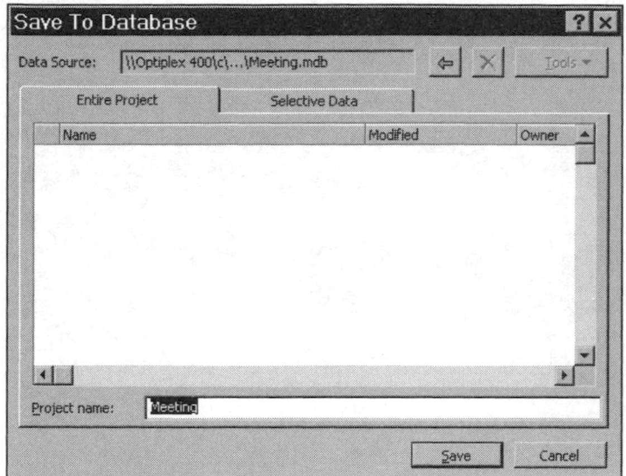


**Figure 20-8:** Use this dialog box to save your project in an Access database.

7. Tell Project whether to export all or some of the data in your project:
   - **To export all the data in your project.** Leave the Entire Project tab selected and type a name for the project in the "Name to give the project in the database" box.
   - **To export only some the data in your project.** Select the Selective Data tab and select the import/export map you want to use for exporting your data.
8. In the Project Name field, type a name that you want to use in Access to represent the data you are exporting.
9. Click Save.

In Access, you can see a list of all projects that you exported to a particular database by viewing the contents of the MSP_PROJECTS table, as shown in Figure 20-9.

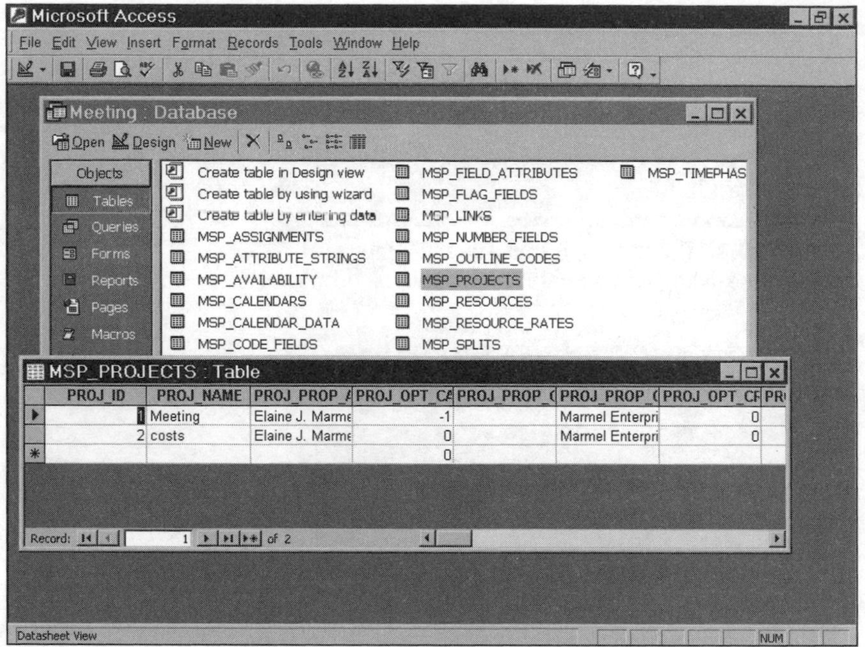


**Figure 20-9:** View the list of projects exported to an Access database by opening the MSP_PROJECTS table.

## Sending Project data to Microsoft Word

Although you can't export Project data directly to Word, you can use the Windows Copy and Paste commands to incorporate Project text or table data in a Word file. For example, you can copy the columns in any table to a Word document. Start in Project and follow these steps:

1. Open the file containing the information you want to incorporate in a Word document.
2. Select the information; you can copy text information from the Notes tab of either the Task Information dialog box or the Resource Information dialog box or, as you see in Figure 20-10, you can copy table columns.
3. Click the Copy button on the Standard toolbar.
4. Open or switch to Word.
5. Position the insertion point where you want the Project information to begin.
6. Click Paste. The Project information appears in Word.

As you can see from Figure 20-11, table information appears in Word as tab-separated columns; using Word's Convert Text to Table feature, you can convert the information into a Word table.

| | Task Name | Fixed Cost | Fixed Cost Accrual | Total Cost | Baseline | Variance | Actual | Remaining |
|---|---|---|---|---|---|---|---|---|
| 1 | ⊟ Conference | $0.00 | Prorated | $3,228.76 | $0.00 | $3,228.76 | $1,948.76 | $1,280.00 |
| 2 | ⊟ Pre-planning | $0.00 | Prorated | $3,028.76 | $0.00 | $3,028.76 | $1,948.76 | $1,080.00 |
| 3 | ⊟ Initial planning | $0.00 | Prorated | $840.00 | $0.00 | $840.00 | $840.00 | $0.00 |
| 4 | Determine bu | $0.00 | Prorated | $600.00 | $0.00 | $600.00 | $600.00 | $0.00 |
| 5 | Invitation list | $0.00 | Prorated | $240.00 | $0.00 | $240.00 | $240.00 | $0.00 |
| 6 | ⊟ Selection | $0.00 | Prorated | $1,108.76 | $0.00 | $1,108.76 | $1,108.76 | $0.00 |
| 7 | Theme | $0.00 | Prorated | $508.76 | $0.00 | $508.76 | $508.76 | $0.00 |
| 8 | Site | $0.00 | Prorated | $600.00 | $0.00 | $600.00 | $600.00 | $0.00 |
| 9 | Keynote spe | $0.00 | Prorated | $0.00 | $0.00 | $0.00 | $0.00 | $0.00 |
| 10 | ⊟ Hire | $0.00 | Prorated | $1,080.00 | $0.00 | $1,080.00 | $0.00 | $1,080.00 |
| 11 | Caterer | $0.00 | Prorated | $360.00 | $0.00 | $360.00 | $0.00 | $360.00 |
| 12 | Bartenders | $0.00 | Prorated | $300.00 | $0.00 | $300.00 | $0.00 | $300.00 |
| 13 | Security | $0.00 | Prorated | $160.00 | $0.00 | $160.00 | $0.00 | $160.00 |
| 14 | Photographe | $0.00 | Prorated | $100.00 | $0.00 | $100.00 | $0.00 | $100.00 |
| 15 | Cleanup crev | $0.00 | Prorated | $160.00 | $0.00 | $160.00 | $0.00 | $160.00 |
| 16 | ⊟ Plan Entertainm | $0.00 | Prorated | $0.00 | $0.00 | $0.00 | $0.00 | $0.00 |
| 17 | Baseball Gar | $0.00 | Prorated | $0.00 | $0.00 | $0.00 | $0.00 | $0.00 |
| 18 | Opera | $0.00 | Prorated | $0.00 | $0.00 | $0.00 | $0.00 | $0.00 |
| 19 | ⊟ Public Relation | $0.00 | Prorated | $0.00 | $0.00 | $0.00 | $0.00 | $0.00 |
| 20 | Alert commu | $0.00 | Prorated | $0.00 | $0.00 | $0.00 | $0.00 | $0.00 |
| 21 | Press releas | $0.00 | Prorated | $0.00 | $0.00 | $0.00 | $0.00 | $0.00 |
| 22 | ⊟ Rent Equipmen | $0.00 | Prorated | $0.00 | $0.00 | $0.00 | $0.00 | $0.00 |

**Figure 20-10:** Select information to copy to Word.

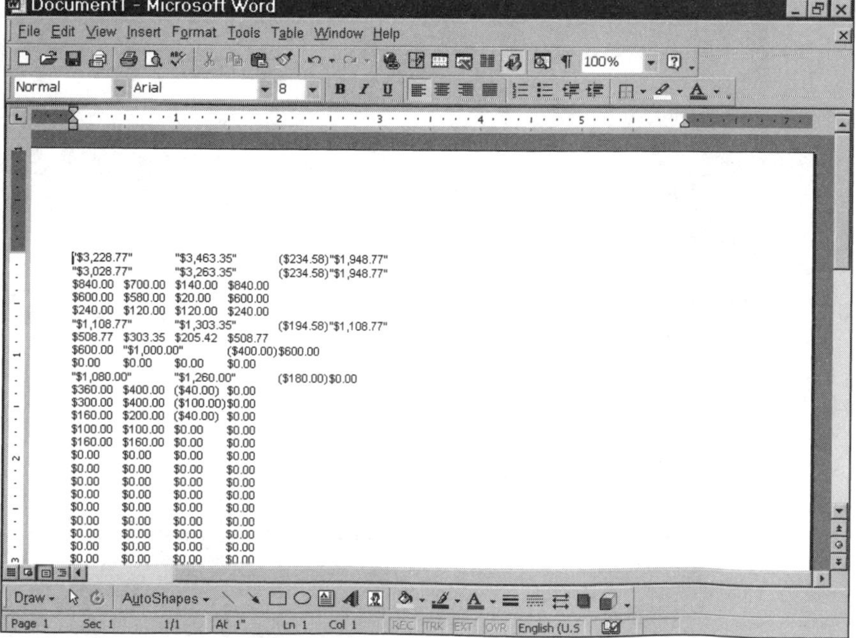


**Figure 20-11:** Project table information as it appears when you copy it into Word

## Exporting Project information to a graphic image

You can create a picture from your Project information and view the picture in any graphics program or save the picture in a Web-compatible file format. When you use the following technique, you copy Project information to the Windows Clipboard; you can copy all or part of any view except the Task PERT, Task Form, and Resource Form views.

1. Select the view of which you want a picture.
2. Tell Project how much of your plan to copy. To copy only a portion of your plan, select the information you want to copy. To copy all visible portions of your plan, click the Copy Picture button on the Standard toolbar. The Copy Picture dialog box appears (see Figure 20-12).

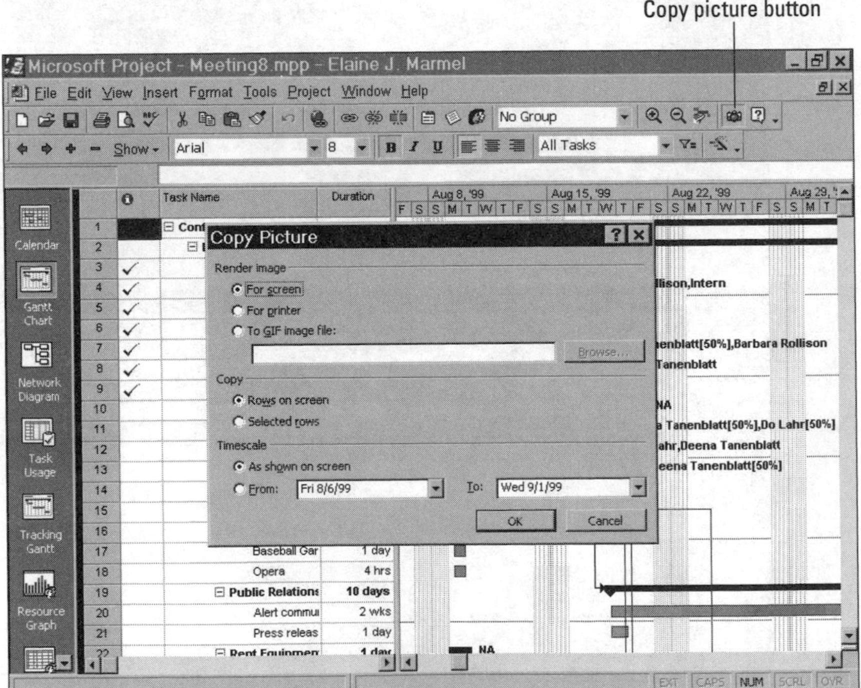


**Figure 20-12:** Use the Copy Picture dialog box to describe how you want to copy the picture.

3. Select an option button to specify how you want Project to copy the picture:
   - **For screen.** Select this to copy the information for display on a computer screen.

- **For printer.** Select this to copy the information for a printer to use.
- **To GIF image file.** Select this to save the information as an image you can use on a Web page and in other programs. Be sure to specify the path and filename in the box below this option.

4. (Optional) If you selected rows before you started this process because you want to copy only those rows, select Selected rows.
5. (Optional) If you want to copy information for a range of dates other than those currently displayed, click the Date option button and then enter From and To dates.
6. Click OK.

To view an image that you copied as a screen or printer image, switch to the program in which you want to display the Microsoft Project information and then paste the picture using the program's Paste command. A copied image in Microsoft Paint appears in Figure 20-13.

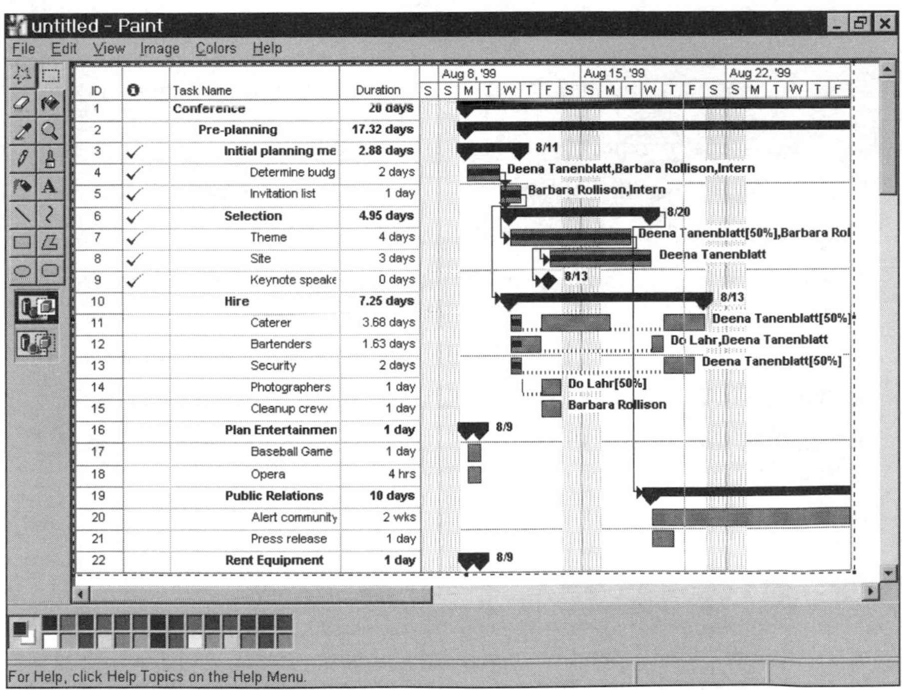


**Figure 20-13:** A Project image pasted into Microsoft Paint

## Exporting to other formats

If you want to export information to a program that can read either text files or Microsoft Project Exchange Files, you can create an export file that the receiving program can read. Text files are a common format and are also called comma-separated values files (CSV). Microsoft Project Exchange format (MPX) is an ASCII, record-based file format.

If the program to which you want to export information supports the Microsoft Access database format (MDB), you should use that format for the best results when you import the information that you exported from Project.

### Exporting to text files

If you have a program that can read either a text file or a CSV file, you can export information from Project to that program. You need to save the information you want to export as either a text file or a CSV file (also called an ASCII, comma-delimited file) in Project.

To export information to a text file, you need to use an import/export map. To ensure that Project information appears correctly in the program into which you want to import it, you may need to create or edit an import/export map.

Follow these steps to export information to a text file:

1. Open the Project file containing the information you want to export.
2. Choose File ⇨ Save As to open the File Save dialog box.
3. Select Text or CSV, whichever format works best in the program to which you're exporting, in the Save as type box.
4. Type a name in the File name box for the file you are exporting.
5. Click Save. The Export Format dialog box appears.
6. Highlight the name of the map you want to use in the "Import/export map to use for exporting" list box.
7. Click Save. Project saves the information.

### Exporting to other project management software

You can use the MPX file format to export Project 2000 information to older versions of Project. Some other project management software packages also support MPX, so if you need to export Project 2000 information to another project management software package, you can save it as an MPX file.

Exporting an MPX file is similar to importing an Excel workbook or an Access database except that you don't use an import/export map. Choose File ➪ Save As. In the File Save dialog box, open the Files of type list box and select MPX. In the File name box, supply a name for the file you want to export. Click Save, and Project saves the file.

The Microsoft Project database (MPD) format is a good format to use whenever possible. MPD has replaced the MPX format, and you can use it with any program that supports either the MPD format or Microsoft Access database formats.

## Saving Project files as Web pages

Suppose you want to include information from your schedule within an HTML document—say, as a page on a company intranet or a corporate Web site. To do so, you have to save the project file in HTML format. In Project you use maps to designate the fields that you want to export.

To save project information in HTML format, follow these steps:

1. Choose File ➪ Save As Web Page to open the Save dialog box.
2. Type a new filename or accept the default of your project filename with the .html extension. Click Save. The Export Mapping dialog box shown in Figure 20-14 appears.

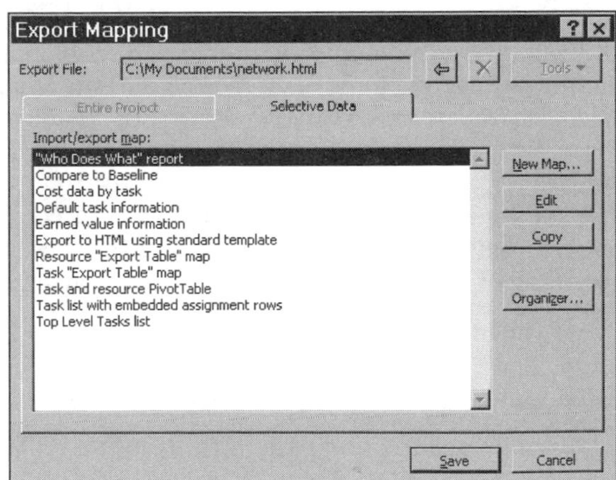


**Figure 20-14:** The Selective data tab enables you to customize maps.

3. Select one of the default maps and click Save or click New Map to open the Define Import/Export Map dialog box shown in Figure 20-15 and display the Options tab. Project generates a map name (such as Map 1 or Map 2) in the Import/Export map name field.

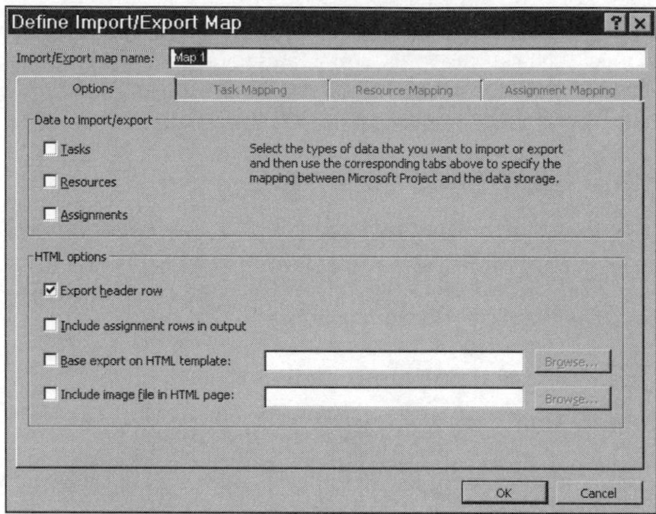


**Figure 20-15:** You can set export options for a new export map here.

You can change the automatically generated map name to make it more informative. For example, you might want to create one map with mostly cost information and another with timing information, and call them "Cost Map" and "Time Map," respectively. This type of naming convention helps everyone using your schedule to locate the right map.

4. Click one or more checkboxes at the top of the Define Import/Export Map dialog box to designate the kind of information to export: Tasks, Resources, or Assignments. Depending on the options you select, additional tabs become available. Use the tabs to specify fields in those categories of data to include in the export file.

5. Click any of the HTML options checkboxes. Here's what they do:
   - **Export header row.** Includes the row of field titles in the HTML file
   - **Include assignment rows in output.** Includes rows that contain information about resource assignments in the file
   - **Base export on HTML template.** Enables you to use a template that applies a predesigned look to the HTML document
   - **Include image file in HTML page.** Enables you to include a graphic file on the HTML document

6. If you selected Tasks as one type of information to save, click the Task Mapping tab. If you chose a different category — Resource or Assignment — click the appropriate tab. Each tab works the same way.

7. Click the text "Click here to map a field." A list arrow appears at the edge of the box.

8. Open the list box to see the drop-down list shown in Figure 20-16.

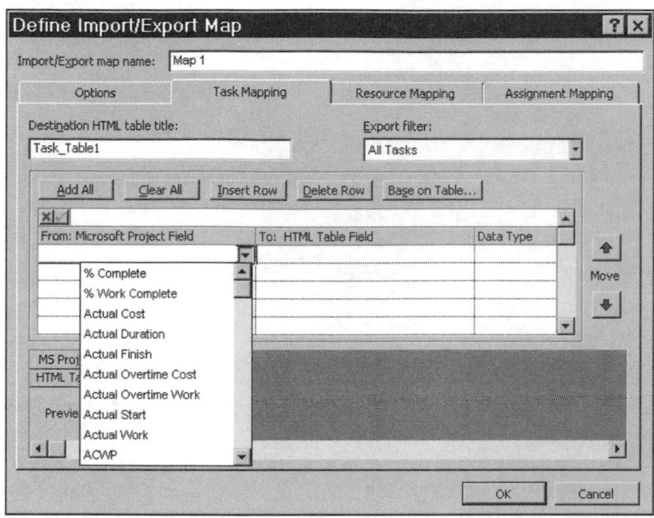


**Figure 20-16:** Build your own maps by using the settings on these tabs.

9. Select a field to include. Project fills in a field name to export to in the HTML file and enters the data type (usually Text).

10. Repeat Steps 9 and 10 to add other fields to your map.

The Task Mapping tab has several shortcuts for building maps. To include all the possible task fields, simply click the Add All button. To apply a filter to tasks to export only critical task information, for example, use the Export filter drop-down list to select a filter. To base the map on fields contained in a Project table, click the Base on Table button and select the table name from the dialog box that appears.

11. Click OK to save the map and then click Save in the Define Import/Export Map dialog box to save the export file.

Figure 20-17 shows a Project file in HTML format. When you save a file in this format, you can publish the file as a Web page using any Web page design and management software.

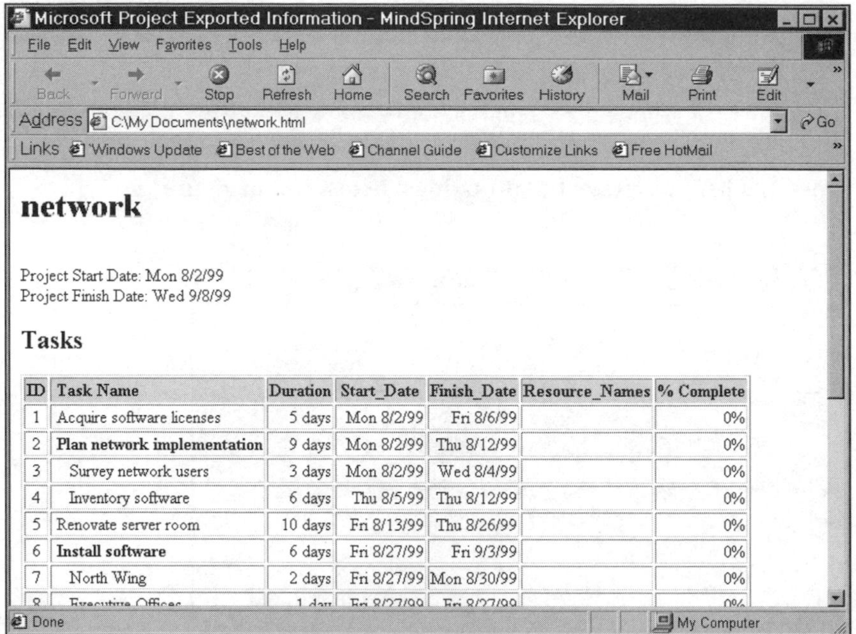


**network**

Project Start Date: Mon 8/2/99
Project Finish Date: Wed 9/8/99

**Tasks**

| ID | Task Name | Duration | Start_Date | Finish_Date | Resource_Names | % Complete |
|---|---|---|---|---|---|---|
| 1 | Acquire software licenses | 5 days | Mon 8/2/99 | Fri 8/6/99 | | 0% |
| 2 | **Plan network implementation** | 9 days | Mon 8/2/99 | Thu 8/12/99 | | 0% |
| 3 | Survey network users | 3 days | Mon 8/2/99 | Wed 8/4/99 | | 0% |
| 4 | Inventory software | 6 days | Thu 8/5/99 | Thu 8/12/99 | | 0% |
| 5 | Renovate server room | 10 days | Fri 8/13/99 | Thu 8/26/99 | | 0% |
| 6 | **Install software** | 6 days | Fri 8/27/99 | Fri 9/3/99 | | 0% |
| 7 | North Wing | 2 days | Fri 8/27/99 | Mon 8/30/99 | | 0% |

**Figure 20-17:** Your Web browser displays Project data saved in HTML format in columns across the page.

# Importing Information

You can bring information into Project from another Project file or from Microsoft Excel, Microsoft Access, or Microsoft Word. You also can import information created in any program that can save text (TXT) files or comma-separated value (CSV) files. When you import a Project file, you actually consolidate two Project files. When you import non-Project files, you use an import/export map to define the data you want to import.

## Inserting another project

When you import one project file into another, you don't use an import/export map. Instead, importing one Project file into another Project file is the same as consolidating Project files, which you learned about in Chapter 17. This section reviews the process of consolidating projects by inserting one project into another project.

When you consolidate project files, you insert one project into another Project file. Each project you insert appears as a summary task in the consolidated project file, as you can see in Figure 20-18. In addition, an icon in the Indicator column tells you, at a glance, that you're looking at an inserted project.

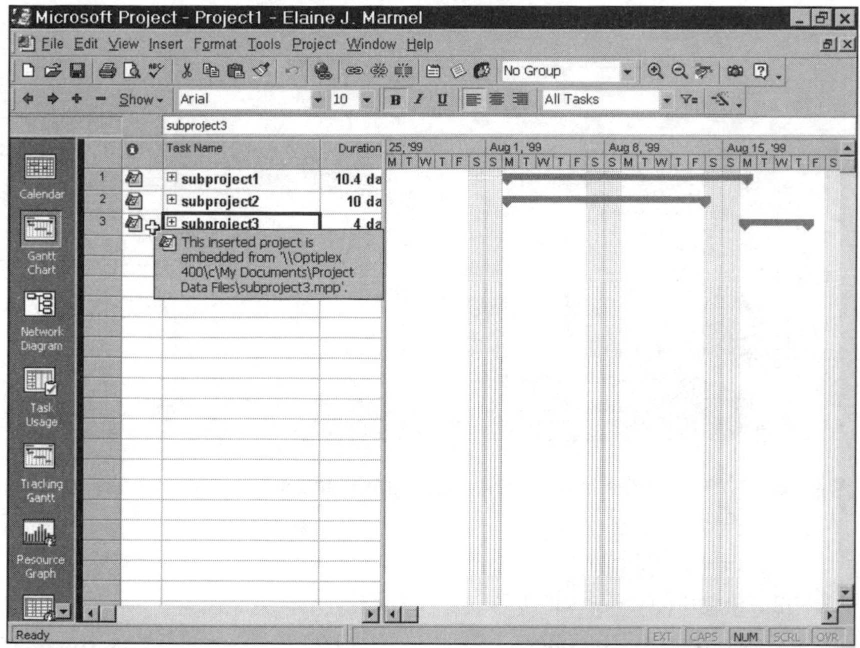


**Figure 20-18:** When you insert one project into another, a special icon appears in the Indicator column.

To insert a project, follow these steps:

1. Open the project into which you want to insert another project.
2. Click Gantt chart in the View bar.
3. Click the Task Name column on the row where you want the inserted project to begin.

When you insert a project, Project places the project immediately above the selected row. Therefore, if your consolidated project already contains tasks, click the task in the Task Name column that you want to appear below the subproject.

4. Choose Insert ➪ Project to open the Insert Project dialog box that you see in Figure 20-19.
5. Use the Look in list to navigate to the folder that contains the project you want to insert.
6. Highlight the file you want to insert.

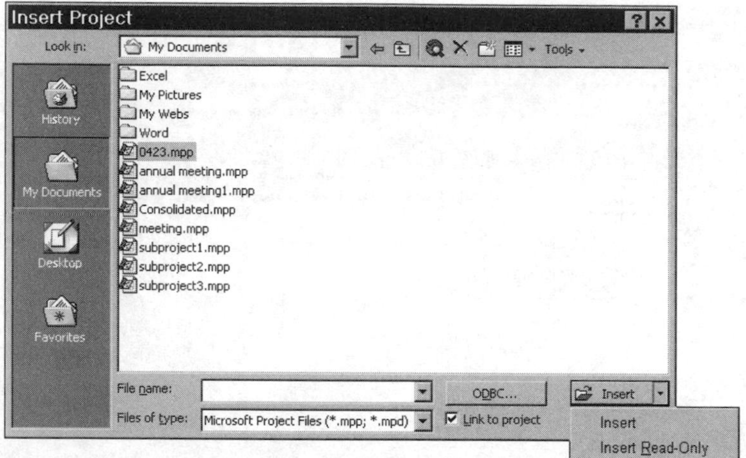


**Figure 20-19:** Use the Insert Project dialog box the same way you use the Open dialog box.

7. Change any inserted project options:
   - If you remove the check from the Link to Project checkbox, the inserted project won't be linked to its source project.
   - If you do not link an inserted project to its source file, any changes you make to the inserted project in the consolidated project file do not affect the source file. Similarly, any changes you make to the source file do not affect the consolidated project file containing the subproject.
   - Under many circumstances, linking the files makes updating easier. When you link an inserted project to its source file, you are creating a link between two files that works like any two linked files in a Windows environment. If you move or rename the inserted project file, you need to update the link in the consolidated project; otherwise, the link won't work.

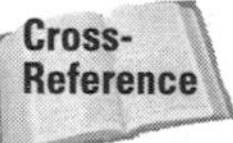


For more information on updating links between Project files, see Chapter 15.

   - If you insert the project as a Read-Only file, the changes you make to the inserted project do not affect its source project.
8. Click Insert. Project inserts the selected file into the open project. The inserted project file appears as a summary task. In Figure 20-20, I've displayed the inserted project's tasks by clicking the outline symbol next to the summary task.

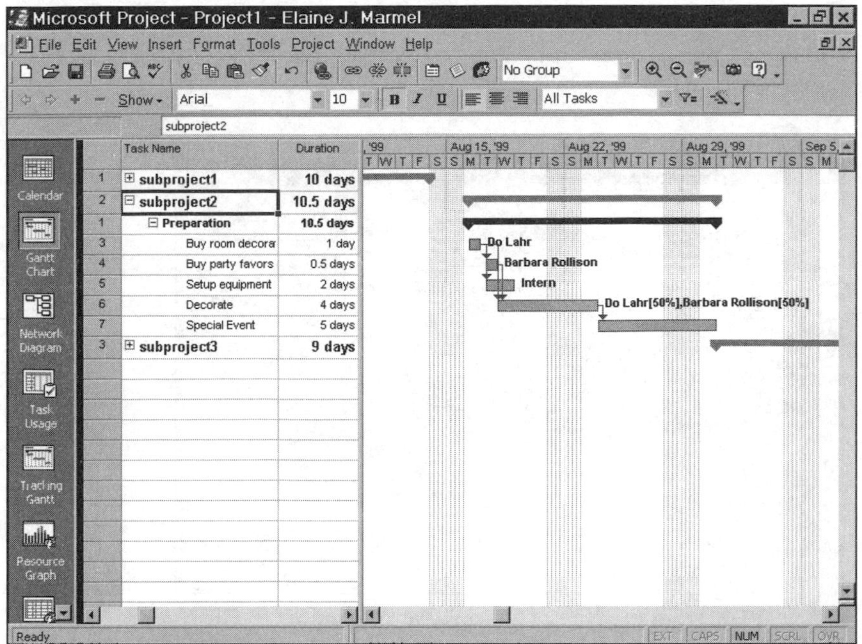


**Figure 20-20:** When you click the outline symbol next to an inserted project's summary task, the tasks of the inserted project appear.

# Importing Office files

You can import information from Excel workbooks or Access databases by using maps that define the way the information should be viewed by Project. You also can include information from Word, but you won't use the import process.

## Bringing Excel workbook information into Project

You can use an import/export map to transfer information from Microsoft Excel workbooks to Microsoft Project files. Project contains predefined import/export maps that tell Project how to treat the information you import. This section shows you how to use a predefined map; earlier in this chapter you learned how to edit a map and create your own map.

You can use any of the existing import/export maps to either import to or export from an Excel workbook, but you cannot import an Excel PivotTable into Project.

1. Choose File ➪ Open or click the Open button on the Standard toolbar.
2. Open the Files of type list box and select Microsoft Excel Workbooks (see Figure 20-21).

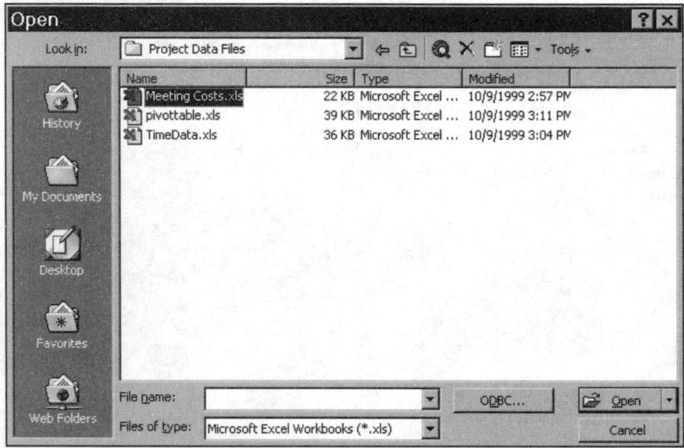


**Figure 20-21:** Set the type of file you want to import to Microsoft Excel Workbooks.

3. Use the Look in list box to navigate to the folder containing the Excel workbook you want to import.
4. Highlight the workbook and click Open. Project displays the Import Mapping dialog box (see Figure 20-22).
5. Select the Selective data option button, and highlight the map you want Project to use while importing your data.
6. Click Open. Project opens the data contained in your Excel workbook in a Project file.

## Bringing Access database information into Project

Importing Access databases into Project is similar to importing Excel workbooks except that you can import all or part of an Access database into a Project file. Again, you use an import/export map to describe to Project the type of data you're importing. If the map you need doesn't exist, you must create it; earlier in this chapter, you learned how to create maps.

To import some or all of an Access database into Project, follow these steps:

1. Choose File ➪ Open or click the Open button on the Standard toolbar.

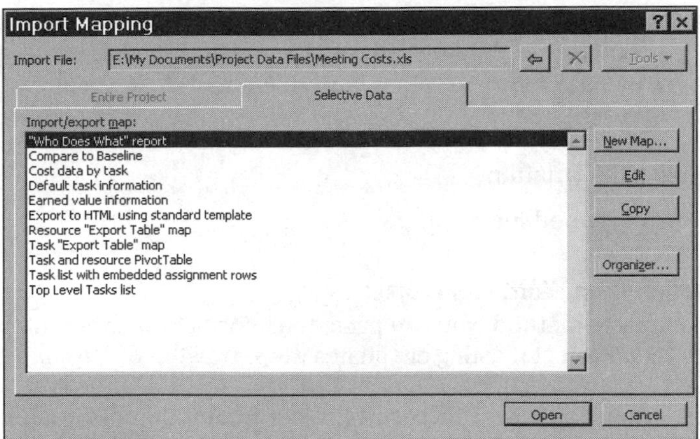


**Figure 20-22:** Use the Import Mapping dialog box to select a map for the imported data.

2. Open the Files of type list box and select Microsoft Access Databases.
3. Use the Look in list box to navigate to the folder containing the Access database you want to import.
4. Highlight the database and click Open. Project displays the Open From Database dialog box (see Figure 20-23).
5. Select a tab to import all or part of the database.
6. Click Open.

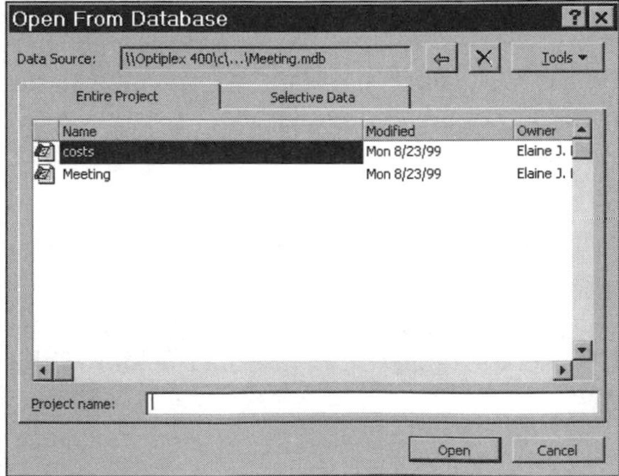


**Figure 20-23:** You can import all or part of the data base into Project from Access.

## Bringing Word document information into Project

Unlike other types of files, you cannot import Word files directly into Project. You can, however, include information in Word documents in a Project file using one of two techniques:

✦ You can paste information.

✦ You can link or embed information.

### Pasting information from Word into Project

When you use the paste method, you can paste the information either into a table view or into a note in Project. Pasting eliminates the extra step of retyping information.

If you paste text into blank rows, Microsoft Project treats the information as new tasks or resources. If you paste information into fields that already contain information, Microsoft Project replaces the information in those fields with the pasted information. However, you cannot paste information into Project fields that contain calculated values, such as calculated values in a cost table.

You can use the following technique to paste information from an Excel workbook into a Project table view, but first you must organize the information in your workbook to match the organization of a Microsoft Project table. For example, suppose you want to paste information into a resource sheet with the Entry table applied. Your workbook has 3 columns, but the resource sheet has 12 columns; and you want to paste the information into Columns 2, 5, and 8. To paste this information, you need to create and apply a table in Project that displays only the fields you intend to paste from your workbook. Make sure that the order and type of columns in the Project table match the order and type of information in the Excel table that you're pasting.

To paste information from Word into a Project table, follow these steps:

1. Open the Word document from which you want to copy information and then copy the information to the Windows Clipboard (see Figure 20-24).
2. Switch to Microsoft Project.
3. Switch to the view into which you want to paste the information. If necessary, use the View bar to click More Views. From the More Views dialog box that appears, select the view you need and then click Apply.
4. Pick the table into which you want to paste information by choosing View ➪ Table ➪ More Tables. Select the table you want from the More Tables dialog box and then click Apply.

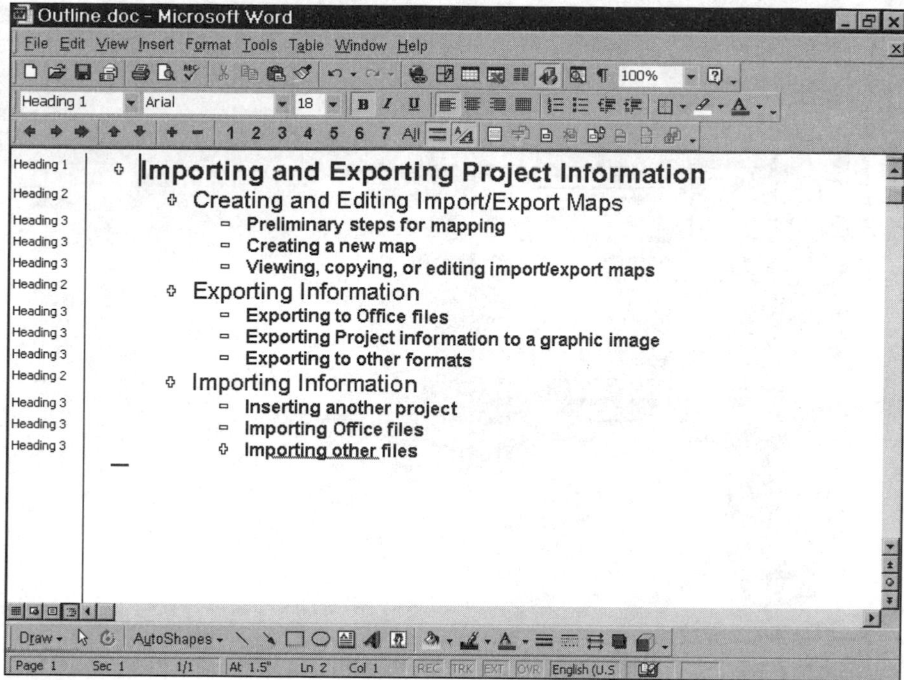


**Figure 20-24:** A Word document you can paste into a Project table

5. (Optional) If the table you select has columns you don't need or is missing columns you do need, then add or hide columns. Also add rows if necessary.
6. Click the first field in which you want information to appear after you paste.
7. Click the Paste button on the Standard toolbar. The information stored on the Windows Clipboard appears in the Project table (see Figure 20-25).

You can paste information from a Word document into a note in Project using the same technique. Copy the information in Word to the Windows Clipboard. Switch to Project and double-click either the task or the resource to which you want to add a note. In the Task Information or Resource Information dialog box that appears, click the Notes tab. Then right-click the Notes area to display a shortcut menu (see Figure 20-26), and choose Paste. The information from Word appears in the Notes area.

### Linking or embedding a Word document in Project

When you link or embed a Word document in Project, you actually insert the document as an object in your Project schedule:

- ✦ When you link a Word document to a Project file, the Project file reflects any changes you make to the Word document.

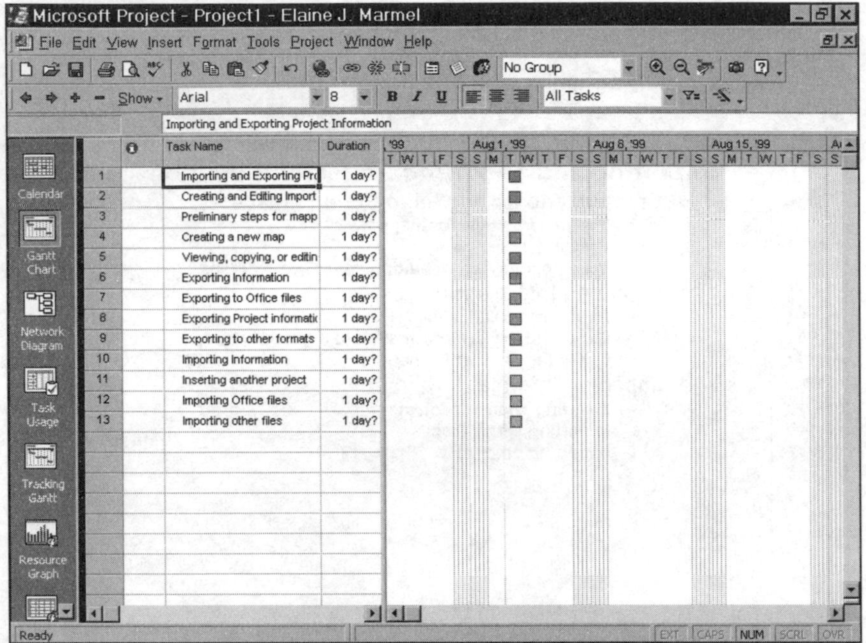

**Figure 20-25:** The information from the Word document appears in Project.

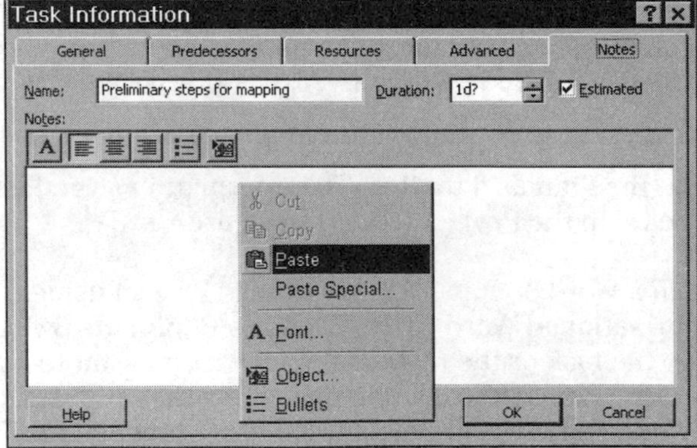

**Figure 20-26:** You can use a shortcut menu to paste information from the Windows Clipboard into a task or resource note.

✦ When you embed a Word document in a Project file, the Project file does not reflect subsequent updates to the Word document.

Project views objects you insert as graphics; therefore, you can link or embed a Word document as a graphic element in any graphics area of a Project file. A graphics area is any area in Project that can display picture information, including task, resource, or assignment notes; headers, footers, and legends in views; headers and footers in reports; the chart portion of the Gantt view; and the Objects box in a task or resource form.

To insert a Word document as a linked or embedded object, follow these steps:

1. Open a Microsoft Project file and display the graphics area into which you want to insert a document.
2. Open the Insert Object dialog box shown in Figure 20-27.

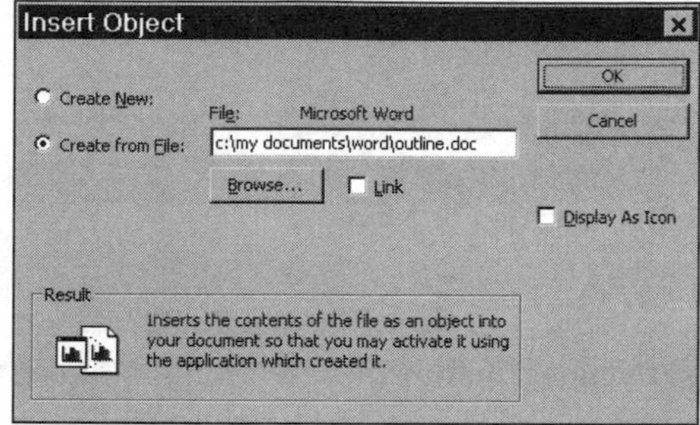


**Figure 20-27:** Use the Insert Object dialog box to link or embed a Word document in a Project file.

To open the Insert Object dialog box in a task, resource, or assignment note, right-click to display a shortcut menu and choose Object. To open the Insert Object dialog box in the Gantt Chart view or Objects box, choose Insert ⇨ Object.

3. Select the Create from File option.
4. Type in the path and filename of the document you want to insert, or click Browse to locate and select the file.
5. Do one of the following:
   - To link the object to the source document, place a check in the Link checkbox.
   - To embed the object, leave the Link checkbox unselected.
6. Click OK. Project displays a graphic image of your file, as you can see in Figure 20-28.

By default, Project displays the contents of the file you insert rather than an icon representing the file. To display the object as an icon, place a checkmark next to Display As Icon.

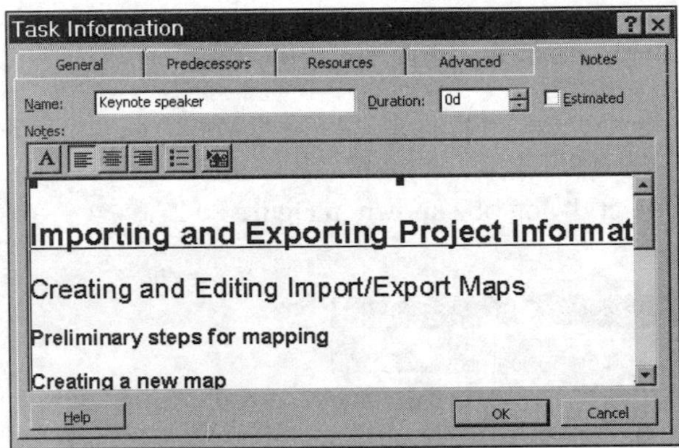


**Figure 20-28:** A Word document inserted as a graphic image in a task note

You can use the handles around the image in the Task Information dialog box to move or resize the image.

You can delete the object by making sure you see the handles surrounding it and pressing the Delete key on your keyboard.

After you click OK, an icon appears in the Indicator column. When you slide the mouse over that icon, however, you won't see the contents of the note because it is a graphic image. Instead, you see a pair of single quotation marks (see Figure 20-29).

## Importing other files

If the information you want to import comes from a program that can produce either text files or Microsoft Project Exchange Files, you can import that information. Text files are a common format and are also called comma-separated values files (CSV). Microsoft Project Exchange format (MPX) is an ASCII, record-based file format.

### Importing Microsoft Project Exchange Files

You can use the MPX file format to import information from older versions of Project into Project 2000. Some other project management software packages also support MPX, so if you need to import information from another project management software package, you can save it as an MPX file and import it into Project.

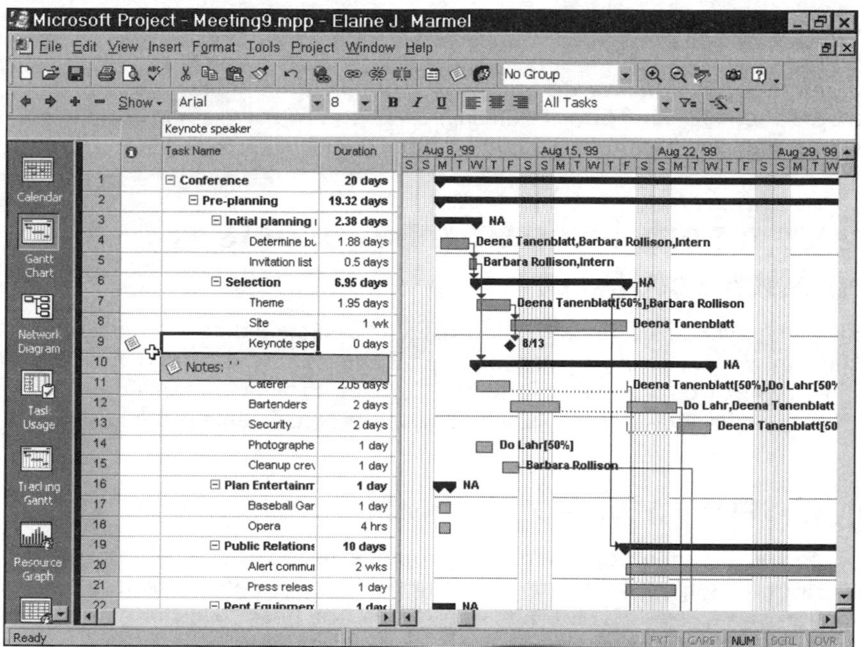


**Figure 20-29:** When you link or embed an object in the note of a task or resource, you can't reveal the contents of the note with the mouse pointer.

Importing an MPX file is similar to importing an Excel workbook or an Access database, except that you don't use an import/export map. Choose File ➪ Open. In the Open dialog box, open the Files of type list box and choose MPX. Use the Look in list box to navigate to the file and click Open.

## Importing text files

If you have a program that can create either a text file or a comma-separated value file, you can import information from that program into Project. You need to save the information you want to import as either a text file or a CSV file in the native program. Again, you use an import/export map to describe to Project the type of data you're importing. If the map you need doesn't exist, you need to create it.

Follow these steps in Project to import the information:

1. Choose File ➪ Open or click the Open button on the Standard toolbar.
2. Open the Files of type list box and choose Text (*.txt) or CSV (*.csv)
3. Use the Look in list box to navigate to the folder containing the file you want to import.
4. Highlight the file and click Open. Project displays the Import Format dialog box.
5. Choose the map you want to use and click Open.

# Troubleshooting

Importing and exporting can be tricky operations. Little things go wrong that cause these operations to fail. This section suggests ways to solve some of the problems you might encounter while importing or exporting.

## Project imports incorrect times in data from Microsoft Excel

In Excel, when you assign a date to a cell, Excel assigns a default time to the cell of 12:00 a.m. You may not see that time, but Excel has attached it to the cell. If the data you import from Microsoft Excel to Microsoft Project contains dates without specific times, Project automatically uses Excel's default time of 12:00 a.m.

## Objects are missing in imported or exported data

If the data you are importing or exporting contains linked or embedded objects, Project does not import or export those objects when exchanging data with Microsoft Excel, Microsoft Access, HTML, MPX, or text files. You need to link or embed the objects again in the file after you complete the import or export operation.

## The export file contains more or less information than expected

The information you find in your exported file depends on the import/export map you select, the table you choose, and the filter you apply. If you export more or less information than you expect, check the map, table, and filter. Choose File ⇨ Save As and specify a filename and file type to display the Export Format dialog box. Highlight the map you want to use and click Edit. Click the appropriate mapping tab; then use the map to inspect the fields you selected for export, the table you selected, and the filter you applied.

## Project imports invalid information

Project checks data you import to ensure that the data types for each field are valid. If necessary, Project may modify the values of some fields to handle inconsistencies.

If Project warns that you are trying to import invalid data, check the import/export map you've selected to make sure you are importing the correct type of information into a Project field. Also check the data in the import file and make sure that the field values are valid and within the acceptable range for the Project field into which you intend to import the data.

### The values of imported information change

This situation is similar to the previous one, where Project determines that the information you're trying to import is invalid. Project checks—and changes if necessary—the data that you import to ensure that the data types and the values for each field are valid. Project may also change data to make sure that it falls within ranges valid for Project fields and won't create inconsistencies between fields that depend on each other. Project also overrides values you attempt to import into calculated fields by replacing the imported data with the calculated value.

### The imported project is empty

As you know, importing depends on the import/export map you select. If you choose the wrong map, no data may import. Also, make sure you're looking at the correct view after importing. If you import task information, you may not see it if you're looking at a resource view.

### Project displays imported information in the wrong fields

When imported information appears in the wrong Project field, you should check the import/export map. Make sure you select the correct map and that the table you used contains the correct fields. Finally, check the mapping of the fields between the import file and your Project file.

## Summary

In this chapter you learned how to import and export information in Microsoft Project. You learned to:

- Create and edit import/export maps
- Export information to Excel, Access, and Word
- Export information to graphics files, text files, HTML files, and other project management software files
- Import information from another project; from Excel, Access, or Word; or from text files
- Solve common problems that occur when you export or import information

✦ ✦ ✦

APPENDIX A

# Project Management Resources

Project management is a detailed methodology and intricate system of requirements that has evolved over many years for various industries and disciplines. Project management as a topic encompasses concepts of leadership and team building, charting and analysis of data, cost and schedule control, and more.

Many useful resources for project management information, tools, and support can help you work with Microsoft Project. This appendix contains five resource categories: Associations, Publications, Education, Online, and Software Products. It provides phone numbers and, when available, address and fax information. As you see from this list, project management is an extremely international discipline. Remember to dial country codes before any phone number outside the United States.

## Associations

The following associations provide support and information for both general and industry-specific project management issues.

- **American Association of Cost Engineers:** Counts among its membership those interested in cost engineering and cost estimating.

  209 Prairie Ave., #100
  Morgantown, WV 26505
  Phone: (800) 858-COST

- **Association of Proposal Management Professionals:** Can assist you in developing proposals for your projects, whether you bid for government or industry contracts. APMP has local chapters as well as a newsletter and task force on Electronic Procurement.

  P.O. Box 970
  111 West 200 South
  Farmington, UT 84025-0970
  Toll Free: (888) 772-9467
  Phone: (801) 451-2323
  Fax: (801) 451-4660

- **Association for Project Management:** Based in England, with chapters in both the United Kingdom and Hong Kong. This association has a certification program for project management professionals.

  Thornton House
  150 West Wycombe Rd.
  High Wycombe
  Buckinghamshire HP12 3AE
  United Kingdom
  Phone: 01494 440090
  Fax: 01494 528937
  E-mail: `secretariat@apm-uk.demon.co.uk`

- **American Society of Quality Control:** Focuses on quality issues in project management. This organization offers certification in a variety of specializations related to quality.

  P.O. Box 3005
  Milwaukee, WI 53201-3005
  Phone: (800) 248-1946

- **The American Project Management Forum:** Brings together executive-level representatives of government agencies and industry to discuss project management-related issues with the intent of improving ties between the project management profession and the United States government.

  PMI-EO
  Phone: (610) 734-3330 ext.1046
  E-mail: `admin@pmi.org`

- **CIPPM:** An international association and center of advanced communication, research, and learning for professional project managers and those interested in project management. CIPPM, founded 1987, is a nonprofit organization based in Ann Arbor, Michigan (United States) at the University of Michigan.

- **Construction Management Association of America**

  Phone: (703) 356-2622
  Fax: (703) 356-6388

- **Educational Society for Resource Management:** (Formerly American Production & Inventory Control Society and still referred to as APICS) Specializes in support and information for those wishing to improve or maximize their resource management skills.

  5301 Shawnee Rd.
  Alexandria, VA 22312-2317
  Phone: (800) 444-2742

- **International Cost Systems Engineering Council:** A global organization that supports those involved in product development and project management.

  1168 Hidden Lake Dr.
  Granite Falls, NC 28630
  Phone: (704) 728-5287
  Fax: (704) 728-0048

- **International Project Management Association (IPMA):** A multinational nonprofit confederation of project management associations based primarily in European countries. It offers international conferences on project management.

  P.O. Box 30
  Monmouth NP5 4YZ
  United Kingdom
  Phone: +44 1594 531007
  Fax: +44 1594 531008
  E-mail: `ipma@btinternet.com`

- **The Japan Project Management Forum (JPMF):** A member-driven, nonprofit organization that promotes project management professionalism in Japan.

  CYD Bldg.
  4-6, Nishi-shimbashi 1-chome,
  Minato-ku, Tokyo, 105-0003, Japan
  Phone: 81-3-3539-4320
  Fax: 81-3-3502-5500
  Web: `www.enaa.or.jp/JPMF/`
  E-mail: `jpmf-adm@enaa.or.jp`
  Secretariat: Kosei Watanabe, Takayuki Kyuno

- **Project Management Institute:** The premier United States project management association. It has chapters across the country, educational programs, a long list of publications, and online discussion forums. In addition, PMI has a monthly magazine called PM Network and a quarterly called Project Management Journal. Its publication, "A Guide to the Project Management Body of Knowledge" (PMBOK Guide), is a bible in the project management world.

  130 South State Rd.
  Upper Darby, PA 19082
  Phone: (610) 734-3330

- **Software Program Managers Network:** Provides information and guidance for those involved in software project management.

  142 N. Central Ave.
  Campbell, CA 95008
  Phone: (408) 378-4700
  Fax: (408) 378-5395

## PMI Special Interest Groups

PMI offers a variety of special interest groups, or SIGs, that focus on different aspects of project management. SIG members are required to pay a small fee to support the group, and all members must also belong to PMI.

These SIGs are either currently available or under consideration:

- Aerospace and Defense
- Automotive
- Design Procurement Construction
- Diversity
- Education and Training
- Environmental Management
- Financial Services
- Government
- Information Management and Movement
- Information Systems
- Manufacturing
- Marketing and Sales
- New Product Development
- Oil, Gas, and Petrochemical
- Pharmaceutical
- Quality in Project Management
- Risk Management
- Service and Outsourcing Projects
- Utility
- Women in Project Management

# Publications

A great many books, newsletters, and journals are devoted to project management and its many facets. Some of the publications in this list are from small presses or associations. You can use the ISBN number, a publishing industry code, to order many of the books from your local bookstore.

## Books

The following books provide guidance on general project management principles and industry-specific project management advice.

- ***The AMA Handbook of Project Management***
  Author: Paul C. Dinsmore
  Publisher: Amacom Books, A Division of AMA
  ISBN: 0-8144-0106-6
- ***Becoming an Indispensable Employee in a Disposable World***
  Author: Neal Whitten
  Publisher: The Neal Whitten Group
  ISBN: 0-13-603812-3
- ***Cost Estimator's Reference Manual***
  Authors: Rodney D. Stewart, James D. Johannes, Richard M. Wyskida, eds.
  Publisher: John Wiley & Sons, Inc.
  ISBN: 0-471-305103
- ***Effective Project Management Through Applied Cost and Schedule Control***
  Authors: James A. Bent and Kenneth K. Humphreys
  Publisher: Marcel Dekker, Inc.
  ISBN: 0-8247-9715-9
- ***Engineering Management***
  Author: Patrick D. T. O'Connor
  Publisher: J. Wiley & Sons
  ISBN: 0-471-93974-9
- ***5-Phase Project Management***
  Authors: Joseph W. Weiss, Robert K. Wysocki
  Publisher: HarperCollins
  ISBN: 0-201-56316-9
- ***Fundamentals of Project Management***
  Author: James P. Lewis
  Publisher: Amacom Books, A Division of AMA
  ISBN: 0-8144-7835-2

- ***A Guide to the Project Management Body of Knowledge***
  Authors: Project Management Institute Standards Committee
  Publisher: Project Management Institute
  ISBN: 1-880410-12-5
- ***In Search of Excellence in Project Management***
  Author: Harold Kerzner
  Publisher: John Wiley & Sons, Inc.
  ISBN: 0-471-29311-3
- ***Managing High-Technology Programs and Projects***
  Author: Russell D. Archibald
  Publisher: John Wiley & Sons, Inc.
  ISBN: 0-471-51327-X
- ***Project Management: Strategic Design and Implementation***
  Author: David I. Cleland
  Publisher: McGraw-Hill Professional Book Group
  ISBN: 0-07-012020-X
- ***Project Management for the 21st Century***
  Authors: Bennet P. Lientz, Kathryn P. Ross
  Publisher: Academic Press
  ISBN: 0-12-449966-X
- ***Project Management Memory Jogger***
  Authors: Karen Tate, Paula Martin
  Publisher: GOAL/QPC
  ISBN: 1-57681-001-1
- ***Practical Risk Assessment for Project Management***
  Author: Stephen Grey
  Publisher: John Wiley & Sons, Inc.
  ISBN: 0-471-93979-X

## Journals and magazines

Many of the associations listed in the first section of this appendix publish magazines or journals. Some of those are listed here, along with a phone number to contact for additional information. Note that many of these publications are available only to members of the organization.

- ***APICS: The Performance Advantage***
  Educational Society for Resource Management
  Phone: (800) 444-2742
- ***Computing Canada*** (regular column on project management)
  Plesman Publications
  Phone: (416) 497-9562

- ***International Journal of Project Management***
  Elsevier Science
  Phone: (212) 633-3730
- ***Journal of Quality Technology***
  American Society of Quality Control
  Phone: (800) 248-1946
- ***Project Management Journal***
  Project Management Institute
  Phone: (704) 586-3715
- ***Quality Engineering***
  American Society of Quality Control
  Phone: (800) 248-1946
- ***Quality Management Journal***
  American Society of Quality Control
  Phone: (800) 248-1946
- ***Technometrics***
  American Society of Quality Control
  Phone: (800) 248-1946

# Education

Educational opportunities exist around the world for certification and degree programs in a variety of project management-related disciplines. Here are just a few:

- **Center for Management and Organization Effectiveness:** Offers workshops relating to coaching and facilitation.

  245 S.E. Madison
  Bartlesville, OK 74006
  Phone: (918) 333-6609
  Fax: (918) 333-5102

- **Louisiana State University:** Offers a week-long seminar through its Department of Executive Education. Go through this seminar to prepare for the PMI certification exam that will earn you the title of Project Management Professional.

  One University Place
  Shreveport, LA 71115-2399
  Phone: (318) 797-5000

- **Project Management Research Network:** Runs out of a university in Austria and supports project management educational programs at many technical schools and universities throughout the world.

  Extraordinariat Projektmanagement
  University of Economics and Business Administration
  Franz Klein-Gasse 1
  1190 Vienna, Austria
  Phone: 0043 1 313 52215

- **The University of Calgary:** (in Alberta, Canada) Has brought together its manufacturing and engineering courses and created a project management area of specialization.

  Project Management Specialization
  Department of Civil Engineering
  The University of Calgary
  2500 University Dr. NW
  Calgary, Alberta, Canada T2N 1N4
  Phone: (403) 220-4816

- **University of New England:** (in New South Wales, Australia) Offers a project management and operations management unit within its MBA degree program. You don't have to fly to Australia to take advantage of these courses (although it's a good excuse to!). The school offers these special programs throughout the world.

  Phone: 61 67 733545
  Fax: 61 67 733461

- **Western Carolina University:** Confers a Masters of Project Management degree from its College of Business.

  College of Business
  Cullowhee, NC 28723
  Phone: (704) 227-7401
  Fax: (704) 227-7414

# Online

You could spend days online and never run through all the project management and project management-associated Web sites. However, here are a few good places to start surfing. Please note that Web sites and addresses change frequently; those listed here were current as this book went to press.

You'll find links to all these sites on the *Microsoft Project 2000 Bible* Web page included on this book's CD-ROM.

- **American Production and Inventory Control Society:** `www.apics.org`
- **Architecture, Engineering, Construction Business Center:** `www.aecinfo.com`
- **Center for Coaching and Mentoring:** `http://coachingandmentoring.com/`
- **Center for International Project and Program Management**: `www.iol.ie/~mattewar/CIPPM`
- **Earned Value Management:** Sponsored by the Office of the Under Secretary of Defense (Acquisition & Technology) Systems Acquisition/Performance Management. `www.acq.osd.mil/pm`
- **FedWorld:** `www.fedworld.gov/`
- **The Project Management Forum:** `www.pmforum.org/newsindx.htm`
- **Project Management Institute:** `www.pmi.org`
- **Project World:** `www.projectworld.com/`
- **Software Program Managers Network:** `http://spmn.com/`

# Software Products

In addition to the excellent software products in demo or trial version form on the companion CD-ROM, here are some other project management tools to investigate:

You'll find the links to all these sites on the *Microsoft Project 2000 Bible* Web page included on this book's CD-ROM.

- **Project Integrator (PI):** Great for working with time and process management issues in a workgroup or team. It has tools for planning, tracking, and reporting on individual resource time expenditures on multiple projects.

  System Solvers, Ltd.
  30685 Barrington Ave., Ste. 100
  Madison Heights, MI 48071-5133
  Phone: (810) 588-7400
  Fax: (810) 588-7170

- **Innate Multi-Project:** Innate Multi-Project extends Microsoft Project to a complete program management system, giving a view across projects, offering resource capacity planning, and supporting your business processes whether top-down or bottom-up.

  Innate, Inc.
  Saracens House, 25 St. Margarets Green
  Ipswich
  Suffolk
  IP4 2BN
  England
  E-mail: mikew@innate.co.uk
  +44 1473 251550

You'll find demos for two other Innate products on the CD-ROM that accompanies this book. Also on the CD-ROM, on the *Microsoft Project 2000 Bible* Web Page, you'll find a link to Innate's web site that you can use to locate and order Multi-Project from Innate.

- **TurboProject:** From International Microcomputer Software, Inc. (IMSI). A higher-end project management software for design, testing, and production.

  IMSI Corporate Headquarters
  75 Rowland Way
  Novato, CA 94945
  Phone: (415) 878-4000
  Fax: (415) 897-2544

  IMSI (UK) Ltd
  IMSI House
  Printing House Lane
  Hayes, Middlesex, England UB3 1AP
  Phone: 0181 581 2000
  Fax: 00181 581 2200

- **Project Administration and Control System (PACS):** The project management portion of a larger financial software suite called Renaissance C/S Financial Applications. If you want to integrate your project costs into your general ledger, check this one out.

  Herkemij & Partners
  Cypresbaan 6
  2908 LT Capelle a/d Ijssel
  The Netherlands
  Phone: 31 10 4580899
  Fax: 31 10 4508233

- **Graneda:** A professional graphics add-on package with which you can create exciting project charts. The application includes extensive printer and plotter drivers for printing your charts.

American Netronic, Inc.
5212 Katella Ave., Ste. 104
Los Alamitos, CA 90720
Phone: (562) 795-0147
Fax: (562) 795-0152

✦ **Artemis:** Offers a bi-directional interface between Microsoft Project 2000 and the Artemis Views enterprise project and resource management solution. Using Artemis MSP Gateway, multiple concurrent project managers can seamlessly exchange project data directly with the Artemis Views enterprise project database. In this way, Microsoft Project becomes a complete enterprise multiproject planning, cost control and resource management solution. With this integration, organizations have the scalability, security, and centralization of the Views client/server architecture, and Microsoft Project users can create projects using predefined project templates, assign available resources from centralized resource pools, and track project progress using integrated timesheets. Best of all, the Artemis MSP Gateway operates as a single tool bar inside Microsoft Project, which gets users up and running quickly.

Artemis Management Systems
6260 Lookout Rd.
Boulder, CO 80301
Phone: (800) 477-6648 (United States and Canada)
(303) 531-3145 (International)
Fax: (303) 531-3140

✦ **Cascade:** An Oracle-based project and finance management tool for senior management. This software is especially helpful in decision analysis for mission-critical projects.

Mantix Systems, Inc.
12020 Sunrise Valley Dr.
Reston, VA 22091
Phone: (703) 715-2450
Fax: (703) 715-2450

✦ **Risk +:** Integrates seamlessly with Microsoft Project to quantify the cost and schedule uncertainty associated with project plans. Anyone familiar with Microsoft Project can easily conduct a sophisticated risk analysis to answer questions such as "What are the chances of completing this effort by 2/28/00?"; "How confident are we that costs will remain below $9 million?"; or "How likely is this task to end up on the critical path?" Single point estimates for task duration and cost tend to be optimistic and provide no insight into the uncertainty associated with a task. With Microsoft Project alone, you are forced to make statements such as "Task X will complete in 10 days." Adding Risk + allows you to make and assess the far more realistic statement, "Task X will take between 8 and 12 days to complete, and most likely about 10 days." With Risk + you are able to identify the high risk areas of your project, determine the likelihood of risk materializing, assess the impact of possible risk, and more importantly, have the information and opportunity to mitigate risk long before it impacts your project.

ProjectGear, Inc.
2522 North Proctor, #37
Tacoma, WA 98406
Phone: (253) 761-9294
Fax: (253) 761-9289

- **SUMMIT Process Management and SUMMIT Ascendant:** Process Management creates Microsoft Project databases (4.*x* through 2000 formats) using the PricewaterhouseCooper SUMMIT method. SUMMIT PM is becoming a Web version this year (SUMMIT Ascendant) and will support the Project 2000 database format at the end of 1999. SUMMIT is a set of information technology methods such as "what and how" to deploy a new large package system or what and how to set up a client-server system. The software products contain these method descriptions and do process management by building Microsoft Project databases from the method's lists of "what to do" and then letting people track the status of tasks and manage their deliverable documents remotely and simultaneously. Microsoft Project fills in the "when" for the project tasks.

  The SUMMIT Center of Excellence
  PricewaterhouseCoopers LLP
  600 Lee Rd.
  Wayne, PA 19087
  Phone: (610) 993-5393

- **Enterprise Project:** A comprehensive software solution for multilevel, multiproject planning, optimization, and reporting. It seamlessly integrates with Microsoft Project to enhance it with a tightly integrated enterprise architecture, adding vital functionality such as dynamic access to enterprise resource pools, a patented skills-based resource scheduling engine, and robust executive reporting and decision support tools. Using Enterprise Project, project managers continue to work with a familiar desktop tool. Enterprise Project functions — such as access to the enterprise resource pools, skills-based search engine, current task loads, and the task status module — are conveniently accessible within Microsoft Project 2000, giving project managers maximum flexibility to rapidly develop optimal project plans.

- **WARP Scheduler:** Also from Enterprise Project, WARP Scheduler automatically performs resource schedule leveling and optimization based on skill qualification, best schedule, lowest cost, and other user-selectable context variables. Its adaptive engine can schedule tens of thousands of tasks in seconds, making it by far the fastest project management solution available on the market today. WARP can automatically and optimally assign resources based on multiple individual skills, dramatically increasing utilization and reducing overhead costs. WARP makes it possible to re-engineer to suit specific management criteria in seconds, providing a big picture of results for every "what if" scenario.

jeTECH DATA SYSTEMS, INC.
5153 Camino Ruiz
Camarillo, CA 93012-8601
Phone: (805) 383-8500
Fax: (805) 383.2830

- **Hans Tørsleff TimeReg:** A time registration system that updates Microsoft Project with Actual Work entered by the individual resource, sparing the project manager the manual update of the project plan and giving more time to the real management of the project.
- **Hans Tørsleff Project Manager:** Allows you to decentralize the planning of the project and resource management but maintain the bird's-eye perspective provided by a centralized project management tool. It includes reporting and a Virtual Project generator.

  Hans Tørsleff Management Systems A/S
  Gl. Kongevej 161
  1850 Frederiksberg C
  Denmark
  Phone: +45 70 20 08 16
  Fax: +45 70 22 08 07
  E-mail: mail@htms.dk
- **Business Engine:** A resource management tool that helps corporations track and manage people, time, and budgets across hundreds of projects. It integrates project, timesheet, and budget information from a variety of resources.

  Business Engine Software Corporation
  100 Bush St., 22nd Floor
  San Francisco, CA 94104
  Phone: (415) 616-4000
  Fax: (415) 616-4008
- **Project InVision 4:** A Web-based project management repository application that allows Microsoft Project users to access Microsoft Project schedules and project-related data or documents across a corporate intranet or the Internet from any computer equipped with a browser. The application's Time Tracking interface allows users to gather their task assignments from across multiple projects and submit weekly timesheets for posting to Microsoft Project schedules. Project InVision 4 is fully customizable, allowing individual workgroups to configure custom fields, define workflow, and integrate templates based on their unique processes and methodologies.

  SME Corporation
  1038 Redwood Hwy B7
  Mill Valley, CA 94941
  Phone: (888) 763-3555

- **Project Control:** Uses a centralized database of information about all your projects to help you control multiple projects. You can update a single project or all your projects from this database. Project Control's document manager works with applications such as Word and Excel to help you track all documents associated with a project.

  Project Control Software
  147 Old Solomons Island Rd.; Ste. 513
  Annapolis, MD 21401
  Phone: (410) 897-0965
  Fax: (410) 897-1135

- **Project Partner:** Functions as an add-on application with Microsoft Project to present the scheduling data in several very useful graphic formats. The three main options include a timescaled network diagram, an earned-value spending curve, and a resource or cash flow by period summary. Project Partner is designed to increase a project team's ability to easily communicate complex project status information.

  Bluewater Project Management Services, LLC
  500 S. 336th Ave., Ste. 204
  Federal Way, WA 98003
  Phone: (253) 874-8884
  Fax: (253) 838-1798

✦ ✦ ✦

# Project Management Worksheet

This appendix provides worksheets that allow you to plan every phase of a project. Feel free to make copies of these pages and fill them in as you work through your project to be sure you've covered all the bases in managing your project.

You'll find a copy of this appendix in the *Microsoft Project 2000 Bible* Forms folder on the CD-ROM of this book in .PDF (Adobe Acrobat) format to help you print and use these forms. You'll also find a copy of Adobe Acrobat Reader if you need it.

## Phase I: Research

In this phase you are gathering information about the scope and goals of your project; determining parameters such as dates, resources, and money available for your project; and specifying deliverables.

1. Ask the following people or groups of people to define the goal of this project. Note any discrepancies in their goal statements and resolve them before you begin planning your project:
   - Your manager
   - Your staff
   - The manager of finance
   - The person who manages the product or service that pertains to your project. For example, if you are setting up a new manufacturing unit, contact the production line supervisor. If you are organizing the move to a new facility, contact the office or facilities manager.

Write the responses here:

________________________________________

________________________________________

________________________________________

________________________________________

**2.** In the space provided, sketch the organizational chart of those who will implement your project. Indicate who reports to whom within your general organization and then specifically for this project (these two hierarchies may differ slightly). Who will expect to receive reports, communications, and deliverables?

**3.** To help you begin to build a project team, list the resources you may have available for your project in the following table, noting each resource's department, expertise, and availability.

Table B-1
**Project Resources Table**

| *Resource* | *Department* | *Expertise* | *Availability* |
|---|---|---|---|
| | | | |
| | | | |
| | | | |
| | | | |
| | | | |

**4.** Research timing for this project and answer these questions:

- How long have similar projects taken in your organization or your experience?

- Are any dates related to your project immutable, such as a yearly inspection by an outside organization or the end of your fiscal year? List them here.

- Rank the priority of the three major areas that typically affect a project: time, quality, and cost. In a crunch, the criteria you rank highest here will take precedence.

  ___ Time

  ___ Quality

  ___ Cost

# Phase II: Planning

In this phase you take some of the information you gathered in Phase I and begin to see how those details will come together to form a project plan that can be the basis of your project schedule.

1. Write a goal statement. This one-sentence description states the desired end result of all the efforts in your project. A sample goal statement might be: "Our goal is to successfully launch a new software product into the marketplace."

   ______________________________________________

   ______________________________________________

   ______________________________________________

2. Write a scope statement. This statement should broadly outline the parameters of your project. A sample scope statement might be: "We will finalize the software according to our internal quality standards and launch it in three major markets by the end of this fiscal year at a cost not to exceed $1.2 million."

   ______________________________________________

   ______________________________________________

   ______________________________________________

   ______________________________________________

   ______________________________________________

**3.** List the major phases of your project:

________________________________________________________________________

________________________________________________________________________

________________________________________________________________________

________________________________________________________________________

________________________________________________________________________

**4.** List any milestones in your project. Milestones are tasks that mark a moment or accomplishment in your project.

________________________________________________________________________

________________________________________________________________________

________________________________________________________________________

________________________________________________________________________

________________________________________________________________________

________________________________________________________________________

________________________________________________________________________

________________________________________________________________________

________________________________________________________________________

________________________________________________________________________

5. Create a contact list for your project, including each resource's name, title, and department; each resource's manager, contact information, hourly rate or fee; and any other information you consider useful. You can create this list in a word processing program, such as Word for Windows, or begin to enter this resource information in Microsoft Project. Use the following entry as a model:

   Resource Name: John Smith
   Title/Department: Engineer/manufacturing department
   Manager: Sally Jones, manufacturing manager
   Phone: (444) 555-1111
   E-mail: `jsmith@org.com`
   Rate: $35 per hour
   Comments: Not available in December due to professional association commitments; assistant is Bob James, ext. 5567

6. Outline the standards you will use for entering information into Microsoft Project, including the following:
   - How will you name resources (by name or title)?
   - Who will track progress and how often?
   - What are your organization's standard work hours and fiscal year? This information enables you to create an accurate calendar in Project.

- What regular reports will you generate and who will they go to?

______________________________________________

______________________________________________

- How will you track and account for overtime?

______________________________________________

______________________________________________

# Phase III: Creating Your Project Schedule

In this phase you enter information to begin building your project. Use this checklist to be sure you are creating a comprehensive and accurate schedule.

## Checklist for creating a Project schedule

- ☐ Enter general project information, such as the project name and start and finish dates.
- ☐ Make any calendar settings for your project based on your organization's work day, week, or year.
- ☐ Enter the names of major phases of your project.
- ☐ Enter the first level of individual tasks in each phase, including task name and timing. If this level task will have subtasks, don't bother to enter timing as the task timing will be derived from subtasks.
- ☐ Enter any subtasks and include timing information.
- ☐ Enter any regularly recurring tasks such as monthly project meetings.
- ☐ Add resource information to individual tasks including costs and availability.
- ☐ Establish dependencies between tasks.
- ☐ Study and resolve resource conflicts using the resource leveling and contouring tools in Project.
- ☐ Determine whether Project is giving you an acceptable finish date. If it isn't, consider any of the following actions:

- Add resources to reduce timing. (However, this action is likely to add costs.)
- Request additional time to complete the project.
- Utilize resource downtime more efficiently.
- Adjust dependencies.
- Start the project earlier.

☐ If possible, add some slack into tasks to allow for delays.

☐ Set up any workgroup resources with whom you will be using Project's TeamAssign, TeamStatus, and TeamUpdate features.

☐ When the project is acceptable, set the baseline and save the file.

# Phase IV: Tracking Your Project

Tracking your project involves entering actual time expended on tasks. Use this checklist to help in tracking projects. Don't forget to set a baseline before beginning to track activity on your project.

## Tracking Procedures Checklist

☐ Enter actual start and finish dates for tasks that have been completed.

☐ Enter resource effort expended on tasks.

☐ Enter actual fees or charges incurred on tasks.

☐ Set remaining durations and percent complete for individual tasks.

☐ Use various tracking views in Project, information about earned value and resource usage, and filters such as critical path to analyze the status of your project. Pay careful attention to how much time and money remains by comparing your original estimates and actual activity on the project.

☐ Make any adjustments necessary to keep your project on track, such as adding or reassigning resources, extending your final deadline, or reassessing the budget remaining to you for the rest of the project based on cost overruns.

☐ Send out TeamStatus and TeamUpdate messages to keep your team informed of project progress.

# Phase V: Preparing for the Next Project

Now that you've completed a project, don't forget to analyze what went on so you can improve on estimating and tracking your next project. Use this worksheet to analyze your complete project.

1. List your baseline start and finish dates and actual start and finish dates for your entire project here:
   - Baseline start: ______________________________
   - Baseline finish: ______________________________
   - Actual start: ______________________________
   - Actual finish: ______________________________

2. Write a statement about the major factor that affected your timing and a conclusion about whether you could have anticipated or avoided that factor. Be honest about your own failings. It's the best way to become better at what you do.

   ______________________________

   ______________________________

   ______________________________

3. Enter your baseline total costs and actual total costs for the project here:
   - Baseline costs: ______________________________
   - Actual costs: ______________________________

4. Write a statement about the major factor or factors influencing your final costs, including what you can do to avoid cost overruns on a future project (or, if you're lucky, what you can do to have similar cost savings on future projects). What did you do or not do to keep costs in line?

   ______________________________

   ______________________________

   ______________________________

5. Analyze how resources performed on your project. Are there people or vendors you would not recommend for use on future projects? Are there people or vendors you feel did exceptionally well? Make a record of them here so that you and others in your company can plan resources for future projects appropriately.

   - Vendor issues on current project:

   ______________________________

   ______________________________

   ______________________________

   - Recommended resources for future projects:

   ______________________________

   ______________________________

   ______________________________

6. List three things you can do more efficiently as a project manager on your next project to improve performance and efficiency:

   ______________________________

   ______________________________

   ______________________________

7. List three things your manager or organization could provide you with to make your next project more successful:

   ______________________________

   ______________________________

   ______________________________

8. List three ways you can improve your tracking procedures on future projects:

______________________________________________

______________________________________________

______________________________________________

9. Write statements of what worked and didn't work in your management of resources in these areas:

   - Communication:

______________________________________________

______________________________________________

______________________________________________

   - Accuracy of time estimates for resources to complete tasks:

______________________________________________

______________________________________________

______________________________________________

   - Resource management:

______________________________________________

______________________________________________

______________________________________________

✦ ✦ ✦

# Available Fields and Functions for Custom Field Formulas

This appendix contains three tables that help you identify the fields and functions you can use when creating formulas to include in custom fields. Table C-1 contains a list of all the Task fields you can include in a formula. I've listed the fields according to the submenu on which they appear when you click the Fields button in the Formula dialog box. Table C-2 contains the same information for Resource fields. In each of these tables, the first column contains a field category. The second column contains either fields within the category or a subcategory. If the second column contains a subcategory, the fields appear in the third column. Table C-3 lists the functions you can include in a formula as well as a description of the function's purpose.

See Chapter 18 for more information on creating formulas in custom fields.

Table C-1
**Task Fields Available for Custom Field Formulas**

| *Category* | *Subcategory or Field* | *Field* |
|---|---|---|
| Cost | Actual Cost | |
| | Actual Overtime Cost | |
| | ACWP | |
| | Baseline Cost | |
| | BCWP | |
| | BCWS | |
| | Cost | |
| | Cost Rate Table | |
| | Cost Variance | |
| | Custom Costs | Cost1–Cost10 |
| | CV | |
| | Fixed Cost | |
| | Fixed Cost Accrual | |
| | Overtime Cost | |
| | Remaining Cost | |
| | Remaining Overtime Cost | |
| | SV | |
| | VAC | |
| Date | Actual Finish | |
| | Actual Start | |
| | Baseline Finish | |
| | Baseline Start | |
| | Constraint Date | |
| | Created | |
| | Custom Date | Date1–Date10 |
| | Custom Finish | Finish1–Finish10 |
| | Custom Start | Start1–Start10 |

| *Category* | *Subcategory or Field* | *Field* |
|---|---|---|
| | Deadline | |
| | Early Finish | |
| | Early Start | |
| | Finish | |
| | Finish Variance | |
| | Late Finish | |
| | Late Start | |
| | Preleveled Finish | |
| | Preleveled SW | |
| | Resume | |
| | Start | |
| | Start Variance | |
| | Stop | |
| Duration | Actual Duration | |
| | Baseline Duration | |
| | Custom Duration | Duration1–Duration10 |
| | Duration | |
| | Duration Variance | |
| | Finish Slack | |
| | Free Slack | |
| | Leveling Delay | |
| | Remaining Duration | |
| | Start Slack | |
| | Total Slack | |

*Continued*

**Table C-1 (continued)**

| Category | Subcategory or Field | Field |
|---|---|---|
| Flag | Confirmed | |
| | Critical | |
| | Custom Flag | Flag1–Flag20 |
| | Effort Driven | |
| | Estimated | |
| | External Task | |
| | Group By Summary | |
| | Hide Bar | |
| | Ignore Resource Calendar | |
| | Level Assignments | |
| | Leveling Can Split | |
| | Linked Fields | |
| | Marked | |
| | Milestone | |
| | Overallocated | |
| | Recurring | |
| | Response Pending | |
| | Rollup | |
| | Subproject Read Only | |
| | Summary | |
| | TeamStatus Pending | |
| | Update Needed | |
| ID/Code | Custom Outline Code | Outline Code1–Outline Code10 |
| | ID | |
| | Outline Number | |
| | Predecessors | |
| | Successors | |
| | Unique ID | |

| *Category* | *Subcategory or Field* | *Field* |
|---|---|---|
| | Unique ID Predecessors | |
| | Unique ID Successors | |
| | WBS | |
| | WBS of Predecessors | |
| | WBS of Successors | |
| Number | % Complete | |
| | Actual Overtime Work | |
| | Custom Number | Number1–Number20 |
| | Objects | |
| | Outline Level | |
| | Priority | |
| Project | Dates | Creation Date |
| | | Current Date |
| | | Default Finish Time |
| | | Default Start Time |
| | | Last Update |
| | | Project Finish |
| | | Project Start |
| | | Status Date |
| | Numbers | Minutes Per Day |
| | | Minutes Per Week |
| | | Resource Count |
| | | Task Count |
| | Text | Author |
| | | Project Calendar |
| | | Subject |
| | | Title |

*Continued*

**Table C-1 (continued)**

| *Category* | *Subcategory or Field* | *Field* |
|---|---|---|
| Text | Constraint Type | |
| | Contact | |
| | Custom Text | Text1–Text30 |
| | Hyperlink | |
| | Hyperlink Address | |
| | Hyperlink Href | |
| | Hyperlink SubAddress | |
| | Name | |
| | Notes | |
| | Project | |
| | Resource Group | |
| | Resource Initials | |
| | Resource Names | |
| | Resource Phonetics | |
| | Resource Type | |
| | Subproject File | |
| | Task Calendar | |
| | Type | |
| Work | % Work Complete | |
| | Actual Work | |
| | Baseline Work | |
| | Overtime Work | |
| | Regular Work | |
| | Remaining Overtime Work | |
| | Remaining Work | |
| | Work | |
| | Work Variance | |

Table C-2
**Resource Fields Available for Custom Field Formulas**

| *Category* | *Subcategory or Field* | *Field* |
|---|---|---|
| Cost | Accrue At | |
| | Actual Cost | |
| | Actual Overtime Cost | |
| | ACWP | |
| | Baseline Cost | |
| | BCWP | |
| | BCWS | |
| | Cost | |
| | Cost Per Use | |
| | Cost Rate Table | |
| | Cost Variance | |
| | Custom Cost | Cost1–Cost10 |
| | CV | |
| | Overtime Cost | |
| | Overtime Rate | |
| | Remaining Cost | |
| | Remaining Overtime Cost | |
| | Standard Rate | |
| | SV | |
| | VAC | |
| Date | Available From | |
| | Available To | |
| | Baseline Finish | |
| | Baseline Start | |
| | Custom Date | Date1–Date10 |
| | Custom Duration | Duration1–Duration10 |
| | Custom Finish | Finish1–Finish10 |
| | Custom Start | Start1–Start10 |
| | Finish | |
| | Start | |

*Continued*

**Table C-2 (continued)**

| ***Category*** | ***Subcategory or Field*** | ***Field*** |
|---|---|---|
| Flag | Can Level | |
| | Confirmed | |
| | Custom Flag | Flag1–Flag20 |
| | Linked Fields | |
| | Overallocated | |
| | Response Pending | |
| | TeamStatus Pending | |
| | Update Needed | |
| ID | Custom Outline Code | Outline Code1–Outline Code10 |
| | ID | |
| | Unique ID | |
| Number | Custom Number | Number1–Number20 |
| | Max Units | |
| | Objects | |
| | Peak | |
| Project | Dates | Creation Date |
| | | Current Date |
| | | Default Finish Time |
| | | Default Start Time |
| | | Last Update |
| | | Project Finish |
| | | Project Start |
| | | Status Date |
| | Numbers | Minutes Per Day |
| | | Minutes Per Week |

| *Category* | *Subcategory or Field* | *Field* |
|---|---|---|
| | | Resource Count |
| | | Task Count |
| | Text | Author |
| | | Project |
| | | Calendar |
| | | Subject |
| | | Title |
| Text | Base Calendar | |
| | Code | |
| | Custom Text | Text1–Text30 |
| | E-mail Address | |
| | Group | |
| | GroupBy Summary | |
| | Hyperlink | |
| | Hyperlink Address | |
| | Hyperlink Href | |
| | Hyperlink SubAddress | |
| | Initials | |
| | Material Label | |
| | Name | |
| | Notes | |
| | NTAccount | |
| | Phonetics | |
| | Project | |
| | Workgroup | |

*Continued*

**Table C-2 (continued)**

| Category | Subcategory or Field | Field |
|---|---|---|
| Work | % Work Complete | |
| | Actual Overtime Work | |
| | Actual Work | |
| | Baseline Work | |
| | Overtime Work | |
| | Custom Start | Start1–Start10 |
| | Finish | |
| | Start | |
| | Regular Work | |
| | Remaining Overtime Work | |
| | Remaining Work | |
| | Type | |
| | Work | |
| | Work Variance | |

**Table C-3**
**Functions Available for Custom Field Formulas**

| Function Category | Function | Description |
|---|---|---|
| Conversion | Asc(string) | Returns an Integer representing the character code corresponding to the first letter in a string |
| | CBool(expression) | Coerces an expression to a Boolean |
| | CByte(expression) | Coerces an expression to a Byte (0–255) |
| | CCur(expression) | Coerces an expression to a Currency value |
| | CDate(expression) | Coerces an expression to a Date |
| | CDbl(expression) | Coerces an expression to a Double |
| | CDec(expression) | Coerces an expression to a Decimal |

| Function Category | Function | Description |
|---|---|---|
| | Chr(charcode) | Returns a string containing the character associated with the specified character code |
| | CInt(expression) | Coerces an expression to a Integer |
| | CLng(expression) | Coerces an expression to a Long |
| | CSng(expression) | Coerces an expression to a Single |
| | CStr(expression) | Coerces an expression to a String |
| | CVar(expression) | Coerces an expression to a Variant |
| | DateSerial(year, month, day) | Returns a Variant (Date) for a specified year, month, and day |
| | DateValue(date) | Returns a Variant (Date) |
| | Day(date) | Returns a Variant (Integer) specifying a whole number between 1 and 31, inclusive, representing the day of the month |
| | Hex(number) | Returns a String representing the hexadecimal value of a number |
| | Hour(time) | Returns a Variant (Integer) specifying a whole number between 0 and 23, inclusive, representing the hour of the day |
| | Minute(time) | Returns a Variant (Integer) specifying a whole number between 0 and 59, inclusive, representing the minute of the hour |
| | Month(date) | Returns a Variant (Integer) specifying a whole number between 1 and 12, inclusive, representing the month of the year |
| | Oct(number) | Returns a Variant (String) representing the octal value of a number |
| | ProjDurConv (expr, durunits) | Converts a numeric value to a duration value in the specified units |

*Continued*

**Table C-3 *(continued)***

| *Function Category* | *Function* | *Description* |
|---|---|---|
| | Second(time) | Returns a Variant (Integer) specifying a whole number between 0 and 59, inclusive, representing the second of the minute |
| | Str(number) | Returns a Variant (String) representation of a number |
| | StrConv(string, conversion, LCID) | Returns a Variant (String) converted as specified |
| | TimeSerial(hour, minute, second) | Returns a Variant (Date) containing the time for a specific hour, minute, and second |
| | TimeValue(time) | Returns a Variant (Date) containing the time |
| | Val(string) | Returns the numbers contained in a string as a numeric value of appropriate type |
| | Weekday(date, firstdayofweek) | Returns a Variant (integer) containing a whole number representing the day of the week |
| | Year(date) | Returns a Variant (Integer) containing a whole number representing the year |
| Date/Time | Cdate(expression) | Coerces an expression to a Date |
| | Date( ) | Returns a Variant (Date) containing the current system date |
| | DateAdd(interval, number, date) | Returns a Variant (Date) containing a date to which a specified time interval has been added |
| | DateDiff(interval, date1, date2, firstdayofweek, firstweekofyear) | Returns a Variant (Long) specifying the number of time intervals between two specified dates |
| | DatePart(interval, date, firstdayofweek, firstweekofyear) | Returns a Variant (Integer) containing the specified part of a given date |

| *Function Category* | *Function* | *Description* |
|---|---|---|
| | DateSerial(year, month, day) | Returns a Variant (Date) for a specified year, month, and day |
| | DateValue(date) | Returns a Variant (Date) |
| | Day(date) | Returns a Variant (Integer) specifying a whole number between 1 and 31, inclusive, representing the day of the month |
| | Hour(time) | Returns a Variant (Integer) specifying a whole number between 0 and 23, inclusive, representing the hour of the day |
| | IsDate(expression) | Returns a Boolean value indicating whether an expression can be converted to a date |
| | Minute(time) | Returns a Variant (Integer) specifying a whole number between 0 and 59, inclusive, representing the minute of the hour |
| | Month(date) | Returns a Variant (Integer) specifying a whole number between 1 and 12, inclusive, representing the month of the year |
| | Now( ) | Returns a Variant (Date) specifying the current date and time according your computer system's date and time |
| | ProjDateAdd(date, duration, calendar) | Adds a duration to a date to return a new date |
| | ProjDateDiff(date1, date2, calendar) | Returns the duration between two dates in minutes |
| | ProjDateSub(date, duration, calendar) | Returns the date that precedes another date by a specified duration |
| | ProjDurValue(duration) | Returns the number of minutes in a duration |
| | Second(time) | Returns a Variant (Integer) specifying a whole number between 0 and 59, inclusive, representing the second of the minute |

*Continued*

**Table C-3 *(continued)***

| *Function Category* | *Function* | *Description* |
|---|---|---|
| | Time() | Returns a Variant (Date) indicating the current system time |
| | Timer() | Returns a Single representing the number of seconds elapsed since midnight |
| | TimeSerial(hour, minute, second) | Returns a Variant (Date) containing the time for a specific hour, minute, and second |
| | TimeValue(time) | Returns a Variant (Date) containing the time |
| | Weekday(date, firstdayofweek) | Returns a Variant (Integer) containing a whole number representing the day of the week |
| | Year(date) | Returns a Variant (Integer) containing a whole number representing the year |
| General | Choose(index, expr1, expr2, expr3) | Selects and returns a value from a list of arguments |
| | IIf(expr, truepart, falsepart) | Returns one of two parts, depending on the evaluation of an expression |
| | IsNumeric(expression) | Returns a Boolean value indicating whether an expression can be evaluated as a number |
| | IsNull(expression) | Returns a Boolean value that indicates whether an expression contains no valid data |
| | Switch(expr1, value1, expr2, value2, expr3, value3) | Evaluates a list of expressions and returns a Variant value or an expression associated with the first expression in the list that is True |
| Math | Abs(number) | Returns a value of the same type that is passed to it specifying the absolute value of a number |
| | Atn(number) | Returns a Double specifying the arctangent of a number |

| *Function Category* | *Function* | *Description* |
|---|---|---|
| | Cos(number) | Returns a Double specifying the cosine of an angle |
| | Exp(number) | Returns a Double specifying *e* (the base of natural logarithms) raised to a power |
| | Fix(number) | Returns the integer portion of a number. If number is negative, Fix returns the first negative integer greater than or equal to number. |
| | Int(number) | Returns the integer portion of a number. If number is negative, Int returns the first negative integer less than or equal to number. |
| | Log(number) | Returns a Double specifying the natural logarithm of a number |
| | Rnd(number) | Returns a Single containing a random number |
| | Sgn(number) | Returns a Variant (Integer) indicating the sign of a number |
| | Sin(number) | Returns a Double specifying the sine of an angle |
| | Sqr(number) | Returns a Double specifying the square root of a number |
| | Tan(number) | Returns a Double specifying the tangent of an angle |
| Microsoft Project | ProjDateAdd(date, duration, calendar) | Adds a duration to a date to return a new date |
| | ProjDateDiff(date1, date2, calendar) | Returns the duration between two dates in minutes |
| | ProjDateSub(date, duration, calendar) | Returns the date that precedes another date by a specified duration |
| | ProjDurConv(expr, durunits) | Converts a numeric value to a duration value in the specified units |
| | ProjDurValue(duration) | Returns the number of minutes in a duration |

*Continued*

| Table C-3 (continued) | | |
|---|---|---|
| ***Function Category*** | ***Function*** | ***Description*** |
| Text | Asc(string) | Returns an Integer representing the character code corresponding to the first letter in a string |
| | Chr(charcode) | Returns a String containing the character associated with the specified character code |
| | Format(expression, format firstdayofweek, firstweekofyear) | Returns a Variant (String) containing an expression formatted according to instructions contained in a format expression |
| | InStr(start, string1, string2, compare) | Returns a Variant (Long) specifying the position of the first occurrence of one string within another |
| | LCase(string) | Returns a String that has been converted to lowercase |
| | Left(string, length) | Returns a Variant (String) containing a specified number of characters from the left side of a string |
| | Len(string \| varname) | Returns a Long containing the number of characters in a string or the number of bytes required to store a variable |
| | LTrim(string) | Returns a Variant (String) containing a copy of a specified string without leading spaces |
| | Mid(string, start, length) | Returns a Variant (String) containing a specified number of characters from a string |
| | Right(string, length) | Returns a Variant (String) containing a specified number of characters from the right side of a string |
| | RTrim(string) | Returns a Variant (String) containing a copy of a specified string without trailing spaces |
| | Space(number) | Returns a Variant (String) consisting of the specified number of spaces |
| | StrComp(string1, string2, compare) | Returns a Variant (Integer) indicating the result of a string comparison |

| Function Category | Function | Description |
|---|---|---|
| | StrConv(string, conversion, LCID) | Returns a Variant (String) converted as specified |
| | String(number, character) | Returns a Variant (String) containing a repeating character string of the length specified |
| | Trim(string) | Returns a Variant (String) containing a copy of a specified string without leading and trading spaces |
| | UCase(string) | Returns a Variant (String) containing the specified string, converted to uppercase |

✦ ✦ ✦

# What's on the CD-ROM

The CD-ROM that accompanies this book contains demos or trial versions of several of the most popular add-on products for use with Microsoft Project. In addition, I've included sample files for three of the most common types of projects for you to use as time-savers when you begin building similar schedules. You'll also find a Web page of links to some Project partners and the forms from Appendix B in Adobe Acrobat Reader (.PDF) format — along with a copy of Adobe Acrobat Reader — so you can easily print the forms and use them.

## Software on the CD-ROM

This appendix describes the contents of the CD-ROM and gives instructions for installing each program on your computer. You can use the trial or demonstration versions of these products to see how they fit your needs. Each listing includes contact information so that you can buy the software directly from the vendor.

In some cases these vendors did not have the fully updated version of their software for Project 2000 ready in time for this book's publication. If you have access to Project 98, you can test the early version and then order the Project 2000 version. If you no longer have access to Project 98, you can contact the companies to get an updated demo or more product information. Also, you'll find WinZip on the CD-ROM, in case you need it to unzip and install any of the products on the CD-ROM.

## Microsoft Project 2000 Bible Appendix B

In the *Forms* folder, you'll find a .PDF file of the forms in Appendix B of this book, which you can use to help you plan your project. PDF files can be read with Adobe Acrobat Reader, which you'll also find on the CD-ROM. If you open the file in Adobe Acrobat Reader, you can easily print the forms.

## Microsoft Project 2000 Bible Web Page

In the *Microsoft Project 2000 Bible* Web Page folder, you'll find a link to the Web page I've compiled of links to the sites of Microsoft Project partners who offer software that enhances Microsoft Project and assistance in using Microsoft Project (see Figure D-1). At several of the Web sites, you'll find Web-based demo products.

**Figure D-1:** A sample of my Web page that you'll find on the CD-ROM of this book.

To use my Web page, connect to the Internet. Then, double-click the My Computer icon on your Windows desktop. Open the *Microsoft Project 2000 Bible* Web Page folder on the CD-ROM and double-click PROJECT 2000.HTM. Click the various links to visit the Web sites and review information.

## Empire TIME

The Windows Support Group, Inc.
150 West 22nd St.
New York, NY 10011
Phone: (212) 675-2500
Web site: www.wsg.com

**Installation instructions:** Choose Start ➪ Programs ➪ Windows Explorer. Make a temporary folder on your hard disk. Then, open the Empire TIME folder on the CD-ROM and double-click the SETUP.EXE file. Follow the onscreen prompts to install the demo version of the program. Installation creates a Demo folder on your hard drive and an Empire TIME Demo group on the Programs menu. You can uninstall the demo by running unInstallSHIELD from the same Empire TIME Demo group.

**Running the program:** To run Empire TIME from the Windows Start menu, choose Programs ➪ Empire TIME Demo ➪ ETDemo.

A multicurrency project time and expense accounting system, Empire TIME can be used for internal chargebacks or external billing. Empire TIME is a high performance, Windows-based client/server system that integrates with Microsoft Project, allowing managers to analyze time, staff assignments, costs and revenue on their projects. Empire TIME distinguishes itself with robust accounting capabilities for tracking and invoicing actual cost and revenue for time, expenses, services and materials.

## Innate Info

Innate, Inc.
Saracens House, 25 St. Margarets Green
Ipswich
Suffolk
IP4 2BN
England
E-mail: mikew@innate.co.uk
+44 1473 251550

**Installation instructions:** You can run this demo software directly from the CD-ROM without installing anything on your disk. You'll need Windows 95, 98, NT, or 2000 and any browser. The demo will run correctly in Internet Explorer 4 or Netscape 4 or later.

**Running the demonstration:** Double-click the My Computer icon on your Windows desktop. Open the Innate folder on the CD-ROM and double-click INDEX.HTM. Follow the onscreen links and prompts to see the demonstration and more information.

Innate Info works with Innate products to publish your data for staff and managers to view as a web of information (via browsers .. or via printers!). Exception reports, progress reports, from top level views to the finest level of detail can all be produced automatically.

## Innate Timesheets

Innate, Inc.
Three First National Plaza
70 W. Madison, Ste. 1400
Chicago, IL 60602
Phone: (312) 781-9674
E-mail: `sales@innateus.com`
Web: `www.innateus.com`

**Installation instructions:** You can run this demo software directly from the CD-ROM without installing anything on your disk. You'll need Window 95, 98, NT, or 2000 and any browser. The demo will run correctly in Internet Explorer 4 or Netscape 4 or later.

**Running the demonstration:** Double-click the My Computer icon on your Windows desktop. Open the Innate folder on the CD-ROM and double-click INDEX.HTM. Follow the onscreen links and prompts to see the demonstration and more information.

Innate Timesheets is a simple-to-use application using the Web or Microsoft Windows. You record time, effort, and progress into a central open database, and Innate Timesheets gives you a wide range of reports and options to link to other corporate systems. You can automatically incorporate and update Microsoft Project plans.

## Milestones, Etc. 5.0

Kidasa Software
1114 Lost Creek Blvd., Ste. 300
Austin, TX 78746
Phone: (800) 765-0167
E-mail: `sales@kidasa.com`

**Installation instructions:** Double-click the My Computer icon on your Windows desktop. Open the Milestones folder on the CD-ROM and double-click the MILESTONES501.EXE file. Follow the onscreen prompts to install the trial version of the program. Note that no serial number is required to install this trial version. When you are asked to enter this number, type **None** and proceed. However, you will need a default printer selected.

**Running the program:** Milestones, Etc. trial version is Project 98–compatible. To run Milestones, Etc. from the Windows Start menu, choose Programs ➪ Milestones, Etc.

Milestones, Etc. is a front end for Microsoft Project. You can enter and manage project data in Milestones and then move (export) it into Project. You can also import Project data to Milestones. This approach enables you to better control the display of some Project data because you can make settings for the number of tasks per page, column and page layout, and OLE linking and embedding.

Milestones, Etc. can also be used as a stand-alone scheduler for creating and updating simple Gantt or timeline schedules without using the resource management features of Project.

## PERT Chart EXPERT

Critical Tools
8004 Bottlebrush Dr.
Austin, TX 78750
Phone: (512) 342-2232
Web: `www.criticaltools.com`

**Installation instructions:** Double-click the My Computer icon on your Windows desktop. Open the PERTChart folder and double-click the setup file.

**Running the program:** This trial version of PERT Chart EXPERT is Project 2000–compatible. When you install this program, you can opt to add a toolbar to Project. Then simply open a Microsoft Project file and either select the PERT Chart EXPERT menu or click the toolbar button to automatically generate a PERT chart. Alternatively, you can open the program from the Windows Start menu. Choose Programs ➪ PERT Chart EXPERT 2000 ➪ PERT 2000. When the program window opens, choose File ➪ Go to Project to open Project 2000.

PERT Chart Expert is a Windows-based application that enables you to create PERT charts from existing Project schedules, text files, or spreadsheets. As an add-on to Microsoft Project, PERT Chart EXPERT integrates with Project to generate presentation-quality PERT chart diagrams such as the one shown in Figure D-2.

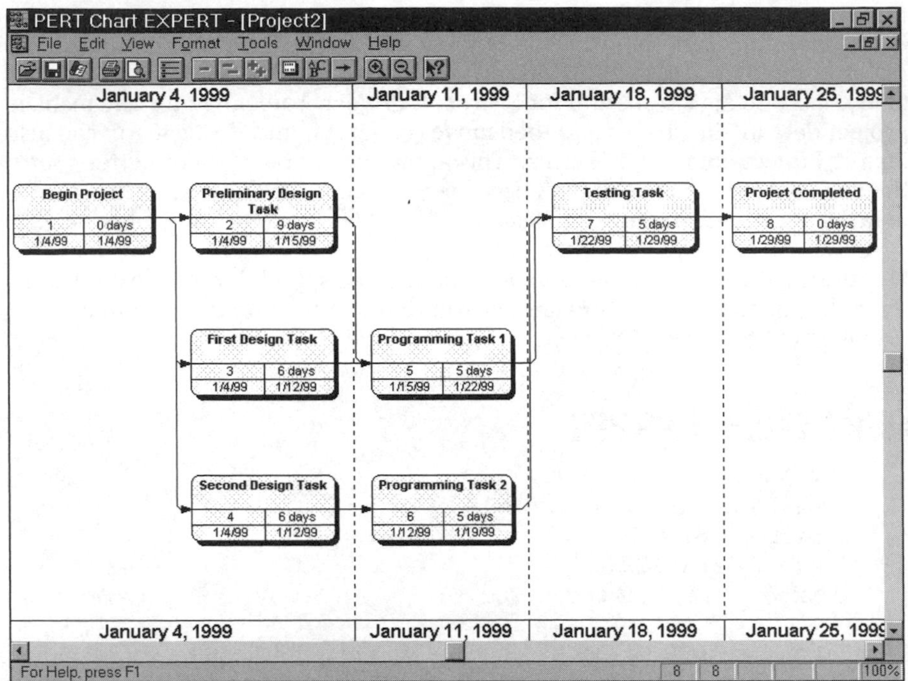


**Figure D-2:** Use PERT Chart Expert to create PERT charts of your Microsoft Project data.

# ProjectCommander Central

Project Assistants, Inc.
2503 Silverside Rd., Ste. 200
Wilmington, DE 19810
Phone: (800) 642-9259
E-mail: `info@projectassistants.com`

**Installation instructions:** Double-click the My Computer icon on your Windows desktop. Open the Project Commander folder and double-click the setup file. When you're asked for a registration code, type **EVALUATE**.

**Running the program:** This trial version of Project Commander is Project 98–compatible only, and as of this writing will not run under Windows 2000. You can open the program from the Windows Start menu. Choose Programs ➪ Project Commander.

ProjectCommander Central combines Microsoft Project's powerful project management engine with a comprehensive and easy-to-use set of functions that make planning, tracking, analyzing, and reporting a snap. Here are just a few of the many features:

- Use ProjectCommander Central to perform project management functions from a single, intuitive interface.
- Use the Task Checklist feature to create a to-do list for the tasks in your project.
- Capture and report on important issues with the Issue Log feature, which is seamlessly integrated within the familiar Microsoft Project desktop.
- With ProjectCommander Central's enhanced Web reporting capabilities, you'll be sharing your most important data on the Internet in no time.

You'll find a fully functional 30-day version of ProjectCommander Central for Project 98 on the CD; you can download the Project 2000 version from the Web at `www.projectassistants.com`.

## Project Kickstart

Experience in Software
2000 Hearst Ave.
Berkeley, CA 94709-2176
Phone: (510) 644-0694
Web: `www.experienceware.com`

**Installation instructions:** From the ProjectKickStart folder on the CD-ROM, double-click the file pkstrial. The opening screen asks whether you want to install Project Kickstart, version 2.02. Click OK and then follow the prompts on the next few screens to designate a program folder for the file.

**Running the program:** This trial version of Project Kickstart is compatible with Project 2000. Open the Project Kickstart folder on your hard drive and double-click the Project Kickstart 2.0 icon. The first screen of this 20-day trial version gives you the option of purchasing the full program or running the trial version. From the main screen you can start to build a project outline with Project Kickstart's easy-to-use tools.

Project KickStart is the fast, easy way to plan and organize your projects. The software's seven-step icons quickly guide you through the process of building a strategic plan. You'll consider project goals, obstacles, resources and other "big picture" issues. Use the Project KickStart "hot-link" icon to transfer your plan into Microsoft Project. Project data will appear in MS Project's Task column ready for scheduling.

Project Kickstart is a front-end planning tool for project managers. With Project Kickstart you can outline your objectives, list things to do, and anticipate major project issues. The software has features to help you brainstorm, strategize, and organize the details of your project before you start to build your project schedule (see Figure D-3). An online planning Advisor and templates for project planning help you formulate your approach to your project. Then you can seamlessly output your data to Microsoft Project.

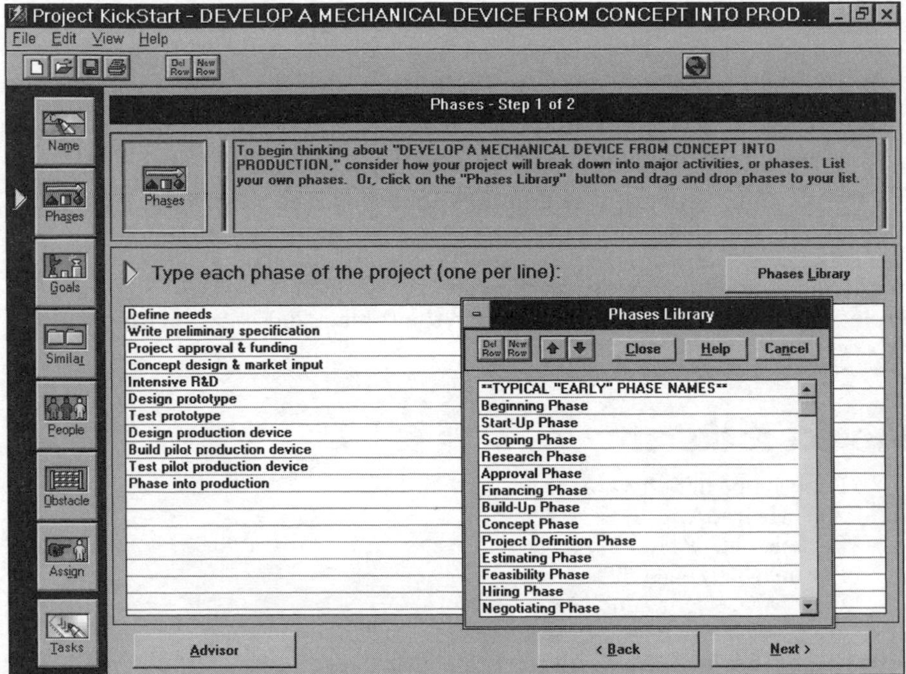

**Figure D-3:** Use predefined lists of project phases to begin to build your Project outline.

# Project Synchronizer

Ira Brown
Project Assistants, Inc.
2503 Silverside Road, Suite 200
Wilmington, DE 19810
Phone: 302-529-5700
Fax: 302-529-7035
Web Site: `www.projectassistants.com`

**Installation instructions:** Double-click the My Computer icon on the Windows desktop. Open the folder named Project Synchronizer and then double-click the setup.exe file. Follow instructions to complete installation. To locate Project Synchronizer after installation, go to C:/Programs/Project Synchronizer.

Project Synchronizer 2000 contains two setup files:

**SetupAdmin** — Contains administrative functions and end user functions. This setup routine should only be executed on the Project Synchronizer 2000 administrator's computer.

**Setup.exe** — Contains only the end user functions. This setup routine should be executed on all end user computers.

After installing Project Synchronizer, the application will be available as a COM AddIn within MS Project 2000. To access COM AddIns, you will need to add the COM AddIns menu option to your standard menu set within MS Project.

1. Select View ⇨ Toolbars ⇨ Customize from the MS Project menu.
2. Select the Commands tab in the Customize dialog box.
3. Select Tools in the Categories window.
4. Select COM Addins in the Commands window and drag this tool onto your standard menu.
5. Close the Customize dialog box.

Project Synchronizer allows you to easily distribute all of your organization's standard Views, Tables, Filters, Reports, Toolbars, Modules and settings to all of your Project users directly from your network, Intranet, or even the Internet. Just add your organization's standard environment to a ".mpp" file, and Project Synchronizer will make sure that each Project user receives all of your latest updates each time they start up Project.

## TeamWork

Project Assistants, Inc.
2503 Silverside Rd., Ste. 200
Wilmington, DE 19810
Phone: (800) 642-9259
E-mail: info@projectassistants.com

**Installation instructions:** Double-click the My Computer icon on your Windows desktop. Open the TeamWork folder and double-click the setup file. When you're asked for a registration code, type **EVALUATE**. You'll also find the TeamWork User Guide on the CD; it uses Adobe Acrobat Reader, which the TeamWork installation routine will volunteer to install. If you don't have Adobe Acrobat Reader, install it when you're prompted so that you can read the TeamWork User Guide.

**Running the program:** This trial version of TeamWork is Project 98–compatible, and as of this writing will not run under Windows 2000. You'll see a Quick Tour of TeamWork when you choose any of the options that appear in the TeamWork group on the Windows Programs menu. Choose Start ⇨ Programs ⇨ TeamWork.

TeamWork is a "Project-centric" process management application. TeamWork provides all of the benefits of process management while working directly within Microsoft Project. You start by building a customized work plan template in Microsoft Project. Incorporate and automate your organization's methodologies as you easily link tasks to all of the intellectual assets required to perform the task. These assets might include detailed methodology steps, Microsoft Word or other document templates, multimedia files such as PowerPoint presentations, hot links to Internet URLs, Excel spreadsheets, Access databases, faxes, and e-mail communications. The only limit is your imagination.

You'll find a fully functional 30-day version of TeamWork for Project 98 on the CD; you can download the Project 2000 version from the Web at www.projectassistants.com.

## TimeSheet Professional

TimeSheet Professional
17950 Preston Rd., Ste. 800
Dallas, TX 75252
Phone: (972) 818-3900
E-mail: tspsales@sageus.com

**Installation instructions:** Double-click the My Computer icon on your Windows desktop. Open the TimeSheet Professional folder and double-click the TSP65EVAL.EXE file. When you're prompted for a password, type **VERSION65TRIALV**. Follow the onscreen prompts to complete installation; I suggest that you install the demo into the default directory of C:\TSP. When you finish, go back to the CD-ROM and, in the Timesheet Professional folder, double-click the TSPMSP.EXE file and allow it to extract three additional files into the same folder where you placed the original installation.

**Running the program:** This single-user version of TimeSheet Professional is Project 98–compatible. To review the program using the sample supplied data, click Start ➪ Programs and double-click the Timesheet Professional for Windows folder. A group of icons will appear; double-click Timesheet Sample Data. To use Project 98 data with the single-user version, you must set up a database connection; instructions for making the database connection can be found in the TIMESHEET README.DOC file also found in the Timesheet Professional Folder on the CD-ROM.

The single-user version includes sample data that highlights the intuitive TimeSheet Professional interface for entering data about resource time (see Figure D-4).

TimeSheet Professional is an easy-to-use front end for tracking of resource time in Microsoft Project. If people working on your project don't have a copy of Microsoft Project, they can enter the time they have spent on various tasks in TimeSheet Professional's simple calendar-like interface. The project manager can then import this information into a Project file, automatically updating resource effort expended on a task-by-task basis. You can also export TimeSheet information on resource time and expenses to a payroll system.

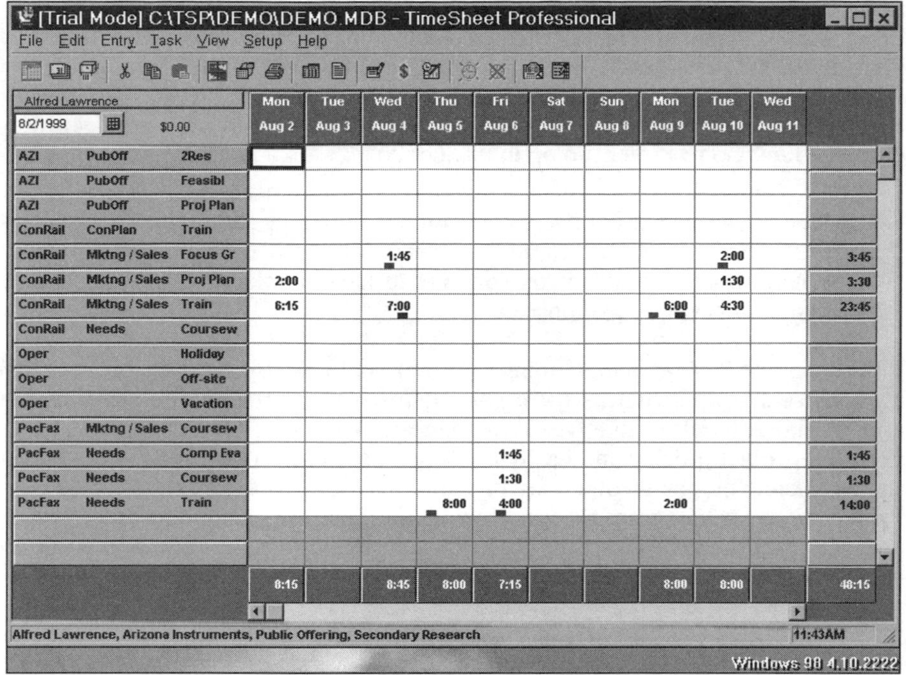

**Figure D-4:** Even people who don't know the first thing about using Project can track their time in TimeSheet.

## WBS Chart for Project

Critical Tools
8004 Bottlebrush Dr.
Austin, TX 78750
Phone: (512) 342-2232
Web: `www.criticaltools.com`

**Installation instructions:** Double-click the My Computer icon on the Windows desktop. Open the folder named WBSChart and then double-click the wd4p2000.exe file. Follow instructions to complete installation.

This setup program needs access to Microsoft Project. If you are accessing Project through a network, you may not have Read/Write access to the Global.mpt file.

**Running the program:** WBS Chart for Project trial version is compatible with Project 2000. When you install the program, you can choose to add a toolbar to Project 2000. Then open Project and simply use the toolbar to run WBS Chart. Alternatively, you can open WBS Chart from the Windows Start menu. Choose Programs ⇨ WBS Chart for Project 2000 ⇨ WBS2000. From the program window, choose File ⇨ Go to Project to open Project 2000.

Depending on your hardware configuration, you may see messages about setup failure. However, because this is a demo, click OK or Continue; the program should install correctly. If you continue to have problems, call the tech support number that will appear onscreen.

WBS Chart for Project is a planning tool that enables you to create projects using a work breakdown structure (WBS) chart. You can use this method to plan, manage, and display projects with a tree-style diagram. With WBS Chart for Project, you can sketch a project quickly and easily by dragging your mouse on the screen. You can then transfer the plans you create in WBS Chart for Project directly to Microsoft Project or to any program that can read a Microsoft Project file format (*.mpp). You can also use WBS Chart for Project to automatically generate presentation-quality WBS charts from existing Microsoft Project files (see Figure D-5).

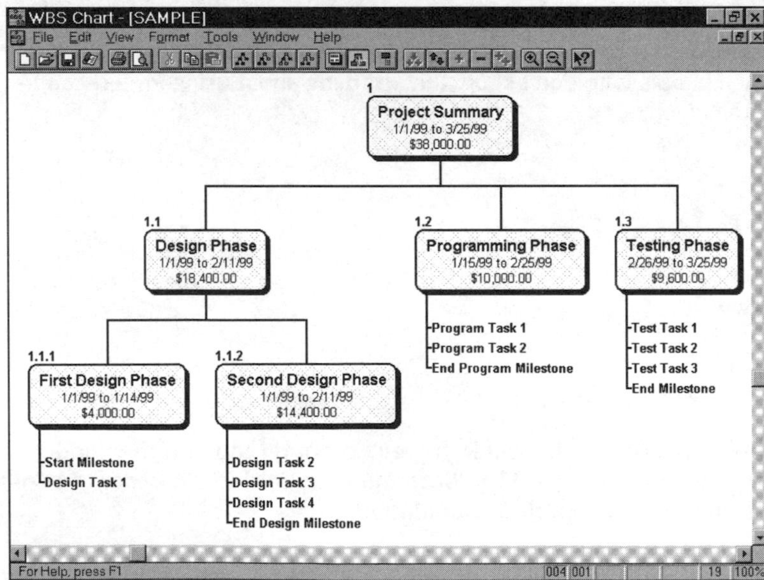


**Figure D-5:** WBS Chart for Project enables you to produce presentation-quality WBS charts from Microsoft Project data.

# Project Sample Files

The CD-ROM also contains three sample files that give you a head start on typical projects. Copy them to your hard disk; open them; save them with your own project name; and then add, delete, and change settings for the various tasks included here. You need to create your own resources and assign them to tasks and add timing and dependency relationships between tasks. The three sample files are as follows:

✦ **Publication sample file (Publish.mpp).** This sample file (see Figure D-6) is useful for any kind of publishing project, from a simple brochure to a product documentation manual. Phases for writing and editing content, design, layout, printing, and distribution give you the basis for your own publishing project.

✦ **Meeting sample file (Meeting.mpp).** Everybody plans meetings. Whether it's a regular weekly staff meeting or your company's annual meeting, this sample file (see Figure D-7) provides the tasks you need to arrange for location, transportation and lodging, invitations, catering, equipment, and speakers.

We've included these files in both Project 98 and Project 2000 formats for your convenience.

Project 2000 comes with some predefined templates on which you can base projects. To use a template, choose File⇨New and click the Project Templates tab. Like my sample files, the templates provide a starting place for projects you enter into Project.

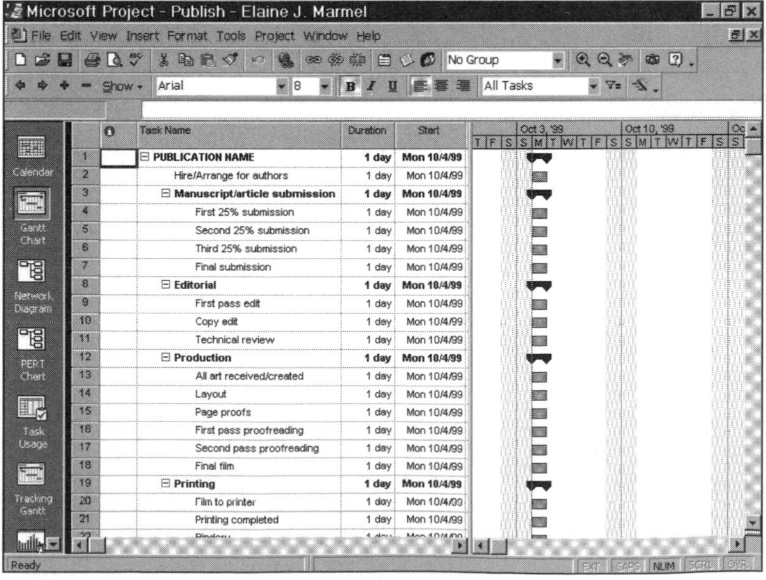


**Figure D-6:** Whether you're publishing product documentation or the company newsletter, many of these tasks will prove useful.

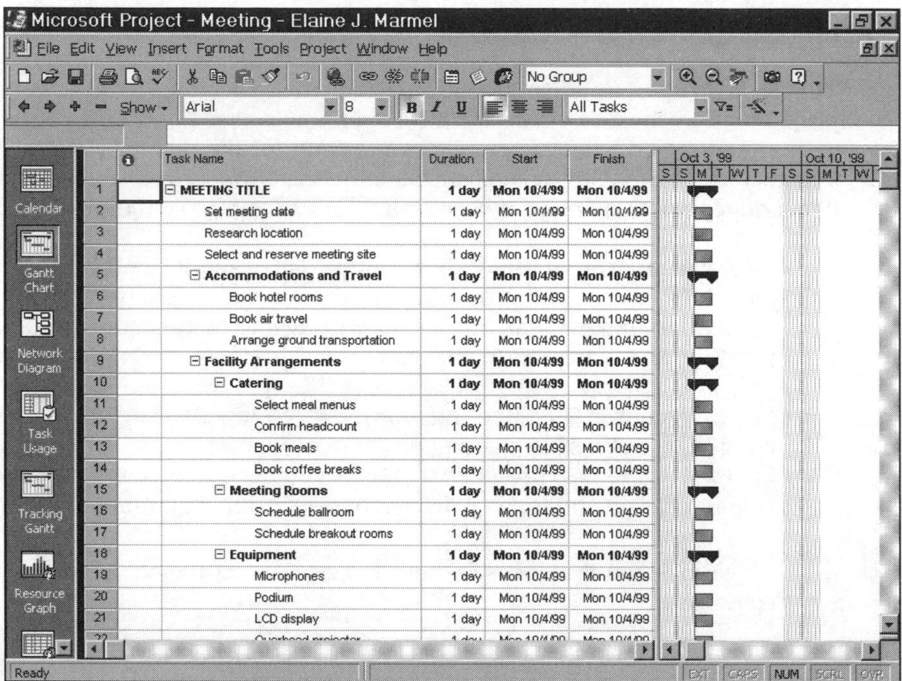


**Figure D-7:** All the details of arranging for meeting space, catering, equipment, and participant transportation and lodging are included here to give you a head start on planning your next meeting.

✦ **Facility sample file (Facility.mpp).** You can use this sample file (see Figure D-8) to set up a new facility or to move to a new space. Tasks include planning space, coordinating movers, managing utilities, and setting up computer networks.

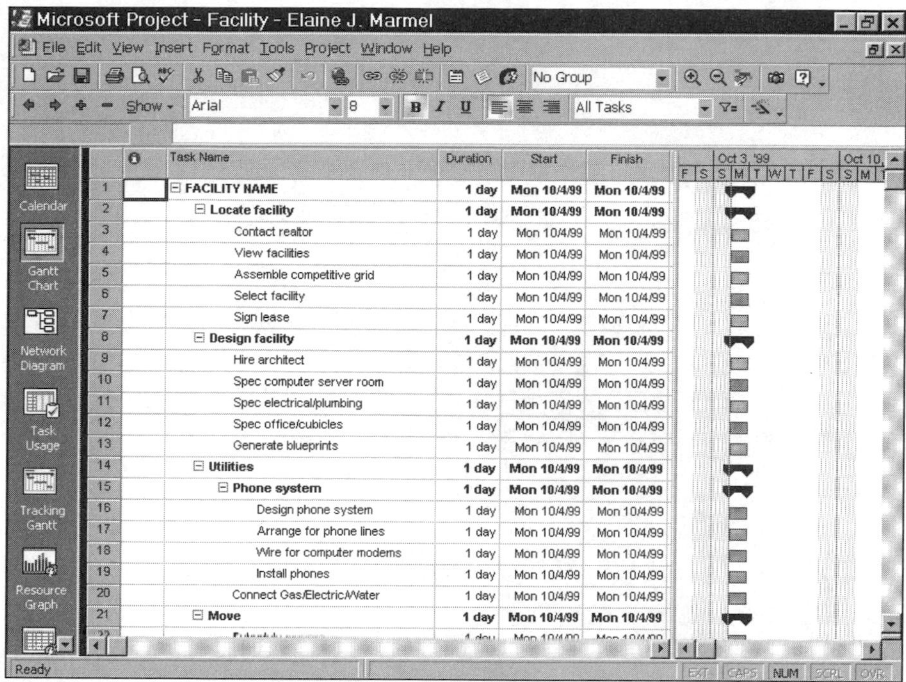


**Figure D-8:** Moving to a new facility or expanding an existing facility is a complex project. This sample file provides the basics.

✦ ✦ ✦

# Project Management Glossary

**ACWP (actual cost of work performed)** Cost of actual work performed to date on the project plus any fixed costs.

**ALAP (as late as possible)** A constraint placed on a task's timing to make it occur as late as possible in the project schedule based on its dependency relationships.

**ASAP (as soon as possible)** A constraint placed on a task's timing to make it occur as early in the project as possible based on its dependency relationships.

**BAC (budget at completion)** The total of planned costs to complete a task (also referred to as *baseline costs).*

**BCWP (budgeted cost of work performed)** Also called *earned value,* this term refers to the value of work completed. A task with $1,000 of associated costs, when 75 percent complete, has a baseline value of $750.

**BCWS (budgeted cost of work scheduled)** The planned completion percentage multiplied by the planned cost. This calculated value reflects the amount of the task that is completed and the planned cost of the task.

**CV (earned value cost variance)** This variance indicates the difference between the planned costs (baseline costs) and the costs taking into account actual costs to date and estimated costs going forward (scheduled costs). The difference between these two values produces either a positive (overbudget) or negative (underbudget) cost variance.

**EAC (estimate at completion)** The total scheduled cost for a resource on a task. This calculation provides the costs incurred to date plus costs estimated for remaining work on the task.

**WBS (work breakdown structure)** Automatically assigned numbers for each task in a project outline that reflect that outline structure. Government project reports often include WBS codes.

**actual** A cost or percentage of work completed and tracked as having already occurred or been incurred.

**actual cost of work performed** See *ACWP.*

**as late as possible** See *ALAP.*

**as soon as possible** See *ASAP.*

**base calendar** The default calendar on which all new tasks are based unless a resource-specific calendar is applied.

**baseline** The snapshot of a project plan against which actual work is tracked.

**baseline cost** The total of all planned costs on tasks in a project before any actual costs have been incurred.

**budget at completion** See *BAC.*

**budgeted cost of work performed** See *BCWP.*

**budgeted cost of work scheduled** See *BCWS.*

**calendar** The various settings for hours in a workday, days in a work week, holidays, and nonworking days on which a project schedule is based.

**circular dependency** A dependency among tasks creating an endless loop that cannot be resolved.

**collapse** To close a project outline to hide subtasks from view.

**combination view** A Project view with the task details showing at the bottom of the screen.

**constraint** A rule that forces a task to fit certain parameters. For example, a task can be constrained to start as late as possible in a project.

**cost** A cost can be applied to a task in a project. The cost of the task may be fixed, or you can apply a cost to a task by assigning resources, which can be equipment, materials, or people with associated hourly rates or fees.

**critical path** The series of tasks that must occur on time in order for the overall project to meet its deadline.

**critical task** A task on the critical path.

**crosstab** A report format that compares two intersecting sets of data; for example, you can generate a crosstab report showing costs of critical tasks that are running late.

**cumulative cost** The planned total cost for a resource to date on a particular task. This calculation provides the costs already incurred on the task plus the costs planned for the remaining, as yet uncompleted, portion of the task.

**cumulative work** The planned total work of a resource on a particular task. This calculation provides the work already performed on the task plus the work planned for the remaining, as yet uncompleted, portion of the task.

**current date line** The vertical line in a Gantt chart indicating today's date and time.

**demote** To move a task to a lower level in the project outline hierarchy.

**dependency** A timing relationship between two tasks in a project. A dependency can cause a task to happen after another task, to happen before another task, or to begin at some point during the life of the other task.

**detail task** See *subtask*.

**duration** The amount of time it takes to complete a task.

**duration variance** A field displaying the variation between the planned (baseline) duration of a task and the current estimated task duration based on activity to date and remaining activity to be performed.

**earned value** Also called *budgeted cost of work performed*. Earned value refers to the value of work completed. A task with $1,000 of associated costs, when 75 percent complete, will have a baseline value of $750.

**earned value cost variance** See *CV*.

**effort driven** An effort-driven task has an assigned amount of effort to complete it. When you add resources to these tasks, the effort is distributed among those resources.

**elapsed duration** An estimate of how long it will take to complete a task based on a 24-hour day and 7-day week.

**estimate at completion (EAC)** The total scheduled cost for a resource on a task. This calculation provides the costs incurred to date plus costs estimated for remaining work on the task.

**expand** Opening a project outline to reveal subtasks as well as summary tasks.

**expected duration** This calculation estimates the actual duration of a task based on performance to date.

**external task** When tasks are linked between projects, Project displays tasks from the external project in the current project. The external task represents the linked tasks without having to leave the current project.

**finish date** The date on which a project will be completed.

**finish-to-finish relationship** A dependency relationship in which the finish of one task depends on the finish of another task.

**finish-to-start relationship** A dependency relationship in which the start of one task depends on the finish of another task.

**fixed cost** A cost that does not increase or decrease based on the time a resource spends on a task. A consultant's fee or permit fee are examples of fixed costs.

**fixed date** A task that must occur on a certain date. Fixed-date tasks do not move earlier or later in the schedule because of dependency relationships.

**fixed duration** The length of time required for a task remains constant no matter how many resources are assigned to it. Travel time is a good example of a fixed-duration task.

**float** See *slack.*

**Gantt chart** A standard project management tracking device that displays task information alongside a chart that shows task timing in a bar chart format.

**gap** See *lag.*

**ID number** The number assigned to a task based on its sequence in the schedule.

**lag** The result of dependency relationships among tasks. Lag is a certain amount of downtime between the end of one task and the start of another.

**leveling** See *resource leveling.*

**linking** Establishing a connection between two tasks in separate schedules so that changes to tasks in the first schedule are reflected in the second. Linking is also a term applied to establishing dependencies among tasks in a project.

**milestone** A task of zero duration that marks a moment of time in a schedule.

**network diagram** A standard project management tracking form that indicates workflow among the tasks in a project.

**node** Boxes containing information about individual project tasks in the Network Diagram view.

**nonworking time** Time when a resource on a project is not assigned to the current task.

**outline** The structure of summary and subordinate tasks in a project.

**overallocation** When a resource is assigned to spend more time than its work calendar permits on a single task or combination of tasks occurring at the same point in time.

**overtime** Any work scheduled above and beyond a resource's standard work hours; overtime work can have a different rate assigned to it than a resource's regular rate.

**percent complete** The amount of work on a task that has already been accomplished, expressed as a percentage.

**predecessor** In a dependency relationship, the task that is designated to occur before, or precede, another.

**priorities** Project uses the priorities you assign to tasks when it performs resource leveling to resolve project conflicts; a higher priority task is less likely than a lower priority task to incur delay during the leveling process.

**progress lines** Gantt chart bars that overlap the baseline taskbar and indicate tracked actual progress on the task.

**project** A series of steps to reach a specific goal. A project seeks to meet the triple constraints of time, quality, and cost.

**project management** The discipline that studies various methods, procedures, and concepts used to control the progress and outcome of projects.

**promote** To move a task to a higher level in a project's outline hierarchy.

**recurring task** A task that is repeated during the life of a project. Typical recurring tasks are regular meetings of project teams or regular reviews of project output.

**resource** A cost associated with a task. A resource can be a person, piece of equipment, materials, or a fee.

**resource contouring** Changing the time when a resource begins work on a task. You can use contouring to vary the amount of work a resource does on a task over the life of that task.

**resource driven** A task whose timing is determined by the number of resources assigned to it.

**resource leveling** A process used by Project to modify resource assignments to resolve resource conflicts.

**resource pool** A group of resources that can be assigned as a group to an individual task (for example, a pool of administrative workers assigned to generating a report).

**roll up** The calculation by which all subtask values are "rolled up" or summarized in a summary task.

**slack** Also called *float.* The time you have available to delay a task before that task becomes critical. You have used up slack on a task when any delay on that task will cause a delay in the overall project deadline.

**split tasks** When progress on a task is interrupted or delayed because the task has been placed on hold, you can split the task into two tasks. When you split tasks, the downtime between the two is not allocated to the total time taken to complete the task.

**start date** The date on which a project begins.

**start-to-finish relationship** A dependency relationship in which one task cannot start until another task finishes.

**start-to-start relationship** A dependency relationship in which the start of one task depends on the start of another task.

**subproject** An inserted copy of a second project that becomes a phase of the project in which it is inserted.

**subtask** Also called a *subordinate task.* A task providing detail for a specific step in the project. This detail is rolled up into a higher-level summary task.

**successor** In a dependency relationship a successor task is scheduled to begin after another task in the project.

**summary task** A task in a project outline that has subordinate tasks beneath it. A summary task rolls up the details of its subtasks and has no timing of its own.

**task** An individual step to be performed to reach a project's goal.

**template** A format in which a Project file can be saved; the template saves elements such as calendar settings, formatting, and tasks. New project files can be based on a template.

**timescale** The area of a Gantt Chart view that indicates the units of time being displayed.

**tracking** The act of recording actual progress in terms of both work completed and costs accrued on tasks in a project.

**variable rate** A shift in a resource's cost that can be set to occur at specific times during a project. For example, if a resource is expected to receive a raise or if equipment lease rates are expected to increase, you can assign variable rates for those resources.

**work breakdown structure** See *WBS.*

**workload** The amount of work any resource is performing at any given point in time, taking into account all tasks to which the resource is assigned.

**workspace** A set of files and project settings that can be saved and reopened together so that you can pick up work on a project or projects at the point at which you stopped.

# Index

## B

## C

*Continued*

# D



*Continued*

## E

## F

## G

## H



## I

*Continued*

## N

*Continued*

## R

*Continued*

## T

*Continued*

*Continued*

## U

## V



*Continued*

## W

# Notes

# Notes

# Hungry Minds, Inc., End-User License Agreement

**READ THIS**. You should carefully read these terms and conditions before opening the software packet(s) included with this book ("Book"). This is a license agreement ("Agreement") between you and Hungry Minds, Inc. ("HMI"). By opening the accompanying software packet(s), you acknowledge that you have read and accept the following terms and conditions. If you do not agree and do not want to be bound by such terms and conditions, promptly return the Book and the unopened software packet(s) to the place you obtained them for a full refund.

1. **License Grant.** HMI grants to you (either an individual or entity) a nonexclusive license to use one copy of the enclosed software program(s) (collectively, the "Software") solely for your own personal or business purposes on a single computer (whether a standard computer or a workstation component of a multi-user network). The Software is in use on a computer when it is loaded into temporary memory (RAM) or installed into permanent memory (hard disk, CD-ROM, or other storage device). HMI reserves all rights not expressly granted herein.
2. **Ownership.** HMI is the owner of all right, title, and interest, including copyright, in and to the compilation of the Software recorded on the disk(s) or CD-ROM ("Software Media"). Copyright to the individual programs recorded on the Software Media is owned by the author or other authorized copyright owner of each program. Ownership of the Software and all proprietary rights relating thereto remain with HMI and its licensers.
3. **Restrictions On Use and Transfer.**

   **(a)** You may only (i) make one copy of the Software for backup or archival purposes, or (ii) transfer the Software to a single hard disk, provided that you keep the original for backup or archival purposes. You may not (i) rent or lease the Software, (ii) copy or reproduce the Software through a LAN or other network system or through any computer subscriber system or bulletin-board system, or (iii) modify, adapt, or create derivative works based on the Software.

   **(b)** You may not reverse engineer, decompile, or disassemble the Software. You may transfer the Software and user documentation on a permanent basis, provided that the transferee agrees to accept the terms and conditions of this Agreement and you retain no copies. If the Software is an update or has been updated, any transfer must include the most recent update and all prior versions.

4. **Restrictions on Use of Individual Programs.** You must follow the individual requirements and restrictions detailed for each individual program in Appendix D of this Book. These limitations are also contained in the individual license agreements recorded on the Software Media. These limitations may include a requirement that after using the program for a specified period of time, the user must pay a registration fee or discontinue use. By opening the Software packet(s), you will be agreeing to abide by the licenses and restrictions for these individual programs that are detailed in Appendix D and on the Software Media. None of the material on this Software Media or listed in this Book may ever be redistributed, in original or modified form, for commercial purposes.

5. **Limited Warranty.**

   **(a)** HMI warrants that the Software and Software Media are free from defects in materials and workmanship under normal use for a period of sixty (60) days from the date of purchase of this Book. If HMI receives notification within the warranty period of defects in materials or workmanship, HMI will replace the defective Software Media.

   **(b)** **HMI AND THE AUTHOR OF THE BOOK DISCLAIM ALL OTHER WARRANTIES, EXPRESS OR IMPLIED, INCLUDING WITHOUT LIMITATION IMPLIED WARRANTIES OF MERCHANTABILITY AND FITNESS FOR A PARTICULAR PURPOSE, WITH RESPECT TO THE SOFTWARE, THE PROGRAMS, THE SOURCE CODE CONTAINED THEREIN, AND/OR THE TECHNIQUES DESCRIBED IN THIS BOOK. HMI DOES NOT WARRANT THAT THE FUNCTIONS CONTAINED IN THE SOFTWARE WILL MEET YOUR REQUIREMENTS OR THAT THE OPERATION OF THE SOFTWARE WILL BE ERROR FREE.**

   **(c)** This limited warranty gives you specific legal rights, and you may have other rights that vary from jurisdiction to jurisdiction.

6. **Remedies.**

   **(a)** HMI's entire liability and your exclusive remedy for defects in materials and workmanship shall be limited to replacement of the Software Media, which may be returned to HMI with a copy of your receipt at the following address: Software Media Fulfillment Department, Attn.: *Microsoft® Project 2000 Bible,* Hungry Minds, Inc., 10475 Crosspoint Blvd., Indianapolis, IN 46256, or call 1-800-762-2974. Please allow four to six weeks for delivery. This Limited Warranty is void if failure of the Software Media has resulted from accident, abuse, or misapplication. Any replacement Software Media will be warranted for the remainder of the original warranty period or thirty (30) days, whichever is longer.

   **(b)** In no event shall HMI or the author be liable for any damages whatsoever (including without limitation damages for loss of business profits, business interruption, loss of business information, or any other pecuniary loss) arising from the use of or inability to use the Book or the Software, even if HMI has been advised of the possibility of such damages.

(c) Because some jurisdictions do not allow the exclusion or limitation of liability for consequential or incidental damages, the above limitation or exclusion may not apply to you.

7. **U.S. Government Restricted Rights.** Use, duplication, or disclosure of the Software for or on behalf of the United States of America, its agencies and/or instrumentalities (the "U.S. Government") is subject to restrictions as stated in paragraph (c)(1)(ii) of the Rights in Technical Data and Computer Software clause of DFARS 252.227-7013, or subparagraphs (c) (1) and (2) of the Commercial Computer Software—Restricted Rights clause at FAR 52.227-19, and in similar clauses in the NASA FAR supplement, as applicable.

8. **General.** This Agreement constitutes the entire understanding of the parties and revokes and supersedes all prior agreements, oral or written, between them and may not be modified or amended except in a writing signed by both parties hereto that specifically refers to this Agreement. This Agreement shall take precedence over any other documents that may be in conflict herewith. If any one or more provisions contained in this Agreement are held by any court or tribunal to be invalid, illegal, or otherwise unenforceable, each and every other provision shall remain in full force and effect.

# CD-ROM Installation Instructions

The CD-ROM attached to the inside back cover of this book contains demos or trial versions of several of the most popular add-on products for use with Microsoft Project. The CD-ROM also contains a Web page with links to the sites of Microsoft Project partners who offer software that enhances Microsoft Project and assistance in using Microsoft Project. At several of the Web sites, you'll find Web-based demo products as well as sample files for some of the most common types of projects.

Appendix D describes the contents of the CD-ROM and gives detailed instructions for installing each program on your computer. You can use the trial or demonstration versions of these products to see how they fit your needs, and each listing in Appendix D includes contact information so that you can buy the software directly from the vendor.